T0377032

FAMILY LIFE IN ENGLAND AND AMERICA, 1690–1820

CONTENTS OF THE EDITION

VOLUME 1
General Introduction
Many Families

VOLUME 2
Making Families

VOLUME 3
Managing Families, I

VOLUME 4
Managing Families, II
Index

FAMILY LIFE IN ENGLAND AND AMERICA, 1690–1820

General Editors
Rachel Cope, Amy Harris and Jane Hinckley

Volume 1
Many Families

Edited by
Jane Hinckley

LONDON AND NEW YORK

First published 2015 by Pickering & Chatto (Publishers) Limited

Published 2016 by Routledge
2 Park Square, Milton Park, Abingdon, Oxon OX14 4RN
711 Third Avenue, New York, NY 10017, USA

Routledge is an imprint of the Taylor & Francis Group, an informa business

Copyright © Taylor & Francis 2015
Copyright © General Introduction Rachel Cope and Amy Harris 2015
Copyright © Editorial material Jane Hinckley 2015

To the best of the Publisher's knowledge every effort has been made to contact relevant copyright holders and to clear any relevant copyright issues. Any omissions that come to their attention will be remedied in future editions.

All rights reserved, including those of translation into foreign languages. No part of this book may be reprinted or reproduced or utilised in any form or by any electronic, mechanical, or other means, now known or hereafter invented, including photocopying and recording, or in any information storage or retrieval system, without permission in writing from the publishers.

Notice:
Product or corporate names may be trademarks or registered trademarks, and are used only for identification and explanation without intent to infringe.

BRITISH LIBRARY CATALOGUING IN PUBLICATION DATA

Family life in England and America, 1690–1820. 1. Families – Great Britain – History – 18th century – Sources. 2. Families – United States – History – 18th century – Sources.
I. Cope, Rachel editor. II. Harris, Amy (Professor of history) editor. III. Hinckley, Jane, editor.
306.8'5'0941'09033-dc23

ISBN-13: 978-1-84893-474-0 (set)

Typeset by Pickering & Chatto (Publishers) Limited

CONTENTS

Acknowledgements	ix
General Introduction	xi
Bibliography	xxv
Introduction	xxxi
Editorial Principles	xliii

Multiple Families
Wills, Estate Papers, Licenses
  Wills of Berkeley Seymour and Jane Seymour   1
    Berkeley Seymour, Will (Written 1744, Proved 1744)   3
    Jane Seymour, Will (Written 1762, Proved 1770)   4
  John Romans, Deed (1766)   5
  Ward Hallowell, Licence [*sic*] to Change his Name to Ward
    Nicholas Boylston (1770)   9
  Jane Parminter, Will (Written 1807, Proved 1812)   13
Letters
  John Drayton, Letter to James Glen (1761)   19
  A. W. Rumney (ed.), *From the Old South-Sea House* (1914)   25
  Chesnut and Cox Families, Correspondence (1797, 1800, 1810)   31
  Lovejoy Family Correspondence (1817–19)   47
Literature
  Anna Letitia Barbauld, *Hymns in Prose for Children* (1781)   55
  Ann Murry, *Mentoria: Or, the Young Ladies Instructor* (1780)   67
  Jane Davis, *Letters from a Mother to her Son, on his Going to Sea: And a
    Letter to Capt. S.* ([1799])   73

Religious Diversity of Families
Parish and Probate
  Church of England, Haselbury-Plucknett, Somerset, Parish Registers   79
  Recusant Returns, Diocese of York (1767, 1780)   87
Petitions and Letters
  William Tennent III, On the Dissenting Petition, House of Assembly,
    Charleston, South Carolina (1777)   95

Zina Baker Huntington Correspondence (1808–13) 107

Literature

Robert Nelson, *An Earnest Exhortation to House-Keepers, to Set Up the Worship of God in their Families* (1739) 125

Anon., *A Persuasive to Family Religion* (1736) 135

Abbé d'Ancourt, 'Of Politeness in Religion, and against Superstition', 'Of Devotion', 'Of Behaviour at Church', *The Lady's Preceptor* (1743) 143

David Muir, *An Humble Attempt toward the Revival of Family-Religion among Christians* (1749) 149

Anon., *Cheap Repository Tracts for Sunday Reading* (1800) 157

Racial Diversity of Families

American Indians and Atlantic Africans

Isle of Wight County, Virginia, Deeds (1720–36, 1741–9) 163

James Dolbeare, Bills of Sale (1732 and 1743) 175

Birth of Negroes, Galbreath Moore Family Bible (1819–56) 179

Lancaster, Pennsylvania Clerk of Courts, Returns of Negro and Mulatto Children (1788–93) 183

Vick Family Deed of Emancipation (1789) 195

John Beall, Will (1803) 199

George Walker, Leeward Plantation Appraisal (1781) 203

John Williams and Elizabeth Williams, his Wife, and their Children, Removal Orders (1818) 211

Dido Elizabeth Belle Davinier 215

Dido Elizabeth Belle, Baptism Record (1766) 219

'The Earl of Mansfield's Will', *Diary or Woodfall's Register* (1793) 219

Dido and John Davinier Marriage Allegation and Bond (1793) 222

Olaudah Equiano, or Gustavus Vassa, 'The African' 225

Olaudah Equiano, *The Interesting Narrative of the Life of Olaudah Equiano, or Gustavus Vassa, the African* ([1794]) 229

Susannah Cullen and Gustavus Vassa, Marriage Certificate (1792) 230

Gustavus Vassa, Will (1797) 231

Anna Maria Vassa, Epitaph (1796) 233

Letters and Literature: England

Daniel Renaud, Commonplace Book Selections from 'The Ladies Oracle', c. 1750 235

Clara Reeve, 'Letter X' and 'Letter XI' 239

Letters and Literature: America

Adolph B. Benson, *Peter Kalm's Travels in North America* (1937) 247

Phillis Wheatley, 'Preface' and 'Letter of Attestation', in *Poems on Various Subjects* (1773) 257

Catherine Sedgwick to Frances Sedgwick (1807) on Elizabeth Freeman – 'Mumbet'	263

Poor Families
Civic and Religious Efforts to Alleviate Poverty: Parish Records

Diocese of Exeter Visitation Records, Stockley Pomeroy (1744)	269
Haselbury-Plucknett, Somerset, Settlement and Removal Papers (1723–1801)	275
Stoke Abbott, Dorset, Bastardy Papers (1780–1820)	287
John Sibley, Settlement Examination (1753)	301
St Katherine Cree Parish Apprenticeship Indentures (1693–1753)	305
Ashton in Makerfield, Lancashire, Census of the Poor (1816)	315
St Ann's Parish (Albemarle County, Virginia), Vestry Book (1772–85)	321

Civic and Religious Efforts to Alleviate Poverty: Literature

London Society for Educating Poor Children in the Protestant Reformed Religion (1782)	325
Hints for the Institution of Sunday-Schools and Parish Clubs, for the Benefit of the Poor (1789)	331
Ferdinando Tracy Travell, *The Duties of the Poor* (1793)	339

Fictive Families
Correspondence, Memoirs and Minutes

Society of Friends, Buckingham Monthly Meeting, Men's Minute Books (1735–98), Women's Minute Books (1670–1822)	357
Sarah Ryan to Mary Fletcher (1762 and 1763)	371
Mary Fletcher, Account of Sarah Lawrence, Methodist Minister (1801)	377

Quaker Fictive Families

Rachel Wilson, Letter to R. Jones and H. Cathrall (1770)	395
Rebecca Jones, Letter to Edward Cathrall (1782)	398

Voluntary Associations 399

Female Society and Female Association of Pennsylvania, Minutes (1805–15)	401
Articles of Association of the Female Hospitable Society (1814)	426

Literature

Articles, to be Observed and Kept by All the Members of the Benevolent Female Society (1790)	439
Clara Reeve, 'Letter XIV' ('The Plan of a Female Community')	445
Elizabeth Bentley, 'On the Renewal of Virtuous Friendship in a Future State. July, 1790'	457

Editorial Notes	461
List of Sources	499

To all my dear family:
Jaren, Emma, Catherine, Ian and Janice

ACKNOWLEDGEMENTS

We have received generous support from our home institution, Brigham Young University. In particular, we'd like to thank the Family Studies Center, the Center for the Study of Europe, the Kennedy Center for International Studies, the Religious Studies Center and the College of Family, Home and Social Sciences for funding support that allowed us to gather documents and hire student research assistants. In addition, the Department of Church History and Doctrine and the History Department provided unstinting material and logistical support. In particular, the help of Patty Smith at the Religious Education Faculty Support Center was instrumental to this project.

Beyond BYU we are also grateful for research and funding support from a Gest Fellowship at Haverford College, a New England Regional Consortium Fellowship at Massachusetts Historical Society and a William Andrews Clark Memorial Library Fellowship at UCLA.

Several colleagues offered advice and recommended resources. In particularly we'd like to thank Dallett Hemphill and Lisa Wilson who offered insight about organization and themes, and who were enthusiastic in their encouragement. Kate Holbrook and Jenny Pulsipher were kind enough to read and comment upon introduction drafts. Karen Auman and Matt Mason were generous with their time, gave insightful input and provided sources for tricky southern-states legal history.

We appreciate the helpfulness of archive staff on both sides of the Atlantic. Scott Jacobs and the staff at the William Andrews Clark Library at UCLA; Peter Nockles at John Rylands Library, Manchester; and Chris Anderson at the Methodist Library, Drew University. We are also thankful for the staff at the London Metropolitan Archives, Gloucestershire Archives, Family History Library, Tulane University Special Collections and New York Historical Society. We are particularly grateful to the Earl of Wemyss and March of Stanway House, who gave permission for Anne Tracy's entire extant diary to be published – for the first time.

This project grew and sprawled until it encompassed nearly everything in sight. Making sense of hundreds of documents covering various social and ethnic groups in two countries, and for over a century, would not have been possible without the diligent help of a bevy of dedicated research assistants. Specifically, we would be remiss if we did not thank Kaitlyn Ayers, Megan Bradford, Bob Call, Anne Clark, Amber Lee Hansen, Rebecca Lofley, Kate Olson, Annalaura Solomon, Rebecca Strein, Brittany Strobelt and Emilee Wolfe. Kim Cantrell's yeoman service as a transcriber, Michael Cope's organization of rekeyed texts, Amy Wallace's rapid-fire scouring of online sources and the attention to detail provided by Sarah Barlow and Rebecca Johnson, deserve special recognition.

This project has been quite the journey for all three of us. It might seem unusual to acknowledge each other, but one of the sweetest benefits of this project has been the association with one other. We spent many hours around our kitchen tables discussing what we had learned about eighteenth-century family life; we found connections and illumination in unexpected places. We hope the reader finds those connections equally illuminating.

GENERAL INTRODUCTION

Amy Harris and Rachel Cope

This series consists of a collection of snapshots of eighteenth-century family life. Like individual photographs, each of the four volumes depicts moments in time, but they do not reflect all experiences for all families in England and America, nor do they illuminate off-camera experiences. Like all snapshots, however, the series does capture a range of familial behaviours and interactions. Some pieces, like formal portraits, have established, almost scripted elements, while other portions illustrate the unexpected and the serendipitous. The collection also shows the possibilities and contours of family life throughout the long eighteenth century and across many regions. In doing so it underscores several themes that run through all four volumes. For example, the malleability of family relationships, whether in fictive ties in Volume 1, or in times of death and conflict in Volume 4, demonstrates families' ability to adapt and even thrive in changing circumstances. Similarly, the practical functions of families in the economic, social and material world are echoed in both courtship and marital concerns found in Volume 2 and in inheritance practices discussed in Volume 3. And, in all volumes, there exists a constant tension between laws and institutions designed to validate, count and measure families, and the actual families whose lived realities did not always sit easily within such standardized measures.

Rationale and Approach

In many ways this series was influenced by the same ideas that inspired one of family history's founding fathers: Lawrence Stone. As he so aptly contended, there were massive transformations between 1500 and 1800 which 'expressed themselves in changes in the ways members of the family related to each other, in terms of legal arrangements, structure, custom, power, affect and sex'.[1] And yet, our volumes also move beyond Stone's rather sterile assertions about family life. Like many other scholars of European and American families who published in the 1960s and 1970s, he saw the pre-modern family as a place of cold-hearted calculation based on survival and devoid of the individuality and affection that typifies modern Western families. The world revealed in these pages is less teleological than that described by Stone; family structures did not move in chronological lock-step from one household type to the next as the wave of modernizing historical change swept them along. Rather, families of all kinds were constantly changing as birth, illness, marriage and death shaped and reshaped their emotional and material realities. In the end, this series arrives at a much more complicated and perhaps even messier place than Stone described – a place where families, in their array of happy success and destructive dysfunction, demonstrate their remarkable adaptability and salience. As Steven Ozment once put it, 'this smallest and seemingly most fragile of institutions ... the family is the great survivor amid the changing ages and cultures'.[2]

In exploring that 'most fragile of institutions', this series draws upon recent developments within the scholarship covering English and American families. Although family history enjoyed heady days of scholarly enthusiasm in the 1960s and 1970s, due to the work of Stone and others, an interest in the subject senesced slightly after 1980. Since the late 1990s, however, there has been a re-flowering of scholarship on families in the eighteenth century. David Kertzer and Marzio Barbagli's three-volume history of European families between 1500 and 2000 demonstrated the varied and expansive family research being conducted.[3] Scholarship on American and British families has similarly expanded beyond the 1960s' and 1970s' demographic interest and focus on marriage and nuclear families to consider kinship more broadly, to incorporate other family relationships, and to consider the significance of fictive family ties.[4] In work heavily influenced by scholarship on women and gender, British and American family history has also come to incorporate studies of violence, childhood, marital status and old age.[5] There has also been an increased recognition of the differences caused by race, region, class and religion.[6] Courses on American and European family history that once emphasized demography now incorporate qualitative work on relationships, power and conflict within families. Additionally, family has been used as a vehicle for understanding the development of everything from the state to democracy and capitalism.[7] In all of this, however, there has been little added to compilations of primary sources. Indeed, to our knowledge, there has not been a compilation of English and American family history sources since the late 1980s; and no compilation of both English and American sources in one series.[8] As excellent as those earlier works are, they were informed by the historiographic questions of the 1970s and 1980s – particularly those associated with debates over the nuclear family and the expression of affection in families. The present series fruitfully builds on this previous work, expands to consider transatlantic comparisons, and engages with the past two decades' scholarship on eighteenth-century families.[9]

The Process

Although this series technically began with the quest to find an array of documents that depicted various aspects of family life in eighteenth-century England and America, its origins can more accurately be traced to snapshots from the lives of three individual women: Catherine Livingston Garrettson, Anne Tracy Travell and Anna Letitia Aikin Barbauld, subjects of research for each of the three editors of this collection. At first glance, Catherine Livingston's personal writings centre on her own conversion experiences, Anne Tracy's diary depicts the life of a young woman in eighteenth-century England, and Anna Barbauld's writings provide an example of female poetry. But a more careful read of the primary sources authored by each of these women reveals experiences that are far more nuanced than those simple summaries suggest. Their writings are not just about their individuality, but also centre on the relationships that mattered to them: parents, siblings, friends, grandparents, aunts, uncles, cousins, children and fellow believers figure into the stories these women had to tell. Catherine Livingston, for example, saw her own conversion experience as a means to lead her loved ones to salvation. A deeper commitment to the divine only expanded her sense of kinship and motivated Catherine to strengthen familial bonds. Similarly, Anne Tracy's diary is not just about her own development. In addition to discussing her personal progress, the diary also highlights her social interactions, the meaningfulness of her sibling relationships, and hints at a future courtship with John Travell. Anne is not just writing about herself, but about the various networks of kin to which she felt drawn. And, finally, Anna Barbauld's poetry is both implicitly and explicitly laced with the relational. The influence of her parents, the support of close friends, and the encouragement of her brother are intricately, even if invisibly, woven throughout the words she penned. Furthermore, the poetry she wrote highlights the diverse and complicated relationships and the varieties of joy and tragedy of which family life is composed.

Ultimately, our in-depth knowledge of Livingston's, Tracy's and Barbauld's writings and lives spurred our thoughts about families on both sides of the Atlantic. They reminded us that families are both simple and complex, that relationships are many and varied, that fictive as well as consanguineal and affinal ties matter, that genealogies can be lateral as well as vertical, that diversity – whether social, economic, racial, religious or other – can challenge and forge familial bonds, that death reshapes all family relationships and alters and obliterates plans, that conflict and tension are inevitable, that violence occurs too often, that questions of power and authority mean different things in different contexts, and that those who are single or childless should be seen as family members and not merely as unconnected individuals.

After identifying a multitude of themes that were woven throughout the writings of the three historical figures that we know so well, we determined to collect a sampling of documents that highlighted similar complexities in eighteenth-century British and American family relationships. Two central driving principles influenced the kind of material we sought to include in this series: first, we wanted our collection to emphasize manuscript sources and, second, we wanted to include a plethora of female voices. Therefore, even though a number of eighteenth-century publications are included in this collection, it does not focus on replicating diaries, autobiographies or other personal material that has been in print. Instead, this series reflects how known and unknown women and men thought about, dreamed about, and managed family life as preserved in archival manuscripts. Additionally, the emphasis on materials written by women is not purely a project of recovery, but is rather meant to underscore that the family was the primary social institution for women in the eighteenth century. While it is true that the eighteenth century also saw the flourishing of women's interests in non-domestic concerns, family life constituted the primary location of most women's work and emotional and financial activities, and thus it is important to consider how women influenced and were influenced by their familial roles and responsibilities.

Given our interest in discovering a variety of family experiences, as well as our goals to locate manuscript sources and to incorporate women's voices into our volumes, we first turned our attention to extensive archival research. Initially, we gathered documents that we were familiar with from previous research, as well as sources we had learned about through careful readings of secondary literature. As a result, our initial gathering efforts, while rich in many regards, tended to reflect our particular research perspectives: we had a significant number of spiritual biographies/autobiographies, poetry, wills and parish records. That round of gathering also tended to encompass the regions where we were most comfortable: New England, British publishing, and southern England. Therefore, after reviewing our initial collection of sources, we assessed the chronological, geographic and racial/ethnic/social coverage and then focused on gathering records that could fill the rather obvious gaps. Although pleased with the amount of coverage the volumes grew to reflect, we acknowledge that we simply could not cover everything that could (or even should) have been included, and that our own research biases are still evident. Since each of us work in areas that have often been neglected by historians of the family – such as spiritual kinship, religious practices, genealogy, and siblinghood – our particular emphases added strength to the series because the documents we have selected allow definitions of the family to expand even further.

After locating the documents that would be included in this series, we turned our attention to the transcription process. Over the course of a few months, we transcribed over half a million words from over two hundred different documents. Each manuscript was transcribed by one individual and then checked by at least one if not two other people. We then organized each transcription into basic categories that we concluded were essential to understanding family life, and which reflected current trends in family historiography. Once the transcriptions were completed, we began writing headnotes and annotations for each of the documents. While in the process of contextualizing these sources, we made a concerted effort to excavate biographic and genealogical details in order to illuminate the document's particular meaning. The Deanery of Ripon cases found in Volume 1 illustrate this point. The Ripon cases address ecclesiastical concerns about sexual misconduct within local parishes. Analysing this document, a manuscript source from the Borthwick Institute at the University of York, involved consulting parish registers via two large online genealogical databases, in order to determine the family situations of those being examined by the Dean's court. It also necessitated exploring an online database of Church of England clergy in order to understand why one parish had an unusually high number of cases. This combination of manuscript sources with genealogical and historical databases is emblematic of the series as a whole.

Each of the steps we engaged in while producing this series involved group effort. We worked together, swapping documents between us as we determined that the content or approach suited one of our specialties more than another; we read drafts of headnotes and reviewed annotations; we queried one another about historiographical debates and discussed how the content from one volume connected with that found in one of the others. Therefore, even though individual names appear on individual volumes, each was a true collaboration and each has all of our fingerprints on its content and framework.

The Structure

As we considered the best ways in which to capture the experiences of numerous families living in a wide range of locations for over a century, we decided to take a volume-level approach to coverage. Indeed, this seemed to be the only way to make the project manageable and to prevent it from growing and evolving into dozens of volumes with hundreds of different themes. *Family Life in England and America, 1690–1820* encompasses four volumes: The Many Families of the Eighteenth Century (Volume 1) covers multiple families, religious diversity, racial diversity, poverty and fictive families; Making Families (Volume 2) focuses on courtship, singleness, marriage and its dissolution, sex and reproduction, and childhood and childrearing; Maintaining and Perpetuating Families (Volumes 3 and 4) consider the themes (3) of household and family economy, sibling experience, and inheritance and genealogy, as well as (4) authority, power, and discontent, violence and conflict, and death and mourning. All of the volumes are arranged thematically and then chronologically within each theme and grouping. The collection of sources reflects recent historiographic trends that have expanded the definition of eighteenth-century families to include friends, fictive relatives, and the multiple family connections beyond spouse and parent-child relationships.

Each volume extends from the late seventeenth century to the early nineteenth century and touches on both northern and southern colonies/states of America and urban and rural England. Additionally, each volume includes information from various religious, ethnic, racial and regional populations. Because each of us worked on each volume, we were also able to make connections between various other documents that either talked about the same families, or that captured similar themes and ideas. Certain large, key collections were particularly helpful in facilitating this. For example, the Allinson Family Papers from the Quaker Collection at the Magill Library at Haverford College figure in several different volumes in this series. Courtship letters, marriage certificates and memorials reflect the many events and individuals that affected specific family relationships as well as the structure of their families. Throughout the various volumes, one can trace Martha Cooper Allinson's development from a young teenager who helped her father, David Cooper, raise her siblings following her mother's death, to a young woman whose father is advising her to marry for companionship or not at all, to a married woman who is mourning her father's death. Similarly, the Fletcher–Tooth Collection from Methodist Archives and Research Centre at the John Ryland's Library at the University of Manchester is woven throughout multiple volumes in this series. This collection captures the importance of fictive ties – the creation of a Methodist family – within a variety of contexts. The relationship between Sarah Ryan, Sarah Lawrence, and Mary Bosanquet Fletcher (and later John Fletcher) not only demonstrates intimate relations between people of faith, but also deals with the role of religious diversity and the influence of violence, conflict and death in shaping and reshaping one's sense of kin. The Papers of the Cox and Chesnut Families, located at the Irvin Department of Rare Books and Special Collections at the University of South Carolina contain a number of letters written between family members, particularly between mother and daughter. Through their correspondence, one can see the formation of multiple families, the role of death and mourning in familial contexts, and the development of the courtship process – life events that both disrupt and create family ties. The Drayton and Glen correspondence, also located at the Irvin Department of Rare Books and Special Collections at the University of South Carolina, reflects the forging and then dissolution of affinal ties. While the two brothers-in-law are intimate friends in Volume 1, doing all they can to help one another in various aspects of professional, social and financial life, their relationship is dissolved in Volume 4 due to tensions over family finances. The

Dolbeare Family Papers from the Massachusetts Historical Society is another collection that is laced through various volumes in this series. In this case, the cruelty of James Dolbeare is evidenced in an abuse warrant, a request for divorce, and in relation to the guardianship of a child. The effect one person can have on dissolving family ties becomes ever-clearer in these manuscripts, since pieces of the story are included in so many different sections of this series. Finally, the Garrettson Family Papers from the United Methodist Archives and History Center at Drew University, in conjunction with the Shippen Family Papers from the Library of Congress, depict the power of sibling relationships when dealing with matters of family tension and conflict. The types of connections just described here underscore the fact that family relationships were multifaceted affairs. In this way, though race and religion each have a section in Volume 1, racial and religious differences are noted throughout the volumes. Similarly, while Volume 4 contains an in-depth discussion of familial conflict, the possibility for discord is evidenced by documents in the other volumes as well.

The series relies heavily on manuscript sources never previously edited or published, supplemented by selected print sources such as sermons and advice literature and out-of-print published diaries and letters. Documents that could be reproduced in their entirety were given priority. When viable, family and personal accounts covering a variety of social and regional backgrounds were used. As far as possible, the original text has been left unchanged. When necessary, abbreviated words were expanded using typical transcription standards, pre-Julian calendar dates have been clarified, and difficult passages have been explained in the headnotes and annotations.

The series' connections to existing digital collections will be particularly useful to scholars and instructors. The personal, unique, and difficult-to-access nature of most of these manuscripts make a great source for those who rely on collections more readily available via large digital databases. While we use some pieces found online, the headnotes and annotations bring these pieces into dialogue with each other – across diverse and rarely connected databases – and with sources found only in archives. Additionally, the reproduction of published English prescriptive works such as sermons, while often available via institutional subscriptions to the *Eighteenth-Century Catalogue Online*, are rendered more useful for study and instruction by putting them side-by-side with records of family practices and with comparative published American works.

Life in the Long Eighteenth Century

While surveys of eighteenth-century society are included in each of the series introductions, as well as the headnotes and annotations composed for each document, they do not individually capture all of the general factors that shaped and influenced family life depicted in these volumes. When considering the collection of family snapshots that are woven throughout this series, therefore, it is important to recognize that each image was taken against a backdrop of other social, political and economic changes. In particular, the shaping of family economics by globalization, the hierarchies of race and gender, and demographic shifts impacted families from all regions.

Families in England and in America earned a living through a variety of means; the families in these pages worked as glaziers, preachers, planation-owners, politicians, authors, artists, farmers and shipwrights. In addition, most families made ends meet by combining these occupations with a variety of home-based industry and food production, much of which was unremunerated. One man's reminiscences of his childhood in eighteenth-century Wales would have been familiar to families on both sides of the Atlantic. When he was a child Richard Jones's family 'faced ... starvation after a disastrous harvest'. He recalled his mother's words to his father:

> 'I'll make a bargain with thee; I'll see to food for us both and the children all winter, if thou, in addition to looking after the horse, the cattle and pigs, wilt do the churning, wash-up, make the bed and clean the house. I'll make the butter myself.' 'How wilt thou manage?' asked my father ... 'I will knit', said she, 'We have wool. If thou wilt card it, I'll spin.' The bargain was struck; my father did the housework in addition to the work on the farm and my mother knitted ... And so it was she kept us alive until the next harvest.'[10]

By the mid-1600s half of the English population were employed in wage labour, but few made enough to survive on since it was seasonal agricultural work. 'Paid work was not, therefore, a living in itself, but simply a vital cash supplement to a subsistence based on the cultivation of cottage gardens and the exploitation of common rights.'[11] Families combined agricultural work with cottage industries that required the labour of all family members. Indeed, long before the eighteenth century most families had come to rely upon a combination of agricultural, home production and cottage industry. For example, David Manner, from whose diary a selection appears in Volume 3, earned his keep by blacksmithing, surveying property lines and writing wills. Even among the gentry, young women contributed to the household economy via handiwork and account management, as Anne Tracy's diary and the recipe books of the Hornyold-Clough women (Volume 3) demonstrate. In speaking of this subject, Steve Hindle has noted, 'by the mid-sixteenth century, perhaps one in six adult males and one in three children and adult women drew their livelihoods from textile production in the cradles of rural industry'.[12] These patterns continued to affect both English and Anglo-American families in the eighteenth century. In America, however, the various colonial contexts shaped a different family labour structure. As Rosemary O'Day described it,

> In the South this [family/household labour system] was based upon, first, indentured white servitude, and second, black slavery, always assisted by family labour; in New England upon family, and secondarily, upon wage labour; in the Middle Colonies ... upon a mixture of immigrant servant and slave labour with family and wage labour.[13]

This series follows this general pattern – there are records of North Carolina indentured labour, Kentucky and South Carolina slavery, and New England family businesses.

This shared responsibility for the household economy did not reduce the gendering and racializing of labour within families and households. In many ways early industrialization and capitalism actually 'increased rather than decreased many women's economic contributions to their households', but that type of labour was simultaneously 'rendered invisible as work'.[14] Additionally, while enslaved people's labour was essential to slave-owning family economics, slaves' ability to form independent households/families was entirely 'at the sufferance of the master'.[15] Mumbet's experience, found in Volume 1, highlights this. She was initially enslaved, but once she was freed she worked for and became part of the Sedgwick family. Eventually she was able to buy and establish her own little home.

In the eyes of the law – both canon and civil – men embodied family power. This was particularly true for Protestant and land-owning men in England and for white and land-owning men in America. The reality, however, was more complicated. Enlightenment ideals and post-Reformation ideas more generally highlighted long-standing tensions between individuality and family governance, between equality and hierarchy.[16] Family negotiation of the division of labour and goods and services rarely matched the simple formulation of family governance found in advice manuals. Each volume's combination of prescriptive literature and accounts of lived experience consistently highlight this gap.

Over the course of the long eighteenth century the advantages men, particularly socially prosperous men, had were consistently questioned and even began to erode. Previous assumptions that disadvantaged dissenting Protestants, Catholics, slaves, freed Blacks, Jews, women, the poor and children were questioned from various political, religious and social groups. By no means were these questions settled by 1820, but if just two examples can be cited, the British abolition of the slave trade and the acceptance of religious, not just Protestant, plurality in America underscore the very different terrain families occupied in 1820 versus 1690. The acceptance of mixed-race Dido Belle in an aristocratic family at the end of the eighteenth century (Volume 1) is just one example of the changing landscape families occupied.

The increased global connections of the eighteenth century meant that more families participated – directly or indirectly – in global markets. Slavery, and the attendant racial mixing it brought to American and English families, was just one of these manifestations. The increased amount of commercial goods and 'comforts' changed the homes people lived in. Household 'stuff' had always been important for household formation, but in the eighteenth century there was more stuff to be had and more cash with which to purchase it. Simultaneously, privacy became increasingly important to notions of personal development and house construction.[17] Globalization also brought a more varied diet and the development of national cuisines. These trends, along with the discovery of inoculation, improved the overall health of the populace, but they also required new kinds of labour from family members – someone had to care for, clean and store all that 'stuff'. The management of household goods and services is highlighted in Volume 3, but the other volumes also reveal how global connections and the increased number of household goods affected families of various social strata. For example, marriage settlements between South Carolina and London gentry provided for the long-term circulation of family wealth and goods across the Atlantic (Volume 1).

Some of that household 'stuff' is what allows this series to reflect so many intimate snapshots of family life. Paper and ink and the space to store them and use them increased over the century. The diarists, letter-writers and authors included in this series benefited from this increased access to the means to record and preserve their thoughts. Additionally, eighteenth-century improvements in transportation and communication, along with expanding educational opportunities and literacy, allowed families to stay in contact across great distances and across time. Letters that flowed between households and diary pages filled with the longings and struggles of individuals survive in greater numbers for all segments of society and for all family members. Without families' greater access to the means of historical preservation we would have no knowledge of Anne Tracy Travell's youthful concerns (Volume 3), Jane Parminter's creation of a cousin-based family (Volume 1), and William Nunwick's failed love affair (Volume 2).

In addition to these general similarities, there were stark differences between America and England and between regions within each country. The importance of slavery and the greater mixing of races and ethnicities in American families have already been mentioned. There were also enormous variations in demographics within and between groups. Both places inherited the Northwest marriage pattern that typified England and much of north-western Europe since the middle ages. The pattern, unique in the pre-modern world, was based on late first-marriage age for women (early-to-mid-twenties instead of mid-teens) and a similarity of ages between men and women at first marriage. Related to these factors was the prevalence of neo-local households upon marriage, instead of joining an existing household as was the norm for early-marriage societies. Additionally, employment patterns reflected a late-marriage age, particularly for women. Young women in north-western Europe left home in their mid-teens for employment just as their brothers did. The economic independence this engendered – in fact required – from both young women and men put their lives on parallel tracks. This, in turn, meant they established homes based more on partnership (though an unequal one) than the more strictly generationally hierarchical households found in southern and eastern Europe. While there were numerous local variations and individuals would experience a variety of household types over their lifetime, this general pattern had already influenced the development of religious, economic, social and political institutions in America and England.[18] Echoes of the north-western marriage pattern can be found throughout this series; Martha Cooper Allinson, who did not marry until she was twenty-eight, was advised by her father not to rush into marriage, but rather to wait to find a spouse who would be an equal (Volume 4). And despite being forty-five when he married, Thomas Sharp's siblings still felt it their duty to insist he and his wife have their own household, instead of continuing to share a home with his brother and sister-in-law (Volume 4).

As hinted at by the example of the Sharp family, marriage was not a given for many people in early modern England. Though the marriage rate fluctuated between 1690 and 1820, before the middle of the eighteenth century as many as 10–25 per cent of the population never married.[19] In the middle of the century rates dropped to 4 per cent, but for those born in the latter half of the eighteenth century and in the early nineteenth century, never-married rates went back up to between 6 per cent and 8 per cent.[20] Those who did marry did so relatively late. For those born in the first half of the eighteenth century, the average marriage age for women was over twenty-six and nearly twenty-eight for men. Marriage ages dropped to just over twenty-three and almost twenty-seven (respectively) in the latter half of the century.[21] The population was young – over 40 per cent throughout the period covered here, were between twenty-five and fifty-nine years old.[22] Despite this overall youthful population, childhood, particularly the first year of life, was fraught with danger. Around 15–20 per cent of children did not survive to their first birthday – though the rate fell as the eighteenth century progressed. Similarly, an additional 11–14 per cent of children died before their tenth birthday. This meant that approximately a third of children did not survive to adolescence.[23] Therefore, eighteenth-century households typically had only 4–5 members. Additionally, older children left home in their teens for employment elsewhere. Volume 4's discussion of death and mourning show the emotional and material impact of these statistics. Similarly, Sarah Drinkwater's will (Volume 2) demonstrates both the expectation that young people would leave home for training and education and the reality that death constantly shaped children's family relationships.

The demographic situation in the American colonies was quite different. Discovering historical demography for colonial and early republic America is also more difficult due to 'inadequate sources' and the 'wide regional variations that existed'.[24] For example, in Massachusetts before 1750 the age at first marriage for men was similar to their English counterparts, but age at first marriage for women was substantially lower, averaging somewhere between nineteen and twenty-three.[25] Virginian and Maryland women similarly married relatively young, as young as sixteen in Maryland before 1700, but Quaker women in the middle colonies married at ages more like English women.[26] While death stalked all eighteenth-century homes, some American colonies faced extreme difficulties. For example, in the middle of the eighteenth century in Christ Church Parish, South Carolina, of those men who lived to their twenty-fifth birthday, 85 per cent would die before their fiftieth.[27] In general, American household-families had more members than English contemporaries, particularly when enslaved members of the household are accounted for.[28]

Overall, in both England and America, the demographic fluidity diminished over the course of the eighteenth century. By the turn of the century both countries were experiencing what has been called the 'demographic transition'. This transition saw the end of 'boom-bust' population fluctuations and the beginning of the sustained population growth that typifies the modern west. Initially this was characterized by a declining mortality rate and booming fertility rate – both legitimate and illegitimate. Overtime, families controlled their fertility and population growth slowed and stabilized.[29] One consequence of this demographic shift for families was that more individuals had living kin throughout their lives. While in the seventeenth century a sixty-year-old English man or woman might expect to have between fifteen and sixteen living relatives (descendants, ancestors and lateral kin), in the eighteenth century they could expect almost twenty-six living relatives.[30] Therefore the families described in this series had a more varied and complicated kinship network to negotiate than their ancestors did.

These impressionistic, broad strokes about family economics and demographics coloured eighteenth-century family life. What follows places a series of intimate snapshots against that broad background to illuminate the way families responded to and shaped the world around them. From Anna Letitia Barbauld writing for the children she didn't have (Volume 1) to the Wentworths flinging sexual insults across the court (Volume 2), and from three generations of Hornyold-Clough women preciously preserving recipes and remedies, ensuring their transmission to future generations (Volume 3) to Martha Allinson conscientiously memorializing her father (Volume 4), we have arranged these snapshots into a picture made visible only with the passage of time. We hope it is a picture they would recognize and appreciate.

Notes
1. L. Stone, *The Family, Sex and Marriage in England, 1500–1800* (New York, NY: Harper and Row, 1977), p. 3.
2. S. Ozment, *Ancestors: The Loving Family in Old Europe* (Cambridge, MA: Harvard University Press, 2001), pp. 111–12.

3. D. Kertzer and M. Barbagli (eds), *The History of the European Family*, 3 vols (New Haven, CT, and London: Yale University Press, 2001-3).
4. A short sampling includes J. Bailey, *Parenting in England c. 1760–1830: Emotions, Self-Identities and Generations* (Oxford: Oxford University Press, 2012); L. Davidoff, *Thicker than Water: Siblings and their Relations, 1780–1920* (Oxford: Oxford University Press, 2012); L. Glover, *All Our Relations: Ties and Emotional Bonds among the Early South Carolina Gentry* (Baltimore, MD: Johns Hopkins University Press, 2000); N. Tadmor, *Family and Friends in Eighteenth-Century England: Household, Kinship, and Patronage* (Cambridge: Cambridge University Press, 2001).
5. C. Daniels and M. V. Kennedy (eds), *Over the Threshold: Intimate Violence in Early America* (New York: Routledge, 1999); K. Wulf, *Not All Wives: Women of Colonia Philadelphia* (Cornell Universitiy Press, 2000); J. Bailey, *Unquiet Lives: Marriage and Marriage Breakdown in England, 1600–1800* (Cambridge: Cambridge University Press, 2003); S. Ottoway, *The Decline of Life: Old Age in Eighteenth-Century England* (Cambridge: Cambridge University Press, 2004); E. Pleck, *Domestic Tyranny: The Making of Social Policy against Family Violence from Colonial Times to the Present* (Champaign, IL: University of Illinois Press, 2004); A. Froide, *Never Married: Singlewomen in Early Modern England* (Oxford: Oxford University Press, 2007); A. Fletcher, *Growing Up in England: The Experience of Childhood, 1600–1914* (New Haven, CT: Yale University Press, 2008).
6. P. Crawford, *The Parents of Poor Children in England, 1580–1800* (Oxford: Oxford University Press, 2010); C. Dallett Hemphill, *Siblings: Brothers and Sisters in American History* (Oxford: Oxford University Press, 2011); S. Pearsall, *Atlantic Families: Lives and Letters in the Later Eighteenth Century* (Oxford: Oxford University Press, 2008).
7. H. Brewer, *By Birth or Consent: Children, Law, and the Anglo-American Revolution in Authority* (North Carolina, 2005); M. S. Hartman, *The Household and the Making of History: A Subversive View of the Western Past* (Cambridge, 2004); R. Perry, *Novel Relations: The Transformation of Kinship in English Literature and Culture 1748–1818* (Cambridge, 2004).
8. For a selection of those earlier works see R. H. Bremmer, *Children and Youth in America: A Documentary History* (Cambridge, MA: Harvard University Press, 1970); L. Pollock (ed.), *A Lasting Relationship: Parents and Children over Three Centuries* (University of New England Press, 1987); Ralph Houlbrooke, *English Family Life, 1576–1716* (Oxford University Press, 1989).
9. For recent related collections of documents covering family life see C. Nelson et al. (eds), *British Family Life, 1780–1914* (London: Pickering & Chatto, 2012); A. Popp (ed.), *Entrepreneurial Families: Business, Marriage and Life in the Early Nineteenth Century* (London: Pickering & Chatto, 2012); and K. Stierstorfer et al. (eds), *Women Writing Home, 1700–1920* (London: Pickering & Chatto, 2006).
10. B. Hill, *Women, Work, and Sexual Politics in Eighteenth-Century England* (New York: Routledge, 1989).
11. S. Hindle, *On the Parish? The Micro-Politics of Poor Relief in Rural England c. 1550–1750* (Oxford: Clarendon Press, 2004), p. 22.
12. Hindle, *On the Parish?*, p. 23.
13. R. O'Day, *The Family and Family Relationships, 1500–1900: England, France, and the United States of America* (New York: St Martin's Press, 1994), p. 192.
14. C. Karlsen, 'Women and Gender', in D. Vickers (ed.), *A Companion to Colonial America* (Malden, MA: Blackwell, 2003), pp. 194–235, on p. 205.
15. E. Fox-Genovese, *Within the Plantation Household: Black and White Women of the Old*

South (Chapel Hill, NC: University of North Carolina Press, 1988), p. 94.
16. M. Hartman, *The Household and the Making of History: A Subversive View of the Western Past* (Cambridge: Cambridge University Press, 2004); A. Harris, *Siblinghood and Social Relations in Georgian England: Share and Share Alike* (Manchester: Manchester University Press, 2012).
17. W. Rybczynski, *Home: A Short History of an Idea* (Penguin Books, 1987), pp. 15–49; R. Sarti, *Europe at Home: Family and Material Culture, 1500–1800*, trans. A. Cameron (New Haven, CT: Yale University Press, 2002).
18. Hartman, *The Household and the Making of History*.
19. For the birth cohorts born between the 1660s and 1670s (and coming of age at the end of the seventeenth century), as many as 25 per cent of the population never married. Though this number is probably exaggerated, considering the lack of surviving marriage records for some people and the unregulated nature of many marriages before Lord Hardwick's Act of 1753, it still reflect a high rate of never-married people. For those born slightly later in the century, and coming of age in the 1710s and 1720s, as many as 15–19 per cent never married. For cohorts coming of age in the 1730s and through the 1750s, the rate of never married was still averaging above 10 per cent. In the middle of the eighteenth century, however, rates dropped significantly – dipping in the 1780s to less than 4 per cent. See E. A. Wrigley and R. S. Schofield, *The Population History of England, 1541–1871, A Reconstruction* (Cambridge: Cambridge University Press, 1989), p. 260.
20. E. A. Wrigley and R. S. Schofield, *The Population History of England, 1541–1871, A Reconstruction* (Cambridge: Cambridge University Press, 1989), p. 260.
21. Laslett, *World We Have Lost*, p. 112.
22. P. Laslett, *World We Have Lost: England Before the Industrial Age*, 3rd edn (New York: Scribner's, 1984), p. 111.
23. Laslett, *World We Have Lost*, p. 112.
24. R. V. Wells, 'The Population of England's Colonies in America: Old English or New Americans?' *Population Studies*, 46:1 (March 1992), pp. 85–102, on p. 87.
25. Wells, 'The Population of England's Colonies in America', p. 88.
26. For Quakers in the middle colonies before 1730 the average age at first marriage for men was 26.5 and 22 for women. Mid-century it was nearly 26 and nearly 23 – and it increased slightly by the end of the century. Virginia's women married between 20 and 22 between 1710 and 1839. There are limited statistics for men, but in at least one county they married before 25 on average. Maryland women married as young as 16 before 1700 and averaged between 18 and 22 for the eighteenth century. The limited data for men before 1750 suggest they married before they were 24 in one county, but the age went up over the century from 23 to nearly 26 on the western shore. Wells, 'The Population of England's Colonies in America', pp. 88–9.
27. L. Glover, *All Our Relations: Blood Ties and Emotional Bonds among the Early South Carolina Gentry* (Baltimore, MD: Johns Hopkins University Press, 2000), pp. 5–6.
28. P. Greven, 'The Average Size of Families and Households in the Province of Massachusetts in 1764 and in the United States in 1790: An Overview', in P. Laslett and R. Wall (eds), *Household and Family in Past Time* (Cambridge: Cambridge University Press, 1972), pp. 549–50.
29. P. P. Viazzo, 'Mortality, Fertility, and Family', in Kertzer and Barbagli (eds), *The History of the European Family*, vol. 1, *Family Life in Early Modern Times* (New Haven, CT, and London: Yale University Press, 2003), pp. 157–87, on p. 157.
30. Viazzo, 'Mortality Fertility, and Family', p. 183.

BIBLIOGRAPHY

Abbott, M., *Family Ties: English Families 1540–1920* (London: Routledge, 1993).

Adams, J., *The Familial State: Ruling Families and Merchant Capitalism in Early Modern Europe* (Ithaca, NY: Cornell University Press, 2005).

Addy, J., *Death, Money and the Vultures: Inheritance and Avarice, 1660–1750* (London: Routledge, 1992).

Andrew, D. T., *Aristocratic Vice: The Attack on Duelling, Suicide, Adultery, and Gambling in Eighteenth-Century England* (London: Yale University Press, 2013).

Aveling, D. H., 'The Marriages of Catholic Recusants, 1559–1642', *Journal of Ecclesiastical History*, 14 (1963), pp. 68–83.

Backscheider, P., *Eighteenth-Century Women Poets and their Poetry: Inventing Agency, Inventing Genre* (Baltimore, MD: Johns Hopkins University Press, 2005).

Bailey, J., 'The History of Mum and Dad: Recent Historical Research on Parenting in England from the 16th to 20th Centuries', *History Compass*, 12:6 (June 2014), pp. 489–507.

—, *Unquiet Lives: Marriage and Marriage Breakdown in England, 1660–1800* (Cambridge: Cambridge University Press, 2003).

Bannet, E. T., *The Empire of Letters: Letter Manuals and Transatlantic Correspondence, 1688–1820* (Cambridge: Cambridge University Press, 2005).

Ben-Amos, I. K., *Human Bonding: Parents and their Offspring in Early Modern England* (Oxford: Oxford University Press, 1997).

Bennett, J. M., and A. M. Froide (eds), *Singlewomen in the European Past, 1250–1800* (Philadelphia, PA: University of Pennsylvania Press, 1999).

Berry, H., and E. Foyster (eds), *The Family in Early Modern England* (Cambridge: Cambridge University Press, 2007).

Block, S., *Rape and Sexual Power in Early America* (Chapel Hill, NC: University of North Carolina Press, 2006).

Brant, C., *Eighteenth-Century Letters and British Culture* (Houndmills: Palgrave, 2006).

Bremner, R. H. (ed.), *Children and Youth in America: A Documentary History, Volume I: 1600–1865* (Cambridge, MA: Harvard University Press, 1970).

Brewer, H., *By Birth or Consent: Children, Law, and the Anglo-American Revolution in Authority* (Chapel Hill, NC: University of North Carolina Press, 2005).

Brown, K. M., *Good Wives, Nasty Wenches, and Anxious Patriarchs: Gender, Race, and Power in Colonial Virginia* (Chapel Hill, NC: University of North Carolina Press, 1996).

Brundage, A., *The English Poor Laws, 1700–1930* (New York: Palgrave, 2002).

Carter, P., *Men and the Emergence of Polite Society, Britain 1660–1800* (Harlow: Pearson Education Ltd, 2001).

Chambers, L., *Liberty, A Better Husband: Single Women in America: The Generations of 1780–1840* (New Haven, CT: Yale University Press, 1984).

Chedgzoy, K., *Women's Writing in the British Atlantic World: Memory, Place and History, 1550–1700* (Cambridge: Cambridge University Press, 2007).

Clement, P., *Welfare and the Poor in the Nineteenth Century City: Philadelphia, 1800–1845* (Rutherford, NJ: Fairleigh Dickinson University Press, 1985).

Cody, L. F., *Birthing the Nation: Sex, Science, and the Conception of Eighteenth-Century Britons* (Oxford: Oxford University Press, 2005).

Connell, R., *Gender and Power: Society, the Person, and Sexual Politics* (Sydney: Allen & Unwin, 1987).

Coontz, S., *Marriage, a History: From Obedience to Intimacy or How Love Conquered Marriage* (New York: Viking, 2005).

Coster, W., *Family and Kinship in England 1450–1800* (Harlow: Longman, 2001).

Cowgill, U. M., 'People of York: 1538–1812', *Scientific American*, 222 (1970), pp. 104–12.

Crawford, P., *Parents of Poor Children in England, 1580–1800* (Oxford: Oxford University Press, 2010).

Crowley, J. E., *The Invention of Comfort: Sensibilities and Design in Early Modern Britain and Early America* (Baltimore, MD: Johns Hopkins University Press, 2001).

Culley, A., *British Women's Life Writing, 1600–1840* (Basingstoke: Palgrave Macmillan, 2014).

Davidoff, L., and C. Hall, *Family Fortunes: Men and Women of the English Middle Class, 1780–1850* (Chicago, IL: The University of Chicago Press, 1987).

Erickson, A. L., *Women and Property in Early Modern England* (New York: Routledge, 1995).

Evans, T., '"Unfortunate Objects": London's Unmarried Mothers in the Eighteenth Century', *Gender & History*, 17 (2005), pp. 127–53.

Fletcher, A., *Gender, Sex and Subordination in England 1500–1800* (New Haven, CT: Yale University Press, 1995).

—, *Growing up in England: The Experience of Childhood, 1600–1914* (New Haven, CT: Yale University Press, 2008).

Foyster, E., 'A Laughing Matter? Marital Discord and Gender Control in Seventeenth-Century England', *Rural History*, 4 (1993), pp. 5–21.

—, *Marital Violence: An English Family History, 1660–1857* (New York: Cambridge University Press, 2005).

Freedman, R., and L. Coombs, 'Childspacing and Family Economic Position', *American Sociological Review*, 31 (1966), pp. 631–48.

Froide, A. M., *Never Married: Singlewomen in Early Modern England*. (Oxford: Oxford University Press, 2005).

Fryer, P., *Staying Power: The History of Black People in Britain* (London: Pluto Press, 1984).

Gerzina, G., *Black London: Life Before Emancipation* (New Brunswick, NJ: Rutgers University Press, 1995).

Gillis, J., *For Better, For Worse: British Marriages, 1600 to the Present* (New York: Oxford University Press, 1985).

Greven, P., *The Protestant Temperament: Patterns of Child-Rearing, Religious Experience, and the Self in Early America* (Chicago, IL: The University of Chicago Press, 1977).

Glover, L., *All Our Relations: Blood Ties and Emotional Bonds among the Early South Carolina Gentry* (Baltimore, MD, and London: Johns Hopkins University Press, 2000).

Harris, A., *Siblinghood and Social Relations in Georgian England: Share and Share Alike* (Manchester: Manchester University Press, 2012).

Hartman, M. S., *The Household and the Making of History: A Subversive View of the Western Past* (Cambridge: Cambridge University Press, 2004).

Hemphill, C. D., *Siblings: Brothers and Sisters in American History* (New York, Oxford University Press, 2011).

Hendricks, M., and P. Parker (eds), *Women, 'Race', and Writing in the Early Modern Period* (London: Routledge, 1994).

Hill, B., *Women Alone: Spinsters in England 1660–1850* (New Haven, CT: Yale University Press, 2001).

—, *Women, Work, and Sexual Politics in Eighteenth-Century England* (Oxford: Basil Blackwell, 1989).

Hilton, M., and J. Shefrin (eds), *Educating the Child in Enlightenment Britain: Beliefs, Cultures, Practices* (Burlington, VT: Ashgate, 2009).

Hindle, S., *On the Parish? The Micro-Politics of Poor Relief in Rural England c. 1550–1750* (Oxford: Clarendon Press, 2004).

—, '"Without the Cry of Any Neighbours": A Cumbrian Family and the Poor Law Authorities, c. 1690–1730,' in H. Berry and E. Foyster (eds), *The Family in Early Modern England* (Cambridge: Cambridge University Press, 2007), pp. 126–157.

Hoffer, P. C., and N. E. H. Hull, *Murdering Mothers: Infanticide in England and New England 1558–1803* (New York: New York University Press, 1984).

Houlbrooke, R., *Death, Religion and the Family in England 1480–1750* (Oxford: Clarendon Press, 1998).

Hudson, L. E., *To Have And To Hold: Slave Work And Family Life In Antebellum South Carolina* (Athens, GA: University of Georgia Press, 1997).

Hufton, O., 'Women and the Family Economy in Eighteenth-Century France' (Paper presented at the Conference of the Society for French Historical Studies at Johns Hopkins University, March 1974).

Hunt, M., 'Wife Beating, Domesticity and Women's Independence in Eighteenth-Century London', *Gender and History*, 4 (1992), pp. 10–33.

Hussey, D., and M. Ponsonby (eds), *Buying for the Home: Shopping for the Domestic from the Seventeenth Century to the Present* (Burlington, VT: Ashgate, 2008).

Jackson, M., *New-Born Child Murder: Women, Illegitimacy and the Courts in Eighteenth-Cen-*

tury England (Manchester: Manchester University Press, 1996).

Johnson, C. H., and D. W. Sabean (eds), *Sibling Relations and the Transformations of European Kinship, 1300–1900* (New York: Berghahn Books, 2011).

Kertzer, D. I., and M. Barbagli (eds), *The History of the European Family: Volume 1 Family Life in Early Modern Times 1500–1789* (New Haven, CT: Yale University Press, 2001).

Kete, M., *Sentimental Collaboration: Mourning and Middle Class Identity in Nineteenth Century America* (Durham, NC: Duke University Press, 2000).

Laslett, P., *The World We Have Lost: England before the Industrial Age* (New York: Charles Scribner's Sons, 1984).

Lawrence, A., *One Family Under God: Love, Belonging, and Authority in Early Transatlantic Methodism* (Philadelphia, PA: University of Pennsylvania Press, 2011).

Lees, L. H., *The Solidarities of Strangers: The English Poor Laws and the People, 1700–1948* (New York: Cambridge University Press, 1998).

Levy, B. *Quakers and the American Family: British Quakers in the Delaware Valley, 1650–1765* (New York: Oxford University Press, 1988).

Mack, P., *Heart Religion in the British Enlightenment: Gender and Emotion in Early Methodism* (New York: Cambridge University Press, 2008).

McCarthy, W., *Anna Letitia Barbauld: Voice of the Enlightenment* (Baltimore, MD: Johns Hopkins University Press, 2008).

Muldrew, C., *The Economy of Obligation: The Culture of Credit and Social Relations in Early Modern England* (New York: Palgrave, 1998).

Nelson, L. P., *Beauty of Holiness: Anglicanism and Architecture in Colonial South Carolina.* (Chapel Hill, NC: University of North Carolina Press, 2009).

Newton, H., *The Sick Child in Early Modern England, 1580–1720* (Oxford: Oxford University Press, 2012).

O'day, R., *The Family and Family Relationships, 1500–1900: England, France, and the United States of America* (New York: St Martin's Press, 1994).

O'Malley, A., *The Making of the Modern Child: Children's Literature and Childhood in the Late Eighteenth Century* (New York: Routledge, 2003).

Ottaway, S. R., *The Decline of Life: Old Age in Eighteenth-Century England* (Cambridge: Cambridge University Press, 2004).

Pahl, J., *Empire of Sacrifice: The Religious Origins of American Violence* (New York: New York University Press, 2010).

Pearsall, S. M. S., *Atlantic Families: Lives and Letters in the Later Eighteenth Century* (Oxford: Oxford University Press, 2008).

Perry, R., *Novel Relations: The Transformation of Kinship in English Literature and Culture, 1748–1818* (Cambridge: Cambridge University Press, 2004).

Pleck, E., *Domestic Tyranny: The Making of American Social Policy against Family Violence from Colonial Times to the Present* (Urbana, IL: University of Illinois Press, 1987).

Pollock, L. A., *Forgotten Children: Parent–Child Relations from 1500 to 1900* (Cambridge: Cambridge University Press, 1983).

Retford, K., *The Art of Domestic Life: Family Portraiture in Eighteenth-Century England* (New

Haven, CT: Yale University Press, 2006).

Reynolds, P. L. (ed.), *To Have and to Hold: Marrying and its Documentation in Western Christendom, 400–1600* (Cambridge: Cambridge University Press, 2007).

Rowlands, M. (ed.), *English Catholics of Parish and Town 1558–1778*, CRS Monograph Series 5 (London: Hobbs the Printers, Ltd, 1999).

Schurer, K., and T. Arkell (eds), *Surveying the People: The Interpretation and Use of Document Sources for the Study of Population in the Later Seventeenth Century* (Great Britain: A Local Population Studies Supplement, 1992).

Stannard, D., *The Puritan Way of Death: A Study in Religion, Culture, and Social Change* (New York: Oxford University Press, 1977).

Stone, L., *Road to Divorce: England, 1530–1987* (New York: Oxford University Press, 1990).

—, *Uncertain Unions: Marriage in England 1660–1753* (Oxford: Oxford University Press, 1992).

Tadmor, N., *Family and Friends in Eighteenth-Century England: Household, Kinship, and Patronage* (New York: Cambridge University Press, 2001).

—, 'Women and Wives: the Language of Marriage in Early Modern English Biblical Translations', *History Workshop Journal*, 62 (2006), pp. 1–28.

Tague, I. H., *Women of Quality: Accepting and Contesting Ideals of Femininity in England, 1690–1760* (Woodbridge, Suffolk: Boydell Press, 2002).

Tate, W. E., *The Parish Chest: A Study of the Records of Parochial Administration in England* (Chicester, West Sussex: Phillimore, 1983).

Taves, A., *Religion and Domestic Violence in Early New England: The Memoirs of Abigail Abbot Bailey* (Bloomington and Indianapolis, IN: Indiana University Press, 1989).

Thompson, H., 'Family Matters', *Eighteenth-Century Studies*, 40 (2007), pp. 476–82. doi: 10.1353/ecs.2007.0033.

Turner, D. M., *Disability in Eighteenth-Century England: Imagining Physical Impairment*, Routledge Studies in Modern British History Series (New York: Routledge, 2012).

Underwood, J. L., and W. L. Burke, *The Dawn of Religious Freedom in South Carolina*. (Columbia, SC: University of South Carolina Press, 2006).

Vickery, A., *The Gentleman's Daughter: Women's Lives in Georgian England* (New Haven, CT: Yale University Press, 1998).

Volo, J., and D. D. Volo., *Family Life in 17th and 18th Century America* (Westport, CT: Greenwood Press, 2006).

Walker, E. C., *Marriage, Writing, and Romanticism: Wordsworth and Austen after War* (Stanford, CA: Stanford University Press, 2009).

Ward, B., M. Bone and W. A. Link (eds), *The American South and the Atlantic World* (Gainesville, FL: The University Press of Florida, 2013).

Weil, F., *Family Trees: A History of Genealogy in America* (Cambridge, MA: Harvard University Press, 2013).

West, E., *Family or Freedom: People of Color in the Antebellum South* (Lexington, KY: The University Press of Kentucky, 2012).

Wilson, A., *The Making of Man-Midwifery: Childbirth in England, 1660–1770* (Cambridge,

MA: Harvard University Press, 1995).

Wilson, L., *A History of Stepfamilies in Early America* (Chapel Hill, NC: University of North Carolina Press, 2014).

Wrightson, K., *Earthly Necessities: Economic Lives in Early Modern Britain*. (New Haven, CT: Yale University Press, 2000).

Wrigley, E. A., and R. S. Schofield, *The Population History of England, 1541–1871, A Reconstruction* (Cambridge, MA: Harvard University Press 1989).

Wrigley, E. A., R. S. Davies, J. E. Oeppen and R. S. Schofield (eds), *English Population History from Family Reconstitution: 1580–1837* (New York: Cambridge University Press, 1997).

Wulf, K., *Not All Wives: Women of Colonial Philadelphia* (Itahca, NY: Cornell University Press, 2000).

Wyatt-Brown, B., *Southern Honor: Ethics and Behavior in the Old South* (New York: Oxford University Press, 2007).

INTRODUCTION

'Family', according to Samuel Johnson, was comprised of 'those who live in the same house'.[1] This mid-eighteenth-century definition of the family as an architecturally delineated group indicates that family was perceived as including more members than the modern concept of the nuclear family. Naomi Tadmor has labelled the eighteenth-century household, 'including its diverse dependents, such as servants, apprentices and co-resident relatives' as the 'household family'.[2] This household family was comprised of people related through blood, such as children, as well as lineage family members like grandparents, uncles, aunts, cousins and other extended kin relations, and people unrelated, but co-resident, who were contractually part of the family, such as servants, apprentices and even a spouse, all of whom may not have resided in the house continuously.[3] The household family, according to Tadmor, 'was an organizational unity that underwent many changes'.[4] This fluid nature of the household family – in other words, who was included or excluded – and in particular the role religion, race and socio-economic conditions played in ordering or disrupting the household family are the topics of 'Volume 1: Many Families' in the *Family Life in England and America, 1690–1820* series.

As an organizational unity, the household family was considered the foundation of English and American, or Atlantic, society.[5] Household families lived in towns and parishes, on plantations, farms and country estates, yet all performed similar roles in household family maintenance. Eve Tavor Bannet described the household family as 'urban and rural society's most basic economic and administrative unit: under the jurisdiction of its master, the household-family was supposed to feed, employ, sustain, socialize, discipline and govern all its members'.[6] Authority-based, the household family was hierarchical, yet open-ended in the varieties of who fulfilled the leadership role when the father was absent or deceased and who the subservient positions, which could be family, servants or friends.[7] The household family took in servants, apprentices and visiting or needy relatives, and sent out fathers to war or on business, children for educational and vocational training or to start their own household family, and unsatisfactory or time-completed dependents. Death constantly altered and affected the household family composition and financial situation.[8] At times, the household family could be geographically separated, even across national borders, but bound together through kinship and correspondence.[9]

Just as kinship ties could bind a family when not living in the same household, so could relationships, bound by similar occupations or shared religious, charitable, ideological or educational beliefs, forge a strong fictive family relationship.[10] These fictive families often cared for each other financially, physically and emotionally, and even named their consanguineal children after each other. Fictive families could include related and/or non-related friends, who either shared living accommodations, or congregated in a person's home, in a religious structure or in a civic building. Just as the household family was bound together under an authority figure, so too was the fictive family organized, formally by charter or informally by agreement, under an administrative body.[11] Under the guidance and governance of the fictive family leader(s), these fictive families were linked through their family calendar of meetings, celebrated anniversaries, social and service gatherings.[12] When fictive families gathered, they often recorded the exchanged, received or dispersed domestic goods, services and monies they provided or collected for each other or for the objects of their common concern; these interactions created a fictive household economy. This economics of instrumental friendship – the give and take of goods and services – as well as the shared purpose or beliefs strengthened the relationships within the fictive family.[13]

The household family also helped each other, either out of affection or duty, or by contract, and in manifold ways. The household family, Bannet noted, 'often functioned as a bank and insurance company for its members'.[14] Fathers provided dowries for or bequeathed moveable property to daughters and provided training for or bequeathed land and capital for yearly incomes to their sons, and provisioned life interests to maintain their widows. When advice or financial assistance was needed, children could turn to their parents or extended kin. When the household family was unable to provide this assistance, ecclesiastical or benevolent groups intervened. These benevolent groups often organized themselves as a household family, under an authority-based relationship and utilizing the language of kinship. Other failures of the household family, particularly in its monitoring and admonitory functions, concerned ministers, moralists, educational and conduct literature writers.[15]

The first section of this volume presents estate and probate records, family correspondence and printed literature about the many kinds of English and American family household formations. Probate proceedings often affected the future fortunes of the household family. 'Wills', according to one historian, 'were the most important documents that most testators would ever draft'.[16] While wills specify the dispersal of a testator's property and to whom, they also reveal a last attempt to set in motion certain actions, such as an adoption or financial security or parity for family members. Legal adoption did not begin in England until the early twentieth century; in the eighteenth century, extended family kinships often provided heirs for childless couples without formal adoption proceedings. Anna Letitia and Rochemont Barbauld adopted her nephew, Charles, the third son of her brother John Aikin. While not becoming a co-resident child in an extended family's household, as did little Charles, Ward Hallowell changed his name to Ward Nicholas Boylston in order to inherit his maternal uncle's considerable fortune. The wills of John Romans, Jane Parminter and siblings, Berkeley and Jane Seymour demonstrate the flexibility of inheritance practices to aid single siblings, unmarried female kin or younger grandsons when estates were not proscribed by freehold rules.

In addition to legal documents that record the many constructions of families, the private correspondence between family members reveals the broad network of kinship relations in families. Letter writing was important kin-keeping work that provided instrumental and emotional support to family members who were geographically separated or dispersed by schooling, service, apprenticeships, indentures, trade, war, emigration, colonization and government appointments; this was called by contemporaries, 'a good correspondency'.[17] Anne Finch, Countess of Winchelsea (see Volume 2), celebrated epistolary communication with her absent husband in her poem, 'To a Friend, in Praise of the Invention of Writing Letters' (1714). Letter writing was so essential to eighteenth-century communication that letter manuals were one of the most purchased, borrowed and handed-down books during the eighteenth century.[18] Siblings sought advice from other siblings, children from parents and parents-in-law, and brother-in-law from brother-in-law upon finances, courtship, health and social problems. Letters between brothers reveal the growing affective expression of male friendship during the late eighteenth and early nineteenth centuries, while letters between brothers and sisters erase or uphold age- and gender-based hierarchies.[19] In the correspondence between John Drayton and James Glen, brothers-in-law communicated regarding shared family concerns. Thomas and William Rumney were orphaned brothers who wrote to each other about courtship and if their maternal uncle, Edward Clark, who had helped rear them, would approve. The Cox and Chesnut correspondence includes a married daughter, her mother and her father-in-law as writers and recipients. Joshua Lovejoy received letters from his brother, father and a fictive brother.

The literature about multiple families demonstrates how writers defined spiritual, affinal and hierarchical relationships that expanded the household family; these writers focused on educating children in their appropriate behaviour to these many family members. Anna Letitia Barbauld instructed her adopted son, Charles, on how to worship God by showing kindness to God's family in *Hymns in Prose for Children* (1781). The young woman's duties and appropriate behaviour towards the hierarchically ordered household and community family were taught by Ann Murry in her popular conduct book, *Mentoria* (1799), while Jane Davis sought instrumental help in the education and care of her seafaring son through letters to the his captain. Though this literature addressed children, it also indirectly provided instruction to parents on how to teach children to apply their religious beliefs in their quotidian interactions with God's family; therefore, these selections of maternal instruction also reveal how religion shaped household family identity.

The influence of religion on family formation and identity is demonstrated in the second section with selections from parish and probate records, petitions, personal letters and the printed word. In the preface to the first volume of *The Family Expositor, or, A Paraphrase and Version of the New Testament* (1739–56), Philip Doddridge explained that his aim was 'chiefly to promote *family religion*'.[20] The belief that the family was the first religious organization was articulated by writers such as the author of *A Persuasive to Family Religion*: 'Families are *societies* of God's *instituting*, and *prior* to all other *societies*: There the *worship of God began*, and for some time was necessarily *confined* to them.' The family, therefore, was considered the religious foundation of Atlantic society.

The leader of the household family, instead of the Anglican minister, became the primary overseer of daily family worship when the Act of Toleration (1689) discontinued mandatory attendance at Anglican services.[21] Ministers and moralists exhorted parents to reinforce daily at home what was taught weekly at church; sermons and other religious literature were extensively purchased, which demonstrates the role religion played in ordering household family practices.[22] The religious writings of Robert Nelson, David Muir and the anonymous author of the *Cheap Repository Tracts for Sunday Reading* educated parents in their roles as spiritual leaders in their household family.

The Toleration Act also allowed certain Protestant dissenting religions to worship publicly; Protestant household families attended houses of worship called churches, chapels or meeting-houses, while Catholics and other faiths had to continue to meet in private.[23] The many religions of eighteenth-century London were noticed by the Scotsman John Breues in the preface to his publication *The Fortune Hunters* (1754):

> As every Sect of Religion is tolerated here, and endeavours to draw over others to their persuasion, so I judge it a duty incumbent upon every one who professes himself a Christian, not to conceal their principles, nor the foundation thereof, but to declare them without disguise or dissimulation. From this principle I unfolded myself to my countrymen, leaving each of them to a liberty of conscience.[24]

This English liberty of conscience was also celebrated by the anonymous author of *A Persuasive to Family Religion*. In America, Zina Baker Huntington wrote letters that revealed her personal quest for religious identity amidst the religious pluralism of the eighteenth century.

Parliamentary acts also affected how the household family, and the Anglican family in particular, celebrated certain family events. The Haselbury-Plucknett parish registers exemplify how household family events, such as birth, marriage and death, were recorded and observed according to Canon law. Across the Atlantic, marriages in South Carolina were also affected by English Canon law, which invalidated any ceremony conducted by a non-Anglican clergyman; William Tennent III, inspired by the American Revolution for political freedom, delivered a petition to the South Carolina Assembly to request religious freedom and to afford all Christian denominations equal religious privileges to marry and own the churches in which their household families worshipped.

Political events, such as the Jacobite Rebellions of 1715 and 1745, rallied Protestant patriotism by uniting dissenting denomations against the Catholic Stuart claimants to the British throne.[25] In his published sermon of 1744, the Dissenting minister, David Muir, praised his patron's 'inviolable Attachment to the Illustrious House of HANOVER, your Aversion to a *Popish Pretender*, and your known Regard for the Welfare of your Native Country'.[26] Muir also continued with a call 'for PROTESTANTS of all Denominations to unite against POPERY, and all its Abettors, who endeavour to disturb the Peace and Tranquility of this Kingdom'.[27] Protestants unified to contain Catholicism, which, despite discrimination, continued publishing Catholic catechisms and other devotional literature to shape Catholic household family identity.[28] The York Diocesan Recusant Returns of 1767 reveal the continued monitoring of Catholic families until the Popery Act of 1698 was repealed in 1829.

Protestant unity against Catholics, however, did not preclude religious diversity within household families. The influential writer of Anglican literature, Robert Nelson, married Lady Theophila Berkeley Lucy, who had converted to Catholicism during her visit to Rome. Theophila remained true to her converted faith, and even published tracts in its defence.

Religious practices also caused rifts within the congregational family. In South Carolina, Anglican churches enacted in microcosm the Atlantic tensions regarding race and family. Louis P. Nelson observed,

> The presence of blacks at the Communion table had significant implications for the community gathered at or in the chancel. In Communion, participants were to approach the table in humility and in full awareness of their sinful state and their dependence on God's mercy. Thus, communicants found that they were for a brief season all in the same state, with no distinctions separating one from another.[29]

While church ritual appeared to transcend socio-economic and racial barriers, slave owners refused to come to the holy table when slaves were received there.[30] Refusing to accept slaves as equal members of church families, which in the New Testament the Apostle Paul described to the Corinthian Christian community as the 'body of Christ', slave-owning societies also defined and treated slave bodies and slave families as different from and inferior to Anglo-American bodies and families.

Changes in the usage of kinship language also occurred in the age of discovery with early modern encounters with foreign peoples. The meaning of 'race' transformed from referring to a lineage family, such as the genealogy of noble families (a 'noble race'), to biological or phenotypical difference.[31] Enlightenment philosophers altered the Medieval *scala naturae*, or the Great Chain of Being, from a spiritually ordered into a naturally ordered hierarchical system.[32] These natural historians such as Carl von Linné proposed that there was a God-given order to Nature that man could identify and classify.[33] This scientific approach to classification now hierarchically ordered the various races according to 'natural' factors such as biology, climate and intellectual capacity.[34] Legitimated by 'scientific' interpretations of racial difference and perceived as economically profitable, the enslavement of Africans was increasingly legalized in the Atlantic colonies of Britain. 'The primary functions of race prejudice', according to Peter Fryer, were 'economic and political'.[35]

The third section of this volume presents documents that reveal how the eighteenth-century concept of race affected household families in Atlantic British cultures. A variety of documents, handwritten or printed, legal or personal, provide insight into the role race played in the formation, dissolution or preservation of the household family: land deeds, deeds of emancipation, bills of sale, family bibles, wills, county and church records, correspondence, poetry, travel writing, commonplace books and conduct books. With few exceptions, these documents indicate how the emergent concept of race defined personal and family identity before considerations of class, abilities or gender. The writings of the Swedish botanist Pehr Kalm reveal his scientific categorizing by race the various people in America he encountered.

One such population Kalm recorded were Native Americans, or as he described them, 'Old Americans', who had sold most of their coastal lands to the white settlers. About a hundred years before Kalm's tour, British colonists forged alliances with the *Haudenosaunee*, or the League of the Iroquois, for mutual survival against the French and other warring native groups.[36] While the Virginian native tribal leaders created a fictive family relationship with the colonial leader, the Virginian colonist perceived the alliance as a contract of utility.[37] By the early eighteenth century, Anglo-American Virginians wanted land for English Protestant families; the Virginia land deeds record Anglo-American expansion for white household families, while circumscribing the tribal lands of the Nottaways.

James Dolbeare's purchase of slaves, John Beall's will, the George Walker Family plantation appraisal, and the Lancaster, Pennsylvania Returns of Negro and Mulatto children all define black slaves as property and indicate the power slaveholders had over the formation of black household families. Slave families could be residentially separated through sales and testator's bequests, valued only as a means to reproduce their slave labour, or be completely unacknowledged in records that only listed slaves according to sex.[38] Though slaves could not legally marry in America, they nevertheless courted, created families and maintained kinship bonds.[39] Slaveholders often supported these family units and even viewed themselves as the father of their plantation family and conscientiously provided for their white and black dependents. Some slaveholders, however, became conflicted in their duties to their plantation family: the enslaved black members of the plantation family should be treated as people not property, yet fathers were expected to provide an inheritance of future income for their white children, but this income was based on the enslaved labour of these black plantation family members.

The tension between slaves' status as property and people is pervasive in the American documents of the Moore family Bible, Jesse Vick's deed of emancipation, the prefatory material to Phillis Wheatley's *Poems* and the Sedgwick family correspondence. All reveal how some slaveholders or abolitionists acknowledged, to varying extents, black household families or included African Americans as members of their white household family. The list of slave births, while not linked to black lineage families, was written down and included along with another list of Galbreath babies in the Moore family Bible. The state of Virginia allowed slaveholders to free their slaves, without prior government approval for a few decades during the late eighteenth century. Significantly, Vick's deed of emancipation states the kinship relation between the two slaves the family had freed. Phillis was bought by a Boston couple still in mourning for the similarly aged daughter who had died the year before; treating Phillis as a household member, the Wheatley's enabled her to write and publish her poetry, despite the challenges posed by her race and gender, and eventually emancipated her. The Sedgwick family was instrumental in assisting Mumbet to obtain her freedom; they also included and referred to her as a member of their household family.

In England, Dido Elizabeth Belle, Olaudah Equiano, or Gustavus Vassa, and John Williams experienced race relations in some significantly different ways from their fellow enslaved Americans. Illegitimate and biracial, Dido escaped the harsh existence of slavery by living with her paternal extended kin's household family, who had her baptized, granted her freedom, and bequeathed her an income sufficient to marry. A double portrait of Dido and her co-resident cousin Elizabeth Murray revealed the unusual relationship between the young women; Paula Byrne opined 'This is, as far as we know, the only portrait of its era to show a white girl and a black one together in a sisterly pose'.[40] Equiano purchased his freedom and capitalized on his ethnicity to attack racist writings, such as Clara Reeve's *Plans of Education* (1792), which in turn were based on the pseudo-scientific categories found in Daniel Renaud's commonplace book. Equiano helped abolition in Britain by publishing his autobiography, which went through several editions; included in this volume is a selection from the eighth edition, which was published after Equiano's marriage to Susanah Cullen. Both Dido and Equiano married inter-racially, which demonstrated that English marriage laws were not influenced by racial prejudice. Equiano's will revealed a husband and father who valued his household family and friends, who, in turn, valued and honoured him: the testamentary guardians of the Vassa orphans most likely paid for the sentimental epitaph composed by an unknown friend for little Anna Maria's grave. The settlement case of the Williams family indicates that black London household families experienced economic challenges and were treated similarly to the white urban poor by parochial authorities. Though not institutionally defined by their race, nevertheless, clerical insertions to legal documents, such as the Williams settlement case and Equiano's marriage record, individually identified these men by their race.

Poor families in English parishes and American towns are the focus of section four. Historians reconstructing the experiences of household families of the poor, who left few personal records like letters, journals or estate records, have turned to parochial and town records to write what Tim Hitchcock described as 'new history from below'.[41] The English Poor Laws (1601–1834) relied upon the parish to administer relief to the 'deserving poor'; while some poor families had little contact with parish officials because of family and friends' assistance, others had constant contact, such as John Sibley, whose settlement examination is included in this section. Some parishes built alms houses and other established charity schools for children. Poor children were apprenticed with parish poor relief funds to live with and work for other household families, and the maintenance of illegitimate poor children was determined through bastardy examinations and bastardy bonds. Settlement certificates provided records of residence for the poor, who could only receive financial assistance from his or her certified parish. Those who applied for poor relief and did not qualify, were resettled elsewhere, as testified in removal papers. As was true for enslaved black household families in America, poor household family relationships could be difficult to maintain because others were invested with greater power over their residential arrangements; the parish overseers could disrupt the household family of the poor by resettling family members in other parishes.[42]

Included in the English poor records are: the Diocese of Exeter visitation records for Stockley Pomeroy, which reveal the state of poor relief in the parish as well as non-parochial charitable efforts; Haselbury-Plucknett, Somerset settlement and removal papers; Stoke Abbot, Dorset, bastardy papers, which demonstrate how rural illegitimacy had changed from punishing mothers to seeking paternity for child support payments; and the parish of St Katherine Cree's pauper apprenticeships, which show urban poor children apprenticed as menial domestic servants, instead of learning a skilled trade. The Ashton in Makerfield's census of the poor in 1816 is remarkable because of the large percentage of poor families trying to subsist on a third of what the average labourer earned.[43] Poor relief in America was based on the English model, but administered primarily by town officials; however, some colonies had retained the English practice of church-administered poor relief, as was the case in Virginia.[44]

The publications about helping poor families highlighted specific situations or particularly pathetic stories.[45] The *London Society for Educating Poor Children* (1782) was an effort to teach poor children reading and, according to gender, a few other academic subjects or training in domestic skills. In *Hints for the Institution of Sunday-Schools* (1789) the author attempted to help establish an organization to provide instrumental familial help to poor orphan girls. Ferdinando Tracy Travell, a rector, published his sermon, *The Duties of the Poor* (1793), in which he defines parental virtues and exhorts poor parents to teach their families to be frugal and industrious.

Charitable institutions, such as the Sunday School for Orphaned Young Women, sought to ameliorate the unexpected misfortune or the perpetually grinding poverty in eighteenth-century society. Men and then women formed voluntary associations in England and America, which were founded according to shared religious or charitable beliefs, or according to occupation. These benevolent or friendly societies acted in the stead of the household family's function of providing insurance and mutual assistance. In the *Articles to be Observed and Kept by All the Members of the Benevolent Female Society*, the language of kinship was used in describing the relationship between the members.

The fifth and final section of Volume 1 contains documents about these fictive families that were formed through spiritual kinships, utopian communities or charitable associations. While some benevolent societies were short-lived, others during their years of association assisted hundreds of needy families. The Female Societies in early Philadelphia were a few of these organizations. In England, the Buckingham Monthly Meetings for men and women detailed the kinkeeping work of consanguineal families within the larger fictive Quaker family of the Society of Friends. Bound by spiritual ties, these men and women designated committees in their meetings to visit Quaker families and assess how they were doing financially and spiritually. In addition to the business of maintaining the large Quaker congregational family, these meetings recorded the procedure for men and women to marry and create their own consanguineal families.

Correspondence, memoir and poetry round out the fictive family section. Several of these fictive families used sororal and fraternal modes of address, which signified, according to C. Dallett Hemphill, that 'sibling relations often served as a metaphor for loving bonds between equals'.[46] Rebecca Jones and Hannah Catherall were able to successfully establish their shared household and sisterhood, and Sarah Lawrence and the Fletcher family created a loving, fictive family. Clara Reeve described her utopian female community in a series of letters that she published as *Plans of Education* (see 'Racial Diversity of Families'). The administrative body for her utopia was called 'A Council of Sisterhood' and the members were to address each other as sister. The strength of fictive ties of friendship is the subject of Elizabeth Bentley's poem, 'On the Renewal of Virtuous Friendship in a Future State' Bentley expressed the hope that her strong bonds of friendship would continue after death.

Many of the documents listed in one section have relevance to others in this volume and in this series. For instance, Dido Elizabeth Belle is treated in the race section, but was reared in a multi-relational home with her extended kin; and while Jane Parminter experienced many variations of a household family, she also created a fictive family with her cousin on their estate. The various documents included in this volume will help the student or researcher appreciate the many kinds of family relationships that shaped and reshaped the Atlantic household family during the long eighteenth century. As Naomi Tadmor observed in *Family and Friends in Eighteenth-Century England: Household, Kinship, and Patronage*:

> it is possible to see that, while by and large many of the broad structural features delineated by pioneering historians hold, there is also evidence to suggest that kinship ties in seventeenth- and eighteenth-century England may have been richer, more complex, and altogether more significant than sometimes estimated.[47]

It is hoped that the study of the materials in all the volumes will enrich future scholarship about the many families of eighteenth-century England and America.

Notes
1. *Dictionary of the English Language* (London, 1755), see 'family'. Quoted in N. Tadmor, *Family and Friends in Eighteenth-Century England: Household, Kinship, and Patronage* (Cambridge: Cambridge University Press, 2001), p. 19.
2. Tadmor, *Family and Friends in Eighteenth-Century England*, p. 19.
3. L. Davidoff and C. Hall, *Family Fortunes: Men and Women of the English Middle Class, 1780–1850* (London: Hutchinson, 1987); A. Kussmaul, *Servants in Husbandry in Early Modern England* (Cambridge: Cambridge University Press, 1981).
4. Tadmor, *Family and Friends in Eighteenth-Century England*, p. 74.
5. S. D. Amussen, *An Ordered Society* (New York, NY: Columbia University Press, 1994); Burchell, 'The Role of the Upper Class in the Formation of American Culture', in R. A. Burchell (ed.) *The End of Anglo-America: Historical Essays in the Study of Cultural Divergence* (Manchester: Manchester University Press, 1991); J. C. D. Clark, *English Society 1660–1832* (Cambridge: Cambridge University Press, 2000); M. R. Hunt, *The Middling Sort: Commerce, Gender, and the Family in England 1680–1780* (Berkeley, CA: University of California Press, 1996); M. B. Norton, *Liberty's Daughters: The Revolutionary Experience of American Women, 1750–1800* (New York, NY: Cornell University Press, 1980); A. Vickery, *The Gentleman's Daughter: Women's Lives in Georgian England* (New Haven, CT: Yale University Press, 2003); R. G. Wilson, *Gentlemen Merchants:*

The Merchant Community in Leeds 1700–1830 (Manchester: Manchester University Press, 1971).
6. E. T. Bannet, *The Empire of Letters: Letter Manuals and Transatlantic Correspondence, 1688–1820* (Cambridge: Cambridge University Press, 2005), p. 38.
7. Tadmor, *Family and Friends in Eighteenth-Century England*, p. 20.
8. T. Arkell et al. (eds), *When Death Do Us Part: Understanding and Interpreting the Probate Records of Early Modern England* (Oxford: Leopard's Head, 2000); P. Laslett, *The World We Have Lost: England Before the Industrial Age*, 3rd edn (New York: Scribner, 1984), pp. 111–12.
9. Bannet, *The Empire of Letters*, p. 40.
10. Tadmor, *Family and Friends in Eighteenth-Century England*, p. 167.
11. A. Harris, *Siblinghood and Social Relations in Georgian England: Share and Share Alike* (Manchester: Manchester University Press, 2012), pp. 112–34.
12. Harris, *Siblinghood and Social Relations in Georgian England*, p. 114.
13. Harris, *Siblinghood and Social Relations in Georgian England*, pp. 116–17.
14. Bannet, *The Empire of Letters, 1688–1820*, p. 40.
15. Bannet, *The Empire of Letters, 1688–1820*, p. 40.
16. C. H. Wilson, 'Slave Ownership in Early Georgia: What Eighteenth-Century Wills Reveal', *Historical Methods*, 44:3 (2011), pp. 121–2. MasterFILE Complete. Web. [accessed 16 December 2014].
17. Bannet, *The Empire of Letters*, p. x.
18. Bannet, *The Empire of Letters*, p. ix.
19. C. Dallett Hemphill, *Siblings: Brothers and Sisters in American History* (Oxford: Oxford University Press, 2011), pp. 67, 83.
20. ODNB.
21. Tadmor, *Family and Friends in Eighteenth-Century England*, p. 158.
22. J. Black, *Eighteenth-Century Britain, 1688–1783*, 2nd end (Houndmills: Palgrave, 2008), p. 136.
23. Black, *Eighteenth-Century Britain*, pp. 128–46; see also W. Gibson. *The Church of England, 1688–1832: Unity And Accord* (London: Routledge, 2001), eBook Collection (EBSCOhost). Web. [accessed 10 December 2014].
24. J. Breues, *The Fortune Hunters: Shewing, (from Experience) 1. How People May Improve their Fortunes, and Raise Themselves in London, by Different and Quite Opposite Ways. II. How Servants, of Various Denominations, May Obtain the Favour of their Masters and Mistresses, the Love of their Fellow Servants, the Esteem of all People, and Gain Preferment. III. Many Useful Instructions and Receipts for a Great Variety of Businesses; as Brewing, Gardening, Making Wines, Dressing a Turtle, and Victuals of all Sorts, &c. &c. IV. The Most Distinguishing Characteristics of the Several Sects and Professions of Religion in This Great City; with Some Queries Proposed to the Atheistical Clubs. V. How Pernicious Some Epidemic Vices Practised in London are to the Welfare of Society; with Proposals for the Suppression thereof. Being a Guide to Such as are Strangers to the Ways and Customs of London. By John Breues, Late of Perth, Merchant, &c* (London, [1754]), Eighteenth Century Collections Online. Gale. Brigham Young University – Utah. [accessed 22 December 2014].
25. Black, *Eighteenth-Century England*, p. 144.
26. D. Muir, *God the Only Saviour of Great Britain, from the Insolent Designs of Spain, France, and a Popish Pretender. Set Forth in a Sermon Preached in Broad-Street Meeting-House, Wapping, April 11th, 1744. being the Publick Fast. By David Muir, M.A.* (London, 1744), Eighteenth Century Collections Online. Gale. Brigham Young University – Utah [ac-

cessed 28 November 2014].
27. Muir, *God the Only Saviour of Great Britain*.
28. F. Blom, J. Blom, F. Korsten and G. Scott, *English Catholic Books 1701–1800: A Bibliography* (Aldershot: Scolar Press, 1996), p. x. Protestant unity against Catholics, however, did not preclude religious diversity within household families. The influential writer of Anglican literature, Robert Nelson, married Lady Theophila Berkeley Lucy, who had converted to Catholicism during her visit to Rome. Theophila remained true to her converted faith, and even published tracts in its defense.
29. L. P. Nelson, *Beauty of Holiness: Anglicanism and Architecture in Colonial South Carolina* (Chapel Hill, NC: University of North Carolina Press, 2009), p. 199. ProQuest ebrary. Web. [accessed 10 December 2014].
30. Nelson, *Beauty of Holiness*, p. 200.
31. M. Hendricks and P. Parker, *Women, "Race," and Writing in the Early Modern Period* (London: Routledge, 1994), p. 2.
32. E. C. Eze, *Race and the Enlightment: A Reader* (Cambridge, MA: Blackwell Publishers, 1997), pp. 4–5.
33. Eze, *Race and the Enlightenment*, p. 10.
34. Eze, *Race and the Enlightenment*, p. 15.
35. P. Fryer, *Staying Power: The History of Black People in Britain* (London: Pluto Press, 1984), p. 134.
36. M. L. Rhoades, *Long Knives and the Longhouse: Anglo-Iroquois Politics and the Expansion of Colonial Virginia* (Madison: Faileigh Dickinson University Press, 2011), p. 13.
37. Rhoades, *Long Knives and the Longhouse*, p. 14.
38. D. Nelson, *The Word in Black and White: Reading "Race" in American Literature, 1638–1867 (Oxford: Oxford University Press, 1992)*, p. xxxviii.
39. L. E. Hudson, *To Have And To Hold: Slave Work And Family Life In Antebellum South Carolina* (Athens, GA: University of Georgia Press, 1997), p. xv. eBook Collection (EBSCOhost) [accessed 13 December 2014].
40. P. Byrne, *Belle: The Slave Daughter and the Lord Chief Justice* (New York: Harper, 2014), p. 4.
41. T. Hitchcock, 'A New History from Below', *History Workshop Journal*, 57 (2004), pp. 294–8.
42. S. Hindle, '"Without the Cry of Any Neighbours": A Cumbrian Family and the Poor Law Authorities, c. 1690–1730,' in H. Berry and E. Foyster (eds), *The Family in Early Modern England* (Cambridge: Cambridge University Press, 2007), pp.126–157, on p. 154.
43. G. Clark, 'Farm Wages and Living Standards in the Industrial Revolution: England, 1670–1850', *Economic History Review*, 54:3 (2001), pp. 475–505, on p. 485.
44. Records from the vestry book of St Anne's Parish, Albermarle County, Virginia and the Boston Overseers of the Poor exemplify the two types of poor relief administration and indicate the effects of poverty on poor household families in America. See Eric Guest Nellis and Anne Deckere Cecere, *The Eighteenth-Century Records of the Boston Overseers of the Poor* (Boston, MA: Colonial Society of Massachusetts, 2001).
45. In *An Apology for the Annual Collections* (1746) Thomas Sharp defended the continued existence of the Corporation of the Sons of the Clergy, founded in 1675 to provide aid to poor clerical families, and in this case, a poor widow's family.
46. Hemphill, *Siblings*, pp. 123, 153.
47. Tadmor, *Family and Friends in Eighteenth-Century England*, p. 112.

EDITORIAL PRINCIPLES

Selection of Texts

The texts selected for inclusion in this collection have been included for balance and for their relative scarcity in modern print form. Texts which are more widely available are referenced within the editorial apparatus but have not been included on the grounds of space. This edition is a selective work as it would be impossible to reproduce every text related to the subject. However, we do believe that the texts included within this edition will be of interest to most scholars or researchers. We hope you will appreciate these principles and ask for your forbearance if we have omitted a favourite text. For more explanation and justification for the inclusion of individual texts please refer to the introductions and headnotes within this edition.

Printed Sources

Every effort has been made to reproduce these texts as closely to the originals as possible without actually replicating the original typography. Original capitalization and punctuation has been retained and only the most significant typographical errors have been amended where they undermine the understanding of the text. Please note that there can be significant variances not only between different editions of texts but also differences between individual extant copies. We have proofed our texts against a single original source and we give details of those in the 'List of Sources' section in this volume. Any variances between our printed text and other original texts have to be considered in this light. The original pagination of the text is indicated by the inclusion of / within the text at the exact point of the page break. Any sections omitted from the text are indicated by [...]. Any other editorial interventions are also contained within square brackets.

Manuscript Sources

Again manuscript sources are transcribed as close to the original as possible, allowing for modern typographical conventions and a degree of standardization of format. Where possible text that is struck through is reproduced in the same way within this edition. Editorial interventions are again noted within square brackets. Please note that as with all manuscript sources there is a degree of editorial judgement and interpretation. Imperfections in the condition of the originals may mean that the original text is not always clear or may be open to more than one reading. In such instances the Editors have used their best abilities to provide the most appropriate reading.

WILLS OF BERKELEY SEYMOUR AND JANE SEYMOUR

Berkeley Seymour, Will (Written 1744, Proved 1744), Bitton, Gloucestershire, proved in the Prerogative Court of Canterbury. The National Archives, PROB 11/735.

Jane Seymour, Will, Woodford, Essex (1762–70), proved in the Prerogative Court of Canterbury. The National Archives, PROB 11/959.

The wills of Berkeley and Jane Seymour, the son and daughter of John Seymour, governor of Maryland (1704–9) and Margaret Bowles, demonstrate several patterns of eighteenth-century family life, particularly about unmarried and childless persons' views on inheritance. First, like nearly 20 per cent of their cohort, neither sibling married nor had children, meaning their views of inheritance differed from those with spouses and children.[1] High rates of never-married adults coupled with the 30 to 40 per cent of children who did not live to see their tenth birthday, made planning for future generations and inheritance a complicated matter.[2] When their father was appointed governor of Maryland, his three surviving children (John, Berkeley and Jane) were adults and they remained in England. Berkeley inherited the Bitton Parsonage when his stepmother died in 1730.[3] If he had had legitimate sons, the parsonage would have easily passed to one of them, but in their absence he, like many unmarried people, considered lateral kin instead of lineal kin. As their sister had died young and their brother John was married and settled, Berkeley passed his possessions to the person most vulnerable to the vicissitudes of financial survival: his single sister.

Jane made a similar decision, but as nearly twenty years had passed by the time she wrote her will, she focused her efforts on her nieces and nephews – favouring, again, the unmarried women. Jana Maria and Esther Seymour and Margaret Bradshaw, who were sisters, were in their fifties or sixties when they eventually inherited from their aunt. Jana Maria Seymour was christened on 6 July 1702 in Oxford and Esther Seymour was christened on 4 June 1717.[4] Margaret Seymour married Peregrine Bradshaw on 22 December 1739 in St Andrew, Plymouth,

Devon.⁵ By the time their aunt died, Jana Maria was unmarried, Margaret was a widow, and Esther might have already been showing signs of mental instability – explaining why they received much larger bequests than the men, or younger (and presumably marriageable) women like Christian, who was only nineteen when her great aunt wrote her will.⁶ Unmarried people often left bequests to other unmarried siblings, particularly sisters, and unmarried women often left legacies to nieces (particularly unmarried ones) in an effort to ameliorate a property and inheritance tradition that disadvantaged women.⁷

Notes

1. A. Froide, *Never Married: Singlewomen in Early Modern England* (Oxford: Oxford University Press, 2005).
2. P. Laslett, *The World We Have Lost: England Before the Industrial Age*, 3rd edn (New York: Scribner, 1984), pp. 111–12.
3. H. T. Ellacombe, *The History of the Parish of Bitton, in the County of Gloucester* (Exeter: Privately printed, William Pollard, 1881), pp. 87–90; A. Baine, *History of Kingswood Forest Including All the Ancient Manors and Villages in the Neighborhood* (London: William F. Mack, Bristol, 1891).
4. Jana Maria Seymour, daughter of John Seymour, christened 6 July 1702, Church of England, St Giles, Oxford, Oxfordshire Parish Registers, 1681–1958, FHL British Film 887486; Esther Seymour, daughter of Dr John and Mrs Elizabeth Seymour, christened 4 June 1717, Church of England, Charles Church, Plymouth, Devon, index and images, *Family Search*, at: https://familysearch.org/pal:/MM9.1.1/KC9X-465 [accessed 1 December 2012]. Other children of John Seymour christened in St Giles, Oxford: John Seymour, christened 7 March 1700; Bowles Seymour, christened 21 October 1707; Berkeley Seymour, christened 2 June 1709. Other children of John and Elizabeth Seymour christened in Charles Church, Plymouth: Phineas Seymour, christened 1 January 1719.
5. A. Broomfield, *Parish Registers for St. Andrew, Plymouth, Devonshire, England: Marriage 1618–1720, 1728–1744/5* (1961), Family History Library British Film 823684, item 6.
6. Church of England, St Winnow, Cornwall, England Parish Registers, 1622–1812, FHL British Film 908076. Seymour, daughter of Bowles and Martha Seymour, christened 27 September 1743.
7. A. L. Erickson, *Women and Property in Early Modern England* (London and New York: Routledge, 1993).

Berkeley Seymour, Will (Written 1744, Proved 1744)

In the Name of God Amen

This is the Last Will and Testament of me Berkeley Seymour of Bitton in the County of Gloucester, Esquire. In the first place I recommend my Soul to the hands of Almighty God, and my Body I commit to the Earth to be decently Interred at the discretion of my Executrix hereinafter named. Item I order and direct that all my Debts which I shall owe at the time of my decease be in the first place fully paid and satisfied out of my Estate. Item I do hereby Give Devise and Bequeath All that my Freehold Lease of the Mannor and Parsonage of Bitton with all Lands, Tenements, Hereditaments and Appurtenances thereunto belonging held by three Lives and all and every my Real Estate whatsoever and wheresoever and also all and singular my Personal Estate of what nature or kindsoever the same is or shall be at the time of my decease unto my Dear Sister Jane Seymour her Heirs, Executors, Administrators and Assigns to her and their own proper use, benefit and behoof forever. And I do hereby constitute and appoint my said dear Sister Sole Executrix of this my will. And Lastly I do hereby revoke all former or other wills by me at any time heretofore made and this only do I Establish as my last Will and Testament In Testimony whereof I have hereunto Set my Hand and Seal the first day of June in the year of our Lord One Thousand Seven Hundred and Forty four. Berkeley Seymour / Signed, Sealed, Published and Declared by the said Testator Berkeley Seymour as and for his last Will and Testament in the presence of us who have hereunto Severally Subscribed our Hands as Witnesses hereto in his sight and Presence and at his request. Tho. Slaughter, E. Bowles. John Atwood.

This Will was Proved at London before the Worshipfull Charles Pinfold, Doctor of Laws, Surrogate to the Right Worshipfull John Bettesworth, Doctor of Laws, Master Keeper or Commissary of the Prerogative Court of Canterbury, lawfully constituted, the Fifth day of October in the Year of Our Lord One Thousand Seven Hundred and Forty four by the Oath of Jane Seymour, Spinster, the Sister of the deceased and Sole Executrix named in the said Will To whom Administration was granted of all and Singular the Goods, Chattels and Credits of the said deceased, being first sword duly to Administer.

Jane Seymour, Will (Written 1762, Proved 1770)

[All capitalization and spelling (except 'niece' which was consistently written 'neice' in the original) is as in the original]

In the Name of God Amen I Jane Seymour of the Parish of Woodford in the County of Essex do make and ordain this my Last Will and Testament in the manner and form following. I desire that my Body may be decently and privately buried in the Churchyard of the said Parish of Woodford in the Morning that my Coffin be covered with white Cloth and that no Bell be told till about half an hour before my Burial and as for my Temporal Estate I Give devise and dispose thereof as follows. I Give and bequeath to my Niece Jana Maria Seymour three Guineas. I Give to my Niece Margaret Bradshaw three Guineas. I Give to my Niece Christian Seymour, daughter of my Nephew Bowles Seymour, one Shilling. I give to my Nephew Berkeley Seymour one Shilling. I Give to my Nephew Phineas Seymour the Picture of my Brother. I Give to the Reverend James Altham Rector of Woodford aforesaid Five Guineas after my debts and Funeral Expenses are paid all the Rest and residue and remainder of my Estate real and Personal whatsoever and wheresoever I Give devise and bequeath to my Niece Esther Seymour and I do hereby Constitute and appoint my said Niece Ester Seymour whole and Sole Executrix of this my Last Will. In Witness whereof I the said Jane Seymour have set my hand and Seal hereby revoking all former wills this twentieth day of September One thousand Seven hundred and Sixty two. The Mark of Jane Seymour. Signed, Sealed, Published and declared by the said Testatrix Jane Seymour as and for her Last Will and Testament in the Presence of us who have Subscribed our Names as Witnesses thereto in the Presence of the said Testatrix. Eliz Dod. J. A. Hainsby. Pierce Dod.

On the Fourth day of July in the year of our Lord one Thousand Seven hundred and Seventy administration (with the will annexed) of the Goods, Chattels and Credits of Jane Seymour late of the Parish of Woodford in the County of Essex, Spinster, deceased was granted to Berkeley Seymour and Margaret Bradshaw, widow, the natural and Lawfull Brother and Sister and two of the next of kin of Ester Seymour, Spinster, a Lunatich the Niece of the said deceased, Sole Executrix and Residuary Legatee named in the said Will for the use and benefit of the said Ester Seymour and during her Lunacy having been First sworn duly to administer.

JOHN ROMANS, DEED (1766)

John Romans, Deed (1766), University of York, Borthwick Institute of Historical Research, Rom. 47.

While John Romans Sr was probably in his eighties when he transferred his property to his grandson in 1766, it was most likely the younger John's coming of age (he turned twenty-one the previous year) that triggered the transfer as much as John Sr's advanced years. John and Elizabeth were the parents of Robert Romans (b. 1707).[1] Robert married Eleanor Swinbank in 1738 and they had four children before his death in 1746.[2] Their son, John, who was born in 1744, is the grandson referenced in the deed. At the time of his grandparents' deaths, John was unmarried (he did not marry until 1775), but he was not the only viable heir of his grandfather. While John Sr did not have any other sons who outlived Robert, Robert had sons older than John Jr. John Jr's older brother was still alive in 1766.[3] If the Romans family followed typical eighteenth-century inheritance practices, John's brother probably inherited their father's property. Families typically compensated younger sons and all daughters with more moveable property and cash and other types of inheritance to offset the practice of giving the bulk of land to eldest sons. John Sr, therefore, might have been compensating his younger grandson, not ignoring or disinheriting his older grandchildren.[4]

Elizabeth, John's wife mentioned in the deed, died in 1769 and John Sr died in 1770.[5] The property would have then transferred to the younger John, as directed in the document. John, the recipient of the property, married Ann Gibson in 1775 and had at least four children (two sons and two daughters). John appears to have still been in possession of his inheritance when he wrote his will in 1800. He passed along his property holdings to his wife and his two sons.[6]

The deed highlights two aspects of eighteenth-century family life. First, it demonstrates how early modern mortality rates (much higher than today) influenced family relationships. Death constantly shaped and reshaped family dynamics and inheritance schemes. The Romans family had lost several members in infancy or childhood (in both generations), but they had also lost several members as young adults – a common experience. Families were fragile affairs – and death of adults in the prime of their earning and childrearing years upset generational expectations.[7] Second, it shows how flexible England's inheritance system was, particularly for those whose land tenure was not governed by rules surrounding freehold estates; it was largely in the hands of individuals and not dictated by statute.[8] Patrilineal descent still mattered, but it was tempered by a sense of justice for all the children.[9] In Yorkshire this was particularly true after 1693 when the custom of York waned, leaving the distribution of personal estate and most forms of land tenure entirely in the hands of the testator.[10] While families with large estates and vast holdings might use the tools of entail, strict settlement and marriage settlements to insure the transfer of property from fathers to elder sons, families with small holdings, such as the Romans, practiced a more pragmatic approach.

Notes

1. Church of England, Cawood, Yorkshire Parish Registers, christening of Robert Romans, son of John Romans, 16 Mar 1707, *England and Wales Christening Records, 1530–1906*; Riccall, Yorkshire Parish Registers, christening of Eleanor Swinbank, 14 November 1714, 'England Births and Christenings, 1538–1975' citing FHL Brit film 599,999, at: www.familysearch.org [accessed 1 December 2014].
2. Church of England, Riccall, Yorkshire Parish Registers, marriage of Robert Romans and Eleanor Swinbank, 22 May 1738, *Yorkshire, England Extracted Parish Records*, at www.ancestry.co.uk [accessed 1 December 2014]. Christenings of Thomas Romans (28 February 1739), Robert (27 September 1741), and John (11 June 1744), 'England Births and Christenings, 1538–1975,' citing FHL British film 599.999; Riccall parish registers, burial of Robert Romans, 14 May 1749, *Yorkshire Burials*, at www.findmypast.com [accessed 1 December 2014].
3. This older brother, also named Robert, remained in Riccall where he married and raised children. He too was a successful yeoman farmer when he died, at age seventy-nine, in 1819. Robert Romans, will, 27 February 1819, York Peculiar Probate Collection, 1383–1883'; Church of England, Riccall, Yorkshire Parish Registers, burial of Robert Romans, 31 August 1819, *Yorkshire Burials*.
4. A. Erickson, *Women and Property in Early Modern England* (New York: Routledge, 1993).
5. Church of England, Riccall Parish Registers, burial of Elizabeth Romans, wife of John Romans, 24 March 1769 and John Romans, 9 May 1770, *Yorkshire, England Extracted Parish Registers*.
6. John Romans of Riccall, Yorkshire, will, 13 March 1800, 'York Peculiar Probate Collection, 1383–1883', at www.findmypast.co.uk [accessed 1 December 2014].
7. P. Laslett, *The World We Have Lost: Further Explored* (Routledge, 2004), pp. 115–16.
8. Erickson, *Women and Property in Early Modern England*, p. 224.
9. T. Arkell et al. (eds), *When Death Do Us Part: Understanding and Interpreting the Probate Records of Early Modern England* (Oxford: Leopard's Head, 2000), p. 65; Erickson, *Women and Property in Early Modern England*, p. 73.
10. Arkell et al. (eds), *When Death Do Us Part: Understanding and Interpreting the Probate Records of Early Modern England*, pp. 19–20.

John Romans, Deed (1766)

John Romans deed of gevet, This Bill of sail I give to my grandson John Romans, 1766
/
KNOW all men by these presents that I, John Romans of Rickall[1] in the County of York, Yeoman for and in consideration of the natural love and affection which I have and bear to my Grand Son John Romans at Rickall aforesaid Husbandman and for and towards his advancement and preferment in the World and also for divers other good causes me hereunto moveing Have given, granted, delivered, ratified, and confirmed and by these presents Do freely clearly and absolutely give, grant, deliver, ratify and confirm unto the said John Romans, my grandson, his Executors, Administrators and assigns All and singular my household goods, Utensils and Furniture. Also all my live goods and Husbandry Geer and all other my goods, chattles, personal estates and effects whatsoever and wheresoever quick or dead, moveable or immoveable of what nature, kind or quality so ever as the same are <of all the same are> standing, being or may be found in or about my Dwelling House Farm Ground and premisses situate at Rickall aforesaid or elsewhere To have and to hold, all and singular the said Household Goods Utensils and Furniture, live goods and Husbandry, Geer and premisses <above mentioned> and every part thereof with the Appurtenances[2] unto the said John Romans, my said Grandson, his Executors, Administrators and Assigns. To the only proper use and behoof of the said John Romans my said Grandson, his Executors, Administrators and Assigns forever and to and for no other use, intent, or purpose whatsoever, Provided always and these presents are upon this Condition that it shall and may be lawful for me the said John

Romans and Elizabeth my wife, for and during our lives and the life of the longer liver of us, peaceably and quietly to have and hold and enjoy all and singular the above Granted premisses without any molestation, suit or trouble of or from the said John Romans my said Grandson or any other person or persons whatsoever, And I the said John Romans all and singular the said premisses unto the said John Romans my said Grand Son, his Executors, Administrators and Assigns <against me the said John Romans> and all other person or persons whatsoever shall and will warrant and forever defend by these presents according to the proviso and condition aforesaid. In witness whereof I the said John Romans have hereunto set my hand and seal the twenty fourth day of December in the year of our Lord one thousand seven hundred and sixty six. John Romans

Sealed and delivered being first duly stampt and also sixpence delivered in the name of possession of the whole in the presence of John Owram, Arthur Benson, Quintin Arom

WARD HALLOWELL, LICENCE [*SIC*] TO CHANGE HIS NAME TO WARD NICHOLAS BOYLSTON (1770)

Ward Hallowell, Ward, Licence [*sic*] to Change his Name to Ward Nicholas Boylston (1770). Boylston Family Papers, 1704–1770, Ms n-4 Box 3 of 86 Folder Jan–June 1770, Massachusetts Special Collections.

'Men without children', according to Helen Berry and Elizabeth Foyster, 'took measures to find different ways of exercising patriarchal manhood'.[1] These childless men assumed paternal roles and asserted patriarchal authority in a variety of ways: philanthropy, as godfather, guardian, or adopted parent. Since legal adoption has been only available in England since 1926,[2] in the eighteenth century, childless, married men often unofficially adopted a child from a relative with several children (see 'Anna Barbauld'). The adoption was usually recognized when the selected nephew or niece was named as the heir in the will. Childless single men also typically named nephews or nieces as their heirs.[3]

The wealthy childless bachelor, Nicholas Boylston, wrote in his will that his nephew, Ward Hallowell, the eldest and probably only child of his sister, Mary, was his heir, provided he change his name.[4] Ward Nicholas Boylston (née Ward Hallowell) born in Boston on 22 November 1747, was the oldest son of Benjamin Hallowell, a Captain, and Mary Boylston.[5] Mary Boylston's family was wealthy enough for her parents, Thomas Boylston and Sarah Morecock, to commission the famous American painter, John Singleton Copley, to paint half-length portraits of each family member: Nicholas, Thomas II, Rebecca, Lucy and Mary.[6] The Boylston family wealth increased with Nicholas's firm, Green and Boylston, which had become extremely successful through consumer imports of textiles, paper, tea and glass.[7] Nicholas's wealth (and perhaps vanity) was sufficient to commission a large-scale replica (full-length) of his portrait, which was unprecedented in Copley's practice.[8] Another replica was commissioned by Harvard University in appreciation for Boylston's bequest to establish a professorship of Rhetoric and Oratory.[9]

The Boylston name had become wealthy and powerful under the influence of Nicholas. While Ward could not have known his fifty-four-year-old uncle would die the following year in August 1771, he did have a great inducement to change his name in 1770 when he married Ann Molineux; Ward mostly likely would have wanted to establish this affinal family relationship under the name which would grant him considerable heritable property and assets for his future heirs. In order to change his name, Ward submitted his petition to the General Court, which was the legislative body of colonial Massachusetts.[10]

Notes
1. 'Childless Men in Early Modern England', in H. Berry and E. Foyster (eds), *The Family in Early Modern England* (Cambridge: Cambridge University Press, 2007), pp. 158–83, on p. 183.
2. A. Teague, *Social Change, Social Work, and the Adoption of Children* (Aldershot: Gower Publishing Company Limited, 1989), p. 2.
3. N. Tadmor, *Family and Friends in Eighteenth-Century England: Household, Kinship and Patronage* (Cambridge: Cambridge University Press, 2001), p. 109.
4. N. Boylston, Will, August 1, 1771, Suffolk County, Docket no. 14979 (Suffolk County Probate Records, vol. 70, pp. 223–5), Archives, Supreme Judicial Court, Boston. Quoted in *John Singleton Copley*, p. 228.
5. Ward may have been the only child, since the two siblings listed for him in various family genealogies have birthdates twenty years later, which would mean his mother Mary would have been thirty-nine when delivering Benjamin Hallowell-Carew, which is not an impossibility, but at the birth of the purported sister, Mary, in 1775, Mary Senior would have been fifty-three years old.
6. C. Rebora, P. Staiti et al., *John Singleton Copley in America* (New Haven, CT: Yale University Press, 2013), p. 222.
7. Rebora, Staiti et al., *John Singleton Copley*, p. 224.
8. Rebora, Staiti et al., *John Singleton Copley*, p. 225.
9. Rebora, Staiti et al., *John Singleton Copley*, p. 228.
10. Available at http://www.sec.state.ma.us/arc/arcgen/genidx.htm#probate [accessed 11 December 2014].

Ward Hallowell, Licence [*sic*] to Change his Name to Ward Nicholas Boylston (1770)

George the Third, by the Grace of God, King of Great Britain, France and Ireland, Defender of the Faith, &: To Our Right Trusty and High Wellbeloved Cousin and Councellor Richard Earl of Scarborough,[1] Deputy to Our Right Trusty and Right—Entirely Beloved Cousin Edward Duke of Norfolk, Earl Marshal[2] and Our Hereditary Earl Marshal of England,[3] Greeting: Whereas Ward Hallowell, of Boston in New England, Merchant, has, by His Petition, humbly represented unto Us, That Nicholas Boylston,[4] His Uncle, by His Mother's Side,[5] has conceived a very great affection for Him, the Petitioner, and has promised to leave Him, at His Death, certain Estates, which are very considerable; That He, the Petitioner, out of Gratitude to the said Nicholas Boylston, His Uncle, to whose Bounty He will be so much indebted / is desirous of changing His Name of Hallowell to that of Nicholas Boylston, and having therefore most humbly prayed Us to grant unto Him, and His Heirs Our Royal Leave and Allowance to change his Name from Ward Hallowell to Ward Nicholas Boylston. Know ye that We, of Our princely Grace and special Favor, have given and granted, and do give and grant unto Him in said Ward Hallowell and His Heirs, full Power, Licence and Authority to change Their Name of Hallowell to that of Nicholas Boylston. And Our Will and Pleasure is that You Richard Earl of Scarborough, Deputy to the said Earl Marshal, to whom the Cognizance of Matters of this Nature does properly belong, do require and command That This Our Concession and Declaration be registered in Our College of Arms, to the End that Our Officers of Arms, and all others, upon Occasion, may take full Notice and have Knowledge thereof. For doing which this shall be a sufficient Warrant Given at our court at St. James's[6] the Twenty First Day of March, 1770, in the Tenth Year of Our Reign.

By His Majesty's Commands,
Weymouth[7]

Registered in the College of Arms, London, in pursuance of a Warrant under the Hand and Seal of Richard Earl of Scarb[o]rough Deputy Earl Marshal, dated 25th March 1770.

    Ralph Bigland, Somerset of Reg.[8]

    Ward Hallowell, Licence to Change His Name to Ward Nicholas Boylston.

JANE PARMINTER, WILL (WRITTEN 1807, PROVED 1812)

Jane Parminter, Will (written 1807, proved 1812), The National Archives, Kew, Prerogative Court of Canterbury and Related Probate Jurisdictions: Will Registers, Class: PROB 11, Piece: 1530.

'A virtuous female superintendent', Amanda Vickery explained, 'was an indispensable member of the genteel Georgian household'.[1] While this virtuous female superintendent was often the mother of the household family, the eldest sister could also perform this role. C. Dallett Hemphill noted that during the early nineteenth century, 'the literature and personal papers alike reveal the triumph of the eldest sister as sibling leader and parental advisor'.[2] This sibling leader would experience a variety of family types within the genteel Georgian household, which was the experience of Jane Parminter (1750–1811).

Jane was the eldest daughter of John Parminter, a wine merchant, and Jane Arboyne. Three more daughters, Mary Ann or Marianne, Elizabeth and Margaret, and two sons, William and John, completed the nuclear family.[3] The oldest three children were born in Lisbon, Portugal, where John the elder had established a bottling factory.[4] While the Parminters were visiting England, the devastating earthquake shook Lisbon on All Saints' Day, 1 November 1755. Jane Arboyne Parminter stayed in England, where the last three children were born, while John split his time between England and Portugal until 1767, when they purchased a home in Devon, England.

When Jane was nineteen, she went to London and lived in her Aunt Margaret Parminter Hurlock's household family. While living with her aunt, Jane's cousin, Richard Parminter, became a widower and sent his young daughters, Mary and Rebecca, to live with the John and Jane Parminter family. When Jane's mother died the following year, Jane returned to Devon in order to care for her younger siblings and her two cousins. In 1779, Mary and Rebecca's father passed away. Though orphaned, Mary and Rebecca were not financially dependent upon their Parminter cousins. In their father's will Mary was bequeathed his 'Estate in Ottery' and Rebecca, 'my House and Gardens situate at Larkbear'.[5]

Within a few years of Mary and Rebecca's becoming co-resident relatives, the John and Jane Parminter household family started to decrease. Older brother William and younger sister Margaret had died before the girls' arrival and, as already noted, in 1773 mother Jane passed away. In 1778, Mary Ann married George Frend and moved to London and two years later father John died. After father John's death, the three remaining siblings (Jane, Elizabeth, John Jr) and the two cousins lived with Mary Ann in London; however, Rebecca died at the young age of fourteen in 1783 and later that year John left for France to establish his career as a merchant.[6] Instead of remaining as co-resident relatives in Mary Ann's house, Jane, Elizabeth and Cousin Mary determined that they would rather travel. On 23 June 1784, they and a female friend from London undertook the traditionally upper-class, young men's activity of travelling on the Continent.[7]

Elizabeth returned from the Grand Tour to create her will on 4 October 1788. In her will, Elizabeth named her surviving siblings, John, Marianne and Jane as her joint trustees, and, instead of bestowing her assets laterally, as was most common for single women, she bestowed her income on her uncle Samuel Parminter for his life.[8] Uncle Samuel was seventy-one years of age at the time Elizabeth wrote her will, and only lived six more years after probate. Perhaps Elizabeth, who suffered from ill-health at an early age, was sympathetic to the challenges of advancing age on her oldest living uncle. Upon Uncle Samuel's death, Elizabeth left the reversion of her fortune to her siblings, and if they died without issue, her fortune would devolve upon all her first cousins: three children of her uncle Samuel, and cousins Joseph and Philip Hurlock, who were the sons of her London aunt.[9] Joseph's daughters, Sophia and Jane, would eventually inherit 'A la Ronde' (Mary and Jane's cottage).[10]

Mary and Jane returned from the Continent in order for the latter to execute Elizabeth's will in 1791. Back in England, Mary and Jane again elected independence, since their inheritances enabled them to establish and support their own household. Mary and Jane decided to build a home based on the basilica of San Vitale, in Ravenna, Italy; they named their octagonal cottage orné 'A la Ronde'. In addition to building their home, the cousins built a non-conformist chapel in 1811, with pointed windows, a four-sided pointed spire, and the inscription 'Some point in view – We all pursue.'[11] The cousins then expanded the church by creating four small almshouses on one side for older, single, and impoverished women, one of whom was expected to teach six pauper girls, who attended the small school that was built on the other side of the chapel. Preference was to be given to Jewish women who had converted to Christianity;[12] when they were in Rome, Mary and Jane had learned about the challenges Jewish women faced when they converted to Christianity.[13]

Bonded by the shared experiences of the death of their parents and siblings, Jane and Mary maintained kinship ties through creating 'A la Ronde' and its charitable institutions. Their final resting places, under the point-of-view chapel, also testified of their dedication to their female community. As the oldest sister, Jane performed kin-keeping work by rearing her younger siblings and orphaned cousins. Jane and Cousin Mary refashioned the Parminter household family by developing an estate through their combined inheritances. At 'A la Ronde' and its dissenting chapel, the cousins created a female utopian community, in which Mary and Jane were able to run their household and estate, and improve the domestic situation of a marginalized few. In her will, Mary named six unmarried female relatives who could inherit 'A la Ronde';[14] Jane's will, transcribed below, demonstrated her commitment to sibling and extended kinship bonds through her bequests.

Notes

1. *The Gentleman's Daughter: Women's Lives in Georgian England* (New Haven, CT: Yale University Press, 1998), p. 128.
2. C. D. Hemphill, *Siblings: Brothers and Sisters in America* (Oxford: Oxford University Press, 2011), p. 154.
3. Available at http://trees.ancestry.com/tree/37628963/family/familygroup?fpid=28658248881 [accessed 24 November 2014].
4. The Story of A la Ronde and its People (National Trust 2011, revised March 2014), at http://www.nationaltrust.org.uk/cs/Satellite?blobcol=urldata&blobheader=applicatio n%2Fpdf&blobkey=id&blobtable=MungoBlobs&blobwhere=1349119204513&ssbi nary=true [accessed 6 November 2014].
5. The National Archives; Kew, England; *Prerogative Court of Canterbury and Related Probate Jurisdictions: Will Registers;* Class: PROB 11; Piece: 1062.
6. The Story of A la Ronde and its People.
7. The Story of A la Ronde and its People.
8. A. L. Erickson, *Women and Property in Early Modern England* (London and New York: Routledge, 1993). N. Tadmor, *Family and Friends in Eighteenth-Century England: Household, Kinship, and Patronage* (Cambridge: Cambridge University Press, 2001), p. 109, n. 20.
9. The National Archives; Kew, England; *Prerogative Court of Canterbury and Related Probate Jurisdictions: Will Registers;* Class: PROB 11; Piece: 1206.
10. The Story of A la Ronde and its People.
11. Available at http://list.english-eritage.org.uk/resultsingle.aspx?uid=1164937 [accessed 6 November 2014].
12. K. Bagshaw, 'Parminter, Jane (1750–1811), Traveller and Designer', *ODNB*.
13. The Story of A la Ronde and its People.
14. The Story of A la Ronde and its People.

Jane Parminter, Will (Written 1807, Proved 1812)

This is the last Will and Testament of miss Jane Parminter of A la Ronde in the Parish of Withycombe-Rawleigh in the County of Devon Spinster[1] I give to my Brother John Parminter[2] the half yearly dividends of my Stock receiv'd Bank Stock and of my stock or property in the three per cent consolidated annuities and of my stock or property in the navy five per cents[3] for and during his life and from and after his decease then I give the said Bank Stock and my stock or property in the navy two per cents unto all and every the his child and children which he shall leave behind him equally to be divided amongst them if more than one and if but one leave to him or ever but if my said Brother should not leave behind him any Child or Children, then after his decease I give the said Bank Stock <& my said stock or property in the 3 p[e]r c[en]t Consol[udated] @ the said stock> or property in the navy five per cents unto my Cousin Mary Parminter of a la Ronde her Exec[utor]s heirs and assigns also I give devise and bequeth unto the said Mary Parminter her avows and assigns for ever all my right and share Estate and interest in and to the messuage[4] and Lands called a la ronde and Great Courtlands[5] in Withycombe Rawleigh aforesaid and all my real Estate whatsoever to hold this said unto her the said Mary Parminter her heirs and assigns for ever also all my goods chattels rights credits personal and testamentary Estate and Effects whatsoever after payment of my debts and funeral Expenses & I give and bequeath unto the said Mary Parminter for her own use and benefit & I make and appoint her Executrix of this my last will and Testament In witness whereof I the said Jane Parminter has & to this my last will and testament set my hand and seal the thirteenth day of January in the forty seventh year of the reign of our Sovereign Lord King George the third by the Grace of God of the united kingdom of Great Britain and Ireland king defender of the faith and in the year of our Lord one thousand eight hundred and seven – Jane Parminter. Signed sealed published and declared by the above named Jane / Parminter the Testatrix as and for her last Will and Testament and in the presence of us who at her request and in the presence of one another have thereunto subscribed our names as witnesses – Ann Lanford W[illia]m Lanford Ja[me]s Edwa[rd] Jackson

Proved at London 1st February 1812 before the Judge by ~~the Judge by~~ the oath of Mary Parminter Spinster the sole Executrix to whom adm[inistrati]on was granted being sworn by Com[missi]on[er] to administer

JOHN DRAYTON, LETTER TO JAMES GLEN (1761)

John Drayton, Letter to James Glen (11 October 1761), James Glen Papers, University of South Carolina Digital Collections, at http://library.sc.edu/digital/collections/glen.html

In the eighteenth century, the term friend typically applied to relatives through either blood or marriage; it was reserved for the closest of ties. Although emotional bonds mattered in such relationships, people also expected their friendships to be 'instrumental'.[1] Indeed, support, protection, advice and material goods were commonly sought and granted as tokens of friendship. Instrumental relationships were particularly evident amongst the gentry class in eighteenth-century South Carolina.[2]

James Glen and John Drayton (see Volume 4) forged a friendship, which proved largely instrumental, when Drayton married Glen's sister, Margaret. Margaret's marriage to Drayton, the lieutenant governor's former son-in-law, served to bolster Glen's dwindling power as governor (1743–60).[3] The bond between Drayton and Glen deepened as Glen provided Margaret's dowry of £5,000 Carolina currency, promoted Drayton's appointment to the South Carolina Council, gave him loans or bonds, entrusted him with the administration of his plantation beginning in 1761 and assisted Drayton's four sons (William 'Billy', Charles, Thomas 'Tommie' and 'Glennie') in their educational pursuits in England.[4]

While political and business motives played a part in forging a friendship between the Draytons and the Glens, their decisions to leave the management of their personal duties (government, plantations and children) in each others' hands suggests that they trusted and respected one another. For example, Glen cared for Margaret and her children (and the children of Dratyon's first and successive marriages) to secure their inheritance in the marriage agreement. Drayton openly shared with Glen his concerns about the plantations, hands, bonds and his children. Glen's care of his nephews consisted of 'offering guidance and money',[5] but he was emotionally invested in their success and often defended them, especially Charles, in response to their father's attacks. Glen even had his step-nephew William confirmed as a noble.[6]

The following letter, written 11 October 1761, demonstrates that the two men considered each other 'best of friends' and 'most affectionate brother[s]' and acted in each other's behalf for over twenty years. Sadly, their friendship ultimately dissolved as a result of Drayton's treatment of Margaret during her illness, the return of Drayton's sons to the Carolinas and Drayton's outstanding debts to Glen (see Volume 4).

Notes
1. N. Tadmor, *Family and Friends in Eighteenth Century England: Household, Kinship, and Patronage* (Cambridge and New York, NY: Cambridge University Press, 2001), p. 177.
2. L. Glover, *All Our Relations: Blood Ties and Emotional Bonds among the Early South Carolina Gentry* (Baltimore, MD: Johns Hopkins University Press, 2000), p. xi.
3. K. Krawczynski, *William Henry Drayton: South Carolina Revolutionary Patriot* (Baton Rouge, LA: Louisiana State University Press, 2001), p. 114.
4. W. Stitt Robinson, *James Glen: From Scottish Provost to Royal Governor of South Carolina*, ed. J. L. Wakelyn (Westport, CT: Greenwood Press, 1996), pp. 125–8.
5. Krawczynski, *William Henry Drayton: South Carolina Revolutionary Patriot*, p. 15.
6. Robinson, *James Glen: From Scottish Provost to Royal Governor of South Carolina*, p. 127.

John Drayton, Letter to James Glen (1761)

[letter Oct 11, 1761]

Dear SirSo[uth] Carolina Octo[be]r 11 1761
   I hearby Congratulate you, and your Lady, on your safe arrival & short passage of five weeks, I hope it was pleasant and agreeable, and may you find all things to your wish. This news we had of Captain Curling, and we were in hopes of letters in him from you, but lo! we are disappointed. Dear Glennie[1] I hope is much better for losing those worms, off Charles Town bar, I pray God, for his safe Recovery from the Small Pox.
   No doubt you will say where is your Bill of Exchange[2] for the money due you from the Public. It is not in my Power to Procure a bill yet, tho' several times presid Mr. Martine the Pay Master, as you directed, he gives me some little hopes, when he Draws, but he says he cant do it till the return of the army who is dayly expected after doing nothing. I refer you to our Gazettes[3] for perticulars. You may depend I shall send that bill the moment it can be had. I dare not go to Town the Yallow fever is their.[4] Poor Mr. Rattray.[5] William Loyd[6] on the bay, Mr. Numan[7] & many others have felt a sacrifice to that destroying fever. they are now no more. I have not yet re[ceive]d the money for your Man Tom. Mr. Bullock[8] wrote me a few days ago, to know in whose hands his Papers was placed. since which I have heard nothing further Rice has been a Drug ever Since you left this.[9] after keeping your rice, with some of my own the whole Summer, expecting a market, a few days ago I was forced to get quit of it (as the new crop was so near at hand) at 37/6 and was paid in the Inclosed Bill of Ex[chan]ge which is equal to 40/ and six months 6 re[ceive]d and that six months, perhaps maybe nine. and no buy on at that tho' 40/ was the nominal price. This bill / Inclosed, is both for your rice, and mine, sold at once. I took mine also in same bill. your past is Sixty five pounds, and five pence Sterling being for your part of the crop made in one thousand seven hundred and Sixty. Exclusive of all Charges as to Plantation Matter, as you will me of acco[un]t adjusted for said Crop. last year was you know a very dog Season, and I think it is very well, considering as I may say put for Eight hands labour. tho' there is one negroe more, but she does nothing being Incapa-

– 21 –

ble, always afflicted with fits, which has so affected her, she is now an Idiot, can, nor, will not do nothing, but only a Charge and Expence.[10] this wench have been so from the first, but now grown worse. I must also acquaint you, about a month ago, you had a loss of a Negroe wench killed by a fall of a tree, clearing ground, so now in fact, these is but Eight of your Negroes with me, and one of them is the wench as above afflicted with the fits, and is good for nothing, as already mentioned. the next year Shair (if no Accidents happens this winter to any of them) will be but for Seven Shairs. lest you may want to know what is become of your nineteen hands,[11] inclosed is a list where they are gone. I gave you or your Lady an acco[un]t how they stood about Eighteen months ago, but since there is a further change as you will find [on the] list. It is not in my Power to help these misforunes tho' pritty great, yet you have lost nothing by the planting Interest if a just calculation were made. Billy Drayton[12] became a Planter but two years ago, and out of twenty odd have lost 9 hands your loss is but six out of nineteen, and in five years; so upon the whole, I have made a calculation, Reckoning the cost of your nineteen negroes a £210. round (tho' one parcel I know cost £220. the other cost but £200. (at an average I call them at £210. with the Interest upon that amo[un]t to but £5600 this November 1761. They / were purchased in November 1756, we will say, you are out of Pocket that sum, to said day above. let us see what negroes remains, we will lay Eight still a live, with the disorderd wench. call them at £250. round tho' seen of them may be worth as negroes sells, near £300. round, but I call it no more then £250 to make up for the sick wench. it will amo[un]t then (for Eight) to £2000. now we are to <take> notice for the five brought down, and deliverd you back again, say Pender Tattamore, Nanny, Tom and Jammie,[13] reckon these at what they cost £210. round, there is then £1050. add this to the £2000. Above is £3050. let us now notice the Several Sums clear paid you for the several years crop made. say for the year 1757 and the Year 1758 paid you £1137.2.11. the Interes on that will amo[un]t to £182. add both Interest and Principle of these two years crop to the £3050. will make the sum £4369.2.11. let us take notice further of the next ball[an]ce paid you for the crop made in the year 1759 is £668. the Interest will be about £52. add both

Principle and Interest to the four thousand three hundred and sixty nine Pound 2/11 will make it amo[un]t to £5089.2.11. now pay your part of this Inclosed Bill of Ex[chan]ge for your part of the crop clear of all charges for the year 1760 is £455.3.0 ½ add this to the above £5089.2.11 will make the sum £5544.5.11 ½ and we will suppose for the crop that is now upon the Ground for your part, four or five hundred Pounds more. Tho' I cant say what it will be. say five hundred pound. that will bring it up to about £6000. and upwards that you still have in hand with the negroes, you sold, and have now remaining. so you see you are against, of upwards of £400. They cost you Interest and all as the Calculation to Nov[embe]r 1761 but £5600. and to the same date, notwithstanding you had bad luck, you have in value for l<a>ying out of the above / £5600. upwards of £6000. as appears etc. think then how much better it would be had you not these misfortunes. I have done the best I can. Deaths, and sickness, I cannot help If I fail of your Expectation I am heartily Sory. I comfort my self you have lost nothing, but neather a gainer. In the Inclosed Bill there is of my money for my Childrens use in England[14] £94.19.7 when added to the £375 you carried, makes up above four hundred and seventy pounds. I should be glad Billy go to the College for about Eighteen months or two years. my wife tells me you use for Sending him Immediate ly out on Mr. Izards acco[un]t that scheeme is hazardous, whether it will succeed or not. If it should not, and Billy should be as Awkard a Lad as Tom Middleton,[15] Son, it will greatly displease me, where as if he was at the College for that time, he may Improve, and that Awkardness wair off and a Genteel behaviour and carage[16] in its stead. as for Charles[17] he may if you approve go with his Brother, or he may be directed at you

Please otherwise, so he comes not out in an Awkard or disagreeable light and if Billy can be Accomplished without going to the College, he need not go, if it is with your approbation, but let him not, at all events come out

before he attains an easy Air, carage & Good behaviour in company al-tho' he stays two years to come. Mr. Izard[18] will not Marry Immediately it will be time enough. I must now beg pardon for troubling you with this long letter. Tomie[19] Presents his Duty, and ask when Uncle and Aunt[20] is coming back. why don't they come to Mr. Drayton[21] will write you. In the meantime, Pray accept my best compliments you & Mrs. Glen[22] and I am Sincerely

Dear Sir

Your Most Affectionate Humble Ser[van]t

J[oh]n Drayton

P.S. The Bill is for £160. S[toc]k drawn on Mess[ers] Buchanan[23] & Simson[24] Merchants in Glasgow.

For Mr. Glen of this Bill £65.0.5
For Mr Drayton of this bill 94.19.7
£160.0.0

Drayton
11th Oct[ob]er
1761

A. W. RUMNEY (ED.), *FROM THE OLD SOUTH-SEA HOUSE* (1914)

A. W. Rumney (ed.), *From the Old South-Sea House, being Thomas Rumney's Letter Book, 1796–1798* (London: Smith, Elder, and Co., 1914), pp. 9–14.

This letter, like many of Thomas Rumney's letters, contains insight into how multiple family members influenced courtship practices. Thomas gives his advice to William, not just about William's interest in Miss Holyoak, but about their uncle's potential approval of the match. Other letters, not included here, touch on Thomas's own matrimonial pursuits. Courtship, even if parents were living, was largely the concern of young people in early modern England. Parental approval mattered, but it was not required by law or custom. Like Thomas and William, siblings were embedded in one another's marriage plans. Because marriage was virtually indissoluble, and often undertaken when one or both parents had died, siblings' positive judgment and support of a potential spouse was key. In this letter, Thomas offers his opinion on William's interest in Miss Holyoak and considers how their uncle would respond to knowledge of her. In the end, all of Thomas's advice and mediation yielded results for William; he married Charlotte Holyoak on 9 July 1799 in Morton Bagot, Warwickshire.[1] Thomas eventually returned to Cumberland to claim his spot as heir of the family holding (his older brother Anthony having died in 1798) and married an Elizabeth Castlehow in 1806.[2]

The Rumney brothers were born and raised in Cumberland. Their parents, William and Mary Rumney, had six children born between 1755 and 1766 – three girls and three boys. Thomas, born 1764, and William, born 1766, were the two youngest children.[3] Their father died when they were very young, in 1769, and their maternal uncle, Edward Clark, also a clergyman, played the role of surrogate father. This 1796 letter between Thomas Rumney and his younger brother, William, comes from Thomas's letter book containing letters he wrote between 1796 and 1798; Thomas also kept some accounts and a diary. Thomas was living in London, working as a clerk at the South Sea House when the letter was written. At this time his brother was a newly ordained priest in Overbury, Worcestershire.[4]

Notes

1. Church of England, Morton Bagot Parish Registers, marriage of Rev. William Rumney and Charlotte Holyoak, Warwickshire County Record Office Engl/2/1152, DR 274, in *Warwickshire Anglican Registers*, index and images, at www.ancestry.co.uk [accessed 1 September 2014].
2. Rumney, *From the Old South-Sea House, Being Thomas Rumney's Letter Book, 1796–1798*, p. 305.
3. A. W. Rumney (ed.), *From the Old South-Sea House, Being Thomas Rumney's Letter Book, 1796–1798* (London: Smith and Elder, 1914), p. xxi.
4. 'William Rumney (CCEd Person ID 122074)', *The Clergy of the Church of England Database, 1540–1835*, at http://www.theclergydatabase.org.uk [accessed 25 August 2014]. William was educated at Queen's College, Oxford and was ordained a priest on 25 July 1795.

A. W. Rumney (ed.), *From the Old South-Sea House* (1914)

London, 11th June, 1796.
Rev. William Rumney

Dear Brother,
I am favoured this morning with your letter of the 9th inst. acknowledging the receipt of and making a general reply to mine of the 25th ultimo. The voluntary remarks respecting Miss Holyoak which yours of the 13th ult. contained were too interesting and affecting to me, to pass over them without particular notice. But be assur'd I have to wish to extort sentiments from you that are at all adverse to your feelings. I spoke from the impulse of the moment.

Your being puzzl'd puzzles me. 'Tis true that it is a matter of the first importance, and of course requires very nice attention, and I shall be very glad to find for the lady's sake, that you pay it all that it deserves.

I am induced from your own account of Miss Holyoak[1] to think very favourably of her upon the whole. As to the term love I do not conceive that either you or I or Miss H. at this period of our lives are likely to be unfortunately bit by it, although I hope none of us are incapable of loving. Admitting Miss H. to stand affected as is represented, is she not entitled to your commiseration and unremitted attention until time produces your avowal, as being a real advocate for her affection or not? The bystander's answer is Yes, surely. I am far from thinking that you have a wish to impose upon the lady, either by engaging her affections, or endeavouring to occupy her whole attention as to connubial matters. But women, though admirably well formed to entertain man, ought to be sparingly smiled upon in their coquettish humours.

The coolness and long face you have put on as second thoughts, in this novel affair, have changed my ideas upon it much, and I now almost despair of having the pleasure of seeing a new sister anything near the time I had mark'd out. £500 on the fall of the male and female Oaks is something, but not tempting without something handsome from some quarter or another to make a suitable beginnings with. I thought the £500 was in the foot of an old stocking of her own, and a sanguine expectation of a noble windfall by-and-by as well as promotion to be obtained in the Church and to crown the whole, the acquirement of the object herself, so well calculated to make domestick life happy, which I hope will always be the primary consideration with you. Look at Old Square Toes as an example. Sharp Nose by her true love, esteem, and affection has done wonders in making his life easy and comfortable, and may be said to have prolong'd it full 12 or 15 years (in considering the general treatment of wives to their husbands). Young men I am every day more and more convinced are most damnably mistaken in forming their plans for comfort in a married state. They adopt notions full of vanity and pregnant with such unattainable matter that when they step into the engagement they find but shadows instead of substance, consequently get baffled and panick struck, and until quite new model'd and beat heartily with the whip of reason and prudence, they are not fit to fill the domestick seat, or claim a common share of tranquility belonging to that society. Since I wrote to you last I have had a letter from Mr. Clark,[2] now, a week since. He mentions your having announced your intention of paying a visit at the Vicarage, but makes no comments upon it necessary for me to repeat to you, but for your own particular government I think it necessary to mention that he tells me he sent you 5 guineas, when you were a candidate for the Living, and perhaps you might extort (as he calls it) 5 more. His letter is very short and says nothing of his own or Mrs. Clark's health. You say you have adjourned paying your respects to the Worthies, but do not say when you think it will suit you to go, which I presume you still intend doing ere long, and I wish the Old South Sea House[3] stood in the way, as I cannot say but I have a wish to have some personal conversation with you respecting the different projects you have in view.

 I beg leave to inform you that in my last letter to my uncle a few days ago, I took some notice of your having cast a sheepish eye at a Miss Holyoak, whom I thought, from the little I knew of her, to be tolerably well calculated to make a comfortable companion for you, and that I supposed he would find you inclined to discuss the matter before him, and pay some deference to his opinion.

 I supposed from your delay in answering my letter, you would be by your uncle's fireside when my letter reached him, and that it would afford you some mirth to find the Cockney talk so freely upon the subject of matrimony. I think it not improbable but that our mutual friend may ask you two or three blunt plain questions, such as—"Who is Miss Holyoak? What are her parents, and what are their circumstances, connections, and disposition towards their daughter? What is there to be laid hold of in hard cash on the Nuptial Day, and what to follow it? Any Church interest in the way? Have you made any professions of love to Miss, and what are your prospects of being happy with her? Can you maintain yourselves in credit according to the cloth upon your back?" I say such sort of questions might come from him, but I am persuaded neither diffidence nor difficulty would arise in your answering, and acquitting yourself like an honest man before him. If you feel a pleasure in encouraging the wish of forming a sound and honourable attachment to Miss H., pump your friends on both sides as to the ways and means for a supply. Miss H.'s friends must of course think of doing something on such an event, and your Reverend Brothers might say in compliment to you on so important and prudent an arrangement—Here's a purse containing so many guineas. I am glad to hear of your success in behalf of your friend, Mr. Martin, at Tewksbury.

Francis is a Johnson and Johnson is a Francis. I hope the dinner Mr. Martin gave the other day afforded you much mirth and enjoyment. Mr. Francis, I am told, attended a dinner party (one day last week given by Mr. Combe, a newly elected member for our City) at the London Tavern, and on his rising to make a formal speech, a cry of Martin, Martin, Martin! prevailed much, and the great man was a little disconcerted. I have pleasure in your calling Mr. Martin friend,[4] and should be glad to hear of your partaking of it more to advantage than the mere treat of roast beef, plum pudding, a glass of wine, etc. I hope to hear a pleasing account of the introduction of his nephew into his new office, and that you have settled your own business with him to advantage. The new Act of Parliament I also hope will afford a pleasant sort of relief. Your next visit into Warwickshire I also hope to hear a particularly good account of. I had a letter from our brother Anthony,[5] dated five weeks ago. It mentioned our mother being pretty well, provisions dear, his intention of managing all his own landed property, his wish to be married, Jemmy Barker of Sparkhead having lost his life in stubbing up an oak tree which fell upon him etc. Farewell, Parson.

Thomas Rumney.

Forwarded on the 14 inst.

CHESNUT AND COX FAMILIES, CORRESPONDENCE (1797, 1800, 1810)

John Chesnut to Mary Chesnut, 6 July 1797, 2 October 1800, 23 August 1810; Esther Cox to James Chesnut, 24 May 1800; Esther Cox to Mary Chesnut, 11 September 1810, 27 September 1810. Papers of the Cox and Chesnut Families, 1792–1858, University of South Carolina Digital Collections, Folder 5: 1 June 1797–11 July 1797, Call Number: Manuscripts Plb 5-FWS-9-2, Folder 9: 14 March 1800–28 October 1800 Call Number: Manuscripts Plb 5-FWS-9-2, Folder 29: 23 August–28 October 1810 from Papers of the Cox and Chesnut Families located in South Caroliniana Manuscripts Division. Call Number: Manuscripts Plb 5-FWS-9-2http://library.sc.edu/digital/collections/coxches.html.

This collection, covering 1797 to 1810, is a sampling from a much larger collection of family papers (see Volume 2). The Chesnut family hailed from South Carolina, but marriage and business took them farther afield and gave them connections to northern states – as evidenced by the letters exchanged here between Camden, South Carolina, Philadelphia and New York. The bulk of these letters are between Mary Cox Chesnut (1775–1864) and her father-in-law, Colonel John Chesnut (1743–1818), who referred to her as his daughter – a common slippage in eighteenth-century usage of kinship terms.[1] There is a letter from Esther Bowes Cox to her son-in-law, James Chesnut (1773–1866), and letters between daughter and mother: Mary and Esther.

The various family members exchanged advice on financial, social and health problems. Taken as a whole, the letters show how family members, both consanguineal and affinal and from various generations, worked together to build a family culture of support and equity. Business matters, an update on the health of a sickly child, the purchase of books for grandchildren, and the discussion of equitable inheritance for daughters are discussed by all family members. Overlaying the details of the letters is a tone of affectionate and intimate friendship among all family members. In this way, the Cox and Chesnut correspondence highlights the importance of affection in the formation and maintenance of eighteenth-century families and their connections to social and economic stability.[2]

Notes
1. Tadmor, *Family and Friends in Eighteenth Century England: Household, Kinship, and Patronage*, pp. 119–22, 163.
2. Pearsall, *Atlantic Families: Lives and Letters in the Later Eighteenth Century*, pp. 15–17.

Chesnut and Cox Families, Correspondence (1797, 1800, 1810)

Mrs. Mary Chesnut
Camden
So. Carolina
Mail-

Phil[Adelphia] 6th July 1797

My dear Daughter

I wrote you a few lines in a hurry before I left Charleston, and since my arrival here I have rec[eive]d a few lines from you (and is the only one received) next post I expect to hear from you all – the letter inclosed for Mrs. Stockton,[1] I expect to deliver the last of next week. I am much pleased with the very friendly and polite attention of your friends here, which in part renders my stay here great agreeable, and makes me feel quite at home, I am Sure you will have no Complaints that I do not Visit them often enough, as I had forgot which of the young Ladies I was to meet with a kiss – to be right and not make a mistake on the wrong side I intend to meet them both in that way, I have only dear Miss Sally yet,[2] and am much pleased with her, we were quite acquainted the first day, the Doct[o]r is tyed fast / to her apron string, I can never Catch him from her side, and as I am fond of siting by her, myself, she generally has one on of each side – the very friendly, and Constant enquiries after you by every one here who calls, or even hears my Name, you may be Sure is very pleasing to me, and I find Ja[me]s[3] also has many friends in this place – I am Sure of a long Conversation about you every day, and as you have promised me that you will not be made vain, I may Venture to tell you how agreeable the Subject is to me equally so with the rest of your friends, almost every time I go to your mothers, I am pretty sure to meet [where] two, or three Ladys there, to enquire after, & talk about Mary, I tell them all how much better you look than your Sister Sally, and that you are as Content, & happy as you can be is possible for you to be absent from your mother & Sister – I sincerely wish that you may continue to enjoy your health through these Warm Months, be carefull not to expose yourself, & Keep as Cool as possible, I think my room would be much Cooler and more Air than yours, pray make use / of it – and if any thing that is proper & Suitable for the Window Curtains, get a Suit Made, if not to be had in Camden, get Ja[me]s to send to Charleston, for such as you think proper. I shall be quite Mortified if you get the fall fever, or any Sickness – that can be avoided by Care – I remain with the Sincerest regard, and esteem

your truly Affectionate father
John Chesnut[4]

as I know you love Writing to your friends, I shall [illeg.] to hear from you very often, tell me the News and Occurrences of Camden –

/

Captain James Chesnut
Camden
South Carolina

Philad[elphia] May 24th 1800-

My dear Sir

I have now another letter of yours, which wou'd have been most agreeable to me – if it had not told me that Mary was again worse – how hard it is for her to be so many weeks helpless – I often sit & fancy I see her looking at her infant & wishing she cou'd wash & dress it – but is forced to let another perform that office – I think I have heard you say that you have excellent Nurses among your black women, & therefore I can't Suppose she has wanted for any help they cou'd give – I pray that your next may inform me she is in a fair way again, & then, however, she may wish to sew, I hope she won't attempt it, there can be nothing worse for her complaint, than using the arm in that way – Tomorrow Mrs. Baldwin is to Sail in the Schooner Minerva – Captain Hughes – all things are on board I believe, she has not call'd yet for the Passage Money – but I expect her every minute, the Captain asks twenty five Dol[lar]s for her Passage, and the same Sum if he feeds her – I thought she had better provide her own Stores, & she agreed to it, & was to call on me for the Cash – I hope they may have a safe Passage – Mr. C. Prichney goes in the same Vessell, & I believe a french Lady – The Box of Maps are on board, but the chairs, by the Mistake of the Maker were put on board of the Schooner Betsy-Holland – Captain Webb – but I have inclosed both Bills of Lading in a letter to Constey Himay & Co. – & recommended Mrs. Baldwin to their care – She has in her trunk a Parcell for Mrs. Alexander – from Mrs. Liston - & a little present from me to each of my grandchildren – Betsy[5] had great pleasure in making the Cap for her little Nephew[6] – Theodosia[7] is still at Harrisburgh – Betsy & I look rather Solitary at our small Table, but we make out to eat our allowance notwithstanding – I find myself much better whithin the Past ten days – my head-ach is not so frequent – Your Solicitude for my comfort, & convenience in having Horses, is truly filial, & I wish I had resolution to encounter the dificulties attending the keeping them – but I don't dare trouble, & I cannot find a person that will take it, without my paying an enormous price – however, I don't quite relinquish the Idea, & your pressing it so much will have great weight with me – It looks whimsical, to drive for a short time, & then lay it down, & I much fear / that wou'd be the case – I intend shortly after Sally releases me from my anxiety for her, to hire a Coach & go to Lancaster – I told Mary in my last that Mr. Barton[8] was ill, he has been extremely so, but is now much better – I believe the arrangement I shall make for the Summer will be, to stay at Lancaster myself – Betsy will either be with me or go to Hoboken, I cannot yet say which – My paper is so thin I must take the other Side / Theodosia is to accompany Mrs. Stockton to the Springs in Sussex for her health. I suppose I shall Shut up my Home, & take my best Servant with me, send my little Susan to Trenton - & do as well as circumstances will permit me – tis indeed a Serious affair to disband ones family every year – We hope The Enemy will not appear this Summer, but we have no Security & ought to be prepared – Sally will lay no Plan for herself – as the Dr. don't seem to be affraid – but if it once makes its appearance, he will hurry her off as he did last year – Now I think of it, let me ask yours & Mary opinion on a Subject which I shall mention separately to each of my children – You know Sally comes to The age of 21 Years on the 10th next July – Her Fathers Will[9] is so worded I believe as to make no other provision against that time, than the interest on the Deferred Stocks of the U.S. – which does not become due 'till 1801, nor payable I believe untill April of that year. Now, we all agree, that it cou'd not have been the intention of Mr. Cox[10] to put one Child on a different footing from the rest – Equity says, she / ought to receive her full Annuity from the time she becomes of age – but I believe the Law wou'd not give it her 'till it arose from the stocks appropriated to her use – She really wants it & I mean to propose to each person concerned, that they authorize me to pay it her, not as a favor, but doing as they wou'd be done unto, as her right, knowing as they all do, that she was not less beloved by her Father than every other Child – Will you read over the Will & give me your opinion – She alone, the Will bears hard upon - & I can only account for it by Mr. Cox's classing the two youngest children together without taking into consideration the difference in their ages – If I cou'd bring this matter about without oppressing her with the weight of obligation, I shou'd be pleased – the Dr. I know wou'd not consent to any writing if he knew of it but I shall not tell them 'till I know the result of my childrens opinions nor then, if it don't accord with my feelings – he has never asked me to advance one dollar for her, & is as any under a limited income as any person cou'd be – his grand Father is very generous, & they are both economists – but I am sure she wou'd like to feel herself a little more independent – I have paid for your Fathers Chair, & charged them to you 3 1/2 Dol[lar]s a Chair,

& I find the freight will be half a Dol[la]r a Chair – Sunday Morning – Mrs. Baldwin call'd last evening for her passage money she is to bring [illeg.] from the Capt[ain] tomorrow morning as the Vessell does not Sail 'till then - & it may be another day or two – I shall pay for all her stores, & advance her a little money, if she requires it, but I will leave the commencement of / her wages to be setled between you & her, she has said nothing to me about it yet – As I shall Dine at the Dr. I must seal & send my letter before I go to Church – but first must thank you for your kind remembrance in sending a Cask of Hams, which I make no doubt will arrive in due time, & shall be distributed agreeable to your intention – I had just sent for a Barrell of Hams to Burlington, which Dr. Rush gladly took, Y paid the Bill, so these will be very acceptable – Did Mary ever hear of her friend Matilda Yeats's being Marry'd to her Cousin, a Mr. Walton – a very proper Match for her – I did not tell her I believe of Miss Hazlehurst's marriage with a Mr. LaTrobe the great Engineer – The Old Lady Lawrence was buried a few days ago – I believe I did mention that her daughter Mrs. Indy Lawrence died about three weeks ago - & Old Mr. Francis a few days after – My most affectionate love to my dear Mary & her sweet children – I hope for a good account of her soon – Compliments to your Father & Family – I am my dear Son –

Yours sincerely E. Cox

/

Mrs. Mary Chesnut
Camden
So. Carolina

Philadelphia 2ᵈ Octo[ber] 1800

The rain preventing me Leaving the City, as intended this afternoon, affords me an opportunity to answer the receipt of my dear Daughter's Letter of the 12ᵗʰ Alt[hough] which I acknowledge I ought to have done Some days ago, but am almost confident you will not accuse me of neglect, when I assure you that you are among the last, (I had like to have said the last) that will experience any from me – and as I have already written this morning have but little to Add – yesterday I spent very agreeably at German Town, after Sitting to Mr. Stewart, I went to the races where Among [the illegible word was struck through] the display of female Beauties, I saw for the first time this trip the Nobillity of Pennsylvania, the <u>excountess</u> / her mother, Satange, tho' the appearance of Ladies, Carriages, & horses was not equal to So. Carolina by any means, but upon the whole pretty Tollerable

I am rather doubtfull by my Saying in my Letters from New York that I intended to Set off for Carolina on the first of October that I shall receive no more Letters from home, which always Contributes to reconcile absence from family, & friends but expect of course, I shall hear through your Mother on my return from Jersey, where I am going to procure two more horses for my Journey, which I now expect, & intend to Commence by the 15th at latest, perhaps Sooner, and hope to hear that Little John[11] has quite recovered his good state of health & Spirits again; ~~and~~ Say to Serena[12] that I expect to See great improvement in her Education when I come home,

I have Just now rec[eived] a Small packet / from your good Little friend Mrs. Kennedy[13] for you, as I know pretty near that it only Contains a pattern for a dress, shall not forw[ard] it 'till I come myself, all your friends here are in good health remember me affectionately to James, the Children & all there at home, & believe me to remain
    Very Sincerely
    Your affectionate father
    John Chesnut

Maj[or] Butler - & his family Set out for Camden to morrow, Doc[to]r Mease & his Lady does not accompany them, they all appear very good friends & quite reconciled – I know you will be attentive to the young Ladys – as they have been so to me.
/
    Mrs. Mary Chesnut
    Camden
    South Carolina

New York – 23rd Aug. 1810

My dear Daughter

I soon got tired of Lebanon & declined to visit Ball Town again – having Purchased a pair of Poneys and a Light Carriage enabled me to travel by land at my ease & Comfort to view the Country as I passed & having Long wished to travel down the east side of the North river by Land I come that rout, and was much gratified with the high Cultivation & beautifull Seats & Prospects as I pass'd down, to be Sure about twenty Miles of the road, was not so pleasant (Called the high lands) very Rocky, rough, & stoney not Capable of that improved Cultivation, that all the rest of my Journey down afforded, on my way I spent One day & night with Chancellor Livingston to View his Merinos (his Hobby at present) where I was received with great hospitallity & attention by himself & family, and particularly so by his Amiable daughter, Mrs. R. Livingston who enquired / very friendly and affectionately after you, both herself and her husband press'd me much to Spend another day with them (which I regret I did not do). She is realy a Charming Woman how does it happen that I cannot be a favorite with the Ladys at Camden as I generally do better & pass pretty well abroad, the tour by Land has been equally fortunate, & Speedy so far, as all my water passages have been this trip I have been Bless'd with perfect health ever Since I left home, have already travel'd four hundred Miles by Land –

I shall go over & pay a visit to your friends before I Leave this City. Mrs. Kinsey tells me that they are all well and now at Hoboken – I purpose to Leave here about a week hence, and to Spend a few days at Brighton (Amboy) now became famous, and greatly resorted by the Gay from hence, & from Philadelphia

On my Arrival here, I had the pleasure to receive Several Letters, three from James – of the 26th July, 2nd and 9th Aug, I expect one or two of his Letters must have Miscarried - & particularly those giving an Account of the [illeg.] in our [illeg.] / that we have from other Carolinians who I meet in almost every Town this year – however by Ja[mes] C[hesnut]- Last Letter, I have reason to hope that the Crops have not been greatly injured with us – as has been represented from Santu & Cayareer

it affords me very great satisfaction to learn that you all enjoy good health at the Sand-hill my Love, & best wishes to Ja[mes] & the Children and remain
    My dear Daughter
    Your very affectionate father
    John Chesnut
/
Mrs. Mary Chesnut
Camden
South Carolina

                                            Philad[elphia] Sept[ember] 1st 1810

My dear Mary –
    Your last gave me great pleasure as it said you were all in good health. I have look'd for the letter as I wished to reply to it particularly shou'd it require it, but I suppose I must have sent it to Sally's as I frequently do when she can't come here, for I cannot find it where it ought to be – and now I will proceed to tell you how we come on here – The Steam Boat performs all that was expected of it, by the Sanguine Owners Robert is Just come down in her, with eighty passengers – They have seldom less than fifty, & sometimes a hundred. Three times a week up to Burdon Town, and three time back to this place. Often on Sunday they go either to Burlington, or Chester & back again – I hope now they will make some profit to replace the Money expanded, but another will be wanted to ply where this will want repairs –
    I shall expect shortly to see your Papa Chesnut, as Sept[ember] has arrived – I have hear'd several times of him lately as a neighbour of ours has been traveling for his health, and met him at Newhaven I believe – Hetty Barton[14] met him in

company, & he mention'd Mr. Chesnut as being a lively fine Old gentlemen, it was Mr. Inskeep, his daughter as with him, and Mr. Claypoole told Hetty too that she had a letter from his daughter in New York, who is at Mrs. Braddock's, full of the praises of Mr. Chesnut – you know all the Young Ladies are charmed with him, he takes care to put them in good humour with themselves – You never mention'd whether I shou'd purchase for you, "Hunter's Sacred Biography" – the oppor[tuni]ty of sending by Mr. Chesnut is so good, I shall send my dear Serena the Tales of fashionable Life, by Miss Edgeworth, and if I thought you had not Miss Moor's Coelebs, I wou'd send that also, but I think you must have it / tis so celebrated, & has gone through so many editions, that I am almost sure you must have read it. tis a serious work, as all hers are, full of good Sentiments, and instructions to Parents, as well as to Bachelors, in search of a Wife – If Mr. Chesnut says you have it not, I will send it – I am sure you will approve the greatest part of it, Notwithstanding some of the reviewers, find fault with it –

Sally Coxe desired I wou'd give her love to you, & say, that though her little family is much better than she was, yet her fears are kept up still – the changeable weather we have lately had, has affected the child much – yet I really think it will be raised, though it may possibly be a Sickly Child all its life, & require extraordinary care – tis a little delicate creature now, that a puff of strong wind wou'd blow over – her others are well – Betsy has this day brought her little family home – she came up a few minutes before dinner, & is to return to Tea with us – hers are both well – Francis Stevens[15] has been with us a week now & will stay some time longer, he is to enter a Counting House this Autumn, having taken his degree in College this Summer – as did Richard – I don't know what Richard means to pursue – John is very industrious geting his Farm in order, & in preparing to raise Merino Sheep, Mr. Harris is still weak & complaining – Julia Stockton has been a long time suffering with the fever and Ague – she cannot shake it off by any means yet tried – I have sent for her to come down here, our City is very healthy – I think the change of air, and the ride down will have a good effect – Mr. Grant has been at the point of Death in New York, Mary was sent for & is there still, I had a letter a few days ago from her in which she says the Drs. have pronounced him out of danger – my last from Theodosia brought a good account – Hetty Barton is in good health and desires her affectionate remembrances to you – As tis near Teatime, I will leave the remaining side of my paper to fill tomorrow – /

Sunday the 2^d

While the family are at Church, I will finish my letter – I generally give you our City News, but excepting Mr. Edward Bard's Marriage, I know very little, that being a great Match, it has of course made a little talk – to the rich Miss Sims – Mrs. Deas may remember Mr. Bard – I don't believe you knew much of him

– a splendid Wedding – but they went off the next day, & have not yet returned – The cool weather will soon bring the company from the watering places, and our City will resume its usual appearance – I am walking about the House, but I do not yet walk out, for I have had a slight attack of my old complaint of pain in the side, but it did not amount to Pleurisy – the Rheumatism in my Arm also troubles me a little, but as I can write with the lame one you you may be sure it is not very bad – only another Memento, that I am very near Seventy years old – I shou'd not mention these circumstances, but to accustom my children to bear them in mind, for I enjoy so many blessings, and any decay is so gentle, that I cannot be too thankfull for these great Mercies – I have every indulgence, that the best of children, and a Competency of this Worlds good, can afford me – think of me always, my dear Mary, as being happy – the separation from you I feel, as I know you do also – but we think alike of it, tis necessary, & Therefore right, and tis our duty to be satisfied, and enjoy the great alleviation to it, of so frequently communicating in this way – shou'd Providence see fit to prolong my life, I may once more see you, and those we all love – I desire to feel easy on that head, and acquiesces cheerfully in every dispensation of the Almighty –

Give my most affectionate love to Mr. Chesnut & all the Children, Compliments & good wishes to all friends – I am my dear Mary – with unabated love – Your affect[ionate] Mother

E Cox

/

Mrs. Mary Chesnut
Camden
South Carolina

Philad[elphia] Sept[ember] 11th 1810

My dear Mary

I rec[eived] yours of the 22d-August, the day after I sent my last – and the next day your Papa Chesnut arrived in good health – He found here Mr. Singletons family, (as I suppose he has told you) Hetty, & Sally waited upon them, and they all drank Tea with me one afternoon, but the old Lady who was unwell – the next day Mr. Chesnut brought a handsome Carriage to the door, & Mr. Reed, myself & Hetty Barton, accompanied him to their lodging – I am delighted with the Old Lady, who talk'd much of you and the children – her Son's daughter is just such a sprightly fine girl as your Mary was when you were here last – Mrs. Browne's Sons are fine looking boys, but Miss Manning I was charmed with, as we all were so affable, unassuming, and every way agreeable, that I was sorry we cou'd not have more of her company – They gave one afternoon to Sally Coxe, & the next day went away – Your Papa went to German Town the next day and this morning came in again, & brought his Carriage to take Sally & Hetty there, but poor Hetty is too Sick to leave her room – Sally has promised to go with him the days after tomorrow, & if Hetty is well enough she will then go, if not Julia Stockton will take her place – She & her sister came down on Saturday, with Francis Stevens Julia is very thin & weak, has a slight touch of her fever some days, but is getting well I think I hope to send her home in a few weeks hence quite well – Hetty Stockton will return to her Mother as soon as Mrs. Barton can be about House again – as I shall not close this letter till next Sunday I hope to be able to say she is as well as ever –

Boudinot Stockton arrived last week from Madeira & Lisbon, He looks fatter & better than he did – He sisters are made very happy by seeing him, and he is going up with Hetty to see his Mother – she has better health ~~than~~ now than for some time past. Mr. Harris is in the same way, sometimes better, sometimes worse – Mr. Grant is recovering very slowly, is still at N. York where he was taken ill, at his brothers – Mary is with him / Mr. Chesnut will have much to relate I suppose, having been to so many places since he left this – I will now put by my letter; it being dinner time

-Saturday the 15th

The day before yesterday, Mr. Chesnut call'd agreeably to promise and took Julia, Sally, Nurse & Child, to her old lodging in German Town they had rain all day yesterday so that they cou'd not ride out, I expect them home to day – Hetty Barton is so far recovered as to walk about the room, probably will go down stairs tomorrow – she has had a small attack of Billious Fever which she almost every Summer has – She desires her best love to you, says she hopes yet to have her ride with Mr. Chesnut in his handsome Carriage –

I am much better than when I last wrote, can walk about House, and manage a little as I used to do – I really feel better for the exersize I have taken – I kept Hetty Stockton to assist me, & Boudinot & Francis Stevens went to Trenton yesterday – Betsy Binney pass'd last evening with us, she desired I wou'd remember her with affection to you – her children are well – Mrs. Bayard has return'd from her Summer's excursion, much benefited by it, as has her Brother Pettit, who is much reduced, by a disorder of the Stomack, he is getting better – Our City has not been sickly, but rather remarkably healthy, the deaths even among the children, are small in comparison to some years, we have had the last five days very warm again, but yesterdays gust, has changed and purified the air, that I expect the hot weather is now over – the verdure is as fine now, as in the spring, we have as much rain –

Mr. Chesnut requested, I wou'd get one of my young folks to chuse some Books for his Grand children – I shall get them next week – He tells me you have Coelebs, and he has already purchased the "Scottish Chiefs," a work very much admired, and which I was going to send you, but as he has them, tis necessary – I shall put in his package, the 2 Vollumes of Fashionable life for my dear Serena, /

and 1 Vol[lume] of Juvenile Poems, for my Grand daughter Mary – I also send the "Maternal Instructress," for whoever you think will be most pleased with it – the 4 Vollumes of "Hunters Sacred Biography," are not on fine paper, but the print is good, and the come much cheaper than those that are elegantly bound – these 4 cost eight dollars, forty Cents, which I shall pay for & charge to your acct. – I wish you may have as much pleasure in reading them as I have had –

Sally & Julia have Just returned from German Town, they bring word that Mrs. Reeds Father was suddenly taken ill – Apoplexy or somethink like it – The family live at German Town – Sally's little girl seems better for the ride, but Julia has a return of her fever – the weather was so damp yesterday it gave it to her – I hope it won't be of any continuance – Miss Molly McCall desires to be affectionately remember'd to you, I sent for her to Tea the day those Ladies were here, on purpose that she might have the pleasure of hearing them talk of you – She and Mrs. Gatliff were both at Sally's with them – they speak of Mrs. Deas's child as being quite a beauty, as well as a fine healthy one – please to give all our remembrances to her, & Mr. [illeg.] – Sunday Morning the 16th – I will now bid you Adieu for this time – Mr. Chesnut did not call here yesterday, being engaged to Dine a few miles out of Town – Sally says he has been in fine spirits ever since they went out, He lodged at the same place they did – Julia is quite bright this morning, and Hetty Barton is so much better as to talk of dining down stairs – We all Join in love to your Mr. Chesnut, and all the children – Francis Stevens is here & says they are all well at home, as he learns by his letters – Tomorrow I shall look for your Usual letter, I hope it will tell me you are quite well – Kiss the dear little ones in remembrance of me – Dear Mary Your affec[tionate] Mother – E. Cox

Dr. Rush's Son John, does not recover so much as they expected, he has been at home, but they were obliged to send him back to the Hospital – Grief has injured Mrs. Rush greatly – what is / the Death of a Child compared to this living Sorrow – He appears now in good health – but his intellect quite destroyed, he is not outrageous, but talks a great deal, and at home was not Manageable – He wou'd not change his clothes or get into Bed – but sat up all night –

/
Mrs. Mary Chesnut
Camden
South Carolina

Philad[elphia] Sept[ember] 27th 1810

My dear Mary –

Your last of the 5th Sept[ember] I am now to reply to, I am glad to find your family all continue well at Sandy Hill, where I suppose you will continue till cold weather – Your Papa Chesnut gave me the pleasure of reading a letter from you to him written since mine – well may I say, the pleasure – for I never saw a more beautifull one, both for Hand writing, & the Sentiments it contain'd – if I had not before known he was one of the best of Fathers, I shou'd have been convinced of it by your letter.

The day before yesterday He left our City, & has warm weather for Travelling – after a two weeks Storm, it has cleared up uncommonly warm – having so many invalids, we had fire all the cool weather, and now we are siting with all the windows & doors open – Mr. Chesnut can give you a good account of my health, for I have not been as well as I am now for seven Months past – I begin to walk out, and ever since Hetty Barton has been Sick I have gone about House, & managed the family as I need to do – He will tell you that Hetty is almost well, that she was down stairs to receive him the two last times he took Coffee with us, and they pass'd their Jokes as usual – she gave him a letter for you, which he said she had better put in the Post Office as he shou'd be so long on the road, but she said no, it wou'd serve to introduce him to you, for as you he had been so long about, you might have forgotten him

I tried to have all my children to meet him the last time he was here, but Betsy was suffering with the tooth-ach, & cou'd not come out – Sally was here, and my four Grand Children of the Stockton Family – but he will tell you all about us, so I will say no more, than that Sally purchased for him five dollars worth of / new Musick – beside what she purchased for you, which also cost five dol[lars], the Irish Melodys were dear – but as they were New, she bought them, and I hope to have the pleasure of hearing my dear Serena, and her Mama also play them – once I thought I shou'd not see you more, but my health is so much amended, that I may still enjoy the hope at least – especially as Mr. Chesnut has given us expectation of your all being here next year – we talked of it often, but as we cannot govern circumstances, we must be content to wait their Issue – I shall charge the five dol[lars] & the eight for Hunter's work, with the last five dollars order'd for Mrs. Baldwin's Mother, to your account with your Fathers Estate – We have lately had seven hundred dollars to pay Catharine Groves for her Life Estate in a small House in Walnut Street, which we sold to Mr. Vallee, having purchased it of Touch Francis 15 years ago to increase the depth of our 5th Street Lots – He gave us a Bond of indemnification against her life, but he has fail'd & is not worth a Copper, her Lawyers brought a charge against us of fourteen hundred dollars, but Mr. Binney talk'd them off, and offer'd seven, which she accepted, and it is paid – Now if we cou'd settle with the Williams's, there would be an end of our difficulties – they demand more than we are willing to pay – and so much time has already been lost, and so much trouble encounter'd, and real difficulties to overcome, that we dread the Law, as it will procrastinate the Sale of the Land,

and bring heavy expenses against it. Mr. Binney has therefore concluded to make a generous offer for their right, and not go into the Matter again – if they accept it, we can then sell, without waiting for their concurrence – we have already lost one year since we obtained the Title tho the Farm has been rented for that time – If they settle it in the way we propose, and which some of their friends also think the best way, I will let you know, and the probable value it will be of to us – In my last I told you of Julia Stockton's being ill here, after her return from German Town, she was much worse, Now she is better again, her ague has not return'd / for a week past, and she is riding out again – Hetty Stockton goes home on Monday, we kept her to help Name the two invalids – Sally Coxe thinks her little girl will get well – it is not yet weaned – that circumstance will, I think, determine her case – I do not think her so well as her Mother does, but yet tis right to wean her, as she has suck'd twenty one Months, and her Nurse begins to feel weak, and sick – Sally is handsomely setled in their Mothers House, and she is now busy in getting her Curtains, Carpet, &c& - fitted to the rooms – she can only furnish one parlor for this year – the Dr. taking the front untill he can build himself a room back for a library – tho the house is large, there being no back buildings, it gives them not many chambers. She takes the best for her own lodging room, & the one on the same floor for a Nursery she has a spare one up two pair of stairs – the Yard is very pleasant with grass & flowering Shrubs and open to the South - I thought I had told you that I consulted Dr. Physick, after talking some time he said he wou'd think of it and call again, which he never has done, I therefore concluded he cou'd do me no good, & did not send again – I find it does not get better, except when my health is strongest, I find less difficulty in swallowing I don't expect a cure, and study to have such soft food, that will nourish me, and is easiest to eat, Soup is a Main part, Dr. Physick was dangerously ill, but has recover'd – I received a letter from Theodosia a few days ago – She and her three children are well – she desires I wou'd particularly mention her love to you – so does Kitty Harris from whom I hear often, she has rather better health this summer, & Mr. Harris is not worse, which is all he can expect, for his situation is still dangerous – Mr. Grant has so far recovered as to come home, Mary is well – As to Mrs. Cunningham, she now signs herself Rachel Noble, and plagues me with her letters – She is still in our Alms House, and has Married one of the Paupers there, (as she says) – I have had much trouble with her – she sometimes continues to get out & I suppose she will come here one day or other – She has been to Dr. / Coxe's & he talk'd with her – and to Mr. Binneys, but he did not see her – Hetty Barton was there and told her a few truths. She cursed her relations one and all but me, & said she wou'd come and see me, Hetty told her she shou'd not see me, & if she attempted to come into the house, she wou'd repent it – hitherto she has received her Pension from England – if she is really Married, I suppose she will get it no more, but as she has said so twice before, and sign'd her Name Carny, I don't think it likely this is a better Marriage – with love to every body – Your affect[ionatel]y

    E Cox

Sunday Morning

    My children, one & all that are with me send their love – poor Julia is afraid you will think she does not intend to perform her promise of writing to you – but you know the Ague is a lazy disorder – she has an Anecdote of Kirkbride Milnar that will surprise you, if you have not already heard it, with respect to Miss Cornelia Rhea, to whom he was engaged to be Married – Kiss all the dear little ones in remembrance of me – To Mr. Chesnut particularly present my love.

    E Cox

LOVEJOY FAMILY CORRESPONDENCE (1817–19)

Lovejoy Family Correspondence (1817–19), Ferris and Lovejoy family papers, Harold B. Lee Library (hereafter HBLL), Provo, UT.

The word 'Friend', Naomi Tadmor explained, 'had a plurality of meanings that spanned kinship ties, sentimental relationships' and 'spiritual attachments'.[1] Eighteenth-century American families maintained friendship bonds through kin-keeping, which, according to C. Dallett Hemphill, 'was a mix of obligation and choice' such as family traditions, socializing, religious worship, and acts of service and assistance.[2] Kin-keeping work was conducted through letters, when a family member left the home. These letters were sent by parents and children, despite their varying levels of literacy, to strengthen bonds with absent relatives.[3] Letters also allowed family members separated by great distances to express their close sentimental affection and attachment to each other.

In addition to the participation of consanguineal families in epistolary kin-keeping, Christians also relied on letter writing to sustain their faith-based family.[4] As canonized examples, the New Testament letters of Paul and other early Church leaders exhorted and strengthened their early Christian brothers and sisters. Eighteenth-century Christians similarly addressed their fellow believers as brother or sister in their letters to signify their egalitarian bond as Christians.[5] The bond of Christian fellowship could be strengthened by correspondence, since, as Clare Brant has noted, 'Letters played out etymological connections between communion, communication and community'.[6] An important communication to a brother or sister in the faith was the account of a fellow believer's death and how the deceased comported him/herself during the final hours.

The first letter below demonstrates the kinship-keeping work of Henry Lovejoy (b. 1775) in communicating brotherly affection to his older brother Joshua (b. 1771).[7] Hemphill noted that the late eighteenth century saw a 'rise of affective expression on the part of brothers' and a 'heightening of male friendship'.[8] Because Henry was shortly to be deployed on a warship, he took the little remaining time he had ashore to communicate his feelings and financial difficulties to his sibling. The brothers were four years apart in age, so although Henry started his letter by addressing his elder brother, Joshua, formally as 'Sir', he concluded with more sentimental language: 'your friend and Brother'.

Joshua Jr also received a letter from his father, Joshua Sr, who addressed his son with even greater affective language than had Joshua junior's sibling, Henry. Joshua Sr had been born in Andover, New Hampshire, on 8 January 1743 or 1744. On 30 April 1769 Joshua married Sara Perkins and they became the parents of ten children.[9] Joshua served in the French and Indian Wars and rose to the rank of second lieutenant in the Eighth Continental Infantry on 1 January 1776. By 1778, the Lovejoys had relocated to Amherst, NH and by 1794 they had moved to Sanbornton, where Joshua served in several civic positions and committees until his death in 1832. While Lieutenant Lovejoy had finally established himself in one place, by 1818 at least half of his children no longer lived in Sanbornton, NH. As an affectionate father, Lieutenant Lovejoy performed kin-keeping work by writing to his oldest son about the health and financial challenges of some of his siblings: Andrew (1772), Jonathan (1780), Warren (1784/5), Lydia (1786) and Mary 'Molly' Lovejoy Taylor (1781/2). Lieutenant Lovejoy also offered instruction; Brant explained, 'Unpublished letters from mothers and fathers show how parents interpreted their role as advisers'.[10]

The final letter below is from William Wing, whose kinship relation to the Lovejoys is undetermined. Wing's letter to Joshua Jr, however, employed the language of familial attachment, either from a biological relationship or fictive Christian fellowship. By writing a letter recounting his wife's death, Wing included the absent family, namely Joshua Jr and Sally, in the shared experience of those who were in attendance. Brant explained that 'Deathbed literature was especially relevant [to devotional letter writing] since it was said that what distinguished Christians from others was, first and last, their confidence in the jaws of death'.[11] Wing's letter, like Joshua Sr's, demonstrates the importance of epistolary correspondence for strengthening friendships with absent family members.

Notes
1. N. Tadmor, *Family and Friends in Eighteenth-Century England: Household, Kinship and Patronage* (Cambridge: Cambridge University Press, 2001), p. 167.
2. C. D. Hemphill, *Siblings: Brothers and Sisters in America* (Oxford: Oxford University Press, 2011), p. 63.
3. C. Brant, *Eighteenth-Century Letters and British Culture* (Houndsmill, Hants: Palgrave, 2006), p. 1.
4. Clare Brant explained how 'To be a Christian was to join a fellowship' that was shared through correspondence, *Eighteenth-Century Letters and British Culture*, p. 312.
5. Hemphill, *Siblings*, p. 83.
6. Brant, *Eighteenth-Century Letters and British Culture*, p. 313.
7. C. E. Lovejoy, *The Lovejoy Genealogy with Biographies and History 1460–1930* (New York: the author, 1930), p. 107, at http://hdl.handle.net/2027/wu.89061962387 [accessed 11 November 2014].

8. Hemphill, *Siblings*, pp. 67, 83.
9. Lovejoy, *The Lovejoy Genealogy with Biographies and History 1460–1930*, p. 106.
10. Brant, *Eighteenth-Century Letters and British Culture*, p. 60.
11. Brant, *Eighteenth-Century Letters and British Culture*, p. 311.

Lovejoy Family Correspondence (1817–19)

[Boston, Mass. 1799.]

    Henry Lovejoy's Letter Dec 28 1799
    Mr Joshua Lovejoy
    Meredith[1]
    Plymouth New Hampshire

Dear Sir,[2] Boston December 21, 1799
    In a few days, I expect to leave this Country and my friends, for we are ordered off for the Havannah,[3] and I hope when you hear from me again, I shall be in better health than I now am; for I have not enjoyed one days health since I have been in Boston which is about four weeks and that is not the worst of my missfortune, for that old enemy which which[sic] always did attend me, attends me still which is want of cash or in the words poverty and the reason is this ever since I have belonged to the Ship I have been keep on Shore by the officers and have been obliged to pay my own expences which has amounted to about fifty dollars which is all the money I rec'd in advance; the loss of which has brought me into a situation not very agreeable to my feelings for it has put me quite out of my calculations: and in consequences of my being to short of / money I am under the necessity of going to sea for a 8 or 10 months voyage not half prepared for one of half the length of time: the difficulties and disadvantages that may attend me in consequences of it you seem not be able to judge, but from the foresight I have of is being by this time some acquainted with the necessary equiptments for such a voyage begin to see the difficulties that I must go through for the event of – or a friend but as it is my fortune so I must take it and make the best of it, it may be that some time, or, other I may see better days if not they are not worth keeping for a person that is one day sick and another disappointed and have been so much of it as I have I think cannot fail to be discouraged. but enough of my misfortunes – for I must close, and believe me to be your friend for I have your welfare as much at heart as I have my own, remember me to all my friends for I have not time to write to / them, being every moment employed

in {tear}ting for the ship, which has hurried me while I have been writing this – I am him with the greatest respect your friend and Brother

> Henry Lovejoy
> To Mr Joshua Lovejoy
> NB, our Capt is a Ignorant Selfconseited and a great Pumpkin

[written on the outside of the letter:] died on the 11th day of July 1800 on board the Mariner Sloop of War off Vera Cruz in S. America. Buried in 20 fathoms Water[4]

> Sandbornton[5] M
> Nh 22–181825
> Mr Joshua Lovejoy Esq-[6]
> Buffalo New York Niagara County[7]

Sandbornton April 18th 1818

Beloved Son

These with my best Love and Affections to you and your Family, hoping you ~~and your Family~~ are in Good health, by the Goodness of God I in joy a midling good State of health my Self I have had Considerable of the Rumitis this Spring but have got much beter of them, your Mother[8] is in a low State of health she keeps about the house but is Very feble Under Goes a Grait deal of pain has a hard dry ~~Coss~~ Cofes, Your Sisters and ther Families are all in Good health Esp[ecially] Taylor & Family[9] are all well I heard from Andrew[10] Jonathan[11] & Warrin[12] in March they were all in the City of New York Warrin's Wife and Children are Most of them at Concord I wish to hear from you I wish you to write to me as Soon as May be how you fare these hard times Whether you are likely to Git any Compinsation from Government for your Losses by the enemy in the time of Our War,[13] I advise you to keep up your Courage and do the best you Can for your Self & Family your Brothers have made grait Ship wrack with there property how they git along I know not the Bankrupt Act[14] has faild in passing in Congress and they must Stay in the State of New York at present. I have no perticular News to write you, Lydia jornis with your Mother and my Self in Love to you and your Wife and Family – from your affectionate Father – Joshua Lovejoy
    Mr Joshua Lovejoy
    /
    Glens Falls
    23rd Nov 1819

Joshua Lovejoy
Buffalo
Glens Falls[15] November 22 1819 –

Dear Brother & Sister in my Last Letter I rote in ~~Curing~~ Curageing Conserning my Wifes Health I was mistaken She has Continued to Grow Weaker Till the 12 Day of this Mont on Which Day She Expired at Ten minits Past four in the Which was Amoust Dreadful Seen for my Self & famaly But I thank God for all Things But more Espekly for the Grace Found With our Savour Some months Before She Departed this Life She Retaind her Sences & Was able to Speak till the Last She Give Every Proof of and Was in Full Belief of going in to the world of Bliss Where all Troubels are over and all happy She Died most Triumphantly She was in Grate Pain the Night She Died one our Before She Left this Life I see She Could not Continue Long I asked her if She new how near She was to her End She Said She Should Now When She Was agoing to Die Do you think Said She that Death Alarms me no it Dose not your father Continues With us and Was at her Bed Side With the rest of the famaly She Gave us all moste noble advice aspesshaly her Children Who ware all in Tears Round her Bed and Escorted us all Not to mourn for her But for our Selves -- / We w[i]sh you to in form Jabesh[16] of the on happy news and my sencere Wish is to here of you Well fair offise Jabesh never wrights I Wish he Woul[d] Your Father is Going to Canan[17] Soon We are all in health one thing Gives me Grate Consolation that is my Children Conduct them Selves Stiddy and mariah[18] Gives Proofs of conducting her Self in the Famaly Concers us Steddy as menny youth at twenty years old We wish you to rite offin

   W[illia]m Wing[19]
   To Joshua Lovejoy & Sally Lovejoy[20]

ANNA LETITIA BARBAULD, *HYMNS IN PROSE FOR CHILDREN* (1781)

Anna Letitia Barbauld, *Hymns in Prose for Children. By the Author of Lessons for Children* (London: Printed for J. Johnson, No. 72, St. Paul's Church-Yard, 1781). ECCO, ESTC Number T053117, ECCO Range 1931.

Legal adoption only became available in England in the early twentieth century.[1] During the long eighteenth century, childless couples had to look to family members for potential heirs. One such couple was Thomas and Catherine Knight, who were in possession of several estates, but childless. After several years of marriage, they approached their distant cousin, George Austen, to ask if they could adopt his third son, Edward, who had accompanied the newlyweds on their honeymoon in 1779.[2] After Thomas Knights' early death, his adopted son and heir, Edward Austen Knight, was able to offer a rent-free cottage on his estate to his mother and two unmarried sisters, Cassandra and Jane Austen. The theologian, chemist and political theorist, Joseph Priestley, had been adopted at the age of nine, by a childless aunt and uncle after the death of his mother.[3] The interfamily adoption of young Charles Aikin by his childless aunt and uncle not only transformed the Barbauld family, but also children's literature.

A year after their marriage, Anna Letitia Aiken (1743–1825) and Rochemont Barbauld were childless and Anna Letitia was looking to her younger brother's family for an adoptable son. John and his wife, Martha (a first cousin), had three boys: Arthur, born in 1773; George, in 1774; and Charles Rochemont, in 1775. Shortly after Charles' birth, Anna Letitia teasingly wrote to John and Martha: 'send him to us, and we will bring him up for a Norfolk farmer ... You may keep him a few months yet before you pack him up in the hamper; and then I desire you will send him with all speed; for you know he is to be mine.'[4] The following year, Anna Letitia petitioned:

> Now I know not what to say to induce you to make us such a gift. Perhaps you will entirely deny it; and then we must acquiesce: for I am sensible it is not a small thing we ask; nor can it be easy for a parent to part with a child ... I would likewise put you

in mind that you would not part with it to strangers; the connexion between you and it would not be broken off: you would see it (I hope), hear of it often; and it should be taught to love you, if it had not learnt that lesson before. Our child must love our brother and sister.[5]

Later that year, the early death of John and Martha's fourth child may have softened their hearts towards parents who lamented the absence of an infant child. The following year, in the summer of 1777, two-year-old Charles went to live with the Barbaulds. Anna Letitia was true to her word, since Charles called Rochemont, 'Father', and continued to refer to John Aikin as father, and most likely called Anna Letitia and Martha, 'Mother'.[6]

Now with a son to care for, Barbauld turned her energies to transform children's educational and devotional literature. After she wrote several *Lessons for Children* (see Volume 2), Barbauld published *Hymns in Prose* (1781). Like *Lessons for Children*, the format of *Hymns in Prose* was printed with the capacities for small children in mind: small books with large type inside large margins, and about fifty words per page. In *Hymns in Prose* Barbauld also accommodated hymnody to small children.[7] Before adopting Charles, Barbauld had composed hymns, some of which were poems that could be set to music and sung by a congregation in a church service; for her boy, Barbauld rejected the formal aspects of hymns, such as stanzas, meter and rhyme scheme, in favour of the liturgical experience of communal reading and reciting of her devotional text.

Hymns in Prose, therefore, was Barbauld's catechism and the doctrine was the universal family of God, for 'he is the parent of all, for he created all' and therefore, 'he loveth all, he is good to all' ('Hymn III'). Barbauld preached Frances Hutcheson's ethics of moral behaviour, from his *Short Introduction to Moral Philosophy* (1753): the individual's compassionate capabilities were developed first in the family and then radiated outwards to offer aid to those, like the 'Negro woman, who sittest pining in captivity' ('Hymn VIII').[8] Barbauld traced Hutcheson's model of enlarged moral empathy in 'Hymn VIII', by starting with the nuclear family, which then expanded to the household family, where all co-resident members were deserving of sympathy because 'they are very closely united, and are dearer to each other than any strangers. If one is sick, they mourn together; and if one is happy, they rejoice together.' Barbauld continued to expand the family by explaining that the household family combined with other household families to form a larger village family, and these combinations replicated and exponentially expanded until these families created the largest family of all, the world.

Hymns in Prose was reprinted twelve times during Barbauld's lifetime, and posthumously reprinted every few years until 1905.[9]

Notes

1.   A. Teague, *Social Change, Social Work, and the Adoption of Children* (Aldershot: Gower

Publishing Company Limited, 1989), p. 2.
2. W. Austen-Leigh and R. A. Austen-Leigh, *Jane Austen: A Family Record*. Revised and Enlarged by Deirdre Le Faye (New York: Barnes and Noble Books, 1989), pp. 40–1.
3. W. McCarthy, *Anna Letitia Barbauld: Voice of the Enlightenment* (Baltimore, MD: Johns Hopkins University Press, 2008), p. 188.
4. Quoted in McCarthy, *Anna Letitia Barbauld*, p. 187.
5. Quoted in McCarthy, *Anna Letitia Barbauld*, p. 188.
6. McCarthy, *Anna Letitia Barbauld*, p. 188.
7. McCarthy, *Anna Letitia Barbauld*, p. 208.
8. McCarthy, *Anna Letitia Barbauld*, p. 211.
9. McCarthy, *Anna Letitia Barbauld*, p. 215.

Anna Letitia Barbauld, *Hymns in Prose for Children* (1781)

PREFACE.

AMONG the number of Books composed for the use of Children; though there are many, and some on a very rational plan, which unfold the system, and give a summary of the doctrines of religion; it would be difficult to find one calculated to assist them in the devotional part of it, except indeed Dr. Watts' Hymns / for Children.[1] These are in pretty general use, and the author is deservedly honoured for the condescension of his Muse, which was very able to take a loftier flight. But it may well be doubted, whether poetry ought to be lowered to the capacities of children, or whether they should not rather be kept from reading verse, till they are able to relish good verse: for the very essence of poetry is an elevation in thought and style above the common standard; and if it wants this character, it wants all that renders it valuable. /

The Author of these Hymns has therefore chosen to give them in prose. They are intended to be committed to memory, and recited. And it will probably be found, that the measured prose in which such pieces are generally written, is nearly as agreeable to the ear as a more regular rhythmus. Many of these Hymns are composed in alternate parts, which will give them something of the spirit of social worship.

The peculiar design of this publication is, to impress devotional feelings as early as possible on the infant / mind; fully convinced as the author is, that they cannot be impressed too soon, and that a child, to feel the full force of the idea of God, ought never to remember the time when he had no such idea – to impress them by connecting religion with a variety of sensible objects; with all that he sees, all he hears, all that affects his young mind with wonder or delight; and thus by deep, strong, and permanent associations, to lay the best foundation for practical devotion in future life. For he who has early been accustomed to see the Creator in the visible appearances of all around / him, to feel his continual presence, and lean upon his daily protection – though his religious ideas may be mixed with many improprieties, which his correcter reason will refine away – has made large advances towards that habitual piety, without which religion can scarcely regulate the conduct, and will never warm the heart.

A. L. B.[2] /

HYMNS in PROSE for CHILDREN.
HYMN I.

Come, let us praise God, for he is exceeding great; let us bless God, for he is very good. /
He made all things; the sun to rule the day, the moon to shine by night.
He made the great whale, and the elephant; and the little worm that crawleth on the ground.
The little birds sing praises to God, when they warble sweetly in the green shade. /
The brooks and rivers praise God, when they murmur melodiously amongst the smooth pebbles.
I will praise God with my voice; for I may praise him, though I am but a little child.
A few years ago, and I was a little infant, and my tongue was dumb within my mouth: /
And I did not know the great name of God, for my reason was not come unto me.
But now I can speak, and my tongue shall praise him; I can think of all his kindness, and my heart shall love him.
Let him call me, and I will come unto him: let / him command, and I will obey him.
When I am older, I will praise him better; and I will never forget God, so long as my life remaineth in me.

HYMN II.

COME, let us go forth into the fields, let us see how the flowers spring, / let us listen to the warbling of the birds, and sport ourselves upon the new grass.
The winter is over and gone, the buds come out upon the trees, the crimson blossoms of the peach and the nectarine are seen, and the green leaves sprout.
The hedges are bordered with tufts of primroses, and / yellow cowslips that hang down their heads; and the blue violet lies hid beneath the shade.
The young goslings are running upon the green, they are just hatched, their, bodies are covered with yellow down; the old ones hiss with anger if any one comes near.
The hen sits upon her nest of straw, she watches / patiently the full time, then she carefully breaks the shell, and the young chickens come out.
The lambs just dropt are in the field, they totter by the side of their dams, their young limbs can hardly support their weight.
If you fall, little lambs, you will not be hurt; there is spread under you a carpet / of soft grass, it is spread on purpose to receive you.
The butterflies flutter from bush to bush, and open their wings to the warm sun.
The young animals of every kind are sporting about, they feel themselves happy, they are glad to be alive, – they thank him that has made them alive. /
They may thank him in their hearts, but we can thank him with our tongues; we are better than they, and can praise him better.
The birds can warble, and the young lambs can bleat; but we can open our lips in his praise, we can speak of all his goodness.
Therefore we will thank / him for ourselves, and we will thank him for those that cannot speak.
Trees that blossom, and little lambs that skip about, if you could, you would say how good he is; but you are dumb, we will say it for you.
We will not offer you in sacrifice, but we will offer / sacrifice for you, on every hill, and in every green field, we will offer the sacrifice of thanksgiving, and the incense of praise.

HYMN III.

BEHOLD the Shepherd of the flock, he taketh care for his sheep, he leadeth them among clear brooks, / he guideth them to fresh pasture; if the young lambs are weary, he carrieth them in his arms; if they wander, he bringeth them back.

But who is the shepherd's shepherd? who taketh care for him? who guideth him in the path he should go? and if he wander, who shall bring him back? /

God is the shepherd's shepherd. He is the Shepherd over all; he taketh care for all; the whole earth is his fold: we are all his flock; and every herb, and every green field is the pasture which he hath prepared for us.

The mother loveth her little child; she bringeth it up on her knees; she nourisheth its body with food; she / feedeth its mind with knowledge: if it is sick, she nurseth it with tender love; she watcheth over it when asleep; she forgetteth it not for a moment; she teacheth it how to be good; she rejoiceth daily in its growth.

But who is the parent of the mother? who nourisheth her with good things, and watcheth over her with tender / love, and remembereth her every moment? Whose arms are about her to guard her from harm? and if she is sick, who shall heal her.

God is the parent of the mother; he is the parent of all, for he created all. All the men, and all the women who are alive in the wide world, are his children; he loveth all, he is good to all. /

The king governeth his people; he hath a golden crown upon his head, and the royal sceptre is in his hand; he sitteth upon a throne, and sendeth forth his commands; his subjects fear before him; if they do well, he protecteth them from danger; and if they do evil, he punisheth them.

But who is the sovereign / of the king? who commandeth him what he must do? whose hand is stretched out to protect him from danger? and if he doeth evil, who shall punish him?

God is the sovereign of the king; his crown is of rays of light, and his throne is amongst the stars. He is King of kings, and Lord of lords: if he biddeth us live, / we live; and if he biddeth us die, we die: his dominion is over all worlds, and the light of his countenance is upon all his works.

God is our Shepherd, therefore we will follow him: God is our Father, therefore we will love him: God is our King, therefore we will obey him. /

HYMN IV.

Come, and I will shew you what is beautiful. It is a rose fully blown. See how she fits upon her mossy stem, like the queen of all the flowers! her leaves glow like fire; the air is filled with her sweet odour; she is the delight of every eye. /

She is beautiful, but there is a fairer than she. He that made the rose, is more beautiful than the rose: he is all lovely; he is the delight of every heart.

I will shew you what is strong. The lion is strong; when he raiseth up himself from his lair, when he shaketh his mane, when the voice of his roaring is heard, / the cattle of the field fly, and the wild beasts of the desart hide themselves, for he is very terrible.

The lion is strong, but he that made the lion is stronger than he: his anger is terrible; he could make us die in a moment, and no one could save us out of his hand.

I will shew you what is / glorious. The sun is glorious. When he shineth in the clear sky, when he sitteth on his bright throne in the heavens, and looketh abroad over all the earth, he is the most excellent and glorious creature the eye can behold.

The sun is glorious, but he that made the sun is more glorious than he. The eye beholdeth him not, for his / brightness is more dazzling than we could bear. He seeth in all dark places; by night as well as by day; and the light of his countenance is over all his works.

Who is this great name, and what is he called, that my lips may praise him?

This great name is GOD. He made all things, but he is / himself more excellent than all which he hath made: they are beautiful, but he is beauty; they are strong, but he is strength; they are perfect, but he is perfection.

HYMN V.

The glorious sun is set in the west; the night-dews fall; and the air which was sultry, becomes cool. /

The flowers fold up their coloured leaves; they fold themselves up, and hang their heads on the slender stalk.

The chickens are gathered under the wing of the hen, and are at rest: the hen herself is at rest also.

The little birds have ceased their warbling; they are asleep on the boughs, / each one with his head behind his wing.

There is no murmur of bees around the hive, or amongst the honeyed woodbines; they have done their work, and lie close in their waxen cells.

The sheep rest upon their soft fleeces, and their loud / bleating is no more heard amongst the hills.

There is no sound of a number of voices, or of children at play, or the trampling of busy feet, and of people hurrying to and fro.

The smith's hammer is not heard upon the anvil; nor the harsh saw of the carpenter. /

All men are stretched on their quiet beds; and the child sleeps upon the breast of its mother.

Darkness is spread over the skies, and darkness is upon the ground; every eye is shut, and every hand is still.

Who taketh care of all people when they are sunk in sleep; when they cannot / defend themselves, nor see if danger approacheth?

There is an eye that never sleepeth; there is an eye that seeth in dark night, as well as in the bright sun-shine.

When there is no light of the sun, nor of the moon; when there is no lamp in the house, nor any little star twinkling through the thick / clouds; that eye seeth every where, in all places, and watcheth continually over all the families of the earth.

The eye that sleepeth not is God's; his hand is always stretched out over us.

He made sleep to refresh us when we are weary: he made night, that we might sleep in quiet. /

As the mother moveth about the house with her finger on her lips, and stilleth every little noise, that her infant be not disturbed; as she draweth the curtains around its bed, and shutteth out the light from its tender eyes; so God draweth the curtains of darkness around us; so he maketh all things to be hushed and still, that / his large family may sleep in peace.

Labourers spent with toil, and young children, and every little humming insect, sleep quietly, for God watcheth over you.

You may sleep, for he never sleeps: you may close your eyes in safety, for his / eye is always open to protect you.

When the darkness is passed away, and the beams of the morning-sun strike through your eye-lids, begin the day with praising God, who hath taken care of you through the night.

Flowers, when you open / again, spread your leaves, and smell sweet to his praise.

Birds, when you awake, warble your thanks amongst the green boughs; sing to him, before you sing to your mates.

Let his praise be in our hearts, when we lie down; let his praise be on our lips, when we awake. /

HYMN VI.

Child of reason, whence comest thou? What has thine eye observed, and whither has thy foot been wandering?

I have been wandering along the meadows, in the thick grass; the cattle were feeding around me, or reposing / in the cool shade; the corn sprung up in the furrows; the poppy and the harebell grew among the wheat; the fields were bright with summer, and glowing with beauty.

Didst thou see nothing more? Didst thou observe nothing beside? Return again, child of reason, for there are greater things than these. / – God was among the fields; and didst thou not perceive him? his beauty was upon the meadows; his smile enlivened the sun-shine.

I have walked through the thick forest; the wind whispered among the trees; the brook fell from the rocks with a pleasant murmur; the squirrel leapt from bough to bough; and the birds sung / to each other amongst the branches.

Didst thou hear nothing, but the murmur of the brook? no whispers, but the whispers of the wind? Return again, child of reason, for there are greater things than these. – God was amongst the trees; his voice sounded in the murmur of the water; his music warbled in the / shade; and didst thou not attend?

I saw the moon rising behind the trees: it was like a lamp of gold. The stars one after another appeared in the clear firmament. Presently I saw black clouds arise, and roll towards the south; the lightning streamed in thick flashes over the sky; the thunder growled at a distance; / it came nearer, and I felt afraid, for it was loud and terrible.

Did thy heart feel no terror, but of the thunderbolt? Was there nothing bright and terrible, but the lightning? Return, O child of reason, for there are greater things than these. – God was in the storm, and didst thou not perceive him? His terrors / were abroad, and did not thine heart acknowledge him?

God is in every place; he speaks in every sound we hear; he is seen in all that our eyes behold: nothing, O child of reason, is without God; – let God therefore be in all thy thoughts. /

HYMN VII.

Come, let us go into the thick shade, for it is the noon of day, and the summer sun beats hot upon our heads.

The shade is pleasant, and cool; the branches meet above our heads, and shut out the sun, as with a green / curtain; the grass is soft to our feet, and a clear brook washes the roots of the trees.

The sloping bank is covered with flowers: let us lie down upon it; let us throw our limbs on the fresh grass, and sleep; for all things are still, and we are quite alone.

The cattle can lie down / to sleep in the cool shade, but we can do what is better; we can raise our voices to heaven; we can praise the great God who made us. He made the warm sun, and the cool shade; the trees that grow upwards, and the brooks that run murmuring along. All the things that we see are his work.

Can we raise our voices up / to the high heaven? can we make him hear who is above the stars? We need not raise our voices to the stars, for he heareth us when we only whisper; when we breathe out words softly with a low voice. He that filleth the heavens is here also.

May we that are so young, speak to him that always was? / May we that can hardly speak plain, speak to God?

We that are so young, are but lately made alive; therefore we should not forget his forming hand, who hath made us alive. We that cannot speak plain, should lisp out praises to him who teacheth us how to speak, and hath opened our dumb lips. /

When we could not think of him, he thought of us; before we could ask him to bless us, he had already given us many blessings.

He fashioneth our tender limbs, and causeth them to grow; he maketh us strong, and tall, and nimble.

Every day we are more active than the former day, / therefore every day we ought to praise him better than the former day.

The buds spread into leaves, and the blossoms swell to fruit; but they know not how they grow, nor who caused them to spring up from the bosom of the earth.

Ask them, if they will tell thee; bid them break forth / into singing, and fill the air with pleasant sounds.

They smell sweet; they look beautiful; but they are quite silent: no sound is in the still air; no murmur of voices amongst the green leaves.

The plants and the trees are made to give fruit to man; / but man is made to praise God who made him.

We love to praise him, because he loveth to bless us; we thank him for life, because it is a pleasant thing to be alive.

We love God, who hath created all beings; we love all beings, because they are the creatures of God. /

We cannot be good, as God is good, to all persons every where; but we can rejoice, that every where there is a God to do them good.

We will think of God when we play, and when we work; when we walk out, and when we come in; when we sleep, and we wake, his praise shall dwell continually upon our lips. /

HYMN VIII.

See where stands the cottage of the labourer, covered with warm thatch; the mother is spinning at the door; the young children sport before her on the grass; the elder ones learn to labour, and are obedient; the father worketh to provide them food: either he tilleth the / ground, or he gathereth in the corn, or shaketh his ripe apples from the tree: his children run to meet him when he cometh home, and his wife prepareth the wholesome meal.

The father, the mother, and the children, make a family; the father is the master thereof. If the family is numerous, and the grounds large, there are servants to / help to do the work: all these dwell in one house; they sleep beneath one roof; they eat of the same bread; they kneel down together and praise God every night and every morning with one voice; they are very closely united, and are dearer to each other than any strangers. If one is sick, they mourn together; and if one is happy, they rejoice together. /

Many houses are built together; many families live near one another; they meet together on the green, and in pleasant walks, and to buy and sell, and in the house of justice; and the sound of the bell calleth them to the house of God, in company. If one is poor, his neighbour helpeth him; if he is sad, he comforteth him. This is a village; see where it stands enclosed / in a green shade, and the tall spire peeps above the trees. If there be very many houses, it is a town – it is governed by a magistrate.

Many towns, and a large extent of country, make a kingdom: it is enclosed by mountains; it is divided by rivers; it is washed by seas; the inhabitants thereof are countrymen; they speak the same / language; they make war and peace together – a king is the ruler thereof.

Many kingdoms, and countries full of people, and islands, and large continents, and different climates, make up this whole world – God governeth it. The people swarm upon the face of it like ants upon a hillock: some are black with the hot / sun; some cover themselves with furs against the sharp cold; some drink of the fruit of the vine; some the pleasant milk of the cocoanut; and others quench their thirst with the running stream.

All are God's family; he knoweth every one of them, as a shepherd knoweth his flock: they pray to him in different languages, but he / understandeth them all; he heareth them all; he taketh care of all; none are so great, that he cannot punish them; none are so mean, that he will not protect them.

Negro woman,[3] who sittest pining in captivity, and weepest over thy sick child; though no one seeth thee, God seeth thee; though no one pitieth thee, God pitieth / thee: raise thy voice, forlorn and abandoned one; call upon him from amidst thy bonds, for assuredly he will hear thee.

Monarch, that rulest over an hundred states; whose frown is terrible as death, and whose armies cover the land, boast not thyself as though there were none above thee: – God is above thee; / his powerful arm is always over thee; and if thou doest ill, assuredly he will punish thee.

Nations of the earth, fear the Lord; families of men, call upon the name of your God.

Is there any one whom God hath not made? let him not worship him: is there / any one whom he hath not blessed? let him not praise him.

[...]
THE END. /

ANN MURRY, *MENTORIA: OR, THE YOUNG LADIES INSTRUCTOR* (1799)

Ann Murry, *Mentoria: Or, the Young Ladies Instructor, in Familiar Conversations on Moral and Entertaining Subjects: Calculated to Improve Young Minds in the Essential, as well as Ornamental Parts of Female Education. The Second Edition, Corrected and Enlarged. Dedicated, by Permission, to the Princess Royal* (London: Printed by Frys, Couchman, and Collier, for Charles Dilly, in the Poultry, 1780), ECCO ESTC Number:T231307, ECCO Microfilm Reel#:Range 14525.

Conduct books for women, according to Naomi Tadmor, were also conduct books about 'friends'.[1] The word, 'Friend', Tadmor explained, 'had a plurality of meanings that spanned kinship ties, sentimental relationships ... occupational connections ... intellectual and spiritual attachments' and 'sociable networks'.[2] A young woman's appropriate behaviour towards this broad spectrum of friendship relationships was categorized and delineated by writers of conduct books. By reading this courtesy literature, young women also received practical and moral instruction on their duties as daughters and their future duties as wives, mothers and widows.[3] Conduct literature written by women, moreover, usually provided an example of powerful and wise maternal governance and intelligent, active girlhood. Mitzi Myers has noted that women who wrote educational literature for young women 'read nurture as power, showing a decided preference for maturity over the childishness male preceptors recommend to women.'[4] Conduct books enlarged a young woman's awareness of her relationships as a member of a household family and of a community.

The appropriate conduct of a young woman to the different members of her household family and to those in her community was articulated by Ann Murry (b. c. 1755, fl. 1816) in *Mentoria; or, The Young Ladies Instructor* (1799). Not much is known about the life of Murry beyond a few particulars: she was born in London, her father was a wine-merchant and she lived near the Tottenham High Cross.[5] *Mentoria* was Murry's first publication and proved so popular it had been reprinted ten times by 1800.[6] In *Mentoria*, Murry's dialogic pedagogy was enacted by two characters: the pupil, Lady Mary, and the teacher, Mentoria.

Murry, as did other female writers, feminized authority figures – transforming the male mentor into her maternal teacher, Mentoria.[7] Murry chose the dialogue form, because 'Dialogue and Fable are generally esteemed the best vehicles to convey instruction, as they lure the mind into knowledge, and imperceptibly conduct it to the goal of wisdom'. This dialogue form could provide a model for mothers on how to instruct their daughters. The knowledge Murry desired to convey was diverse: subjects in *Mentoria* ranged from truth, grammar, civility, geography, history, Sabbath observance, the Spartan form of government, astronomy and adversity. This selection is from the tenth dialogue, which was entitled, 'On the relative Duties of Life; in which the obligations we owe to our fellow-creatures are compared to those due to our Creator, and traced in regular gradation; but more especially considered ...'.

Notes
1. N. Tadmor, *Family and Friends in Eighteenth-Century England: Household, Friendship and Patronage* (Cambridge: Cambridge University Press, 2001), p. 245.
2. Tadmor, *Family and Friends in Eighteenth-Century England*, p. 167.
3. 'Writings on Education and Conduct: Arguments for Female Improvement', n V. Jones (ed.), *Women and Literature in Britain 1700–1800* (Cambridge: Cambridge University Press, 2000), pp. 25–45, on p. 26.
4. M. Myers, 'Impeccable Governesses, Rational Dames, and Moral Mothers: Mary Wollstonecraft and the Female Tradition in Georgian Children's Books', *Children's Literature*, 14 (1986), pp. 31–59, on p. 54.
5. 'Ann Murry', English Poetry 1579–1830: Spenser and the Tradition, at http://spenserians.cath.vt.edu/authorrecord.php?action=GET&recordid=33749 [accessed 23 October 2014].
6. Murry wrote a sequel later in 1799, but it was not as successful as *Mentoria*.
7. Myers, Impeccable Governesses, Rational Dames, and Moral Mothers', p. 34.

Ann Murry, *Mentoria: Or, the Young Ladies Instructor* (1780)

DIALOGUE X.
WEDNESDAY. On the relative Duties of Life, with a general Exhortation to Virtue.

[...] Lady *Louisa*.
Why are they called *relative Duties*?

Mentoria.[1]
Because they comprehend the different classes and degrees of duty, respect, or love, which are due to those who are connected with us, either by blood, friendship, or dependence; such as parents, brothers, sisters, masters, servants, and friends. This Duty is so diffusive, it may be traced in regular gradation, from the monarch who sits on the throne, to the most inconsiderable of his subjects. I shall therefore confine myself to the consideration of those particular branches, which seem best suited to your age, and station in life.

Lady *Mary*.
I hope, my dear Mentoria, you will explain each of these branches separately.

Mentoria.
With great pleasure, my dear Lady Mary. The Duty we owe to our *parents*, bears a near resemblance to that which is due to our Creator; / as it consists of gratitude, obedience, and love. The blessings of our creation, preservation, and redemption, produce religious faith, and impel the mind to adore and worship the Cause from whence they proceed. In like manner, as we derive our existence from our earthly parents, and owe our safety and improvement to their tenderness and love (which, in the helpless state of infancy, we could not acquire by any other means) we are bound to render them the tribute of gratitude, by paying implicit obedience to their commands.[2]

[...]

Lady *Louisa*.

Pray, Mentoria, what is our Duty to our *brothers* and *sisters*? I suppose we are to love and be kind to them.

Mentoria.

You are bound to respect those who are older than yourself; and to instruct and protect / those who are younger. You should treat them on all occasions with tenderness and love; nor ever seek an opportunity to dispute with, or tease them. Be also particularly cautious to set a good example, to excite emulation in those who are your elders, and to afford a pattern worthy of imitation to those who are younger.[3]

[...]

Lady *Mary*.

Masters, I think, is the next branch you are to consider. What kind of Respect, or Duty, do we owe to them. /

Mentoria.

Superiority, of whatever quality it consists, demands Respect, whether it proceeds from the possession of virtue, knowledge, or power, in the superlative, or greatest degree. Your masters therefore are entitled to receive every mark of attention you can possibly shew. You should never consider them as your equals, which will prevent any levity of conduct in their presence. You are all indispensably bound to attend to their instructions, which you will retain and profit by, if you acquire the habit of treating them with deference and politeness.

Lady *Louisa*.

I wish to know, how you would have us behave to our *servants*, my dear Mentoria.

Mentoria.

With humanity and condescension: you should always remember, notwithstanding they are your inferiors, they are your fellow-creatures, and in your conduct towards them, equally avoid haughtiness and familiarity. Maintain your own dignity, nor ever lose it, by permitting a servant to joke with you, or partake of your recreations:[4] such proceedings are not the effect of humility, but of a depraved / taste, and meanness of spirit. There are some persons so fond of superiority, they choose to associate with those who are beneath or dependent on them, for no other reason, than the opportunity it affords them of gratifying their inclinations without control or reproach.

Lady *Mary*.

We may command our servants, I suppose, to do every thing we like!

Mentoria.

This right, my dear Lady Mary, extends no farther than the bare discharge of their duty, and ought to be exercised with caution and discretion. We should never lay an injunction on them, which appears not possible, or convenient for them to perform; and be ever ready to accept any reasonable excuse for the non-performance. Let us in this, as in every other instance, incline to the side of mercy: let us break the bonds of servitude, and ease our dependents of every oppressive yoke.

Lord *George.*

How should we conduct ourselves to our *friends*, my dear Madam? /

Mentoria.

We are ever inclined to perform acts of kindness to those we style our friends. This duty is so diffusive, and the motives so numerous, which urge us to the discharge of it, there requires but little to be said on this branch; more especially, as in a former discourse I enumerated the mutual obligations of friendship. I shall therefore proceed to point out the goodwill we owe to the human species, without limitation or exception. The philanthropy I mean to recommend, is not only a Duty, but a Virtue. Those who exercise it in the superlative degree, must possess benevolence, moderation, and steadiness; and be wholly exempt from arrogance, malice, or prejudices, either personal or national: they must be inclined to redress the grievances of the distressed, comfort the afflicted, and clothe the naked;[5] to which they should be alone impelled by the dictates of the Christian religion, and the force of their own feelings: neither should they wish or expect any reward, but what arises from the consciousness of having performed their duty.

[...] Lady *Louisa.*

Are there any other Duties, my good Mentoria?

Mentoria.

It is necessary, for the good of the community, that there should be subordination in the different classes of mankind. I shall consider them under the heads of Superiority, Equality, / and Inferiority; which, I hope, will enable you to form a just conception of the several states. Superiority requires the persons who possess it, to act with dignity and caution; to exercise their authority with moderation and justice; and to dispense their favours to those who appear most deserving of them.

Lady *Louisa.*

What is our Duty to our Equals?

Mentoria.

Like most other Duties, they are reciprocal, and consist of a mutual exchange of kind offices, and general good-will. As this state equally excludes profound respect and implicit obedience, it is necessary to point out the medium which should be preserved between these extremes, in order to make the cement of friendship binding. Undue familiarity proverbially produces contempt: we have also scriptural authority, that where servile fear is, there can be no love, as love casteth out fear.[6] From which it may be inferred, our deportment towards our Equals ought to be tinctured with the respect due to our Superiors, and the condescension and freedom authorised to our Inferiors; which is productive of the pleasing / compound, usually called *Politeness*.[7] Without the due observance of this amiable quality, the friendly intercourse of society degenerates into Barbarism and Incivility!

Lady *Mary*.

The state of Inferiority is the next branch you are to explain. I know, persons in that class are required to be obedient.

Mentoria.

This obedience is limited; as they should ever avoid flattering the weakness and imperfections of their Superiors, and in all their actions make a distinction between servility and respect. From the dependence of their state, it is necessary they should conform to the will of their rulers, in every instance which is not repugnant to reason or conscience.

Lady *Mary*.

But how will these rules regulate our conduct, my good Mentoria?

Mentoria.

You must be actuated by the precept enjoined by our Saviour, "To do to others, as you would they should do unto you."[8] You / must therefore pursue the same conduct to your Inferiors, as you would that your Superiors should to you; and pay the same deference to those above, as you expect to receive from those beneath you. To persons who are on a level with yourself, you should perform such services, as seem most acceptable and necessary to the sphere of life in which you move. Be courteous to all, haughty and imperious to none. Be not high-minded, but condescend to those of low estate; and you will be respected by the great, and reverenced by the humble.

JANE DAVIS, *LETTERS FROM A MOTHER TO HER SON, ON HIS GOING TO SEA: AND A LETTER TO CAPT. S.* ([1799])

Jane Davis, *Letters from a Mother to her Son, on his Going to Sea: And a Letter to Capt. S. By an Inhabitant of Congleton. Dedicated, by Permission, to Sir Richard Hill, Bart., M. P. The Second Edition* (Stockport: Printed by J. Clarke, [1799]), pp. 29–33. ECCO, ESTC Number N019975, ECCO Range 11710.

The title of 'friend' carried many meanings during the eighteenth century; in addition to designating kin, Naomi Tadmor explained that '"friend" was also used to refer to a wide range of non-related supporters, such as patrons, guardians, employers, and other allies'.[1] As friends, these non-related supporters could act in the place of kin, especially when there was a service expectation.[2] These useful friends also expanded the nuclear family's instrumentality of caring for children by acting *in loco parentis* either contractually through an indenture, service or guardian relationship or fictively as an interested friend or godparent. The godparent and fellow denominational friends also expanded the nuclear family through a shared religious community.[3] The vehicle through which the extended family worked was the letter. Eve Tavor Bennet explained the importance of letters to maintaining 'a good correspondency' among 'the many families and friends that schooling, apprenticeships, service, indentures, urbanization, emigration, trade, war, government posts and colonization, separated and dispersed'.[4]

In *Letters from a Mother to her Son on his Going to Sea: A Letter to Capt. S.*, Jane Davis relied upon the language of friendship to solicit paternal guidance from 'Captain S' for her young son, who was a sailor trainee on his ship. Davis's son would have been at least fourteen years old, but could have been as young as nine when he was bound to maritime service.[5] The practice of young boys living and working on board ship was introduced in 1676; young boys of 'good family' were allowed on board as a 'Volunteer'.[6] In the mid-eighteenth century, the London Marine Society was established to help provide pauper boys apprenticeships as naval servants as well. That the Davis's had a higher social standing than the London poor was evident in the type of educational studies she asked the captain to oversee.

Davis also wrote the captain to help remind her young son to avoid unnecessary danger. Having a son apprentice on a British ship during a time of war would increase the anxiety of separation for a concerned parent. Davis indeed confessed her fears about her son; in the preface to the third edition of her *Letters* Davis wrote: 'Convinced of the shortness and uncertainty of life, which renders it extremely probable I might never see my son again in this world, I was prompted to offer such advice as appeared to me best calculated to promote his essential happiness'.[7] Davis's letter to her son blended practical and pious advice; Clare Brant has noted, 'When older children took up dangerous professions, many parent were torn between solicitude for their person and concern for their conduct'.[8] In her letter, Davis expressed concern for her son's devotional conduct by reminding him to pray and to seek help and guidance from his religious friends.

Davis' letters testify to her concern and affection for her son, a concern that authorizes maternal involvement. 'Letter-writing', according to Brant, 'gave mothers a voice and some authority, a much more active role' and in the case of Davis, a more public role through publishing.[9] Davis's *Letters* provided models for other mothers during wartime on how to express their maternal concerns for and to their absent sons.

Notes

1. N. Tadmor, *Family and Friends in Eighteenth-Century England: Household, Friendship, and Patronage* (Cambridge: Cambridge University Press, 2001), p. 167.
2. Tadmor, *Family and Friends in Eighteenth-Century England*, p. 179.
3. Tadmor, *Family and Friends in Eighteenth-Century England*, pp. 161, 168.
4. E. T. Bannet, *The Empire of Letters: Letter Manuals and Transatlantic Correspondence, 1688–1820* (Cambridge: Cambridge University Press, 2005), p. x.
5. R. Pietsch, '"Ships" Boys and Youth Culture in Eighteenth-Century Britain: The Navy Recruits of the London Marine Society,' *Northern Mariner/Le Marin du Nord*, XIV: 4 (October 2004), pp. 11–24, on p. 13.
6. A. Stenzel, *The British Navy* (London: T Fisher Unwin, 1898), at books.google.com [accessed 23 December 2014].
7. J. Davis, *Letters From a Mother to her Son, on his Going to Sea: And a Letter to Capt. S. By an Inhabitant of Congleton. Dedicated, by Permission, to Sir Richard Hill, Bart., M.P.*, 3rd edn (Stockport, [1799]), *Eighteenth Century Collections Online.*, Gale. Brigham Young University – Utah, available at http://find.galegroup.com.erl.lib.byu.edu/ecco/infomark.do?&source=gale&prodId=ECCO&userGroupName=byuprovo&tabID=T001&docId=CW3305773957&type=multipage&contentSet=ECCOArticles&version=1.0&docLevel=FASCIMILE [accessed 5 December 2014].
8. C. Brant, *Eighteenth-Century Letters and British Culture* (Houndmills: Palgrave, 2006), p. 68.
9. Brant, *Eighteenth-Century Letters and British Culture*, p. 60.

Jane Davis, *Letters from a Mother to her Son, on his Going to Sea: And a Letter to Capt. S.* ([1799])

LETTERS from A MOTHER TO HER SON, ON HIS GOING TO SEA:
and *A LETTER TO CAPT. S.*
BY AN INHABITANT OF CONGLETON.
Dedicated, by permission, *TO SIR RICHARD HILL, BART., M. P.*[1]
Hear counsel, and receive instruction, that thou mayest be wise in thy latter end. Prov. xix. 20.
THE SECOND EDITION. *STOCKPORT;* PRINTED BY J. CLARKE. /

TO *Sir Richard Hill, Bart., M. P.*
    MOST HONORED SIR;

    The character you bear for piety, charity, benevolence, and philanthropy, can receive no additional lustre by any eulogium I can bestow; nevertheless, the experience I have had of your friendship and kindness excites my gratitude, and demands my warmest thanks: at the same time I am induced to offer this public testimony to your / merit, since few, in your elevated situation, so eminently adorn the christian profession.

    I have nothing to plead in vindication of this my first attempt, but must solicit your kind indulgence, and that of a generous Public, – but more especially of the Ladies and Gentlemen of Congleton, to whom I consider myself under innumerable obligations, – hoping you will make every allowance for Letters written in haste, under great and accumulated bodily affliction, and encumbered with the concerns of a numerous infant family,[2] therefore destitute of the embellishments of rhetoric, or refinements of art, to recommend them; and only dictated by maternal solicitude for the welfare of a beloved child, separated from his parents at a very early age. The sincerity of the intention / with which they are penned will, I humbly hope, be some compensation for their defects and imperfections. Requesting this indulgence and candour from you, and the Public,

    I am,
    honored Sir,
    your obliged,

obedient,
humble servant,
JANE DAVIS. /
[...]
Liverpool. /

LETTER II.
TO CAPT. S.
Congleton, Dec. 2nd, 1798.
Sir;

Relying implicitly on the good opinion, which our very worthy friend Mr. F. entertains of you, and the character he gives you, we have sent our son, who is a beloved child, for your approbation; / hoping you will treat him with all possible care, and lenity, making every allowance for his youth and inexperience: but his ignorance of maritime affairs will soon be removed, I doubt not, by your kind and friendly instructions, and his own assiduity and diligence; for he is willing to be taught, and very industrious.

I should consider myself particularly obliged, if you would take the trouble to desire him not to venture into unnecessary danger. I am well acquainted with his enterprizing spirit, which, under prudent restrictions, may / one day render him conspicuous in the service of his country, and redound to the honor of his instructor. To hazard life, or health, or limbs, where the duties of our station do not absolutely demand our exertions, cannot be denominated true courage; a virtue which I know he is ambitious to possess. Properly to cultivate, and improve this temper, I leave, Sir, entirely to your care and management, persuaded that you will do every thing conducive to his advantage, and my comfort.

His youth and volatile disposition may incline him to neglect / the study of useful learning. I hope, Sir, you will therefore be so obliging as to order him to employ his leisure time in Writing and Accompts,[3] and not totally to forget the Latin tongue, in which he made some proficiency during the time he studied it.

I do not for a moment doubt that you will give all necessary attention to his health and comfort. To your kind and friendly care I therefore commit him, praying for the blessing of God in your protection, preservation, and prosperity.

Mr. D. unites in respectful / compliments to Mrs. S. Accept the same yourself from,
Sir,
Your obedient,
humble servant,
J. DAVIS. /

LETTER III.

Congleton, Dec. 10th, 1798.
My dear Child;

You are now on the verge of being separated from your native country, your tender parents, and all your dear relations and friends. Permit me to offer a word of advice, which you will probably pay a particular regard to now, as you are deprived of the advantage of personal conversation. For alas! we seldom / know the value of our privileges except by their loss; and as you cannot now apply, as formerly, for advice, or counsel, or direction, let me beg of you to pay attention to what I now write, assured that I have no motive in view but your welfare, and that I feel deeply interested in all that concerns you.

And first let me entreat you, if ever you hope to meet me, at the last great day, to our mutual comfort, that you pay a daily, and indeed a continual, regard to God who made you, and therefore has a right to your adoration and / worship. Much have you seen of his great goodness and amiable perfections; much you may yet see of his amazing power, which can only be known to seafaring persons. Do not, then, my dear child, on any account, neglect to recommend yourself to his protection every morning and night. Life at best is very precarious, but a sailor's life is particularly so. Keep up an habitual sense of his presence, which will tend to deter you from acting contrary to his will, and be a support and consolation to you in time of danger or distress; and, after all the / storms of life are finally over, you will anchor in the port of peace, that haven where everlasting "rest remains for the people of God".[4]

Let me beg of you to cultivate an agreeable, and courteous demeanor; be ready to oblige every person, as far as may be in your power; but be careful never to expose yourself to unnecessary danger. Our life, health, and limbs, ought never to be wantonly trifled with, since, if we run into dangers where the duty of our station does not require our exertions, we have no right to expect the blessing of Providence, nor / can we consistently pray for God's protection.

Neglect not to improve yourself in useful learning, particularly Writing and Accompts. I would not wish that you should neglect the Latin language, which you have taken so much pains to acquire. You will one day, perhaps, experience it's utility, in enabling you to acquire with greater facility, some knowledge of the French, should you ever be favored with an opportunity of learning it.

And let me entreat you to bear in mind the relationship you bear to your parents, who have hither-to / brought you up with great tenderness and expense. Embrace every opportunity of convincing us that our labor has not been, altogether, in vain. Write as often as opportunity will permit, as that will be the only compensation for the loss of your company.

To the protection and blessing of God, your father and myself desire to commit you; persuaded that he is able to keep you, in the midst of danger and surrounding death; and convinced that his eye will be upon you, his ear open to you, and his power engaged to preserve and defend you. /

Your brothers beg their love; and you may rest assured of the affection and prayers of

Your loving Mother. /

[...]

If you go to Falmouth our excellent friend the Rev. Mr. W. will be glad to see you I am sure; and I think it will give you pleasure to meet a gentleman who truly respects your parents. Indeed, I should be happy in a similar opportunity. We spent many / delightful hours in his company at M., and it would give me real satisfaction, once more to converse with him here. It is certainly one of the greatest pleasures I know, to meet with a friend after a long absence. Often do I think it will form no inconsiderable part of our happiness in the world of glory, when ministers shall again behold their people, and the people again unite, with their beloved ministers, in ascribing salvation to God and the Lamb,[5] throughout the countless ages of a blissful eternity. If you, my dear Thomas, are spared / to return again, I shall with more pleasure receive you than I can express. Country, home, relations, and friends will appear to you doubly valuable after being absent from them, though for a short time; and more especially if you are called to encounter difficulties in your voyage; rest will then appear inexpressibly sweet. So it is with christians. That hope which they enjoy, is as an anchor of the soul, keeping them near to Christ, amidst the storms of life. The prospect of rest animates them to endure the trials and afflictions of this imperfect / state with some degree of patience, knowing that the time is rapidly approaching, when they shall bid a final adieu to trouble, in all the various forms it now assumes; and then they shall enjoy permanent tranquillity, and unfading happiness in that heavenly country, where no storm shall interrupt our peace, no fears alarm, no affliction assail us. For neither sickness, nor pain, nor death, nor parting (so painful to our feelings in the present state) will be permitted to enter there.[6] There may I meet with you, my beloved child, and spend a glorious eternity / with the redeemed of the Lord. There may I meet your father and each of your brothers. So will be completed the felicity, the everlasting felicity of

Your most
affectionate Mother,
JANE DAVIS.

CHURCH OF ENGLAND, HASELBURY-PLUNKNETT, SOMERSET, PARISH REGISTERS (1680s, 1754, 1813)

Church of England, Haselbury Plunknett, Somerset, Parish Registers (1680s, 1754, 1813), Family History Library Brit film 1526637, original at Somerset Record Office 88360378, 51920 HRP, 87 20.

Haselbury-Plucknett, Somerset was a small village on the Exeter–London road. Its population never exceeded a few hundred when these records were kept. Note that poor law records from this parish appear in a later section of this volume (see 'Poor'). These snippets from Church of England parish registers for Haselbury-Plucknett highlight legal changes that affected how family events were recorded and celebrated between the late seventeenth century and the early nineteenth century.

The Act of Toleration (1689) allowed various nonconformist Protestant groups to worship freely and ended the required attendance at Anglican services. The act represents an increased official acceptance for (Protestant) religious diversity. This gave families of various Protestant sects official sanction for more varied religious familial rituals. For families who remained in the Established Church, laws passed by Parliament shaped how their religious-familial events were celebrated and given official seal of approval. The Haselbury-Plucknett registers demonstrate the impact of three such parliamentary statutes: the Burial in Woollen Acts (1666–80), Lord Hardwicke's Act (1753), and Rose's Act (1812).

The example from 1689 shows that burials were done in accordance with the Burial in Woollen Acts (1666–78) – meaning that all but plague victims and those too poor to afford a wool shroud, were buried in wool. The acts were passed in an effort to encourage domestic production and sale of wool, but unintentionally they influenced how the church recorded deaths and how families experienced death and burial. By requiring families to purchase woollen shrouds and swear before a Justice of the Peace that the deceased had been buried in wool, and imposing a £5 fine for noncompliance, the state inserted itself into the ritual.[1]

The second example, marriage records from 1754, demonstrates the state's power, via the church, to codify familial practices. Lord Hardwicke's Marriage Act of 1753 standardized legal marriages in England and Wales in an effort to reduce the number of clandestine marriages. It was the culmination of centuries of debate and disagreement between state, church and family tradition about what constituted a legitimate marriage. In practice, it also required that the vast majority of marriages be solemnized in the Established Church if the couple wanted their marriage to be valid and legal. To be considered legal, marriages now had to be performed by an ordained minister of the Church of England, either by banns or license, and had to take place in front of two witnesses. It enforced a minimum residency requirement for the couple (at least one of them had to have lived in the parish where they married for the previous three weeks) and required parental consent for those under twenty-one. In this way the state enforced one standard marriage ritual – sometimes at odds with families' religious preferences and practices. It is notable, however, that Quakers and Jews, whose own marriage ceremonies were so radically different from the Anglican services, were exempt from the requirement.[2] The example here includes the language printed in the newly required books – language stipulating the strict organization and content of marriage records. It also contains entries from the banns books – which lists the three weeks' announcements prior to the marriage. Some of the banns entries are not duplicated in the marriage records either because the couple married in a different parish, or because the marriage did not take place.

Similarly, Rose's Act of 1812 required a standardization of Anglican baptism and burial records. While this did not affect other denominations – beyond those who were buried in Anglican churchyards – it meant that the recording of baptism and burial would be systematic. With the requirement to use separate pre-printed books for each event, it was bureaucratic in purpose, but it ultimately shaped the recording of family religious rituals. They now included information about occupation, age and residence that was not required before 1813. In this way it enforced categories onto rituals previously recorded with the minimal information relevant to the ceremony: the date, and the name of the child and parent(s) in a baptism record or the name of the deceased in a burial record. The shift between free-form register and the printed books is obvious in the selection from 1812 and 1813 christenings and the 1813 burials (though apparently the new baptism book did not arrive in Haselbury until February of 1813).

Notes
1. R. Houlbrooke, *Death, Religion and the Family in England, 1480–1750* (Oxford: Oxford University Press, 1998), pp. 341–3.
2. The exemption put both groups into an awkward legal position – as their marriages might still be considered invalid. J. Mews (ed.), *The Law Journal Reports for the Year 1900. The Chancery Division of the High Court of Justice*, volume 69 (London, 1900), p. 721.

Church of England, Haselbury-Plunknett, Somerset, Parish Registers (1680s, 1754, 1813)

The Register booke of Hasleberge-Plucknet in the County of Somerset of all those if were buryed in Woolen since the late Act of parliament in the case provided from August Hie 1st in the yeer 1678
    [1689]

Mr. Constantine	Joane the wife of John Brown buryed Octob 24
Mr. Constantine	Allice the daughter of Wm Gardener buryed Dec 15
Mr. Constantine	Sarah Gooden was buryed Jan 29
Mr. Constantine	Elizabeth Padimore was buryed Marc[h] 16
–	Eliz[abeth] Padimore buryed [illeg.] 1696

/

Register of BURIALS Hasslebury SOMERSET January 1764
The Register of Burials in Haslebury for the Year 1764

William Son of William & Thomasin Strong	March	4
Anne Clench Widow	–	25
William Pitcher Labourer	May	30
John Walker Labourer	–	27
Mary Daughter of Daniel Gardner	June	10
Sarah Baulch Maiden	July	2
Alice Wife of John Gumber of Hinton St. George	–	12
Antony Son of Antony & Eliz Way	–	22
Mary Hutchings Maiden	Augst	9
Elizabeth Ham Widow	Sep	16
John Son of John & Eliz Pool	Octob	17
Elizabeth wife of Mr. John Draper	Nov	14

/
REGISTER OF BURIALS IN THE PARISH OF Haselbury IN THE COUNTY OF Somerset. London: Printed by GEORGE EYRE and ANDREW STRAHAN, Printers to the King's most Excellent Majesty. *In pursuance of the Act of Parliament,* 52 Geo. III. Cap. 146. *(passed 28*th *July* 1812*) a Copy of which is prefixed to the Register of Baptisms.*

BURIALS in the Parish of Haselbury in the County of Somerset in the Year 1813.

Name.	Abode.	When buried.	Age.	By whom the Ceremony was performed.
James Bishop No. 1. 22nd Jany	Crewkerne	1813	3	John Allen
John Perry No. 2.	Haselbury	18 Feby	1	John Allen
John Clench No. 3.	Haselbury	3 June	60	John Allen
Elizabeth Perry No. 4.	Haselbury	11 July	25	Thomas Price
Hannah Robins No. 5.	Haselbury	29 July	68	John Allen
Charlotte Jeffery No. 6.	D[itt]o	30 Octr	3	John Allen
Anne Hallett No. 7.	D[itt]o	11 Novr	1	John Allen
John Pitt No. 8. 27 Jany	D[itt]o	1814	78	John Allen

Register OF BAPTISMS Hasslebury
   [written faintly on the fly leaf of the Baptism record:]
   Woman Return Thanks for their Safe deliverey in Child birth May 18 <u>1753</u>
   Anne Newman
   Joan [illeg.]
   Sarah Pitt ---------------- 6
   Susan Elliott ------------
   Eliz Gardner ------------ 6
   Hanna Robbins -------- 6

The Register of Baptisms in Hasslebury for the Year 1764 Rob Pearson Curate
   /
Thomas Son of John & Joan Denry   Janry   15

Robert Son of Thomas & Annabella Robbins	-	30
Mary Daughter of William & Catherine Robbins	-	30
Molly Gibbs a base born Child of Molly Pitt	-	30
William Son of William & Joan Clarke	Febry	7
John Hallett Son of John & Mary Sherwood	March	11
Anne Daughter of Abraham & Thomasin Wilkins	May	13
Peter Son of Griffin & Joan Williams	June	17
Abraham Son of William & Susanna Dix	June	17
Elizabeth Daughter of Thomas & Bridget Ham	June	17
John Son of John & Eleanor Coalfields	July	12
Henry Son of Joseph & Mary Tracy	-	10
Anne Daughter of Isaac & Eliz: Baker	-	29
Edward Son of John & Grace Petwin	Augst	19
William Son of George & Anne Butcher	-	26
Sarah Daughter of Francis & Joan Gardner	Sepr	18
Elizabeth Daughter of John & Susanna Hawkwell	-	30
Jane Daughter of John & Sarah Perry	Octobr	21
Mary Daughter of John & Mary	Novr	14

Rob Pearson Curate
/
Baptisms 1812

Caroline D[aughte]r of Willm & Ann Adams	February	9
Amy D[aughte]r of John & Mary Meecham	-	-
Sarah D[aughte]r of Geo & Ann Hallett	-	23
Mary D[aughte]r of Wm & Sarah Tytherleigh	-	20
Thomas Son of Jos & Ann Bishop	March	15
William Son of Thos & Mary Sealy	-	-
Ann D[aughte]r of Richd & Elizabeth Handfield	-	27
Ann D[aughte]r of John & Jeane Gillingham	April	12
Geo[rge] Son of William & Ruth Bartlett	May	10
Elizabeth of Jona of Tomason Eastment	-	17
John Son of Anthony & Mary Brown	August	2
Ann D[aughte]r of Hannah Williams a Base Born	-	9
Hanah D[aughte]r of Robert & Mary Farle	Septemr	13
Rose D[aughte]r of Thos & Eliz Tytherleigh	October	11
Precilla D[aughte]r of Charles & Elizabeth Regain	-	18
Lavinia D[aughte]r of Samuel & Rose Robins	-	30

/
1813

John Son of Joseph & Priscilla Gillingham	Feby	7th
John Son of Thomas 7 Elizabeth Jeffery	Feby	14
Joseph Son of Jonah & Ann Rendall	–	14
Mary Daughter of Jonah & Ann Rendall	–	14

Page 1.
BAPTISMS solemnized in the Parish of Haselbury in the County of Somerset in the Year 1813.

When Baptized.	Child's Christian Name.	Parents Name.	Christian Surname.	Abode.	Quality, Trade, or Profession.	By whom the Ceremony was performed.
1813. 7th Feby No. 1	John Son of	Joseph Priscilla	Gillingham	Haselbury	Shopkeeper	John Allen
14 Feby No. 2.	John Son of	Thomas Elizabeth	Jeffery	Haselbury	Labourer	John Allen
14 No. 3.	Joseph Son of	Jonah Ann	Rendall	Haselbury	Labourer	John Allen
14 No. 4.	Mary Daughter of	Jonah Ann	Rendall	Haselbury	Labourer	John Allen
28 No. 5.	Mary Daughter of	William Sarah	Tytherleigh	Haselbury	Butcher	John Allen
28 No. 6.	John Son of	Ann	Tytherliegh Illegitimate	Haselbury	Single Woman	John Allen
14 March No. 7.	Susan Daughter of	Joseph Mary	Holman	Haselbury	Labourer	John Allen
23 May No. 8.	Jesse Son of	Joseph Ann	Andrews	Haselbury	Baker	John Allen

/
BAPTISMS solemnized in the Parish of Haselbury in the County of Somerset in the Year 1813.

When Baptized.	Child's Christian Name.	Parents Name.	Christian Surname.	Abode.	Quality, Trade, or Profession.	By whom the Ceremony was performed.
1813. 28 May No. 9.	Thomasin Daughter of	John Alice	Robins	Haselbury	Labourer	John Allen
10 June No. 10.	Edward Charles Son of	Edward & Rachel	Shore	Coasson Parish of Chardstock	Miller	John Allen
10 No. 11.	Nathaniel Son of	Thomas Fanny	Shore	Haselbury	Miller	John Allen
4 July No. 12.	Ann Daughter	Thomas Joan	Bartlett	Haselbury	Labourer	Thomas Price
4 July No. 13.	Joseph Son of	Joseph Ann	Bishop	Haselbury	Labourer	Thomas Price
1 August No. 14.	John Son of	William Rose	Jeffery	Haselbury	Labourer	John Allen
15 August No. 15.	Jane Daughter of	Thomas Anne	Newbery	Haselbury	Labourer	John Allen
29 Aug No. 16.	Julia Daughter of	Jacob Grace	Denty	Haselbury	Labourer	John Allen

/

BAPTISMS solemnized in the Parish of Haselbury in the County of Somerset in the Year 1813.

When Baptized.	Child's Christian Name.	Parents Name.	Christian Surname.	Abode.	Quality, Trade, or Profession.	By whom the Ceremony was performed.
1813. 26 September No. 17.	Jane Daughter of	John Mary	Perry	Haselbury	Labourer	John Allen
10th October No. 18.	George Son of	Robert Sarah	Champ	Haselbury	Labourer	John Allen
17th October No. 19.	Hannah Daughter of	Anthony Mary	Bartlett	Haselbury	Labourer	John Allen
5th December No. 20.	Samuel Son of	Thomas Ruth	Perry	Haselbury	Labourer	John Allen
1814 2 Jany No. 21.	Mary Daughter of	Robert Grace	Felt	Haselbury	Labourer	J Allen
30 Jany No. 22.	Elizabeth Daughter of	Mark Esther	Whorrowd	Haselbury	Labourer	J Allen
13 Feby No. 23.	Charles Son of	Joseph Charlotte	Coombs	Haselbury	Labourer	J Allen
19th Feby No. 24.	Edward Son of	William Sarah	Randal	Haselbury	Labourer	J Allen

RECUSANT RETURNS, DIOCESE OF YORK (1767, 1780)

Recusant Returns, Diocese of York (1767, 1780), Borthwick Institute, University of York, Ep.Rec.Ret. 1780/569.

The Popery Act of 1698 enforced a more muscular form of Catholic discrimination within England. Though parts of the Act were not always fully enforced (especially over time) Catholicism was still an oppressed religion until a series of Catholic relief acts were passed between 1771 and 1793 and until the Popery Act was repealed in 1829. Recusants – originally a term that meant those who refused to profess loyalty to the Church of England, but in practice a term that generally applied only to Catholics – were more common in the north than in southern England. In the early eighteenth century the presence of Catholics in northern England retained its sharp and political edge that it had inherited from the seventeenth-century political-religious conflicts. This was especially true around the two Jacobite rebellions in 1715 and 1745. By the 1760s, however, the tone and content of oppression of northern Catholics had moved away from the punitive measures stipulated in penal codes from the 1690s through the 1720s.[1] Instead, the effort was to find and remove 'busy' Catholic priests and to leave 'quiet and peaceable' priests in place.[2]

As the York diocesan count of recusants from 1767 demonstrates, somewhere around 40 per cent of parishes in northern England had recusant families, though the archbishop was clear to point out that those numbers did not reflect a serious increase in the number of Catholics in the Diocese of York. This account reflects overall trends in the monitoring of Catholic families, who tended to come from wealthier segments of society (see 'Multiple Families'). While the law still discriminated against them (barring them from the universities, from office-holding and subjecting them to double payments of the land tax, for example), its strict enforcement began to decline in the latter half of the eighteenth century. This was aided by the declining fears about Catholic attempts to overthrow the Crown as the possibility of a French-backed Stuart claimant to the throne disappeared.

Recusant returns often recorded the name, family members, ages and occupations of Catholics within each parish. This document shows the statistical list made from compiling those returns for the entire diocese of York. Before the general diocesan count, Ripon's report shows the type of information the local vicars gathered and submitted to the diocesan officials. The report shows an interest in the gender and age demographics as a way of measuring whether Catholic families were growing. The number of priests was also counted in order to measure the geographic spread of Catholic worship.

Notes
1. H. Aveling, *Northern Catholics: The Catholic Recusants of the North Riding of Yorkshire, 1558–1790* (London: Geoffrey Chapman, 1966), pp. 365–6.
2. H. Aveling, *Northern Catholics: The Catholic Recusants of the North Riding of Yorkshire, 1558–1790* (London: Geoffrey Chapman, 1966), p. 379.

Recusant Returns, Diocese of York (1767, 1780)

Ripon Markington Ingerthorpe
Within the Town and Liberties of Ripon (exclusive of the Chapelries from which a particular Return is sent in by their respective Ministers) there appear to be eighty nine Papists; Witness our Hands this thirty first Day of August 1780

Richd Browne
J. Godmond
vicars

His Grace the Archbishop of York}
/
An Account of the Number of Papists or Reputed Papists in the Diocese of York, taken from the Returns of the Clergy to the Archbishop's Enquiry in the Year 1767 in Obedience to His Majesty's Commands, & the Order of the House of Lords of the 22nd of May 1767.

Arch-deconry	Dean-ries	Under 18		From 18 to 50		Above 50		Total
		Males	Females	Males	Females	Males	Females	
York	City of York	76	126	121	196	38	85	642
	Ainstie	155	155	200	208	75	91	884
	Craven	118	96	90	117	30	29	480
	Doncaster	159	159	149	169	34	56	726
	Pontefract	44	55	62	68	17	30	276
Total in the A[rch] Deaconery of York		552	591	622	758	194	291	3008

Arch-deconry	Dean-ries	Under 18		From 18 to 50		Above 50		Total
East Riding	Buckrose	4	2	2	1	1	0	10
	Dickering	7	4	12	10	3	6	42
	Harthill	48	59	60	80	30	26	303
	Holderness	81	62	94	115	32	29	413
Total in the A[rch] Deaconery of E[ast] Riding		140	127	168	206	66	61	768
Cleveland	Bulmer	76	63	95	114	24	28	400
	Cleveland	167	184	203	234	98	105	991
	Rydal	29	35	38	55	26	13	196
Tot[al] in y[e] A[rch] Deaconry of Cleveland		272	282	336	403	148	146	1587
Nottingham	Bingham	16	9	14	11	3	6	59
	Newark	1	5	3	5	4	3	21
	Nottingham	17	24	23	29	20	18	131
	Retford	86	76	68	94	25	17	366
Tot[al] in the A[rch] Deaconry of Nottingham		120	114	108	139	52	44	577
Jurisdiction Of Ripon		43	47	41	59	21	27	238

Arch-deaconry	Deaneries	Under 18		From 18 to 50		Above 50		Total
D[ean] & Chap[t]er Peculiars in The N[orth] Riding		5	8	4	6	5	4	32
Jurisdiction of Haxham		57	38	68	78	23	34	318
Jurisdiction of Southwell		3	8	3	4	1	2	21
Total in the Diocese of York		1192	1235	1350	1653	510	609	6549
Diocese and Isle of Man		5	4	12	14	4	5	44

/

Jan[uary] 4 1768.

Number of Parishes & chapelries in the Diocese of York, including Peculiars

	Parishes		**Papists 1767**	**Priests**
City of D[eacon]ry of	York	25	642	9
	Ainsty	82	884	4
	Craven	37	480	3
	Doncaster	91	742	3
	Pontefract	72	276	3
Archd[eacon]ry of York		307	3024	22
D[eacon]ry of	Buckrose	26	10	0
	Dickering	52	42	0
	Harthill	77	303	2
	Holderness	54	413	2
Archd[eacon]ry of East Riding		209	768	4

	Parishes		Papists 1767	Priests
D[eacon]ry of	Bulmer	71	400	3
	Cleveland	66	991	7
	Rydal	48	196	2
Archd[eacon]ry of Cleveland		185	1587	12
D[eacon]ry of	Bingham	53	59	0
	Newark	39	21	0
	Nottingham	45	139	1
	Retford	61	366	2
Archd[eacon]ry of Nottingham		198	585	0
Jurisdiction of Ripon		8	238	1
D[itt]o of D[ea]n & Cha[pte]r of York in N[orth] Riding		12	32	0
D[itt]o of Southwell		29	21	0
Hexhamshire		8	329	3
	Total	956	6584	45
According to Mr. Mackley the Reg[ist]er Book in 1762		Parishes & Chapelries	Papists	Priests

/

Number of Papists or reputed Papists in the Diocese of York, including Peculiars

[Sir William] Dawes A[rch]b[isho]p	[Lancelot] Blackburne	[Thomas] Herring	[Robert Hay] Drummond	
1706 [sic]	1735	1743	1767	
194	249	1705	642	In the City of York

734	898		2382	Rest of ye Archdeaconry of York
497	431	533	768	Archd[eacon]ry of East Riding
1399	1262	1642	1587	Archd[eacon]ry of Cleveland
308	383	482	585	Archd[eacon]ry of Nottingham
215	196	364	270	238 In the Jurisdiction of Ripon
				32 in D[itt]o of ye Dean & Chapter of York in the Parishes not included here the forgoing Lists.
27 included in Notes			21	In ye Jurisdiction of Southwell
107	107	286	329	In Hexhamshire in Northumb[erland]
3481	3526	5042	6584	Total in the Diocese of York
	{above 18, and under 50	1359}		{In the Isle of Mann there are
Males	{under 18	1200}	3071 Males	{17. Parishes
	{above 50	512}		{44. Papists
	{above 18, and under 50	1658}		{no Parish in ye Island
Females	{under 18	1241}	3513 Females	{13, out of the 17 Parishes have no Papists
	{above 50	614}		{Souls computed at 20,000
			6584	

N[ota]B[ene] There are	389	Parishes & Chapelries	that have Papists.
	553		that have no Papists.
	9		that have made no Returns: & probably have no Papists.
	5		Craike return'd in Durham Diocese; & Massam w[i]th Kirkby Malze[a]rd, Hartwith C[um Winsley] & Middlesmore[sic] C. Returned in Chester Diocese.
	<u>956</u>}		

The Lists of 1706, 1735, & 1743 seem to be very imperfect, & those of 1767, perfect: so that the Increase is not so great as appears at first sight; probably not above one third in the last sixty years.[1]

N[ota]B[ene] when the Computation is by families, as in the Lists of 1743; a Family is computed at 5 Persons.

WILLIAM TENNENT III, ON THE DISSENTING PETITION, HOUSE OF ASSEMBLY, CHARLESTON, SOUTH CAROLINA (1777)

> William Tennent III (11 January 1777), On the Dissenting Petition, House of Assembly, Charleston, South Carolina, Travel Journal and Album of Collected Papers of William Tennent III (1740–1777), University of South Carolina Manuscripts Division, Digital Collection, at http://digital.tcl.sc.edu/cdm/ref/collection/wtj/id/378

'Family identity', according to Louis P. Nelson, 'was linked to denominational identity' in eighteenth-century South Carolina.[1] Families of many denominations made South Carolina their home and enjoyed religious freedom during the seventeenth century; the Fundamental Constitution of 1669 stipulated that any seven persons could unitedly form their own church and any other religious denomination must declare a belief in and publicly worship God.[2] However, a series of legislation, culminating in the Church Act of 1706, led to the establishment of the Anglican Church as the government's official religion.[3] In March 1711, the first Anglican church building was constructed in South Carolina by an act of the General Assembly – following Parliament's act earlier that year to fund the construction of fifty Anglican churches in London.[4] South Carolina was divided into ten parishes, which doubled by the 1760s, and clergy were sent to administer parish duties, such as determine poor relief, oversee church worship and perform marriages, by the London-based Society for the Propagation of the Gospel in Foreign Parts.[5] After 1706, Dissenting faiths could not own church property, and their brides and grooms needed a Church of England minister to post their banns and perform their marriage ceremony in order to have a legally recognized marriage.[6] The scarcity of Anglican ministers in remote areas meant that couples either cohabitated 'in sin' without any religious marital ceremony, or worse, were married illegally by a non-Anglican minister. The state-controlled religion, James Lowell Underwood observed, 'undermined the stability of families and the legitimacy of children'.[7]

By the mid-eighteenth century, Evangelical Protestants, primarily Baptists and Presbyterians, swelled the number of dissenting churches (which previously had been mainly Congregationalists) in South Carolina, thus widening the disparity between the economic and civic advantages enjoyed by the Anglican Church and the disadvantages of the more populous Dissenting faiths.[8] The speech by William Tennent III (1740–77) to the General Assembly below initiated the disestablishment of the Anglican Church as the state religion in South Carolina, which was enacted when the South Carolina state Constitution was ratified in 1790.[9] Tennent was descended from a long line of Presbyterian ministers: William III was the son of William Tennent Jr, a Presbyterian minister in Freehold, New Jersey, and Catherine van Burgh Noble; he was the grandson of William Tennent Sr, an educator and member of the Presbyterian clergy, and Katherine Kennedy, the daughter of a Presbyterian minister.[10] The Tennent family emigrated from Ireland to Pennsylvania in 1718, where William Sr established the 'log college' in Neshaminy, Pennsylvania. William Jr studied under his father and later, in New Brunswick, New Jersey, under his older brother, Gilbert. William III received degrees from Princeton and Harvard before he married Susan Vergereau in 1764; they had five children. In 1772, William III arrived in Charleston, South Carolina, to minister to the Independent Church.[11] As a member of the General Assembly, Tennent was present at the reading of the Declaration of Independence in Charleston on 5 August 1776.[12] Tennent's revolutionary fervour for political freedom informs his language in petitioning for religious freedom for families and future posterity.

Notes

1. L. P. Nelson, *Beauty of Holiness: Anglicanism and Architecture in Colonial South Carolina* (Chapel Hill, NC: University of North Carolina Press, 2009), p. 187, at ProQuest ebrary [accessed 10 December 2014].
2. J. L. Underwood and W. L. Burke, *The Dawn of Religious Freedom in South Carolina* (Columbia, SC: University of South Carolina Press, 2006), p. ix.
3. According to *The Edinburgh Encyclopaedia, conducted by D. Brewster* (Edinburgh, 1830): 'The law of England is adopted, with a few variations, as the common law of South Carolina' (p. 492).
4. Nelson, *Beauty of Holiness*, pp. 16–17.
5. Nelson, *Beauty of Holiness*, pp. 4–5.
6. A neighboring colony, North Carolina, also tried to abolish the state sponsorship of the Anglican Church in 1769. L. Maren Wood. 'Marriage in colonial North Carolina', at http://www.learnnc.org/lp/editions/nchist-colonial/4079 [accessed 13 December 2014].
7. Underwood and Burke, *The Dawn of Religious Freedom in South Carolina*, p. 28. Underwood and Burke also noted that cohabited couples could have been considered married according to common-law.
8. Nelson, *Beauty of Holiness*, p. 8.
9. Nelson, *Beauty of Holiness*, p. 336.
10. ODNB.
11. William Tennent (1740–77) Papers, South Caroliniana Library, University of South Carolina.

12. Tennent also has connections with individuals in this volume. In his courtship of Susan, he was assisted by her cousin, Elias Boudinot, whose wife was a member of the Female Association of Philadelphia (see 'Fictive Families'). Tennent corresponded with Selena Hastings, the Countess of Huntingdon, regarding their mutual support of George Whitfield, who had established the Bethesda Orphanage in Savannah, Georgia; further up the coast, in Boston, Phillis Wheatley composed an elegiac poem about Whitfield's untimely death, which she respectfully sent to the countess (see 'Racial Diversity'). Tennent travelled with John Drayton (see 'Multiple Families') to convert Tories to the American patriot cause.

William Tennent III, On the Dissenting Petition, House of Assembly, Charleston, South Carolina (1777)

Mr. Tennent's Speech
On the Dissenting Petition, delivered in the house of Assembly, Charleston South Carolina, January 11th 1777
Mr. Speaker

I am much concerned, lest an unfavorable construction should be put upon any word that may fall from me in the course of this debate, as reflecting upon the respectable members of the Church of England. I wish Sir, to be understood as bearing the Gentlemen of that Church, a very high respect.

None that now exist have been the Authors of that which we complain of: with the generosity of sentiment, that now prevails; with the same enlightened minds, I am persuaded they never would have been the authors. I dissent from the Church of England, it is true; but I trust, it is upon the most liberal grounds: when I oppose its establishment, I do not mean to oppose the Church itself. I would equally oppose the establishment of any other, though I admired its constitution ever so much. I firmly believe that this petition arises from an unextinguishable love to the free & equal rights / of mankind, & not from a dislike to one denomination of Christians, more than another. And Sir, while a love to freedom & equality in the grand sentiment that inspires all ranks of Men, in this great contest; while you feel an unconquerable spirit of freedom, animating you to all these measures, how can you find in your heart to blame those who risk their all, & stand with you in the foremost rank of zeal & danger, if they should only desire to secure to themselves & children, the same privileges that you enjoy? You must pardon them, if, sensible of the injuries that have been done them in times past, while we mutually groaned under a foreign yoke, & anxious for the complete freedom & happiness of their posterity, they should improve the important moment of forming a Constitution for this most righteous purpose.[1]

And now Sir, I beg leave to offer a few of those reasons which induce me to oppose the religious establishment of any one denomination of Christians in this State, under our new Constitution. 1st My first & most capital reason, against all religious establishments is, that they are an infringement of religious liberty. Religious establishments, as far as they operate, do interfere with the rights of private judgements & conscience: in effect, they amount to nothing less, than the Legislature's taking the consciences of men into their own hands, & taxing them at discretion. We contend, that no Legislature / under Heaven, has a right to interfere with the judgement & conscience of men, in religious matters, if their opinions & practices do not injure the state. The rights of conscience are now too generally understood, to make it needful to take much pains to convince mankind that they appertain to an higher tribunal, & that the objects of human legislation, are quite of a different nature. The State may give countenance to religion, by defending & protecting all denominations of Christians, who are inoffensive & useful. The State may enact good laws for the punishment of vice, & the encouragement of virtue.

The State may do anything for the support of religion, without partiality to particular societies or imposition upon the rights of private judgement. But when the legislative authority of the State, sets itself up as a judge in Church controversies, & proceeds by law, to declare this systim of opinions right, & that wrong; when it proceeds to lay hardships upon the professors of the one, while it lavishes its bounties on the other, & that while both are equally useful & inoffencive – I say, in this, it not only mistakes the proper objects of legislation, but is chargeable with manifest injustice. No Legislature upon earth, has a right to do such a thing; nay, we contend, that such a right cannot possibly be communicated to them. I can communicate to my representative, a power to dispose of part of property, for the security of the remaining part: I may give him a right / to resign a part of my personal liberty to the obligation of good laws, as a means of preserving the rest, -- but cannot, -- I say it is out of my power, to communicate to any man on earth, a right to dispose of my conscience, & to lay down for me what I shall believe & practice in religious matters. Our judgement & practice in religious matters, is not like our purse; we cannot resign them to any man or set of men on earth; & therefore, no man or set of men on earth, either has, or can have, a right to bind us in religious matters. The rights of conscience are unalienable, & therefore, all the laws to bind it, are, ipso facto, null & void. Every attempt of this kind is tyranny, let it be made by whatever body of men, & in whatever age: Of all tyranny, religious tyranny is the worst, & men of true sentiment, will scorn civil, where they cannot enjoy religious liberty. And now Sir, permit me to take a short view of religious establishments, & see, whether they do not, more or less, bear hard upon the rights of private judgement, & partake, in greater or smaller degrees, of this worst of tyranny.

On all hands it will be acknowledged, that those establishments are of this nature, which lay heavy penalties upon those who refuse to conform to them. Can you form an idea of more horrid cruelty exercised upon the rights of conscience, than that which imposes fines, imprisonment & death, upon those who presume to differ from the established religion? /

You Sir, look back with horror upon the history of such savage cruelty, -- the more cruel, as it has ever been exercised under the colour of law. Of the same nature, though differing somewhat in the degree of their cruelty, are those establishments, which incapacitate good subjects, who differ from the speculative opinions of the State. Judgement & conscience, in these matters, is, or ought to be, as independent of our will, as our height or colour. They are formed by the circumstances of the time in which we live, by the manner of our education, by the capacity of our mind, & the degree of evidence. Would not that prince be esteemed a cruel Tyrant, who should ordain, that every man of six feet high, & of a sandy complexion, should be excluded from the rights of Citizens? An assembly of two hundred Senators, who could ordain, that good citizens should be deprived, on account of their inoffensive opinions, would be two hundred times as cruel. 2^d The next kind of establishment that we meet with, is, that which none obtains in this State. I shall speak cautiously of it, but I shall take the liberty to speak freely, & shall only mention facts.

Its chief characteristics are, that it makes a legal distinction between people of different denominations, equally inoffensive; it taxes all denominations, for the support of the religion of one; it only tolerates those that dissent from it, while it deprives them of sundry privileges which the people of the establishment / enjoy. I say it makes a legal & odious distinction between subjects equally good. The law knows & acknowledges the society of the one, as a Christian Church; the law knows not the other Churches.[2]

The law knows the Clergy of the one, as Ministers of the Gospel; the law knows not the Clergy of the other churches, nor will it give them a license to marry their own people.[3] Under this reputedly free government, licenses for marriage are even now refused by the Ordinary,[4] to any but the established Clergy. The law makes provision for the support of one Church, -- it makes no provision for the others. The law builds superb Churches for the one, -- it leaves the others to build their own Churches: the law, by incorporating the one Church, enables it to hold estates, & to sue for rights: the law does not enable the others to hold any religious property, not even the pittances which are bestowed by the hand of charity for their support. No dissenting Church can hold or sue for their own property at common law. They are obliged therefore to deposit it in the hands of Trustees, to be held by them as their own private property, & to lie at their mercy.

The consequence of this is, that too often their funds for the support of religious worship, get into bad hands, & become either alienated from their proper use, or must be recovered at the expence of a suit in Chancery.[5] These are important distinctions indeed, but these are not all. The law vests the Officers of the Church of England with power to tax not only / her own people, but all other denominations within the bounds of each respective parish, for the support of the poor: an enormous power![6] Which ought to be vested in no one denomination more than another. Greater distinctions still! Where there are parishes the law throws the whole management of elections, that most inestimable of all the rights of freemen! into the hands of Church Officers exclusively. And why all this inequality?

Why does the law thus favor one, & bear hard upon every other denomination of Christians? The reason is only to be found in the spirit of the times when this unequal establishment was framed, & in the Machiavelian[7] policy of the British government; which ought not any longer to take place in this Country. But that which shows much of the injustice & oppression of the present establishment, is the tax which it makes all other denominations pay to the support of the religion of one.[8] It puts its hand into the pocket of nine denominations, all equally pretending to the merit of good subjects & citizens, to bestow upon one & support its dignity.

Sir! is this consistant with our first notions of justice & equality? And here, it matters not whether the religious tax is equally levied upon the people at large, or whether it is paid by a general duty. The treasury is the equal property of all denominations in the state, & if it comes out of the treasury, it comes in effect out of their pocket. / [...]

Sir, you may say, that the doors of the established Church are open equally to all denominations, & that all may equally enjoy the benefit of it. I have heard of such an argument. But besides that it is notorious, that what the public has paid for, in some instances has been converted into private property, & become the real estate of individuals, it would here be extremely natural to ask, how a rational Dissenter can enjoy the benefit of the Establishment? The only answer that I can give to such a question is a very short one: he must do it at the expence of his own private judgement & conscience. 'But Dissenters are tolerated; there is a free toleration: does any man impose upon them? who prevents their worshipping as they please?' I answer. In this respect they stand upon the same footing with the Jews.[9] Nobody molests them. But would it, Sir, content our brethren of the Church of England, to be barely tolerated? that is, not / punished for presuming to think for themselves. Is a bare toleration sufficient for the majority of a free State? of a free State that expects to gain its liberties by the sword? Would not a bare toleration be viewed by our brethren with infinite disdain; is this equality? Sure the justice of this house, now unfettered by British violence, will not permit the continuance of such a monument of inequality. 3^d There are some who entertain an idea of keeping up the Establishment, merely as a matter of religious superiority, without taxing other denominations. But they seem to forget, that every reason for which they desire the superiority by Establishment, operates as an abridgement of religious liberty. For when a Man presumes to follow his own judgement in religious matters, & refuses to conform, he must at lease submit to this inferiority, or rather bear the reproach of the law, as not being on a level with those that are Christians in its esteem. Still there remains injustice, & a foundation for dissatisfaction. For Sir, let it be remembered, that there are many Dissenters in this State, who care but little for the money that it costs them to support the Church of England. They value much more their religious, their unalienable rights, than the expence. Sir, you very well know, that it was not the three pence on the pound of tea, that roused all the virtue of America.[10] It is our birth right that we prize. It is a full & undiminished freedom in the exercise of our own judgement, in all religious matters, / profit, for a mere title of pre-eminency without emolument, is it worth while to have a bone of endless contention in the State, & to maintain these odious distinctions? 4th There is a proposal, Mr Speaker, to establish all denominations by law, & to pay them all equally. This Sir, may operate as a scheme of division, but in practice it must appear equally absurd & impossible.

Absurd, as the establishment of all religions would in effect be no establishment at all. It would destroy the very end of an establishment, by reducing things just to the same state they would be in without it, with this disadvantage, that large bodies of men who could not obtain Church Officers, might be oppressed, by being obliged to pay for that which they received no benefit from. But it would be found impracticable, as people of different sentiments live intermingled, & there could be no possible distinction of Parishes, so as to accommodate different denominations. But if the Establishment must from time to time conform itself to the prevailing party in each Parish or District, there would not only be the same ground for complaint that there now is, but it would prove the means of everlasting strife. And indeed I am afraid that the expense would be found upon trial insupportable. Sir, it is impracticable in this State to establish all denominations, & it is only thrown out to amuse us. But to admit the establishment of a few dissenting Churches, in preference to all others, as a / means to make them acquiesce! It is too big with injustice to procure the consent of an honest man. Let us all have equal privileges or nothing. Equality or Nothing! ought to be our Motto. In short, every plan of Establishment, must operate as a plan of injustice & oppression; therefore, Sir, I am utterly against all Establishments in this State. Leave each Church to be supported by its own members, & let its real merit be all its pre-eminence. Thus while you give proper scope for a laudable emulation, you take away all complaint of injustice, & build your State upon the solid foundations of equity & righteousness. If these arguments have failed to weigh at other times, they ought now to have amazing weight, / that a refusal of justice would not damp their ardour, if not utterly disarm them? Do they ask any more than what they have an absolute & indefeasible right to enjoy? Sir, these are rights which they cannot possibly relinquish. Their claim is founded in eternal justice, & this stands confessed by their most violent opposers. They must pay an equal share of that tax which independency will cost you, they must spill a greater share of blood, & therefore they cannot, I say they cannot consent to the smallest inferiority in privileges either civil or religious.

But Sir, in the present case, the claims of good policy join those of common & confessed justice. Religious Establishments discourage the opulence & cramp the growth of a free State. Every fetter, whether religious or civil, deters people from settling in a new country. Take off every unnecessary yoke, & people of all denominations & professions will flock in upon you with all their arts & industry. If a spirit of toleration raised the United Provinces to such a pitch of glory & grandeur, by inviting people from every quarter [of] Europe; if an entire equality has made Pennsylvania the emporium of America, to the immortal honour of its wise legislator; what good effects may not be expected from the same spirit of laws in this State. That State in America which adopts the freest & most liberal plan will be the most opulent & powerful, & will well deserve it. Sir, as a narrowness in these matters is the disgrace of the human mind, so is it the / disgrace of any system of laws whatever. I could wish to draw the attention of the house to another important motive, that is, the future peace & happiness of this State. Grant this petition, & the foundation of religious discord is eternally removed. It is inequality that excites jealousy & dissatisfaction.

Make your laws partial towards people of any one set of opinions, suppose it only in philosophy, & you entail immortal strife & debate upon your Children. If all your people are equally free & happy, it will be no matter who is in or who is out, i.e. in respect to denomination. Where the people have a full voice in legislation, the case is vastly different from what it has been in times past, while royal violence stood ready to support the claims of injustice. Gentlemen of the Church of England, should methinks, be as much concerned to obtain the prayer of this petition as any others. The course of things is very uncertain. None know where numbers & interest may carry matters in future time. Some have unjustly accused Dissenters with an intention to establish themselves. It was partly that accusation that gave birth to the petition before you. But if the Gentlemen of the Church of England do really apprehend danger of such a mortifying issue in process of time, sure they of all men ought to be most anxious so to fix the basis of the Constitution, as for ever to prevent it: I mean by making it a foundation article, that there never / shall be any such Establishment. This is the only security of the Church of England, as well as of other Churches.

The Church has long had the advantage; she has reaped uncontrolled, the emoluments of the State; she has subsisted on the abridgement of the equal privileges of others; she has flourished by aid of their property. Let the time past suffice.

With the new constitution, let the day of justice dawn upon every rank & order of men in this State. Let us bury what is past for ever. We even consent, that the estate which she has for a Century past been drawing more or less from the purses of all denominations; an estate of no less value than three hundred & eighty thousand pounds, remain in her quiet possession, & be fixed there. Let her only for the future cease to demand pre eminence. Let her freely consent that others enjoy the same privileges, in every respect, with herself.

This is all we ask; we seek no restitution. After the vast sums partially expended by the State upon one denomination, all the others ask not a farthing to be returned to them. Let her be contented with her superb Churches, her spacious burying grounds, her costly parsonages, her numerous glebes, & other Church estates, obtained in a great degree from the public purse, while not a farthing has been granted to other Churches; & let her not now insist upon such glaring partiallity any longer. But it is impossible to do justice to this great cause by confining myself to a narrow / compass [...] Should not the Constitution take care of the religious as well as civil liberties of the People? Or do you think the former of less importance than the latter? When these questions are properly answered, I then beg leave to ask; if this matter is not now attended to, will not the Church of England be established by law under the new Constitution, & become the constitutional Church? If so, then will not all these oppressions which have been groaned under heretofore, be constitutional in this free state? And is this a matter of small moment to the major part of the People? And must they sit still out of mere compliment? Must they compliment away their freedom in this manner,& not only suffer, but even lend their aid, by putting their own hands to it, with the sanction of the People at large? It is strange that Gentlemen can expect it.

How can we answer our neglect to our constituents, who expect that we shall make them free? How can we answer it to our posterity, who even now ought to rise in our imagination, & demand of us to / leave them free? This is the natural time, & this is the only time. Things ought to be done in their proper season. And Gentlemen may pretend what they please, if they are averse to grant justice in the present season of it, if they are unwilling to do it now, they will be more so by & by. One thing I am sure of, they will have fewer motives to engage them to do it by & by. He that is disposed to do justice, is willing to do it without delay. The old maxim is good, to delay justice is to deny it.

Sir, at this time, all ranks of people more sensibly feel the claims of justice, than they will hereafter. They now feel the rod of oppression: & there is nothing like suffering to bring us to our senses. They are now struggling against arbitrary power. They can now realize the hardship. Let these times pass, & ease will naturally lull them into an in attention to the rights of mankind. That this is a proper time the example of other States confirms. [...]

That this is the proper time is plain, as the People are now waiting to see what they have to expect, for what it is they are to waste their treasure & their blood? They are ready to do it cheerfully, if they may with certainty expect to be made & kept as happy as their brethren. They ask no favors; they ask only the common rights of Mankind. By some it is said to be dangerous / to grant this request at the present time. They own it is just thought to be. No Member, say they, in the House will deny it; but the time is dangerous. But Sir, are we indeed reduced to that situation, that it is dangerous to do common justice? [...] Will the danger arise from the Church of England? I cannot think it. It is too harsh an imputation upon the Gentlemen of that Church. They will not endanger the state on account of that which they know & universally allow to be just. I cannot, I will not admit the supposition. Sir, I have the pleasure of knowing too many of them to think so.

Many of them have signed the petition. Many more have declared their sentiments in the most liberal terms.

There is too much Catholicism[11] & love to liberty among them. They don't desire any longer to oppress their brethren. They profess a generous disdain of the thing. They have property sufficient to maintain their own Clergy liberally; & if the State did not take it off their hands, I believe they would do it more liberally than it is now done. If the Dissenters did not apply now, it might by & by be retorted upon them, & that with great justice: / 'You have had a hand in framing the Constitution, as well as we. The Church of England is the constitutional Church, by your own act & deed. Why did you not make your opposition in proper time? Why so much out of season? Why endeavour to subvert what your own hands have reared?' Sir, we should be dumb; or what is as bad, we should justly lie under the charge of some species of sedition. Sir, we mean to act a rational & constitutional past. And now Sir, it only remains to be seen whether this legislative body, now by God's goodness, free from the chains of foreign compulsion, will rectify the errors of less happy times: whether they will rise in the annals of this important age, by showing a temper superior to all illiberality & oppression.

Will you Sir, comply with the demands of common justice? Will you make all your People equally free & happy? Do you desire to put an effectual end to all religious broils & contentions forever? Will you strengthen your own hands in defence of your bleeding Country? Do you wish to enrich it by an influx of healthy inhabitants from every quarter of the world? Would you secure yourself from the fetters of any one Denomination, with which the uncertainty of time may inundate this Country?

Will you give to every Denomination the best security of future religious freedom & happiness that the nature of the case admits? Grant them the prayer of the Petition: grant it / in substance, if not in the very expressions: Let it be a foundation article in your Constitution, 'that there shall be no establishment of one religious denomination of Christians in preference to another. That none shall be obliged to pay to the support of a worship in which they do not freely join.' Yield to the mighty current of American freedom & glory, & let our State be inferior to none on this wide Continent, in the liberality of its laws, & in the happiness of its People.

ZINA BAKER HUNTINGTON CORRESPONDENCE (1808–13)

Zina Baker Huntington Correspondence (1808–13), Zina Brown Card Family Collection, LDS Church History Library, Salt Lake City, UT.

The Second Great Awakening (1790–1840s) was a Protestant Revival movement that occurred in antebellum America. Although scholars have considered the impact of this movement in a variety of locations, particular heed has been given to the intensity of the revivals that occurred in upstate New York. Historian Whitney Cross brought attention to the uniqueness of the region by arguing that it had been 'burned over' by every religious, political and social enthusiasm that emerged during the Jacksonian era. Influenced by Cross's foundational work on the Burned-Over District, subsequent historians continued to examine the 'bizarre social experiments' and 'new religions' that emerged in upstate New York in the early nineteenth century.[1] This scholarship typically connected the noted religious intensity to changing economic and demographic conditions occurring in this region at the time.[2]

Suggesting that class analysis is both 'suggestive' and 'insightful' but also 'incomplete' when studying the Burned-Over District, Mary Ryan complicated the social history of revivalism in antebellum America with her contention that 'the history of class and religion was hopelessly entangled with questions of family and gender'.[3] Many young women, for example, became involved in churches and moral reform societies, and went to great effort to 'convert and to rehabilitate' their own husbands and children.[4] In the process of shaping belief and behaviour within their homes, women also formed and fostered friendships with one another, thus demonstrating the relational nature of religious conversion and commitment. Zina Baker Huntington serves as one example of a woman whose life demonstrates the role religion played in influencing and shaping a variety of relationships both within and without the home.

On 2 May 1786, Oliver and Dorcas Baker welcomed twin daughters, Zina and Lina, into their home in Plainsfield, New Hampshire. In the Baker household,

Dorcas, who would ultimately give birth to twelve children, focused on domestic tasks, while Oliver worked as one of the first physicians in New Hampshire.

As a young woman, Zina assisted her mother with chores: cooking, cleaning, sewing, spinning, weaving and needlework shaped a significant part of her daily routine. But, her life was not consumed entirely by such laborious tasks. Zina developed intellectual as well as practical skills; she also cultivated familial and social relationships. Reading, writing and religious engagements – private and public activities in early New England – allowed young women such as Zina to form reading circles as well as other groups that promoted intellectual and spiritual engagement and fostered friendship.[5]

Religion also played an influential role in young Zina's life. Because the religious revivals that permeated society during that time period spread from location to location, the quest for conversion became a common phenomenon. Young women, in particular, accepted religion following their growing sense of conviction.[6] The spiritual seeking this environment encouraged shaped Zina's early religious interests.

On 28 November 1805, nineteen-year-old Zina married William Huntington Jr, son of William and Presendia Lathrop Huntington. Consequently, Zina moved from her parent's home in Plainfield, New Hampshire to the Huntington home in Watertown, New York.[7] In Watertown, Zina created a home of her own, established a social network, and attended church. Like her mother, she would spin, weave, plant and cook; she also assisted her husband in his business endeavours. As Zina became a mother, she taught her children – she would eventually give birth to ten – to read the Bible, sing hymns and play musical instruments.[8]

Despite her busy schedule, Zina found time to worship and to reflect upon religious topics. She attended Sunday services, as well as the Baptist and Methodist revivals that prospered in upstate New York in the early nineteenth century. Family deaths, particularly those of some of her own children, enhanced her desire to attain salvation. In addition to worrying about her own spiritual state, Zina cultivated religiosity in the lives of her husband and children.

Much of what is known about Zina Baker Hutington's role as a religious seeker is gleaned from a series of letters she wrote to her mother, Dorcas Baker, between 1806 and 1829. This 'silent conversation', as Martha Bradley calls this correspondence, details Zina's inner and outer worlds: the words she penned disclose the patterns of life within her family (birth, death, marriage), domestic chores, farm responsibilities and social functions. The central theme of these letters, however, does not pivot around the mundane concerns woven throughout Zina's daily routine. She is searching for, thinking about, experiencing and sharing her growing sense of religious understanding. Indeed, her longing to find the pathway to salvation, and to share it with others, is woven throughout each of the letters she writes.

Zina began writing to her mother shortly following her marriage and move to Watertown. In her first letter, she reported that William and she had arrived safely at their home and assured her mother of the kindness of her in-laws. Zina then recalled, 'I went to meeting last Sunday and there was quite a full meeting they had very good singing'.[9] This sentence intimated the central theme of the letters Zina would write for over two decades.[10] During this period, she carefully recorded the rise and decline of religious revivals in Watertown and neighbouring communities, lamenting times of religious 'stupidity' and rejoicing when 'there is revivals of religion all around us some places a few drops and other places a plentiful shower'.[11] But preceding and even exceeding her recollections of the revivalism so prevalent in nineteenth-century New York is Zina's discovery and continuing development of her religious self and her commitment to using those experiences to benefit others. Like other nineteenth-century women, her personal writings reflect a 'remapping' of her spiritual 'aspiration and identity'. She uses her letters to express how revivalism paved the pathway of her personal spiritual progress – a pathway she believed would ultimately lead to salvation.[12]

Zina's communication with her mother makes it clear that she continually pondered upon soul-searching questions because she feared she was 'more cold and indifferent than is agreeable'.[13] While in her early twenties, for example, she reflected upon the meaning of redemption through the atonement of Jesus Christ. Aware of the evolutionary nature of her spiritual consciousness, she concluded, 'I must tell you I have a little hope of myself much better than ever before'.[14] Hoping to continue progressing spiritually, Zina attended some of the Methodist and Baptist revival meetings taking place in her neighbourhood; and, when a preacher was unavailable on Sundays, she met with other members of the community for singing and worship.[15]

Like many of her female contemporaries, Zina also worried about the spiritual welfare of those she loved. She lamented their disinterest in religious matters and hoped and prayed that their hearts would change. She explained to her mother that she longed to sprinkle her family with the 'drops of grace and mercy' she had experienced in her quest for religious understanding. Her perseverance would eventually pay off. On 5 March 1817 she wrote, 'O what reformations we hear of from almost all parts of the earth' – reformations that would have a powerful presence in her home. To her delight,

> this God and the Saviour of our souls (which are spirits) has I trust appeared under the roof of my dwelling in a particular manner and has opened the eyes of my husband ... has given him strength to flee to the Saviour and to make his peace with God.[16]

On another occasion, she noted:

> Our eldest daughter, Presendia, has experienced the saving change of heart, I believe. She is 11 years of age last September and our little girl, Adaline, she is six last August. She has had remarkable exercises indeed for such a child, but known to God are all our hearts, and we ought to rejoice that we are in his hands.

Eventually, Zina, William and their children joined the Presbyterian Church.[17] She believed the Lord had, indeed, 'visited [her] family with his good spirit'.[18]

Over time, however, Bible study convinced Zina and William that Presbyterianism was not identical to the gospel found in the New Testament. As a result, they again assumed the role of active religious seekers. In the early 1830s, Joseph Wakefield, a Mormon missionary, stopped at the Huntington home, and gave the family a copy of the Book of Mormon. After reading this text, both Zina and William decided to join this church.[19] They were baptized in the spring of 1835.

Notes

1. W. Cross, *The Burned-Over District: The Social and Intellectual History of Enthusiastic Religion in Western New York, 1800–1850* (Ithaca, NY: Cornell University Press, 1950), p. 270; C. Johnson, *Islands of Holiness: Rural Religion in Upstate New York, 1790–1860* (Ithaca, NY: Cornell University Press, 2012), p. 2; M. Barkun, *Crucible of the Millennium: Burned-Over District of New York in the 1840s* (Syracuse, NY: Syracuse University Press, 1986), p. 4; P. E. Johnson, *A Shopkeeper's Millennium: Society and Revivals in Rochester, New York, 1815–1837* (New York: Hill and Wang, 1978), p. 4.
2. Johnson, *A Shopkeeper's Millennium*, p. 4.
3. M. Ryan, *Cradle of the Middle Class* (Cambridge, MA: Cambridge University Press, 1983), p. 12.
4. Ryan, *Cradle of the Middle Class*, p. 12; S. Stephan, *Redeeming the Southern Family: Evangelical Women and Domestic Devotion in the Antebellum South* (Athens, GA: University of Georgia Press, 2011), p. 21.
5. M. Kelley, 'The Need of their Genius: Women's Reading and Writing Practices in Early America', *Journal of the Early Republic*, 28:1 (Spring 2008), pp. 3–7.
6. N. F. Cott, 'Young Women in the Second Great Awakening in New England', *Feminist Studies* 3:½ (Autumn 1975), pp. 15–18.
7. Watertown, located in northern New York State, was settled just four years prior to Zina's arrival. It became the seat of Jefferson County. It was in Adams, Jefferson County, where famed revivalist Charles G. Finney had his conversion experience in 1821. See G. M. Rosell and R. A. G Dupius (eds), *The Memoirs of Charles G. Finney: The Complete Restored Text* (Grand Rapids: Zondervan Publishing House, 1989), pp. 16–26. Also M. Perciaccante, *Calling Down Fire: Charles Grandison Finney and Revivalism in Jefferson County, New York, 1800–1840* (Albany: State University of New York Press, 2003), p. 17.
8. M. S. Bradley and M. B. F. Woodward, *Four Zinas: A Story of Mothers and Daughters on the Mormon Frontier* (Salt Lake City: Signature Books, 2000), pp. 5–9.
9. Zina Baker Huntington, Letter to Dorcas Dimick Baker, 18 February 1806, Watertown, New York, in Zina Card Brown Family Collection, 1806–1972, archives, historical department, The Church of Jesus Christ of Latter-day Saints, Salt Lake City, Utah (hereafter LDS Archives).
10. Historian Martha Sonntag Bradley made the following comment, 'These letters ... are filled with the disappointments and trial's of Zina's life, the changing seasons, the births and deaths of her children and loved ones, and her husband's business. But it is religion – Zina's preoccupation with matters of the spirit – that color the pages of these letters.' See, M. Sonntag Bradley, '"Seizing Sacred Space": Women's Engagement in Early Mormonism', *Dialogue: A Journal of Mormon Thought*, 27:2 (Summer 1984), pp. 57–70, on p. 57.

See also Bradley and Woodward, *4 Zinas*.
11. Bradley and Woodward, *4 Zinas*, p. 4, notes that stupidity is Zina's 'favorite metaphor for religious malaise or spiritual numbness'. The words 'stupidity' and 'dullness' are used regularly in nineteenth-century journals, diaries, correspondence, periodicals and memoirs when referring to times of religious stagnation. For example, Zina Baker Huntington, Letter to Dorcas Dimick Baker, Watertown, New York, 30 August 1811, LDS Archives. In addition, Martha Tomhave Blauvelt notes that the use of the word stupid draws on traditional Calvinist language for spiritual dullness. See M. Tomhave Blauvelt, *The Work of the Heart: Young Women and Emotion, 1780–1830* (Charlottesville, VA: University of Virginia Press, 2007), p. 152. In contrast, the words, 'shower', 'drops' and 'dew' are used in reference to religious growth and success. Zina Baker Huntington, Letter to Dorcas Dimick Baker, 6 June 1813 (Watertown, New York, LDS archives); Zina Baker Huntington, Letter to Dorcas Dimick Baker, 8 June 1822 (Watertown, New York, LDS archives).
12. J. B. Gillespie, 'The Clear Leadings of Providence: Pious Memoirs and the Problems of Self Realization For Women in the Early Nineteenth Century', *Journal of the Early Republic*, 5:2 (Summer, 1985), pp. 197–221, on p. 198.
13. Zina Baker Huntington, Letter to Dorcas Dimick Baker, 18 January 1811 (Watertown, New York, LDS Archives).
14. Zina Baker Huntington, Letter to Dorcas Dimick Baker, 7 August 1808 (Watertown, New York, LDS Archives).
15. Zina Baker Huntington, Letter to Dorcas Dimick Baker, 9 August 1809 (Watertown, New York, LDS Archives). Caleb Burnham's barn was located four miles from the Huntington home. It was known as the 'Religious Society of Watertown' and served as the village's first church. See Bradley and Woodward, *4 Zinas*, p. 28.
16. Zina Baker Huntington, Letter to Dorcas Dimick Baker, 5 March 1817 (Watertown, New York, LDS Archives).
17. In 1822, Zina described a plethora of revivals that were occurring in Watertown, and the impact they had on her young daughters, Prescendia and Adaline. See, Zina Baker Huntington, Letter to Dorcas Dimick Baker, 8 June 1822 (Watertown, New York, LDS Archives).
18. Zina Baker Huntington to Dorcas Baker, 8 June 1822, Watertown, New York.
19. The official name of the Mormon Church at its founding in 1830 was the Church of Christ. In 1838, the name was changed to The Church of Jesus Christ of Latter-Day Saints.

Zina Baker Huntington Correspondence (1808–13)

[punctuation and some capitalization added]
Watertown, February 8, 1807

Honored parents it is with pleasure I sit down this evening to converse with you tho we are at a great distance farther than we have ever yet been. The road was not so long as I expected we had a verry agreeable journey[1] , we was on the road nine days, had agreable weather all the way I caught a verry bad cold on the road which lasted a short time my new father[2] was verry kind and I suppose I should not had produce enough to preserve my health. I suppose you will want to know every particular about my affairs and feelings as to my mind. I felt it quite contented and happy I live verry agreeable. My new Mother[3] I like verry well. I believe she is a verry nice woman, and all the family I like verry well they live in peace.[4] I went to meeting last Sunday and there was quite a full meeting they had verry good singing.[5] I have been a visiting two evenings and have found verry agreeable people. I found on the road Co. Prices wife she that was Ruth Grant[6] we had verry agreeable time she took the high scrapes at tolland[7] and said she would give a large sum to you and told me if ever I wrote back to give her Greatest respects to you. I have not anything verry especial to write that I now recollect it has been quite sickly but I believe the sickness has abated. We are all well at present. I want to hear from you. I hope you will write the first opportunity. As to everything else I know nothing about, it is now later in the evening and my eyes are some sore yet the next time I write perhaps I shall write more so I conclude wishing to know your health hoping you enjoy it perfectly well. My best respects to all the family wishing you all well. ADIEU.[8] Zina Huntington

P.S. I expect we shall live by ourselves next fall and I shall stand in great need of some help and I want daddy[9] should come and see us in the fall and try to {tear} us a little &c

My friends I should wish to converse with you but time and distance will not admit—I suppose you would wish to know something respecting our Business—which is not yet determined. I expect that we shall work together this summer and then I expect to work by my Self—I wish to say more but time failes

But must leave you to happier Scenes than to present these short lines—My best respect to all the family.

Wm. Huntington, Jr.[10]

[...] /

Doct Oliver Baker
Plainfield
New Hampshire State
to be left at the post office in Windsor, Vermont/

August 7 1808

My Honored Parents.[11] Once more I am permitted to write to you and inform you that I am on the land with the living and blest with health and prosperity while Zina[12] is now growing as this beneath [illeg.] were fear it is drawing, oh the feelings of my poor sister I can never know them only by experience, but oh the soul how low is that. Pray for her soul. Oh {smudge} prayers is that the Lord Jesus ... be better to her than parents {smudge} husband and children, but if I could but know that it is was well with her and she felt resind what a comfort what a satisfaction that dreadful sting wanted to be taken away, I can look of my two children and try to realize her feelings but alas tis in vain, oh my heart akes[13] for her but more for her soul, but do not think that I have forgot you my dear parents, my heart feels as tho it would burst out of my bosom, but may we not forget God [illeg.] this is the work of his hands, but remember that tho we are at such a distance we can call on the same God and I hope we have it all, altogether I wish we might all feel to give her up willingly and cheerfully into the hands of him who gave her and to give up our selves and our children. I beg of you my parents to be reconciled to put your trust [illeg.] and go to him for support. She is better than children if you have but a faint hope of her it better than worlds, I suppose you will want to know how I feel in my mind. I have been a growing stupid[14] this some time and would sometimes look of myself and wonder and be astonished. Last winter I had trials about myself and about baptism. I was at meeting one Sunday and there was a considerable number of children baptized and as quick as it was mentioned how beautiful it looked I thought then it was right. I was so affected that it was perceived I had talked several they knew my / situation, had talked with me there was no particular thing that I could tel that convinced me but I was satisfied, there was one woman asked me afterwards how it felt. I told her I was satisfied but how I could not tel. She said the wind bloweth where it listeth and ye hear the sound there of &c. I had a great trial about being sick. I concluded that I should not live and that I was not prepared and that I could not endure it but at once I felt as tho it was not too hard and was nothing to what

Christ went through to redeem our sins and I could say no more but felt reconnected. I believe in some measure I cannot write half my feelings but I must tel you I have a little hope of myself much better than ever before but mourn for me that I live no better than I do and pray for me that I may, and pray that my heart may not be deceived my feelings I keep to myself pretty much that have told them to William[15] once and some of them to some others this church has no preacher we have no preaching only and in a while a minister comes along. But Methodists are plenty they preach every Sunday but I hope it is all for the best. My babe[16] was born the 26 of May he is a very nice boy more heartier than Chauncy and good natured we are all well enjoy good health and myself better than common and have ever since I have him here one here named Dimmick Baker when he was one week old, when he was born he weighed almost 11 pound you wanted I should write what you brought one pair of cards handkerchief sheet linen three pieces of woolen sheets petticoats some calico a great mess of dried apple and green ones a little ship and a little bag full all and a good mes of yams 8 dollars a blanket I thought I was rich I can never be to thankfull, if we live a few months longer I hope I shall tel you by the word of my mouth if we live and are well we shall see you next winter {tear} [li]ves are spared /

I cannot write many particulars our blessings all goes on well as we can expect. I live quite agreeable not one word of difficulty has ever past yet tho I have some little small trials not worth mentioning I wrote that little letter but can write none more but as much as this. She is a strange creature. I put no dependence in her but according to my own judgme but it is all peace for it shall be I can write but little in one at present I have got to be about as large as my mother you would be surprised when you see me I will measure around the lower part of my body and round my arms and put it into this letter so that you may see and not be scared when you see me. How I want to see you all but I O Lina I fear I never shall see I entreat of you to write just as soon as you receive this letter and do remember I feel anxious to hear. I received your letter yesterday. It was put in the post office 6 of August but the date of the letter came of with the seal so that I could not see it I have not much more to write only it is a general time of health we shall fetch both of our boys, if we come with 2 horses [illeg.] sends will come we have not concluded whether we shall come with one or two tel them all I long to see them and Wm[17] sends his love and respects to you all tho I am at such a distance do not think I have forgot you because I do not write oftener but pardon me and I will try not to neglect it so long again and hope you will write oftener.

So Adieu and beg that the Lord will preserve your lives all that is alive until I can see you all more. Oliver S. Dorcas [illeg.]
Zina Huntington /

You must be seen and let one of the girls come home with me without fail the mail does not come in until Friday

Dorcas Baker

Plainfield

N... Hampshire S ..../

Jan 18, 1811

Honored and beloved friends, It is with the greatest regard I write to you, not knowing your situation but the impression is that your lives are all yet spared. I address you once more in this silent way this being the only way that I can converse with my friends. I think I feel to sympathize with you in sickness and trouble, how do you feel, all of you, do you rightly eye the hand of God in all his dealings towards you – to my Mother[18] in particular. Now sit down, calm and composed and reflect why are these things so, do you have suitable reflections. I feel sometimes to with myself there it seems as tho I could reconcile you, but alas it must be the convincing power of the almighty, it disturbs my affection at the first perusal of the news, but on a few moments reflection my mind was at peace everything appears right and just. My feelings are such as my pen cannot describe, neither could my tongue and sometimes I think I have that comfort that the world cannot give nor take away. I do not know but I am deceived tho at times I feel willing to rest easy about that, I think my greatest concern is that I may live more to the glory of God. I feel more cold and indifferent than is agreeable. I hope you all enj[oy] heavenly comforts and if you don't, do not delay improving the time in this life, for we see our dissolution fast approaching. O how many calls and invitations which will add to our condemnation if we reject them, I have but little time to write. I hope you all will feel reconciled and will exercise great fortitude and calmness in whatever you are called to meet with in this world of reflection – we live in our families verry agreeable. I enjoy myself much better than I can ask or even think to the bearer will tel you whatever you wish to know better than I can write. I can write no more at present only add that my desire is that you may come and see us once while we live in this world. My best wishes attend you and my feelings for you I cannot express. Do write to me the first opportunity. I feel anxious to hear. We all enjoy good health at present.
    Zina H.

Dorcas Baker
Plainfield New Hampshire

to be left at the post office at Windsor, Vermont /

Watertown
August 30, 1811

Honored and beloved friends, It is of hope with some affection that I now sympathize with you on a solemn occasion, being well satisfied our Honored Father[19] is no more, & my beloved Mother this name draws tears from my eyes alas; is he no more, one of our number drops away after another and I am yet spared and placed alone from you all first to hear the Death of a sister[20] and next of a father. O that I could behold all your faces once more but I ought to be thankful for this great privilege of conversing with my tender Mother and brothers and sisters I am yet spared to speak to you once more in this silent way.[21] Therefore let my speech be to warn and advise you to prepare to follow our near and tender Father you all behold the messenger of death which seems to hover around your windows and there you behold with your eyes, O my near friends, I hope you will no longer delay to attend to these things if you have not I hope you have, some of you.[22] And I hear that Dorcas thinks she has embraced Christ. It gives me no small consolation. I write as tho my Father was dead and has no other expectations but if he is not tel him I can go to the throne of grace with him. I hope there he will give up all to God and feel safe to put his trust there. I come short of all my duties therefore do remember me in all your petitions, each one. O my feelings are such as I cannot describe and what are yours, my mother. I hope you are composed and resigned to the will of God. I hope that your will is swallowed up in his will. I hope this is a good season to your soul. I want to have you calm and composed and guided by God for comfort and I feel as tho I knew there was comfort / there. I must write some concerning our affairs here. It has been considerable sickly, there is some sickness. Our families are all well. I enjoy a verry good state of health and all my family Presenda went alone at ten months, is a large, fair child there has a great many children died at the village of Watertown[23] and Women lost 3 children and her husband. All the family she had, her husband died last and I was at his funeral and O how she felt she was helpless and had to be carried from the grave in a chair, a scene how distressing. It is a dull time as to religion. I am dull myself. I am surprised at myself, it is late in the evening and I cannot write much more. It seems as tho we have prospered as to this worldly things, I am pestered for a girl. I want one of my sisters verry much. I want you should send a note to me if I can have one and try to send me one of them. I want you should write to me as soon as possible. I must draw to a close, wishing you all the happiness that this world can afford. Give my respects to all enquiring friends. O how I wish to see you all. This is from your affectionate child and sister.
Zina Huntington

Honored Parent, Brothers and Sisters – I say parents but expect our father is no more – if that be the case. Let us link one of old in reality say the bond gave and he now sees fit in his kind providence to take from us and Blessed be the Lord – my friend, we here experienced the loss of a dear child and affectionate Mother – we think to remember you / in the hour of trouble – if our father is alive when this received, remember me to him. I ask his prayers for me as a sinner in the Eyes of the Lord. My friend I am well though somewhat fatigued with labours. I this minute have come in from melting a batch of my potash – it is now eleven o'clock at night. One word to Oliver respecting his note. I received of him against one Laban Lewis – I am doing the best I can with him. He is a poor man, has had sickness. I received a letter from him {tear} and informed he – he would do the best he could – and asked me not to see him – that if I did [illeg.] should come [illeg.] limits – I think [illeg.] he went for grain or that {smudge} wheat was for {smudge} in the course of one year – money try newer way [illeg.] since this corn was settled – you wished Zina to come and see you this fall, but not possible. We halve a great family – one man by the year two by the job, halve boarded Marietta Burr the school keep four months and are mutch herried – and for the present cannot tell when we can – come times are hard – this from yours.[24] &c. Wm. Huntington

   Dorcus Baker
   Plainfield
   New Hampshire /
   Watertown, Jan 20th, 1812

Honored Mother, Brothers and Sisters, I once more attempt to improve a privilege which we all to much neglect. I thought when E of Phim—was here that I would write soon but business crowded along from time to time so that I have neglected it, the flattering myself that Sementha[25] would come over here this winter which has in a great measure detained me from writing and has still some hopes yet, tho I do not know of any way but feel sure that it would be for your good to come here and I give it as my best advice for you to come here as soon as possible, we are not likely to move out of this place, we have made a purchase near Burrs Mills[26] one half Mile from there. There is a verry nice barn and they say a verry good log house which if I live I expect to see how it will feel to live in a log house of our own and if I should live I invite you all to come and see me and my family. We are all well and the neighbors round us, at the harbor it has been verry sickly among the Soldiers and is yet there has been several Deaths there this week past, you live where you do not see the effects of war, we have had some alarms this season past.[27] One day in particular the streets were filled with men and women, no one felt easy at home, there was a girl in this neighborhood that came from Westland that day, she said the women would stand in the door with their husbands, come crying, some holding their husbands all in tears, the vessels were in sight on the hill about one mile from here, where I went to see, but they had just gone out of sight as I got there, as for my part I was somewhat composed altho I knew that he was likely to be killed as anyone / but still I was not distrest as I suppose some were, my opposition to the proclamation of war has distrest me sometimes, I have never informed myself with politics any great until this disgraceful and abominable war has commenced and thus you see my feelings, so amen to this.[28] I would inform you that Lyman Cary and family arrived last week, his situation is better known to you than to me, it is evident here. Enoch has got home and they are all here but what they are doing I cannot tel but do not expect they will starve at present. John will not have much to do with them, he has but one child now and that is all I can say this month or two – and now I must write concerning this property I had last winter, I will state to you the true situation, in the first place as I suppose you know that one shoe broke long before I got home and after a while he went to get it mended and before he got home it smashed all down to the ground and so it has been until a little while ago we undertook to get it mended and finally it had to all be made new except the biggest part of the bone. The old mare we have kept, she got kut not agreat while after I got home which cost some thing, we had but little hopes of her for some time but finally recovered and as soon as it come warm weather she began her capers and continued until the snow came, almost every time that I have made her somebody must lead her away and do the same when I come home. One Sunday I got on to her 4 times before I could get home and so she has carried on all summer. She has had no colt. We have been at 20 shillings expense to have her have one next summer but the appearance is that it is to no purpose. Her age is known here as well as there, and now are these things considered. What is this property worth, you said you would give five dollars if she did not have a colt and it is no way likely she ever will and now I want something done that is about right and as I have stated to you the fact you can do something / near what is right and this is what I shall expect you to do, and I shall expect you to write your mind as soon as you receive this and make up your judgment. I shall be willing to take the sum of money proposed this winter, with an addition of what is right, I should be glad to have the business settled, if it cannot be, it will be the best way to return the property and that will end it. I trust I do not want more than what is right and expect you feel the same—I hope these few lines will find you all enjoying the greatest blessing. That is, health, I would inform you Sementha[29] a little about the old queen. She has lost her power in a great degree the society is moved from Converses to Dean Sawyers and Dean Fellow and wife is now determined to leave the church at all events they all begin to see and finally she is not one amongst us all the rest and united except Mrs. Lambson and I think as great a union among the church as I have seen at any time at the no great attention to religion, we have a hired Minister at this time, I was at meeting first Sabbath, he preached very as to the state of my own mind, I confess I am stupid,[30] I am nationally convinced that it is all the same tho,[31] I don't feel it at this time, therefore all you who have an interest at the throne would remember me and mine. I have enough of this world's good to be comfortable if I could but enjoy the exercise of religion. I think that is an addition to this world comfort. I wish I had room and time to write more but you see it fails. Perhaps there is some particulars you would be glad to know as there often is from you, but I hope Sementha you will come and fetch them this winter. I must tel you I should be verry glad to have you come next month. I can write no more so Adieu[32] at present and perhaps forever, give my love to all enquiring friends and accept of the greatest love to yourselves.

Zina Huntington, Presendia[33] was over here the other day and said she should be verry glad to have you come over here.

Widow Dorcas Baker,
Plainfield
New Hampshire /

Watertown, June 18th 1813

My Mother, Brothers and Sisters, I once more speak to you in this silent way for it is alone the goodness of God that I am now spared to improve this opportunity. I will begin at the first of our news. Last February the 11 day I was taken sick and had a fine boy wt.[34] about ten pounds and in one week I broke out with the measles and in that week I was quite sick, had two or 3 doctors but no one knew my case, nor I myself for I had not been exposed, except just going into a store which I had no idea that I had seen anyone that had them, my babe was taken into the other room and took a verry bad cold and brot on a sore mouth and was verry sick, had fits two or three days and expired the day before it was 3 weeks old, the next day after it was buried I was not able to set up much after that, set up for 3 only weeks but could do no work.[35] I could get no strength, a distress at the stomach, an uncommon lameness in my arms and then grew worse and sent for a doctor. He came and doctored me first for the spleen after finding I was not so much troubled with that he tried for worms and finding that want the case, he was at a stand and I finding myself fail wanted another doctor – sent to Brownville, got doctor Farley that married Hannah Hinkly of Tolland he came, said my case was clear, it was the effects of the measles, I was then so that I could not lie still in the bed. / My flesh was all the time trembling and twitching, this doct. Came and bled me, gave me some pukes[36] and in three weeks was so that

I was carried to his house and staid 2 weeks and then came home and gained slowly about 3 weeks ago. My girl[37] went away and since that I have done my chores myself. Some days ago I got a verry bad cold and have now some cough but hope I shall be better. I have now one more serious affair to make mention to you i.e. my children took the measles from me and Dimmick, the one that has been trouble with his eyes they fell into his eyes and have not been well since, what to do for him we do not know. We have done everything almost that we can but too much purpose. His eyelids he cannot lift up, he cannot bare the light, he must have the room dark, and verry much confined to me, he grows verry poor and appears some time to be quite sick and what to do with him now we do not know. I wish you could tel us—and as to my mind I suppose you will want to know. I must tel you that in the first week of my sickness I did not think I could live but could not feel that resignedness that I wanted too, I continued in this situation for 5 or 6 weeks. I felt all the time as tho I should die one sunday all at once as it were something seemd to change my mind if I am not deceived I felt willing to die I could [illeg.] to my family.

Sept. 3, 1813, you will here see that it is some time since I began this letter. I was soon taken sick again, but was not verry sick, then Dimmick grew worse, was verry sick, could not see any for a long time, about 3 weeks ago I found a woman that made an excellent / salve, it was our minds to try this salve on his eyes, after wearing it one week I thought I could perceive a little alteration so that we agreed to keep it on a little longer, and the end of last week I was convinced they was a little better, and we continue it now and find it really helps them. I examined them today and found that he could open them halfway which has not been done since last March nor even so much as the light of one pane of glass to be open in the room since last March and now but a few weeks since I was obliged to hold him in my lap or rock him in the cradle and none must take him but Wm or myself, yesterday was cloudy and today I have had two windows in the kitchen uncovered and the first day for six months and I now feel some hopes of him. I would mention that his pain {tear} his eyes has been such that he would dance and scream that his hands and spat his head and seem like one distracted, therefore you cannot wonder that I tell you that my flesh has not been so low since the first summer I came into the country. I must leave you to ponder upon this subject – and mention a few things, our health are all good at present. I can spend my days working Esq. Hunt family are all well except Hyrum he has a course of fever but now is on the mend it is tolerable healthy here last winter and spring a remarkable dying time as to religion general time of coldness which I hope is lamented by every good Christian – we moved here last april and I feel verry contented we have not made a bad swap respecting war, it does not trouble me any. I do not feel any afraid of Indians or of being disturbed not at all. I expect you heard of a battle in June or July which was distressing indeed.[38]

I could stand and small arms and cannon hear every round distinct a continual roar but my being unwell and Dimmick being sick I pursuaded Wm not to go until we had heard the battle a while /

Widow Dorcus Baker
Plainfield
Favor by Mrs. Hutchins, N. H. /
March

Honored Mother Brothers and Sisters with pleasure I embrace this opportunity of a moments time to convey a few ideas, it is tolerable healthy in this place, our family are all well and all our connection and as to religion in this place it is not so dull and stupid[39] a time as it has been sometimes, there does not seem to be that appearance of a reformation[40] in this place as there was a little time ago. If we have reason to bless God for a few drops of his grace and mercy and likewise to pray for more of what reformations we har of from almost all parts of the earth, I think we have reason bless even the name of the living God, I want to hear of each and every one of you, that you are all a walking in that strait and narrow path that leadth to life in Louville[41] and Denmark[42] there is a great work going on and we hope it will spread and overshadow us.[43] I would inform you my dear friends that this God and the Saviour of our souls which are Spirits has I trust appeared under the roof of my dwelling in a particular manner and has opened the eyes of my husband to see his dreadfull situation by nature and to realize his transgressions and has given him strength to flee to the Saviour and to make his peace with God.[44] I wish my dear friends that you could know his trials. I tell you I think I am a living witness to the power grace and mercy of God. Wm[45] is about to join the Church, he feels a determination to be faithful and do {smudge} duty as far as he can see / he has enjoyed his mind verry well ever since he obtained a hope which was about November, I think. I cannot certain tel the time, if I had time I would write his Experience but my time was set by Wm. Taylor not over 2 hours, as to my own feelings, I can tel you that I have enjoyed my mind Extremely well for about ten months, am why it is so I cannot tel I have been astonished at the Condescension and goodness of God toward me while I am so full of sin and even do that which I would not do that God should shine upon me and give me comfort and peace of soul, that comfort that the world cannot give nor take and I think I feel to bless his holy name, it has appeared sometimes as tho I must call upon every one to praise God. I now inform you my dear friends that my hope is as an anchor to the soul both sure and steadfast and that my faith is strong, I think sometimes I am fitting for the approach of some great event that hope I shall ever be prepared for all that awaits me and ever feel reconciled to Gods will and rejoice in his government. I could write

much more but time and fear would fail as Wm. Taylor went past here and said he should be gone about two hours, that little Book you sent me by Ambrose[46] I carried it to our meeting and read it and it stired them all to a desire to follow the example and we have not far from one hundred that belongs to the society. I feel verry glad you sent it. I am much disappointed indeed that Lodema[47] has not come over here this winter, I think it a great pitty that you cannot and see me once. I feel sorry Brother Dimmick that you cannot come over here and bring our sister. You are heaping up riches but remember that you cannot enjoy them but a little while at the longest and you can carry none of them with you. How do you know what you may profit if you should come and see us once, as I want Lodema you should seek an opportunity and be sure and come. I cannot think you would be sorry. We are {tear} to build a nice stone house early / this spring and we are quite well prepared. We have our stone all on the shed but verry few we have lumber enough to finish all off and it is all paid for so far and we have a good yoke of oxen tor [illeg.] ing time. We are in comfortable circumstances as yet. Wm. sends his compliments to you all, I hope sometime to see you all but do not know when adieu at present.[48]
    Zina Huntington

If Wm Taylor does not come back this way I shall send it in the mail or some way

Watertown March 10 [1818]

Beloved Mother brothers and Sisters, once more I am permitted thro the kindness of providence to speak to you in this silent way.[49] I would inform you that we are all in good health. I have no knews in particular to write it a general time of health in this place as to religion, it is neither a stupid time[50] as to that in this place or neighbourhood but there is attention in places all around here. I have to lament my own weakness and stupidity but hope the cause is equally as near and dear to me if I cannot enjoy some comfort from the holy spirit, I think my enjoyments are faint indeed if I had time I could write much more but my babe[51] being but ten days old and being weary, having company this afternoon and no time to write but this evening I cannot write but little, my little son is not well, has a sore mouth and my nurse went away today and I must be excused from writing much at this time. I would inform you that we enjoy ourselves verry well at present, I hope you will come and see us before long. I long to see you all my dear friends. I will once more ask you the question, why do you not come and see me once before you die. Remember you cannot carry anything with you out of this world, I beg of you to write the first opportunity I want to hear from you all verry much, give my respects to all enquiring friends, So adieu[52] at present.
    Zina Huntington

If you have any dried apples to spare I wish you would send me a few.

ROBERT NELSON, *AN EARNEST EXHORTATION TO HOUSE-KEEPERS, TO SET UP THE WORSHIP OF GOD IN THEIR FAMILIES* (1739)

> Robert Nelson, *An Earnest Exhortation to House-Keepers, to Set Up the Worship of God in their Families. With Daily Prayers for Morning and Evening* (London: Printed and sold by M. Downing, in Bartholomew-Close near West-Smithfield, 1739), pp. 3–20, ECCO, ESTC Number T225141, Ecco Range 13126.

'How ought religious differences to be debated among Christians?' queried Robert Nelson (1656–1715) in his popular publication, *A Companion for the Festivals and Fasts of the Church of England* (1704). Nelson answered: 'without throwing scorn and contempt upon those that oppose us', 'without railing and injurious reflections', 'without detracting from the real worth of our adversaries' and 'without ever suffering our passions to vent themselves under a pretence of zeal for God's Glory'.[1] Nelson's liberal views towards religious differences probably stemmed from his own family experience. Nelson was born in London, the only surviving child of John Nelson, a merchant, and Delicia Roberts.[2] John died soon after Robert's birth, and Delicia's brother, Sir Gabriel Roberts, also a merchant, became the boy's testamentary guardian.[3] After Nelson left Trinity College, Cambridge, without taking his degree, he embarked on a tour of the Continent and in Rome, Nelson met Lady Theophila Lucy, a young widow and a daughter of George Berkeley, the first Earl of Berkeley.[4] After their return to England, Robert and Lady Theophila married on 23 November 1682.

When Lady Theophila was in Rome, she had been converted to Catholicism by a prominent English Catholic, Cardinal Philip Howard.[5] After her marriage, Lady Theophila wrote but did not publish under her name, *A Discourse concerning a Judge of Controversy in Matters of Religion, Shewing the Necessity of such a Judge* (1686), which sparked a Protestant response from William Sherlock, the Dean of St Paul's. Perhaps in reply to his wife's Catholic beliefs, Nelson wrote *Transubstantiation contrary to Scripture; or, the Protestant's Answer to the Seeker's Request* (1688). Though the Nelson family was divided according to religious affiliation, according to Alexander Chalmers's entry in his biographical dictionary, 'Her change of religion made no change in his affections for her'.[6]

Nelson's extended family experience may have also contributed to his career as a writer of religious literature. Prior to Robert and Lady Theophila's marriage, her Berkeley family had endured several scandals. Lady Theophila's sister, Lady Mary, had been accused of having an affair with the Duke of Monmouth by her husband, Forde Grey, Earl of Tankerville and Lord Grey of Warke. Then, on 6 November 1682, Lord Berkeley filed a writ *de homine replegiando* against this son-in-law, Lord Grey, whom he suspected of seducing and abducting his other daughter, Lady Henrietta; Lord Grey was found guilty, but no punishment was recorded.[7] The trial was sensational enough that Aphra Behn based her *Love Letters between a Nobleman and his Sister* (1684) on Lady Henrietta and Lord Grey's affair.[8] Though not biologically related to Lady Henrietta, Lord Grey became her brother and she his sister when he married her sister Lady Mary, in accordance within the language of kinship and the Levitical definition of incest from the Bible.[9]

Lord Grey's flagrant disregard for marital fidelity by engaging in an incestuous relationship with his sister was the type of licentious behaviour that concerned the Church of England leadership. Their response was to create the Society for Promoting Christian Knowledge (SPCK) in 1698. The preamble to the SPCK's charter stated that 'gross ignorance of the Christian religion' was responsible for the 'growth of vice and immorality'.[10] An important counteractive to irreligion the SPCK promoted was devotional literature and since Robert Nelson had not taken a degree at Cambridge, he was encouraged to write tracts as a layman to promote Protestant religiosity. His popular publication, *Festivals and Fasts*, was a catechism to explain the Anglican liturgical calendar, and was probably written as a complementary family devotional text to his earlier publication, *An Earnest Exhortation to House-Keepers, to set up the Worship of God in their Families* (1702).

The selection below taken from *An Earnest Exhortation* demonstrates Nelson's concern regarding the moral climate of his culture and the importance of proper religious instruction and catechizing in families. Nelson derived his perception of children from Calvinist and contemporary views: children were wilful, deceitful and corrupted by sin. Catechizing the child, according to Ian Green, 'was a means of both enforcing proper discipline on a child and providing the knowledge of God's will which was a prerequisite of salvation'.[11] Therefore, in the prayer for a child, Nelson used the language of the Anglican Prayer Book catechisms taught at school.[12] Nelson's *An Earnest Exhortation* was reprinted twelve times during the eighteenth century.

Notes
1. Quoted in W. Gibson, *The Church Of England, 1688–1832: Unity And Accord* (London: Routledge, 2001), p. 244, *eBook Collection (EBSCOhost)* [accessed 28 November 2014].
2. *ODNB*.

3. 'Nelson, Robert', in A. Chalmers, *The General Biographical Dictionary*, 32 vols (London: J. Nichols and Son, 1812–1817 [online database]. Provo, UT, USA: Ancestry.com Operations Inc, 2010.
4. http://thepeerage.com/p2841.htm#i28404 [accessed 6 December 2014].
5. Both Robert and Lady Theophila corresponded with Bossuet, the Bishop of Meaux; however, Nelson, unlike his wife, never converted to Catholicism.
6. 'Nelson, Robert', *The General Biographical Dictionary*.
7. *ODNB*.
8. Greaves, 'Grey, Ford'. In his will, Lord Grey left his estate to his daughter, Mary, a financial bequest to Henrietta in a codicil, and nothing to his wife, who survived him by almost eighteen years.
9. N. Tadmor, *Family and Friends in Eighteenth-Century England: Household, Kinship, and Patronage* (Cambridge: Cambridge University Press, 2001), p. 145.
10. Quoted in J. Black, *Eighteenth-Century Britain, 1688–1783*, 2nd edn (Houndmills: Palgrave, 2008), pp. 136, 144.
11. I. Green, *The Christian's ABC: Catechisms and Catechizing in England c. 1530–1740* (Oxford: Clarendon Press, 1996), p. 209.
12. Green, *The Christian's ABC*, p. 170.

Robert Nelson, *An Earnest Exhortation to House-Keepers, to Set Up the Worship of God in their Families* (1739)

An Earnest EXHORTATION TO House-keepers.
To the Parents and Masters of Families.

THE great Decay of *Piety* in this corrupt and degenerate Age, is very much owing to the shameful Neglect of many Parents and Masters, in not instructing their Children, and those under their Charge, / in the Principles of Religion. Were Childrens Minds early seasoned with the main Points of Christianity, and were they and Servants rightly informed in their Duty towards *God,* their *Neighbour,* and *themselves,* much of that *Lewdness* and *Debauchery,* which we groan under, and still complain of, would vanish and disappear. I beg you therefore, as you value your own Souls, and the Souls of those committed to your Charge; as you have any Consideration for the Publick Good, or Concern for the Prosperity of your own Families, that you would use your best Endeavours to bring up your Children in the Fear and Nurture of the Lord, and to make your Servants God's Servants.

You are obliged to this both from Duty and Interest; for the Power and Authority God has given you over others, is a Talent entrusted with you for their Good; and you must certainly give a strict Account at the Day of Judgment, what Use you have made of it, and how you have exercised it.[1]

Besides, by instilling Virtue and Piety into your Children and Servants, / you take the best Method to secure the Obedience and Tractableness of your Children, and the Diligence and Fidelity of your Servants. For, when all is done, the Duties of mutual Relation stand most firm upon Principles of Religion.

Let it be your Care therefore, that your Children be taught to read, and then to learn the *Church Catechism,* with some short Prayers for Morning and Evening, which you must oblige them constantly to use. Be very severe with them if they tell Lies, or betake themselves to pilfering Tricks, or lightly use the Name of God, especially if they swear by that Sacred Name; or offend against Modesty, by any filthy or obscene Words or Actions. Your Authority ought to influence and restrain them, till their Reason can discover the Advantages of Piety, and the Folly and Ingratitude of sinning against God, and breaking his holy Commandments. Indulgence in these Cases may be of a fatal Consequence; for by letting the Reins of Government hang loose, Children will abandon themselves to the Conduct of their Passions, which they / are most inclined to follow; and you will quickly repent that Fondness, which, by dear-bought Experience, will be found to have ruin'd your Children. Never omit carrying them with you to Church on the Lord's Day, and see that they behave themselves reverently at the Publick Worship.[2] But what I chiefly designed to recommend to you at present was, to set up the *Worship of God in your Families*, by the constant performing of Morning and Evening Prayer, and by reading a Psalm[3] and Chapter in the New Testament, before you begin that holy Exercise. This will be the best Means to preserve a Sense and Spirit of Religion in your Families: By this Method they will be constantly put in mind of their Duty; for the Matter of it is contained in such Prayers; and what we ask of God, we are obliged to use our utmost Endeavours to obtain:[4] And upon this Condition, God promises the Influences of his Grace, which (provided we do our best) will always be ready to assist and strengthen us in the doing and suffering his holy Will.[5] /

There are many Helps to this Purpose in several Books; but for fear none of them may have come to your Hands, I thought fit to make this Provision for you by it self. If you, or any one in the Family, can read, let him or her take the *Bible*, and gravely read a *Psalm*, and a *Chapter* in the *New Testament*, and then distinctly and reverently on your Knees, offer up the following *Prayers to Almighty God*. And whatever Objections you may have, as to your Worldly Affairs, in a Morning; I am sure in the Evening you have Leisure enough for this Purpose. Let your Children get by Heart the two Prayers that are added for them; and stand by them sometimes, that they may learn to pray seriously and devoutly. When they are of a fit Age, go with them to your Minister, and desire him to prepare them for Confirmation, and afterwards for receiving the blessed Sacrament.[6] /

A Morning Prayer for a Family.

GREAT and Glorious Lord God! we pray thee to look down from Heaven, the Habitation of thy Holiness and thy Glory, upon us vile and sinful Creatures. Have Mercy upon us, O Lord, and *according to the Multitude of thy tender Mercies, blot out all our Transgressions*: And do thou keep it for ever in the Purpose and Resolution of our Hearts, to serve and fear Thee for the future, and to keep all thy Commandments always, that it may be well with us for ever. We pray Thee, to this end, to write thy Laws in our Hearts, and to put thy Fear into our inward Parts, that we may never depart from Thee.

Grant us the Grace of thy Holy Spirit, to become every Day better; to reform and amend whatever is amiss in the Frame and Temper of our Minds, or in the Course and Actions of our Lives; to enable us to mortify our Lusts; to govern our Passions, and to order our whole Conversation aright; / to assist us in all that is good; to keep us from all Evil, and to preserve us to thy heavenly Kingdom. We pray Thee to instruct us in all the Particulars of our Duty, which we owe to

Thee and our Neighbour: *That we may herein exercise our selves always to have Consciences void of Offence both towards God and towards Man;*[7] that we may love Thee, the Lord our God, with all our Hearts, with all our Souls, and with all our Strength, and may love our Neighbour as our selves; and whatever we would that Men shall do unto us, that we may do likewise unto them.[8]

And let the Grace of God, which hath appeared unto all Men, and brings Salvation, teach us, that *denying Ungodliness and worldly Lusts, we may live soberly, righteously, and godly, in this present World, waiting for the blessed Hope and glorious Appearance of the great God and our Saviour Jesus Christ, who gave himself for us, that he might redeem us from all Iniquity, and purify unto himself a peculiar People, zealous of good Works.*[9]

And we pray Thee make us sensible of our own Frailty, of the Shortness / and Uncertainty of this Life, and of the Eternity of the next; to make us careful so to live, as we shall wish we had done when we come to die. Let our Loins always be girded about,[10] and our Lamps burning,[11] and we our selves like unto Men that wait for their Lord.

Extend thy Goodness to the whole World; let thy Way be known upon Earth, and thy saving Health among all Nations. Bless, we pray Thee, our Governors in Church and State, make them useful and serviceable to thy Glory, and the publick Good. We implore thy Mercy in Behalf of our Relations, Friends, and Benefactors; forgive our Enemies and teach us to do Good unto them.

We offer unto thee our hearty Praises for all thy Mercies bestowed upon us from Time to Time; for making us Christians; for preserving us the Night past, and the rest of our Lives, from innumerable Accidents and Dangers. Let all thy loving Kindness have this Effect upon us, to make us better, and to lead us to Repentance. And all we beg for Jesus Christ his Sake; in whose / blessed Name and Words we conclude our imperfect Prayers, saying, *Our Father,* &c.

May the Grace of our Lord Jesus Christ, the Love of God, and the Fellowship of the Holy Ghost, be with us this Day, and evermore. *Amen.*

An Evening Prayer for a Family.

O God, who art the Giver of all good Gifts, and the Father of Mercies, we thine unworthy Servants entirely desire to praise thy Name for all the Expressions of thy Bounty towards us. Blessed be thy Love, that gave thy Son to die for our Sins, to put us in a Way of being happy, if we would obey Thee; and after all the wilful Refusals of thy Grace, still hast Patience with us, and hast added this one Day more to all we have mis-spent already, to see if we would finish the Work Thou hast set us to do, and fit our selves for eternal Glory. /

Pardon, good Lord! all our former Sins, and all our Abuses of thy Forbearance; for which we are now sorry at our Hearts; and give us Grace to lead more holy Lives, and to be more careful in improving all future Opportunities. Make thy self present to our Minds, and let thy Love and Fear rule in our Souls in all Places, and upon all Occasions.

Keep us chaste in all our Thoughts; temperate in all our Enjoyments; humble in all our Opinions of our selves; charitable in all our Speeches of others; meek and peaceable under all Provocations; sincere and faithful in all our Professions; and so just and upright in all our Dealings, that no Necessity may force, no Opportunity in any kind [illeg.] us to defraud, or go beyond our Neighbours.

When Thou bestowed Good on others, let us not envy, but rejoice in it; and when thou addest any to our selves let us own thy Mercy, and humbly thank Thee for it. Afford us convenient Supplies in all our reasonable Necessities, and protect us against the Approach of / all Dangers; make us diligent in all our Business, and give such Success to our Endeavours, as thou seest most expedient for us.

Teach us contentedly to submit, and not to repine at any thing that comes upon us by the Allotment of thy wise Providence. And whilst we are in this World, and have manifold Concerns in it, suffer not our Hearts to be too much set upon it, but always fix our Eye upon the blessed Hope of things above. And we pray Thee make all the things of this World minister to it; and make us careful above all things to fit our Souls for that pure and perfect Bliss, which thou hast prepared for all that love and fear Thee, in the Glories of thy Kingdom.

Charge thy holy Providence with us this Night; make our Sleep safe and refreshing to us. Fit us for our great Change, that it may not surprize us unawares; but that having led holy Lives, we may be happy in our Deaths, and have Comfort and well-grounded Hope in Thee. /

Extend thy Grace to all Men in all Places; to our Governours both in Church and State; to High and Low, Rich and Poor; to all that pray for it, or need it in these Kingdoms. Bless all our Friends, Relations and Benefactors.[12] Forgive our Enemies, give them Hearts to fear Thee, and to be reconciled to us. Supply us, and all others, with whatsoever Thou seest proper for us, for Christ his Sake: In whose blessed Name and Words we still recommend our selves unto thee, saying, *Our Father,* &c.[13]

May the Grace of our Lord Jesus Christ, the Love of God, and the Fellowship of the Holy Ghost, be with us all this Night, and evermore. *Amen.*

A Morning Prayer for a Child.

GLORY be to Thee, O Lord! for all the Blessings I daily receive from Thee; for thy particular Preservation and Refreshment of me this Night past. /

Teach me to believe in Thee, to fear Thee, and love Thee with all my Heart; to worship Thee, and give Thee thanks; to honour thy holy Name, and to serve Thee truly all the Days of my Life.

Make me to love my Neighbour as my self; and to do to all Men as I would they should do to me. Make me obedient to my Parents, and all my Governours in Church and State.

Grant, O Lord! that I may order my self lowly and reverently to all my Betters; that I may hurt no Body by Word or Deed; that I may keep my Hands from picking and stealing, and my Tongue from Evil-speaking, Lying, and Slandering;[14] that I may demean my self with Temperance, Sobriety, and Chastity; that I may never covet and desire other Mens Goods, but learn and labour truly to get my own Living, and to do my Duty in that State of Life unto which it shall please Thee, O Lord, to call me. And all this I beg for the Merits of Jesus my Saviour; in whose holy Words I sum up all my Wants, saying, *Our Father,* &c. /

ANON., *A PERSUASIVE TO FAMILY RELIGION* (1736)

Anon., *A Persuasive to Family Religion: And the Obligation Christian Parents are Under to the Religious Education of their Children. With A Collection of Some Texts of Scripture for the Use of Children. By the Author of The Advantages of Closet Religion. To Which is Added, Some Forms of Prayer* (London: Printed for Richard Hett, at the Bible and Crown in the Poultry; and sold by T. Cadell, Bookseller, in Bristol, 1736), pp. 3–11, ECCO, ESTC Number T079346, ECCO Range 3749.

'Theological writings', according to Clare Brant, made up 'probably the greatest percentage of eighteenth-century print culture in general and epistolary writings in particular'.[1] In a society where how and not if it was best to worship was of great import, sermons and other devotional literature were extensively purchased.[2] The amount of theological writings published and purchased demonstrated the important role of religion in shaping personal and familial practices and identity. Religious letters by religiously minded laypeople, Brant further explained, 'were an important means of establishing spiritual authority'.[3] Theological treatise and Christian letter combined in an anonymous author's publication of *A Persuasive to Family Religion: And the Obligation Christian Parents are Under to the Religious Education of their Children ...* (1736).

The same year that *A Persuasive to Family Religion* was published also marked the third edition of the anonymous writer's *The Necessity and Advantages of Closet Religion. By a Private Christian* (1727).[4] The term 'closet religion' hearkened to earlier devotional books, such as the Anglican *The Common-Prayer-Book* (1689). These prayer books by religious leaders and concerned Christians testified to the importance of the domestic space to replicate and reinforce the rituals of the religious space. The emphasis upon parents as teachers of devotional behaviour to their children domesticated spiritual authority.

In the text of *A Persuasive to Family Religion* reproduced here, the writer began with an appeal to 'Dear Fellow-Citizens', which established an epistolary familiarity to discuss religious behaviour more intimately than the published sermon; the letter format implied a personal conversation about family prayer rather than the public preaching in a church. The author then established a dichotomy between the benefits of family religion and the deleterious effects if ignored or abandoned, which resembled the terrible fates William Hogarth had recently painted and engraved in his popular 'progress paintings' of the harlot (1732) and the rake (1733–5).

Notes

1. C. Brant, *Eighteenth-Century Letters and British Culture* (Houndmills: Palgrave, 2006), p. 283.
2. J. Black, *Eighteenth-Century Britain 1688–1783*, 2nd edn (Houndmills: Palgrave, 2008), pp. 134–6.
3. Brant, *Eighteenth-Century Letters and British Culture*, p. 31.
4. Private Christian, *The Necessity and Advantages of Closet Religion. By a Private Christian* (London, 1727), *Eighteenth Century Collections Online*. Gale. Brigham Young University – Utah, 10 December 2014.

Anon., *A Persuasive to Family Religion* (1736)

A PERSUASIVE TO Family Religion.
Dear FELLOW-CITIZENS,

THE *abounding* of *vice* and immorality, notwithstanding the *vigorous* endeavours of a number of *generous* souls, associated for putting our excellent laws in execution, by the most *legal,* and *prudent* methods, is justly lamented by *good men* of *all Persuasions.* Blessed be God *some success* they have; but *how small,* to what might be expected in so *righteous* a cause! Must not this put *a serious* mind on the enquiry, whence it *comes about?* And can it be resolved into / any cause more evident than this, *the neglect of family worship?* God is forgotten in our families! He is shut out of our houses! Of how many is that character most just, they *live as without God in the World?* As if *he* stood in no Relation to them, nor expected any regard from them! As if *self-sufficient* and *unaccountable!* That this should be true of *any,* yea, of *so many families* in this *great City*; That our *religion* should be *confined* to *publick worship*; That we should *satisfy* ourselves with *once a week* going to church, and, in a *customary manner,* attending on God's worship there, and all the week behave as if this were the utmost required of us, is *lamentable!* Were this neglect universal, I should fear, in a little time, even *publick worship* would be *set aside* too; and so all appearance of religion banished from among us.

That this *neglect* should befriend *vice* and *immorality,* is no wonder: It has a natural tendency to it. When *branches* of a prayerless family are *transplanted into families* of their own, the mischief of *bad example* is too evident: As their fathers did, so do they; the *sin* is, as it were, hereby *entailed,* and the neglect propagated. Surely *true love* and *tenderness* to our *posterity* should excite parents to *family religion,* as the most effectual means to spread *religion in the world*; agreeable to our *prayers,* if we know what we say, when we beg *God's kingdom may come.*

Families are *societies* of God's *instituting,* and *prior* to all other *societies*: There the *worship of God began,* and for some time was necessarily *confined* to them. But as the world / increased, Men formed themselves into *communities*; and, then *publick worship* took place: *men then began to call on the name of the Lord*; which, I take, was the *original* of *publick worship.* But sure it cannot be imagined, that this should *supersede family worship*. The *great God stands related* to us in *every capacity: duty* and *homage* is owing to him in *every relation*. As *single* persons, 'tis express'd, by *solitary worship*; as *families* by *family worship*; as communities by *publick worship*.

In my *converse* I have met with but few persons, that have *disputed the obligation to this duty*: Men usually *defend* or excuse their *neglect*, by pleading *inability* or *modesty*. As to the first, 'tis with me *astonishing*; since we live in a day that *abounds* with *helps* of that kind. *Numerous* are our excellent *books of devotion*, and easily *procured* by a willing mind; in which persons, who *chose them*, may find *forms* suitable to the *principal occasions* of life: and, as for others, by *practice* with these *helps*, they may soon *acquire* such an *habit*, as to enable them, tho' persons of *mean abilities*, to perform in a *manner above contempt*; and as they have to do with *a merciful God*, who will make *gracious* Allowances, requiring no more than he gives; if the *heart is upright*, they may be assured, that when they do their *best*, tho' 'tis but *mean*, thro' the *interposal* of the great High-priest[1] it shall find *acceptance*.

As for *shyness*, or *false modesty*, (for so I must call it) shall *prophane families*, without a *blush*, affront God Almighty, *by oaths* and *curses*, ridicule all *religion*, and esteem this / *Gentleman-like*, *a point of good breeding*; *prosess* themselves, without *shame*, in the *interest of the devil*, promoting his *kingdom*, by *example*, *encouragement*, and *influence*? And shall profess'd christians be *asham'd* to tell the world they are *engaged in the opposite interest*? that they are on *God's side*? *subjects* of his *kingdom*? And that therefore, as *families*, they *pay* him *homage*? How *awful* are those words of our *Lord!* – *him that is ashamed of me before men, of him will I be ashamed before my father and his holy angels*.[2]

CITIZENS,

Suffer me to *expostulate!* 'tis not about a *rite* or *ceremony:* 'Tis whether God Almighty shall be *acknowledged* by *christian protestant families*: whether *family sins* shall be *lamented*, and pardon implored: whether *family mercies* shall be *supplicated*, and *family judgments deprecated:* In a word, whether God shall be *owned* by us for the *fountain and spring* of all the good, we either *have*, or *want*? – How *strict* is our *dependance* on this *great* and *good God!* Is he not our *constant benefactor;* continually doing us *good?* does he not *load* us with *his benefits?* live we not on his *constant over-flowing bounty?* is he not *more* to us than all the *world* beside? 'Tis because *his compassions do not fail, that we are not consumed.* Should he *shut* up himself from us, what a *wilderness* would the *whole creation* be to us; without any one *able*, or *inclined* to *relieve* us! Every thing is to us no other than what he is pleased to make it. He *spreads* our *table*, and *gives* us our *daily bread*. /
The *ease, health, content, and quiet* we enjoy in our *families* is owing to his *beneficence:* we could have no *comfort* in our *nearest relatives;* shall find no *faithfulness* in our *servants* and *dependants;* have no *success* in our *undertakings;* the *best laid*

design will prove *abortive* and *mischievous,* if he withholds *counsel* and *blessing.* There is no *safety* in our *goings out* and *comings in:*³ a thousand Accidents we and ours are exposed to, one of which may create the greatest Discomfort in our families. And what *security* have we from these, but in the *divine protection?* 'Tis the *blessing of the Lord makes rich,*⁴ without which the most diligent hand can do nothing. We may labour and toil all our days, *rise up early, sit up late, and eat the bread of carefulness,*⁵ and, after all, put our earnings into a *bag* with *holes.*

But with what *christian boldness* may a man that comes from *family worship,* having therein *asked counsel* and *blessing* of God, *engage* in any *lawful* business; and *without terror* go forth into a world of *snares* and *temptations,* having put *himself* and *family* under the *protection* of a *powerful providence,* encouraged by that promise, *he shall give his Angels charge concerning thee, to keep thee in all thy ways?*⁶

What an aptness has this practice to make the world better? has it not a tendency to *promote religion* in our *relatives;* and so (as to some) to put an end to that *too common complaint* of *undutiful children,* and *unfaithful servants?* Religion heartily embrac'd makes persons better in every relation: and if it *mends families* it will *mend the world.* /

Take but a view of many *prayerless families,* especially those of *persons of figure* in the world. What an uncomfortable aspect do they yield! *God* being *shut out,* what *fills up* his *room?* Instead of *prayer* and *praise, oaths* and *execrations;* instead of *reading the scriptures, plays* and *romances, profane songs* and *ballads;* instead of *religious converse, cards* and dice; instead of *order* and *regularity, revelling, luxury* and *excess;* oftentimes the *night* turn'd into *day,* and the *day* into *night.* Of too many families it may be said, they are but a *herd of beasts,* living to no higher purposes than the capacity of a *brute* would answer.

Look into *praying families,* what *order,* what *peace,* what *enjoyment* of *themselves!* how delighting, even to standers-by, to behold them *bowing the knee* to Almighty God, and *morning* and *evening* offering up the daily *sacrifice* of *prayer* and *praise!* It seems a faint Resemblance of the great family in the blissful world above, that innumerable company of perfected Spirits, that are *ever* worshipping before the throne.

As to those who keep up *solitary worship,* and also attend on *publick,* yet neglect *family worship;* who, I am persuaded, are very few; I would ask them, whether they do not think, that their families are more likely to meet with God's blessing and presence in publick, when with them they have seriously implored his blessing, than when they have neglected it, and suffer those under their care to rush into publick worship, without any previous thoughts on what they are going about, which family / prayer would probably excite? *Religious Duties* have that *dependence* one on another, *publick* on *private,* and *private* on *publick,* that where either is *statedly,* or *wilfully neglected,* the other is to little purpose *attended to.*

I cannot but think, that the Man that makes *conscience of closet religion,*⁷ cannot find in his heart to *neglect family religion.* He that has *tasted that the Lord* is *gracious*,[8] and that *'tis good to draw nigh to God*,[9] will engage in every Duty, wherein that *taste* is to be *improv'd* and *heightened*. Religion *seated in the heart*, surely, will be *set up in the house*.

The hopes I have of the sobriety and piety of the rising generation is confined to *praying families:* from them only can it be rationally expected, that religion should be abetted, and the cause of God in the world supported.

I cannot conclude, without a grateful Remark on the happy posture of our publick affairs. We have our *religious* and *civil liberties secur'd* unto us, *by law;* our *king interesting* himself in the *happiness* of all his *subjects*. Look abroad in the world, where will you find a people under our *happy circumstances?* we seem the *envy* of all our *neighbours*. Our *Bibles* are in our *hands;* we have liberty to *use* them, and *understand* them for *our selves;* we may attend on God's publick worship *according, to our own consciences;* we may sing his praises, and call on his name *in our families,* in which none can disturb us without *becoming criminal*. What would our *suffering brethren* in *France, Piedmont*, the *Palatinate*,[10] and at *Thorn*,[11] give to be in our happy state! Now / does this *deserve no acknowledgment* from us and our families? How *base* and *disingenious* to the great God, who has so remarkably *distinguish'd* us, and given us the happy prospect of having these invaluable blessings *transmitted* to our dear posterity, should we still continue of the number of those families, *that call not on his name*.

If any, from a sense of duty, should resolve, through divine assistance, to set up, and keep up God's worship in their families, it is my advise, that they be called together as soon as possible in the morning, before business comes in to divert; and early in the evening, before sleepy hours; and let nothing but absolute necessity postpone it. With prudence and forecast this may be easily done; and, if you are in earnest, you will do it: that it may be at such hours, as that, through heaviness it may not be mockery, without the exercise of the *mind* and *soul,* which must accompany all reasonable and acceptable service. In order to this, I would with some warmth, caution my fellow-citizens against a very pernicious practice, both to soul and body: I mean clubs, and appointments. A practice I could with, were less encouraged by such, whose character, one would think, should set them out of danger of falling into it. There's scarcely any thing has given a more mortal wound to family religion than this. Oh! the time that is hereby wasted! families neglected! God's worship set aside, or, which is much the same, postponed to sleepy hours! A time when persons are unfit for the affairs of life. But this is not all the mischief: the usual conversation at such places of resort, the temper of spirit there contracted, / assures me, they are in a high degree sinful, and ought to be discouraged and avoided by all, who would with honour support the christian character.

I dare appeal to any who frequent such places, whether they can reflect on what was there said, and done, without self-reproach. What a low opinion must such persons have of family worship? who for the sake of such company, and such conversation, can set it aside, or spoil it by rendering it mock-service.

I have observ'd, this practice naturally diverts, the mind from what is serious, by being so accustomed to what is vain and trifling: the *mind* so fill'd with what it last convers'd with, that there is no room for a serious thought; that, at length, they have turn'd their back upon the concerns of their *souls*, and the eternal world, and it may be, stept into *the seat of the scorner*.[12] For a person to come from such a place, at a very late hour, and call his family to prayer (this is fact) when himself scarcely able to utter an intelligible word. Horrid insolence! What notion must such a creature form of a divine being? Surely, a practice which leads to such a profanation, must affright every one who would pay a due regard to that glorious Being, before whom the highest angel is represented as vailing his face.

Oh that I had but my wish! that some, yea many families, may set up this *delightful* and *gainful* practice: this would be a *better security* to our many national blessings, than *walls* or *bulwarks, armies* or *navies:* the Almighty *God* himself would be our defence, and dwell amongst us. And *thrice happy is that people whose God is the Lord.*[13] / [...]

ABBÉ D'ANCOURT, 'OF POLITENESS IN RELIGION, AND AGAINST SUPERSTITION', 'OF DEVOTION', 'OF BEHAVIOUR AT CHURCH', *THE LADY'S PRECEPTOR* (1743)

Abbé d'Ancourt, 'Of Politeness in Religion, and against Superstition', 'Of Devotion', 'Of Behaviour at Church', *The Lady's Preceptor. Or, a Letter to a Young Lady of Distinction upon Politeness. Taken from the French of the Abbé d'Ancourt, and Adapted to the Religion, Customs, and Manners of the English Nation. By a Gentleman of Cambridge* (London: Printed for J. Watts, 1743), pp. 3–8, ECCO, ESTC Number T068927, ECCO Range 11641.

'For all the complications of eighteenth-century religion', explained Clare Brant, 'letter-writers of different faiths frequently described themselves as writing as Christians'.[1] The universal aspects of shared religious beliefs applied to a larger audience than would a particular denomination addressing its adherents. Brant also observed that these ecumenical letter writers clarified 'a context for exchanges between people' so that 'their letters served a community'.[2] This universal Christian letter-writing identity was inscribed in a published letter by a French Abbot, which was then translated and adapted by a Anglican Cambridge gentleman: *THE LADY's PRECEPTOR. OR, A LETTER TO A YOUNG LADY of DISTINCTION UPON POLITENESS* ... (1743). The community the Abbé d'Ancourt addressed was genteel women ('Lady of Distinction'). The title also indicated the kind of letter these young genteel women would be reading, since a 'Preceptor' was a 'book of instruction in a particular art, subject, etc.', *The Lady's Preceptor* was a women's conduct book about courtesy.[3]

Until the end of the seventeenth century, the majority of conduct books were addressed to governing men and described the aristocratic masculine ideal. *The Lady's Preceptor* participated in the increasing number of conduct books addressed to aristocratic women; the author dedicated the book to 'her Highness, the Lady Augusta', who was the eldest daughter of Frederick, the Prince of Wales, and his wife Augusta. Although directed towards an aristocratic female, *The Lady's Preceptor* constructed a female identity at odds with courtly behaviour.

This new ideal of femininity became more prominent by the mid-eighteenth century, because at this time, as Nancy Armstrong noted, 'the number of books specifying the qualities of the new kind of woman had well outstripped the number of those devoted to describing the aristocratic male'.[4] These conduct or courtesy books were promoted as ideal reading material for aristocratic down to the middling sort of young women; for instance, to meet the public demand for conduct literature, *The Lady's Preceptor* was reissued in seven editions by 1762.

The popularity of conduct books contributed to its protean form, such as a French Catholic's letter to an English princess on polite femininity. Kathryn Sutherland explained,

> In the course of the eighteenth century, the conduct book absorbed aspects of socially and generically diverse earlier forms – devotional writings, the marriage manual, works on household economy and recipe books – to create a composite character-kit, incorporating practical advice on the duties of womanhood, on reading, dress, and desirable accomplishments, with moral instruction on less palatable issues, like the regulation of the affections and the control of moods, and with categories of virtuous identity, as daughter, wife, mother, widow.[5]

In this selection of *The Lady's Preceptor* the author defined the appropriately regulated behaviour of young women in public and private religious observance.

Notes
1. C. Brant, *Eighteenth-Century Letters and British Culture* (Houndmills: Palgrave, 2006), p. 281.
2. Brant, *Eighteenth-Century Letters and British Culture*, p. 281.
3. 'preceptor, n.' (*OED*).
4. N. Armstrong, *Desire and Domestic Fiction: A Political History of the Novel* (Oxford: Oxford University Press, 1987), p. 62.
5. 'Writings on Education and Conduct: Arguments for Female Improvement', in V. Jones (ed.), *Women and Literature in Britain 1700–1800* (Cambridge: Cambridge University Press, 2000), pp. 25–45, on p. 26.

Abbé d'Ancourt, 'Of Politeness in Religion, and against Superstition', 'Of Devotion', 'Of Behaviour at Church', *The Lady's Preceptor* (1743)

THE LADY's PRECEPTOR. OR, A LETTER TO A YOUNG LADY *of* DISTINCTION UPON POLITENESS. Taken from the FRENCH of the ABBÉ *D'ANCOURT*, And Adapted to the RELIGION, CUSTOMS, and MANNERS of the *ENGLISH* NATION. By a GENTLEMAN of CAMBRIDGE.
– – – Adorn'd
With all that Earth or Heaven could bestow,
To make her amiable: – On she came,
Grace was in all her Steps, Heav'n in her Eye,
In every Gesture Dignity and Love.
MILTON.[1]
LONDON: Printed for J. WATTS: And Sold by B. DOD at the *Bible* and *Key* in *Ave-Mary-Lane*, near *Stationers-Hall*.
MDCC XLIII. /

Of POLITENESS *in* RELIGION, *and against* SUPERSTITION.

THE first and most important of all the Instructions I beg leave to present you with, Madam, is that which relates to your Duty towards Heaven. Religion is the Knowledge of what is required of / us from our Creator, communicated to the Mind by Reason and Revelation, and rooted in the Heart by Divine Affection. 'Tis a Principle which soars above mere Nature, in order to search out and adore the Lord of Nature; and whereby we are instructed how, by a due Submission to his Laws, and by the Practice of Justice, Gratitude, and the other Virtues required of us in his revealed Will, to secure to our selves that eternal Felicity which the same Revelation gives us an Assurance of. The whole Conduct of yourself through Life ought to be regulated by Religion; every Movement of your Mind, your Thoughts, Talents, Manners and Studies should be agreeable to that, and should be all employ'd in the Service of the Supreme Being, not only as the Prince of all Perfections, but likewise as the ultimate End which we ought to aspire after in order to Happiness. A young Lady without Piety, and a religious

Reverence towards Heaven, is a kind of Monster[2] in the World. You ought to love GOD then from the Motives of Obligation and Gratitude, and to fear at the same time the Severity of his Justice; but be sure to avoid entertaining any of those gloomy and enthusiastical[3] Apprehensions of him which represent him always in Wrath, and with his Thunder about him, for the Destruction of Mankind. As you had the Felicity of being born a Christian, you have all the Reason in the World to rely on his Mercy, and to throw off those servile Terrors which only tend to diminish that Affection towards him, which you should above all things preserve in Purity and Vigour.

I shall not say any thing to you, Madam, with regard to the Duties of Conscience; that is the Business / of a Spiritual Tutor rather than of a *Worldly Sage*, you have sometimes been pleased to stile me: You'll however permit me just to hint my Sentiments upon what appears right or wrong to me in the common Practice of Devotion.

Of DEVOTION.

NOTHING is more hidden than true Devotion, it being lodged entirely in the Heart, whilst the false and affected is quite the Reverse, studying nothing but Exteriors in order to appear what it is not, and assuming an Authority of reforming every thing but itself. I would advise you to have a particular Guard against People of this Character; Hypocrisy is in high Mode and Practice amongst us at present, and it requires no small Degree of Sagacity not to be deceived by it, or mistake it for its opposite Virtue.

However good and wise you may naturally be, yet be sure always to remember that the Moral Virtues, without Faith and Religion, are Branches lopt from the Parent Tree, and will in the End wither and perish; and therefore make it a chief Business in your Youth to be well grounded in the Articles and Principles of your Profession.

Of BEHAVIOUR *at* CHURCH.

TO behave with Modesty,[4] Madam, is requisite every where in a young Lady, but more particularly at Church; I would therefore advise you against the fashionable Practice of gazing about to find People to curtsy to; though when others make the same Compliments to you, I would have you return 'em without laughing or talking. The church is not a Place / for courtly Ceremonies; 'tis a Temple set apart for the Service of the Supreme Author of all Things, where nothing should enter but Respect, Silence, and Devotion; fly therefore all those other Distractions which are quite the Opposites to these Duties, remembering always that whatever Incense is offered up by the Tongue is unprofitable and vain, unless the Heart and Mind entirely concur with it.

During the Time of Sermon always behave with Gravity and Attention, which is a thing too much neglected by young Ladies of this Age, who come to Church merely to see and be seen, and would be ashamed of nothing so much as to remember even the very Subject that the Gentleman in the Pulpit had been upon; sometimes indeed they will vouchsafe to attend a little, but 'tis only in order to make ill-natured Remarks on the Preacher, and to shew how much better Criticks than Christians they are. This may sit well enough on an Atheist or Free-thinker, but is insupportable in a young Lady, who ought to manifest Respect and a Desire of Information. You are not obliged to pass Judgment upon the Performance, but rather to profit by it. Another Particular allied to this, which I would at the same time caution you against, is the attempting to dogmatize, or form Difficulties with regard to Religion, which is a dangerous Undertaking, and often carries People farther than they at first imagined. Neither is it the Business of one of your Sex, Madam, to concern themselves about the Rites and Ceremonies of the Church she adheres to, nor to separate from the Established Worship through a Spirit either of Opposition or affected Delicacy, as if what was common was beneath / her Regard, and did not keep pace with her more refined and exalted Piety.

DAVID MUIR, *AN HUMBLE ATTEMPT TOWARD THE REVIVAL OF FAMILY-RELIGION AMONG CHRISTIANS* (1749)

David Muir, *An Humble Attempt toward the Revival of Family-Religion among Christians* (London: Printed for the Author, and Sold by J. Oswald at the Rose and Crown in the Poultry, Cheapside, 1749), ECCO, ESTC Number T091605, ECCO Range 5786.

During the eighteenth century, the concept of a family could include a household unit comprised of a nuclear family and co-habitant dependents such as servants and apprentices.[1] While this household family was bound not only by ties of blood and marriage, but also by co-residence, both types of families were also organized under some form of authority.[2] This authority figure, or head of the household, was expected to direct household management, provide and administer household finances, and oversee household religious observance.[3]

This paternal authority figure also permeated ecclesio-political discourse. As Naomi Tadmor explained: 'Notions of fatherhood were also significant in perceptions of monarchic government. Though it was the subject of so many political and philosophical controversies, the idea of paternal and sacrosanct monarchy did not disappear from eighteenth-century social thought.'[4] The ecclesio-political description of paternal monarchy indicated that during the eighteenth century there was little divide between religious writing and political polemic.[5] David Muir (*c.* 1708–80) used this ecclesio-political perception of kingship to characterize the influence of the father upon household family devotion in his sermon, *An Humble Attempt Toward the Revival of Family-Religion among Christians* (1769). Muir was the minister of the Wapping Presbyterian Church for forty years, and the dissenting church was known as Mr Muir's Meeting House.[6]

Muir's title to his sermon evoked an earlier sermon by another Dissenting minister, the hymn-writing Isaac Watts, who published *An Humble Attempt toward the Revival of Practical Religion among Christians, and particularly the Protestant Dissenters* (1731). While Watts directed his treatise first to Dissenting ministers and then to 'Disciples', Muir widened his audience by addressing fathers of the household family.

Notes

1. N. Tadmor, 'The Concept of the Household-Family in Eighteenth-Century England', *Past and Present*, 151 (May 1996), pp. 111–40, on p. 112, at http://www.jstor.org/stable/651207 [accessed 26 December 2014].
2. N. Tadmor, *Family and Friends in Eighteenth-Century England: Household, Kinship, and Patronage* (Cambridge: Cambridge University Press, 2001), p. 20.
3. Tadmor, *Family and Friends in Eighteenth-Century England*, pp. 24–5.
4. Tadmor, *Family and Friends in Eighteenth-Century England*, p. 158.
5. W. Gibson, *The Church of England, 1688–1832: Unity And Accord* (London: Routledge, 2001), eBook Collection (EBSCOhost) [accessed 10 December 2014], p. 5.
6. http://www.mocavo.com/Fasti-Ecclesiae-Scoticanae-the-Succession-of-Ministers-in-the-Church-of-Scotland-From-the-Reformation-Volume-7/660502/517 [accessed 28 November 2014].

David Muir, *An Humble Attempt toward the Revival of Family-Religion among Christians* (1749)

AN Humble Attempt TOWARD THE REVIVAL OF FAMILY-RELIGION AMONG CHRISTIANS.
By DAVID MUIR, *A. M.*
LONDON: Printed for the Author, and Sold by J. OSWALD at the *Rose and Crown* in the *Poultry, Cheapside*. M,DCC,XLIX. /
GOVERNORS AND HEADS of FAMILIES
Urged to the Practice of Family-Religion,
FROM JOSHUA xxiv. 15.[1] last Clause.

– *But as for me and my House, we will serve the* LORD.

THE lamentable Decay of FAMILY-RELIGION, in the present Age, shall be my Apology for some Discourses on this Subject. And, as your Souls, my dear Brethren, are in a peculiar Manner committed to my Care; and I lie under the strongest Obligations to contribute all in my Power to save them from final Ruin, I expect your most favourable Ear, your closest Attention; while from a Consciousness of the Duty I owe to my great Lord and Master, / to you, the People of my Charge, and to my own Soul, I give you fair Warning both of your Sin and Danger, if found negligent, cold and careless, in the Discharge of *Family-Religion*. I am sensible there are some of you who make Conscience of this Duty; would to God, I could say you all did so: But alas! I have too great Reason to fear, there is but little *Family-Religion* in many of your Houses: Notwithstanding the great God has built you Tabernacles,[2] you have not erected Altars[3] in them for him, and you do not pay him that Family Worship that is his Due. And therefore I look upon myself as too nearly concerned in this Matter, to pass it over in Silence: Yea, I should be justly chargeable with Unfaithfulness to God, to you, and myself, did I not exert my utmost Endeavours to remedy this fatal Evil, by exhorting you who are negligent to a more conscientious Performance of this your Duty, and to quicken you who are cold and indifferent to a more vigorous Discharge of it.

[...] The Practice of Family Religion is peculiarly incumbent on all Heads and Governors of Families.

The Method in which I shall treat of this Subject is this,

I. To open up the Nature of this Duty.

II. To mention a few of the many and strong Obligations that lye upon all concerned to practise it. /

III. To enquire, Whence is it, that such a general and woful Neglect of *Family-Religion* prevails at this Day? And then,

IV. To conclude all with such Addresses to several Sorts of Persons, as are very suitable to the Subject under our present Consideration.

I. Let us consider and open the Nature of the Duty mentioned in my Text. Now, this Part of our Task will be the more easily performed, if we suffer ourselves to reflect, that every Family-Governor sustains a threefold Character, *viz.* of a PROPHET,[4] to instruct his Family in all the Branches of useful Knowledge, especially in those which tend most to perfect their Nature, and to promote their great and ultimate End, the Glory of God and their final Happiness: Of a PRIEST, to discharge every Act of Family-Worship, especially to pray with and for his Houshold: And in fine, of a KING,[5] to direct, govern and provide for them all the Necessaries of Life. Thus I think the great and important Duty in my Text divides itself into three Branches, to which I shall now speak in their Order.

I. The Duty of every Parent or Head of a Family lies in instructing his Children and / Servants in all useful Knowledge, especially in that which tends most to promote the Glory of God and their final Happiness, in whatever is necessary to their being the faithful and obedient Servants of God in this Life, and the happy Possessors of a glorious Life of Immortality, when Time shall be no more [...] All Heads of Families should teach their Children and Servants, that it is owing, entirely owing to *Christ*'s meritorious Righteousness, that any of *Adam*'s sinful Race[6] are restored to the Favour of God in this World, and finally saved in the next [...] That every Governor should, according to his Capacity, teach those of his House, the Truths both of Natural and Revealed Religion [...]

2. To that which relates to his Priestly Character, his setting up and maintaining the Worship of God in his Family [...] And 'tis not to be questioned, that every Family ought to be a Church, wherein the great God should have solemn Worship and Adoration paid him.

In order, therefore, that every Family-Governor may discharge this Part of his Duty, let him carefully attend to, and study to practise the following Things:

(1.) He must be careful to read the Sacred Scriptures to those of his House [...] so it in a special Manner becomes all Heads of Families to instruct those under their Care, in the Knowledge of the Word of God, which is singularly adapted and every Way suited to the Purposes of Light and Grace, of Knowledge and Holiness [...]

(2.) He must pray with and for his Houshold [...] Hence 'tis, that the best of Family-Governors, in all Ages, have been indefatigable in the Performance of this Part of Family-Religion. [...] But to put this beyond all Doubt, we read frequently of our blessed Saviour's being alone, praying with his twelve Disciples, which was then his little Family.⁷

[...] For are there not Family-Mercies, which all in the House are jointly concerned to pray for, when wanted? And to make grateful Acknowledgments and suitable Returns for, when received? Are there not Family-Afflictions and Crosses, which they are in common concerned to pray against? And are there not Family-Sins which call for sincere Confessions and deep Humiliations? Surely there are. And what then can be more reasonable and just, more decent and comely, than to behold whole Families joining together in Prayer; to see those who live and love, eat and drink together, wrestling at the Throne of Grace together! [...]

(3.) The singing of Psalms, Hymns, or spiritual Songs, I think, should be brought in as a third Part of Family-Worship. It is too evident to be denied, that this Part of Worship is wofully neglected, even in many Families where the two former are carefully and conscientiously performed [...] For, when [Jesus] had eat the *Passover* with his Disciples, who were his Family, and instituted the Sacrament of his Supper, he concluded all with an Hymn of Praise to his heavenly Father. This was the last Time he had an Opportunity of performing Family Worship, when, you see, singing of Psalms was not forgotten. And surely we cannot copy after a better Pattern, than that of our dearest Lord.

3. To the Regal Part of every Master of a Family's Duty [...] every Head of a Family has particularly three Things to do:

(1.) To make all proper and necessary Provision for the Maintenance of his Houshold. He should take special Care of the Bodies and temporal Welfare of all who stand in a Family-Relation to him; and this Care must be suitable to his Abilities, and sufficient to the Ends of a useful and comfortable Life [...] to contribute their utmost Endeavours for the Support and Comfort of their Children and Servants. But,

(2.) Every Head of a Family should use his pious Counsels, proper Reproofs, and seasonable Corrections, to preserve those under his Care from every evil and wicked Way. Parents and Governors of Families should rule their Houses well, and keep their Children and Servants in Subjection, with all Gravity and becoming Authority [...]

(3.) [...] Vice is so very infectious, that one wicked Person may soon corrupt the Morals of others in the Family: Yea, Children and Servants, who descend from the Loins of the best Parents, have a corrupt Quality in them, derived from guilty *Adam*, which renders them susceptible of vicious Impressions, and makes them liable to be easily corrupted [...] And therefore such Considerations as these should awaken in Parents and Masters a due Concern for the Welfare of their Families, not only by giving them all proper Instruction, and daily admonishing them, but likewise by taking Care what Company they keep, and especially that there be none suffered to live with them in the same House, who are openly wicked and profane [...]

1. [...] Doth not Reason tell you, that God is the Author and Constituter of Families [...] Seeing, therefore, God in his Providence has brought you into a Family-Relation, built you Tabernacles, and committed Children and Servants to your Care; seeing he superintends the Affairs of your Families, preserves them from innumerable Evils, and supplies them with all needful Good, shall you not be chargeable with the utmost Ingratitude, if you lay not yourselves out to instruct and govern them, after such a Manner as may promote the Glory and Honour of your kind Benefactor? [...] But,

2. If Gratitude to your best Friend and most bountiful Benefactor, will not move you to the Practice of this Duty; methinks, Love and Pity to your Children and Servants should constrain you to it [...]

3. If neither of the above Arguments will prevail with you; yet let that powerful / and constraining Motive of Self-Interest constrain you to practise Family-Religion. All Parents and Masters of Families have a special Interest of their own, in the Welfare and Happiness of their Children and Servants; and therefore, the powerful Motive of Interest, the strong Principle of Self-Love, so deeply rooted in our Natures, should prevail with us Parents and Masters, to take all imaginable Care of our respective Households. [...]

4. [...] All Parents and Heads of Families / should consider, there is a Day coming, when they must be accountable for every Child and Servant under their Care; and according as they have performed or neglected their Duty towards them, receive a suitable Reward. [...]

1.[...]. the ill Formation of Families at the first, by unsuitable Marriages and Relations [...] is ever like to prove an unhappy Match; and what more unsuitable than to join the pious and the / profane, the well educated and well disposed Person with the loose and profligate? [...] I cannot, therefore, but look upon this as one of the chief Causes of that criminal Neglect of Family-Religion at this Day; and I can't but heartily wish, and earnestly beseech all unmarried Persons, who have any Regard for the Glory of God, the Interest of *Christ*, and their own temporal and eternal Welfare, to chuse such a one for their nearest Relation, as will chearfully and willingly engage in the Service of the Lord [...]

2. [...] Praying is the best Way to get the Gift of Prayer, and by doing your Duty you will acquire fresh Courage, and attain a greater Fitness and Ability to perform it.

[...] And lastly. May I not affirm, that the great Neglect of Family-Worship, that is but too visible at this Day, is owing to the lamentable Decay of serious Religion, and great Abatement of Zeal in Family-Governors. [...] I therefore beseech you, both for your own Sake, and the Sake of your Families, seriously to weigh this Matter, and allow it to have such an happy Influence upon you, as to engage you for the future vigorously and carefully to maintain the Practice of Family-Religion. [...]

2. I beg Leave to address myself to you who are the Children of pious Parents, and have been blessed with a religious Education; you who have heard many a wise Counsel and compassionate Advice drop from your Parents Lips, and from the Fondness of their pious Hearts [...] O how truly thankful should you be to the great and the best of Beings, for the Privileges of your Birth and Education! While some glory in the Antiquity of an illustrious House, and in being the Descendants of great and noble Ancestors, you may glory in being the Children of the Covenant made with *Abraham* and his Seed.[8][...] But, if I should be mistaken, give me Leave to tell you, that if there be a hotter Place in Hell[9] than another, you may expect to be lodged there. Therefore think, O think, before it be too late, what must be the Consequence of forsaking the Lord God of your Fathers. Are you willing to be eternally banished from all your godly Relations, at as great a Distance as between Heaven and Hell? [...]

3. Suffer me next to turn my Address to such Parents and Heads of Families who live in the woful Neglect of this important Duty recommended in my Text [...] How strangely and wickedly careless are ye of the immortal Interests of your own Offspring and Servants, and the Interest of God in them? [...] Your Children and Servants are given you in Charge to be brought up for the Lord, and therefore sad and uncomfortable will your Day of Reckoning be, if, through your Carelessness, they die in their Iniquities [...] In order, therefore, to prevent such a heavy Accusation being brought against you another Day by your Children and Servants, let me beseech you to fall in with good *Joshua's* Resolution in my Text, and serve the Lord with your respective Households. I proceed, /

4. To address myself to the Children of irreligious Parents; such Parents as do not serve and worship God in their Families. I confess, your Case is very deplorable, and much to be pitied, seeing your Lot is cast in such Families as have not so much as the Form of Godliness; seeing you are the Offspring of such unnatural Parents, as are at no Pains to take Care of your truest and everlasting Interests; seeing you have the worst Example set before you, and are taught by your Parents Practice to neglect your immortal Concerns, and to transmit to your own Posterity all these Inconveniencies, which you yourselves lie under [...] Shall your whole Family perish, from Generation to Generation? God forbid! O then let there be, at least, one Heir of Heaven in your Line. And if your Parents should be so wicked, as rather to discourage than to countenance and assist you in this great Concern; you must remember, that Father and Mother, your nearest and dearest Relations, must all be forsaken for *Christ* and Salvation:

5. Suffer me to address myself to such as may have Intentions of soon entering into a new Family-Relation [...] I beseech you, my Friends, to consider this, and

before-hand to put on this pious Resolution, that as soon as God in his Providence brings you into such a Relation, you and your Household will serve the Lord [...]

6. and lastly; I can't help thinking but this Subject affords Matter of Address, to such of you who, by the Providence of God, are in the Condition of Servants. You have heard the great Advantage that attends Family-Religion, and of Consequence what a Loss it must be to live in a Family where God is not worshipped, and where, tho' there may be Food enough for the perishing / Body, there is none for the immortal Soul: Methinks, therefore, this should engage you to be very careful in the Choice of the Place you go to, that it be a House where God is served and worshipped, and the Blessing of the Lord is most likely to dwell [...]

ANON., *CHEAP REPOSITORY TRACTS FOR SUNDAY READING* (1800)

Anon., *Cheap Repository Tracts for Sunday Reading. To Which are Added, Some Prayers for Individuals and for Families. A New Edition* (London: Sold and printed by Bye and Law, 1800), pp. 356–61, ECCO, ESTC Number T184326, ECCO Range 10538.

The late eighteenth century was a period of political turmoil fomented by the American and French Revolutions. As a countermeasure to the radical street literature found in pamphlets and broadsides, the Church of England responded with anti-revolutionary, religious literature; Beilby Porteus, the Bishop of London, urged Hannah More and others to write what became known as *Cheap Repository Tracts*.[1] These *Cheap Repository Tracts* were written and distributed to the same audience as Thomas Paine's *Rights of Man*. Whereas Paine's *Rights of Man* advocated republicanism and social welfare for the poor; the *Cheap Repository Tracts* responded by promoting 'budget-conscious, frugal, investment model, stressing the deferral of happiness, self-restraint, and reliance on paternalistic benefaction'.[2] Paine had insisted that the two parts of his *Rights of Man* (1790–2) be combined and sold in cheap editions in order to be affordable to the labouring classes;[3] therefore, the *Cheap Repository Tracts* were sold monthly for ½ d. or 1d., and were distributed to 'cottages, workshops, coal pits, and public houses'.[4]

Over two million tracts were bought in the first year of the *Cheap Repository* publications and were also sent to the Americas, Sierra Leone and the West Indies.[5] 'Though their influence on their intended audience cannot be measured', as S. J. Skedd notes, the *Cheap Repository Tracts* were the acknowledged 'safe reading of the poor'.[6] Thus, through the *Cheap Repository Tracts* the poor family became included in purchasing and reading the devotional literature of the eighteenth century. The *Cheap Repository Tracts* were published between 1795 and 1799, after which the Religious Tract Society, founded in 1799, grew to prominence.

In the tract reproduced here, the writer explains the duties of poor parents to oversee the religious observance of prayers in their families.

Notes
1. *ODNB*.

2. P. Demers, *The World of Hannah More* (Lexington, KY: University Press of Kentucky, 1996), p. 109.
3. M. Philp, 'Thomas Paine', in E. N. Zalta (ed.), *The Stanford Encyclopedia of Philosophy* (Winter 2013 edition), at http://plato.stanford.edu/archives/win2013/entries/paine/ [accessed 19 November 2014].
4. Demers, *The World of Hannah More*, p. 112.
5. Demers, *The World of Hannah More*, p. 110.
6. Skedd, 'More, Hannah', *ODNB*.

Anon., *Cheap Repository Tracts for Sunday Reading* (1800)

PRAYERS TO BE Used by a Child or Young Person – By a Grown Person – By the Master or Mistress of a Sunday School – And by the Master or Mistress of a Family.

ADDRESS TO INDIVIDUALS ON THE SUBJECT OF THE FOLLOWING PRAYERS.

THERE are many persons, it is to be feared, who do not accustom themselves to pray at all, than which there cannot be a greater proof of irreligion. Some of these may plead, perhaps, that they have never been taught to pray, or at least that they have no suitable prayer provided for them. To such persons an opportunity is now given of beginning what they cannot but allow to be a good custom, for who can deny that it is a good custom, or rather, indeed, that it is a bounden duty to call day by day on the God who made them.

There are other persons who oblige themselves / daily to say over the Lord's Prayer[1] only, and, perhaps, also the Belief.[2] This is often done in a very formal and superstitious manner. The Lord's Prayer is undoubtedly a most excellent pattern for our daily prayers, but it does not appear to have been given by Christ as the only form of Prayer that was to be used; and, it is worthy of remark, that when he uttered it, he took occasion to warn his disciples against the vain repetitions used in prayer by the Pharisees.[3] It is to be feared that even the Lord's Prayer has become a vain repetition in these days, not through any fault in the Prayer itself, but through the unthinking, and, perhaps, over frequent way in which some people use it. Possibly a new form may supply some new thoughts, and may serve to awaken the sort of people I am speaking of to a sense of the true meaning and use both of the Lord's Prayer, and of Prayer in general.

ADDRESS TO PARENTS.

IT is hoped that there can be little occasion to inform parents, that they ought to teach their children to pray. A short Prayer, fit for persons of twelve or fourteen years of age, is here supplied. The same Prayer may serve both for morning and evening, and the memory, therefore, will be little burthened by learning it by heart. Before children entirely leave their father's house, it is desirable that, instead of the Child's Prayer, they should learn by heart the Morning and Evening Prayer for a Grown Person which follows. /

To Heads of Families.

IF all Masters and Mistresses of Families[4] would ask each of their servants what is the custom in respect to daily Prayer, and would supply them, if there seems occasion, with the Morning and Evening Prayer for a grown Person, which they will find in this Tract, it is plain, I think, that much benefit might arise, through the blessing of God, both to Masters and Servants: for a Servant's duty to his Master is one of the things which these Prayers will teach.

Address to Masters and Mistresses of Schools.

YOU are desired to take notice, that the Prayer for a Sunday School is intended to be used only on a Sunday. The Prayer for an individual may, by merely changing the word *I* into *we*, and the word *me* into *us*, be made to suit a Daily School, and indeed it may be made to suit some Families also. Some of the Family Prayers may also suit Sunday Schools.[5]

On Family Prayer.

THE advantages of Family Prayer are many, and they are very plain. The Master of a family (or the Mistress in his absence) by devoutly reading a Morning and Evening Prayer to his Family, instructs both his children and servants in their duty, accustoms them to prayer, makes an open profession of his own religion, brings himself under an obligation to observe a consistent, that is a religious conduct during the day; and above all, let it be remarked, he draws down the blessing / of God on himself and his household. Several Prayers are here offered to Masters and Mistresses of Families, and they who have not yet been used to Family Prayer, have now, therefore, an opportunity to beginning [sic] this good custom; and in doing it, may God grant them his blessing!

General Directions, applicable chiefly to the Case of Private Prayer.

FIRST, before you proceed to your private prayers, endeavour to compose your thoughts, and then examine yourself for a few moments. Ask yourself in the morning, for instance, what are likely to be the duties and trials of the day that is before you, and in the evening, reflect what have been the sins of the past day. By doing so, you will be enabled to apply the words of your prayer more particularly to your own case, and possibly also you may thus be led to add a few words of your own to what you have got by heart, and by degrees you may thus be inclined to enlarge your daily petitions more and more in your own words, and thus you may learn to pray more and more in spirit and in truth.

Secondly, When about to pray, endeavour to lift up your heart to God for the help of his Holy Spirit; for the Scripture tells us, that it is "the Holy Spirit that helpeth our infirmities."[6] Many people complain of great coldness and indifference while engaged in prayer, and there are few who are not conscious of this in a greater or less degree. Let all then begin, by imploring God's Holy Spirit to assist them in praying as they ought. There cannot be a better introduction to every / kind of prayer, than a few secret words first uttered to this effect from the heart.

Thirdly, Beware of wandering thoughts, when engaged in prayer. To this end let every struggle be made, and let it be seriously impressed upon you, that God is now present in an especial manner, and that all absence of mind which is allowed and indulged is a great affront to his Majesty.

Fourthly, But besides being attentive, take care that you are also sincere in your prayer. Ask yourself often, whether you mean what you say while you are praying, and whether you sincerely and earnestly wish the thing that you ask. Accustom yourself not to attend to the mere found of your words, but to the sense; and if you do not well understand any part of the prayers here offered you, endeavour to get what is difficult explained before you repeat it. Some persons have been known to say prayers day by day, almost every word of which, they have contradicted by their whole conversation and conduct. What a terrible hypocrisy is this! A man's prayers may either be the greatest blessing to him, or the most grievous sin, according to the manner in which he performs them.

Fifthly, Endeavour not only to be sincere in your prayers at the moment when you offer them, but endeavour also, that the same spirit which animates your prayers, may animate your whole life. To this end, examine your life often by means of your prayers. Try whether all your maxims in life, your common speech and your several tempers, as well as your open conduct, / agree with the prayers which you use. The sincerity which God requires of you is not a momentary sincerity, it is not a short lived and changeable feeling, which is forgotten when you go into the world. The remembrance of what you have been praying for in the morning should follow you into the field, or the shop, and should influence your conduct all the day long.

Lastly, Consider whether God answers your prayers. If you pray aright, depend upon it your prayers will be heard and answered; your tempers will be subdued, your temptations weakened, and your whole mind will be rendered pious if you really pray that it may be so; and if this be not the case, you may reasonably suspect that your prayers have not been such as they ought. If you pray aright, depend upon it, you will improve in every respect; you will gain more humility, more tenderness of conscience, more fear of God, more pleasure in his worship, and more happiness in his service, and also more conscience in Christ, and probably more hope of salvation, in proportion to the earnestness and sincerity of your prayers to God to this effect, for these are all the gifts of that Holy Spirit which God hath promised to them that ask it.[7]

ISLE OF WIGHT COUNTY, VIRGINIA, DEEDS (1720-36 AND 1741-9)

Isle of Wight County, Virginia, Deeds (1720–36 and 1741–9), Isle of Wight County Deed Book 7, 1744–7 (Richmond, VA: Southside Virginian Pub. Co.: Orders to W.L. Hopkins, *c.* 1994).

Native American and Anglo American interactions during the seventeenth and eighteenth centuries in Virginia were conducted from two differing approaches to relationships. In Virginian tidewater native communities, the *mamanatowick*, or head chief, would adopt the Anglo-American leader into his fictive family.[1] While the native tribes viewed their alliance partners as brothers, the Virginians valued the Iroquois Confederation only for their military utility.[2] By the eighteenth century, however, the Virginians sought to control the native groups, not to coexist.[3]

This controlling approach was evident in colonial Virginian encounters with the Nottoways, an Iroquoian speaking tribe, who lived in Isle of Wight County along the shores of the James River.[4] In 1726, the colonial government kept the Nottoways under surveillance because of 'a suspected transgression'.[5] In terms of the Nottoway lands, the Virginia Assembly honoured the 1662 legislation that granted 'peaceful Indians' property rights.[6]

The land deeds of the early eighteenth century reflected the change effected by Sir William Gooch, Virginia's lieutenant governor, from the seventeenth-century headright system, that granted 50 acres per immigrant to Virginia, to much larger land grants for Protestant families.[7] This change, according to Alfred A. Cave, revealed the transformation of Anglo-Indian relations over land use 'from a ritual of peace to an instrument of imperialism'.[8]

Notes
1. M. L. Rhoades, *Long Knives and the Longhouse: Anglo-Iroquois Politics and the Expansion of Colonial Virginia* (Madison, NJ: Faileigh Dickinson University Press, 2011), p. 14.
2. Rhoades, *Long Knives and the Longhouse*, p. 14.
3. L. Scott Philyaw, *Virginia's Western Visions: Political and Cultural Expansion on an Early American Frontier* (Knoxville, TN: University of Tennessee Press, 2004), p. 39.
4. Rhoades, *Long Knives and the Longhouse*, p. 42.

5. Philyaw, *Virginia's Western Visions*, p. 39.
6. A. A. Cave, *Lethal Encounters: Englishmen And Indians In Colonial Virginia* (Santa Barbara, CF: Praeger, 2011), p. 141, eBook Collection (EBSCOhost) [accessed 12 December 2014].
7. Cave, *Lethal Encounters*, p. 181. This was the 1734 law that all Deeds must be acknowledged, proved and recorded.
8. Cave, *Lethal Encounters*, p. 182.

Isle of Wight County, Virginia, Deeds (1720–36 and 1741–9)

THIS INDENTURE[1] Tripartite made the Twenty forth day of March in the year of our Lord one Thousand Seven hundred [thirty-six] King Edmunds,[2] James, Harrison, Peter, Wansake Robin, Frank, Wonoak Rigin, Robin Scholler, Sam,[3] [Chie]f men of the Nottaway Indians[4] of the first Part John Simmons[5] of Isle wight County. Tho[ma]s Coche and Benj[amin] Edwards[6] [of the County of Surry] Gent[lema]n of the Second Part and Coll. John Simmons of the County of Isle of White – of the third Part. Whereas [by one]

Act of the Gen[era]l Assembly made at a Session lately held at Williamsburgh in the Eighth year of the Reign of our Lord George the Second King of Great Brittain Intituted an Act to Enable the Nottaway Indians to Sell Certain Lands[7] therein Mentioned and for discharging the Indian Interpreters it is [among] other things Enacted that the Chief men of the Nottaway Nation are impowered to make Sale of all or any part of a Certain Circular Tract of land[8] of Six Miles diameter lying and being on the Northside of Nottaway River in the County of Isle wight by and with the Consent of the said John Simmons Tho[ma]s Coche and Benj[amin] Edwards who are by the said Act appointed Trustees to See the said Act duly Executed and after any Agreement made for the Sale of any Part of the said land so as Such part do not Exceed four hund[re]d Acres to any one person it shall and may be lawfull for the Said Chief were together with the Trustees aforesaid or the Survivors or Survivor of them to Seal and deliver a feofm[en]t[9] to the Purchaser who immediately after the Execution thereof shall pay down to ye said Chief men the Purchase money for w[hi]ch a Receit shall be likewise Endorsed on the deed and any feofm[en]t So Executed and perfected and afterwards acknowledged or Proved by the Oaths of three Witnesses and Recorded in the Court of the said County [of] Isle wight where the lands lye shall be Sufficient in law to pass the fee Simple Estate of Such lands and the Purchaser or Purchasers [thereof] his or there heirs or Assigns shall for Ever hold and Enjoy the Same free and discharged from all Claims of the Nottaway Nation [and their posterity any thing in an Act] of the Gen[era]l Assembly made in the fourth year of the Reign of the late Queen Anne [instituted an Act for preventing] of Misunderstandings between the Tributary Indians and other his Majesties Subjects of this Colony and dominion [and for a free and open] Trade with all Indians whatsoever or in any Other Act of the Gen[era]l Assembly Contained to the Contrary hereof in any wise Notwithstanding as [in] the Said Act among Other things more fully is Contained.

Now This Indenture Witnesseth that the said King Edmunds, James, Harrison, Peter, Wanoak Robin, Frank, Wanoak Robin jun[io]r, Robert Scholler, Sam, Cockarous Tom & Cherrino the Chief men of the Said Nottaway Indians by and with the Consent of the said John Simmons Tho[ma]s Cocke and Benj[ima]n Edwards Testified by their being made parties to these presents for and in Consideration of the Sum of Fifteen pounds Current Money to the [said] Chief men in hand paid the Receit whereof is hereby acknowledged have granted bargained Sold Enfeofed[10] and Confirmed and by these presents do grant bargain Sell Enfeoff and Confirm unto the Said Coll. John Simmons his heirs and Assigns Three hundred and Ninety Acres parcell of ye said Circular Tract of Land bounded as followeth Beginning at a white Oake on the East Side of the East Side of the Atsamoosock Swamp a Corner of No. 1 Thence by the line of No. 1 East Three hundred Thirty Six pole to a Hickory, thence North one hundred and forty pole to {smudge} {smudge} West Three hundred Ninety four pole to alive Oak by the side of Atsamaosock aforesaid and down the Various Courses of the Run of the Said Swamp to the Beginning it {smudge} As by the Survey and Platt of John Allen Gent[lema]n Surveyer of the said County of Isle wight doth and may appears and all the Estate Right Title and Interest of the said Nottaway Indians in and to the Same. To have and to hold the said land with ye appurtinances unto the Said Col. John Simmons his heirs and Assigns to the only use and behalf of the said Coll. John Simmons his heirs and Assigns for Ever yielding and paying to his Majesty his heirs and Successors the yearly {smudge} Rents due for the said Land In Witness whereof the said parties have hereunto Set their hands and affixed their Seals the day and year above Written

    SethTho[mas] Davis   J Simmons   King Edmunds

James Stanton	Tho[ma]s Cocke	James
J Gray	Benj[ami]n Edwards	Harrisson Peter
Wine Oak Robin		
frank		
Wine Oak Robin		
Robert Scholar		
James		

Mem[orandum] that on the twenty fourth day March in the year of our lord One thousand seven hundred & Forty seven peaceable & great possession and season of the land with in Mentioned was had & taken by the Chief {smudge}

{smudge} Nottaway Nation within Mentioned and by thence declared to the within Named John Simmons Gentl[eman] to him his heirs Assignes for Ever According to the forme & Effect of the within Mentioned {smudge} Indenture Recd of the within Named John Simmons the just sum of fifteen pounds the purchase money within mentioned

    Tho[mas] Davis   King Edmunds
    James Stanton   James
    J Gray   Harrison
    Peter
    Wine Oak Robin
    Frank
    Wine Oak Robin
    Robin Scholar
    Sam

At a Court held for Isles of Wight County Feb[rua]ry 12th 1746
    within Indenture of Feofment with the above Livery and Seisin[11] and Reciept between the Chief Men of the Nottaway Indians of the one Part John Simmons Gent[lema]n of the other Part was proved by the Oath of Thomas Davis James Stanton and Joseph Gray the Witnesses thereto and Ordered to be Recorded
    Test Ja[mes] Baker CCler[k]
/

THIS INDENTURE Tripartite Made the 30th Day of March: In the Year of our Lord one Thousand Seven Hundred and Forty five Between Waynoak, Robin, Frank, Roger, Sam, Chorens, Tom, Doct[o]r Tom, Walt Cockrous Tom, Scipere, Jack Will Jo[h]n Turner & Chief Men of the Nottoway Indians of the first Part James Baker, John Person & Richard Blow Jun[io]r of the County of Isle of Wight Gent[leman] of the Second, Part, and Timothy Sharp of the County afores[ai]d of the third Part WHEREAS by one Act of <the> General Assembly made at a Session lately held at Williamsburg in the Eighteenth Year of the Reign of our Lord George the Second King of Great Britain Intituted an Act to enable the Nottoway and Nansemond Indians to Sell Certain Lands, And for other Purposes therein & Mentioned. It is among other things Enacted that the Chief Men of the Nottoway Nation are impowered to Sell Five Thousand Acres of Land being Part of a Tract of Land of Six Miles Square lying and being on the South side of Nottoway River in the afores[ai]d County of Isle of Wight, And Between the Western Boundary of their said Land & Buck Horn Swamp. By and with the Consent and Approbation of James Baker, John Person & Richard Blow Jun[io]r who are by the s[ai]d Act. Appointed Trustees to see the said Act duly Executed And after any Agreement made for the s[ai]d Lands or any Part thereof it shall and may be Lawfull for the Chief Men of the s[ai]d Nation together with the Trustees afores[ai]d or the Survivors or Survivor of them to Seal and Deliver a Feoffment and to make Livery and Seisen upon the Land to be Indorsed upon such Feoffment to the Purchaser, who immediately after the Execution thereof shall Pay down to the said Trustees (for the Uses and Purposes herein Expressed) the Purchase Money for which a Receipt shall likewise be Indorsed on the Deed. And any Feoffment so Executed and Perfected and afterwards Acknowledged or Proved by the Oaths of three Witnesses and Recorded in the Court of the s[ai]d County of Isle of Wight where the Lands lie shall be Sufficient in Law to Pass the Fee Simple Estate of Such Lands so by them Sold. And the Purchaser or Purchasers thereof his or their Heirs or Assigns shall forever hold and enjoy the same freed and Discharged from all Claims of the Nottoway Nation and their Posterity, Anything in one Act of the General Assembly made in the Fourth Year of the Reign of the late Queen Anne Instituted an Act for Preventing of Misunderstandings Between the Tributary Indians and other her Majest[ies] Subjects of this Colony and Dominion and for a free and open Trade with all Indians whatsoever or in any other Act of the General Assembly contain'd to the Contrary hereof in any wise Notwithstanding as in the s[ai]d Act among other things more fully is Contained NOW THIS INDENTURE WITNESSETH That the s[ai]d Waynoak Robin, Frank, Roger, Sam, Cherens, Tom, Doct[o]r Tom, Walt Cockrons Tom, Sciper, Jack Will, John Turner - - The Chief Men of the Nottoway Indians by and with the Consent of James Baker, John Person, & Richard Blow jun[io]r Testified by their being made Parties to these Presents for and in Consideration of the Sum of Thirty four Pounds <five Shillings> Current Money to the s[ai]d Trustees in hand Paid the Receipt whereof is hereby Acknowledged HAVE Granted, Bargained, & Sold, Enfeoffed and Conformed, And by these Presents Do Grant, Bargain, & Sell Enfeoff & Conform unto the s[ai]d Timothy Sharp his Heirs and Assigns One Hundred & Siventy Acres Parcel of the afores[ai]d Tract of Land And Bounded as followeth BEGINING at a Gum by the side the Cabbin Branch thence 82d W 22, Pole to three Trees Cropt inwards a Corner of No F. thence S:5d E 84 Pole to a pine a Corner of No L thence by No L N:70d E280. Pole to a Blk oak Corner of No M. thence by No M:E:N:E 32 Pole to a Hickory, thence N:75 E40 Pole to a Pine a Corner of No D: by the side the Cabbin Br[an]ch thence by No D N:60 W154, Pole to a Gum over the Run of the Cabbin Branch afores[ai]d thence up to Various Courses of the Run of the s[ai]d <Branch to the Begining> as by the Survey and Plot of James Baker Gent[leman] Surveyor of the s[ai]d County of Isle of Wight doth and may Appear, And all the Estate, Right, Title, & Interest of the s[ai]d Nottoway Indians in and to the same TO HAVE AND TO HOLD The s[ai]d Land with the Appurtenances unto the s[ai]d Timothy Sharp & his Heirs and Assigns for Ever. Yealding and Paying to his Majesty and his Successors the like Quitrents[12] as are Paid by Persons obtaining Grants for Land from his Majesty IN WITNESS whereof the s[ai]d Parties have hereunto set their Hands and Affixed their Seals the Day and Year above Written

   Signed Sealed & Delivered
   In Presence of }Ja[mes] Baker   Skiper S   Frank C
   James Ridley   John Person   John Robin   Roger C
   Jordan Thomas   Watt B   Waynoak Robin
   Tho[ma]s Jarred   Cherrons N   Doct. Tom
   Jo[h]n Turner   Sam
   Jack Will
   Cockrous Tom
/

MEMORAND[U]M That on the 30th Day of March In the Year of our Lord One Thousand Seven Hundred and Forty five Peaceable & Quiet Possession & Seison of the Land within Mentioned was had and taken by the Chief Men of the s[ai]d Nottoway Nation within Mentioned and by them Delivered to the within Named Timothy Sharp to hold to him his Heirs & Assigns for Ever According to the Form and Effect of the within Mentioned Indenture.

   In Presence of
   Skiper S   Frank
   John G   Robin Roger
   Watt   Waynoak Robin
   Cherins   Doct[o]r Tom
   Jo[h]n Turner   Sam

   Jack Will
   Cockraus Tom

Rec[eiv]ed of the within Named Timothy Sharp the Just Sum of Thirty four Pounds five shill[ings] Current Money, the Purchase Money within Mentioned.

   In Presence of
   Ja[mes] Baker   Skiper S   Frank
   John Robin   Roger
   Watt Waynoak   Robin

   Cherens MDoct[o]r Tom
   Jo[h]n Turner   Sam
   Jack Will
   Cockraus Tom
   Nottoway Indians to Sharp
   Nov 12 1747 }Deed

At a Court held for Isle of Wight County November 12th 1747. The within Indenture of Feofment with the above Livery and Seisin and Receipt, from the

Chief Men of the Nottoway Indians to Timothy Sharp; was Proved by the Oath of James Ridley, Jordan Thomas and Thomas Jarrell Gent[leman] the Witnesses thereto, and Ordered to be Recorded

Test Ja[mes] Baker & CCler[k]

/

to The Begining as by the survey and Plat of James Baker Gent[leman] surveyor of the said County of Isle of Wight Doth and may Appear and All the Estate Right Title and Entrust of the said Nottoway Indians in and to the same To HAVE AND TO HOLD the said Land with the Appurtenances unto the said Williams Sawrey J[unio]r his hiers and Assigns to the Only Use and Behoof of the said Willam Sawrey J[unio]r his heirs and Assigns for Ever Yealding and Paying to his to his Majesty his heirs and successors the Yearly Interests Due for the said Land IN WITNESS whereof the said Parties to These present have Unto at their hands and Afficted their seals the Day & Year Afore

Written J Simmons

~~In Presence of~~

Ja[mes] Baker	John Turner Frank
Tho[ma]s Cocks	Jo[h]n Robin Roger
B Edwards Skiper	Cockraus Tom
Watt Jack Will	

/

Nottoway Indians to Sawrey Jun[ior]

April 28 1746 }Deed

Mind that in the 28th Day of March In the year of our Lord in as Peaceable and Quiet Possession and Seisin of the Land within Mentioned was had and Taken by the Chief men of the Nottoway Nation Within Mentioned and by them Delivered to the Within Named William Sawry J[unio]r to hold to him his heirs and Assigns for Ever According <to> the form and Effect of the Within

Written Indenture

In Presence of Franks

Ja[mes] Baker	Roger
J Gray	Cockraure Tom
Benj[amin] Clements	Jack Wit
Jo[h]n Turner	
Jo[h]n Robin	
Skiper	
Watt	

Rec[iev]ed of the within Named William Sawrey the Just Sum of Twenty five Shill[ings] Current Money the Purchase Money within Mentioned

Ja[mes] Baker	J Simmons
E[d]m[un]d Tayler	Tho[ma]s Cocke

J Gray   B Edwards
Benj[ami]n Clements
/

This Indenture Tripartite made the 28th Day of March in the Year of our Lord one Thousand seven hundr[e]d and forty six Between Waynoak Robin, Frank Roger, Sam Cherins, Tom Doct[o]r <Tom Watt, Cockrous Tom, Skiper, Jack, Will, John Turner> Chief men of the Nottoway Indians of the first Part John Simmons of the County of Isle Wight Tho[ma]s Cocke and Ben. Edwards of the County of Surry Gent[leman] of the Second Part & William Sawrey Jun[io]r of the County of Isle Wright of the Third Part, Whereas by one Act of a Gen[tlemen] Assembly made at a Session lately held at W[illia]msburgh in the Eighth Year of the Reign of Our Lord George the second King of Great Brittain Intituted an Act to Enable the Nottoway Indians to Sell Certain lands Therein Mentioned and ford is charging the Indians Interpretor it is among Other things Enacted that the Chief men of the Nottoway Indians are Impowered to make Sale of all or any Part of a certain Circular Tract of land of Six Miles Diameter lying and being on the North Side of Nottoway River in the County of Isle Wight by and with Consent of the said John Simmons Tho[ma]s Cocke & Benja[min] Edwards Who are by the Said Act Appointed Trustees to see the Said Act duly Executed and after any Agreement made for the Sale of any Part of the the Said Land So as such part do not Exceed four Hundred Acres to any One Person it shall and May be Lawfull for the said Chief men together With the said Trustees Aforesaid Or the survivors or survivors of them to seal and Deliver a ffeofment to the Purchaser Who Immediately after the Execution Thereof shall Pay Down to the Chief in the Purchase Money for Which a Receipt shall be Likewise Endorsed on the Deed and any Feeofment so Executed and Perfected and afterwards Acknowledged or Prov'd by the Oaths of three Witnesses and Recorded in the Court of the said County of Isle Wight Where the Lands lye shall be sufficient in Law to pass the fee simple Estate of such Land and the Purchasers or Purchasers thereof his Or their Heirs or Assigns shall for Ever hold and Enjoy the same free and Discharged all Claims of the Nottoway Nation and Their posterity and things in an Act of the Gen[era]l Assembly made in the fourth Year of the Reign of the Late Queen Ann Intituated an Act for Preventing of Misunderstanding between the Tributary Indians and Other his Majesties Subjects of this Colony and Dominion and for a free Open Trade With all Indians Whatsoever or in any Other Act of the Gen[era]l Assembly Contain'd to the Contrary hereof in any Wise Notwithstanding as in the s[ai]d Act among Other things more fully Contain'd Now This Indenture Witnesseth that the s[ai]d Waycoak, Robin Frank, Roger Sam, Cherens, Tom, Doct[o]r Tom <Watt, Cockraus Tom, Skipper Jack Will, Jo[h]n Turner> the Chief men of the Nottoway Indians by and with the consent of the S[ai]d John Simmons Tho[ma]s

Cocks & Ben Edward Testified by there being Made Parties to these presents for and in Consideration of the sum of Twenty five Shillings Curr[en]t Money to the Chief men in hand paid the Receipt Whereof is hereby Acknowledged have Granted bargined sold Enfeoffed and Confirmed & by These presents do Grant Bargin sell Enfeoff and Confirm Unto the said William Sawrey J[uni]or his heirs and Assignes Two hundred and fifteen Acres of L. Parcell of the s[ai]d Circular Tract of Land Bounded as followeth Beginning at Thre trees Chopt Inwards by the side of the flat Meadow branch a Corner of William Sawrey John Simmons J[unio]r and Rich[ar]d Parker the Younger thence Down the Corses of the said Branch to a Pine a Corner of the said Parkers thence by his lines North Twenty Degrees West sixty four pole to a gum then Nort<h>west One hundred fifty four pole to a small Red Oack A corner of Rich[ar]d Parker J[unio]r Thence by his line West One hundred & Twenty Eight pole to thre Trees Chopt Inwards in the Nottoway Indians Outside line Thence by the said Indians line North and be East One hundred & forty Eight pole to a Pine a Corner of Rich[ar]d Hines Thence by the said Hines line south sixty One Degrees East Three hundred & forty six pole to a Lightwood post a Corner of the aforesaid William Sawreys Thence by the said Sawreys lines south forty Degrees West One hundred & forty Two pole to a pine and south Twenty Degrees East One hundred & Twenty Pole
/

At a Court held for Isle of Wight County April 28 1740

The Indenture of Feofment hereunto annexed with Livery and Seizin and Receipt thereon Indorsed from the the Chief Men of the Nottoway Indians of the ones Part to William Sawrey Jun[io]r of the other Part was Proved by the Oaths of Joseph Gray, Etheldred Taylor and James Baker Gent[leman], and the same is Ordered to be Recorded.

Test Ja[mes] Baker CCler[k]
/

Deed from Moses Newsum to Tho[mas] Barkam for 150 Acres land bear[in]g date 22 July 1745 on the south side of Notoway River

Deed from Tho[mas] Barkam to Solomon Newsum for 190 land bearing date 27 May 1745. on the south side of a Nottoway River

Deed from Thomas Barkam to Benja[min] Barkam for 50 Acres land bearing date 4th day of May 1748 on the South side of Nottoway River

Deed from Charles Barkam to John Fort for 100 Acres land bearing date 7th Sept 1747. part of a patent[13] granted to Charles Barkam bearing date 25th July 1746 (divided from a larger tract)

Deed from Charles Barkam to Christoper Foster for 120 Acres land bearing date 2 Oct 1747 Part of Patent granted to Ch[a]r[les] Barkam dated 25th July 1748.

I can find no conveyance from Tho[mas] Barkam to Jo[h]n Watkins, nor from the s[ai]d Watkins to Holladay Fort, as is mentioned in the Memo[randum] sent by W Urquhart

Deed from Benj[ami]n Barkam to Tho[mas] Barkam for 190 Acres land dates 4 Sept 1748

J Young

R[ecorde]d the Clerk 3/ for this W Urquhart

/

Sir,

Be kind enough enough to send me a Patent granted to Charles Barkam dated 25th July 1746. If there is a Patent in your office from Benjamin Barkam to the s[aid] Barkam for 190 Acres send it.

I am &c.

Windsor

[sideways]

Certificate from the Cl[er]k IWight County For Mr Newsum

/

Ralph Vickers's Patent for 85 Acres Isle of Wight

Exam[ine]d

Rec[eive]d

Executed

George the Second by the Grace of God of Great Britain France and Ireland King Defender of the Faith &c To ALL TO WHOM these Presents shall come Greeting KNOW YE that for divers good Causes and Considerations but more especially for and in Consideration of the Sum of TEN SHILLINGS of good and lawful Money for our use paid to our Receiver General of our Revenues in this our Colony and Dominion of Virginia WE HAVE given granted and confirmed and by these Presents for us our Heirs and Successors Do give grant and confirm unto Ralph Vickers one certain Tract or Parcel of Land containing eighty five Acres lying and being in the County of Isle of Wight on the South side of Black Water Swamp and bounded as follo[wet]h, to wit. BEGINNING at a Maple by the side of the said Swamp Then North sixty Degrees West twenty Poles to a Maple [th]ence South eighty Degrees West forty two Poles to a Gum by the edge of the Low Grounds of the said Swamp Then by the various Courses of the edge of the said Low Grounds to a black Walnut Then North eighty Degrees East seventy six Poles to a Gum then South fifty five Degrees East twenty four Poles to a Gum Then South thirty Degrees East forty Poles to an Ash Then South by Poles to a Gum by the side of black Water Swamp aforesaid Then down the various Courses of the Run of the said Swamp to the beginning With all Woods Underwoods Swamps Marshes Low Grounds Meadows Feedings and his due share of all Veins Mines and Quarries as well discovered as not discovered within the bounds aforesaid and being Part of the said Quantity of eighty five Acres of Land and the Rivers Waters and Water Courses therein contained together with the Privileges of Hunting Hawking Fishing Fowling and all other Profits Commodities and Hereditaments whatsoever to the same or any Part thereof belonging or in any wise appertaining To HAVE HOLD Possess and Enjoy the said Tract or Parcel of Land and all other the before granted Premises and every Part thereof with their and every of their Appurtenances unto the said Ralph Vickers and to his Heirs and Assigns forever to the only use and behoof of him the said Ralph Vickers his Heirs and Assigns forever {tear}ld of us our Heirs [and su]ccessors as of our Mannor of East Greenwich in the County of Kent in free and common Soccage[14] and not in Cupite[15] or by Knights Service[16] YIELDING AND PAYING unto us our Heirs and Successors for every fifty Acres of Land and so proportionately for a lesser or greater Quantity than fifty Acres the Fee Rent of one Shilling Yearly to be paid upon the Feast of Saint Michael the Arch Angel and also Cultivating and Improving three Acres Part of every fifty of the Tract above mentioned within three Years after the Date of these Presents Provided always that if three years of the said Fee Rent shall at any Time be in Arrear and Unpaid or if the said Ralph Vickers his Heirs or Assigns do not within the Space of three Years next coming after the Date of these Presents Cultivate and Improve three Acres Part of every fifty of the Tract above mentioned Then the Estate hereby granted shall Cease and be Utterly determined and hereafter it shall and may be lawful to and for us our Heirs and Successors to grant the same Lands and Premises with the Appurtenances unto such other Person or Persons as we our Heirs and Successors shall think fit IN WITNESS whereof we have caused these our Letters Patent to be made WITNESS our Trusty and Welbeloved Thomas Lee Esq[uire] President of our Council and Commander in Chief of our said Colony and Dominion at Williamsburgh Under the Seal of our said Colony the fifteenth Day of December one thousand seven hundred and forty nine In the twenty third year of our Reign.

Thomas Lee P

JAMES DOLBEARE, BILLS OF SALE (1732 AND 1743)

James Dolbeare, bills of sale of slaves, Dolbeare Family Papers 1685–1745, MassHS, Box 1 of 7, Folders 1655–1725, 1726–32, 1733–34, 1742–4.

In the seventeenth century, Massachusetts became the first New England colony to allow slavery and by the eighteenth century, Boston had the greatest concentration of slaves in the colony.[1] When the Northern slave trade was at its peak in the 1720s and 1730s, the private sale of slaves was solicited via newspaper advertisements, and listed among the sale of household furniture or books.[2] In early eighteenth-century Boston, there was no legislation to protect enslaved black families, so children could be sold away from their parents, and parents separated from their spouse and offspring. With tragic irony, James Dolbeare (see Volume 4) purchased a slave on 9 March 1732, and most likely took Loran away from his consanguineal kinship family, just three months before he created an affinal kinship marriage to Mary Valentine.[3] Likewise, little Rose was also separated from her family when Dolbeare purchased her on 3 June 1743.

The bills of sale reproduced here, then, are the sad documentation of the dissolution of household families for enslaved black Americans, as well as troubling testaments to the treatment of people as property. As property, twenty-one-year-old Loran, in comparison to five-year-old Rose, must have been rather valuable because £90 was among the highest prices quoted at a time when slaves typically cost £40.[4]

Notes
1. I. Berlin, *Many Thousands Gone: The First Two Centuries of Slavery in North America* (Boston, MA: Harvard University Press, 1998), p. 58.
2. Berlin, *Many Thousands Gone*, p. 58.
3. James Dolbeare and Mary Valentine Marriage, 16 June 1732, Boston, Massachusetts, 'Massachusetts, Town and Vital Records, 1620–1988,' www.ancestry.org [accessed 9 October 2014].
4. L. J. Greene, *Negro in Colonial New England, 1620–1776* (New York: Columbia University Press, 1942), p. 318.

James Dolbeare, Bills of Sale (1732 and 1743)

Bill of Sale for Negro Loran 1732 March 9th From William Richardson to James Dolbeare for £90

To ALL PEOPLE unto whom this Present Bill of Sale shall come. William Richardson[1] of Lancaster within the County Of Worcester and Province of the Massachusetts Bay in New England Yeoman Sendeth Greeting KNOW YE That I the Said William Richardson for and in Consideration of the Sum of Nintey Pounds[2] In good Publick bills of Credit of the Province aforesaid to me in hand at and before the Ensealing and Delivery of these Presents well and truly Paid by James Dolbear of Boston within the County of Suffolk and Province aforesaid Brazier[3] the Receipt whereof I Do hereby Acknowledge HAVE Granted Bargained and Sold And by these Presents Do Grant Bargain Sell and Confirm unto the Said James Dolbear My Negro man Named or Called Loran aged Twenty one years or thereabouts TO HAVE AND TO HOLD the Said negro man Loran unto the Said James Dolbear his Executors Admin[istrat]ors And Assignes to his and their only Proper Use benefit and behoof for ever. And I the Said William Richardson for my Self my /
    Executors & Administrators Do hereby Covenant and agree to and with the Said James Dolbear his Executors Administrators and Assignes to WARRANT AND DEFEND[4] The Said negro man Loran unto the Said James Dolbear his Executors Administrators And Assignes for Ever against the Lawful Claims and Demands of all and Every Person and Persons whatsoever IN WITNESS whereof I have herunto Sett my hand and Seal the Ninth Day of March Anno Dom[in]i 1732 And in the Fifth year of His Majesty's Reign
    Signed Sealed & Deliv[ere]dWilliam Richardson
    In presence of}
    Ezek[ia]l Goldthwait
    Antho[ny] Woulf

Received on the Day of the Date hereof of [*sic*] the aforenamed James Dolbear's the sum of Ninety pounds Being the Consideration money before Expressed William Richardson

£90
/

Know all Men by these presents That I Nathaniel Brown of Boston in the County of Suffolk Tayler in Consideration of the sum of Fifty Nine pounds of Ten[de]r to Me paid by James Dolbeare of said Boston Braisier thereat whereof I do hereby Acknowledge

Have and by These presents Do Sell assigne and make Over unto the said James Dolbeare his heires Ex[ecutor]s Adm[inistrator]s & Ass[igne]s forever a Certain Negro girl called Rose aged about five Years and Slave for her life To hold Said Negro to the Said James Dolbeare his heires Exe[cutor]s Adm[inistrator]s & Assigne[s] to his and their proper Use and behoofe forever and I do avouch myself at the Time of the Ensealing and Untill the delivery of these presents to be the lawfull owner of s[ai]d Negro and that I have good right to sell her as afores[ai]d and that free of all demands whatso[eve]r And I further Covenant And Agree to and with the said James Dolbeare his heires Exe[cutor]s Administrators & Ass that if Said Negro shall happen to dye in his or their Custody In Six months from the date hereof that then I myself Ex[ecutor]s or Adm[inistrator]s shall and Will pay to the s[aid] James Dolbeare his Ex[ecutor]s Adm[inistrator]s or Ass[igne]s the Sum of Fifty Nine Pounds Inevitable Accidents Excepted In Wittness Whereof I have hereunto Set my hand and Seale the 3d of June 1743
Present

Nathaniel Brown
W Mistry
Jo H Lawrence

BIRTH OF NEGROES, GALBREATH MOORE FAMILY BIBLE (1819–56)

Birth of Negroes, Galbreath Moore Family Bible (1770–1856), Moore Family Notes (1770–1950), HBLL, Brigham Young University, Provo, UT. MSS 1306.[1]

Colonial Americans who could afford or had inherited family Bibles inscribed their family history within the pages of this religious book. The material practice of recording genealogical information during this time varied from writing the family record on the inside cover or on a specific page of the Bible, or inserted on a separate leaf.[2] Later, in the post-revolutionary war decades, American ownership of family Bibles increased dramatically along with American publications of the religious text:[3] in 1781 Robert Aitken published the first complete English-language Bible in Philadelphia; in 1790 the first Catholic Bible was printed by Carey, Steward & Co, also in Philadelphia; and in 1791 Isaac Collins printed in New Jersey one of the most typographically correct Bibles.[4] Collins acknowledged that the Bible editing was a family endeavour, since he paid his children £1 if they found typographical mistakes; a daughter purportedly read the proofs eleven times.[5] Also during the 1790s, printers of family Bibles in the United States began to include preprinted blank family records in order to accommodate American genealogical practices.[6] François Weil has observed that American records of ascendants and descendants in their family Bibles 'reveal how Americans relied on genealogy to define and reinforce their individual and collective identities, as well as to situate themselves and their families in time by inclusion and by exclusion of others'.[7]

The genealogies listed below demonstrate how information in family Bibles simultaneously included and excluded family members. The Galbreath family record was written on a blank leaf of paper, as was the list of slave births; the latter had ledger-like hand-drawn lines between each name. The Galbreath record of births included the date, year and the infant's full name, while the list of slaves only preserved the birthdate, year and forename. The unknown genealogists' listing of the names of both white and slave births demonstrated his or her interest in each individual's place in the household family; both sheets would have been inserted into the family Bible – the Galbreath list to record the white progeny, and the slave list to record black births as genealogy but also as an accounts record in the household or plantation family.[8]

Notes
1. The Galbreath family genealogy was inherited by Elizabeth Augusta Galbreath (8 October 1830–1914), who was born in Christian, Kentucky, and married John William 'Buck' Moore (Oct 1830–1900). http://trees.ancestry.com/tree/47072485/person/7008617952/citation/24269924127?pg=32772&pgpl=pid [accessed 4 December 2014].
2. F. Weil, *Family Trees: A History of Genealogy in America* (Cambridge, MA: Harvard University Press, 2013), p. 33.
3. Weil, *Family Trees*, p. 41.
4. 'Chronological History of the Bible – 18th Century', at http://clausenbooks.com/bible1800.htm [accessed 15 December 2014].
5. J. Tebbel, *A History of Book Publishing in the United States* (New York, NY: R. R. Bowker Company, 1972), vol. 1, p. 183.
6. Weil, *Family Trees*, p. 48.
7. Weil, *Family Trees*, p. 3.
8. Weil recorded two examples of families recording their genealogy in an account book: Abigail Langley recorded her marriage to Robert Hargroves, their children, her parents' deaths and the births of her slaves; Philip Turpin recorded his family's marriages and births (p. 32).

Birth of Negroes, Galbreath Moore Family Bible (1819–56)

1770
March 2d} Margarat Galbreath[1] Born
1771
July 4th} John Galbreath Born
1773
June 30th} Malcolm Galbreath Born
1780
[F]eb[ruar]y 2d} Elizabeth Galbreath Born
1782
Nov[em]b[e]r 1st} Dan[ie]l Galbreath Born[2]
1785
Jan[uar]y 6th} James Galbreath Born
1787
Nov[em]b[e]r 30th} Duncan Galbreath Born
{tear}
July 7th} Peter Galbreath Born
1792
{illeg}ry 25th} Barbra Galbreath Born
1795
March 11th} Marron Galbreath Born[3]
1798
May 5th} Mary Galbreath Born
1805
March 5th} Duncan Blue Born March 5th 1805
Marron Blue Sunday 24th of August 1806
March 9th 1808 Effie Ann Blue Born
/
Birth of Negroes
Benjamin	June	1819
Charlotte	May	1823

Margarett	June	1828	
Joseph	June	1835	
Henry		1831	
Jake	July	1839	
John	April	1841	
Lucy	May	1845	
George		1840	
Edmond	Dec	1846	
Hannah	May	1848	
Thomas	Mar	1852	
Daniel	Sept	1855	
Silvy	Octo	1856	
Owen	Aug	1857	
Mary Ann	May	1859	Died 1860
Allice	Jany 16th	1860	

LANCASTER, PENNSYLVANIA CLERK OF COURTS, RETURNS OF NEGRO AND MULATTO CHILDREN (1788-93)

Lancaster, Pennsylvania Clerk of Courts, Returns of Negro and Mulatto Children and Index of Slaves, 1788-1793, FHL 1433968.

Antislavery in America began in Pennsylvania as early as 1688 when German Quakers drafted the Germantown Quaker Petition Against Slavery.[1] In 1744 Philadelphian Quakers initiated a ban of slavery among their members and formed the earliest American abolitionist society, called 'the Society for the Relief of Free Negroes unlawfully Held in Bondage'.[2] This Society expanded its membership beyond Quakers and transformed into the 'Pennsylvania Society for Promoting the Abolition of Slavery, and the Relief of Free Negroes, Unlawfully Held in Bondage' (PAS) in 1784. The goals of the PAS were twofold: to end the importation of slaves into Pennsylvania and improve the conditions of blacks through education and employment in order to prepare them for freedom.[3]

On Wednesday, 1 March 1780, the Pennsylvania legislature passed 'An Act for the Gradual Abolition of Slavery'. Section 1 of the Act stated: 'It is not for us to enquire why, in the creation of mankind, the inhabitants of the several parts of the earth were distinguished by a difference in feature or complexion. It is sufficient to know that all are the work of an Almighty Hand.' Acknowledging the humanity of slaves and desiring to promote 'universal civilization,' the framers of the Act declared that 'all persons, as well Negroes and Mulattoes as others, who shall be born within this state from and after the passing of this act, shall not be deemed and considered as servants for life, or slaves.'[4] These children would become indentured servants instead of slaves, and would be bound in service until their twenty-eighth birthday. Any slaveholder of slaves born before the Act was to submit to the clerk of the peace of the county, or to the clerk of the court of record of the city of Philadelphia, their full name, occupation, where they currently resided and the following information about their slave's child(ren): name, age and sex. The slaveholder also paid the clerk a two-dollar fee per slave. If a slaveholder neglected to file this information by 1 November 1780, he forfeited the ownership of his slaves.

Because slaveholders found loopholes to circumvent certain articles of the Act (e.g. taking a pregnant slave to give birth across state lines, selling slaves to out-of-state slaveholders or profiting by building slave ships), on 29 March 1788 'An ACT to explain and amend an act, entitled "An Act for the Gradual Abolition of Slavery"' was passed. In the amendment fines were assigned to various violations and the requirement that any child born to a slave or 'servant for term of years' mother after 1 March 1780 must be registered by the slaveholder with the appropriate Clerk of Peace or Clerk of the Court where they reside. These records had to be submitted by 1 April 1789 and thereafter within six months of the birth of each subsequent child; the penalty for negligence in filing was the immediate emancipation of the unregistered child(ren).[5]

The two Acts made reference to the deleterious impact of slavery upon black families. In the 1780 Act, the second section acknowledged that slavery 'has cast them into the deepest afflictions, by an unnatural separation and sale of husband and wife from each other and from their children.' A resident of Lancaster, County, Colonel Alexander Lowry was a member of the 1780 legislature and a slaveholder; nevertheless, he 'took strong ground against the separation of slave families, and made most urgent appeals to the Legislature to insert a clause in the law, then under discussion, to prevent families from being divided and sold to different masters.'[6] More than just lamenting the denied rights of slaves to maintain kinship-based households, these legislators limited the slaveholder's power over slave families, since the master or mistress could not separate spouses, or children from parents at a distance greater than ten miles without the testified consent of the slave.

These 'Returns of Negros' were filed with the Clerk of the Peace for Lancaster County from 1788 to 1793. The gradual abolition of slavery appeared to be slowly reducing the number of enslaved children in Lancaster: out of the fifty-nine extant returns between 1788 and 1793, twenty-eight were filed during the month of March in 1789, but only nineteen were filed between 1 April 1789 and 7 October 1793.

Notes
1. Quaker Protest Against Slavery in the New World, Germantown (PA) 1688, Haverford College Special Collections, at: http://tripod.brynmawr.edu/record=b3309321~S12 [accessed 23 December 2014].
2. B. C. Tomek, *Colonization And its Discontents: Emancipation, Emigration, And Antislavery In Antebellum Pennsylvania* (New York, NY: New York University Press, 2010), p. 19, eBook Collection (EBSCOhost) [accessed 17 December 2014].
3. Tomek, *Colonization And Its Discontents*, p. 7.
4. An Act for the Gradual Abolition of Slavery (1780), section 3, at http://www.ushistory.org/presidentshouse/history/gradual.htm [accessed 17 December 2014].
5. Available at http://www.ushistory.org/presidentshouse/history/amendment1788.htm [accessed 17 December 2014].
6. F. Ellis and S. Evans, *History of Lancaster County, Pennsylvania, with Biographical Sketches of Many of its Pioneers and Prominent Men* (Philadelphia, PA: Everts & Peck, 1883), p. 71.

Lancaster, Pennsylvania County Clerk, Returns of Negro and Mulatto Children (1788–93)

A return of Negro's belonging to James McColly of Salisbury Township Lancaster County farmer for the purpose of being registered agreeably to the Directions of an Act of Assembly of this commonwealth made for the Gradual Abolition of Slavery[1]

My Boy Samuel was Seven years old the twenty forth of February in the year of our Lord one thousand seven hundred and eighty Eight

My Girl Truth was five years old the fifteenth Day of December Seventeen hundred and eighty seven

June 7th 1788

James McCally being duly sworn

To the truth of the above Entry

June 7th 1788

James McCally

For me
John Hubly Cl[er]k[2]

/

James Clemson's Entry of Negroe Children

August 9th 1788

Julia Negro girl Born ye 7 day of May 1780 Pompy Negro boy Born ye 17 of June 1785 Both the property of James Clemson of Salisbury Township Lancaster County

James Clemson

Agust ye 9 1788

James Clemson was duly sworn to the truth of The above Entry the {tear} Aug[us]t 1788 for me John Shelby Cl[er]k

/

Thomas Edwards's Entry of a Mulattoe & a Negroe Child.

August 16th 1788

I Thomas Edwards of the Borough of Lancaster and Countey of Lancaster inkeeper do Certify that I am owner of a molatta female Child named Dina one year old born of anegro Slave Named Jude and also of <negro> a meal Child named Jere one year old Born of anegr[o] Slave Named Reach who both ther mothers was Regalerly entred by Christafel Reiglert in the offece of this Countey the mothers and Children now in my possesion Both mothers Slaves for life the Children to Serve until the age of twenty Eight years of age[3] Eage agreable to the act of General assembley made in such Casses for the Gradual abolition of Slavery and I now Return the aforsaid molatto and Negro Child as my Servents aged as above to <be> Registered according to Law witness my hand and Sell

Thomas Edwards [Seal]

Lancaster August the 16th 1788
 To John Hubley Esq[ui]r[e] Clark
 of the Court for the Countey
 of Lancaster
 Thomas Edwards was duly sworn to the Truth of the above Entery – Lan[caste]r August 16th
 [be]for[e] Me
 John Hubley Clk
 /
 William Smith's Entry of a Mulattoe Child

August 30th 1788
 I William Smith of Earl Township County of Lancaster Farmer, do Enter one Mallatto Boy Named Benn – which was Born the Nineteenth day of December 1787 and belongs to my Daughter Margaret Smith which is under Age and Lives with me as Witness my hand this Thirteenth day of August Anno. Dom[ini] 1788
 W[illia]m Smith
 William Smith was duly sworn to the Truth of the above Entery

August 30th 1788
 [be]for[e me] John Hubley
 /
 Robert Wallace's
 Ent<r>y of Negroe Children
 November 5th 1788
 [written upside down:]
 1788
 Return of Negroes

Robert Wallace of Earl Township, Lancaster County Yeoman, agreeable to an Act of Assembly inacted the twenty ninth Day of March 1788, Begs leave to return to you one Negroe ~~Girl~~ Boy named Ned aged about four years & eight months, one other Negroe Boy named Peter aged about two years & eight months and likewise a Negroe Girl nd Abbe aged about four months,
Robert Wallace
To John Hubley Esq[uire]
November 5th 1788
Robert Wallace sworn (U[plifted] H[and]) to the truth of the above return Nov[embe]r 5th 1788
[be]for[e me] John Hubley
/
James [sic] McComant's Entry of a Mulattoe Child

November 13, 1788
Isaac McCormant of Salsburry Township Lancaster County yeoman agreeable to an act of Assembly enacted the twenty ninth of March 1788 Beggs Leave to Return one Malatto Boy named Mingo aged about ten months his mother Bet Being a slave Entred in the Clerks office for said County wit my hand this 13th of November 1788
Isaac McComant
Isaac McCamant was duly sworn to the truth of the above Return Nov[embe]r 13th 1788
[be]for[e] me
John Hubley
/
Robert Spears's Entry Of a Negroe & a Mulattoe Child

January 9th 1789
I Robert Spears of the Township of Hempfield in the County of Lancaster Yeoman Do hereby return That (to the best of my Knowledge), Prince a Negroe Male Child Son of <Negroe> Debe a Female Slave was born on the ninth Day of May in the Year of our Lord One thousand Seven hundred & Eighty three, and that David a Mulatoe Male Child another Son of the Said Negroe Debe was born on the third Day of May in the Year of our Lord One thousand Seven hundred and Eighty six. and also that their said Mother was duly registered by me at Lancaster on the ninth Day of October 1780. pursuant to the act "for the Gradual Abolition of Slavery" and that the aforesaid two Children are my Property and liable by the Act aforesaid to serve until they shall severally arrive to the age of twenty eight years. Witness my Hand the Ninth Day of January Anno Domini 1789

Robert Spear
To John Hubley Esquire Clerk of the Peace}
For the County of Lancaster}
Robert Spear affirmed to the Truth of this Return & Entry the 9th Day of January 1789
[be]for[e] Me.
John Hubley
/
In pursuance of an Act of Assembly of the State of Pennsylvania I John Hubley Clerk of the Peace for the County of Lancaster residing in the Borough of Lancaster do hereby enter and return that (to the best of
my knowledge) Hannah a Mulato female Child the Daughter of Negro Juddy a Female Slave, was born on or about the twelfth day of June on thousand seven hundred and eighty seven: And that her said Mother Juddy was duly entered and Registered by me at Lancaster on the 9th day of October 1780 as a Slave, persuant to the Act "for the gradual abolition of Slavery" and that the aforesaid Mulatoe Child Hannah is my property and liable to serve until She arrives to the age of twenty eight years.

– Witness my Hand this 26th day of February 1789
John Hubley
John Hubley Esq[ui]re was duly sworn to the truth of the above
Return or account, before us the Subscriber President of the Court of General Quarter Sessions of the Peace[4] for the County of Lancaster
This 26th day of February 1789
John Hubley
/
James Old Esq[ui]re Entry of Negroe Children
March 3d 1789
The following is a true list of the ages & sixes of young negro Children born since March 1780 and to be recorded according to a late Act Passed 29th March 1788 belonging to James Old Esq[ui]re Iron Master of Carnarvan Township Lancaster County Viz:

Philis	Female	Aged	5 years	10 mo[nths]
Frank	Male	aged	5 years	3 months
Pheoby	Female	Aged	4 years	3 mo[nths]
Fann	ditto	Aged	2 years	9 mo[nths]
Sall	ditto	Aged	2 years	6 mo[nths]
Mark	Male	Aged		10 mo[nths]
Hannah	Female	Aged		9 mo[nths]

Witness my Hand this 3d day of March 1789
James Old
James Old Esq[ui]re was duly sworn to the truth of the above return 3d March 1789 [be]for[e] me
John Hubley
Cl[er]k
/
Henry Skiles's Entry of a Molattoe Child
March 22d 1789
The Return of Henry Skiles of the Township of Salisbury in the County of Lancaster & Commonwealth of Pennsylvania of a Mullatto male Child <belonging to him> named Abel who was born the 2d day of April 1787 for the purpose of being registered agreeably to the laws of this Commonwealth made for the gradual Abolition of Slavery March 22d 1789
Henry Skiles
Sworn & Subscribed
before me Ead[em] Die[5] John Hubley
/
Margaret Patterson's Entry of Molattoe Children
March 24th 1789
I James Patterson of Raphoe Township, Lancaster County do hereby return to the Pruthonitors[6] [sic] office for said County, a Mullatto Wench named Dinah, born in the fourteenth Day of October in the year of our Lord, one thousand seven hundred and eighty one, being the Child of a Negroe Wench named Hannah, who was legally entered in said Office; Likewise A Mullato boy call'd Tom born the twenty second day of December, in the year of our Lord one thousand seven hundred and eighty three, being the Child of the aforesaid Negroe. Likewise a Mullatto Wench call'd Deb, born the third day of April, in the year of our Lord one thousand seven hundred and eighty seven, being a Child of the aforesaid Negroe
March 23d 1789Marget Patterson
Wife of James Patterson
Margaret ~~Mary~~ Patterson swor'n To the truth of the above Return March 24th 1789
John Hubley
/
Phoebe Frazer's Entry of Negroe Children
March 25th 1789
I Pheby Frazer of the Township of Little-Britain and County of Lancaster Farmer do hereby return That (to the Best of my Knowledge) George a Negro male Child son of Hannah a Female Negro Have for Life was Registered at Lan-

caster the 14th Day of October 1780 s[ai]d George was born on the forth Day of July in the year of our Lord one thousand seven hundred and Eighty five and that the afforesaid Negro Child is to be Required persuant to an Act of General Assembly of Pennsylvenia for the gradual Abolition of Slavery and which Child is my Property and liable by the Act afforesaid to serve untill he shall arive to the age of twenty Eight years

    Witness my hand this 25th day of March A[nno] Dom[ini] 1789
    The mark of
    Phobe P Frazer
    To John Hubly Esquire}
    Cleark of the peas for the}

County of Lancaster}
Pheby Frazer swor'n to the truth Of the above Return and Entry the 25th day Of March 1789
    [be]for[e] me
    John Hubley
    Cl[er]k
    ~~February 1789~~
    /
    Ann Middleton's Entry of a Negroe Child

March 27th 1789

In pursuance of an Act of Assembly of the State of Pennsylvania I Ann Midelton (Spinster) of Donegall Township and County of Lancaster do hereby enter and Return that (to the best of my knowledge) Barbara a female Child the Daughter of Negroe Jean a Slave was born about the 29th Day of January One Thousand Seven Hundred and Eighty Six and that her Said Mother Negroe Jean was duly Entered & Registered by John Midelton at Lancaster as a Slave pursuant to the Act for the Abolition of Slavery and that the Aforesaid Negroe Child Barabara is my property and liable to Serve untill She arives to the Age of twenty eight years – Witness my hand this 27th Day of march 1789

    Ann Middleton was dulyher
    swor'n to the truth of the aboveAnna + Midelton
    Return. March 27th 1789mark
    [be]for[e] me
    John Hubley
    Cl[er]k
    /
    William Steele's Entry of a Negroe Child

March 30th 1789

In Pursuance of an Act of Assembly of Pennsylvania I William Steel of the Townshiop of Drumore in the County of Lancaster Tanner Do hereby enter and return That (to the best of my Knowledge) Maria a Negroe Female Child the Daughter of Negroe a Female Slave was born on the Twenty fifth Day of December in the Year four Lord One thousand Seven hundred and Eighty one and that her said Mother was duly entered & registered by Patrick Ewing Esquire (whose Property she was) at Lancaster as a Slave, pursuant to the Act "For the Gradual Abolition of Slavery" And that the aforesaid Negroe Child

Maria is my Property and liable to serve until it shall arive to the Age of Twenty eight years – Witness my Hand the Thirtieth Day of March in the Year of our Lord One thousand Seven hundred and Eighty nine

To John Hubley Esquire Clerk of}
the Peace for the County of Lancaster}William Steele

William Steel was duly sworn by uplifted Hand to the truth of the above Return & Entry the 30th Day of March Anno Domini 1789

Before me
John Hubley
Cl[er]k of the Peace
/
Hugh Peden's Entry of a Molattoe Child

March 31st 1789

[sideways:]
Hugh Peden was duly swor'n to the writtin Return March 31
1789 [be]for[e] me
John Hubley
Cl[er]k of the P[eace]

I Hugh Peden of the township of Rapho and County of Lancaster and State of Pensylvania Farmer do say that my Mallata boy Bob was born of a mallata women on the Seventeenth Day of October one thousand Seven Hundred and Eighty three and I do Certify the Above to the Just and true to the best of knowledg

this 30th Day of March 1789
Hugh Peden
/
Joseph Work's Entry of a Negroe Child

May 1st 1790[7]

In Pursuance of an Act of Assembly of the State of Penn[sylvani]a I Joseph Work of Donegal Township Lancaster County Farmer, do hereby en[t]er &

return that Charity, a Negroe <or Mullato> Female Child was Born on or about the Second day of November Last. and that the said Negroe Childs Mothers name is Alice and is Registered as the Law directs and that the Afforesaid Negroe Child is my Property and Liable to serve Untill she arrives to the Age of Twenty Eight Years Witness my hand this 1st day of May A[nno] dom[ini] 1790

    Jos[eph] Work

To John Hubley Cl[er]k of the Peace for Lancaster County
Joseph Work was duly swor'n to the truth of the above return
May 1st 1790
[be]for[e] me
John Hubley
/
Elizabeth Ramey's Entry of a Negroe Child

Decem[be]r 14th 1791
    Lancaster

County of} Personally appear'd before me the Subscriber one of the Justices of the peace for s[ai]d County Elisabeth Ramsey of Bart Township in s[ai]d County and upon her affirmation saith that in the Night of the fourteenth Day of November Last there was born in her house by her Negro wench Hester which is a Slave by law and Duly Enter'd a Male Negro Child which she names Bristo and Desires he may be Recorded agreeable to Law Dec[embe]r 13th 1791 I allow it to my Daughter Isabella

    Done before me Witness my hand & seal} Elisabeth Ramsey
    Andew Work
/
William Conkle's Entry of a Molatoe Child

June 1st, 1792

In persuant of an act of General Assembly of the State of Pennsylvania I William Conkle of Bart Township in the County of Lancaster Blacksmith do hereby enter and Return Hannah (a Molatoe) Female Child daughter of Negro Sib a Female Slave was born on the third day of January in the year of our Lord One Thousand Seven hundred and Ninety two and that her said Mother Sib was duly Entered and Registered at Lancaster as a Slave persuant to the act "for the gradual abolition of Slavery["] and that the aforesaid Molatoe Child Hannah is my Property and Liable to Serve untill it Shall arrive to the age of Twenty Eight years. Witness my hand the first day of June in the year of our Lord One Thousand Seven hundred and Ninety two

    William Conckel
    To John Hubley Esq[uir]e }

Clerk of the peace for the}
County of Lancaster}
William Conkle was}
duly Sworn by the }
uplifted hand To the}
Truth of the above Entry}
[be]for[e] me
John Hubley
Cl[er]k of the Peace
/

October 7th 1793
 David Cook
 In Pursuance of an Act of Assembly of the State of Pennsylvania I David Cook of the Township of Donigal in the County of Lancaster Farmer, DO hereby enter and return that Juliet a Negroe female child the Daughter of Negroe Rose a Female Slave, was born on the Twelfth Day of April in the Year of our Lord one thousand seven hundred and ninety three, and that her said Mother Rose was duly entered & Registered in Lancaster County as a Slave pursuant to the Act for the gradual abolition of Slavery, and that the aforesaid Negroe Child Juliet is my Property and liable to serve untill she shall arive to the age of Twenty eight Years Witness my Hand the Seventh Day of October in the Year of Our Lord One thousand
 Seven hundred & Ninety three.
 David Cooke
 To John Hubley Esq[uir]e Cl[er]k of the Peace for Lancaster County
 David Cook was duly sworn upon the Evangelists of Almighty God to the Truth of the above Entery and Return the Seventh Day of October 1793
 John Hubley
 Cl[er]k of the Peace

VICK FAMILY DEED OF EMANCIPATION (1789)

Vick Family Letter of Emancipation, Southampton, Virginia (1789), Archival Manuscript, HBLL MSS SC474.

Virginia was the first colony to establish slave codes as early as the mid-seventeenth century. By abandoning English common law, which dictated that a father conferred his status upon his child, Virginian lawmakers determined that children received their status from their mother, in order to ensure that children of female slaves and free white fathers remained slaves.[1] In May 1782, however, the House of Delegates finally acknowledged the Baptist, Methodist and Quaker antislavery petitions when they passed 'An Act to Authorize the Manumission of Slaves', which, according to Andrew Levy, was 'the most liberal antislavery bill in its history'.[2] Before this act, it was illegal for slaveholders to emancipate their slaves without legislated approval; now the act allowed slaveholders to liberate their slaves if two witnesses certified the 'instrument of emancipation' in the county court: the fee was five shillings.[3]

The 'instrument of emancipation' in Virginia that freed the greatest number of slaves by an individual slaveholder in American History was filed by Robert Carter III.[4] As a slaveholder, Carter considered himself the 'father' of his nuclear, biological family, and of his household and plantation family of slaves; he wrote about 'the Whites & black[s] in our families here.'[5] But between May 1782 and September 1791, Carter faced a dilemma: he felt 'tolerating Slavery indicates great depravity'; however, his sons and sons-in-law did not share his antislavery opinions and as their lineage father, Carter would be expected to protect their inheritance, which was dependent upon slave labour.[6] On 5 September 1791, Carter filed what he called a 'Deed of Gift' at the Northumberland District Court, in which he outlined the emancipation of all his slaves, which numbered over four hundred and fifty.[7]

Another 'instrument of emancipation' was entered by Jesse Vick, who was born in Southampton County, Virginia around 1755 as the second son of Simon and Patience Vick. Vick's deed of emancipation was unusual in that no mention was made of Rose or Simon being too infirm, too old or too young to work for their owners, which was another prerequisite listed in the 1782 act.[8] Vick's deed of emancipation also redefined Rose and Simon's family relationship since they were now a free black family instead of heritable property.

Vick's next extant civil record was his will, which he wrote in 1827. The only mention of slaves was in his bequest to his wife: 'First. I lend to my Wife all my Lands and Negroes during her life or widowhood'.[9] Vick's attitude towards emancipation and slavery appeared to mirror the ambivalence of Virginians in general; Eva Sheppard Wolf noted that

> slaves were persons whom owners might wish to reward with freedom even if they did not view freedom as a natural right for blacks, and at the same time slaves were valuable property in a society that viewed protecting property rights as one of the highest functions of the law.[10]

This ambivalence hardened into a repudiation of the liberal 1782 emancipation law by the early nineteenth century; an 1806 law forced emancipated slaves to leave Virginia, which most likely separated the free from their enslaved family members and any community networks for subsistence.[11] Even if Vick had wanted to emancipate more slave families or individuals as the father of his plantation family, he would have had considerably diminished power to do so in 1827 than he did in 1789.

Notes

1. E. S. Wolf, *Race and Liberty in the New Nation: Emancipation in Virginia from the Revolution to Nat Turner's Rebellion* (Baton Rouge, LA: Louisiana State University Press, 2006), p. 2.
2. A. Levy, *The First Emancipator: The Forgotten Story of ROBERT CARTER the Founding Father Who Freed His Slaves* (New York, NY: Random House, 2005), pp. 101, 117.
3. Levy, *The First Emancipator*, pp. 101, 118.
4. Levy, *The First Emancipator*, p. xii.
5. Levy, *The First Emancipator*, pp. 125–6.
6. Levy, *The First Emancipator*, pp. 125–6.
7. Levy, *The First Emancipator*, p. xi.
8. Levy, *The First Emancipator*, p. 101.
9. Available at http://files.usgwarchives.net/va/southampton/wills/v200j8wl.txt [accessed 2 December 2014].
10. Wolf, *Race and Liberty in the New Nation*, p. 31.
11. Wolf, *Race and Liberty in the New Nation*, p. 35.

Vick Family Deed of Emancipation (1789)

A Court Continued and held for the County of Southampton the 11th day of Sept 1789 This Deed[1] for the affirmed to by Jesse Vick[2] & ordered to be recorded

L. Vick & al:
To }Emancipation
Rose &
September 11th 1789 –
Proved by the oath of J. W. Cathon & by the affirm[atio]n of Jesse Vick & or

Recorded

Copied
/

We the subscribers of the County of Southampton Virginia having under our care Two Negroes (Family) One woman named Rose aged about fifty years also Simon Aged about thirty years – whome we have heretofore held as Slaves but do hereby emancipate and set free, and we do for our selves our heirs – Executors and administrators relinquish all our rights titles Interests and claims and Pretinsions of Claims whatsoever either to their Persons or to any estate they may have after Acquire; the abovesaid Rose and Simon to enjoy their full freedom without any interruption from us or from any person claiming for by or under us,[3] In Witness whereof we have hereunto set our Hands and seals this 27th day of the first Month One Thousand seven Hundred and Eighty nine

Signed and Sealed in the presense of}
Jesse Vick affir[me]d Lenrie Vick {Seal[4]
William <his>X<mark> Newsom Pilgrim Vick {Seal
Josah W. Cathon Joshua Vick {Seal
Sarah <her>+<mark> Vick {Seal Giles <her>+<mark> Vick {Seal
Piety <her>+<mark> Vick {Seal

JOHN BEALL, WILL (1803)

John Beall, Will (6 October 1803), Wilkes County, Georgia, Georgia, Probate Records, 1742–1990, Wilkes County, 1790–1852. 1803 John Beall will.

Wills, like emancipation deeds, revealed to a lesser extent 'the tension between the view of slaves as persons and the view of slaves as property.'[1] This tension was articulated civically later in Georgia than in Virginia; slavery in Georgia was not legalized until 1752. The colony of Georgia had been previously established as a place for the British 'worthy poor' and European-persecuted Protestants to reinvent themselves as productive and/or non-discriminated members of society by producing luxury goods such as wine and silk for the British empire. Slave labour was perceived by the Trustees for Georgia as depriving their poor of the morally-salubrious effects of small farm labour.[2] Therefore, slavery had been legally banned in Georgia by the trustees of the colony in 1735, but pressure from neighbouring South Carolina plantation owners desiring to expand into Georgia contributed to its legalization less than twenty years later.[3] To accommodate plantation growth, Wilkes County was created in 1777 from former Cherokee and Creek Indian lands.[4]

John Beall was born in Montgomery, Maryland, in 1760 and sometime afterwards moved to Wilkes County, Georgia to start a plantation.[5] In his will, Beall, as was typical for eighteenth-century Georgia landowners, left his wife a maintenance instead of an estate in 'fee simple', which would have given her ownership and hence power to bequeath it according to her desires.[6] Charles Hooper Wilson noted that testators primarily bequeathed commodities to women, and land and the overseeing of young children's education to men.[7] Wilson also observed that 'some will authors referred to slaves by name, suggesting they regarded their slaves as more than mere possessions.'[8] Otherwise, slaves were listed like chattel – such as in Thomas Carter's will – who bequeathed his estate, 'consisting of Negroes, cattle, horses, hogs, sheep, etc.'[9] In these wills Wilson also pointed out the importance of differentiating between black names:

> It suggests that some slave owners thought of their slaves as simply being more human than did other slave owners. This is because they bestowed names on their slaves that

were essentially unremarkable by the standards of the day. However, slave owners that bestowed unusual names on their slaves (e.g., names of powerful Greek gods) often did so to lampoon them and to reiterate the irony of their bound condition.[10]

That Beall perhaps viewed himself as the patriarch of his white and black plantation family could be evident in the way he has bequeathed his wife and children the ordinarily-named slaves somewhat separately from the heritable land and commodities.

Notes

1. E. S. Wolf, *Race and Liberty in the New Nation: Emancipation in Virginia from the Revolution to Nat Turner's Rebellion* (Baton Rouge, LA: Louisiana State University Press, 2006), p. 31.
2. C. H. Wilson, 'Slave Ownership In Early Georgia: What Eighteenth-Century Wills Reveal', *Historical Methods*, 44:3 (2011), pp. 115–26, on p. 120. MasterFILE Complete [accessed 16 December 2014]. See also B. Wood, *Slavery in Colonial Georgia 1730–1775* (Athens, GA: University of Georgia Press, 1984), pp. 1–11.
3. Wilson, 'Slave Ownership In Early Georgia', p. 121.
4. *The Handybook for Genealogists: United States of America*, 10th edn (Draper, UT: Everton Publishers, 2002), at: https://familysearch.org/learn/wiki/en/Wilkes_County,_Georgia#cite_note-Handybook-1 [accessed 16 December 2014].
5. Available at http://trees.ancestry.com/tree/44909445/person/6276360439 [accessed 16 December 2014].
6. Wilson, 'Slave Ownership In Early Georgia', p. 118.
7. Wilson, 'Slave Ownership In Early Georgia', p. 119.
8. Wilson, 'Slave Ownership In Early Georgia', p. 122.
9. Quoted in Wilson, 'Slave Ownership In Early Georgia', p. 122.
10. Wilson, 'Slave Ownership In Early Georgia', p. 122.

John Beall, Will (1803)

In the name of God Amen, The sixth day of October in the Year of our Lord God Eighteen hundred and three I John Beall[1] of Wilkes County[2] in the State of Georgia Planter, being very sick and weak in ~~I~~ Body but of perfict Mind and memory, thanks be given unto god therefore Calling unto mind the Mortality of my Body. And knowing that it is appointed for all men once to die. Do make and or claim this my Last Will and testament, that is to Say Princepally, and first of all I give and recommend my Soul into the hands of God that gave it and for my body I recommend it to the earth, to be buried in a Christian like and Decent manner, at the ~~direction~~ discrition of my Executor nothing doubting but at the general Resurrection I Shall receive the Same again by the mighty Power of God, and as touching Such worldy Estate wherewith I have pleased God to bless me in this Life, I give devise,[3] and despose of the Same in the following manner and form – I give and bequeath to my <dearly> beloved Wife Mary ~~Bell~~ Beall[4] a Certain Negro Woman named Leannes During the life of my Wife and also to have her Maintainance out of the plantation and stock during her life and the Contents of the tract of land and plantation utinsels and House hold furniture[5] also that I do give to Joseph Beall and Nathan Beall what they Can make out of the Land and Stock over and above which he'll maintain the family and School[6] Polley and ~~Lloyd~~ Lloyd to two of ~~my~~ Sons Joseph and Nathan Beall I make and ordain my only and sole Executors and to make what they Can over and above the aforesaid maintenance untill my son ~~Lloy~~ Lloyd Beall Shall Come at age out of the aforesaid property – I give to my Daughter Betsey Beall[7] and to the Heirs of her Body a negro Girl / by the name of Mariah. I give to my Daughter Harriet ~~Bell~~ Beall and to the Heirs of her body to Negro Girl by the name of Charity. I give to my Daughter Rachel Beall and to the Heirs of her body a negroe Boy by the name of Samuel. I give to my Daughter Polley Beall and to Heirs of her body a Negroe Equal with the rest if the said Leannes have another Child it is to be for Polly Beall if not, there must be one bought with some of the stock I give ~~unto~~ to my Son Lloyd Beall A Negroe boy by the name of Reason also a Hone Saddle ~~and Bridle~~ and my Dwelling Plantation and Land that Pretains thereto unless the place should be Sickly and the Executor Should dee[m] Cause to Sell this and buy Lloyd another Habitation with the same money. I give my Son Joseph Beall at the Death of his mother a Negro Woman by the name of ~~Leannes~~ Leanne also I give to My Four Daughters A horse and Saddle, and feather beds and furniture each at the time of their marriage I give to my Son John ~~Bell~~ Beall one feather bed and furniture more than what he has had & no more I acknowledge this to be my last Will and Testament. Signed sealed and delivered in the presence of us

John Beall LS
Test
Richard Rivear[8]
Daniel Gafford

I do hereby Certify that the above and foregoing is a True Copy from the original June 19th 1807 –

John Hatieay fer
D Farrell C. C. Ordy

GEORGE WALKER, LEEWARD PLANTATION APPRAISAL (1781)

George Walker, Leeward Plantation Appraisal in Berney Family, Slave Lists (1784), London Metropolitan Archives (hereafter LMA), London, United Kingdom, 4301.A.001.

Slavery began in Barbados in 1627 and sugar was exported as early as 1646.[1] In 1689, the British agent for Barbados wrote, 'Of all the Things we have occasion for, *Negroes* are the most necessary, and the most valuable.'[2] The '*Negroes*' were the necessary implements in producing sugar for British profit in the triangle trade. The other necessary component for the production of sugar in Barbados was financial credit extended by commission agents in London until the first successful crop had been produced.[3] West Indian plantation owners increased their profits by expanding plantations and acquiring more male slaves; therefore the increased material goods enjoyed by the often-absentee planter's kinship family were purchased at the expense of the creation or perpetuation of black kinship families.[4]

Two writers, Richard Ligon and Hans Sloane, who recorded their observations of British West Indian slavery in the late seventeenth and early eighteenth centuries respectively, noted the existence of slaves living in family units, and strong, affectionate bonds between mothers and their infants in Barbados.[5] Later in the century, however, Michael Craton noted, 'planters became more callous and indifferent to slaves' social arrangements.'[6] Plantation owners viewed their slaves as ready-made or replaceable tools in the production of sugar.

In the deed below, slaves were recorded entirely as property in the slave society of Barbados. The inventory of slaves was catalogued between the lists of canes and cattle. As chattel, the slaves named in the deed were listed according to sex and not family units.[7] At the time of the deed, Craton explained, 'West Indian families were probably at a low point of integration' since 'conjugal unions were rare and impermanent, and the majority of infants lived with single mothers or grandmothers.'[8] Slave marriage in the British West Indies would not be legally encouraged until the 1820s.

Notes

1. P. Fryer, *Black People in the British Empire: An Introduction* (London: Pluto Press, 1988), p. 6.
2. Quoted in P. Fryer, *Staying Power: The History of Black People in Britain* (London: Pluto Press, 1984), p. 16.
3. Fryer, *Black People in the British Empire*, p. 6.
4. Fryer, *Black People in the British Empire*, p. 11.
5. M. Craton, 'Changing Patterns of Slave Families in the British West Indies', *Journal of Interdisciplinary History*, 10:1 (Summer, 1979), pp. 1–35, on p. 28, at http://www.jstor.org/stable/203299 [accessed 25 December 2014].
6. Craton, 'Changing Patterns of Slave Families in the British West Indies', p. 30.
7. Trinidad required slaves to be listed in families, but Michael Craton observed that many Bahamian plantation owners voluntarily listed their slaves according to families. Craton, 'Changing Patterns of Slave Families in the British West Indies', p. 5, at http://www.jstor.org/stable/203299 [accessed 25 December 2014].
8. Craton, 'Changing Patterns of Slave Families in the British West Indies', p. 30.

George Walker, Leeward Plantation Appraisal (1781)

First Schedule to which the annexed Deed[1] refers.

Barbadoes,

At the request of the Honourable Frenans Moe[2] Esquire Trustee to the Estates of George Walker[3] Esquire We have this day met upon and appraised the Leeward Plantation belonging to the said George Walker agreeable to the under mentioned

Two hundred and fifty seven Acres of Land with the Buildings in their present Condition and all Plantation Utensils together with Provisions of all kinds} 7710

Twenty nine Acres of young Canes growing thereon at £12 per acre 348

Negroes Viz.

Men 34 in Number

				£	s	d
Anthony	80		Brought up	895		
Great Willey	25		Bunty	35		
Prince	15		Marris	65		
-Larosoe	80		Ffanniah	80		
Dirk blind			Johnny	50		
Bowman	50		Quominah	60		
Harry	5		Samson	75		
Jupiter	60		Abel	80		
Addoe	20		Offah	60		
Quomin	75		Sammy	75		
Hector	75		Dego	60		
Odipus	80		Tim	65		
Robin	70		Marlbrough	70		
Quow	60		Tom Bowman	60		

			£	s	d
Jemsy	70	Jemmy	70		
Orrorrow	60	Quominah	55		
Little Willey	70	Tim Davis	15		
Carries up	895	Great Addoe at Guinea	1870		

Women 38 in Number

			Brought up	370	
Great Ubbah	45	Esther	55		
Mosom	35	Ubbah	70		
Great Dennis	40	Cumbah	70		
Bussey	30	Dinis	70		
Moll	30	Banbah	50		
Gracey	25	Phebah	60		
Sue	40	Mueco	70		
Hagar	35	Phillis	65		
Peggy	35	Rinah	70		
ffrances	35	Rose	65		
Carried up	370	Carried up	1015	9928	

Women continued	£	s	d	Brought up		9928
Brought up	1015			Brot up	1415	
Chinan	20			Nellys Ubbah	65	
Benah	25			Betty Phillis	65	
Hog Nanny	65			Pen Betty	70	
Little Marget	55			Sary	65	
Betty	60			Ms Nanny	70	

Women continued	£	s	d	Brought up		9928
Easter	25			Sally Harris	60	
Quashebah	30			Mumas Sally	60	
Penelope	50			Hannah	60	
Jenny	45			Great Marget	5	
Carried up	1415			Carried up	1935	1935

Boys forty one in Number

Harry	55
Tom Dich	60
Jupiter	50
Money	50
William	50
Jemmy	60
Asam	40
Frank	45
Joe	35
Cudjoe	35
Buckey Sambo	30
Tom Turkey	30
Neddy	35
George	45
Billy Marnis	5
Little Jemsey	15
Cumberland	5
Toney	25
Will Gibbes	25
John Morrison	20
Dickey	20
Ned Morrison	15
Carried up	930

Bro[ugh]t up	930	
Odipus	50	
Jack Crip	45	
Ben	40	
Mulatto Ned	45	
Richard	10	
Pearcy	25	
Fanuiah Sam	10	
Mo. Tim	30	
Billy Boroman	12	
William	15	
Cambridge	5	
Kitt	7	10
Mily Joe	10	
Harry	10	
Hector George	5	
James Henry	7	10
Ampouah	5	
Tom Moore	5	
Thomas	5	
	1092	1392
		12955

/
Girls forty in Number

Eley	65
Molly	65
Aubat	5
Easter	55
Violet	60
Banbat	30
Mimken	35
Betty Peter	65
Rosy	45
Betty Chinen	25
Katey	40

Charlotte	70	
Mary Will	50	
Mary Ann	60	
Amy	35	
Jenny	30	
Lucy	20	
Nanny Joan	30	
Saminat	25	
Katamat	30	
Pegg	25	
	865	
Brought up	865	
Pamelia	20	
Maria	20	
Nancy	20	
Nanny	10	
Lucy	15	
Coco	15	
Hagar	25	
Sabinat	10	
Emily	10	
Cumbat	10	
Nelly	7	10
Hannah Grace	12	
Dutches	5	
Franky	7	10
Elsy	7	10
Comelia	5	
Hagar	5	
Bussy Ubbat	10	
Nanny Grace	5	
	1084	10
Land and Negroes	14039	10

Twenty nine Head of Cattle at twelve pounds	348		
Thirteen Hogs Valued to	6	18	9
ffourteen Head of Sheep at ffifteen Shillings	10	10	
	365	8	9
	365	8	9
One hundred and ten Gallons of Rum at three Shillings	16	10	
Two hundred and Fifty Gallons of Melasses at two Shillings	25		
Two Potts of Sugar {illeg.} four hundred and twenty pounds Mel[a]ss[es] at fforty per cent and one hundred and twenty Pounds Clayed[4] at Seven pence half Penny Per	12	3	
	53	13	0
	53	13	
Amount	14458	11	9

Given under our hands the above sum of fourteen thousand and four hundred and Fifty eight pounds Eleven Shillings and nine pence this twenty ninth day of June one thousand seven hundred and Eighty One

    Signed
    Abraham Cumberbatch[5] – Samuel Hinds
    Cumberbatch Sober[6]
    Benjamin Seale[7]
    John Boyce

JOHN WILLIAMS AND ELIZABETH WILLIAMS, HIS WIFE, AND THEIR CHILDREN, REMOVAL ORDERS (1818)

John Williams and Elizabeth Williams, his Wife, and their Children, Removal Orders (1818), Middlesex Sessions of the Peace: Court in Session, LMA, London.

By the eighteenth century, the black inhabitants of London had formed what Gretchen Gerzina described as 'a thriving black community.'[1] While some black Londoners were able to enjoy prosperity or at least a comfortable income, many often impoverished black immigrants from the Revolutionary war, who had fought for Britain with the promise of emancipation, did not.[2] Unfortunately for the black poor who moved to the slums in the city of London, the 1731 Lord Mayor's proclamation had barred them from learning a trade, lest they deprive the white poor from employment.[3]

In 1786 some philanthropists organized the Committee for the Relief of the Black Poor, and with their collected funds created a hospital and distributed food.[4] When the Committee ran out of funds, they turned to another proposed solution: the emigration of the black poor to Sierra Leone.[5] The idea was to treat the black poor similarly to white criminals and paupers, who, since the passing of the 1718 Transportation Act, had been sent to America (see also 'John Beall, Will').[6] A year later, the ships sailed for Sierra Leone where the colony foundered (see also 'Olaudah Equiano, or Gustavus Vassa'). With colonization no longer a viable option, the black poor had to petition for parochial relief along with their fellow white paupers. Peter Fryer noted that by the mid-nineteenth century, black Britons 'no longer thought of themselves as constituting a distinct black community. They were part of the British poor.'[7] Therefore the information about the Williams family on the preprinted certificate of removal indicated only their economic status and residency (see also 'Poor Families'). The Williams' ethnicity was only noted by a clerk in the manuscript notation on the back.[8]

Notes
1. G. Gerzina, *Black London: Life Before Emancipation* (New Brunswick, NJ: Rutgers Uni-

versity Press, 1995), p. 23.
2. Gerzina, *Black London*, pp. 18–19, 23–4.
3. Gerzina, *Black London*, p. 19.
4. Gerzina, *Black London*, p. 140.
5. Among the group leaders to establish this new community was a twenty-five-year-old seaman named John Williams, from Charlestown, Massachusetts (Gerzina, *Black London*, p. 145).
6. Available at: http://www.oldbaileyonline.org/static/Punishment.jsp [accessed 17 December 2014].
7. Quoted in Gerzina, *Black London*, p. 203.
8. For explanation of removal certificates and other poor law procedures, see 'Poor Families'.

John Williams and Elizabeth Williams, his Wife, and their Children, Removal Orders (1818)

MO/SP/1818/12/004
[in manuscript on the back]
44. John Williams & wife & child
Midd[lese]x General Session[1] Decr[ee] 1818
St. Marylebone Midd[lese]x agt.
St. Margaret Westm[inste]r
Brief for Appellants
Mr. Adolphus
{illeg.}
John Adolphus
Appeal allow was to the man – order confirmed as to the Woman & Child
Greenwell Lloyd
Appell[a]n[t] Jobs
Negro – slave
Wife & Child –
she settled by service in St. Mary-le-bone
/

To the Churchwardens and Overseers of the Poor of the Parish of SAINT MARGARET,[2] in the City and Liberty of Westminster,[3] and to the Churchwardens and Overseers of the Poor of the Parish of Saint Marylebone[4] in the County of Middlesex –

Middlesex, and the City and Liberty of *Westminster*} to Wit

WHEREAS Complaint hath been made unto Us, Two of His Majesty's Justices of the Peace acting in and for the County, City and Liberty aforesaid (One whereof being of the *Quorum*) by the Churchwardens and Overseers of the Poor of the said Parish of *Saint Margaret*, That John Williams & Elizabeth his wife & their Child Eliza aged four months – lately intruded and came into the said Parish of *Saint Margaret*, and become chargeable to the same; We the said Justices, upon Examination of the Premises upon Oath, and other Circumstances, do adjudge the same to be true, and do also adjudge the Place of the last legal

Settlement of the said John Williams & Elizabeth his Wife & their said Child Eliza to be in the said Parish of Saint Marylebone in the County of Middlesex –

THESE are therefore, in His Majesty's Name, to require You, the said Churchwardens, and Overseers of the Poor of the said Parish of *Saint Margaret*, on Sight hereof, to remove and convey the said John Williams & Elizabeth his Wife and their said Child Eliza from and out of your said Parish of *Saint Margaret*, to the said Parish of Saint Marylebone and their deliver unto the Churchwardens and Overseers of the Poor there, or to some or one of them, together with this our Order, or a true Copy hereof, who are hereby required to receive and provide for them according to Law. Given under our Hands and Seals this 26th Day of October One Thousand Eight Hundred and eighteen.

Sa. Marshland
[Seal]
M Prestney
[Seal]

DIDO ELIZABETH BELLE DAVINIER

Dido Elizabeth Belle, Baptism Record (20 November 1766), St George's Church, Bloomsbury, LMA P82/GEO1/001.[1]

'The Earl of Mansfield's Will', *Diary or Woodfall's Register*, Saturday, 20 April 1793, issue 1274, 17th–18th Century Burney Collection Newspapers, Gale Document Number: Z2000306912.

Dido and John Davinier Marriage Allegation and Bond (6 November 1793), St George, Hanover Square and St Martin's in the Fields, LMA DL/A/D/24/MS10091E/106.[2]

In her study of black Londoners, Gretchen Gerzina observed, 'A far smaller number than their male counterparts, black women's transference to Britain carried proportionately more weight', which could describe the possible influence of Dido Elizabeth Belle's indirect influence upon the British Abolition movement.[3] By sending his bastard biracial daughter to live with her paternal kinship family in Britain, instead of selling her as a slave in the Atlantic colonies, Sir John Lindsay, a naval officer, privileged lineage over law, convention over profit. Lindsay entrusted his daughter, Dido Elizabeth Belle to the care of his maternal grand-uncle, Lord Mansfield. Perhaps love for his great-niece, Dido, influenced Lord Mansfield in his 1772 Somerset decision, which was perceived by many as abolitionist (see also 'Phillis Wheatley'). Certainly Dido had gained his confidence and concern sufficiently to receive legal emancipation and also several financial bequests in his will. From her lineage and household family, Dido enjoyed a comfortable financial and domestic situation, which enabled her to avoid a life of dependent poverty and instead to create her own household family through marriage.

Not much is known of Dido's life before she came to Lord Mansfield except that her parents probably met when Lindsay was stationed in the West Indies and had taken Maria Belle from a Spanish ship; Dido would have been born either in 1760 or 1761.[4] The earliest record of Dido's residence in England was her baptism entry at the age of 5 on 20 November, 1766, which was also the last evidence of Maria's existence. Paula Byrne surmised that Dido was baptized at the behest of Lord and Lady Mansfield when she came to live with them in their home in Bloomsbury, which was in the same area of London where Dido was baptized. Byrne also suggested that the name Elizabeth might have been given to Dido at that time, which 'would have been a powerful sign of her adoption into the Mansfield family,'[5] but it would be equally likely that Lindsay may have already given her the name in the hope that Elizabeth Finch Murray, Lady Mansfield, would care for his illegitimate daughter.[6]

Elizabeth and William Murray, first earl of Mansfield, had been unable to have children; their heir was Murray's nephew, David Murray, the son of William's older brother.[7] When David, now Lord Stormont, was the ambassador to the Habsburg dynasty in Vienna, he married a young German widow, Henrietta Frederica de Berargaard.[8] Two daughters were born – the younger died in infancy and the mother soon afterwards. Little Elizabeth Murray was six when she was sent to the Murrays around 1766, which was also the time that Dido went to live with the Murray family.[9] The childless Murrays now had the care of two grand-nieces.

Dido's position in Lord Mansfield's household may have started out similarly to other illegitimate white relations: not completely family, and not quite a servant.[10] Dido cared for the dairy, which was a female servant's chore, and service of some sort was often expected of illegitimate family members;[11] but the dairy was also one of Lady Mansfield's favourite domestic employments.[12] The affection the Murrays displayed towards the illegitimate and mixed-race Dido was noted by the former governor of Massachusetts, Thomas Hutchinson (see also 'Phillis Wheatley'); when Hutchinson visited Lord Mansfield, he was horrified to see that Dido was included in the family.[13] In his will, Lord Mansfield ensured that Dido's future relationship with her kinship family was not as property by legally emancipating her (otherwise the heir could have treated her as a slave), but as a financially secure member. Perhaps Lord Mansfield knew that when Dido's father, Sir John Lindsay died in 1788, he only provided for his widow and his two other natural children: a son, John, and a daughter, Elizabeth.[14] To compensate, Lord Mansfield included codicils to his will with increasing financial bequests to Dido. Lord Mansfield's sister, Lady Margery Murray, who also lived at Kenwood, similarly remembered Dido with a financial bequest in her will.[15] Dido's comfortable financial situation enabled her to marry John Davinier in St George's, Hanover Square, London, which was 'one of the most fashionable churches in greater London.'[16] Marrying by an expensive license instead of by banns also revealed her well-connected status. Dido gave birth to twin sons, Charles and John in 1795, and Edward William in 1802.[17] Dido died in 1804.

Notes
1. London Metropolitan Archives, Saint George, Bloomsbury, Register of Baptisms, Jan 1730–Oct 1775, P82/GEO1/001. Ancestry.com. *London, England, Baptisms, Marriages and Burials, 1538–1812* [online database]. Provo, UT, USA: Ancestry.com Op-

erations, Inc., 2010. Original data: *Church of England Parish Registers, 1538–1812*. London, England: London Metropolitan Archives.
2. www.ancestry.com. *London and Surrey, England, Marriage Bonds and Allegations, 1597–1921* [online database]. Provo, UT, USA: Ancestry.com Operations, Inc., 2011. Original data: *Marriage Bonds and Allegations*. London, England: London Metropolitan Archives.
3. G. Gerzina, *Black London: Life Before Emancipation* (New Brunswick, NJ: Rutgers University Press, 1995), p. 76.
4. *ODNB*.
5. P. Byrne, *Belle: The Slave Daughter and the Lord Chief Justice* (New York, NY: Harper, 2014), pp. 94–5.
6. Lindsay apparently sired another illegitimate daughter, also named Elizabeth, in Scotland.
7. Byrne, *Belle*, p. 89. Elizabeth was also friends with Mary Delaney (see Volume 4) and Lady Mary Wortley Montagu (see Volume 2).
8. Byrne, *Belle*, p. 91.
9. Byrne, *Belle*, p. 92.
10. Gerzina, *Black London*, p. 88.
11. N. Tadmor, *Family and Friends in Eighteenth Century England: Household, Kinship and Patronage* (Cambridge: Cambridge University Press, 2001), p. 186.
12. Byrne, *Belle*, p. 169. See also 'Clara Reve, "Letter XIV"'.
13. Byrne explains that Dido was invited to drink coffee with the family after dinner, which may seem that she had been treated differently, but Byrne interprets this as the family protecting her from 'stares and questions – or worse, the contempt of people who might look down on her for her colour and illegitimacy'. Byrne notes that Hutchinson 'knew the gossip about her "history"' and 'that she was an object of fascination in London society' and by inviting Dido to drink coffee the Murrays 'were not ashamed of her, and wanted to show visitors that she was part of the family' (*Belle*, p. 176).
14. *ODNB*.
15. *ODNB*.
16. Byrne, *Belle*, p. 229.
17. S. Minney, 'The Search for Dido', *History Today*, 55:10 (October 2005), pp. 2–3.

Dido Elizabeth Belle, Baptism Record (1766)

Baptized November 1766
20 Dido Elizabeth D[aughte]r of Bell[1] & Maria his Wife[2] Aged 5 Y[ears]

'The Earl of Mansfield's Will', *Diary or Woodfall's Register* (1793)

THE EARL OF MANSFIELD's WILL.[3]

    WHEN it shall please GOD to call me to another state to which of all I now enjoy, I can only carry the satisfaction of my, own conscience, and my firm reliance upon his goodness, through JESUS CHRIST, with regard to what I must leave behind, I William Earl of Mansfield[4] declare my last Will and Testament to be as follows: – I desire to be buried privately, and from the love I bear to the place of my early education, I wish it to be in Westminster-Abbey[5] – I give to each of my nieces, Ann and Marjory,[6] Six Thousand Pounds each, and after the decease of my dear Wife[7] I, give to each Three Hundred Pounds a Year during their lives and the whole Six Hundred Pounds a Year to the survivor during her life, – I give to my Niece Elizabeth Murray[8] the sum of Ten Thousand Pounds – I give to each of the Children of Sir David Lindsay[9] One Thousand Pounds, – I leave to Sir John Lindsay,[10] in memory of the love and friendship I always bore him, One Thousand Pounds – I leave to his Sister my Niece, Mrs. Murray,[11] Five Hundred Pounds for a Ring. – I continue to my Sister Margaret[12] what I now allow her at her time of life she wants – nothing more. – I give to Mr. John Way,[13] who has long served me in many capacities with great ability and the strictest integrity, the sum of One Thousand Pounds – To my servants Thomas Douse, Fifty Pounds a year during his life – To Mrs. Cooper and George Wilkinson, Three Hundred Pounds each. To Thomas Wilkinson all my wearing apparel and One Hundred Pounds. To George Walker, John Lloyd and Betty Kendall, One Hundred Pounds each. To Daniel Inwin, Fifty Pounds. To each of my other Servants, male *or* female, as have lived with me above five years, I give three years wages. To the rest I leave one year's wages. All the above Legacies to persons now in my service, are, provided they continue in my service to the time of my death. – I confirm to Dido Elizabeth Belle her freedom,[14] and after the decease of my dear Wife I give her One Hundred Pounds a year during her life. – I hope the Dutchess Dowager of Portland[15] will let my Picture by Vanlo[16] hang in her room, to put her in mind of one she knew from her infancy, and always honoured with uninterrupted confidence and friendship. – I give to Lady Mary Milbank[17] and Lady Charlotte Wentworth,[18] Two Hundred Pounds each, to be laid out in some memorials of me, – I desire Lord Kinnoul, the Archbishop of York, and the Bishop of Worcester,[19] to accept One Hundred Pounds each, as a token of my remembering them with the warmest sentiments of affection. All the rest of my Real and Personal Estate of what kind, nature or tenure soever, I give to my dear Wife during her life without impeachment of waste, and that she may not think herself under any restraint in the enjoyment of Chattles which are consumed by using, such as carriages, liquor, horses, cows, hay, implements, I give her the absolute property of all such, such power also to convert to her own use while she lives, any part of the Household Goods, Furniture or Plate; I also give her the sum of One Thousand Pounds. – I give to Lady Stormont[20] my best Diamond Ring, to Lady David Lindsay[21] my second, and to Lady John Lindsay[22] my third Diamond Ring, which I hope they will wear for my sake. – After the death of my dear Wife, I leave my whole Real and Personal Estate of what nature or kind soever to my Nephew David Viscount Stormont,[23] his Heirs, Executors and Administrators. He can best judge whether any and what future settlements should be made after his death in his own family. I appoint my Wife and Lord Stormont Executors of this my Will.

In witness whereof, I have hereunto set my hand and seal, this 17th of April, 1782.

MANSFIELD. (L.S.)

Signed, sealed and published by the within named Earl of Mansfield, as and for his last Will and Testament, in the presence of us who have hereunto set our hands at his request, in his presence and in the presence of each other.

BENJAMIN THOMAS.

SAMUEL PLATT,

JOHN JORDAN.

In addition to what I have given my Nieces, Anne and Margery[24] by my above Will, I hereby leave to each the sum of Two Thousand Pounds. My old servant John Minshut ought not now to want assistance after what I have done for him, but lest he should I leave him Fifty Pounds a year during his life.

MANSFIELD.

9th 08. 1783.

In addition to what I have given my Nieces Ann and Marjory, by my above Will and Codicil, I give to each the sum of Two Thousand Pounds; and I further give to John Way; to whose care and fidelity I owe the preservation and increase of my property, One Thousand Pounds.

MANSFIELD.

20th May, 1784.

[...]

I desire Rings may be sent the Chancellor, Master of the Rolls and Judges. I leave to my Nieces Ann Marjory each of my carriages as they can use. I leave them my Liquor, and the Household Goods and Linnen *which* shall be in my Collar and House in Lincoln's-Inn-Fields at the time of my death. My Plate I leave them the use of during their lives and the life of the Survivor.

MANSFIELD.

[...]

What I have given upon the marriage of my niece Elizabeth,[25] is in full satisfaction of her legacy.

Besides the annuity, I give Dido the sum of Two Hundred Pounds to set out with.

May 5, 1786. I give to each of my nieces, Anna and Margery, Two Hundred Pounds a year more during their lives, and the whole to the survivor during her life.

I give to creditable and reputable persons families or children in distress, the sum of Five Hundred Pounds to be distributed by my nieces, or the survivor, according to their conscience and discretion.

I give to Thomas Douse, Fifty Pounds a year more during his life, in case he be living with me at my decease.

I give to Mrs. Murray, of Henderland, Five Hundred Pounds more – I do not literally mean she should buy a ring.

MANSFIELD.

May 12, 1786.

May 17, 1786. I declare this to be a Codicil to my last Will, which Will is written in one sheet of paper, the four pages completely filled. I think it right, considering how she has been bred, and how she has behaved, to make a better provision for Dido, I therefore give her Three Hundred Pounds more.

I give to Edward Hunter an excellent servant, the sum of one hundred pounds.

I give to my nieces Anne and Margery, the *absolute* property of my plate.

[...] I leave to William Coch, fifty pounds. All, legacies to persons in my service, or employment, are upon condition they continue in such service or employment till my death.

1st November 1786. I cannot too often express my satisfaction with the service of Mr. John Way, as a small token of my constant remembrance and lasting

approbation, I give him One Thousand Pounds more, and recommend my family to his service, assistance, and friendship. His able and upright advice will be of the greatest use; I owe much to his careful and wise management. With what I have before given to the said John Way, I leave to him Five Hundred Pounds a year during his life. 25th November, 1786.
MANSFIELD.
I mean that he should coutinue to act for Lord Stormont as he has done for me in the management of my Rents, Securities and Effects, but I leave this to his Honor, of which I have no doubt, and do not make it a condition. Republished this day, *Sept.* 12, 1788, and often before.
MANSFIELD.
Kenwood, Sept. 27, 1788.
If my Lord Stormont should happen to die before he has made a disposition or declaration of his mind, my intention is, that my Estate should be deemed to have been directed to have been limited so as to go after the death of Lady Stormont, with my Title and Peerage of
MANSFIELD.
[...]

Dido and John Davinier Marriage Allegation and Bond (1793)

[Punctuation added]
Diocese of London}
   6th October Nov – 1793
   Appeared personally John Davinier[26] and made Oath, that he is of the Parish of Saint Martin in the Fields in the County of Middlesex a Bachelor Aged Twenty one Years and upwards – and intendeth to intermarry with Dido Elizabeth Belle of the Parish of Saint George Hanover Square in the same County a Spinster above the age of Twenty one Years[27] and that he knoweth of no lawful Impediment, by Reason of any Pre-Contract, Consanguinity, Affinity, or any other lawful Means whatsoever, to hinder the said intended Marriage, and prayed a Licence[28] to solemnize the same in the Parish Church of Saint George Hanover Square aforesaid and further made Oath, that the usual Place of Abode of him her the said Dido Elizabeth Belle She Appeare hath been in the said Parish of Saint George Hanover square for the Space of four Weeks last past. John Davinier
   Sworn before me, Geo. Harris surrogate

/
Know all Men by these Presents, That We, John Davinier of the Parish of Saint Martin in the Fields in the County of Middlesex, Servant are hereby become bound unto the Right Reverend Father in God, Beilby by Divine permission, Lord Bishop of London,[29] in the Sum of Two Hundred Pounds of good and lawful Money of Great-Britain, to be paid to him the said Right Reverend Father in God, or his lawful Attorney, Executors, Successors or Assigns; For the good and faithful Payment of which Sum, we do bind ourselves, and both of us, jointly and severally, for the Whole, our Heirs, Executors and Administrators, firmly by these Presents. Sealed with our Seals. Dated the 6th Day of ~~October~~ Nov[embe]r in the Year of our Lord 1793.

The Condition of this Obligation is such, that if hereafter there shall not appear any lawful Lett or Impediment, by Reason of any Pre-Contract, Consinguinity, Affinity, or any other lawful Means whatsoever; but that the above bounden John Davinier Bachelor and Dido Elizabeth Belle Spinster may lawfully solemnize Marriage together, and in the same afterwards lawfully remain and continue for Man and Wife, according to the Laws in that Behalf provided: And moreover, if there be not at this present Time any Action, Suit, Plaint,[30] Quarrel, or Demand, moved or depending before any such lawful Impediment between the said Parties: Nor that either of them be of any other Parish or Place, nor of any better Estate or Degree, than to the Judge at granting of the Licence is suggested. And by him sworn to.

And lastly, if the said Marriage shall be openly solemnized in the Church, or Chapel in the Licence specified, between the Hours appointed in Constitutions Ecclesiastical confirmed,[31] and according to the Form of the book of Common Prayer, now by Law established,[32] and the above bounden John Davinier do save harmless and keep indemnified the above-mentioned Right Reverend Father in God, his Chancellor and Surrogates, and all other his Officers and Ministers whatsoever, by Reason of the Premises; then this obligation to be void, or else to remain in full Force and Virtue. John Davinier

Sealed and Delivered in the Presence of ACOwen

OLAUDAH EQUIANO, OR GUSTAVUS VASSA, 'THE AFRICAN'

Olaudah Equiano, *The Interesting Narrative of the Life of Olaudah Equiano, or Gustavus Vassa, the African. Written by Himself* (Norwich: Printed by the author, 1794). Eighth edition enlarged, pp. 333–5, 358–60. ECCO, ESTC Number T136630, ECCO Range 3549.

Susannah Cullen and Gustavus Vassa, Marriage Certificate (17 April 1792), Soham Cambridgeshire, FHL.

Gustavus Vassa, Will (1797), The National Archives, Kew, Prerogative Court of Canterbury and Related Probate Jurisdictions, PROB 1, Piece: 1289.

Anna Maria Vassa, Epitaph (1796), St Andrew's Church, Chesterton, Cambridge[1]

While Southern American colonies passed laws against interracial marriages during the late seventeenth century, in England the occurrences of interracial marriage were 'far too common' for Gretchen Gerzima to include them in her study of eighteenth-century black Londoners.[2] 'Mixed-race marriages' Gerzima noted, 'tended not to be seen as problematic to the English because they primarily occurred among the lower working classes.'[3] Nevertheless, English writers – primarily pro-slavery – expressed fears similar to many Atlantic colonists that the purity of white people would be tainted by interracial marriage.[4]

An outspoken proponent for marriage choice, regardless of skin colour, was found in Olaudah Equiano (*c.* 1745–97). In a review of a pro-slavery pamphlet for the *Public Advertiser*, Equiano countered, 'Why not establish intermarriages at home and in our Colonies? and encourage open, free and generous love, upon Nature's own wide and extensive plan, subservient only to moral rectitude, without distinction of the colour of a skin?'[5] Equiano's argument, based on Enlightenment appeals to Nature's laws, also reflected the late eighteenth-century sentimentalism toward courtship and marriage. Equiano's commitment to freedom of marital choice probably stemmed from his horrible experiences of being separated from his family by force and sold into slavery.

Equiano was probably born in eastern Nigeria, and was the youngest son of seven surviving children of a village elder;[6] Equiano's ability to and opportunities for maintaining kinkeeping relationships with his family ended when he – at the age of 11 – and his sister were kidnapped and sold into slavery.[7] In Virginia, Equiano was purchased by Michael Pascal, a British naval lieutenant who mockingly renamed him Gustavus Vassa – after a fifteenth-century Swedish King.[8] By 1766, however, Equiano had purchased his freedom, worked a variety of jobs and travelled to many countries. In 1786, Equiano was appointed the commissary of provisions and stores for the 'resettlement' scheme of the black poor to Sierra Leone (see also 'Williams Settlement').[9] Vigilant in performing his duties, Equiano soon discovered that a government agent was embezzling the funds. Though the Navy Board accepted Equiano's testimony against the embezzler, they still dismissed him because he had lobbied too much on behalf of his fellow black Britons.[10] The one positive outcome from his involvement with the Sierra Leone scheme was Equiano's prominence as a public figure.

Equiano was able to utilize his high-profile status to lobby for abolition. Nine 'Sons of Africa' wrote a letter to the *Diary* newspaper in support of abolition in 1787. The newspaper, the *Public Advertiser* ran articles and reviews by 'Gustavus Vassa the African.'[11] The sobriquet 'the African' highlighted his racial identity as a spokesperson for abolition, as he continued to write and speak against slavery. Equiano described the degrading experience of slavery when he published his autobiography using his African name, his slave name and his sobriquet: *The Interesting Narrative of the Life of Olaudah Equiano, or Gustavus Vassa, the African* (1789).[12] *The Interesting Narrative* was so popular, eight editions were published during Equiano's lifetime. Equiano lectured tirelessly for abolition, pausing only to court and marry Susannah Cullen (*c.* 1761–96) in 1792.

Equiano's marriage was reported in several London newspapers. In the *General Evening Post* the announcement highlighted Equiano's involvement in abolition and his subsequent fame:

> On Monday the 9th instant Gustavus Vassa, the African, well known in England as the champion and advocate for procuring a suppression of the slave trade, was married at Soham, in Cambridgeshire, to Miss Cullen, daughter of Mr. Cullen, of Ely, in the same county in presence of a vast number of people assembled on the occasion.[13]

Equiano's celebrity and higher socioeconomic status was also indicated on his marriage certificate: he married Susannah by special license (see also Dido Elizabeth). Oddly, however, the curate entering the information referred to Equiano's sobriquet parenthetically with an indefinite article, either betraying his need to record this as an interracial marriage, or revealing an imprecise acknowledgment of Equiano's celebrity status.[14]

Olaudah and Susannah had two daughters: Anna Maria and Joanna. Susannah died first, in 1796, and had written a will; a married woman could only write a will with her husband's consent, which indicated Equiano's egalitarian and loving treatment of his wife.[15] Perhaps Equiano's experiences as a slave enlarged his empathy toward his wife's subordinate legal position as a married woman. Tragically, starting with Susannah's death in 1796, the family was be reduced to only Joanna by 1797. Joanna alone inherited her father's wealth when she came of age.

The documents below are an extract from the eighth edition of *The Interesting Narrative* (1794) which includes Equiano's description of his religious beliefs, his failed attempt to be sent as a missionary and his marriage to Susannah. The transcript of his marriage certificate precedes the epitaph for Anna Maria; the anonymous poet employed the typical Augustan rhymed iambic pentameter couplets to compose this sentimental tribute to the young girl.

Notes
1. Available at http://trees.ancestry.co.uk/tree/31080769/person/12488423511/photox/006de799-356f-4408-9095-0dee20024f3c?src=search [accessed 23 May 2014].
2. G. Gerzima, *Black London: Life Before Emancipation* (New Brunswick, NJ: Rutger's University Press, 1995), p. 22.
3. Gerzima, *Black London*, p. 21.
4. P. Fryer, *Staying Power: The History of Black People in Britain* (London: Pluto Press, 1984), pp. 108–9; Gerzima, *Black London*, p. 103.
5. Quoted in Fryer, *Staying Power*, p. 108.
6. Fryer, *Staying Power*, p. 103.
7. *ODNB*. Early records of Equiano also list him as a native of South Carolina.
8. Fryer, *Staying Power*, p. 103.
9. Fryer, *Staying Power*, p. 105.
10. Fryer, *Staying Power*, p. 106.
11. Fryer, *Staying Power*, p. 108.
12. James Walvin explained that *The Interesting Narrative* was 'a record of his own experiences or was composed from the recollections of enslaved Africans whom he met'.
13. *General Evening Post*, April 19, 1792–April 21, 1792, Issue 9137. *17th–18th Century Burney Collection Newspapers* [Accessed 8 December 2014].
14. In contrast to Equiano's high profile marriage, Dr Samuel Johnson's Jamaican servant and heir, Francis Barber, married a local English woman by banns on 28 January 1773: 'also in Trust to be applied, after paying my Debts, to the Use of Francis Barber my Man Servant a Negro in such Manner as they shall judge most fit and available to his Benefit' (Guildhall, St Dunstan in the West, Register of Marriages, 1762–79, P69/DUN2/A/01/Ms 10354/2). His marriage entry contains no reference to his natal ethnicity. Available at http://www.nationalarchives.gov.uk/pathways/blackhistory/work_community/transcripts/will_johnson.htm [accessed 9 December 2014].
15. See S. Staves, *Married Women's Separate Property in England, 1660–1833* (Cambridge, MA: Harvard University Press, 1990); A. Erickson, *Women and Property in Early Modern England* (London: Routledge, 1993).

Olaudah Equiano, *The Interesting Narrative of the Life of Olaudah Equiano, or Gustavus Vassa, the African* ([1794])

Behold, God is my salvation; I will trust, and not be afraid, for the Lord Jehovah is my strength and my song; he also is became my salvation.

And in that day shall ye say, Praise the Lord, call upon his name, declare his doings among the people. Isa. xii. 2. 4.[1]

EIGHTH EDITION ENLARGED.

NORWICH: Printed for, and Sold by the AUTHOR.

1794.

PRICE FOUR SHILLINGS. *Formerly sold for 7s.* [*Entered at Stationers' Hall.*]

/

CHAP. XII.

Different transactions of the author's life till the present time [...] – *His marriage – Conclusion*

Such were the various scenes which I was a witness to, and the fortune I experienced until the year 1777. Since that period, my life has been more uniform, and the incidents of it fewer than in any other equal number of years preceding; I therefore hasten to the conclusion of a narrative, which I fear the reader may think already sufficiently tedious.

I had suffered so many impositions in my commercial transactions in different parts of the world, that I became heartily disgusted with the seafaring life, and was determined not to return to it at least for some time. I therefore once more engaged in service shortly after my return, and continued for the most part in this situation until 1784.

Soon after my arrival in London, I saw a remarkable circumstance relative to African / complexion, which I thought so extraordinary that I beg leave just to mention it: A white negro woman, that I had formerly seen in London and other parts, had married a white man, by whom she had three boys, and they were every one mulattoes, and yet they had fine light hair. In 1779, I served Governor Macnamara,[2] who had been a considerable time on the coast of Africa. In the time of my service I used to ask frequently other servants to join me in family prayer; but this only excited their mockery. However the Governor understanding that I was of a religious turn, wished to know what religion I was of; I told him I was a protestant of the church of England, agreeable to the thirty-nine articles of that church;³ and that whomsoever I found to preach according to that doctrine, those I would hear. A few days after this we had some more discourse on the same subject; when he said he would, if I chose, as he thought I might be of service in converting my country men to the Gospel-faith, get me sent out as a missionary to Africa.⁴ [...] /

Since the first publication of my Narrative, I have been in a great variety of scenes in many parts of Great Britain, Ireland and Scotland, an account of which might well be added here; but this would swell the volume too much, I shall only observe in general, that, in / May 1791, I sailed from Liverpool to Dublin where I was very kindly received, and from thence to Cork, and then travelled over many counties in Ireland. I was every where exceedingly well treated, by persons of all ranks. I found the people extremely hospitable, particularly in Belfast, where I took my passage on board of a vessel for Clyde, on the 29th of January, and arrived at Greenock on the 30th. Soon after I returned to London, where I found persons of note from Holland and Germany, who requested of me to go there; and I was glad to hear that an edition of my Narrative⁵ had been printed in both places, also in New York. I remained in London till I heard the debate in the House of Commons on the Slave Trade, April the 2d and 3d.⁶ I then went to Soham in Cambridgeshire, and was married on the 7th of April to Miss Cullen, daughter of James and Ann Cullen, late of Ely.

Susannah Cullen and Gustavus Vassa, Marriage Certificate (1792)

No 220} ~~Gustava~~ Gustavus Vassa (an African)⁷ of the Parish of St. Martin in the Fields in the Co[unty] of Middlesex Bachelor, and Susannah Cullen of this Parish Sp[i]n[ste]r were Married in this Church by Licence⁸ from Dr Commons this seventh Day of April in the Year One Thousand seven Hundred and ninety two By me Cha[rle]s Hill Curate⁹

This Marriage was solemnized between Us
{Gustavus Vassa
{Susanah Cullen
In the Presence of {Francis Bland
{Thomas Cullen¹⁰

Gustavus Vassa, Will (1797)

In the the Name of God Amen. I Gustavus Vassa of Addle Street Aldermanbury[11] in the City of London[12] Gentleman being sound in Mind and Body and in perfect Health and firm in my belief of a future state in the Death and Corruption of the Body and hopeful in the rise of the Soul depending in the Mercy of God my Creator for forgiveness of my Sins Give devise and Bequeath unto my ffriends John Audley and Edward Ind[13] both of Cambridge Esquires All my Real and Personal Estate of what nature kind or sort soever either in possession reversion, remainder or expectancy (and which Estate and Property I have dearly earned by the sweat of my Brow in some of the most remote and adverse Corners of the whole world to solace those I leave behind me) To hold to them the said John Audley and Edward Ind the Executors administrators and assigns in Trust, that they, the said John Audley and Edward Ind shall and do receive and take the Produce and Profits arising from my Estate both real and personal and apply the same or a sufficient part thereof towards the Board Maintenance and Education of my two infant[14] daughters Anna Maria[15] and Johanna Vassa[16] until they shall respectively attain their respective ages of twenty one years then upon this further Trust that from and after their attaining their said age of twenty one years equally to be divided between / them share and share alike but if either of them shall happen to die then I give and bequeath the share of her so dying to the survivor of them but in case of the decease of both my children before they arrive at their said age of twenty one years then and in that case I give devise and bequeath the whole of my Estate and Effects hereinbefore given one Moiety[17] thereof to the Treasuror and directors of the Sierra Leone Company[18] for the use and Benefit of the School established by the said Company at Sierra Leone and the other Moiety thereof to the Treasurer and Directors of the Society instituted at the Spa Fields Chapel[19] on the twenty second Day of September one thousand seven hundred and ninety five for sending Missionaries to preach the Gospel in Foreign parts & I hereby give and bequeath unto the said John Audley and Edward Ind the Sum of ten pounds each and I do hereby nominate Constitute and appoint the said John Audley and Edward Ind Executors of this my last will and Testament hereby revoking and making void all and every other will and declare this to be my last will and Testament in Witness whereof I have hereunto set my Hand and Seal this twenty eigth day of May in the year of our Lord one thousand seven hundred and ninety six, Gustavus Vassa Signed sealed published and declared by the above named Gustavus Vassa as and for his last will and Testament in the presence [o]f us who at his request and in his presence have subscribed our Hands as witnesses thereto, Elizabeth Melliora Cross No. 9 Adam Street[20] J. Gillham No. 9 Adam Street Adelphi,[21] George Streetin Clerke to Mr Gillham.

The Schedule or Inventory of the principal part of my Estate and Effects which I am possessed of at the time of making this my will Two acres of Copyhold[22] Pasture Ground with the appurtenances thereunto belonging situate lying and being in Sutton and Mepal in the Isle of Ely and County of Cambridge[23] which devolved to me my Heirs or Assigns after the decease of Mrs. Ann Cullen[24] of Fordham in Cambridgeshire by the last Will and Testament of my late wife Susanna Vassa[25] and I have Mrs. Cullen's Bond for one Quarter of her worth one Annuity of James Parkinson Esquire[26] of the Leverian Museum Blackfriars Road[27] in the County of Surry of the yearly value of Twenty six Pounds thirteen Shillings and eight pence one other Annuity of Francis Fokes and Frances his wife[28] of Pleasant Passage near Mother Red Caps Hampstead Road in the County of Middlesex of the yearly value of Fifty eight / Pounds two shillings and eight Pence One other annuity of Mrs Ann Seborne of Westwell[29] in the County of Oxfordshire the yearly value of one hundred Pounds all payable Quarterly Three hundred Pounds derived to me by an Assignment of the Lease of Plaisterers Hall[30] situate in Addle Street No. 25 in the City of London Sundry Household Goods and Furniture wearing apparel and Printed Books at Present in the premises at Plaisterers Hall The Sum of Three hundred Pounds at present undisposed of and since other Property as I may in future annuities I do hereby desire my Executors to Insure the Lives on which the several annuities are granted at the assurance office in Bridge street Blackfriars The deeds of which Estate are lodged in the Possession of James Gillham Attorney No. 9 Adam Street Adelphi or with Messrs Down Thornton and comp[an]y Bankers Bartholomew Lane in the City of London Gustavus Vassa Witnesses Eliz[abe]th Melliora Cross J[ame]s Gillham George Streetin Clerke to Mr Gillham

This Will was proved at London with a Codicil the eighth day of April in the year of our Lord one thousand seven hundred and ninety seven before the worshipful Charles Coste Doctor of Laws Surrogate of the Right Honourable Sir William Wynne Knight Doctor of Laws Master or Commissary of the Prerogative Court of Canterbury[31] lawfully constituted by the Oaths of John Audley and Edward Ind Esquires the Executors named in the said will to whom administration of all and singular the Goods Chattels and Credits of the deceased was granted then having been sworn duly to administer.

Anna Maria Vassa, Epitaph (1796)

Near this Place lies Interred –
ANNA MARIA VASSA
Daughter of GUSTAVUS VASSA the AFRICAN
She died July 21, 1797
Aged 4 Years
Should simple village rhymes attract thine eye,
Stranger, as thoughtfully thou passest by,[32]
Know that there lies beside this humble stone
A child of colour haply not thine own.
Her father born of Afric's sun-burnt race,
Torn from his native fields, ah foul disgrace;[33]
Through various toils, at length to Britain came ...
Espous'd, so Heaven ordain'd, an English dame,
And followed Christ: their hope, two infants dear.
But one, a hapless Orphan, slumbers here.
To bury her the village children came.
And dropp'd choice flowers and lisp'd her early fame:
And some that lov'd her most, as if unblest,
Bedew'd with tears the white wreath on their breast:
But she is gone and dwells in that abode
Where some of every clime shall joy in God.

DANIEL RENAUD, COMMONPLACE BOOK SELECTIONS FROM *THE LADIES ORACLE* (*c*. 1750)

Daniel Renaud, commonplace book selections from *The Ladies Oracle*, *c*. 1750. William Andrews Clark Memorial Library, UCLA, MS 1977.007.

Commonplace books were used in the early modern period to help readers remember passages from books and periodicals. They could also contain household memorandum, recipes and remedies. Some were kept by individuals, while others were kept by several generations within the same family (see also Volume 3, 'Household Economy'). In this way, they helped early modern people organize and retain knowledge.[1] They were used by young and old, by the wealthy and the middling sort, and by men and women. Their malleable nature – there was no one, right way to keep a commonplace book – meant that their contents reflect a particular individual's interpretation of her or his reading.

Daniel Renaud was a rector in Whitchurch, Hertfordshire from 1728 until his death in 1772. Born in Switzerland in 1697, he immigrated to England as a youth. He entered Brasenose College, Oxford in 1716, receiving his BA in 1720 and his MA in 1723. He became rector of Whitchurch in 1728 and married Christiana Button at Misterton in Leicestershire that same year.[2] Together they had six children, at least one of whom followed his father's footsteps into the clergy. Renaud was a prolific record keeper, compiling an account book and family memoranda in addition to this commonplace book (see also Volume 2, 'Courtship'). He worked diligently to record family events and accounts, often editing and refining the text years after events.[3] His account book, of which he made two copies, and the commonplace book were both produced in the 1750s and 1760s, while his notebook covered 1730–69.[4]

In this commonplace book composed between 1751 and 1763, Daniel Renaud extracted passages about racial differences from *A Ladies Oracle*. It is not clear the precise publication he refers to, since the title and the answers do not match a specific book known to have been published in the seventeenth or eighteenth centuries. The question he extracted, however, is found in *A Ladies Diary* from 1749. As this annual publication posed questions in one year's volume and answered them in the next, it is possible that the remainder of the content copied by Renaud came from a volume no longer extant.[5] Though not technically about families, the text shows a typical eighteenth-century attempt to apply scientific explanations of plant and animal hereditary to racial differences among people. The text emphasizes a racialized sense of nation and difference, and overlaps with Enlightenment ideas of racial hierarchy. Scientific and Enlightenment impulses that led to the categorization of the natural world overlapped with discussions of human evolution and social organization. As Emmanuel Eze asserted, 'Enlightenment philosophy was instrumental in codifying and institutionalizing both the scientific and popular European perceptions of the human race'.[6] Renaud's account shows precisely this overlap of eighteenth-century science and reasoning, and racial understandings of human differences.

Notes

1. V. Burke, 'Recent Studies in Commonplace Books', *English Literary Renaissance*, 43:1 (February 2013), pp. 153–77.
2. J. Foster, *Alumni Oxonienses: The Members of the University of Oxford, 1715–1886*, 00 vols (Nendeln/Liechtenstein: Kraus Reprint Limited, 1968), vol. 3, p. 1186; Church of England, marriage of Daniel Renaud and Christiana Button, 1728, *Leicestershire, England Extracted Parish Registers*, available at www.ancestry.co.uk [accessed 1 December 2014].
3. K. Harvey, *The Little Republic: Masculinity and Domestic Authority in Eighteenth-Century Britain* (Oxford: Oxford University Press, 2012), p. 141.
4. Daniel Renaud, Account Books, 1752, 1769, William Andrews Clark Memorial Library, UCLA, MS 1977.008 and MS 1977.009; Daniel Renaud, notebook, 1730–69, Hertfordshire Record Office A98/1.
5. *The Ladies Diary, or Woman's Almanack, for the Year of Our Lord, 1749* (London: A. Wilde, 1749), p. 43, Princeton University Library, accessed via www.googlebooks.com [accessed 1 December 2014].
6. E. C. Eze, *Race and the Enlightenment: A Reader* (New Jersey: Wiley-Blackwell, 1997), p. 5.

Daniel Renaud, Commonplace Book Selections from *The Ladies Oracle* (*c.* 1750)

21 Q. It is clear from the Nature of human Existence (Without Revelation) That there must be a first human Fair unborn, as well as first Pairs & distinct Models of all Animal Species & vegetable Kinds, ungenerated, at Creation: How therefore is the Negro Race accounted for, of opposite Colour to the Whites? and how the Swarthy Indians of a Hue betwixt both? seeing they are distinguish'd by their Hair from the Molatto People of Wooly Covering, produced from Whites & Blacks: And these appearances without Supposing more first Models than one Pair?
Ans. It is observ'd by Surgeons & Anatomists, that the skins of Whites & Blacks are tinctur'd by the Liquors respectively secreted by the Cuticular Glands. Hence may be inferr'd that the various colour'd Skins of the human Species proceed form the Texture of the Cuticular Glands & Colour of the Liquor secreted by them. And by the like Analogy the Spots & Colours of all Animals, as well as of all vegetables Whatsoever proceed from the Juices respectively separated immediately under their Surfaces. That hot Climates contribute to the Tawny Complexion is certain, but cou'd never produce Black from White, or Tawny from Black is equally certain, since the East Indies & America, inhabited by tawny Indians coverd w[i]th Hair are both as hot as Africa inhabited by Blacks & Wooly Molattos, the last produc'd of Blacks & Whites, therefore it may be inferr'd, that the Blacks & Whites & also Indians were either three distinct originals, adapted to the
/
Respective Climates they were appointed to inhabit

by the Great Creator (an Argument of the Trinity)
or else, seeing that the Whites have always had Dominion
over the rest, the Tawny & Black might spring from
them by the like Cause to that w[hi]ch transform'd Moses's
Rod into a Serpent.

CLARA REEVE, 'LETTER X' AND 'LETTER XI'

Clara Reeve, 'Letter X' and 'Letter XI', *Plans of Education; with Remarks on the Systems of Other Writers. In a Series of Letters between Mrs Darnford and her Friends* (London: Printed for T. Hookham and J. Carpenter, New and Old Bond-Street, 1792), pp. 76–96, ECCO, ESTC Number T110125, ECCO Range 1299.

'The primary functions of race prejudice,' according to Peter Fryer, 'are economic and political.'[1] British racism spread from seventeenth-century Barbados (see also 'George Walker, Leeward Plantation' in 'Racial Diversity of Families') as an oral tradition, to print in England by the mid-eighteenth century.[2] Those who spread the ideology of racial inferiority were those who would receive the most economic benefit – namely the plantocracy, who were the slave merchants and sugar planters of the British Caribbean colonies.[3] Writers like James Grainger in his poem *The Sugar Cane* (1764), extolled British imperialism and dehumanized slaves into plantation tools, or sturdy yet sportive livestock:

> When therefore such
> Thou buy'st, for sturdy and laborious they,
> Straight let some learned leach strong medicines give,
> Till food and climate both familiar grow.
> Thus, tho' from rise to set, in Phoebus' eye,
> They toil, unceasing; yet, at night, they'll sleep,
> Lap'd in Elysium; and, each day, at dawn,
> Spring from their couch, as blythsome as the sun'[4]

The influence of plantocracy writings had firmly entrenched racism in Britain by the 1770s.[5] Therefore a 19 August 1788 article in the *Morning Chronicle*, by 'Civis' (Latin for citizen), could refer to the literary accomplishments of 'Gustavus Vassa, Ignatius Sancho, &c.' as evidence of trained tricksters, and not of racial equality.[6] In addition to dismissing African literary ability, proslavery writers utilized pseudo-scientific racist explanations to justify slavery; non-white populations were incapable of self-rule because of perceivable and classified biological differences (see also 'Daniel Renaud').[7]

British fears of slave rebellions, racial intermarriage and the pollution of white culture reached fever pitch by the 1790s (see also 'Olaudah Equiano').[8] In this climate, Clara Reeve (1729–1807; see also 'Clara Reeve, Letter XIV') published *Plans of Education, with remarks on the systems of other writers, in a series of letters between Mrs. Darnford and her friends* (1792). In this epistolary educational treatise, Reeve utilized contemporary racist arguments when describing the feared results of abolition, the lives of slaves and the phenotypical categories of slaves. Reeve's justification against supporting abolition also employed the pious domestic sentiment: 'charity begins at home.' The home that concerned Reeve was of the poor white family, who deserved assistance more than enslaved negroes.

Notes
1. P. Fryer, *Staying Power: The History of Black People in Britain* (London: Pluto Press, 1984), p. 134.
2. Fryer, *Staying Power*, p. 134.
3. Fryer, *Staying Power*, p. 135.
4. J. Grainger, *The Sugar-Cane: A Poem. In Four Books. With Notes. By James Grainger, M.D. &c.* (London, 1764), *Eighteenth Century Collections Online*, Gale, Brigham Young University (Utah), at http://find.galegroup.com.erl.lib.byu.edu/ecco/infomark.do?&source=gale&prodId=ECCO&userGroupName=byuprovo&tabID=T001&docId=CW3315187933&type=multipage&contentSet=ECCOArticles&version=1.0&docLevel=FASCIMILE> [accessed 8 December 2014].
5. Fryer, *Staying Power*, p. 161.
6. Fryer, *Staying Power*, p. 163.
7. E. C. Eze, *Race and the Enlightment: A Reader* (Cambridge, MA: Blackwell Publishers, 1997), pp. 4–5, 10, 15; Fryer, *Staying Power*, pp. 165–7.
8. Fryer, *Staying Power*, p. 161.

Clara Reeve, 'Letter X' and 'Letter XI' (1792)

LETTER X.

MRS. DARNFORD TO LADY A –.

MY DEAR LADY,

I WILL suppose that you have recovered from the fatigue of my late investigation, and are prepared to go on with me in my progress through the rest of my subject.

I have led you from the top of a high hill, down into a spacious valley, from whence we can fall no lower. The rich and the proud look down with disdain from their high habitations, but we will not doubt to find many beautiful flowers, fruits, and herbs; we shall also find many noxious weeds, which we will endeavour to eradicate, that the herbs of value may thrive the better.

Fenelon[1] divides his nation into seven orders of men; after which he speaks of an eighth, which he calls slaves. Whom does he mean, think you? – Surely, not the peasantry; they ought not to be slaves; they are not so with us; but I fear, in his time, they were little less in France; and he could not foresee that a time should come, when they should be delivered from the yoke of tyranny, and become freemen.[2]

There have been in all times and all countries a set of men in the most abject state of servitude, and it rested with their masters to render their situation tolerable or miserable. In some countries they made the captives they took in war perform their most servile offices. The Spartans kept a whole district in this state of slavery, to do such offices as they held too mean for the citizens of Sparta. – I speak of the Helotes,[3] whose treatment was at least as bad as the negroes receive from their masters in the sugar islands.[4]

The Romans treated their slaves more liberally; they distinguished those of superior merit from the herd of men. They gave to young men of talents the best education; they raised them to offices of trust, and sometimes made them their companions.

They were frequently freed entirely from servitude; and the number of freedmen, became almost equal to the denizens.

In the History of the Jews, we find that a whole nation, or rather the inhabitants of a small district, were condemned to be hewers of wood and drawers of water to the children of Israel.[5]

There were also slaves of another kind among the Jews, as household servants; and they were enjoined to treat them with humanity.

In all the Eastern countries, it has always been common to have many slaves; / in all great cities they have slave markets, where both men and women are bought and sold like cattle, and how they shall be treated, depends entirely upon the purchasers. Cervantes gives an account of their treatment in his admirable Don Quixotte; and, under feigned names, relates the adventures of himself and his companions during their slavery at Algiers, particularly in the charming story of the Captive.

In Spain and Italy there are societies of charitable persons, for the redeeming of Christian captives in Turky and other Mahometan countries; this charity reflects honour upon its donors.

If thousands of Europeans are in actual slavery, and tens of thousands in a state of oppression, does it not seem a strange kind of Quixottism, to demand an abolition of the slave trade to Africa, and the emancipation of the negroes? There / are among us a set of men who are engaged in this cause, and who pursue it with an ardour and perseverance that would do honour to a better; for surely they have made choice of improper objects on which to exercise their charity. – I have heard and read all the arguments on both sides; and, upon a fair and impartial survey and consideration, it appears to me, that if they could carry their points, they would be injurious to the commerce of this land, and no benefit to the objects they wish to relieve.

I have been assured, both by natives of the West Indies, and by those occasionally resident there, that the accounts given by the patrons of the negroes are in some instances false, and in most of the others highly exaggerated. That they are, in general, much happier there than in their native country; that the grief and sullenness they shew, when they are first carried over, / is owing to an apprehension that they are saved only to be killed and eaten; and that, when this is cured, they soon recover their health and spirits; – that they are lazy and obstinate beyond conception, and must be governed by strict discipline; that they are malicious and revengeful, and, if they had the power, would be cruel.

If their masters were cruel enough to inflict stripes and torments upon them, merely to gratify their humours, their interest would forbid it; but it is to be hoped, this can scarce ever happen. – Englishmen were never reckoned cruel, though there may have been some instances of it, as there have of the most exalted virtues in the negro race; but these do not characterize a whole nation. It is degrading our country and countrymen, to suppose them guilty of wanton cruelty to their slaves, and then to reason / upon it, as if it were generally true. Could our enemies speak worse of us than our brethren have done?

If what the West Indians assert be true, that every negro has a little spot of ground, and is allowed time to cultivate it; that from these the markets are supplied with vegetables; that from the produce of these, they are allowed to have merry meetings of their own race, with music, dancing, and other recreations; – that those who are careful and prudent frequently save money enough to purchase their freedom; if these things be true, and they have not been yet disproved, surely it would be better if the gentlemen engaged in the negro cause would turn the current of their charity into another channel, and leave this matter as they found it.

That "Charity begins at home," is a proverb too often abused by selfish and / avaricious people to cover their sordid dispositions; but, in the case before us, it will bear a more generous application. I will, under shelter of this proverb, presume to point out some objects of Charity at home, that claim attention from the public in general, and every generous and worthy mind.

The first objects I would bring before them, should be *poor children* of all denominations. Poor children put out to parish nurses; poor children apprenticed by the parish, to people but one degree less paupers than themselves; to chimneysweepers, to basket-makers, to spinners, throwsters, weavers, &c. &c.

Let a Committee of Enquiry be appointed from the charitable society, who have taken the African negroes under their protection. Let them enquire how these poor children are treated; how they are cloathed and fed: let them direct how / they shall be brought up, so as to become useful members of the community, and put out properly and likely to produce this effect. Let them institute schools of industry, to promote a reformation of manners of the lower orders of men; which are of as much importance as the manners of the great.

In all cities and great towns, there are numbers of poor children walking about half naked, hungry and wretched, without any visible means of support. Those who can regard human nature, under this humiliating appearance, have followed them into lanes and allies, in the outskirts of the towns, into miserable hovels and cottages, that could hardly keep out the wind and rain. Their parents without any trade or calling for the most part: – they do not care to confess how they live, nor what they design for their children; / but, most probably, they are destined to beggary or stealing, perhaps both. Human nature here is degraded to its lowest state, even below slavery. I will suppose the Committee abovementioned to pick up these wretched creatures; to purchase some old house, run to ruin, for them to repair and make it habitable, and to found a school of industry. I would clothe them in the most ordinary materials, if it were in coarse canvas, it would be better than rags and filthiness. They should wear wooden shoes, not such as the peasants wear in France, but such as I have seen made for the prisoners in the lately erected gaol for the county of Suffolk. The upper part is of a thick, strong leather, the sole is like the board of a wooden clog or patten, and the upper part is nailed all round. I have wished to found a trade for this article, and to send / them to all the bare-footed children which I have met in my walks in the outskirts of a certain town. I would have these children brought up to hard labour, and qualified to get an honest livelihood. They should cultivate a piece of ground, to provide them with vegetables of every kind, which might produce the chief part of their food.

As the youths grew up, and they had strength sufficient, they might assist as porters at wharfs and quays, or help sawyers and sellers of timber and other works. In harvest time, they should be let to work in the fields, at small prices; and by the time they grew to manhood, they might be able to earn an honest living.

Behold my first and lowest Plan of Education! – which I dedicate with unfeigned respect to those gentlemen, who / have taken the negroes under their protection. I perceive and admire their generous intentions; and have no doubt that they are at least equally ready to assist their own countrymen, who claim and deserve their notice, and solicit their charity.

I should add, that according to my Plan, these paupers are not to be taught to write or read; being rescued from extreme poverty, they are to be hewers of wood and drawers of water, and to be thankful for their deliverance; but they are to be taught their duties to God, their neighbours, and themselves; and to attend the service of the church regularly, and to use private devotions every morning and evening; and to know that no undertaking can succeed without the blessing of Heaven. When they enter into life and can maintain themselves, they should be enjoined to contribute their *mite,* though ever so little, to the support / of their brethren, whom they leave in the situation they have just quitted.

Here I shall conclude this letter, hoping to hear from your ladyship soon, with your remarks on my performance.

I am now, and at all times, your ladyship's obliged and obedient servant,

FRANCES DARNFORD. /

LETTER XI.

LADY A – TO MRS. DARNFORD.

Do not be angry with me, my dear Mrs. Darnford! – it is so natural to communicate our pleasures to those we love best, that I could not forbear shewing your letters to Lord A –. He was surprised to find you so deep in knowledge of a national kind, and pleased to see you entering so warmly into the best interests of mankind. He is pleased that you have defended a due subordination of rank, and that you do not wish the boundaries thrown down, and all men put upon a level; because he thinks, that in their different degrees and occupations men are most useful to each other, and that the result is the harmony of the whole.

My lord says, he can strengthen your / arguments against the emancipation of the negroes, by two considerations; the first is, the present consequences; the second, the future. The first seems to be already coming forward; namely, that the negroes, being apprized of the steps that have been taken here in their favour, are preparing to rise against their masters, and to cut their throats. We have heard of very late rebellions, that have, with difficulty, been crushed, and we may expect to hear of more daily.

The second consequence to be expected is, that when the great point shall be carried for them, they will flock hither from all parts, mix with the natives, and spoil the breed of the common people. There cannot be a greater degradation than this, of which there are too many proofs already in many towns and villages.

The gradations from a negro to a white / are many: first, a black and a white produce a mulatto; secondly, a mulatto with a white produce a mestee; thirdly, a mestee and a white produce a quadroon, a dark yellow; the quadroon and a white, a sallow kind of white, with the negro shade, and sometimes the features. All these together produce a vile mongrel race of people, such as no friend to Britain can ever wish to inhabit it.

These considerations should be recommended to the patrons of the Black Bill of Rights; perhaps they may not have reflected upon these points, and the mischiefs they contain.

The king of the French, when he was king of France, banished all the negroes from his country; it would be wise to do so in Britain, while it is yet in our power.

You are to understand this reasoning to / proceed from my lord; who says farther, that he has no doubt to call the negroes an inferior race of men, but still a link of the universal chain, and, as men, entitled to humanity, to kindness, and to protection; and he thinks, their masters ought to be amenable to the laws, if they overwork, or otherwise ill-treat them.

If we have known an Ignatius Sancho, and a Phillis Wheatly [sic], they are exceptions to the general rules of judgment, and may be compared with a Bacon and a Milton, among the most civilised and refined of the race of Europeans.

Thus much is for my lord, and as a return for your thoughts, which you have communicated to us. For myself, I have travelled with you through all your gradations to the bottom of the valley; and shall be happy to climb up again with you; for I perceive you mean to ascend by the same gradation, and to give us your / Plan of Education for each, as you go along.

[...]

I am, dear Madam,
Your obliged and affectionate friend,
LOUISA A –.

ADOLPH B. BENSON, *PETER KALM'S TRAVELS IN NORTH AMERICA* (1937)

Adolph B. Benson, *Peter Kalm's Travels in North America. The English Version of 1770* (New York, NY: Wilson-Erickson, 1937), pp. 129–30, 142–3, 204–11.

This selection from the Swedish botanist, Pehr Kalm (Peter Kalm in English translation), describes the racial and ethnic differences he discovered during his journey around America in 1750. Kalm notes the different forms of home construction diet and agricultural practices that were had among the Indians, Germans, Jews, Swedes, Africans (both enslaved and free) and English families he encountered. While his account is clearly coloured by his personal perspective and the racist and nationalist attitudes of the day, it opens a small window on the domestic arrangements of Americans of various ethnic backgrounds and highlights the interactions that crossed ethnic boundaries.

Kalm was a staunch follower of fellow Swedish botanist, Linnaeus. With Linnaeus's encouragement and the backing of the Swedish government, Kalm made a three-year journey (1748–51) around Pennsylvania, New York and Canada recording not just the plant and animal life he observed, but also the varieties of human behaviour and living conditions. Upon his return to Sweden he published an account of his findings, *En resa til Norra America* (A Journey to North America), between 1753 and 1761. The English translation was published in 1770, with additional editions in French, Dutch and German appearing in the nineteenth century.

Adolph B. Benson, *Peter Kalm's Travels in North America* (1937)

The Jews. Besides the different sects of Christians, many Jews have settled in New York, who possess great privileges. They have a synagogue, own their dwelling-houses, possess large country-seats and are allowed to keep shops in town. They have likewise several ships, which they load and send out with their own goods. In fine, they enjoy all the privileges common to the other inhabitants of this town and province.

A daughter of one of the richest Jews had married a Christian after she had renounced the Jewish religion. Her sister did not wish / either to marry a Jew, so went to London to get a Christian husband.

During my residence in New York, both at this time and for the next two years, I was frequently in company with Jews. I was informed among other things that these people never boiled any meat for themselves on Sunday, but that they always did it the day before, and that in winter they kept a fire during the whole Saturday. They commonly eat no pork; yet I have been told by several trustworthy men that many of them (especially the young Jews) when travelling, did not hesitate the least about eating this or any other meat that was put before them, even though they were in company with Christians. A young rabbi read the divine service, which was partly in Hebrew and partly in the Rabbinical dialect. Both men and women were dressed entirely in the English fashion; the former had their hats on, and did not once take them off during the service. The galleries, I observed, were reserved for the ladies, while the men sat below. During prayers the men spread a white cloth over their heads, which perhaps is to represent sackcloth. But I observed that the wealthier sort of people had a much richer cloth than the poorer ones. Many of the men had Hebrew books, in which they sang and read alternately. The rabbi stood in the middle of the synagogue and read with his face turned towards the east; he spoke however so fast as to make it almost impossible for anyone to understand what he said.

[...]

Treatment of Germans. Though the province of New York has been inhabited by Europeans much longer than Pennsylvania, yet it is not be far so populous as that colony. This cannot be ascribed to any particular discouragement arising from the nature of the soil, for that is pretty good, but I was told of a very different reason which I shall mention here. In the reign of Queen Anne, about the year 1709, many Germans came hither, who got a tract of land from the government on which they might settle. After they had lived here for some time, and had built houses and churches and cultivated fields and meadows, their liberties and privileges were infringed upon, and under several pretences they were repeatedly deprived of parts of their land. This at last roused the Germans; they returned violence for violence, and beat those who thus robbed them of their possessions. But these proceedings were looked upon in a very bad light by the government: the leading Germans being imprisoned, they were very roughly treated and punished with the utmost rigor of the law. This however so exasperated the rest, that the greater part of them left their houses and fields and went to settle in Pennsylvania. There they were exceedingly well received, got a considerable tract of land, and were granted great privileges in perpetuity. The Germans not satisfied with being themselves removed from New York, wrote to their relations and friends and advised them if ever they intended to come to America not to go to New York, where the government had shown itself so inequitable. This advice had such influence that the Germans, who afterwards emigrated in great numbers to North America, / constantly avoided New York and kept going to Pennsylvania. It sometimes happened that they were forced to go on board such ships as were bound for New York; but they had scarcely got on shore, when they hastened on to Pennsylvania, right before the eyes of all the inhabitants of New York.

The Dutch Settlers. But the lack of people in this province may likewise be accounted for a different manner. As the Dutch, who first cultivated this section, obtained the liberty of staying here by the treaty of England, and of enjoying all their privileges and advantages without the least limitation, each of them took a very large piece of ground for himself, and many of the more powerful heads of families made themselves the possessors and masters of a country of as great territory as would be sufficient to form one of our moderately-sized, and even one of our large, parishes. Most of them being very rich, their envy of the English led them not to sell them any land, but at an excessive rate, a practice which is still punctually observed among their descendants. The English therefore, as well as people of other nations, have but little encouragement to settle here. On the other hand, they have sufficient opportunity in the other provinces to purchase land at a more moderate price, and with more security to themselves. It is not to be wondered then, that so many parts of New York are still uncultivated, and that it has entirely the appearance of a frontier-land. This instance may teach us how much a small mistake in a government can hamper the settling of a country.

[...]

Servants. The servants which are employed in the English-American colonies are either free persons or slaves, and the former, again, are of two different classes.

1. Those who are entirely free serve by the year. They are not only allowed to leave their service at the expiration of their year, but many leave it at any time when they do not agree with their masters. However, in that case they are in danger of losing their wages, which are very considerable. A man servant who has some ability gets between sixteen and twenty pounds in Pennsylvania currency, but those in the country do not get so much. A maidservant gets eight / or ten pounds a year. These servants have their food besides their wages, but they must buy their own clothes, and whatever they get of these as gifts they must thank their master's generosity for.

Indenture. 2. The second kind of free servants consists of such persons as annually come from Germany, England and other countries, in order to settle here. These newcomers are very numerous every year: there are old and young of both sexes. Some of them have fled from oppression, under which they have labored. Other have been driven from their country by religious persecution, but most of them are poor and have not money enough to pay their passage, which is between six and eight pounds sterling for each person. Therefore, they agree with the captain that they will suffer themselves to be sold for a few years on their arrival. In that case the person who buys them pays the freight for them; but frequently very old people come over who cannot pay their passage, they therefore sell their children for several years, so that they serve both for themselves and for their parents. There are likewise some who pay part of their passage, and they are sold only for a short time. From these circumstances it appears that the price on the poor foreigners who come over to North America varies considerably, and that some of them have to serve longer than others. When their time has expired, they get a new suit of clothes from their master and some other things. He is likewise obliged to feed and clothe them during the years of their servitude. Many of the Germans who come hither bring money enough with them to pay their passage, but prefer to be sold, hoping that during their servitude they may get a knowledge of the language and character of the country and the life, that they may the better be able to consider what they shall do when they have gotten their liberty. Such servants are preferable to all others, because they are not so expensive. To buy a negro or black slave requires too much money at one time; and men or maids who get yearly wages are likewise too costly. But this kind of servant may be gotten for half the money, and even for less; for they commonly pay fourteen pounds, Pennsylvania currency, for a person who is to serve four years, and so on in proportion. Their wages therefore are not above three pounds Pennsylvania currency per annum. These servants are, after the English, called *servingar* by the Swedes. When a person has bought such a servant for a certain number of years, and has an intention to sell him again, he is at liberty to do / so, but is obliged, at the expiration of the term of servitude, to provide the usual suit of clothes for the servant, unless he has made that part of the bargain with the purchaser. The English and Irish commonly sell themselves for four years, but the Germans frequently agree with the captain before they set out, to pay him a certain sum of money, for a certain number of persons. As soon as they arrive in America they go about and try to get a man who will pay the passage for them. In return they give according to their circumstances, one or several of their children to serve a certain number of years. At last they make their bargain with the highest bidder.

3. The *negroes* or blacks constitute the third kind. They are in a manner slaves; for when a negro is once bought, he is the purchaser's servant as long as he lives, unless he gives him to another, or sets him free. However, it is not in the power of the master to kill his negro for a fault, but he must leave it to the magistrates to proceed according to the laws. Formerly the negroes were brought over from Africa, and bought by almost everyone who could afford it, the Quakers alone being an exception. But these are no longer so particular and now they have as many negroes as other people. However, many people cannot conquer the idea of its being contrary to the laws of Christianity to keep slaves. There are likewise several free negroes in town, who have been lucky enough to get a very zealous Quaker for their master, and who gave them their liberty after they had faithfully served him for a time.

At present they seldom bring over any negroes to the English colonies, for which were formerly brought thither have multiplied rapidly. In regard to their marriage they proceed as follows: in case you have not only male but likewise female negroes, they may intermarry, and then the children are all your slaves. But if you possess a male negro only and he has an inclination to marry a female belonging to a different master, you do not hinder your negro in so delicate a point, but it is of no advantage to you, for the children belong to the master of the female. It is therefore practically advantageous to have negro women. A man who kills his negro is, legally, punishable by death, but there is no instance here of a white man ever having been executed for this crime. A few years ago it happened that a master killed his slave. His friends and even the magistrates secretly advised him to make his escape, as otherwise they could not avoid taking him prisoner, and then he would / be condemned to die according to the laws of the country, without any hopes of beings saved. This leniency was granted toward him, that the negroes might not have the satisfaction of seeing a master executed for killing his slave. This would lead them to all sorts of dangerous design against their masters, and to value themselves too much.

The negroes were formerly brought from Africa, as I mentioned before, but now this seldom happens, for they are bought in the West Indies, or American Islands, whither they were originally brought from their own country. It has been found that in transporting the negroes from Africa directly to these northern countries, they have not such good health as when they come gradually, by shorter stages, and are first carried from Africa to the West Indies, and from thence to North America. It has frequently been found, that the negroes cannot stand the cold here so well as the Europeans or whites; for while the latter are not in the least affected by the cold, the toes and fingers of the former are frequently frozen. There is likewise a material difference among them in this point; for those who come immediately from Africa, cannot bear the cold so well as those who are either born in this country, or have been here for a considerable time. The frost easily hurts the hands or feet of the negroes who came from Africa, or occasions violent pains in their whole body, or in some parts of it, though it does not at all affect those who have been here for some time. There are frequent examples that the negroes on their passage from Africa, if it happens in winter, have some of the limbs frozen on board the ship, when the cold is but very moderate and the sailors are scarcely obliged to cover their hands. I was even assured that some negroes have been seen here who had excessive pain in their legs, which afterwards broke in the middle, and dropped entirely from the body, together with the flesh on them. Thus it is the same case with men here as with plants which are brought from the southern countries, before they accustom themselves to a colder climate.

The price of negroes differs according to their age, health, and ability. A full grown negro costs from forty pounds to a hundred of Pennsylvania currency. There are even examples that a gentleman has paid a hundred pounds for a black slave at Philadelphia and refused to sell him again for the same money. A negro boy or girl of two or three years old, can hardly be gotten for less than eight / or fourteen pounds in Pennsylvania money. Not only the Quakers but also several Christians of other denominations sometimes set their negroes at liberty. This is done in the following manner: when a gentleman has a faithful negro who has done him great services, he sometimes declares him independent at his own death. This is however very expensive; for they are obliged to make a provision for the negro thus set at liberty, to afford him subsistence when he is grown old, that he may not be driven by necessity to wicked actions, or that he may fall in charge to anybody, for these free negroes become very lazy and indolent afterwards. But the children which the free negro has begot during his servitude are all slaves, though their father be free. On the other hand, those negro children which are born after the parent was freed are free. The negroes in the North American colonies are treated more mildly and fed better than those in the West Indies. They have as good food as the rest of the servants, and they possess equal advantages in all things, except their being obliged to serve their whole lifetime and get no other wages than what their master's goodness allows them. They are likewise clad at their master's expense. On the contrary, in the West Indies, and especially in the Spanish Islands, they are treated very cruelly; therefore no threats make more impression upon a negro here than that of sending him over to the West Indies, in case he will not reform. It has likewise been frequently round by experience that when you show too much kindness to these negroes, they grow so obstinate that they will no longer do anything but of their own accord. Therefore a strict discipline is very necessary, if their master expects to be satisfied with their services.

In the year 1620 some negroes were brought to North America in a Dutch ship, and in Virginia they bought twenty of them. These are said to have been the first that came hither. When the Indians, who were more than numerous in the country than at present, saw these black people for the first time, they thought they were a real breed of devils, and therefore they called them *manito* for a long while. This word in their language signifies not only god but also devil. Some time before that, when they saw the first European ship on their coasts, they were quite convinced that God himself was in the ship. This account I got from some Indians, who preserved it among them as a tradition which they had received from their ancestors. Therefore the arrival of the negroes seemed to have / confused everything; but since that time, they have entertained less disagreeable notions of the negroes, for at present many live among them, and they even sometimes intermarry, as I myself have seen.

The negroes have therefore been upwards of a hundred and thirty years in this country. As the winters here, especially in New England and New York, are as severe as our Swedish winter, I very carefully inquired whether the cold had not been observed to affect the color of the negroes, and to change it, so that the third or fourth generation from the first that came hither became less black than their ancestors. But I was generally answered that there was not the slightest difference of color to be perceived; and that a negro born here of parents who were likewise born in this country, and whose ancestors, both men and women had all been blacks born in this country, up to the third or fourth generation, was not at all different in color from those negroes who were brought directly from Africa. Hence many people concluded that the negro or his posterity did not change color, though they continued ever so in a cold climate; but the union of a white man with a negro woman, or of a negro man with a white woman had an entirely different result. Therefore to prevent any disagreeable mixtures of the white people and negroes, and to hinder the latter from forming too great opinions of themselves, to the disadvantage of their masters, I am told there was a law passing prohibiting the whites of both sexes to marry negroes, under the pain of almost capital punishment, with deprivation and other severer penalties for the clergyman who married them. But that the whites and blacks sometimes copulated, appears from children of a mixed complexion, which are sometimes born.

It is likewise greatly to be pitied that the masters of these negroes in most of the English colonies take little care of their spiritual welfare, and let them live on in their pagan darkness. There are even some who would be very will pleased [with negro enlightenment], and would in every way hinder their negroes from being instructed in the doctrines of Christianity. To this they are led partly by the conceit of its being shameful to have a spiritual brother or sister among so despicable a people; partly by thinking that they would not be able to keep their negroes so subjected afterwards; and partly through fear of the negroes growing too proud on seeing themselves upon a level with their masters in religious matters.

Several writings are well known which mention that the negroes / in South American have a kind of poison with which they kill each other, though the effect is not sudden, and take effect a long time after the person has taken it. The same dangerous art of poisoning is known by the negroes in North America, as has frequently been experienced. However, only a few of them know the secret, and they likewise know the remedy for it; therefore when a negro feels himself poisoned and can recollect the enemy who might possibly have given him the poison, he goes to him, and endeavors by money and entreaties to move him to deliver him from its effects. But if the negro is malicious, he not only denies that he ever poisoned him, but likewise that he knows an antidote for it. This poison does not kill immediately, as I have noted, for sometimes the sick person dies several years afterward. But from the moment he has the poison he falls into a sort of consumption state and enjoys but few days of good health. Such a poor wretch often knows that he is poisoned the moment he gets it. The negroes commonly employ it on such of their brethren as behave well [toward to whites], and beloved by their masters, and separate, as it were, from their countrymen, or do not like to converse with them. They have likewise often other reasons for their enmity; but there are few examples of their having poisoned their masters. Perhaps the mild treatment they receive, keeps them from doing it, or perhaps they fear that they may be discovered, and that in such a case, the severest punishments would be inflicted on them.

They never disclose the nature of the poison, and keep it inconceivably secret. It is probable that it is a very common article, which may be had anywhere in the world; for wherever the blacks are they can always easily procure it. Therefore it cannot be a plant, as several learned men have thought, for that is not to be found everywhere. I have heard many accounts here of negroes who have been killed by this poison. I shall only mention one incident which happened during my stay in this country. A man here had a negro who was exceedingly faithful to him, and behaved so well that he would not have exchanged him for twenty other negroes. His maser likewise showed him a peculiar kindness, and the slave's conduct equalled that of the best servant. He likewise conversed as little as possible with other negroes. On that account they hated him to excess, but as he was scarcely ever in company with them they had no opportunity of conveying the poison to him, which they had often tried. However, on coming to town during the fair (for he lived in the country) some other negroes invited him to drink with them. At first he would not, but they pressed him till he was obliged to comply. As soon as he came into the room, the others took a pot from the wall and pledged him, desiring him to drink likewise. He drank, but when he took the pot from his mouth, he said: "what beer is this? It is full of ..." I purposely omit what he mentioned, for it seems undoubtedly to have been the name of the poison with which the malicious negroes do so much harm, and which is to be met with almost everywhere. It might be too much employed to wicked purposes, and it is therefore better that it remains unknown. The other negroes and negro-women began laughing at the complaints of their hated countryman, and danced and sang as if they had done an excellent thing had at last won the point so much wished for. The innocent negro went away immediately, and when he got home asserted that the other negroes had certainly poisoned him: he then fell into decline, and no remedy could prevent his death.

PHILLIS WHEATLEY, 'PREFACE' AND 'LETTER OF ATTESTATION', IN *POEMS ON VARIOUS SUBJECTS* (1773)

Phillis Wheatley, 'Preface', and 'Letter of Attestation', *Poems on Various Subjects, Religious and Moral. By Phillis Wheatley, Negro Servant to Mr. John Wheatley, of Boston, in New England* (London: Printed for A. Bell, 1773), pp. 5–8, ECCO, ESTC Number T153734, ECCO Range 1280.

In the eighteenth century, the household family included the biologically-related nuclear family, as well as the contractual members, such as servants and other co-resident dependents.[1] When a co-resident member of the family was a slave, however, he or she occupied the paradoxical position of being a person who was part of the household family, but also being property that was part of the household family's goods. In Boston, Massachusetts, the Wheatley household family included a female slave who became the 'earliest international celebrity of African descent'.[2]

Before becoming a celebrity and part of the Wheatley household family, Phillis Wheatley (c.1753–84) had been born into a family that lived in the Gambia region of West Africa; because she left no written record of her life, specific details about Wheatley's kinship family are unknown. Wheatley was around seven years old when she was purchased by John for his wife, Susanna Wheatley, and renamed after the ship that brought her to America, the *Phillis*.[3] When Phillis joined the Wheatley household family, Susanna and John had two living children – twins Mary and Nathaniel – and had buried three others – John, Susanna and Sarah – who had died in childhood. Vincent Carretta surmised that Susanna chose the young girl, instead of the more able-bodied older women, because of sentimental reasons: 'Bought at almost exactly the same age Sarah had been when she died, the future Phillis Wheatley may have appealed to Susanna and John Wheatley as a surrogate for their late beloved daughter, their last-born child'.[4]

Wheatley as replacement child may explain that while Phillis was legally a slave, her actual lived experience was closer to being treated as a person rather than only as property. The Wheatleys lived in New England, where laws regarding slaves, who were often called 'servants for life', treated them as property but also, in some activities, as people, since slaves had the right to be baptized, to marry and to acquire literacy.[5] Education, however, was dependent upon the master's generosity. While the Wheatley's white children would most likely have attended a 'petty' or elementary school, Phillis, as a slave, would not have been able to attend; as the attestation below states, Phillis learned 'Without any Assistance from School Education'. The Wheatleys, however, did not prevent Phillis from developing her literary skills as a member of their household family. The attestation explains that Phillis' education came from 'only what she was taught in the Family'. John C. Shields opined that the Wheatleys' daughter, Mary, who was six years older than Phillis, was the most likely candidate to have taught her to read.[6] Shields also posited that Phillis learned Latin and received some tutoring in writing poetry from the neighbor across the street, Mathew Byles.[7]

In a few of her letters, Wheatley revealed her feelings about her relationship with her household family. In a letter to a friend in Newport, Wheatley explained, 'I have been in a very poor state of health' and thus she had been living 'in the country for the benefit of its more wholesome air'. This indicates that her household family made arrangements for the benefit of Wheatley's health, which could be motivated either from monetary investment in the further use of the slave they bought or, more likely in Phillis' case, from goodwill towards a household family member.[8] In a letter to another African American, Obour Tanner, Wheatley related her sorrow over the death of her mistress and described it in familial terms: 'let us imagine the loss of a parent, sister, or brother, the tenderness of all these were united in her'.[9] Wheatley continued describing her household family:

> I was a poor little outcast & a stranger when she took me in: not only into her house, but I presently became a sharer in her most tender affections. I was treated by her more like her child than her servant; no opportunity was left unimproved of giving me the best of advice; but in terms how tender! how engaging![10]

Wheatley's household family encouraged and assisted her to publish her poetry. Her first well-known publication was an elegy about the unexpected death of the Methodist preacher, George Whitefield, when he had come to Boston in October 1770. Whitefield was friends with the Methodist leaders John and Charles Wesley, and most importantly was the privy chaplain to Selina Hastings, countess of Huntingdon. Wheatley had written to the countess and included a copy of her elegy. When Wheatley was unable to find a publisher willing to print her collection of poetry, her publishing career became a transatlantic venture. In 1773, through the influence of the countess, Wheatley came to London with John and Susanna's son, Nathaniel Wheatley, to secure publication of her poems, which made her the first African-American woman to publish a collection of poetry.[11]

While in England, Phillis met Granville Sharp (see also Volume 4), who most likely enlightened her about the recent Somerset decision, which determined that 'as soon as any slave sets foot upon the soil of England he becomes free'.[12] Once Wheatley returned to Boston, she received her freedom; Wheatley wrote to David Wooster a brief account of her manumission: 'Since my return to America my Master, has at the desire of my friends in England given me my freedom'.[13] Later, Wheatley explained that her master granted her freedom 'at [Susanna's] desire'.[14] Wheatley continued to live with the Wheatley family until she married John Peters, a free African American in 1778; six years later, Phillis died in childbirth. All three of Phillis's and John's children died in infancy.

The prefatory materials to Wheatley's first published poetry collection below reveal the vexed situation of female slaves in the household family and also in print culture. In the title, Wheatley's race and occupation were listed as 'Negro Servant', followed by the name of her employer/owner. Other labouring poets published their poetry during the eighteenth century, but their race and the name of their household employer were rarely included in the architexture (title) of their writing. A contemporary of Wheatley's, Ann Cromartie Yearsley (1753–1806), published her poems under her own name and with the occupational description of 'a Milkwoman of Clifton, near Bristol' but never with the name of her employer or employers.[15] Because Yearsley and other labouring poets wrote and published without the 'Disadvantage of serving as a Slave', the titles to their works signified their class status, but not their race or their subservient relationship to a household family.

The 'Preface' below also revealed Wheatley's familiarity with the gendered publishing conventions of the female writer. Wheatley, like white female poets, reassured her readers that no domestic duty was shirked while composing poetry: 'The following Poems were written originally for the Amusement of the Author, as they were the Products of her leisure Moments'. Furthermore, Wheatley presented herself as a non-professional poet, and that only 'at the Importunity of many of her best, and most generous Friends' was she induced to publish her works. These sentiments were found in many prefaces to poetry written by women of the labouring and middle classes during the eighteenth century.

The 'Attestation', which was signed by eighteen Boston dignitaries, further inscribed the challenges of Wheatley's race, labouring status and gender to write and publish poetry. Other labouring female poets wrote poems defending their literary abilities, and Yearsley even invited judges to watch her compose a publishable poem, but no white labouring poet – male or female – was ever interviewed by eighteen men to determine if s/he had the knowledge to compose the kind of poetry s/he wrote.

Notes
1. N. Tadmor, *Family and Friends in Eighteenth-Century England: Household, Kinship, and Patronage* (Cambridge: Cambridge University Press, 2001), p. 19.
2. V. Carretta, *Phillis Wheatley: Biography of a Genius in Bondage* (Athens, GA: University

of Georgia Press, 2011), p. ix.
3. *ODNB*.
4. Carretta, *Phillis Wheatley*, p. 14.
5. Carretta, *Phillis Wheatley*, p. 15.
6. *ODNB*.
7. *ODNB*.
8. Letter to Arbour Tanner, Boston, 19 July 1772, in *The Collected Works of Phillis Wheatley*, ed. J. C. Shields (Oxford: Oxford University Press, 1988), p. 165.
9. *The Collected Works of Phillis Wheatley*, p. 177.
10. *ODNB*.
11. *The Collected Works of Phillis Wheatley*, pp. vii, 229.
12. *ODNB*.
13. *The Collected Works of Phillis Wheatley*, p. 170.
14. *The Collected Works of Phillis Wheatley*, p. 184.
15. For example, *Poems, on Several Occasions. By Ann Yearsley, A Milkwoman of Bristol* (London, 1785).

Phillis Wheatley, 'Preface' and 'Letter of Attestation', in *Poems on Various Subjects* (1773)

POEMS ON VARIOUS SUBJECTS, RELIGIOUS AND MORAL.
BY
PHILLIS WHEATLEY,
NEGRO SERVANT[1] to Mr. JOHN WHEATLEY,[2] of BOSTON, in NEW ENGLAND.
LONDON:[3] Printed for A. BELL, Bookseller, Aldgate; and sold by Messrs.
COX and BERRY, King-Street, *BOSTON.*
MDCCLXXIII. /

PREFACE.

THE following POEMS were written originally for the Amusement of the Author, as they were the Products of her leisure Moments. She had no Intention ever to have published them; nor would they now have made their Appearance, but at the Importunity of many of her best, and most generous Friends;[4] to whom she considers herself, as under the greatest Obligations.

As her Attempts in Poetry are now sent into the World, it is hoped the Critic will not severely censure their Defects; and we presume they have too much Merit / to be cast aside with Contempt, as worthless and trifling Effusions.

As to the Disadvantages she has laboured under, with Regard to Learning, nothing needs to be offered, as her Master's Letter in the following Page will sufficiently shew the Difficulties in this Respect she had to encounter.

With all their Imperfections, the Poems are now humbly submitted to the Perusal of the Public. /

The following is a Copy of a LETTER sent by the Author's Master to the Publisher.

PHILLIS was brought from *Africa* to *America*, in the Year 1761, between Seven and Eight Years of Age. Without any Assistance from School Education, and by only what she was taught in the Family,[5] she, in sixteen Months Time from her Arrival, attained the English Language, to which she was an utter Stranger before, to such a Degree, as to read any, the most difficult Parts of the Sacred Writings, to the great Astonishment of all who heard her.

As to her WRITING, her own Curiosity led her to it; and this she learnt in so short a Time, that in the Year 1765, she wrote a Letter to the Rev. Mr. OCCOM, the *Indian* Minister,[6] while in *England.*

She has a great Inclination to learn the Latin Tongue,[7] and has made some Progress in it. This Relation is given by her Master who bought her, and with whom she now lives.

JOHN WHEATLEY.
Boston Nov. 14, 1772. /

To the PUBLICK.

AS it has been repeatedly suggested to the Publisher, by Persons, who have seen the Manuscript, that Numbers would be ready to suspect they were not really the Writings of PHILLIS, he has procured the following Attestation, from the most respectable Characters in *Boston*, that none might have the least Ground for disputing their *Original.*

WE whose Names are under-written, do assure the World, that the POEMS specified in the following Page,* were (as we verily believe) written by PHILLIS, a young Negro Girl, who was but a few Years since, brought an uncultivated Barbarian from *Africa*, and has ever since been, and now is, under the Disadvantage of serving as a Slave in a Family in this Town. She has been examined by some of the best Judges, and is thought qualified to write them.[8]

His Excel'ency THOMAS HUTCHINSON, *Governor,*[9]
The Hon. ANDREW OLIVER, *Lieutenant-Governor.*[10]
The Hon. Thomas Hubbard,[11] *The Rev.* Charles Chauncy, *D.D.*[12]
The Hon. John Erving,[13] *The Rev.* Mather Byles, *D.D.*[14]
The Hon. James Pitts,[15] *The Rev.* Ed. Pemberton, *D.D.*[16]
The Hon. Harrison Gray, *The Rev.* Andrew Elliot, *D.D.*
The Hon. James Bowdoin,[17] *The Rev.* Samuel Cooper, *D.D.*
John Hancock, *Esq;*[18] *The Rev. Mr.* Samuel Mather,[19]
Joseph Green, *Esq; The Rev. Mr.* John Moorhead,[20]
Richard Carey, *Esq;*[21] *Mr.* John Wheatley, *her Master.*

N. B. The original Attestation, signed by the above Gentlemen, may be seen by applying to *Archibald Bell*, Bookseller, No. 8, *Aldgate-Street.*

---

* The Words "following Page," allude to the Contents of the Manuscript Copy, which are wrote at the Back of the above Attestation.

CATHERINE SEDGWICK TO FRANCES SEDGWICK (1807) ON ELIZABETH FREEMAN – 'MUMBET'

Catherine Sedgwick to Frances Sedgwick (1807), Robert Sedgwick Family Papers, Massachusetts History Society MS N-851, Box 77 of 117, Folder 24.

John Winthrop's 26 February 1638 journal entry, which notes that the ship, *Desire*, had returned from the West Indies with 'some cotton, and tobacco, and negroes, etc., from thence', suggests that the slave trade began relatively early in Massachusetts history.[1] By 1644, Boston merchants initiated the triangular trade: they imported slaves directly from Africa, sold these slaves in the West Indies and then brought sugar home in order to make rum.[2] For a time, Boston served as the primary port of departure for slave ships; eventually, however, Rhode Island replaced Massachusetts as the centre of the slave trade.[3]

Many wealthy families and tradesmen in colonial Boston used slaves and indentured servants to help them with their various responsibilities. Most of these slaves lived with their owners and had at least some direct contact with their owners' families.[4] The Massachusetts courts allowed slaves to own some property, to keep any wages they made from work completed on their own time and to receive trial by jury, legal counsel and some forms of legal protection.[5] Notwithstanding examples of legal protection, legislation controlled slaves' daily lives: for example, laws defined curfew, marriage arrangements, travel, trade, shopping and ownership of livestock.[6]

Although some slaves in colonial Massachusetts sought freedom – some ran away, others sought manumission and still others attempted to obtain freedom through a legal petition, or sued for freedom based on a contractual agreement with the slave owner or on the premise of a natural right to freedom – slavery persisted in this area throughout most of the eighteenth century.[7] In the century's latter decades, however, two court cases, *Brom & Bett v. John Ashley, Esq.* and a series of trials relating to Quock Walker, resulted in the abolition of slavery in the 1780s in response to the new Massachusetts Constitution.[8]

Elizabeth Freeman (Mumbet) was the first slave to be freed in Massachusetts as a result of this Bill of Rights being added to the 1780 state constitution. Born into slavery in approximately 1742, Mumbet and her younger sister, Lizzie, were owned by Peter Hogeboom – a Dutchman who lived in Claverack, Columbia County, New York.[9] Hogeboom gave the two girls to John Ashley of Sheffield, Massachusetts, when Ashley married his daughter, Annetje.

Different reasons have been given for Mumbet's quest for freedom. Family legend, for example, suggests that Mumbet decided to seek freedom after Annetje attempted to strike Lizzie with a shovel. Mumbet blocked Annetje from being able to do so, but in the process was injured herself and never regained full use of her arm.[10] Catharine Maria Sedgwick, on the other hand, reported that Mumbet decided to seek freedom after listening to a public reading of the Declaration of Independence.[11] Whatever the motivation, Mumbet asked the prominent Stockbridge Attorney, Theodore Sedgwick, to help her secure her freedom in 1781. Legal action began in the spring of that same year when Mumbet and a male slave, known as Brom, filed a suit for freedom against their owner, John Ashley. Because Ashley refused a writ of replevin – 'a court order to return or release unlawfully obtained property' – he was ordered to appear before the Court of Common Pleas in Great Barrington on 21 August 1781.[12] In this context, Theodore Sedgwick argued that the newly ratified Massachusetts Constitution made slavery illegal when it stated:

> All men are born free and equal, and have certain natural, essential, and unalienable rights; among which may be reckoned the right of enjoying and defending their lives and liberties; that of acquiring, possessing, and protecting property; in fine, that of seeking and obtaining their safety and happiness.[13]

Sedgwick's argument proved convincing, and the jury agreed that Mumbet and Brom should be freed and that Ashley should pay trial costs as well as an additional thirty shillings in damage. Although Ashley initially appealed the decision to the Supreme Judicial Court of Massachusetts – then the highest court in the Commonwealth – he decided to drop the appeal before it even reached the court. This is likely because decisions made in relation to the Quock Walker trials made it clear that no Massachusetts court would consider slavery legal under the new constitution.[14] Thus, *Brom & Bett v. John Ashley, Esq*, became a very important legal case within Massachusetts's history.[15]

After being granted her freedom, Mumbet became the paid domestic servant of Theodore and Pamela Sedgwick. Mumbet was 'a noted midwife and nurse'[16] and thus served as a 'nurse' or governess to the Sedgwick children[17] and later to the oldest Sedgwick, Eliza's, children. The Sedgwick family loved and respected Mumbet and came to consider her part of their family. The youngest daughter in the Sedgwick family, and well-known author of domestic novels, Catharine

Maria, wrote an account of Mumbet's life. Within this manuscript, Sedgwick details Mumbet's experiences as a slave, her fight for freedom and her lifelong service to the Sedgwick family, including her defence of the Sedgwick house from a small mob during Shay's Rebellion in 1787. As a result of her employment with the Sedgwick family, Mumbet became financially independent and eventually purchased a small home of her own.

Mumbet passed away on 28 December 1829. Catherine wrote several tributes to her, as did the other Sedgwick siblings and people in the surrounding community. In particular, they made note of her great character and uprightness.[18] Wrote one member of the Sedgwick family, 'If there could be a practical refutation of the imagined superiority of our race to hers, the life and character of this woman would afford that refutation.'[19]

Her epitaph, written by Charles Sedgwick, captures the role she played within the Sedgwick family circle. It reads:

> ELIZABETH FREEMAN, known by the name of MUMBET died Dec. 28 1829. Her supposed age was 85 years. She was born a slave and remained a slave for nearly thirty years. She could neither read nor write, yet in her own sphere she had no superior nor equal. She neither wasted time, nor property. She never violated a trust, nor failed to perform a duty. In every situation of domestic trial, she was the most efficient helper, and the tenderest friend. Good mother fare well.[20]

Mumbet is buried next to Catharine Maria Sedgwick in the family plot in Stockbridge, Massachusetts. She is the only non-Sedgwick buried in the 'Sedgwick Pie': a series of concentric circles of family headstones with Theodore and Pamela Sedgwick in the centre.[21]

The fictive bonds that define the relationship between Mumbet and the Sedgwick family are captured in a letter written in 1807 by Catharine Maria Sedgwick to her brother Frances. Catharine recounts family matters, including the well-being and activities of Mumbet. Catharine knew it would comfort Frances to know that 'Mumbet is with Eliza at present, and is very well – She has renewed this winter the exercise of her kind care towards Eben'.

Notes
1. R. S. Dunn, J. Savage and L. Yaendle (eds), *The Journal of John Winthrop, 1630–1649* (Cambridge, MA: Harvard University Press 1996), p. 246.
2. P. R. Emert, *Colonial Triangular Trade: An Economy Based on Human Misery* (Carlisle, MA: History of Compass, 1970).
3. O. Reiss, *Blacks in Colonial America* (Jefferson, NC: McFarland and Company, 1997), p. 29.
4. L. J. Greene, *The Negro in Colonial New England, 1620–1776* (New York, NY: Columbia University Press, 1942).
5. Available at http://www.masshist.org/endofslavery/index.php?id=58 [accessed 20 November 2014].
6. Greene, *The Negro in Colonial New England, 1620–1776*; G. H. Moore, *Notes on the*

History of Slavery in Massachusetts (New York, NY: D. Appleton & Co., 1866), p. 51, at http://www.masshist.org/endofslavery/index.php?id=58 [accessed 20 November 2014].
7. Available at http://www.masshist.org/endofslavery/index.php?id=55 [accessed 20 November 2014].
8. G. Nash, *The Unknown American Revolution: The Unruly Birth of Democracy and the Struggle to Create America* (New York, NY: Penguin, 2005), p. 408.
9. Approximately twenty miles south of Albany.
10. H. Felton, *Mumbet: The Story of Elizabeth Freeman* (Lincoln, NE: University of Nebraska Press, 1970), p. 12.
11. Available at http://www.masshist.org/database/viewer.php?old=1&item_id=587 [accessed 20 November 2014].
12. Available at: http://www.masshist.org/endofslavery/index.php?id=54 [accessed 20 November 2014].
13. Available at http://press-pubs.uchicago.edu/founders/documents/bill_of_rightss6.html [accessed 20 November 2014].
14. T. DiCanio, 'The Quock Walker Cases (1781–3): The Abolition of Slavery and Negro Citizenship in Early Massachusetts', *The Journal of Negro History*, 53 (April 1968), pp. 12–32; Piper, Emilie; Levinson and David, *One Minute a Free Woman: Elizabeth Freeman and the Struggle for Freedom* (Salisbury, CT: Upper Housatonic Valley National Heritage Are, 2010).
15. Moore, *Notes on the History of Slavery in Massachusetts*, p. 51.
16. Nash, *The Unknown American Revolution*, p. 409.
17. C. Sedgwick, 'Slavery in New England', *Bentley's Miscellany* (London: 1853), pp. 417–24, on p. 422.
18. Felton, *Mumbet: The Story of Elizabeth Freeman*, p. 9; C. Sedgwick, *The Power of her Sympathy: The Autobiography and Journal of Catherine Maria Sedgwick*, ed. M. Kelley (Boston, MA: Massachusetts Historical Society and Northereastern University Press, 1993), p. 70.
19. Nash, *The Unknown American Revolution*, p. 409.
20. Available at http://www.masshist.org/database/viewer.php?item_id=547&pid=15 [accessed 20 November 2014].
21. Available at http://www.masshist.org/database/viewer.php?item_id=547&pid=15 [accessed 20 November 2014].

Catherine Sedgwick to Frances Sedgwick (1807) on Elizabeth Freeman – 'Mumbet'

Stockbridge 25 Dec 1807

Dear Sister

Notwishstanding all my natural languor & ernestness, which is now very much encreased by a cold & fever I have deemed it my duty to delay no longer answering your last and very excellent letter on Friday the 18th in the evening Eliza again became the joyful Mother of a living child, and the light first beamed on Miss Frances Susan Pomeroy - the lady You know of course possesses great talents and great virtues both natural and acquired, but as my skill in the nature of babies is not very profound, You will expect from me neither a picture of her personal charms nor a delineation of her moral qualities – The mother is to all seeming perfectly well – The child weighed when a day & a half old about 7 lb with its cloathes on. I believe my dear sister that Harry has told you as much about the youthful stranger as there is to tell; often exhausting the only subject by expatiating on which I should hope to communicate much pleasure he has resigned to me a worn out pen a dry inkstand, and finally a forlorn hope – Little Ebb is by my side, and spares no pains in dictating everything, that in his opinion will amuse you – Notwithstanding the fertility of his inventions, does not at all accellerate my progress in my letter and I fear his / most "polished efforts" committed to paper would lose half their beauty where they of necessity lose the varied and soft tones of his voice, and the concomitant lustre and sweetness, that emanates from ~~the~~ beautiful eyes – I should be solitary indeed without this little charmer, who is very often my only companion, and I may wish must add, my only solace for many long hours secluded & alone in this eastroom, this very place which has so often seemed the favorite resort of "mirth and youthful jollity" is now during a great part of the day almost deserted, Eben and myself being the sole occupants – I frequently, perhaps too frequently review the scenes ~~that have~~ through which we have passed in this home, endeared by a thousand ties of love and gratitude – Here we have mutually shared the approving smiles and caresses of the fondest parents, the tenderest affections of the best Brothers; and here, my beloved Frances, my dearest Sister, have we together shared every opinion, every thought, everything that elevated us with joy, or depressed us with sorrow. But now separated, and afflicted, all all scenes fled — Do not my Sister misunderstand me, I should be ungrateful beyond measure if although robbed of some blessings, I did not feel ~~the~~ pleasure from the possessions of others — Your letters since they are all that I can now have of you, are inestimable to me – You my dear Frances are the only person from whom I have received a single line since my return – I have sometime <u>hoped</u> that as Susan knew how much a letter from her would gladden my heart, she would make an effort to gratify me – Her friends in / New York are very numerous, and probably occupy all her attentions, as all my solicitations through the medium of your letters have as yet been ineffectual – I should once more regret them, but I fear vainly — Papa has not yet returned from Northampton – He was very well when we heard from him — He found a great deal more business, and more troublesome than he expected, so that he will probably be detained there nearly all next week – Eliza has so far been remarkably well – It is exactly one week this evening since she was confined. She has not yet seen your letter, but has most affectionately enquired after you. We often together think of you, and I <u>always</u> my dear frances think {tear} Charles is very well and begs to be affectionately remembered to you and Mr Watson – Mumbet is with Eliza at present, and is very well – She has renewed this winter the exercise of her kind care towards Eben –

I beg my dear Frances that you will remember me affectionately to my Brother – Kiss the children for me – I have absolutely promised Eliza to go and see her this afternoon, and I shall therefore spare you with a shorter letter than usual – my love to Matilda –

Believe me my dear Frances most aff[ectionat]ely yours CMS –
Eben has kindly shaded my letters, with his blots —

DIOCESE OF EXETER VISITATION RECORDS, STOCKLEY POMEROY (1744)

Diocese of Exeter Visitation Records, Stockley Pomeroy (1744), Exeter Record Office, Devonshire, Chanter 225a.

In the eighteenth century, the Church of England made regular enquiries into the state of affairs in each individual parish (see also 'Religious Diversity'). The bishop would send pre-printed questionnaires to the parish priests, who would complete the form and then return it to the bishop, or travel to a nearby parish to answer the questions. The answers were then bound and kept in the diocesan archives. This particular example from Stockley Pomeroy, a Devonshire village, shows the reach of non-parochial charitable and poor relief efforts. While the Established Church administered poor relief – such as rent or food assistance – various charitable and religious societies established alms houses and provided for education of poor children. By the latter half of the eighteenth century, friendly, volunteering and charitable organizations were heavily involved in social reforms throughout the country. Though an older tradition, they expanded as population growth and industrialization stretched the limits of parish poor relief. These societies worked to alleviate poverty by funding medical care or education, or to form friendly societies that would provide support for their members.[1] Their presence in a parish would have mattered to the local Anglican minister, who was involved with parish poor relief, and the bishop who would have been interested in the resources within his diocese.

Notes
1. E. K. Wallace, 'The Needs of Strangers: Friendly Societies and Insurance Societies in Late Eighteenth-Century England', *Eighteenth-Century Life*, 24:3 (2000), pp. 53–72.

Diocese of Exeter Visitation Records, Stockley Pomeroy (1744)

To the *Minister* of the *Parish* of Stockley Pomeroy in the *Deanry* of Cadbury.

Good Brother,

In order to obtain a proper Knowledge of the present State of my Diocese, which, I am sensible, I cannot have without the Assistance of my Reverend Brethren, I have sent you the following Queries, with vacant spaces left for you to insert your Answers as you can. I desire that this Paper, with the Answers inserted, may be return'd, sign'd by yourself, at my approaching Primary Visitation, and may be deliver'd either to the Register, or to my Secretary. And because it is possible that some Man's Answer in this Matter may be construed an Accusation of himself, I promise that no such Answer shall be used as Evidence against any Person subscribing.

I heartily recommend both yourself, and your Labours in the Church of GOD, to the Divine Favour and Blessing, and am,

Reverend Sir,
Your very affectionate Brother
Queen's-Square, *near* N. EXON.[1]
The Park, Westminster,
May 15, 1744.

I. What Number of Families have you in your Parish? Of these how many are Dissenters? And of what Sort or Denomination are they? Is there any licenced or other Meeting-House of Dissenters in your Parish? Who teaches in such Meeting-House?

Answ. We have about forty families in our parish, & only one dissenter of the Presbytarian Persuasion who behaves quietly & peaceably. we have no meeting <house> in our Parish.

II. Is there any Publick or Charity School, endowed or otherwise maintain'd, in your Parish? What Number of Children are taught in it? And what Care is taken to instruct them in the Principles of the Christian Religion, according to the Doctrine of the Church of *England*, and to bring them duly to Church, as the Canon requires?

Answ. We have no Publick, or Charity School endowed: But we have an old Master who teaches Children to read, & write at so much per week – by whose means, & the assistance of their Parents, & Masters the Children are well instructed in the Church Catechism according to the Doctrine of the Church of England & are brought to Church Sundays & holid[ays.]

III. Is there in your Parish any Alms-house, Hospital, or other charitable Endowment? Have any Lands or Tenements been left for the Repair of your Church, or other pious Use? Who has the Direction of such Benefactions? Do you know or have you heard of any Abuses or Frauds committed in the Management of them?

Answ. We have an Alms-houes in our parish but not Endowed. We have no Lands or Tenem[ents] left for the repair of our Church, or other pious use: But we have seventy pounds in money given by divers Persons for [the] use of the poor, who have the in{obscured by binding} yearly viz such as have no pay of the par[ish] it list in several farmers hands on Sing{obscured by binding} have heard of no Abuses hitherto in ye Manage[ment]

IV. Do you reside personally upon your Cure, and in your Parsonage House? If not, where do you reside? And what is the Reason of your Non-Residence?

Answ. I reside Personally upon my Cure, & in my Parsonage house.

V. Have you a residing Curate? What is his Name? Is he duly qualified according to the Canons in that Behalf? Does he live in your Parsonage-House? What allowance do you make him?

Answ. I have no Curate.

VI. Do you perform Divine Service at any Church besides your own?

Answ. No, unless to assist A sick, or absent friend in his necessity.

VII. On what Days is Divine Service perform'd in your Church? If not twice every Lord's-Day, with a Sermon in the Morning, for what Reason?

Answ. We have prayers, & A Sermon every Sunday twice A day: And prayers every holiday, & A Sermon on such days as require it.

VIII. How often in the Year is the Holy Sacraments of the Lord's Supper administered in your Church?

Answ. At least six times every year.

May it please y[ou]r Lordship/

Having here [a] vacant space, I thought it proper, & my duty humbly to re{obscured} unto y[ou]r Lordship that two timber trees growing upon the h{obscured} [t]hat fences the Church-yard were lately cutt down by a farmer {obscured words} since dead, & appropriated to his own use. The farmers cla{obscured} tree w[hi]ch grow upon that part of the hedge w[hi]ch each of {obscured} obleidg'd to repair, but by what right I know not neither am {obscured}lily to consult that matter with them, but I thought it {obscured} pilily to represent ye matter to y[ou]r Lordship least any detriment {obscured words} accrew to my Successor. My Plow is in y[ou]r Lor[d's] Gift.

IX. How many Communicates are there in your Parish? How many of them usually receive? In particular, How many were there, or whereabouts might be the Number of them who Communicated at *Easter* last past?

Answ. Ours is but A smal parish so that the greatest Number that I ever had of Communicants at once never reach'd forty. There were above thirty last Easter who receiv'd the Sacrament: But (except on the great festivals) I have not much above half the number.

X. At what particular Times, and how often, are the children catechiz'd in your Church? Do your Parishioners send their Children and Servants who have not learn'd their Catechism to be instructed by you.

Answ. Every Sunday for about A quarter of the year successively in the beginning of the long days in Spring & Summer. And at proper intervals during the whole year the Parishioners send their Children, & Servants duely to be instructed by me.

XI. Have you any Chapels within your Parish? What are the Names of them, how far are they distant from the Parish Church, and by whom are they serv'd? Have you any Chapel in Ruins, in which no Divine Service is perform'd?

Answ. We have no Chapel within our Parish. May it please y[ou]r Lordship/ this is A true answer unto y[ou]r Lordships Queries according to ye best of my Present knowledge. witness my hand.

Rich[ar]d Foot Minister[2]

It would be, at this Time, a further Satisfaction to me, if you would write down for me upon this Paper, the Dates of your Institution (or Collation) *and Priest's Orders, after the Manner of the* Specimen *herunto added.*

Specimen.

'Chagford R. – JOSHUA HAYTER, A.B. *inst.* Sept. 29. 1742. *Presb.* Sept. 19. 1742. Tho. Oxon.'

Stockley-Pomeroy R. – Richard Foot A.M. Coll:Decem[ber] 6 1737. Presb: May 27th 1711. Offspring Exon.

HASELBURY-PLUCKNETT, SOMERSET, SETTLEMENT AND REMOVAL PAPERS (1723–1801)

Haselbury-Plucknett, Somerset, Settlement and Removal Papers (1723–1801), FHL Brit film 1596989, citing Somerset Archives and Local Studies D/P/ha.pl/13/3.

This selection of removal and settlement papers from Haselbury-Plucknett (see also 'Religious Diversity') highlights the connection between familial poverty and the bureaucratic state. The examinations and removals show poor families and individuals being asked to provide employment histories, give an account of their birth and parentage, and assert the validity of their marriages. While anyone who applied for relief might be subjected to questions about their familial and employment past, it was more common for widows with children or single people in search of employment to be examined. Additionally, the records reference the practice of apprenticing poor children with parish poor relief funds (see also 'St Katherine Cree').

Examinations were exceptional records – most people who resided in a parish for many years and with whom the overseers or churchwardens were acquainted would have received relief without having to establish their settlement in the parish. Therefore, many of these documents represent the most marginalized and isolated members of a parish. For many poor families, the majority of whom never had examination or removal records produced, they relied upon each other, some assistance from the parish and support from neighbours and friends.[1]

Notes
1. S. Hindle, *On the Parish? The Micro-Politics of Poor Relief in Rural England c. 1550–1750* (Oxford: Oxford University Press, 2004).

Haselbury-Plucknett, Somerset, Settlement and Removal Papers (1723–1801)

Somersett [to wi]tt

To the Churchwardens & Overseers of the poor of the p[ar]ish of Haselbury plucknett in the S[ai]d County to Convey and to the Churchwardens & Overseers of the poor of the p[ar]ish of Halstock in the County of Dorsett and to every & either of them to receive & obey THESE

WHEREAS upon the Comp. of the Churchwardens & Overseers of the poor of the p[ar]ish of Haselbury plucknett afores[ai]d unto us whose Names and Seales are hereunto Sett two of his Ma[jes]ties Justices of the peace for the s[ai]d County of Somersett (and one of the Quorum) that Sarah Guppy wid[ow] Hannah[,] Jane & Joanna her three Children came lately to dwell in the parish of Haselbury plucknett by virtue of a Legal Certificate mid^l the hands and Seales of the Churchwardens & overseers of the poor of the s[ai]d p[ar]ish of Halstock well Attested & allowed as the Law directs & are Now becomes Chargeable to the s[ai]d p[ar]ish of Haselbury plucknett Wee upon Examination of the premises do find & adjudg the same to be true and do also adjudg that the last place of their Legall Settlem[en]t is at the p[ar]ish of Halstock afores[ai]d These are therefore in his Ma[jes]ties Name to require you the Churchwardens & Overseers of the poor of the p[ar]ish of Haselbury plucknett afores[ai]d to Convey the Sayd Sarah Guppy Hannah Jane and Joanna her three Children from the s[ai]d p[ar]ish of Haselbury plucknett to the s[ai]d p[ar]ish of Halstock & them there to deliver to the Churchwardens & overseers of the poor of the p[ar]ish of Halstock afores[ai]d or to one of them with a true Coppy of this s[ai]d ord[e]r Showing the originall who are hereby required to receive & provide for them the s[ai]d Sarah Guppy Hannah Jane & Joanna her three Children as Inhabitants of their s[ai]d p[ar]ish of Halstock untill Such time as they Shall be from there discharged by due Course of Law given und[e]r o[u]r hands & Seales this 21th day of August Anno Dom[ini] 1723

    Philip Sydenham
    [seal]
    W[illiam] Harfin

[seal]
/
Somersett

To the Churchwardens and Overseers of the poor of the parish of Haselbury Plucknett in the s[ai]d CountyThese.

We whose hands and Seals are hereunto subscribed and sett Churchwardens and Overseers of the poor of the Parish of Crewkern in the said County of Somerset do hereby in Pursuaded of the late Act of Parliament in that behalf made Certifie [un]der law own and acknowledge that John Phelps who is gone from our said Parish of Crewkern, to your said Parish Haselbury Plucknett, is an Inhabitant legally settled in our said Parish of Crewkern and shall be received back again as such whensoever he shall become chargeable to your said Parish of Haselbury Plucknett; An witness whereof we have hereunto put our hands and seals this twenty six day of October Annoq[ue] Dom[ini] 1723

Signed sealed certified and   Witt Bryne[seal]Church-
acknowledged in the Presence   Will[ia]m Paul [seal]wardens
of us
W[illia]m Rowe   Eliz[abeth] Speed [seal]
Hon J[ame]s Pemny   Mary Morefield [seal]
[seal] Overseers of the poor

We whose hands are hereunto subscribed two of his Ma[jes]ties Justices of the Peace for the said County of Somersett (Quorum mem[ber]) do allow and approve of the above written Certificate Witness our hands the 26th day of October anno Dom[ini] 1723

W[illia]m Pitt
Geo[rge] Speks
/

To the Church Wardens and overseers of the poor of the parish of HassleburyPluckett in the County of Somersett afores[ai]d

Somersett (to witt) we whose names and Seals are hereunto Sett being the said churchwardens and overseers of the poor of the Parish of merriott in the Said County (do according to the direction of the statute in Such case made and provided) hereby certifye unto you the officers of HassleburyPlucknett aforesaid That wee do own and acknowledge Charles Patten to be am Inhabitant and parishioner Legally settled within our said Parish of Merriott dated the twenty third day of September 1738

Sealed and delivered in presence of
Joseph Patten   Robert Beck [seal]
William Phelps   The Mark of
23rd of September 1738 Mattew + Rendel [seal]

allowed by in H. Palmer
John Robbard

Wee his Majesty's Justices of the Peace who allowed of the above Certificate do also certifye that Joseph Patten - one of the witness who attested the Execution of the Said Certificate hath made with before and these he did see the Church warden and overseer whose names and Seales where the said Certificate Subscribed and Sett severally signs and Seals the said Certificate And that the names of the said Joseph Patten and William Phelps - whose names are above subscribed as witnesses to the Execution of the s[ai]d certificate are of then own proper hath writeing sealed the twenty third - day of September 1738

H. Palmer
John Robbard
/
Somerset To wit

To the Churchwardens and Overseers of the Poor of the Parish of Haselbury Plucknet in the County of Somerset. These.

To that Churchwardens & Overseers of the Poor of the Parish of Crewkern in the County of Somerset whose Names are Hereunto subscribed

Do prove out to the Late Acts of Parliament in that behalf made Hereby Certify Declare Own & Acknowledge that John Wills Son of John Wills deceased who is Lately bound apprentice to Thomas Gange of the Parish of Haselbury Plucknet for an Inhabitant Legally settled in the Parish of Crewkern and shall be Received and taken back as Such Whensoever he shall be any ways Burthensom or Chargeable to the Said Parish of Haselbury Such his apprenticeship to the Contrary Notwithstanding. In Witness Whereof We have hereunto set our Hands Seals this Twentieth Day of June in the Eighteenth year of the Reign of our Sovereign Lord George the Second and in the year of our Lord 1744

Signed Sealed Delivered
in the Presence of his —
Sam[ue]l Roper
Hon[erable] Henry Roper
Edward Smith[seal]Churchwardens
William Cobbson[seal]
Robert Hillard[seal]Overseers
Sam[ue]l Palmer[seal]

We whose Names are Hereunto Subscribed Two of his Majesties Justices of the Peace for the Said County (One whereof is of the Quorum) Do allow approves of the above written Certificate Witness our Hands the Day & year Abovewritten
Per Poalett

James James Manstod
/
Somerset (to wit)

The Examination of Ann Butcher of Haselbury Plucknett in the said County widow Taken the 5th day of August 1755.

Who upon her Oath saith that upwards of thirty years ago she was lawfully married to Henry Butcher her late Husband deceased was then lived at North Perrott in the s[ai]d County, and saith she does not recollect ever to have heard her husband say any thing relating to his settlement but knows his Parents resided in North Perrott afores[ai]d, and never heard her Husband was a parishioner elsewhere and saith she had a Son (by her said Husband) & born in the said parish of North Perrott near thirty years since (christened Henry) and when her said son was about four or five years old, her Husband went to Sea and therefore took her son and removed into the Parrish of Haselbury Plucknett aforesaid, and her son was there hired by one Hackwell to quill for him far three pence a week wages, and continued in his service for the space of one year and upward, but might have left the s[ai]d Hackwell's service at the end of any week and after he left the service of the s[ai]d Hackwell he entered into the service of one John Body of North Perrot aforesaid Broadweaver and continued therein till he attained the age of twenty one years at weeks wages and during the whole time he return'd nightly and lodged in this Examinants house a Hassellbury Plucknett afores[ai]d, but five years of the time he so served the said John Body were by and under a written agreement between him and his master whereby he engaged to serve the s[ai]d John Body the term of five years after the rate of Certain sums agreed on to be weekly wages but at all that time lodged every night at Haselbury Plucknett as aforesaid and this Examinant further saith that her said son at the Age of twenty years enlisted into his Majestys Service as a soldier and whether he hath since done anything to gain a settlement she knew not.

Sworn before
H: Robbard   The mark of the
J:s Uttermares   s[ai]d Ann Butcher
a true Copy+
/

I hear/have perused ye Examination of Ann Bucher relating to ye Letter of her Son, & I think that if the fact can be proved that he [illeg.] Served Mrs. Body of Parrot under Such agreement as she has set forth in her Examination, & during ye time of Such Service that he lodged with her at Haslebury, that Such Service at Parrot, Lodging at Haslebury, will gain him a Letter at Haslebury, but as this Point is at a clear one, and as the agreement in writing Lehson Body & ye Son when produced may alter the case, & as the proof of a Settlement at Haslebury is intirely incumbe[n]t on ye Parish of Ilmister, and as ye Expence of an appeal will be very inconsiderable (& Parish of Haslebury having to witness it) I sho[ul]d advise them to run ye Hazard of an appeal to the order of Removal, as their Chance of Success (all ye Circumstances of this case considered) will be far from a bad one

Rich[ar]d Brodrepp
24^(th)Sep[tembe]r 1755.
/
[seal]
Somerset (to wit)

To the Churchwardens and Others, the Overseers of the Poor of the Parish of Haselbury Plucknett *in the* said County *to Convey: And to the Churchwardens and Overseers of the Poor of the Parish of* Malmsbury in the County of Wilts[hire] *to Receive and Obey These*

WHEREAS Complaint hath been made, by you the Churchwardens and Overseers of the Poor of the Parish of Haselbury Plucknett aforesaid, unto Us whose Hands and Seals are hereunto set Two of his Majesty's Justices of the Peace, in and for the county of Somerset aforesaid, that Mary Adams Single-woman lately intruded herself into your said Parish of Haselbury - Plucknett there to inhabit as a Parishoner contrary to the Laws relating to the Settlement of the Poor, and is likely to - become chargeable to your said Parish of Haselbury Plucknett WE, therefore upon due Examination and Enquiry made into the Premises aforesaid, upon Oath do find and adjudge the same to be true, and we do also adjudge that the last Place of the legal Settlement of her the said Mary Adams was and is in the Parish of Malmsbury aforesaid. These are therefore in his Majesty's Name, to order and require you the Churchwardens and Overseers of the Poor of the Parish of Haselbury Plucknett aforesaid, that you, some, or one of you, do forthwith Remove and Convey her the said Mary Adams from your said Parish of Haselbury Plucknett to the Parish of Malmsbury aforesaid, and her deliver to the Churchwardens and Overseers of the Poor, or some, or one of them there, together with this our Order, or a true Copy thereof. And you the Churchwardens and Overseers of the Poor of the Parish of Malmsbury aforesaid, are likewise hereby required in his Majesty's Name to receive and provide for her the said Mary Adams as an Inhabitant of your said Parish of Malmsbury untill from thence she shall be discharged by due course of Law. Given under our Hands and Seals the Thirteenth Day of September in the fifth Year of the Reign of our Sovereign Lord George the Third by the Grace of God, of *Great-Britain, France* and *Ireland*, King, Defender of the Faith, and so forth, and in the Year of our Lord One Thousand, Seven Hundred and Sixty five

[seal]
Westmorland
[seal]

T[h]o[mas] Phelips
/
Somerset (to wit)

To the Churchwardens and Others, the Overseers of the Poor of the Parish of Hasselbury Plucknett in the said County to Convey: And to the Churchwardens and Overseers of the Poor of the Parish of Middle Chinnock in the same County to Receive and Obey These.

WHEREAS Complaint has been made, by you the Churchwardens and Overseers of the Poor of the Parish of Hasselbury - aforesaid, unto Us whose Hands and Seals are hereunto set, two of his Majesty's Justices of the Peace, in and for the County aforesaid, (one of Us of the *Quorum*,) that Elizabeth Harvey Singlewoman lately intruded herself into your said Parish of Hasselbury there to Inhabit as Parishioner, contrary to the Laws relating to the Settlement of the Poor, and is likely to - become Chargeable to your said Parish of Hasselbury Plucknett WE therefore upon due Examination and Enquiry made into the Premises aforesaid, upon Oath do find and adjudge the same to be true, and we do also adjudge that the last Place of the legal Settlement of her the said Elizabeth Harvey was and is in the Parish of middle Chinnock aforesaid. THESE are therefore in his Majesty's Name to Order and Require you the Churchwardens and Overseers of the Poor of the Parish of Hasselbury Plucknett aforesaid, that you, some, or one of, you, do forthwith Remove and Convey her the said Elizabeth Harvey from your said Parish of Hasselbury Plucknett to the Parish of Middle Chinnock aforesaid, and her deliver to the Churchwarden and Overseers of the Poor, or some, or one of them there, together with this our Order, or a true Copy thereof. And you the Churchwardens and Overseers of the Poor of the Parish of Middle Chinnock aforesaid, are likewise hereby Required in his Majesty's Name to Receive and Provide for her the said Elizabeth Harvey as an Inhabitant of your said Parish of Middle Chinnock until from thence she shall be discharged by due Course of Law. Given under our Hands and Seals the 19th Day of June in the 16th Year of the Reign of our Sovereign Lord George the 3rd by the Grace of God of *Great Britain, France,* and *Ireland,* King, Defender of the Faith, and so forth, and in the Year of our Lord One Thousand, Seven Hundred, and ~~Sixty~~ Seventy Six.

[seal]
I Philips
[seal]
T Thyrdford
/
County of Somerset (to wit)}

To the Churchwardens and Overseer of the Poor of the Parish of Wincanton in the said County of Somerset to execute and convey.

And to the Churchwarden and Overseer of the Poor of the Parish of Hasselbury Plucknett in the said County to receive and obey -

FORASMUCH as Complaint hath been made unto us whose hands and Seals are hereunto Subscribed and not two of his Majesty's Justices of the Peace of and for the said County of Somerset (whereof one is of the Quorum) by you the Churchwardens and Overseers of the Poor of the said Parish of Wincanton in the said County of Somerset That Elizabeth Brown Spinster lately cause and intruded into the said Parish endeavouring there to settle as an Inhabitant thereof contrary to Law and having any way acquired or obtained any legal Settlement therein and being likely to become chargeable there{smudge} We do upon due Examination adjudge the said Complaint and Premises to be true; And we do farther upon the Examination of the said Elizabeth Brown taken upon her Oath adjudge that the said Elizabeth Brown was last legally settled in the said Parish of Haselbury Plucknett in the County of Somerset aforesaid -

THESE are therefore in his Majesty's Name to require order and command you the said Churchwardens and Overseers of the Poor of the Parish of Wincanton or some or one of you forthwith to remove and convey the said Elizabeth Brown from the said Parish of Wincanton unto the Parish of Haselbury Plucknett aforesaid and her to de{smudge} to the Churchwardens and Overseers of the Poor there or to some or one of them (together with this Order or Duplicate or a true Copy hereof) who is and are hereby required to receive and provide for her as the Law directs And how of you are not to fail. Given under our Hands and Seals the Thirty first day of March in the Twenty fifth Year of the Reign of our Sovereign Lord George the Third King of Great Britain and so forth and in the Year of our Lord One Thousand Seven Hundred and Eighty five

JA Melliar [seal]

Sam[ue]l Ordington[seal]

/

Somerset County

To the Churchwardens and others, the Overseers of the Poor of the Parish of Pendormer-in the said county of Somerset to convey; and to the Churchwardens and Overseers of the Poor of the Parish of Hasselbury Plucknett in the said county to receive and obey. These.

WHEREAS Complaint has been made by you the Churchwardens and Overseers of the Poor of the Parish of Pendormer-aforesaid unto us, whose Hands and Seals are hereunto set, two of his Majesty's Justices of the Peace in and for the county aforesaid (one of us of the Quorum), that Elizabeth Mullins Widow lately intruded herself into your said Parish of Pendormer there to inhabit as a Parishioner contrary to the Laws relating to the Settlement of the Poor, and is become chargeable to your said Parish of Pendormer - WE therefore, upon due Examination and Enquiry made into the Premises aforesaid, upon oath do {ink stain} adjudge the same to be true, and we do also adjudge, that {ink stain} Place of the legal Settlement of her the said Elizabeth Mullins was and is in the Parish of Hasselbury Plucknett aforesaid. THESE are herefore, in his Majesty's Name, to order and require you the Churchwardens and Overseers of the Poor of the Parish of Pendormer aforesaid, or some or one of you, forthwith to remove and convey her the said Elizabeth Mullins from your said Parish of Pendormer to the Parish of Hasslelbury Plucknett aforesaid, and her deliver to the Churchwardens and Overseers of the Poor, or some or one of them, there, together with this our Order, or a true Copy thereof. And you the Churchwardens and Overseers of the Poor of the Parish of Hassellbury Plucknett aforesaid, are likewise hereby required, in his Majesty's Name, to receive and provide for her the said Elizabeth Mullins as Inhabitant of your said Parish of Haselbury Plucknett-until from thence She shall be discharged by due Course of Law. GIVEN under our Hands and Seals the thirty first Day of December in the 25th Year of the Reign of our Sovereign Lord George the Third by the Grace of God of Great Britain, France, and Ireland, King, Defender of the Faith, and so forth, and in the Year of our Lord

One Thousand, Seven Hundred, and Ninety four

Pd. Phelips[seal]

W[ilia]m Phelips[seal]

TAUNTON: Printed and Sold by T. NORRIS

/

Somerset, (to wit.)

To the Churchwardens and others, the Overseers of the Poor of the Parish of Hasselbury Plucknett in the said county of Somerset to convey; and to the Churchwardens and Overseers of the Poor of the Parish of Wincanton in the said County to receive and obey. These.

WHEREAS Complaint has been made by you the Churchwardens and Overseers of the Poor of the Parish of Hasselbury Plucknett aforesaid, unto us, whose Hands and Seals are hereunto set, two of his Majesty's Justices of the Peace in and for the county aforesaid (one of us of the Quorum) that Elizabeth Parsons lately intruded herself into your said Parish of Hasselbury Plucknett - there to inhabit as a Parishioner contrary to the Laws relating to the Settlement of the Poor, and is become chargeable to your said Parish of Hasselbury Plucknett. We, therefore, upon due Examination and Enquiry made into the Premises aforesaid, Upon said do find and adjudge the same to be true, and we do also adjudge that the last Place of the legal Settlement of her the said Elizabeth Parsons was and is the Parish of Wincanton aforesaid. THESE are therefore in his Majesty's Name, to order and require you the Churchwardens and Overseers of the Poor of the Parish of Hasselbury Plucknett aforesaid, or some or one of you, forthwith to remove and convey her the said Elizabeth Parsons from your said Parish of Hasselbury Plucknett to the Parish of Wincanton aforesaid and her deliver to the Churchwardens and Overseers of the Poor, or some one of them, there, together with this our Order, or a true Copy thereof. And you the Churchwardens and Overseers of the Poor of the Parish of Wincanton aforesaid, are likewise hereby required, in his Majesty's Name, to receive and provide for her the said Elizabeth Parsons as an Inhabitant of your said Parish of Wincanton until from thence she shall be discharged by due Course of Law. GIVEN under our Hands and Seals the 24th Day of April - in the 29th Year of the Reign of our Sovereign Lord George the Third by the Grace of God of Great Britain, France, and Ireland, King, Defender of the Faith, and so forth, and in the Year of our Lord. One Thousand, Seven Hundred, and ninety nine.

W. Philips[seal]
C. Philips[seal]
/
[seal]

STOKE ABBOTT, DORSET, BASTARDY PAPERS (1780–1820)

Stoke Abbott, Dorset, Bastardy Papers (1780–1820), Dorset History Centre, PE/STA: OV/4/2, digital images at www.ancestry.co.uk.

The time period covered by these records captures a particular moment in parish attitudes toward illegitimacy. In earlier centuries, officials attempted to discover a man's guilt or innocence, and in the nineteenth century they were more concerned with punishing mothers. In the eighteenth century, however:

> authorities were less concerned with men's innocence or guilt than in finding a man who could pay maintenance and so absolve the parish ratepayers. By the later eighteenth century, authorities were more determined to make 'fathers' pay maintenance than to punish mothers.[1]

Illegitimate children and their mothers were a constant concern to parish officials. An economic and educational system that disadvantaged women meant that unmarried women with children were always financially vulnerable. The women and children that appear in these examples are a small sample of children conceived or born outside of marriage. Most parents married before, or shortly after the birth of a first child.[2] Though how local parishes recorded illegitimacy changed over time, it appears that throughout the early modern period, rates of illegitimacy never rose above 5%.[3] Those recorded here represent an extraordinary effort on the part of the parish to determine who would be liable for the child, should his or her parents be unable, or in the case of absent fathers, unwilling to support the child.

Notes
1. P. Crawford, *Parents of Poor Children in England, 1580–1800* (Oxford: Oxford University Press, 2010), p. 111.
2. P. Laslett, *Family Life and Illicit Love in Earlier Generations* (Cambridge: Cambridge University Press, 1977), pp. 128–30.
3. Crawford, *Parents of Poor Children in England, 1580–1800*, p. 31.

Stoke Abbott, Dorset, Bastardy Papers (1780–1820)

DORSET.} THE voluntary Examination of Agnes Endicott of Stoke Abbas singled Woman, taken on Oath before me T.R. Drewe one of his Majesty's Justices of the Peace in, and for the said County this 6th day of March in the Year of our LORD one thousand eight hundred and ~~one~~ nine.

Who saith That she is with Child, and that the said Child is likely to be born a Bastard, and to chargeable[1] to the said Parish of Stoke Abbas and that Thomas Gollop of Bridport in the County of Dorset Flax dresser is the Father of the said Child.

Taken and signed the day}The Mark of
And year above written,}+
Before me}Agnes Endicott
T. R. Drewe
/
Feb[ruar]y 4th 1788
Stoke Abbas
Order in Bastardy on
William Brinson ak Miller
& Martha Seal.
~~5/ not paid~~
Feb 4, 1788
[left upper corner:]
10-9-2
9-8

———
15
/
Dorset.

To wit.} The Order of Sir William Oglander Bar[one]t & Tho[ma]s Rose Drewe Esq[ui]re two of his Majesty's Justices of the Peace for the said, County of Dorset, and both residing next unto the Limits of the Parish Church of Stoke Abbas in the said County of Dorset, made the fourth Day of February 1788 concerning a female Bastard Child lately born in the said Parish of Stoke Abbas in the said County of Dorset, of the Body of Martha Seal Singlewoman

Whereas it hath appeared unto us the said Justices, as well upon the Complaint of the Churchwardens and Overseers of the Parish of Stoke Abbas aforesaid, as upon the Oath of the said Martha Seal that she the said Martha Seal on or about ~~on~~ the 22d Day of October last past, was delivered of a female Bastard Child within the said Parish of Stoke Abbas in the said County of Dorset, and that the said female Bastard Child is become chargeable to the said Parish of Stoke Abbas and likely so to continue, And that William Brinson ak Miller of Beamister in the said County has on Son of John Brinson did beget, and is the Father of the said Bastard Child.

AND whereas it hath been duly proved before us on Oath, That the said William Brinson al[ias] Miller hath been duly summoned to appear before us this Day, to the End that we might examine into the Cause and Circumstances of the Premises, and hath appeared accordingly, but hath assigned no sufficient Reason why he should not be deemed the Father of the said female Bastard Child.

WE therefore, upon Examination and Consideration of the Cause and Circumstances of the Premises, as well upon the Oath of the said Martha Seal as otherwise, do hereby adjudge the said William Brinson al[ias] Miller to be the reputed Father of the said Bastard Child,

AND thereupon we do order, as well for the better relief of the said Parish of Stoke Abbas as for the Sustenance and Relief of the said Bastard Child, that the said William Brinson al[ias] Miller shall, and do, immediately upon Notice of this our Order, pay, or cause to be paid to the Churchwardens and Overseers of the Poor of the said Parish of Stoke Abbas or to some or one of them, the Sum of One Pound and ten Shillings for and towards the lying-in of the said Martha Seal and the Maintenance of the said Bastard Child, to the time of making this our Order.

AND we do hereby also further order, that the said William Brinson al[ias] Miller shall likewise pay, or cause to be paid, to the Churchwardens and Overseers of the Poor of the said Parish of Stoke Abbas for the Time being, or to some or one of them, the Sum of One Shilling & three Pence weekly, and every Week, from the Date of this our Order, as well as for the Relief of the said Parish of Stoke Abbas as also for and towards the Keeping, Sustenance, and maintaining the said Bastard Child, for and during so long time as the said Bastard Child, shall live and be chargeable to the said Parish of Stoke Abbas.

AND we do further order, that the said Martha Seal shall also pay, or cause to be paid unto the said Churchwardens and Overseers of the Poor of the said Parish of Stoke Abbas the Sum of 9 d^2 weekly, and every Week for so long as the said Bastard Child shall live, and be chargeable to the said Parish of Stoke Abbas except such time as she the said Martha Seal shall keep, nourish and maintain the said Bastard Child with the allowance aforesaid from the said William Brinson al[ias]. Miller.

Given under our Hands and Seals the fourth Day of February in the Year of our Lord 1780

W Oglander
[Seal]
T.R. Drewe
[Seal]

/
Stoke Abbas
Orders in Bastardy on James Bird and Ann Kerslake
Oct[obe]r 17th 1791 James Bird was served with this order by John Udal Overseer
/
Dorset.

To wit.} The Order of Tho[ma]s Rose Drewe Esq[ui]r[e] Henry Sherive Dr of Laws two of his Majesty's Justices of the Peace for the said County of Dorset, and both residing next unto the Limits of the Parish Church of Stoke Abbas in the said County of Dorset, made the fifth Day of September 1791 concerning a male Bastard Child lately born in the said Parish of Stoke Abbas in the said County of Dorset, of the Body of Ann Kerslake Single Woman.

Whereas it hath appeared unto us the said Justices, as well upon the Complaint of the Churchwardens and Overseers <of the Poor> of the Parish of Stoke Abbas aforesaid, as upon the Oath of the said Ann Kerslake that she the said Ann Kerslake on the 11th Day of June now last past, was delivered of a male Bastard Child within the said Parish Stoke Abbas in the said County of Dorset, and that the said male Bastard Child is become chargeable to the said Parish of Stoke Abbas and likely so to continue, And that James Bird of Beamister in s[ai]d County Victualler did beget, and is the Father of the Said Bastard Child.

AND whereas it hath been duly proved before us on Oath, That the said James Bird hath been duly summoned to appear before us this Day, to the End that we might examine into the Cause and Circumstances of the Premises, aud hath appeared accordingly, but hath assigned no sufficient Reason why he should not be deemed the Father of the said male Bastard Child.

WE therefore, upon Examination and Consideration of the Cause and Circumstances of the Premises, as well upon the Oath of the said Ann Kerslake as otherwise, do hereby adjudge the said James Bird to be the reputed Father of the said Bastard Child.

AND thereupon we do order, as well for the better relief of the said Parish of Stoke Abbas as for the Sustenance and Relief of the said Bastard Child, that the said James Bird shall, and do, immediately upon Notice of this our Order, pay, or cause to be paid to the Churchwardens and Overseers of the Poor of the said Parish of Stoke Abbas or to some or one of them, the Sum of One Pound

& two Shillings for and towards the lying-in of the said Ann Kerslake and the Maintenance of the said Bastard Child, to the time of making this our Order.

AND we do hereby also further order, that the said James Bird shall likewise pay, or cause to be paid, to the Churchwardens and Overseers of the Poor of the said Parish of Stoke Abbas for the Time being, or to some or one of them, the Sum of One Shilling & six pence weekly, and every Week, from the Date of this our Order, as well as for the Relief of the said Parish of Stoke Abbas as also for and towards the Keeping, Sustenance, and maintaining the said Bastard Child, for and during so long time as the said Bastard Child, shall live and be chargeable to the said Parish of Stoke Abbas.

AND we do further order, that the said Ann Kerslake shall also pay, or cause to be paid unto the said Churchwardens and Overseers of the Poor of the said Parish of Stoke Abbas the Sum of Nine pence weekly, and every Week, for so long as the said Bastard Child shall live, and be chargeable to the said Parish of Stoke Abbas except such time as she the said Ann Kerslake shall keep, nourish and maintain the said Bastard Child with the allowance aforesaid from the said James Bird

Given under our Hands and Seals the fifth Day of Sept[embe]r in the Year of our Lord 1791

/

Bast[ard]y
Stoke Abbas
Orders on John Hann & Ann Kerslake 1798
March 27 1798
Excute this order with John Hann Benjamin Welmar Overseer

/

Dorset.}

To wit.} THE ORDER of Sir W[illia]m Oglander Bar[one]t & Jno Munden LLD two of his Majesty's Justices of the Peace for the said County of Dorset, and both residing next unto the Limits of the Parish Church of Stoke Abbas in the said County of Dorset, made the 5th Day of March 1798 concerning a male Bastard Child lately born in the said Parish of Stoke Abbott in the said County of Dorset, of the Body of Ann Kerslake Singlewoman

Whereas it hath appeared unto us the said Justices, as well upon the Complaint of the Churchwardens and Overseers of the Poor of the Parish of Stoke Abbas aforesaid, as upon the Oath of the said Ann Kerslake that she the said Ann Kerslake in ~~on~~ the Month ~~Day~~ of January 1795 ~~last past~~, was delivered of a male Bastard Child within the said Parish of Stoke Abbott in the said County of Dorset, and that the said male Bastard Child is become chargeable to the said Parish of Stoke Abbott and likly so to continue. And that John Hann of ~~Stoke Abbas~~ the same place Lab[oure]r did beget, and is the Father of the said Bastard Child,

AND whereas it hath been duly proved before us on Oath that the said John Hann hath been duly summoned to apear before us this Day to the end that we might examine into the Cause and Circumstances of the Premises, and hath appeared accordingly, but hath assigned no sufficient Reason why he should not be deemed the Father of the said male Bastard Child.

WE therefore, upon examination and consideration of the Cause and Circumstances of the Premises, as well upon the Oath of the said Ann Kerslake as otherwise do hereby adjudge the said John Hann to be the reputed Father of the said Bastard Child.

AND thereupon we do order, as well for the better relief of the said Parish of Stoke Abbas as for the Sustenance and relief of the said Bastard Child, that the said John Hann shall and do immediately upon Notice of this our Order pay or cause to be paid to the Churchwardens and Overseers of the Poor of the said Parish of Stoke Abbas or to some or one of them, the Sum of Six Pounds for and towards the lying in of the said Ann Kerslake and the Maintenance of the said Bastard Child, to the time of making this our Order.

AND we do hereby also further order that the said John Hann likewise pay, or cause to be paid to the Churchwardens and Overseers of the Poor of the said Parish Stoke Abbas for the time being, or to some or one of them, the Sum of one shilling & three pence weekly, and every Week, from the Date of this our Order, as well as for the Relief of the said Parish of Stoke Abbas as also for and towards the Keeping Sustenance and maintaining the said Bastard Child, for and during so long time as the said Bastard Child shall live and be chargeable to the said Parish of Stoke Abbas.

AND we do further order that the said Ann Kerslake shall also pay or cause to be apid unto the said Churchwardens and Overseers of the Poor of the said Parish of Stoke Abbas the Sum of Nine Pence Weekly and every Week, for so long as the said Bastard Child shall live, and be chargeable to the said Parish of Stoke Abbas except such time as she the said Ann Kerslake shall keep, nourish and maintain the said Bastard Child with the allowance aforesaid from the said John Hann

Given under our Hands and Seals the 5th Day of March in the year of our Lord 1798.

W Oglander [Seal] J. Munden [Seal]

/

Dorset.

To Wit.} THE ORDER of Tho[ma]s Rose Drewe Esq[ui]re & Henry Sherive LLD two of his Majesty's Justices of the Peace for the said County of Dorset, and both residing next unto the Limits of the Parish Church of Charmouth in the said County of Dorset, made the second Day of Sept[embe]r 1799 concerning a female Bastard Child lately born in the said Parish of Charmouth in the said County of Dorset, of the Body of Elizabeth Norman Singlewoman whilst residing there under a Suspended order of Removal from thence to Stoke Abbas in the same county and which s[ai]d order was suspended on acco[un]t of the illness of the said Elizabeth Norman

Whereas it hath appeared unto us the aid Justices, as well upon the Complaint of the Churchwardens and Overseers of the Poor of the Parish of Charmouth aforesaid, as upon the Oath of the said Elizabeth Norman that she the said Elizabeth Norman on the 11th Day of July last past, was delivered of a female Bastard Child within the said Parish of Charmouth in the said County of Dorset, and that the said female Bastard Child is likely to become chargeable to the said Parish of Stoake Abbas and ~~likely~~ so to continue. And that James Govier of Charmouth also Servant did beget, and is the Father of the said Bastard Child.

AND whereas it hath been duly proved before us on Oath that the said James Govier hath been duly summoned to apear before us this Day to the end that we might examine into the Cause and Circumstances of the Premises, and hath appeared accordingly, but hath assigned no sufficient Reason why he should not be deemed the Father of the said female Bastard Child.

WE therefore, upon examination and consideration of the Cause and Circumstances of the Premises, as well upon the Oath of the said Elizabeth Norman as otherwise do hereby adjudge the said James Govier to be the reputed Father of the said Bastard Child.

AND thereupon we do order, as well for the better relief of the said Parish of Stoke Abbas as for the Sustenance and relief of the said Bastard Child, that the said James Govier shall and do immediately upon Notice of this our Order pay or cause to be paid to the Churchwardens and Overseers of the poor of the said Parish of Stoke Abbas or to some or one of them, the Sum of twelve shillings and six pense for and towards the lying in of the said Elizabeth Norman and the Maintenance of the said Bastard Child, to the time of making this our Order.

AND we do hereby also further order that the said James Govier likewise pay, or cause to be paid to the Churchwardens and Overseers of the Poor of the said Parish of Stoke Abbas for the tine being, or to some or one of them, the Sum of one shilling & three pence weekly, and every Week, from the Date of this our Order, as well as for the Relief of the said Parish of Stoke Abbas as also for and towards the Keeping Sustenance and maintaining the said Bastard Child, for and during so long time as the said Bastard Child shall live and be chargeable to the said Parish of Stoke Abbas.

AND we do further order that the said Elizabeth Norman shall also pay or cause to be paid unto the said Churchwardens and Overseers of the Poor of the said Parish of Stoke Abbas the Sum of Nine Pence Weekly and every Week, for so long as the said Bastard Child shall live, and be chargeable to the said Parish of Stoke Abbas except such time as she the said Elizbeth Norman shall keep, nourish and maintain the said Bastard Child with the allowance aforesaid from the said James Grovier

Given under our Hands and Seals the 2 Day of Sept[embe]r in the year of our Lord 1799

T.R. Drewe [Seal] H. Sherive [Seal]

/

Dorset.

TO WIT.} THE ORDER of Francis John Browne Esquire & John Munden L.L.D. two of his Majesty's Justices of the Peace for the said County of Dorset, and both residing next unto the Limits of the Parish Church of Stoke Abbas in the said County of Dorset, made the fourth Day of May concerning a female Bastard Child lately born in the said Parish of Stoke Abbas in the said County of Dorset, of the Body of Mary Pearce

Whereas it hath appeared unto us the said Justices, as well upon the Complaint of the Churchwardens and Overseers of the Poor of the Parish of Stoke Abbas aforesaid as upon the Oath of the said Mary Pearce, that she the said Mary Pearce on the thirteenth Day of April last past, was delivered of a female Bastard Child within the said Parish of Stoke Abbas in the said County of Dorset and that the said female Bastard Child is become chargeable to the said Parish of Stoke Abbas and likely so to continue. And that John Hann of Stoke Abbas aforesaid Weaver did begat, and is the Father of the said Bastard Child.

And whereas it hath been duly proved before us on Oath that the said John Hann hath been duly summoned to appear before us this Day to the end that we might examine into the Cause and Circumstances of the Premises, and hath appeared accordingly, but hath assigned no sufficient Reason why he should not be deemed the Father of the said female Bastard Child.

WE therefore, upon examination and consideration of the Cause and Circumstances of the Premises, as well upon the Oath of the said Mary Pearce as otherwise do hereby adjudge the said John Hann to be the reputed Father of the said Bastard Child. And thereupon we do order, as well for the better Relief of the said Parish of Stoke Abbas as for the Sustenance and Relief of the said Bastard Child, that the said John Hann shall and do immediately upon Notice of this our Order pay or cause to be paid to the Churchwardens and Overseers of the Poor of the said Parish of Stoke Abbas or to some or one of them, the Sum of One Pound for and towards the lying in of the said Mary Pearce and the Maintenance of the said Bastard Child, to the time of making this our Order.

AND we do hereby also further order that the said John Hann likewise pay, or cause to be paid to the Churchwardens and Overseers of the Poor of the said Parish of Stoke Abbas for the time being, or to some or one of them, the Sum of One Shilling & Eight Pence weekly, and every week, from the Date of this our Order, as well as for the Relief of the said Parish of Stoke Abbas as also for and towards the Keeping Sustenance and maintaining the said Bastard Child, for and during so long time as the said Bastard Child shall live and be chargeable to the said Parish of Stoke Abbas

AND we do further order that the said Mary Pearce shall also pay or cause to be paid unto the said Churchwardens and Overseers of the Poor of the said Parish of Stoke Abbas the Sum of Ten Pence Weekly and every Week, for so long as the said Bastard Child shall live, and be Chargeable to the said Parish of Stoke Abbas except such time as she the said Mary Pearce shall keep, nourish and maintain the said Bastard Child with the allowance aforesaid from the said John Hann

Given under our Hands and Seals the fourth Day of May in the Year of our Lord 1807

F.J. Browne [Seal]
J Munden [Seal]
/
4th May 1807
Stoke Abbas
John Hann }
&Bastardy
Mary Pearce}
Orders
/
Aug[us]t 1809
Stoke Abbas
Endicott}
and }
Gollop}
Orders in Bastardy
1809 Sep[tembe]r 16th Sarve'd Thomas Gollop with Coppiy of This Order: by Geo[rge] Payne Overseer
/

Dorset.

TO WIT.} THE ORDER of Thomas Rose Drewe Clerk & John Munden L.L.D. two of his Majesty's Justices of the Peace for the said County of Dorset, and both residing next unto the Limits of the Parish Church of Stoke Abbas in the said County of Dorset, made the seventh Day of August 1809 concerning a female Bastard Child lately born in the said Parish of Stoke Abbas in the said County of Dorset, of the Body of Agnes Endicott singlewoman

Whereas it hath appeared unto us the said Justices, as well upon the Complaint of the Churchwardens and Overseers of the Poor of the Parish of Stoke Abbas aforesaid as upon the Oath of the said Agnes Endicott, that she the said Agnes Endicott on the seventh Day of May last past, was delivered of a female Bastard Child within the said Parish of Stoke Abbas in the said County of Dorset, and that the said female Bastard Child is become chargeable to the said Parish of Stoke Abbas and likely so to continue. And that Thomas Gollop of Stoke Abbas of Bridport in s[ai]d County Flaxdresser did beget, and is the Father of the said Bastard Child.

And whereas it hath been duly proved before us on Oath that the said Thomas Gollop hath been duly summoned to appear before us this Day to the end that we might examine into the Cause and Circumstances of the Premises, and hath appeared accordingly, but hath assigned no sufficient Reason why he should not be deemed the Father of the said female Bastard Child.

WE therefore, upon examination and consideration of the Cause and Circumstances of the Premises, as well upon the Oath of the said Agnes Endicott as otherwise do hereby adjudge the said Thomas Gollop to be the reputed Father of the said Bastard Child.

And thereupon we do order, as well for the better Relief of the said Parish of Stoke Abbas as for the Sustenance and Relief of the said Bastard Child, that the said Thomas Gollop shall and do immediately upon Notice of this our Order pay or cause to be paid to the Churchwardens and Overseers of the Poor of the said Parish of Stoke Abbas or to some or one of them, the Sum of one Pound and Thirteen Shillings for and towards the lying in of the said Agnes Endicott and the Maintenance of the said Bastard Child, to the time of making this our Order.

AND we do hereby also further order that the said Thomas Gollop likewise pay, or cause to be paid to the Churchwardens and Overseers of the Poor of the said Parish of Stoke Abbas for the time being, or to some or one of them, the Sum of Two Shillings weekly, and every week, from the Date of this our Order, as well as for the Relief of the said Parish of Stoke Abbas as also for and towards the Keeping Sustenance and maintaining the said Bastard Child, for and during so long time as the said Bastard Child shall live and be chargeable to the said Parish of Stoke Abbas

AND we do further order that the said Agnes Endicott shall also pay or cause to be paid unto the said Churchwardens and Overseers of the Poor of the said Parish of Stoke Abbas the Sum of one shilling Weekly and every Week, for so long as the said Bastard Child shall live, and be Chargeable to the said Parish of Stoke Abbas except such time as she the said Agnes Endicott shall keep, nourish and maintain the said Bastard Child with the allowance aforesaid from the said Thomas Gollop

Given under our Hands and Seals the seventh Day of August in the Year of our Lord 1809

T.R. Drewes [Seal]
J Munden [Seal]

/
The order of J Judby in Bastardsey Stoke Abbott
/

COUNTY OF

Dorset} The order of S[i]r Will[ia]m Oglander Bar[one]t & F[ranci]s Jo[h]n Browne Esq[uire] two of his Majesty's Justices of the Peace in and for the said County, one whereof is of the Quorum, and both residing next unto the Limits of the Parish Church within the Parish of Stoke Abbas in the said County, made the seventh Day of February One Thousand Eight Hundred and fourteen concerning a female Bastard Child lately born in the Parish of Stoke Abbas aforesaid, of the Body of Mary Lacey

WHEREAS it hath appeared unto us the said Justices, as well upon the Complaint of the Churchwardens and Overseers of the Poor of the said Parish of Stoke Abbas as upon the Oath of the said Mary Lacey that she the said Mary Lacey on the eleventh Day of September now last past, was delivered of a female Bastard Child at Stoke Abbas in the Parish of Stoke Abbas in the said County, and that the said Bastard Child is become chargeable to the said Parish of Stoke Abbas and further that Thomas Tidby of Litten Cheney in the County of Dorset Lab[ourer] did beget the said Bastard Child on the Body of her the said Mary Lacey And whereas the s[ai]d Thomas Tidby being now before us the s[ai]d Justices to answer to the Premis truth assigned no sufficient Reason why He sho[ul]d not be Named the Father of the s[ai]d bastard Child

We therefore, upon Examination of the Cause and Circumstances of the Premises, as well upon the Oath of the said Mary Lacey as otherwise, do hereby adjudge him the said Thomas Tidby to be the reputed Father of the said Bastard Child – And thereupon we do order, as well for the better Relief of the said Parish of Stake Abbas as for the Sustention and Relief of the said Bastard Child that the said Thomas Tidby shall and do forthwith, upon Notice of this our Order, pay or cause to be paid to the said Churchwardens and Overseers of the Poor of the said Parish of Stoke Abbas or to some or one of them, the Sum of Eight Shillings and six Pence for and toward the Lying-in of the aid Mary Lacey and the Maintenance of the said Bastard Child to the Time of making this our Order, and for the Charges and Expences incurred prior to he said Order of Filiation being made, and incident to the obtaining of the said Order, as ascertained on Oath.

And we do also hereby further order that the said Thomas Tidby shall likewise pay or cause to be paid to the Churchwardens and Overseers of the Poor of the said Parish of Stoke Abbas for the Time being, or to some or one of them, the Sum of Two shillings, sixpence weekly and every Week from this present Time, for and towards the Keeping, Sustenation, and Maintenance of the said Bastard Child for and during so long Time as the said Bastard Child shall be chargeable to the said Parish of Stoke Abbas

And we do further order, that the said Mary Lacey shall also pay or cause to be paid to the said Churchwardens and Overseers of the Poor of the said Parish of Stoke Abbas for the Time being, or to some or one of them, the Sum of One shilling (3) weekly and every Week, so long as the said Bastard Child shall be chargeable to the said Parish of Stoke Abbas in Case she shall not nurse and take Care of the said Child herself.

Given under our Hands and Seals the Day and Year first above-written.
[along the left margin:]
[Seal]
W Oglander
[Seal]
F.J. Browne
Langdon, Printer, Sherborne.
/
Order Basterday
Jno. Ivory &
Jane Shiner
Stoke Abbott
/

COUNTY OF

Dorsett} The Order of S[i]r Will[ia]m Oglander Bar[one]t Jno. Munden L.L.D. two of his Majesty's Justices of the Peace in and for the said County, one whereof is of the Quorum, and both residing next unto the Limits of the Parish Church within the Parish of Stoke Abbas in the said County, made the sixth Day of February One Thousand Eight Hundred and fifteen concerning a female Bastard Child lately born in the Parish of Stoke Abbas aforesaid, of the Body of Jane Shiner single Woman.

WHEREAS it hath appeared unto us the said Justices, as well upon the Complaint of the Churchwardens and Overseers of the Poor of the said Parish of Stoke Abbas as upon the Oath of the said Jane Shiner that she the said Jane Shiner on the Day of November now last past, was delivered of a female Bastard Child at Stoke Abbas in the Parish of Stoke Abbas in the said County, and that the said Bastard Child is become chargeable to the said Parish of Stoke Abbas and further that John Ivory of Stoke Abbas in the County afores[ai]d Lab[ore]r did beget the said Bastard Child on the body of her the said Jane Shiner

And whereas the said John Ivory is now before us the said Justices, to answer to the Premises, but hath assigned no sufficient Reason why he should not be deemed the Father of the said Bastard Child.

We therefore, upon Examination of the Cause and Circumstances of the Premises, as well upon the Oath of the said Jane Shiner as otherwise, do hereby adjudge him the said John Ivory to be the reputed Father of the said Bastard

Child And thereupon we do order, as well for the better Relief of the said Parish of Stoke Abbas as for the Sustentation and Relief of the said Bastard Child that the said John Ivory shall and do forthwith, upon Notice of this our Order, pay or cause to be paid to the said Churchwardens and Overseers of the Poor of the said Parish of Stoke Abbas or to some or one of them, the Sum of One Pound two Shilling for and towards the Lying-in of the said Jane Shiner and the Maintenance of the said Bastard Child to the Time of making this our Order, and for the Charges and Expences incurred prior to the said Order of Filiation being made, and incident to the obtaining of the said Order, as ascertained on Oath.

And we do also hereby further order that the said John Ivory shall likewise pay or cause ot be paid to the Churchwardens and Overseers of the Poor of the said Parish of Stoke Abbas for the Time being, or to some or one of them, the Sum of twenty Pence weekly and every Week from this present Time, for and towards the Keeping, Sustentation, and Maintenance of the said Bastard Child for and during so long Time as the said Bastard Child shall be chargeable to the said Parish of Stoke Abbas

And we do further order, that the said Jane Shiner shall also pay or cause to be paid to the said Churchwardens and Overseers of the Poor of the said Parish of Stoke Abbas for the Time being, or to some or one of them, the Sum of ten pence weekly and every Week, so long as the said Bastard Child shall be chargeable to the said Parish of Stoke Abbas in Case she shall not nurse and take Care of the said Child herself.

Given under our Hands and Seals the Day and Year first above-written.
[written in the left margin:]
[Seal]
J Munden
[Seal]
W Oglander
Landon and Son, Printes, Sherborne.
/
John Caddy
Dr to the Overseers of Stoke Parish
1819 March 0 to March 6 1820 52 Weeks at 15d: £3 5s 5d
March 8:1820 to Jan[uary] 31: 1821: 47 Weeks at D:2 18 9
£6 3 9

JOHN SIBLEY, SETTLEMENT EXAMINATION (1753)

John Sibley, Settlement Examination (1753), Mosterton, Dorset, Poor Law Records, Dorset History Centre PE/MSN: OV 3/2, digital image www.ancestry.co.uk.

In 1753 parish officials in Mosterton in Dorset examined John Sibley about his settlement. John had encountered the administration of poor relief long before 1753, however. It is possible that this was the same John Sibley, son of Richard of Mosterton, who in 1723 was apprenticed to a carpenter in Haselbury-Plucknett in Somersetshire.[1] In 1723, however, John was already well known to the overseers. John had arrived in Mosterton in 1709 along with his parents and his six siblings when the parish of Bradford Peverell removed the family in December of that year.[2] The Bradford Peverell parish registers reveal more about the Sibley family that made the forced fifteen-mile journey. John was christened on 2 December 1702 in Bradford Peverell. He was the seventh child, though only six were living – his seven-year-old sister had died six months before his birth. By the time the family was removed to Mosterton, John was seven years old and had been joined by two younger siblings.[3] Despite the typical language that the family had 'lately come' to Bradford Peverell and were likely to be chargeable, the family had christened all nine children and buried one in Bradford.[4] Despite Bradford Peverell's fears, the Sibleys did not immediately descend into parish relief. Instead Richard Sibley began to pay a one shilling rate as soon as he arrived, and until his disappearance from the rate payers' list in 1717. Though the Sibleys never received relief from Mosterton, the parish officials must have known the background when they apprenticed John in 1723. Therefore, by the time parish officials questioned fifty-one-year-old John in 1753 he had already connected with the administration of the Poor Laws. In fact, poor relief bureaucracy had been a constant in his life.

Notes
1. John Sybley, 7 February 1753, Settlement Examination, Mosterton, Dorset (Mosterton, Dorset Records of the Overseers of the Poor, Mosterton Online Parish Clerk, online database at http://www.opcdorset.com/MostertonFiles/MostertonOverseers.htm [accessed September 2009]); Mosterton Apprenticeship Indentures, Salt Lake City, Family

History Library (hereafter FHL) British Film 1596045, item 25.
2. Richard Sybley, 23 December 1709, Removal Order from Bradford Peverell to Mosterton, Dorset (Mosterton, Dorset Records of the Overseers of the Poor, Mosterton Online Parish Clerk, online database at http://www.opcdorset.com/MostertonFiles/MostertonOverseers.htm [accessed September 2009]); Mosterton, Dorsetshire Churchwardens, Account Books, 2–6 January 1710, FHL British Film 1526228, item 5.
3. R. Grosvenor Bartelot, *The Parish Register of Bradford-Peverell Co., Dorset, 1572–1800*, FHL British Book 942.33 V26br.
4. Mosterton, Dorset Overseers of the Poor, Removals to the Parish, FHL British film 1596045, item 39.

John Sibley, Settlement Examination (1753)

Dorset To wit}The Examination of John Sybley – now residing in the Parish of Mosterton in the County of Dorset taken on Oath before we one of his Majesty's Justices of the Peace for the County aforesaid the 7th: Day of February 1753 (touching the Peace of his last legal Settlement.) Who Saith that he was born in the Parish of Bradford

in the County of Dorset – as he was Informed by his Parish; The father saith that his Father was a Parishioners in Mosterton as {tear} this Examinant; when he was about fifteen or sixteen Year {tear} {con}sent and agreed with Robert Watts of the Parish of Broa{dwindsor} of Dorset in Service by the Week and lived with {tear} there he went to Lower Kingca{smudge}le and hired {tear} one Thomas Hooper for a Years Service and lived wi{tear}[hi]m Six months & received for his half years Service, then he came back, and hired himself for one years service with his former master Robert Watts of Broadwindsor and continued with him four Months; And he hath not done any Act or Acts whereby to gain a legal Settlement but as above.

The Mark of
                    John + Sibley
Taken and sworn the Day and Year above Before me.
John Tucker

ST KATHERINE CREE PARISH APPRENTICESHIP INDENTURES (1693–1753)

Parish Apprenticeship Indentures (1693–1753), Saint Katherine Cree: City Of London, LMA P69/KAT2/B/038/MS07701/001.

For children whose parents had died, or who were unable to provide for their offspring, the parish might pay for a child to be apprenticed to another family in the parish or elsewhere (see also Volume 2, 'Childhood'). Ideally, this meant a poor child benefited from gaining a skilled trade. In practice, however, many children were apprenticed as cheap domestic servants. This was true for boys as well as girls, as domestic labour was 'relatively ungendered'.[1] If children or youth were apprenticed to another parish they might inherit a lifetime of marginal settlement and a constant interaction with poor relief officials in several parishes – as already mentioned in the examination record for John Sibley.

While most children apprenticed by the parish were boys, girls could also be apprenticed. Such was the case with Elizabeth Osborne in 1694, in an indenture included here. She was apprenticed to female lacemakers, much like the young Sarah Drinkwater was apprenticed to a dressmaker (see also Volume 2, 'Childhood').[2] Like Sarah Drinkwater, Elizabeth might have been apprenticed when her parents died. However, poverty meant that parish officials sometimes assumed parental roles even when parents were living[3] Her indenture describes her as poor, but does not clarify whether her parents were living. It is possible that her age (she was twelve years old) and her parents' poverty combined to motivate parish officials to apprentice her out. By doing so they hoped to have her become financially independent from both the family and the parish – both during the term of the apprenticeship and ideally for the rest of her life.

While Elizabeth Osborne was apprenticed to women in a field dominated by women, Frances George's indenture show she was apprenticed to a male upholsterer. It is possible she learned the trade as the 1713 indenture requires, but as with many parish apprenticeships, it is also quite likely that she really became an unpaid domestic servant. This was because 'domestic work was almost always a central feature of girls' apprenticeships'.[4] Even for Benjamin Anderson, a boy apprenticed to a woman (a merchant tailor) in 1707, there was no guarantee he would learn the trade; his social status may have trumped his gender and he too might have been employed more as a domestic servant than an apprentice.

Most of the children and young people apprenticed by the parish were 'parish children' – foundlings discovered within the parish boundaries who were given a name (often reflecting the street or neighborhood where they were 'taken up'), baptized and then given to a parishioner to care for. The parish typically remunerated the families that cared for such children. Where possible the christenings for the following apprentices have been discovered and are included in the annotations.

Notes
1. C. Steedman, 'The Servant's Labour: The Business of Life, England, 1760–1820', *Social History*, 29:1 (Feb 2004), pp. 1–29, on p. 15.
2. Girls and young women, even those apprenticed by their parents and not the parish, were generally apprenticed in fields dominated by women – particularly lacemaking, dressmaking and shopkeeping. A. M. Froide, *Never Married: Singlewomen in Early Modern Europe* (Oxford: Oxford University Press, 2005), p. 91.
3. P. Crawford, *Parents of Poor Children in England, 1580–1800* (Oxford: Oxford University Press, 2010), pp. 193–239.
4. P. Humfrey, 'Introduction', in P. Humfrey (ed.), *The Experience of Domestics Service for Women in Early Modern London* (Farnham: Ashgate, 2011), p. 5.

St Katherine Cree Parish Apprenticeship Indentures (1693-1753)

Thomas Jewry[1] to James Horworth for 8: Years or from 20:76:1694

This Indenture made the six and twentieth day of September in the Sixth year of the Reigne of our Soveraign Lord and Lady W[ilia]m and Mary by the Grace of God of England Scotland ffrance and Ireland King and Queen Defenders of the ffaith &c Annoque Dom[ini] 1694 Witnesseth that John Moss and John Lingard Church wardens of the Parish of St. Katharine Cree church als[o] Christchurch London in the Citty of London. And also the said John Moss and Thomas Cage Overseers of the Poor of the Said Parish by and with the consent of one of their Majesties Justices of Peace of the Said Citty whose Name is hereunto subscribed, have put & placed, & by these p[re]sents do put & place Thomas Jewry a poor Child of the said Parish Apprentice to James Howarthy of the p[ar]ish of St. Andrew Holborn in Cou[nty] Middl[esex] Taylor with him to dwell and serve from the day of the date of these presents unto the full end and term of Eight Years from thence next ensuring and fully to be compleat and Ended – During all which term the said Apprentice his said Master faithfully shall serve in all lawfull businesses according to his power, wit and ability, and honesty, orderly, and obediently in all things demean and behave himself towards his said Master and all his during the said term. And the said James Holworth doth covenant and grant for himself his Executors and Administrators to and with the said church wardens and overseers, and every of them, then and every of their Executors and Administrators, and their and every of their Successors for the time being by these p[re]sents, that he - the said James Holworth the said Apprentice, in the Art and Trade which he now useth shall teach and Instruct or cause to be taught and instructed. And shall and will during all the term aforesaid, find, provid[e] and allow unto the said Apprentice meet competence and sufficient Meat, Drink, Apparel, Lodging Washing and all other things, necessary and fit for an Apprentice. And also shall and will so provide for the said Apprentice, that he be not any way a charge to the said Parish or the Parishioners of the same, but of and from all charge shall and will save the said Parish and Parishioners harmless and indempnified during the said term. And at the End of the said term shall and will make provide, allow and deliver unto the said Apprentice double Apparel of all sorts, ~~good and new~~, that is to say, a good new suit for the Holy dayes and another for the Working dayes. In Witness whe[re]of the p[ar]ties abovesaid to these p[re]sent Indentures interchangeably have put their Hands and Seales the day and year above written.

Sealed and delivered in the p[re]sense of
Tho[mas] Butler
George Liddell
JS:e Samull Dashwood Kn[igh]t: One of the Justices of the peace of the said Citty & Ald[er]man of the Ward of Algate aforesaid do (as much as in us lies) consent to The putting forth of the abovesaid Thomas Jewry Apprentice according to the intent and meaning of the Indenture abovesaid.
James Holworth [seal]

/

Elizabeth Osborne[2] for 7: Yeares to Sarah Colwith & 29:7 1694

This Indenture made the six and twentieth day of September in the Sixth year of the Reigne of our Soveraign Lord and Lady W[ilia]m and Mary – by the Grace of God of England Scotland ffrance and Ireland King and Queen Defenders of the ffaith &c Annoque Dom[ini] 1694 Witnesseth that John Moss and John Lingard - Church wardens of the Parish of St. Katharine Cree church als[o] Christchurch London in the City of London. And also the said John Moss and Thomas Cage Overseers of the Poor of the Said Parish by and with the consent of one of their Majesties Justices of Peace of the Said City whose Name is hereunto subscribed, have put & placed, & by these p[re]sents do put & place Elizabeth Osborne a poor Child of the said Parish Apprentice to Sarah Colwith of London Widdow and Martha Colwith of Lond[o]n Spinst[e]r with them to dwell and serve from the day of the date of these presents unto the full end and terme of Seven Years from thence next ensuring and fully to be compleat and ended – During all which term the said Apprentice her said Mistresses faithfully shall serve in all lawfull businesses according to her power, wit and ability, and honesty, orderly, and obediently in all things demean and behave herself towards her said Mistresses and all theirs during the said term. And the said Sarah Colwith & Martha Colwith ~~doth~~ covenant and grant for themselves their Executors and Administrators to and with the said church wardens and overseers, and every of them, then and every of their Executors and Administrators, and their and every of their Successors for the time being by these p[re]sents, that they - the said Sarah & Martha the said Apprentice, in the Art of Lacemaking which they us[eth] shall teach and Instruct or cause to be taught and instructed. And shall and will during all the term aforesaid, find, provid[e] and allow unto the said Apprentice meet competence and sufficient Meat, Drink, Apparel, Lodging Washing and all other things, necessary and fit for an Apprentice. And also shall and will so provide for the said Apprentice, that she be not any way a charge to the said Parish or the Parishioners of the same, but of and from all charge shall and will save the said Parish and Parishioners harmless and indempnified during the said term. And at the End of the said term shall and will make provide, allow and deliver unto the said Apprentice double Apparel of all sorts, ~~good and new~~, that is to say, a good new suit for the Holy dayes and another for the Working dayes. In Witness whe[re]of the p[ar]ties abovesaid to these p[re]sent Indentures interchangeably have put their Hands and Seales the day and year above written.

    Sealed and delivered in the p[re]sense of
Tho[mas] Butler
George Liddell
JS:r Samuell Dashwood K[nigh]t One of the Justices of the peace of the said Citty & Ald[er]man of the Ward of Algate aforesaid do (as much as in us lies) consent to The putting forth of the abovesaid Elizabeth Osborne – Apprentice according to the intent and meaning of the Indenture abovesaid.
                  John Moss [seal]
                  [seal]
                  [seal]
    The marke of the said Elizabeth C Osborne [seal]

/

This Indenture Witnesseth, That Benjamin Anderson Son of Benjamin Anderson – late of the parish of Saint Catharine Creed Church London doth put himself Apprentice to Ann Cope - Citizen and *Merchant Taylor* of *London*, to learn her Art, and with her (after the manner of an Apprentice) to serve from the date hereof unto the full end and term of Seven years from thence next following, to be fully compleat and ended. During which term, the said Apprentice, his said Mistress faithfully shall serve, her Secrets keep, her lawful Commandments every where gladly do. He shall do no Damage to his said Mistress, nor see to be done by others; but that to his power he shall let, or forthwith give warning to his said Mistress of the same. He shall not waste the Goods of his said Mistress, nor lend them unlawfully to any. He shall not commit Fornication, nor contract Matrimony within the said Term. He shall not play at Cards, Dice, Tables, or any other unlawful Games, whereby his said Mistress may have any Loss: with her own Goods or others, during the said term, without license of his said Mistress, he shall neither Buy nor Sell. He shall not haunt Taverns or Play-houses, nor absent himself from his said Mistress's service day nor night unlawfully: But in all things as a faithful Apprentice, he shall behave himself towards his said Mistress and all hers, during the said term. And the said Mistress, her said Apprentice in the same Art which she useth, by the best means that she can, shall teach and instruct, or cause to be taught and instructed, finding unto her said Apprentice, Meat, Drink, Apparel, Lodging, and all other necessaries according to the Custom of the City of *London*, during the said Term. And for the true performance of all and every the said Covenants and Agreements, either of the said Parties, bindeth himself unto the other by these presents. In Witness whereof, the Parties above-named, to these Indentures Interchangeably have put their Hands and Seals, the ninth day of January in the fi[f]th Year of the Reign of our Sovereign Lady Anne, Queen {obscured by seal} [of *Eng]land, &c, Anno Dom*[*ini*] 1707

     Ye mark of Ann Cope
       C [seal]

Thomas Ange
/

Hanah Synagogue[3]
 Inden[ture] to James palmer
 April 13th 1711
  Rec'd the day w Q in written of the w Q in written Richd Penny & Robert Gill

This Indenture made the thirteenth day of Aprill in the Tenth year of the Reigne of our Soveraign Lady Anne by the Grace of God of Great Britain, ffrance, and Ireland Queen Defender of the ffaith &c Annoque Dom[ini] 1711 Witnesseth that Rich[ard] Penny and Robert Gill – Church wardens of the Parish of St. Cath[erine] Cree ch[urch] in the Citty of London. And the Overseers of the Poor of the Said Parish by and with the consent of her Majesties Justices of Peace of the Said City whose Names are hereunto subscribed, have put & placed, & by these p[re]sents do put & place Hannah Synagogue a poor Child of the said Parish Apprentice to James Palmer of Great St. Bartholomews in Cou[nty] Middl[esex] clothwork Lon[don] with him to dwell and serve from the day of the date of these presents for the term of seven years from thence next ensuring & fully to be compleat and Ended – During all which term the said Apprentice her said Master faithfully shall serve in all lawfull businesses according to her power, wit and ability, and honesty, orderly, and obediently in all things demean and behave herself towards her said Master and all his during the said term. And the said James Palmer doth covenant and grant for himself his Executors and Administrators to and with the said church wardens and overseers, and every of them, then and every of their Executors and Administrators, and their and every of their Successors for the time being by these p[re]sents, that he – the said James Palmer the said Apprentice, in the Trade & business which he now useth shall teach and instruct – And shall and will during all the term aforesaid, find, provid[e] and allow unto the said Apprentice meet competence and sufficient Meat, Drink, Apparel, Lodging Washing and all other things necessary and fit for an Apprentice. And also shall and will so provide for the said Apprentice, that she be not any way a charge to the said Parish or the Parishioners of the same, but of and from all charge shall and will save the said Parish and Parishioners harmless and indempnified during the said term. And at the End of the said term shall and will make provide, allow and deliver unto the said Apprentice double Apparel of all sorts, good and new, that is to say, a good new suit for the Holy dayes and another for the Working dayes. In Witness whe[re]of the p[ar]ties abovesaid to these p[re]sent Indentures interchangeably have put their Hands and Seales the day and year above written.

    Sealed and delivered in the p[re]sense of
Thomas Jenkinson
Will[ia]m Jobsoll
      We whose Names are subscribed Justices of the peace of the
        Citty aforesaid do (as much as in us lie) consent to
   The putting forth of the abovesaid Hannah Synagogue Apprentice
   According to the intent and meaning of the Indenture abovesaid.
           Tho[mas] Abney
           Ja[mes] Bateman
                        Rich[ard] Penny [seal]
                        Robert Gill [seal]

/

St. Katharine Creed Church
   Frances George[4]
   Indenture of Apprenticeship September 16 1713

This Indenture made the sixteenth day of September in the Twelfth year of the Reigne of our Soveraign Lady Ann – by the Grace of God of Great Britain, ffrance, and Ireland Queen Defender of the ffaith &c Annoque Dom[ini] 1713 Witnesseth that Hillory Barton and Richard Smith – Church wardens of the Parish of St. Katharine Creed Church in the City of London. And Richard Penny and William Bush Overseers of the Poor of the Said Parish by and with the consent of h[er] Majesties Justices of Peace of the Said City whose Names are hereunto subscribed, have put & placed, & by these p[re]sents do put & place ffrances George a poor Child of the said Parish Apprentise to Thomas Careless of the parish of St. Sepulcher London upholsterers with him to dwell and serve from the day of the date of these presents for and during the full End and term of seven years next ensuring fully to be compleat and Ended – During all which term the said Apprentice said M[aster] faithfully shall serve in all lawfull businesses according to her power, wit and ability, and honesty, orderly, and obediently in all things demean and behave herself towards her said Master and all his during the said term. And the said Thomas Careless doth covenant and grant for himself his Executors and Administrators to and with the said church wardens and overseers, and every of them, then and every of their Executors and Administrators, and their and every of their Successors for the time being by these p[re]sents, that he the said Thomas Careless the said Apprentice, in the art and mystery of an upholsterer w[hi]ch he now useth - shall & will teach and instruct or cause to be taught – And shall and will during all the term aforesaid, find, provid[e] and allow unto the said Apprentice meet competence and sufficient Meat, Drink, Apparel, Lodging Washing and all other things necessary and fit for an Apprentice. And also shall and will so provide for the said Apprentice, that she be not any way a charge to the said Parish or the Parishioners of the same, but of and from all charge shall and will save the said Parish and Parishioners harmless and indempnified during the said term. And at the End of the said term shall and will make provide, allow and deliver unto the said Apprentice double Apparel of all sorts, good and new, that is to say, a good new suit for the Holy dayes and another for the Working dayes. In Witness whe[re]of the p[ar]ties abovesaid to these p[re]sent Indentures interchangeably have put their Hands and Seales the day and year above written.

Sealed and delivered in the p[re]sense[sic] of
Robert Hartford
Thomas Jenkinson Parish Clerke

Tho[mas] Careless [seal]

We whose Names are subscribed Justices of the peace of the
City of London aforesaid do (as much as in us lie) consent to
The putting forth of the abovesaid ffrances George Apprentice
According to the intent and meaning of the Indenture abovesaid.
Tho[mas] Abney
Sam Stanier

/

Anne Gray[5] Indentures

This Indenture made the Twenty ffirst Daye of July Anno Dom[ini] 1716 and in the Second Year of the Reign of our Sovereign Lord George, by the Grace of God of Great Britain, ffrance and Ireland, King Defender of the ffaith, &c. Witnesseth that John Burkham Solomon Hall *Churchwardens* of the parish of St. Katherine Cree Church in the Citty of London and George Collingwood Overseers of the Poor of the Said Parish by and with the Consent of two of Her[sic] Majesties Justices of the Peace of the Said Citty whose Names are hereunto Subscribed, have put and placed, and by these Presents do put and place Ann Gray a poor Child of the said parish Apprentice to William Logalt of the parish of St. Gilesis in the ffeailds with him to Dwell, and Serve from the Day of the Date of these Presents, until the Expiration of Eight years according to the Statute in that Case made and provided. During all which Term the said Apprentice her said Master faithfully shall serve, in all lawfull Businesses, according to her Power, Wit and Ability; and honestly, orderly, and obediently in all Things demean and behave herself towards her said Master and all his during the said Term. And the said William Logalt doth Covenant and Grant for himself his Executors and Administrators, to and with the said Church-warden and Overseers of the Poor and every of them, their, and every of their Executors and Administrators, and their, and every of their Successors, for the time being by these Presents, That he the said William Logalt shall teach the said Apprentice in the Art of Huss[w]ifry - shall teach and instruct, or cause to be taught and instructed, and shall and will during all the Term aforesaid, find, provide and allow unto the said Apprentice meet, competent and sufficient Meat, Drink, Apparel, Lodging, Washing, and all other things, necessary and fit for an Apprentice. And also shall and will so provide for the said Apprentice, that she be not any way a Charge to the said parish or parishioners or to the Domestification - of the same, but of and from all Charge shall and will save the said parish & parishioners and will hold harmless and indempnified, during the said Term, and at the end thereof, shall and will make, provide, allow and deliver, unto the said Apprentice Double Apparel of all Sorts, Good and New (that is to say) a good New Suit for the Holy-Days, and another for the Working-Days. In Witness whereof the Parties abovesaid to these Present Indentures, interchangeably have put their Hands and Seals, the Day and Year above-written.

Sealed and delivered in the presence of
Ann Hartford
Thomas Jenkinson parish Clerke
We whose Names are Subscribed two of His Majesties Justices of the Peace of the Citty of London - Do consent to the putting forth of the abovesaid Ann Gray Apprentice according to the Tenor, true intent and meaning of the Indenture abovesaid.
Charles Peer Mayor
Sam Stanier

William Loggat [seal]

/

Ja[mes] Crawforth [seal]

This Indenture made the Eleventh day of August Anno Dom[ini] 1718 and in the Fo[u]rth Year of the Reign of our Sovereign Lord George, by the Grace of God of Great Britain, ffrance and Ireland, King Defender of the ffaith, &c. Witnesseth That Francis Gregory John Morton Church-Wardens of the parish of St. Katherine Cree alias Christ Church London in the County of Midellsex - and James Crawforth Overseers of the Poor of the Said of St. Katherine Cree by and with the Consent of two of His Majesties Justices of the Peace of the Said County (Quorum) whose Names are hereunto Subscribed, have put and placed, and by these Presents do put and place Prissillia Pumps[6] - a poor Child of the said parish Apprentice to John Hoggs of St. Mary Southwarks in the County of Surr[e]y and with him to Dwell, and Serve from the Day of the Date of these Presents, until the said Apprentice shall Accomplish the full Age of Twenty One yeairs - according to the Statute in that Case made and provided.

During all which Term the said Apprentice her said Master faithfully shall serve, in all lawfull Businesses, according to her Power, Wit and Ability; and honestly, orderly, and obediently in all Things demean and behave herself towards her said Master and all his during the said Term. And the said John Hogg doth Covenant and Grant for himself his Executors and Administrators, to and with the said Church-warden and Overseers of the Poor and every of them, their, and every of their Executors and Administrators, and their, and every of their Successors, for the time being by these Presents, That he the said John Hogg - shall teach the said Apprentice in the Art of Ironing and Hus[w]ifry shall teach and instruct, or cause to be taught and instructed, and shall and will during all the Term aforesaid, find, provide and allow unto the said Apprentice meet, competent and sufficient Meat, Drink, Apparel, Lodging, Washing, and all other things, necessary and fit for an Apprentice. And also shall and will so provide for the said Apprentice, that she be not any way a Charge to the said parish or parishioners - of the same, but of and from all Charge shall and will save the said parish and parishioners and will hold harmless and indempnified, during the said Term, and at the end thereof, shall and will make, provide, allow and deliver, unto the said Apprentice Double Apparel of all Sorts, Good and New (that is to say) a good New Suit for the Holy-Days, and another for the Working-Days. In Witness whereof the Parties abovesaid to these Present Indentures, interchangeably have put their Hands and Seals, the Day and Year above written.

    Sealed and Delivered
    in the presence of
    Sam[ual] Wall
    James Holme
    Wittness Thomas Jenkinson parish Clerke
    We whose Names are Subscribed two of His Majesties Justices of the Peace of the aforesaid (Quorum) Do consent to the putting forth of the abovesaid Prisslia Pumps Apprentice according to the Tenor, true intent and meaning of the Indenture abovesaid.
                W[illia]m Lewen Maior
                Sam Stranier

                                      John Hogg [seal]

ASHTON IN MAKERFIELD, LANCASHIRE, CENSUS OF THE POOR (1816)

Ashton in Makerfield, Lancashire, Census of the Poor (1816), FHL British Film 1701023, items 1–2, original at Warrington Library, Archives and Museum, WMS 735 Sibson Papers, Brym End Census of the Poor.

A census of the poor was not a typical part of English poor relief. However, there was nothing typical about 1816. Often termed the 'year without a summer' the year saw unprecedented crop failures due to drastic temperature drops throughout most of the northern hemisphere (at least partially attributed to the massive eruption of Mount Tambora in Indonesia in 1815). Medieval and early modern England had experienced repeated crop shortages, but by 1800 crop production had become more stable and short-term crop failures had ceased to produce widespread famine and starvation.[1] This overall stabilizing in crop yields meant, however, that the crop failures of 1816 were even more stark and catastrophic.

In the midst of this crisis and its attendant social unrest, the parish of Ashton in Makerfield in Lancashire conducted a census of the poor. Ashton, including the village of Haydock, lies near Wigan and was a growing manufacturing village in the early nineteenth century. In 1816 it had between 4,500 and 5,000 inhabitants.[2] The census reveals a stark reality. It is not the number of people who were sick or unemployed despite being able to work that is striking, it is that so many families lived on less than 4 shillings a week, or about £7.80 per year. Typical winter wages in northern England between 1815 and 1819 were nearly 2 shillings per day (or 12 shillings in a six-day work week), meaning Ashton's poor were trying to live on a third of what an average labourer was earning.[3]

Notes
1. B. M. S. Campbell and C. Ó Gráda, 'Harvest Shortfalls, Grain Prices, and Famines in Preindustrial England', *Journal of Economic History*, 71:4 (December 2011), pp. 859–86.
2. 1811 and 1821 census returns for Ashton in Makerfield, cited in J. Croston (ed.), *The History of the County Palatine and Duchy of Lancashire by the Late Edward Baines, Esq.*, 5 vols (J. Heywood, 1891), vol. 4, p. 347, Google Books [accessed 1 December 2014].
3. G. Clark, 'Farm Wages and Living Standards in the Industrial Revolution: England, 1670–1850', *Economic History Review*, 54:3 (2001), pp. 477–505, on p. 485.

Ashton in Makerfield, Lancashire, Census of the Poor (1816)

36

Name and Residence	Edward Curliff Burton
Belongs to what Parish: and what parochial Relief.	Haydock a
Number employed: in what Trade: and by whom.	1 Waggoner 12/ by T. Leigh Esq[ui]re 2 Drawers 3/
Number able to work, who are unemployed;	0
and Trade of each:	
By whom dismissed; and why.	
Any Sick; and what Allowance from Sick Club.	0
Number of Family: and Age of each.	7 Age 38 38 13 10 & 3 1
Weekly Earnings, and Income, of whole Family.	14/
Moral Charcter of Family, and other Remarks	no Quilt

/
37

Name and Residence.	John Greenall Burton
Belongs to what Parish: and what parochial Relief.	Bartonward 0
Number employed: in what Trade; and by whom.	1 Collier 15/} JLegh Esq[ui]r[e] 2 Drawers 8/}

Name and Residence.	John Greenall Burton
Number able to work, who are unemployed; and Trade of each:	0
By whom dismissed; and why.	
Any sick; and what Allowance from Sick Club	0
Number of Family, and Age of each.	7 Age 37 38 17 12 5 4 1
Weekly Earnings, and Income, of whole Family.	23/
Moral Character of Family, and other Remarks.	

/
158

Name and Residence.	Robert Chisnall Stanley Mill
Belongs to what Parish: and what parochial Relief.	Parr 0
Number employed: in what Trade; and by whom.	1 Laboarer 12/Mr Arrell
Number able to work, who are unemployed; and Trade of each:	0
By whom dismissed; and why.	
Any sick; and what Allowance from Sick Club	0
Number of Family, and Age of each.	5 Age 30 29 5 4 2
Weekly Earnings, and Income, of whole Family.	12/
Moral Character of Family, and other Remarks.	2 Blankets

/
159

Name and Residence.	Nathan Atherton Stanley Mill
Belongs to what Parish: and what parochial Relief.	Parr0
Number employed: in what Trade; and by whom.	1 Laboarer 12/ Mr. Greenall
Number able to wrok, who are unemployed; and Trade of each:	0
By whom dismissed; and why.	
Any sick; and what Allowance from Sick Club	0
Number of Family, and Age of each.	6 Age 29 32 8 7 3 1
Weekly Earnings, and Income, of whole Family.	12/
Moral Character of Family, and other Remarks.	2 Blankets

/

State of the Poor in Haydock

Families who have nothing to live upon	Who have less per head than one Shilling, a Week to live upon	Less than two Shillings	Less than three Shillings	Less than four shilling	Numbers of Persons unemployed & able to work	Average of the whole
1	1	10	23	14	20	284 Persons have each two Shillings & seven peace a Week to line upon.

ST ANN'S PARISH (ALBEMARLE COUNTY, VIRGINIA), VESTRY BOOK (1772–85)

St Ann's Parish (Albemarle County, Virginia), Vestry Book, 1772–85, FHL US/Can Q 925.5482 K2s, Reproduced from the original in the Henry E Huntington Library and Art Gallery.

In England, parish relief was administered by church wardens and overseers of the poor, but in Virginia this work was done by the vestry (twelve men and the minister) who, along with the churchwardens, managed the maintenance of the church and the gathering and disbursement of any payments. Earlier payments were often in kind – typically in tobacco – instead of in cash, but the same here from 1772 shows payments in cash.[1] This sample comes from near the end of Anglican poor relief in Virginia. After the Revolution the Anglican Church ceased to be a state church, and by 1780 its poor relief system had been completely dismantled or converted to county civil control (see also 'William Tennent III').[2] Despite abundant resources, poverty in Virginia was still 'endemic', leading an unknown person to write in the St. Anne vestry book, 'Lord have mercy upon the POOR'.[3] The vestry members gathered each fall to record the year's expenses, so the amounts listed here are annual payments to poor families.

Notes
1. J. K. Nelson, *A Blessed Company: Parishes, Parsons, and Parishioners in Anglican Virginia, 1690–1776* (Chapel Hill, NC: University of North Carolina Press, 2001), p. 70.
2. H. Mackey, 'The Operation of the English Poor Law in Colonial Virginia', *Virginia Magazine of History and Biography*, 73:1 (January 1965), pp. 29–40.
3. Nelson, *A Blessed Company*, pp. 83, 369 (n. 98).

St Ann's Parish (Albemarle County, Virginia), Vestry Book (1772–85)

Vestry Book Belong[ing] to the Parish of St. Ann's Commenct the 25th September In the Year of our Lord God. 1772. Lord have mercy upon the Poor Order that W. Peter Clarkson be reappointed President & Cornel[ius] Schink ~~Clk~~ & provided to lay Such Sums for indigent & Charitable persons as in their Judgments were objects – viz

    NE district

To Peter Clarkson	for John Newcom	£3.10.0
To ditto. ditto	for Catherine Leach	5.0.0
To ditto. ditto	for Frances Martin	8.0.0
To ditto. ditto	for Zachariah Tammons	5.0.0
To ditto. ditto	for Runsom Alphin	+12.0.0
To Wille: Dalton	for Patience Beaver	5.0.0
To ditto. ditto	for Willi: White	5.0.0
To ditto. ditto	for Peter Shephard (for confer)	7.0.0
To ditto. ditto	for Sam[ue]l Munday	5.0.0
To Willi: Meriwether	for Morgan & wife	+12.0.0
To ditto. ditto	for Tourniwell Johnson & Grand Daughter	5.0.0

S.W.

To Samuel Black	for Margeret Colman	9.0.0
To ditto. ditto	for Eliza[beth] Carter	7.0.0
To ditto. ditto	for Eliza[beth] Horner	4.0.0
To ditto. ditto	for John Houswright	+9.0.0
To Willi: Woods	for John Elum	6.0.0

To ditto. ditto. Jun[io]r	for Geo[rge] Dudley	10.0.0
To Richard Harrison Jun[io]r	for Geo[rge] Dudley	6.0.0
To ditto. ditto.	for John Harris	8.0.0
To ditto. ditto.	for Sarah Barnet	7.0.0
To Joel Harris	for Elise Ballow	9.0.0
N.W. district		
To Charles Goodman	for Willi: Denton & wife	15.0.0
To ditto. ditto.	for Ann Orsburm & 8£&20/to Goodman}	9.0.0
To ditto. ditto.	for Mary Pritt	9.0.0
To ditto. ditto.	for Sam[ue]l Fowler	8.0.0
To Thomas Fritwell	for Th[oma]s Gardner	8.0.0
To ditto. ditto.	for John Shiflet	6.10.0
To ditto. ditto.	for Th[oma]s Shiflet & Wife	5.0.0
To ditto. ditto.	for David Epperson	3.0.0
To Joel Harris	for Richd. Becket	3.0.0
To ditto. ditto.	for Jeremiah Jacobs	9.0.0
To Charles Goodman	for Widow Phelips	2.0.0
		£225.0.0

LONDON SOCIETY FOR EDUCATING POOR CHILDREN IN THE PROTESTANT REFORMED RELIGION (1782)

London Society for Educating Poor Children in the Protestant Reformed Religion ... Having Met in Red Cross Street ... the First Day of August, 1782 ... Have Come to the Following Resolutions (London: R. Denham, 1782), ECCO, ESTC Number T0128247, ECCO Range 6936.

Established to ensure that the children of the poor were educated in proper reformed Protestant religion, the London Society for Educating Poor Children seems not to have survived beyond its initial attempts in 1782 (see also 'Religious Diversity'). It intended to pay for instructing children older than seven, of both sexes, with a guarantee of two years' education. In this way, it reflected common themes in eighteenth-century educational theories.[1] Primary education was a patchwork of approaches and schools in eighteenth-century England. In addition to the expensive grammar schools for the better-off boys, there was a variety of village schools, parish schools, dame schools and ad hoc schooling in the homes of ministers or school masters and mistresses. Poor girls and boys had access to basic catechetical instruction, as well as basic reading – writing was taught separately and might not have been regularly taught to poor children, particularly poor girls. The education of girls as well as boys was a common preoccupation of eighteenth-century educators and reformers. However, the

> education received by poor children throughout the early modern period ... was premised on basic gender biases: the curriculum for girls contained fewer academic subjects, often taught to a less advanced level to allow for training in domestic arts, particularly sewing.[2]

Notes
1. I. Green, *Humanism and Protestantism in Early Modern English Education* (Burlington, VT: Ashgate, 2009).
2. M. Hilton and J. Shefrin (eds), *Educating the Child in Enlightenment Britain* (Burlington, VT: Ashgate, 2009), p. 9.

London Society for Educating Poor Children in the Protestant Reformed Religion (1782)

LONDON SOCIETY FOR Educating Poor Children IN THE PROTESTANT REFORMED RELIGION.

POPERY Being replete with IDOLATRY and SUPERSTITION†,

AND the WORD of GOD having denounced dreadful Curses against IDOLATRY: AND the Papists in the present Day being very assiduous in propagating their wicked and superstitious Tenets amongst the Children of the Poor,

* Whereby King, Lords, and Commons, declare that the Invocation or Adoration of the Virgin Mary, or other Saint and Sacrifice of the Mass, as used by Papists, are *superstitious* and *idolatrous*.

A NUMBER OF PROTESTANTS

Having met in Red Cross Street, on Thursday the first day of August, 1782, and having taken into their serious consideration the most effectual method in their power to prevent the spreading of POPERY, and that they may bear their testimony against IDOLATRY, have agreed to form a Society for the Education of poor Children in the PROTESTANT REFORMED RELIGION, and therefore have come to

The following RESOLUTIONS, Viz.

I. THAT a Society be formed called the *'London Society, for educating Poor Children in the Protestant reformed Religion.'*

II. That a subscription be immediately opened to bear the expence of educating poor children, of both sexes, and all denominations, in the *Protestant reformed Religion*, who shall be thought proper objects of this charity.

III. That this Society do meet the second Thursday in every month (or oftener if occasion shall require) to receive subscriptions, and transact other necessary

---

*   See statute 30. Car. 2. Stat. 2. Cap. 1.statute 30. Car ... Cap. 1: statute from the thirtieth year of Charles II's reign. This specific statute was the 1678 Test Act – one in a series of Test Acts that imposed conforming with the Established Church in order to hold public or clerical offices in England.

business of the charity. And that there be four general quarterly meetings in every year, *viz.* the second Thursday in January, the second Thursday in March, the second Thursday in June, and the second Thursday in September. And that seven members be sufficient to constitute a general meeting.

IV. That a Treasurer be annually chosen out of this Society, and a Secretary, and fifteen Committee Men, quarterly; five of whom shall be sufficient to form a board for transacting of business.

V. That at all general meetings no member shall vote but those present, (except Ladies who subscribe) and every thing shall be determined by a majority of votes, or by ballot. If in any case the majority on the vote appears doubtful, such ballot to be entered on immediately and finished; and where the numbers are equal, the chairman then presiding to have the casting vote.

VI. That no person be permitted to subscribe to this charity, unless he be known by two or more of the Society to be a Protestant.

VII. That whoever shall give to this charity eight shillings a year, shall be deemed a subscriber, and the subscriptions may be paid monthly or quarterly, at pleasure. Any donation to be received at any time by the Treasurer or Secretary, and at the monthly meetings.

VIII. That in case of the death or resignation of the Treasurer, Secretary, Schoolmaster, or Schoolmistress, a special general meeting shall be called within two weeks, for the choice of another.

IX. That proper persons (who are Protestants) be appointed to teach such children as shall become objects of this charity, in the *Protestant reformed Religion*; and in such way as shall be most agreable to the subscribers in general. The Boys to be taught reading, writing, and arithmetic. The Girls to be taught to read, write, few, mark, *&c.*

X. That no children be admitted to this charity but those who are nominated by the subscribers, and approved of by the Committee. And every subscriber of one guinea a year, is to be at liberty to nominate one child; the said subscibers to take their turn to nominate according to the time of subscribing. And that any two yearly subscribers of ten shillings and six-pence each, may join in nominating a child. And that any three yearly subscribers of eight shillings each, may also join and nominate a child ; and that such nomination shall be in rotation, according to the time of subscribing. And that no child shall be admitted under the age of seven years.

XI. That all children admitted to this charity shall be educated for two years: at the expiration of which term, provided the subscriptions will admit, and the Society judge it necessary, then those children shall continue in the School so long as the Society shall judge fit.

XII. That the subscribers shall be at liberty till the second Thursday in January, 1783, to admit such number of children as they shall think proper, according to the subscriptions : but after that time no children shall be admitted, but at the four general quarterly meetings.

XIII. That the Committee for the time being shall examine into the character and conduct of the person or persons who may be intrusted with the education of the children, and report the same to the Society at every quarterly meeting.

XIV. That the Master or Mistress, neglecting to pay due attention to the instruction of the children, or for any great misbehaviour, shall, on the report of the Committee at the next quarterly general meeting, be discharged, and a special general meeting be called as soon as possible, for the choice of another.

XV. That the Master or Mistress shall be paid for the instruction of the children every quarter, *viz.* on the 29th day of September, the 25th day of December, the 25th day of March, and the 24th day of June.

XVI. That if any child, who shall be admitted into this charity, shall behave contrary to the rules, which shall be given to the parents or friends of such child at the time of admission, the Committee shall request the attendance of such parents or friends at their next meeting, when such parents or friends shall be admonished to comply with the rules of the charity. And in case of the non-attendance of such parents or friends, or the continued misbehaviour of any such child, then, and in either of the said cases, such child shall, by the Committee, be dismissed the school.

XVII. The teachers of such children shall keep an account of the children's attendance, and report the same to the Committee every month.

XVIII. That all the children, educated by this Society, shall, every Lord's day, both morning and afternoon, go to such place or places of worship as shall be appointed by the Society at a general quarterly meeting, unless a sufficient reason shall be given to the Schoolmaster, by the parents or friends of such child or children, for omitting thereof.

XIX. That there be no fixed number of children in the before mentioned school, it being the intention of this Society to educate, in the *Protestant reformed Religion*, as many as the subscription shall allow.

XX. That the children who are educated by this Society, shall be supplied with books, &c. according to the different stages of their education, at the expence of the Society, and the discretion of the Committee.

XXI. That after each yearly or quarterly meeting, the names and places of abode in writing, of the officers and receivers of subscriptions, shall be sent to every subscriber to this charity.

XXII. That the hours of transacting the business of this Society shall be from seven o'clock until nine in the evening, after which time no business shall be transacted.

XXIII. That no article or rule for governing of this charity, shall be made without the approbation and consent of the majority at a general quarterly meeting, except such as are made before the first meeting in the year of our Lord 1783.

XXIV. That if this Society shall have a sufficient fund, *they shall contribute to the support of any other similar Society in England.* And the accounts of this Society shall be subject to be audited by three delegates from any such similar society.

SUBSCRIPTIONS *to this Charity, are received by the* TREASURER, Mr. THOMAS MORLEY, Westmoreland Buildings, Aldersgate Street. *And by the* SECRETARY, Mr. JOSHUA BANGS, Lyons Inn.
LONDON: PRINTED BY R. DENHAM, No. 20, SALISBURY SQUARE, FLEET STREET. /

HINTS FOR THE INSTITUTION OF SUNDAY-SCHOOLS AND PARISH CLUBS, FOR THE BENEFIT OF THE POOR (1789)

> *Hints for the Institution of Sunday-Schools and Parish Clubs, for the Benefit of the Poor. Chiefly Intended for the Middle Ranks, Whose Benevolence May Induce Them to Attend to These Useful Institutions. To Which Are Added, Some Rules for a Female Society, As Established in York: By the Author of the Poor Child's Friend* (York: W. Blanchard, 1789), ECCO, ESTC Number T028247, ECCO Range 6936.

The Sunday School Movement brought together educational and religious concerns for children that flourished in late eighteenth- and nineteenth-century England and America. Various denominations offered weekly religious instruction, and by the 1830s they provided the bulk of working-class education and educated a million and a half students in England.[1] The schools might be attached to a denomination, or social or charitable organization. They 'provided a basic religious education, one that was often informed by the late eighteenth-century emphasis on salvation through faith, which owed so much to Methodist influence'. They typically taught reading and, in some schools, writing.[2]

This document describes a society that would go one step further than Sunday schools and other local educational efforts. It was established particularly for poor girls, to build on an education they might have received at Grey Coat or spinning schools. A Blue Coat school (for training poor boys) and a Grey Coat school (for training poor girls) were established in York in 1705.[3] Similar institutions existed in London as well. Despite the spinning schools and Sunday schools, however, there were still many 'parentless and friendless' young women in a 'very forlorn state'. The women who organized the society determined to allow these young women to join the society in order to provide for them in times of need or illness.

Notes
1. K. D. M. Snell, 'The Sunday-School Movement in England and Wales: Child Labour, Denominational Control and Working-Class Culture', *Past and Present*, 164 (August 1999), pp. 122–68, on pp. 125–6.
2. Snell, 'The Sunday-School Movement in England and Wales: Child Labour, Denomina-

tional Control and Working-Class Culture', p. 129.
3. R. W. Unwin, 'Tradition and Transition in Market Towns in the Vale of York', *Northern History* (1981), pp. 72–116.

Hints for the Institution of Sunday-Schools and Parish Clubs, for the Benefit of the Poor (1789)

RULES and ORDERS,
TO BE STRICTLY OBSERVED AND KEPT BY
The Members of a Female Society,
Instituted the first day of August, 1788, at York.

THE Ladies who have promoted this Association being particularly interested about the welfare, of the poor Girls who are the objects of it ; and moreover, taking into consideration the very forlorn state of young females that are parentless and friendless, have determined to make them the offer of being formed into a Society, of which, for its further support and encouragement, they will themselves become Members.

The Objects of this Association are,

In the first place, By the contributions of the Members, during health, to form a Fund towards their support in sickness;– and, in the second place, after the term of their education is elapsed, to retain still within the sphere of useful influence such young persons as having been brought up / in the Grey-Coat, or Spinning-Schools, shall chuse to avail themselves of the proposed Institution, for the sake of preserving and improving the good principles and habits which, it is hoped, they may have gained there; as well as for their relief in time of sickness–It is the purpose of the Ladies to subscribe also towards a *second* fund, which shall likewise operate for the benefit of the poorer members, in exigencies towards which the *first* fund principally formed of their own subscriptions, cannot extend. The distributions from this second fund, they will reserve entirely to their own direction and in their own power: The following Rules and Articles therefore relate to the *first* fund only; in respect to which all the poorer members will have votes, equally with the ladies, their patronesses.

RULE I.

THAT the Members of this Society shall pay 2s. 6d. entrance-money, and shall be entitled to receive a copy of these Rules.

RULE II. Four quarterly meetings shall be held, viz. on May-Day, the first of August, and on Martinmas and Candlemas[1] Days, at the SPINNING-SCHOOL in Little Alice Lane, between the hours of eleven and twelve o'clock in the morning, for the purpose of collecting the contributions of / the members; at which time each member, whose wages do not reach 3l. per year, shall pay one shilling towards raising a sum for the purposes hereafter specified. But every member, whose wages amount to 3l. or upwards, shall pay 1s 6d and if any member shall neglect to pay her contribution-money at one of such meetings, she shall forfeit 6d. and unless she shall discharge all arrears at the next or second meeting after such forfeiture has been incurred, she shall from that time be excluded from the Society.

RULE III. That no young person shall be elected a member, but such as are of a healthy constitution, and have behaved well in their respective schools; the intention being to exclude all prophaneness and immorality, in order that the christian character may be improved, in health, as well as the body supported and relieved, in sickness.

RULE IV. That every member who has been duly elected, and paid her contribution-money for one half year, and shall be afflicted with any such illness as shall wholly disable her from discharging the duties of her service, and shall give notice thereof to one of the Stewardesses for the time being, the Stewardess shall, within the space of twenty-four hours, either in person or by deputy, visit such indisposed member; and if her illness / shall be found to be real, then, whether she be continued in her place (unless her master and mistress should be able and willing to take the whole expence of hiring an assistant upon themselves) or is removed elsewhere, she shall receive out of the public stock of this Society, the weekly sum of 4s. during the continuance of her illness, reserving, however, this exception–that if she can be admitted as a patient in the County Hospital, the shall then only receive is per week during her stay there: And in the *former* case, the 4s. shall not be extended beyond the period of six months. But if such illness should continue longer than six months; or if any member should become blind or lame, or labour under any illness, which, although it should not wholly disable per from contributing towards her own maintenance, yet should prevent her continuing in service; then she shall, upon notice given as before-mentioned, receive the weekly sum of 2s. during the continuance of such illness, provided it does not, as in the case of the 4s. payment, continue longer than six months.

RULE V. Every member who has continued such for three years, and has behaved well during that time, shall be rewarded with the sum of 5s. to be laid out in some article of wearing apparel, to be worn by / her on the future days of meeting; and every member who has continued such for seven years, and behaved well, shall be intitled to the sum of 20s. to be applied to the same purpose, and worn as a mark of honor.

Rule VI. Every member not resident in York, must send a certificate signed by the minister or churchwardens at the place where she resides, or by her attending apothecary, signifying her indisposition and the nature of it, to one of the Stewardesses for the time being, and upon her recovery shall give notice thereof; and if any member shall be found guilty of having feigned an illness, or of procuring a false certificate, with an intent to impose upon either of the Stewardesses, she shall be excluded from this Society

Rule VII. Any member chusing to continue such after her marriage, shall, upon paying her subscription as before-mentioned, be entitled to all the benefits arising from this Institution, with this exception only– that this Society cannot provide for such illnesses as may be the more immediate effects of child bearing; nevertheless, in order to give some aid in cases of extreme difficulty and danger, certified to be such by the attending surgeon, to one of the Stewardesses for the time being, the Stewardess shall / at her discretion have the power of applying the sum of 10s. 6d. out of the public stock, for the relief of such extraordinary distress.

Rule VIII. That all gifts and benefactions to this Society shall be added to the joint stock, and considered as a part thereof.

Rule IX. If any member shall continue such for forty years, she shall afterwards be exempted from all further contributions, if the state of the fund will then admit of it, and shall nevertheless be intitled to all the advantages arising therefrom.

Rule X. If any member, after her admission, shall become guilty of any scandalous crime, or of any such misconduct as shall directly tend to the dissolution of this Society, she shall not be admitted to any future meeting, except for the purpose of vindicating her own character; and if she fail of doing this at the next following meeting, it shall be in the power of the majority of the members then present to exclude her altogether from this Society, as a disreputable and unworthy member.

Rule XI. That no stranger shall be admitted into the Society-Room without the consent of the Stewardesses; and of such as are admitted, it will be expected that before they leave the room, they give what they deem a decent contribution towards the / purposes of this Association–not less than 6d. nor more than half a crown.

Rule XII. That for the government of this Society, two ladies shall be elected Stewardesses for one year ; that at the termination of that period, one only of the ladies first elected shall be requested to continue in office for a second year, for the sake of putting this part of the Institution into a proper train,–it being intended that in future both the Stewardesses shall continue in office *two* whole years; but that only one shall be chosen each year, to the end that there may be always one in office who can inform her colleague in respect to any necessary particulars relating to the Society of which she may be ignorant One of the Stewardesses to be chosen from among the ladies who visit the Grey-Coat, and the other from among the patronesses of the Spinning-School; and the poorer members who want relief, are to apply to the lady who is Stewardess in behalf of that School in which such Member has been educated.

RULE XIII. That there shall be provided a box with two locks and two key and that therein the cash, books, and paper shall be deposited: That one of these key shall be kept by each Stewardess. And either of them shall neglect, in person or be deputy, to attend with the key of the So- / ciety-box on each of the four appointed days of meeting, by the hour of eleven in the morning, in order to receive the contribution-money of the members, she shall forfeit 2s. 6d. to the Society box; also, if either of the keys should happen to be lost, the Stewardess to whom for the time being it belonged, shall find a new one at her own expence. That the box shall be kept at the Grey-Coat School, and shall not be opened but by the two Stewardesses, in the presence of each other; or, in case of the unavoidable absence of one of them, in the presence of some one by her appointed to be her representative; together with a third person, who may be one either of the honorary, or common members of this Society.

RULE XIV. Whenever the money shall amount to 5l. or upwards, the sum, if in the opinion of the Stewardesses it can be spared, shall be deposited in some place of greater safety, which shall-be by them, and the majority of the other members present at a quarterly meeting, approved of for that purpose; the sum of two guineas being always previously placed in the hands of each of the Stewardesses, for the purposes of the Society, each of them giving a note of hand for the same to be deposited in the / box of the Society; and whenever the contribution-money shall amount to 20l. or upwards, over and above the necessary and contingent expences and payments of the Society; then such money shall, from time to time, be placed out at interest, upon such security as shall be previously approved of at a meeting of a majority of the members of this Society, which security shall, from time to time, be taken in the name of the Stewardesses for the time being, and be deposited immediately in the Society-box.

RULE XV. That from time to time, as it may become necessary, a Clerk shall be chosen by a majority of the members of this Society, who shall continue in office during his good behaviour, and shall be paid for his trouble annually on the 1st of August; and if he shall neglect to attend any of the stated meetings, he shall forfeit 2s. 6d. to the public stock.

RULE XVI. That all new rules and orders that may be made for the better regulation of this Society, shall be previously presented in writing by some of the members to one of the Stewardesses, and shall by her be delivered in to the Society, and read at three of the quarterly meetings, before it can be adopted, and shall then be admitted or rejected, as a majority of the members / present at the last meeting shall agree; if then admitted, it shall pass into a law, and be registered as such in the books of the Society, and shall from that time be binding upon all the members.

Rule XVII. That if either of the Stewardesses for the time being, shall neglect to visit, in person or by deputy, as here required, any sick member, she shall for every such omission forfeit one shilling to the box.

Rule XVIII That every act of the Society, to which such a mode of decision is applicable, shall be determined by ballot.

Rule XIX. That all pecuniary forfeitures shall be paid at the next meeting of the Society after such forfeitures have been incurred; and that whoever shall neglect to pay her forfeiture, shall from that time be excluded from the Society, unless a majority of the members at the following meeting shall think proper to restore her.

Rule XX. That if any member shall either publicly or privately promote the dissolution of this Society, or shall propose to divide among them, the joint stock, or any part thereof, unless she shall be joined by ninety-five of the other members, she shall be excluded from the Society, and from all the benefits arising therefrom. /

Rule XXI. That every honorary member shall have the privilege of introducing one other member, although she may {illegible} have been educated in either of the Schools as before specified; provided she be a young woman of healthy constitution, and of good character, and she, upon paying her contribution, and conforming to the rules in {the} manner as the others, shall be entitled to all the privileges arising from the Institution.

FINIS.

FERDINANDO TRACY TRAVELL, *THE DUTIES OF THE POOR* (1793)

Ferdinando Tracy Travell, *The Duties of the Poor; Particularly in the Education of their Children, in an Address from a Minister to his Parishioners* (London, 1793), British Library, 224.c31 (excerpts).

As mentioned in the examination of John Sibley, claimants on poor relief increased in number during the eighteenth century. In addition to official parliamentary action via the Poor Laws, there were a variety of charitable, personal and religious responses to this seemingly ever-expanding poverty. Most political and religious thinkers considered poverty an aspect of divine will or a social given. While it was the duty of the wealthy to provide assistance to the 'deserving poor', it was the duty of the poor to be thrifty and hard-working; there were few who argued that poverty itself needed to be eradicated.[1] The responses gathered here show a concern for poor families that are focused on particular situations or particular objects of charity.

Ferdinando Tracy Travell, a native of western Oxfordshire and educated at Oxford, was rector of Upper Slaughter in Gloucestershire from 1764 until his death in 1808.[2] In 1789 he donated £167 in stock to the local Sunday school – an investment that continues to produce income dedicated to local education.[3] This published sermon went through five editions between 1793 and 1799. Most of it is about the kind of virtues parents should have; it is only the last section that discusses how parents in poorer families should teach their children. Travell recognized that many of his parishioners were of 'humble station'. He admonishes them to be industrious and frugal, because just surviving, he recognized, took constant labour.

Notes
1. R. Ashcraft, 'Lockean Ideas, Poverty, and the Development of Liberal Political Theory', in J. Brewer and S. Staves (eds), *Early Modern Conceptions of Property* (London and New York, NY: Routledge, 1996), pp. 43–61.
2. Ferdinando Tracy Travell (CCEd Person ID 209858) in *The Clergy of the Church of England Database, 1540–1835*, at http://www.theclergydatabase.org.uk [accessed

1 December 2014]. His mother's diary (Anne Tracy Travell) is included in Volume 3, Household Management.
3. 'Upper Slaughter', in C. R. Elrighton (ed.), *A History of the County of Gloucester*, 00 vols (London: Victoria County History, 1965), vol. 6, pp. 134–42, at www.british-history.ac.uk [accessed 10 December 2014].

Ferdinando Tracy Travell, *The Duties of the Poor* (1793)

The Duties of The Poor

My Friends and Neighbours,

The near relation which I have so long borne to you, as your Minister, and the kind manner in which you have, all in your turns, often received my advice and instructions, convinces me that you will not be displeased with any attempt of mine that may prove useful to you. It is my inclination, as well as my duty, to render you every service in my power: but as increasing infirmities and advancing years may probably make me less and less capable of giving you public instruction, I have chosen this method of pointing out to you your various duties: partly as a mark of my regard for you, / but still more in the hopes, that by having my advice conveyed to you in this manner, you will frequently dwell upon it, and endeavour heartily to put it in practice.

However unable I may be to be useful to you in the public service of the Church, it by no means lessens my obligation to serve you in private; it does indeed greatly increase it; and I may fairly apply the words of the prophet Samuel, and say,* God forbid that I should sin against the Lord, in ceasing to pray for you; but I will teach you the good and the right way. Only fear the Lord, and serve him in truth with all your heart; for consider how great things he hath done for you. Highly blameable should I be, if I did not offer up to God my prayers for you, and endeavour, to the best of my power, still to instruct you in your duty. And when you consider, how great are the blessings you all receive from God, you cannot but confess your obligation to obey his laws, as his true and faithful servants.

It is not for his own sake that God requires our obedience; we can add nothing to his / happiness, nor take away any thing from it: but it is one of the strongest motives to a good and useful life, that we thereby consult our own real happiness; – our happiness in this world, as well as in the next.

In order therefore to assist your endeavours towards the attainment of so important a point as your present and future happiness, I shall lay before you some of the chief duties belonging to your situation in life; by the due perfor-

---

* 1 Samuel xii. 23, 24.

mance of which, you may generally insure comfort to yourselves, together with the approbation of God and you own consciences.

You are most of you placed in that humble station, which requires constant labour and activity, for the maintenance of yourselves and your families: the first duty therefore which I shall recommend to you, is Industry.

We are all sent into life to act our several parts, some to labour with the head, others with the hands, but no man was intended to be idle. Many of those, who are blessed with large and affluent fortunes, are obliged to act a very laborious part; and even they who are the most independent, must find some business or / occupation for themselves, if they would preserve their health, or have a relish for any enjoyment. – But to you, who must labour for your daily bread, industry is absolutely necessary: you will not be the only sufferers by the neglect of it; when you are idle, your children must be starving. An interruption from labour by sickness, only for a few days, will be severely felt; and if idleness be added to those accidental hindrances, which all must sometimes feel, distress and ruin must be the consequence.

But these are not the only bad effects of a want of industry; all habits grow stronger by indulgence, and if idleness once become habitual, both the mind and the body will be less inclined to labour: still, subsistence must be procured; and if a man will not work for his bread, he must either rely upon the bounty of others, or he will too probably be induced to steal, or take it by force. I scarcely need point out to you the misery of such as procure a wretched subsistence by begging, or the wickedness of those who live by theft and plunder; I would rather lead your minds to the consideration of the comfort which you may enjoy from a habit of honest industry, and a due use of / those means which God has put in your power. The wife Providence of God has allotted to mankind a variety of ranks and stations, all contributing to the general good of the whole. While you are laboring for the maintenance of your families, you are fulfilling a principal part of the duties of that station in which his goodness has placed you, and you lay a claim to his future kindness and protection. Besides, they who are industrious, will seldom fail to meet with encouragement and assistance; charity is never happier than in bestowing her bounty upon those who will be sure to make a good use of it.

In order to make your industry more useful, you must not neglect to add to it Frugality. The most ample fortune may be dissipated, without some attention to ceremony; but with frugality and proper management, a very slender income may be enough, and to spare. In times of difficulty, the utmost industry will sometimes be scarce sufficient to supply the wants of a numerous family; and if the little that comes in be wasted, or applied to improper purposes, it is easier to foresee, than to prevent, the / ruinous effects which must follow. It is surprising to observe the difference between one poor family and another, where the income is equally small, and there is an equal number of children; now this difference is owing to frugality and good management in one family, and an entire neglect of it in the other. In one case we see the children decently clothed and fed, with clean and healthy countenances, reflecting credit on the good conduct of their parents, whose dwelling, however small and mean, is a pattern of neatness. In the other case, we are offended every step we take, all is confusion and disorder, rage and filth; and we can scarce be persuaded, that the two families have the same means of subsistence.

In times like the present, when vanity and show have so much influence over every rank, the plain duty of frugality will be too apt to be neglected: - neither the food, nor clothing, which our own country can supply, will be thought sufficient, even by those who are put to difficulties to procure wither. But surely the necessities of nature should be satisfied, be the fare ever so plain and homely, before far-fetched luxuries be sought for; and the parent /would be highly blameable, who, in order to trick out one of her children in flaunting ornaments, should pinch the rest of them in food and decent clothing.

But besides the absolute necessity of frugality to your present comfort and support, you will gain a lasting advantage from it, if it enable you to lay up something against the time of sickness or old age. Much cannot be expected to be done in this way by those who have families to maintain; but when times and seasons are favourable, a little foresight and good management may enable even them to save something that may prevent their being burthensome to the public. They, who have only themselves to support, will be unpardonable if they do not look forward to the decline of life, when, without such prudent foresight, they may be forced to depend upon charity for subsistence.

I will just add too, that you should remember the parable of the widow's mite; they who are poor themselves, may find still poorer, to whom the most trifling assistance will be acceptable: We are told in Scripture, that if we have much, we must give plenteously, but if we have little, we must do our diligence gladly to give of that little; / for by that means we shall gather to ourselves a good reward in the day of necessity.*

To industry and frugality must be added a strict regard to Honesty in all your dealings. – This is required by the positive law of God, nor will the laws of man dispense with the breach of it. I shall not, I believe, be mistaken in saying, that dishonesty, of some kind or other, is a sin, which the lower classes of people are too apt to commit. This perhaps may arise in some measure from their ignorance, and from being accustomed to see trifling instances of this kind overlooked and unpunished. But if dishonesty be sinful, as it undoubtedly is, the smallest instance of it is so in its degree: and when once we allow ourselves to go beyond the bounds of strict truth and honesty, we know not where we shall stop. It is from small beginnings that every sin first takes its rise, and therefore it is of the utmost consequence that these should be firmly resisted. The most deter-

---

* Tobit iv 8,9.

mined villains, who have forfeited their lives for their dishonesty, little thought to what / shocking lengths they should be carried, when once they left the strait path of uprightness. -- But the progress of every vice is rapid, and quickly hurries men on to the commission of crimes, which in the beginning they could not have thought of without trembling. Whenever therefore you are tempted in the smallest degree to be dishonest, either in buying or selling, in defrauding your neighbor of his property, or in pilfering any thing that does not belong to you; firmly resist the temptation in the first instance, resolve to banish from your minds every thought of deceit and fraud, every secret desire of unjust gain. The inward consciousness of upright behavior, and the having preserved your peace of mind unbroken, will give you a satisfaction which all the ill-gotten treasures in the world could never bestow.

But besides this, the old maxim, that honesty is the best policy, will seldom fail to stand good . If the crooked arts of dishonesty and fraud do sometimes appear to succeed, there is no depending upon them, and the world in general will steadily oppose them. But the honest man will be sure to find friends; all men of worth and principle will be ready to take his part, and / to encourage and assist him in those difficulties and distresses, to which all are unavoidably subject.

One kind of honesty, which I would particularly recommend to you, is a strict regard to the due performance of whatever is committed to your trust. The man who is diligent in his master's work, no longer than when his eye is upon him; who only waits for his absence to slacken his industry, deserves not the character of an honest man; he certainly robs his master of his time, and if he continues to indulge that idle disposition, will too probably be induced, when opportunity offers, to rob him of his property.

The next duty I shall point out to you is Sobriety. --- The practice of this is as necessary to your well-being as any of the former duties, nor indeed can they well subsist without it. Industry and frugality can never be effectually maintained without a strict attention to sobriety; and if intemperance become habitual, it is to be feared, that even honesty will sometimes yield to the strength of the temptation. If the utmost you can earn by constant labour be barely sufficient for the decent maintenance of your / families, you can surely very ill spare any part of it for the ale-house. Your time is, or ought to be, so fully employed the whole week, that you can have no leisure for going there, except on a Sunday; and that is the most unfit day of all for the purpose. When you have been spending the former part of the day in attending the public worship of God, in thanking him for his continual mercies, in begging his blessing upon your honest labours, and in beseeching him to keep you from evil of every kind; will you plunge yourselves headlong into the midst of evil; will you run the risk of losing all the good you got at church, by frequenting the company of those who seldom think of God, or speak of him, but by taking his holy name in vain? You cannot be ignorant how improper such a conduct would be.

But besides the great impropriety of frequenting the ale-house on a Sunday, and the loss of time in doing it on the other days of the week, consider how much it exposes you to the dangers of evil company. If a sober and honest man be sometimes seen in public-houses, it is well known that they who constantly frequent them are rarely men of respectable characters; / and it is there that the plans are commonly laid for the robbing and plundering their neighbours. If you are ever so well disposed when you go there, you know not into what mischiefs you may be led before you part; one cup draws on another, a false shame induces you to do like the rest, and when once you are heated with liquor, and have lost your reason, you may commit such actions as you will bitterly repent of all your life.

Another ill consequence of the want of sobriety, is the fatal effects it produces upon the health, injuring the constitution, depriving a man of that strength and activity upon which he depends for his livelihood, and laying a foundation for those diseases, which frequently cut him off before his time, and leave a wretched family to lament his folly and imprudence.-- They who are not accustomed to see the miseries of the poor in large manufacturing towns, cannot fully judge of the sad effects which are produced by a habit of drinking; they are such, as should make the poor in the country very thankful for their situation, and very careful to avoid a practice so full of misery and ruin. / Closely connected with sobriety is Chastity, a virtue strictly commanded by God's laws, and the neglect of which produces infinite misery and distress .Most of the evils which men bring upon themselves, are owing to the want of keeping their passions in due subjection; if we do not get the mastery over us. A habit of chastity, in particular, should be formed from early youth, and parents should be very attentive to keep their children within the strict bounds of decency, both in their words and actions.

The breach of chastity is not only a heinous offence against the strict law of Christianity, which requires a purity of thought, of conversation, and of behavior; but it is followed by a loss of character, and by a train of evils, destructive of every comfort and happiness.—They, who have offended in this way in their youth, and have been drawn into a sinful connexion before marriage, are too apt to think they make full amends by marrying the partners of their guilt; but they must shew a long course of good behavior, before they can regain the good opinion of the world; and with respect to the forgiveness of God, both for this and / every other offence against chastity, they must know that they can lay no claim to it, but by a hearty repentance ,and a thorough change of life. The best method which parents can take to preserve their children from this sin, is to cultivate in them a strict regard to the sacred law of God, to keep them constantly and usefully employed, and as soon as they are able to maintain themselves, to procure for them decent services of trades: nothing is so great an encouragement to vice as idleness; and experience has often shewn the ill consequences of suffering children that are grown up to loiter at home with their parents, instead of their being sent out into the world to be usefully employed.

Another duty, which I shall recommend to you, is Contentment; a duty required from men of every station, and without which there can be no true happiness. As most of you are placed in a low situation of life, and are sometimes exposed to the sufferings of poverty and want, you may perhaps imagine, that the practice of this duty cannot be much be assured, that God is not partial in the distribution of his / blessings to mankind, and that every station has the means of happiness, and consequently of contentment in its power. You have not, indeed, the luxuries of the rich, their splendid equipages, their costly tables, their gaudy apparel; you have not the full command of your time, nor can you afford to waste it in folly and idleness. But you have at least as good health as they have; and when it is otherwise, charity has provided abundant assistance. Your own industry can supply you with the necessaries of life, and by frugality and good management, with many of the comforts of it too. When seasons are unfavorable, and difficulties press upon those who have numerous families, they will be likely to meet with assistance, if their past good conduct entitle them to it. – God will raise up friends for those who reverence his laws, or as David happily expresses it, I have been young and now am old, and yet saw I never the righteous forsaken, nor his seed begging their bread.* Then, consider the cares and anxiety which riches bring with them, the dangers to which they frequently expose men, / and the imaginary and teasing wants which they create: consider this, and you will not envy the uncertain possession of them, but will daily bless the goodness of God, for having placed you in a station, where you have the means of having yourselves and your children happy; where yu are free from many of the temptations to which others are exposed, and where your being constantly employed is of itself a source of happiness, which your betters have too often cause to envy you.

In order to render contentment still easier to you, I shall advise you to add to is Humility, which is a temper of mind suited to the weak and dependent nature of man, closely connected with the mild duties of Christianity, and with the station in which you are placed. Pride and haughtiness are very offensive and disgusting, wherever they are seen; but they are particularly unbecoming is those, who must work for their bread, and who are often indebted to the bounty of others for their subsistence. It is absolutely necessary for the general good of society, that there should be various orders and degrees of men; society indeed cannot subsist / without it; there must be some to govern, and some to be governed; there must be some to procure food and clothing for themselves and others, and there must be some to employ them, and to reward their labours.

---

*   Psalm xxxvii. 25.

Strange and wild notions have been spread abroad of late, as if it were designed by Providence that all mankind should have power of distinction above the rest; such absurd opinions serve only to create confusion, and to make the lower orders of people discontented with their station. Were it possible for such a scheme to take place, your condition would be far from being bettered by it; famine and disease, rapine and misery, would be the lamentable consequence of it. Learn then to be content with your present useful stations; respect those whose talents and situation make them your superiors; check that pride of heart which would lead you to envy and discontent; and endeavor to cultivate that humility which is well pleasing in the fight of God, which will gain you the esteem of your neighbours, and make you valuable members of the community. / A most important duty to be added to the rest, is Charity, that amiable virtue, which so particularly distinguishes the Christian religion. By charity I do not mean the giving of alms, for that is only a small branch of it, and few in comparison are able to practice it: but I mean benevolence, compassion, loving-kindness, and a desire to do all the good in your power. Some of the lower class of mankind are apt to complain, that, however will disposed they may be, they have no opportunities of doing good; as if so godlike a virtue as charity were only in the reach of the great, or wealthy.

It is a great mistake to suppose, that you are not capable of assisting the poor, because you cannot spare any thing to relieve their necessities; in fact, you may be extremely assistant to each other, by kind advice, by friendly consolation, by wholesome instruction, by visiting and attending one another in sickness and distress, by rejoicing with them that do rejoice, and weeping with them that weep.* These are the truest kinds of charity, and such as every one may have frequent opportunities of practicing.
/
What a happy world would this be, if every man followed the golden rule, of doing to others what we would have them do to us. -- Take this for your guide, and you will never be at a loss how to act, you will never want means of doing good. Leave this rule to your children, as the most valuable legacy you can bequeath them. Teach them by your example, as well as by your lessons, that to do good is the chief business of life, and that if they will indeed be the disciples of Christ, they must have love one to another. How directly contrary to this benevolent disposition do we sometimes find the behavior of the poor: instead of taking pleasure in the exercise of kindness and charity, they are too apt to indulge a spirit of envy and jealousy, of malice and slander. They seem to grudge their neighbours any little favours and advantages which they may happen to possess; they take a malicious pleasure in their misfortunes; and never appear so happy as when they are spreading false and slanderous reports against

---

* Rom. Xii. 15

the innocent and unwary, and blackening the characters of those who have had the misfortune to slip. Want and poverty surely should give milder and more affectionate feelings! / I have spoken pretty fully on the duties you owe to yourselves, and to your neighbours, but have not yet particularly mentioned those you owe to God: in general, however, these duties are so closely connected, that by fulfilling the one, we fulfil the other also. We can seldom do more acceptable service to God, than by shewing kindness to one another, and doing the duties of our station. But piety has its claims as well as benevolence; and since we have received so much from God, we ought to make him all the return in our power. When we consider the numberless blessings bestowed upon us, we cannot surely refuse our gratitude to the great Author of them. It was He that called us into being, and made us capable of enjoying happiness, and made us capable of enjoying happiness, and of being useful in the world. It is He that hath given us health and strength, and hath preserved us from a multitude of evils; and whose Providence continually watches over us for good. But beyond all this, it is He that hath redeemed us from sin and death, and made us capable of eternal happiness in his heavenly kingdom.—Justly therefore may He expect that our heart should be full of gratitude for such undeserved / mercies; that we should reverence his holy name and his word, and pay a strict obedience to the laws of so good a God.

To believe in God's Providence, to love him for his goodness, and to be fearful of offending him, are so plainly our duty, that one should think nothing would easily prevent us from the practice of them. But we are such weak and frail creatures, and are so liable to act contrary to our duty and true happiness, that we have need of every means to keep us stedfast in the right path. It is upon this account, therefore, that prayer is so necessary a duty; being a confession of our own weakness, an acknowledgment of God's power to help us, a claim upon his goodness to give us the aids of his grace, and an incitement to us to use our best endeavours to second his divine assistance.

Let me intreat you then to persevere in the habitual practice of prayer; fail not, every morning and evening, to thank God for his mercies, to implore his forgiveness, to beg his blessing upon your honest labours, and his protection from evil of every kind. The doing this constantly will take up very little time, and you will find infinite benefit from it, especially / if you make your families join in it. But remember, however short your prayers are, you must endeavour to repeat them with attention, and above all, to conform your lives to them; for this is the true end of prayer, to make us holy, that we may be happy.

In addition to private and family devotion, one day in seven you are called upon to join in the united prayers of the congregation; to the due performance of which God has promised his peculiar blessing. So important as this duty is, you will not surely let a slight excuse ever prevent your going to church; and if the younger part of your family require some attendance at home, the elder part may take their turns, so that each of the family may attend divine service at least once in the day.

But going to church, though it be a principal, is by no means the only part of your duty on the Sabbath: you will then have leisure to look back upon the week past, to repent of any thing you may have done amiss, and to make firm resolutions against it for the future: you will have time to visit your sick neighbours, and to instruct your children, as well as to / partake with them of that domestic enjoyment which is the great sweetener of life. The due observance of the Sabbath does not require and sourness of severity of manners, nor to be shut up from society; when the public and private duties of the day have been duly performed, the conclusion of it may well be spent in pleasant walks, in sober and cheerful conversation; neither of which will be rendered the less pleasant, nor the less cheerful, by reflections on God's bounty in furnishing the beauties of the spring, the blessings of harvest, the variety of flowers with which the fields are clothed, the numberless animals which contribute to the food and use of man, or those splendid lights which hang like lamps in the heavens, and make some amends for the absence of the fun. The wonderful works of creation are a subject of astonishment, both to the learned and the ignorant, and lead the mind to the contemplation of that awful Being, who spake and it was done, who commanded and it stood fast.[*]

/
I have now gone through the several duties I proposed to point out to you, except the Education of your Children. This is a subject of so much consequence, not only to parents, but to the world in general, that I have deferred to consideration of it to the last, in order to give you more full directions with respect to it. Great complaints are made of the wickedness of the present age, and that mankind are growing more and more profligate; -- I am rather inclined to doubt, whether this is so much the case as it is represented to be: corrupted as human nature is, vice will at all times too much prevail, and it will put on different appearances, according to the manners and fashion of the times. Perhaps the case may be, that there is at present less deceit in the world than there may sometimes have been, and therefore, wherever there is vice, it will be sure to appear. However that may be, it is too true that there is always a great proportion of wickedness, and therefore it concerns us all to endeavour to stop the course of it, as well by our own example, as by our influence over others. / It is a common saying, that the world would soon be better, if every one would mend one; that is, himself: this is true, no doubt, but the effect of it is more to be wished than expected; for when sin is become habitual, it is no easy matter to shake it off; and though all may wish others to amend themselves. Our chief hopes, therefore, must be from the rising generation; from those whose minds are yet untainted by evil habits, and

---

[*] Psalm xxxiii. 9.

are ready to receive every good impression that can be made upon them. That you all love your children, cannot admit of a doubt; nature hath taken effectual care of that, by implanting in you such strong affections towards them; but the best proof you can give of your love, is to bring them up in the way most likely to make them happy, and to teach them to do their duty to God and their neighbor.

I have laid down rules for the government of yourselves, most of which will be of use in the management of your children; but in order to be more particular, the first thing I would advise you to teach them, is Obedience. It is a / long time before young people are at all capable of conducting themselves; and their minds want full as much assistance from us as their bodies. Who would not blame a parent, that, for want of due care of a child in infancy, should suffer it to lose the free use of its limbs? And how fatal would be the neglect, in suffering the will to grow crooked and preserve, and obstinately to follow its own headstrong fancies. To prevent this growing evil you cannot begin too soon; even before your children can speak, it will be necessary to put some restraint upon their desires, and to accustom them to submit their will to yours. It is wonderful with how much ease the generality of children may be managed, if they are begun with early. Do not then let a false tenderness, and the fear of a little more trouble, prevail upon you to delay this necessary talk; it must be done at some time or other, for you sake as well as theirs; and if the foundation be early and happily laid, every thing will go on smoothly. Your children, having at first obeyed you from habit, will soon be induced to do it from a sense of duty, and from good principle. The improper indulgence of children is, after all, but a kind / of self-indulgence, and, like other selfish passions, requires to be corrected.

It is very common to hear parents complain, as their children grow up, that they are obstinate and untractable: -- they, who will be persuaded to check them betimes, which may be done with all possible love and tenderness, will seldom have these complaints to make, but will find a present, as well as future, reward from their habit of compliance.

After obedience, the next thing to be taught children, is the Command of Themselves, or, in other words, the proper government of their passions. Few things are of more importance than this; for it is from the hurtful indulgence of the passions, that most of the evils of life take their beginning; so that if you check them at the fountain-head, and betimes accustom your children to keep them under, you thereby put them in the way of stopping one of the greatest causes of future mischief and misery. There is as much difference, it is true, between the natural temper of men's minds, as there is in the shape and form of their bodies; and after all the pains that can be taken, something / of the original disposition will still remain. – But if the temper be attended to very early, and the child be led by degrees into a habit of checking and restraining its own unruly will, it is astonishing what a change may be wrought; greater indeed than most of us are aware of, or than they, who are unwilling to take the pains, may be inclined to believe. One great advantage of self-command is this, that it is useful in every circumstance of life, so that if a habit of it be obtained in one instance, there will be the less difficulty in gaining it in another: the child that has been long accustomed to check the first risings of anger, will a proportionable ease in restraining those unruly passions, which are the attendants of a riper age.

I have purposely mentioned obedience, and self-command, as necessary for the good of children even before the sense of their Duty to God; both because the practice of those will prepare the way for this duty, and as they may and ought to be taught them, long before they can have any notion of the Deity, and of their obligations to Him. But you cannot too soon give them such notions of God and religion as their / tender age is capable of: and as their laborious life, and the humble station is which they will generally be placed, will put it out of their power to understand the more difficult parts of religion, you must be careful to enforce the practice of it as early and as habitually as possible. We are all strangely governed by custom and habit, especially by such habits as we have learnt in our earliest years: be sure then not to neglect giving them that habit, which is the most important of all others. -- Teach them to love God, and to adore his fatherly goodness in giving them their daily bread, and providing them with many of the comforts of life. Direct them to put their chief confidence in him, and to make his will the guide of their lives. Teach them to fear his displeasure, to reverence his name, to keep holy his Sabbath, to frequent his church, to pray to him daily, and to consider themselves as always in his presence. – Give them such habits as these, and do not fear their wanting the knowledge of religion; they will feel the comfort of these habits as long as they live, and will bless your memory for them, long after you are at rest in the silent grave. /

With the duties we owe to God, are closely connected those by which we are bound to one another; and indeed, these are required of us in scripture, as the proof of our love to God: – He that loveth not his brother whom he hath seen, how shall he love God whom he hath not seen?* Let it therefore be one of your first cares, to sow in the hearts of your children the good seeds of brotherly kindness, of mutual good-will, and universal benevolence; the tender affections towards each other, which nature has planted in them, must be cherished and encouraged; but you must teach them not to limit their regard to their relations only, but to look upon all mankind as one great family, with whom they are intimately connected, and to whom they owe every good office that is in their power. Nothing is more opposite both to the precepts and spirit of Christianity, than that envy and jealously, those secret grudgings, and open repinings at the welfare and success of their neighbours, which too many are apt to entertain.

---

* 1 john, iv. 20.

Would you then discharge one of your principal duties as a parent? Be earnest / to stifle, in your children, every emotion of malice and ill-will, every tendency you can perceive in them towards a narrow selfish temper. Endeavour to make them sensible, that by promoting their neighbour's happiness, they will greatly increase their own; and that by so doing they will best secure the favour of God, who hath taught us, that 'all our doings without charity are nothing worth.'

The next point I would recommend to you, is to be very strict with your children in the article of Speaking the truth. Few things are of so much consequence as this; honesty, fidelity, and character, all depend upon it; and therefore every means must be employed to make the practice of it easy and familiar to them. Let reward be sure to follow speaking the truth, and punishment never fail to be the consequence of telling lies, and yu will quickly gain your point. Even when they are guilty of faults, if they are willing to own them, you must not be backward in forgiving them; it will encourage an open behavior, and you will gain their confidence by it, which will be sure to give you a happy influence over them. — The / good effects of constantly speaking the truth will appear in every part of their lives; they will just in their dealings, true to their promises, and faithful in the discharge of every duty. Whereas a habit of lying will produce hypocrisy and deceit, it will lay the foundation of fraud and dishonesty, and too probably lead the way to the commission of the most notorious crimes.

Diligence and Industry are very important in every situation of life, but they are particularly necessary to those who are to earn their daily bread by the labour of their hands. Be sure then to give your children a habit of industry as early as you can; neglect no opportunity of employing them in whatever is suitable to their years and strength: though they earn ever so little, it will at least keep them from doing mischief, and will in time give them such a habit if industry, as they will find the benefit of, all their lives after. Teach them also to be doubly diligent when no eye overlooks them, and to be particularly careful of whatever is committed to their charge. / Bringing them up thus early to labour, need not prevent a proper attention to their learning. Some time there will necessarily be, before they are capable of bodily labour; – if that time be carefully spent in teaching them to read; and if at the least busy seasons of the year they are properly employed in improving their little stock of knowledge, it will be the fault of their parents if they have not learning sufficient for their humble station in life, and to enable them to read and understand the plain parts of their duty, in the word of God. The institution of Sunday Schools is admirably suited to this purpose, as well as to the important one of making children regularly attend the service of the church; and tends more that any thing to prevent that dreadful profanation of the Sabbath, to which so many unhappy wretches owe their ruin. If parents will second this good institution by sending their children regularly; and will endeavour to keep up the spirit of it in their own management of them, during their absence from the school; the best effects may be expected to follow from it, and a lasting foundation be laid of decency, morality, and religion. /

Thus have I endeavoured to lay before you some of the chief points to be attended to in the education of your children; a habit of obedience and self-command, – a sense of the duty they owe to God and their neighbor, – a constant regard to truth and honesty, – diligence and industry in their several callings, – and such a proportion of learning as is suited to their station in life. In addition to these several points, only one thing more is necessary, but that is the most important of all: – I mean, your own examples. As a picture makes a more lasting impression than a mere description, so does example recommend more powerfully than precept. Let parents take ever so much pains in teaching and correcting their children, few good effects can be expected to follow their lessons, unless they enforce them by their own practice. In vain can you expect your children to obey the divine laws, if they see you live in a habit of disobedience to them. In vain will you correct them for lying or pilfering, if they find you regardless of your word, or trying to defraud and overreach one another. In vain can you hope that they will check their passions, when you indulge your own with out limit or restraint. /

Let this consideration then be an additional call upon you, to a faithful discharge of every part of your duty; consider, that not only your own happiness depends upon it, but the happiness of those also, who are, as it were, a part of yourselves. All who are convinced of what is most undoubtedly true, that *Godliness hath the promises of this life, as well as of that which is to come*, [*] can never want motives to a truly Christian life: but how is the obligation increased, when we consider the influence which our example will have upon our children; and that, according to our good or ill conduct and behavior, we are promoting their future happiness or misery.

If then you do indeed love your children, and earnestly wish to make them happy, both in this world and the next; the best proof you can give of it, and the most effectual means you can take for it, is to set them a good example in every part of your own life and practice; and then you may expect to reap the fruits of it by the honesty and piety of theirs. Children / are usually the greatest blessings or the greatest curses of life: that they are the one or the other, in great measure depends upon those who have the care of them in their youth; there may be some exceptions to this observation, but it will generally be found to hold good. What a shock would it prove in your declining years, should you live to be the miserable witnesses of the profligacy of your own offspring! At that period of life, when you are preparing to leave the world, and have need of every comfort that you have been the means of bringing children into the world, only to make them wretched: that you have neglected the cultivation of their minds, when it would have been an easy and a pleasing talk; and by your ill-times indulgence

---

* 1 Timothy iv. 8.

have suffered their vices to take such deep root, that you have now nothing left but to deplore the fruits of them. The ingratitude and misconduct of a child is a calamity that bears very hard upon a parent, to whatever cause it may be owing; but nothing would give it so keen an edge, as to be conscious that the blame must / justly be laid upon your own negligence, or ill example.

On the other hand, how will it calm the soul of the dying parent, to feel that he has done his duty in that near and tender relation! How will it smooth the rugged path of death, to think, that he has been an instrument in God's hand of bringing a pious and virtuous family into the world, and of enabling them to be serviceable in it. His situation in life, perhaps, may permit him to leave them but a small share of this world's goods; but he will not need to be anxious on that account, having early taught them, that a *small thing that the righteous hath, is better than great riches of the ungodly;** and having amply stored their minds with the good principles of religion and honesty, which will procure them a happiness that the world can neither give nor take away.

I have now pointed out the several duties which I intended to recommend to you; they are in general of such a nature, that the bare mention of them is sufficient to shew the / necessity of living in the constant practice of them. Scarcely a day can pass that you are not called upon to exercise the duties of industry, frugality, honesty, sobriety, chastity, contentment, humility, and charity. Pious affections towards God, and earnest prayer to Him, with firm resolutions of obeying his laws, are duties of continual obligation; and they, who have children, can never want motives to bring them up in the fear of God, and in the habits of virtue and usefulness. All these are such plain and simple duties, that they require no learning to comprehend them; they lie open to every understanding, and are suited to men of every station.

It is also of the utmost importance to remark, that the habitual practice of these duties is the surest means of promoting your happiness here, as well as of laying the foundation of it for the world to come. Virtue must ever be, in great measure, its own reward, and vice its own punishment. Whoever wishes to enjoy those calm, composed, and lasting pleasures, which are the object of every wife man's hopes: whoever wishes to preserve his body, as far as is in his power, free from pain and disease, and to / keep his mind undisturbed by violent passions and headstrong desires: whoever wishes to gain the approbation of his neighbours, his conscience, and his God, let him sincerely and heartily endeavour to conform his life to the precepts of religion, and patiently submit to that light and easy yoke which the Gospel imposes; and then he may hope to obtain the present rewards of such a conduct.

---

*   Psalm xxxvii. 16.

But besides the present happiness of a virtuous course, it must be remembered, that human life, at the longest, is but of short duration; and when a few more suns have risen and gone down, you will receive your final summons, and must appear before that awful tribunal, from whence there is no appeal. Of how great consequence then is it, that you should be able to stand before your judge with a consciousness of having endeavoured, to the utmost of your power, to discharge the duties of your station.

It is indeed upon the mercies of God and the merits of our blessed Redeemer, that every man must depend, after all, for his final acceptance with God: For by grace are ye saved, through faith; and that not of yourselves; it is the gift / of God.* Nevertheless, though it is God which worketh in you, both to will and to do of his good pleasure;† it is also your duty to use your best endeavours in assisting to work out your own salvation, and to second the aids of God's grace by a strict attention to the duties of morality and religion.

When you are stretched upon the bed of sickness, and the vanities of life are closing fast upon you, nothing will give you so much comfort, as the reflection that have not spent an idle, and an useless life, or set a vicious and profligate example to others; but have labored to perform faithfully the talk which God allotted you. Whereas the thoughtless, the idle, and the wicked, will then feel the bitter reproaches of conscience, and will vainly wish for a return of those precious hours, which they wasted in sin and folly, regardless of their own happiness, and despising the gracious intentions of Providence.

---

*   Ephef. Ii.8.
†   Phil. Ii. 13.

SOCIETY OF FRIENDS, BUCKINGHAM MONTHLY MEETING, MEN'S MINUTE BOOKS (1735–98), WOMEN'S MINUTE BOOKS (1670–1822)

Society of Friends, Buckingham Monthly Meeting, Men's Minute Books (1735–98), Women's Minute Books (1670–1822), Buckinghamshire Record Office, NQ/4/3/1.

Monthly Meetings were composed of Quakers (Friends) in good standing from each of the local worship meetings established within a specific jurisdiction.[1] Those involved in this grouping of meetings, which were divided into men's meetings and women's meetings, met monthly for administrative purposes. In between each meeting, committees from the women's and the men's meetings visited and observed various Quaker families, conducted marriage inspections and consulted with those whose conduct – often for financial and behavioral reasons – was deemed questionable.[2] In addition to disciplining those in need of correction, members of these committees also visited and cared for the poor and unfortunate, reviewed community business and encouraged 'holy conversation' by 'identifying and disowning "carnal talk" and by organizing life for the rule of the world'.[3]

One of the primary purposes of the Monthly Meeting was 'their elaborate marriage discipline'; indeed, historian Barry Levy explains, those involved in these meetings spent the bulk of their time controlling 'the formation of new households and thereby the primary environments in which children grew'.[4] Because Quakers considered the creation of new families so important, prospective couples had to obtain permission for courtship, and then later marriage, from parents and other close relatives. Upon being granted permission to wed from their families, the couple then had to announce their intent to marry before the men's and women's monthly meetings. Following this public announcement, the meetings organized two committees, each composed of two 'well-established Friends', to 'investigate the "clearness" from prior ties and particularly the "conversation" of the man and woman (two women investigated the woman, two men the man)'.[5] The couple would attend the next monthly meeting to hear the committees' decision, which was typically favourable.[6] Shortly thereafter, the marriage ceremony took place, often in the meeting house, attended by the woman's family.

Quakers believed that marriage took place 'directly before God'; nonetheless, those in attendance served as witnesses and thus signed the marriage certificate.[7] After establishing their own household, the newlyweds would also be visited and inspected by members of the women's and men's monthly meetings. This suggests that they were being recognized as an extension of the larger Quaker family. As one Quaker observed 'a church is ... made up of living stones, living members, a spiritual household'.

> It is of this living church that we really learn in the records of the Monthly Meetings for discipline and business ... The lives of the members of meeting were known to one another almost as those of one family and the overseers ... as the most careful and solicitous parent could be ... as lenient and long suffering as a wise and tender parent.[8]

The Minute Books kept by members of the Monthly Meeting in Buckinghamshire, Pennsylvania, not only reflect the fictive ties that bound Quakers together as spiritual kin, but also detail the formation and perpetuation of the consanguineal Quaker families who resided in that specific jurisdiction. In the early eighteenth century, Quaker settlers in Buckingham travelled eighteen miles to the township of Falls for their monthly meetings. In 1720, they requested their own monthly meeting while attending the Falls Quarterly Meeting.[9] The Men's Buckingham Monthly Meeting was established shortly thereafter; three years later, the women's meeting was likewise established. The construction of the society's 1768 meetinghouse became a model of the 'doubled' monthly meeting, or the monthly men and women's meetings.[10]

The Buckingham Society is unique in that it is among the few groups (the others are also located in Bucks County, Pennsylvania) to record disciplinary actions against women in the women's minutes rather than the men's. Although this does not necessarily mean that women in other areas lacked power, members of the Buckingham Monthly Meeting broke an established pattern and expanded female responsibilities by doing so.[11]

Notes

1. B. Levy, *Quakers and the American Family: British Settlement in the Delaware Valley* (Oxford: Oxford University Press, 1988), p. 131.
2. Levy, *Quakers and the American Family: British Settlement in the Delaware Valley*, p. 131.
3. Levy, *Quakers and the American Family: British Settlement in the Delaware Valley*, p. 131. See also *The Two Hundredth Anniversary of Buckingham Monthly Meeting, Buckingham Township, Bucks County, Pennsylvania: Fifth Day, Eighth Month, Sixteenth, 1923.* (Philadelphia, PA: Walter H. Jenkins, 1923), p. 21.
4. Levy, *Quakers and the American Family: British Settlement in the Delaware Valley*, p. 132.
5. Levy, *Quakers and the American Family: British Settlement in the Delaware Valley*, p. 132.
6. Levy, *Quakers and the American Family: British Settlement in the Delaware Valley*, p. 133.

7. Levy, *Quakers and the American Family: British Settlement in the Delaware Valley*, p. 133.
8. 'History of Buckingham Meeting', pp. 15–19.
9. J. D. Marietta, *The Reformation of American Quakerism, 1748–1783* (Philadelphia, PA: University of Pennsylvania Press, 2007), pp. 15–19.
10. 'A Brief History of the Meetinghouse of Buckingham Monthly Meeting', *Buckingham Friends Meeting* (2008), at https://sites.google.com/site/buckinghamfriendsmeeting/Home/meetinghouse [accessed 19 January 2015].
11. Marietta, *The Reformation of American Quakerism, 1748–1783*, pp. 28–9.

Society of Friends, Buckingham Monthly Meeting, Men's Minute Books (1735–98), Women's Minute Books (1670–1822)

[COVER OF BOOK]

Women's meeting Hogshaw-house and Biddlesolon 1678–1762
1678
This Book belongeth to the Womens meetings At Hogshaw house[1] for the keeping an account of what money is & effected for the wiseife those that our poor and other necessary occasions as need shall we givene
[...] /
the 25 day of the 5 mo[nth] 1720[2]
John hemens and hannah Ashby layd their intencon of marige before the meeting and sarah hingo and Jane Ashby was desired to make in quire consarn hur clernes[3]
the 29 day of 6: mo[nth] 1720[4]
John hemens and hanah Ashby layd ther intenzon <of marig> the second time before the wimens meeting and find in nothing but clernes thay was left to ther librty to prosed acordin to the good order of truth
[...] /
the 26 of the 12 mo[nth] 1721[5] thomas hull And Jane cubidg layd ther intonshon of ~~of~~ taking each other in maridge before the womens meeting the first time & Elizabeth gray & Ann haugood[6] was desired to look in to ther clearness
the 26 day of the first 1722[7]
gorge Culluge and Susan rands laid their in tention the second time and shee was found Clear and was left to thou libert acording to truth
the 26 day of the first month 1722[8]
Thomas hull and Jane Culidye laid their in tene of marage the scond time before the women meeting And shee was found Clear was left to their liberty acording to procee<d> the good order of truth
[...]/
The 31 of the 12 month 1753[9]

Thoams Ball are Ann Cots Said thare intenshens of taking Each other in mareige the first time Sarate hinson Mary Gray are desired to Look into there Clearness [...] /

The 29 of the 9 month 1755[10]

Thomas Gilbey and Hannah intentions Laid Thear inshentes of Taking Each other in mareige the Fust Time sarah Hiseon Ann Ball are Disired to Look into Ther clarness

The 27 of the 10 Month 1755[11]

Thoams Gilbey and Hannah Uincon Leaid ther intenshens of taking Each other in marige the secent time Before Frinds and was Found clear and was Left to perccead a cording to truth

[...] /

At a Quarterly Meeting Held at Wickham[12] the 7th of the 14th Month 1761[13] the Receaved a Minute from the Mens Meeting which is as Follows Viz

The Meeting Understanding That at Some Monthly Meetings there is no Regular Womens Meeting kept, Therefore it is Strongly Reccomended from This Meeting that Regular Womens Monthly Meetings may be Established in all the Monthly Meetings In order that a Womens Quarterly Meeting[14] may be Established in This County. Copies of this Minute Are Desired to be Sent to Each Monthly Meeting

Quarterly Meeting 7th of ye 4th Month 1761[15]

It is Requested That This Minute and also The Advice & Queries May Be Recorded in The Monthly Meeting Books in order to be Read And the Queries Answered at Least Once a Quarter, and the Answers Brought in Writing to the Quarterly Meeting

/

From the Yearly Meeting[16] in London 1755

It is with Real Concern This Meeting Observs that Notwithstanding The Establishing Womens Meetings for Discipline hath been Strongly Recommended By Divers Minutes of preceding Yearly Meetings and Their Service Clearly Set forth Yet a Dificiency Appears in Sundry Counties We therefore Earnestly Intreat That Quarterly Monthly And Two Weeks Meetings Do take the Said Minutes into their Serious and Weighty Consideration and Agreeably to those Advices In a Spirit of Brotherly Love and Godly Concern for the Prosperity of Truth Tenderly to Encourage And Assist Women friends in the Establishment of Womens Two Weeks Monthly and Quarterly Meetings Where any Dificiency Appears, where They may wait for Divine-Wisdom to Direct Them and as it Appears Such Meetings Where they Are Held, have been of Great Service to the Society in General And to the Youth in Particular it is Our Earnest Desire That our Sisters in the Truth whome Providence hath Endued with Spiritual Gifts may Come up to the Help of their Brethren in the Discipline of the Church and

in order that the Service of Womens Meetings May be the More Extencive it is Recomended that Each Monthly Meeting of Women friend Depute Representatives to attend the Service of their Quarterly Meeting Who may be furnished with Answers to the following Queries.
/
The Queries

1st Are Meetings for Worship and Discipline duly Attended and Do friends[17] Avoid all Unbecoming Behaviour therein

2d Are Love and Unify presarved Amongst You and Do you Discourage All Talebaring and Detraction?

3rd: Is it your Care By Example and Precept to Train up your Children in a Godly Conversation and in frequent Reading the Holy Scriptures as also in plainness of Speech
Behaviour and Apparel?[18]

4th: Do you Bear a Faithful and Christian Testimony Against the Receiving or Paying Tithes[19], Priests Demands and those called Church Rates?

5 Are friends Careful to avoid all vain Sports places of Diversion and Gameing?

6:th Are friends just in their Dealings and Punctual in fulfilling their Engagements?

7:th Is Early Care Taken Timely to Advise and Deal with Such as may appear Inclinable[20] to Marry Contrary to the Rules of our Society
/
8th How are the Poor amongst you provided for, and what care is taken for the education of their Offspring[21]

9th Have you ten or more faithful Friends Deputed in each particular Meeting to have the oversight thereof and is care taken when any thing appears amiss, that the Rules of our Discipline[22] be put in practice;
[...] /
At our Monthly Meeting held at Chackmore[23] 29 of the 3 Month[24], the Ansers to the Queries are drawn up and sent to the Quartley meeting by our Friend Thomas Ball.

-	£	s	d
Collected	0	1	9
In Stock	0	4	9

at our Monthley Meeting held at Chackmore the 26 of the Forth Month. our Answers were Excepted We received the Epstle from the ye Womens yearly Meeting at York, Witch we hope to <endever> put in practise

-	£	s	d
Collected	0	5	3
In Stock	0	10	0

At our monthely Meeting Helt at Clakmor 31 of the Fift month ware

Coleted 3s3d	0	3	3
In Stok	0	13	3

At our monthely meeting Helt At chackmor 21 at sixt month our ancers ware Dron up and sent By our Frind Ann Batt

-	£	s	d
ware colite 1s3d	0	1	3
in Stok	0	14	6

[...]
[NQ 4/3/2]

Women's Meeting Buckingham[25] 1793–1822

/1

At our Monthly Meeting of Women Friends held at Nash[26] 27th of 9th Month 1793[27] was present Ann Coles, Hannah Harden and Ann Pettifer and others, this Meeting Queries[28] were read and written answers prepared, read, and signed in order to go to the ensuing Quarterly Meeting to which the following Friends are appointed Representatives, Ann Coles, and Elizabeth Harden.

	£	s	d
Collected	0	7	3
Stock in hand	0	2	0

This Meeting concludes, and our next is intended to be held at Buckingham at the usual time. Signed by Martha Coles Clerk[...]

/7

this Meeting Concludes and our next is intended to be held at Buckingham at the usual time signed by Martha Coles clerk

At our Monthly Meeting of Women Friends held at Buckingham the 30th of 7 Month 1794[29] was present. Ann Coles Ann Southam and Ann Collins and others. the Friends appointed to attend the Quarterly meeting did attend.

The Yearly Meeting Epistle[30] from London and likewise that from America was read to our edification.

Collected	0	3	3
Stock in hand	<u>0</u>	<u>11</u>	<u>9</u>

This Meeting concludes and our next is intended to be held at this place at the usual time Signed by Martha Coles Clerk

At our Monthly Meeting of Women Friends held at Buckingham the 27th of 8th Month 1794[31] as a present Ann Southam Mary Edwin Ann Harding and others. At this meeting Joseph Coles and Joanna Beven hath declared their intention of Marriage and a Certificate was produced[32] of Joanna Parents consent.

/8

Ann coles and Ann Southam is appointed to to [sic] enquire into Joanna Beven's Conversation and Clearness of all others respecting Marriage.[33]

Collected	0	5	6

Sent to Mary Turner 7th 6th out of the Collection by Ann Coles

	£	s	d
Stock in hand	<u>0</u>	<u>9</u>	<u>9</u>

This Meeting concludes and our next is intended to be held at Nash at the usual time signed by Martha Coles Clerk

At our Monthly Meeting of Women Friends held at Nash the 24 of 9th Month 1794[34] was present Ann Southam Hannah Harden Ann Pettifor and others. at this Meeting Joseph Coles and Joanna Bevan continued their intention ot Marriage, and on due enquirey being made don't find but they are clear of all others, therefore they are left at liberty to solemnise their intended marriage when it may be convenient. At this Meeting we was favord with the Company of Sarah Dillin. This Meeting Queries /9 were read and written answers prepared, and signed in order for the ensuing Quarterly Meeting to which the following Friends are appointed representatives, Ann Coles, & Martha Coles.

Collected	0	4	6
Stock in hand	0	14	3

This Meeting concludes and our next is intended to be held at Buckingham at the usual time signed by Martha Cole Clerk

[...]

At our Monthly Meeting of Women Friends held at Buckingham 28th of the 1st Month 1795[35] was present Frances Gilkes Ann Southam Ann Coles and others. the Friends appointed to attend the Quarterly Meeting did attend.

The Minute respecting visiting Martha Greaves continued

Collected	0	3	6
Stock in hand	0	3	6

/12

This Meeting concludes and our next is intended to be held at this place at the usual time. Signed by Martha Coles Clerk

At our Monthly Meeting of Women Friends held at ~~Buckingham~~ Nash 25th of 2[d] Month 1795[36] was present Ann Coles Elizabeth Coles and others.

	£	s	d
Collected	0	2	9
Stock in hand	0	6	3

This Meeting concludes and our next is intended to be held at Buckingham at the usual time Signed by Ann Pettifor Clerk this time

At our Monthly Meeting of Women Friends held at Buckingham the 25th of 3[d] Month 1795[37] was present Ann Coles, Ann Southam Frances Gilkes and others. our answers to the Queries have been drawn up in this Meeting, in order for the ensuing Quarterly Meeting to which the following Friends are appointed representatives Ann Southam and Mary Butcher We received a Certificate from the Mens Meeting[38] /13 respecting Sarah Carter being written the compass of our Monthly Monthly [sic], to which the following Friends are appointed Ann Coles Sen[io]r and Frances Gilkes collected 0 7 6 Sent Cathrine Greg 5s out of the Collection Stock in hand 0 9 9 <and Elizabeth Browett 5s> This Meeting concludes and our next is intended to be held at this place at the usual time signed by Ann Coles Clerk Junior this time.[...]/

Men's Meeting Book:
Chackmore 1735–1779 and Chackmore and Buckingham 1780–1798

[NQ 4/1/2 Men's Meeting Book]
Chackmore 1735–1779

This Book is for the sarvise[39] of Friends belonging to the Monthly meeting Called Bidlesdon Meeting[40] but now kespt at Whitlebury[41] or Chackmore[42] in the County of Buck's[43] which said Meeting is apinted to be kept on the last second day of every month for the well ordery of the Church of God in those parts

the first month in ye year 1735

/

A Copy of the ussall Questans asked at the yearly Meeting as the now stand in ye yearly meeting Book

1st: An account what present Prisoners thou are?
2: How mainy discharged since Last Year & when & how
3 How many died Prisoners
4 How many Publick Friends died
5 How many meet[in]g Houses Bult & Ho[w many] Meet[in]g now settled:
6 How do frinds prosper in the Truth and doth any Convincement. Appear and how friends are in Unity and How former Advice of this meeting is observed and practised relating to their Godly Cair for the good Education of their Children in the way of Truth in Plainess of Habit and Speech?
7 How are the Several other Advices of this meet[in]g been put in Practice particularly that against recovering or paying of Tithes and do you keep a Particular Record of all ye Sufferings and Prossentions ye happen anyone County
8 How are the Poor amongst you provided for & what care is taken for ye Education of thire Offspr<ing> in our me[eting] and Quarterly meeting books
9 Do your Quarterly and Mo[nth]ly Meeting take care to see that none under our Professon defrad the King of any of his Customs or duty Excise / or in any wise incurage the Running of Goods[44] by lying or vending such good and do the severly reprehend and Testifie against all such offenders and their unwarantable and Unlawfull Actions 24:4 mo[nth]:1735
[...] /
1743 taking into Concidation the affair of Rich Colling Paying no Rent for his house Friends agreed to draw up a paper to be handed by all our Colecting members as anagrement for puting them out of their hous by due Cours of law

6 mo 1[45] At the mens Mo[nth]ly Meeting held at Chackmore John Campion made Report that Greogry darby and he was at the Quarterly Meeting and brot the yearly Epistle and an Epistle in manuscript which was ordered to read at willsbury and Chackmore and a small Book: cost 1s4d which was orderd to be paid for out of the Colection mony, Friend handed a paper of agreement to brrn Rich[ar]d Collings out of his hous by Law

7 mo 6[46] At the Mens monthly Meeting held at Chackmore John Campion made Report that he had an oportunity of Speaking with Mary Gilbert Conserning her keeping Company with on that is not a Br[other][47] Tho[mas] Cabbidge was desired to Speak to Alex Haugood Concerning her micarig of being married by the Preist aginst her ffriends Consent.
[...] /
1744 John Haugood brought half a years Rent which John Vincent had Rec[eive]d of John Shot due at Mickellmars being 14 Shill[in]g for ye hous belonging to Friend at Whitlebury and had allowed him one Shilling out of ye Rent which he had paid for the window Tax <from> Last year Friends understanding that Georg Cubbidge Continues very Same and in want of help this meeting agreed to send him one Pound out of the Colection mony as a Token

9 mo 26[48] At the mens monthly meeting held at Chackmore John Vincent brot a bill of Charge for for [sic] Repars done at Witlebury come to 8s6d was paid out of the Colection mony this meeting Rec[eive]d an account from Oxfordshire of Ten months Charg of the Widow Simkins which come to 3£4s6d one our Part Friends defer the Colecting of the mony till next meeting Friends agree to send George Cubbidge 4 Shilling as a Token out of the colection mony

10 mo 31[49] At the Mens Monthly Meeting held at Chackmore John Gray made Report that he had paid H: Sandwell fifteen Shilling for half a years Rent for this hous and had Rec[eive]d 9s6d and a bill of Charg to come to 9s6d for Repairing the thatching of this hous of John Welch which made / <1744> made up f<if>teen Shill[ings] for half a years Rent due at Michlmars and Jo[h]n Gray was paid ye 5s6d out of ye Colection mony and John Welch had a Recept Tho[ma]s Cubbidge and John Gray was apinted to go to the Quarterly meeting Friends agreed to send George Cubbidge 5s out of the Colection mony at a Token

At this meeting friends agreed upon a Privit Coloction to defray[50] the Charges of the widow Simkins and Pay for a Load of Straw of John Haugood which come to 8s6d for ye Reparing of ye Thatching of this meeting hous John Haugood was desired to yee to the Colection of it and send the widow Simkins mony into Oxfordshire[51]

11 mo 28[52] At the mens monthly meeting held at Chackmore Tho[mas] Cubbidge and John Gray made Report of this being at the Quarterly meeting John Haugood and Tho[mas] Cubbidge made Report that they had Gother the mony a[g]reed upoon Last meeting which come to 3£15s0d and sent the widow Simkins mony into Oxfordshire and John Haugood was paid 8s6d for his Load of Straw which in all was 3£13s0d the 2 Shill[ing]s Remainder was paid into this Meeting Stok Friends agreed to send Georg Cubbidg 5 Shilling out of the Colection Mony as a token

/
1753
[...]

26[th] 3 month 1753[53] At the mens monthly meeting held at Chack<moore> Colected 4s John Haugood and John Gray Wars apointed to Go to the Quarterly meeting[54]

30th 4 month 1753[55] at the mens monthly meeting held at Chackmoore Colected 4s John Haugood made Report that John Gray and his being both at the Quarterly meeting at the same meeting John Vincent broght a bill for work and palling at Whittelbury 2 pounds 7s 5 penc which wars paid oute of the meeting Stock

[...] at the mens monthly meeting held at Chackmoore Wars present T[h]o[ma]s Ball John Gray T[h]o[ma]s Grimes W[illia]m Colles at the same meeting colected 7 at the same meeting T[h]o[ma]s Grimes Broght his Suferings

for Tithes Gret and Small Taken by Warant Granted by Richard Lounds of Winsllow[56] an John Lord of Draiton Justisses taken by T[h]o[ma]s King Tithe Renter and W[illia]m King Constabell Both of Nash in the County of Bucks and in the parish of Whadon 9 pounds 17 Shillings and all without his concent
/

at the same meeting T[h]o[ma]s Ball and W[illia]m Colles wars apointed to Go to the Quarterly meeting at Wickham and to Cary the State of the meeting and the ansers to the select meeting with them

[...]/

20:6 month 1764[57]

at the mens monthly meeting held at Chackmoore Wars present T[h]o[ma]s Ball John Gray John Haugood John Eaton at this meeting John Haugood made Report that T[h]o[ma]s Ball and he had Drawe'd up a Testimeny aCording to friends Desier concerning Thomas Eatons misconduct which wars here Red and ordered to be Red at the Close of a first Days meetings at this meeting Colected 5s 6 penc at the same meeting John Haugood Broght 14 Shillings from Sarah Scott for half a years Rent Due for the Dwelling house the 25 of the 3 month 1764[58] at Wittellbury at this meeting John Haugood made Report that he had paid Sarah Scott 3s for Reparing the Windowes and sum Leveys and wars paid againe oute of the Colection mony John Haugood and Samuell Colles are appointed to Go to the Quarterly meeting at Sherington[59] / at our mens monthly meeting held at Chackmoore

30:7th month[60]

wars present J[oh]n Haugood T[h]o[ma]s Ball J[oh]n Eaton at this meeting John Haugood made Report that the Testimony Drawed up against Tho[ma]s Eatons misconduct Concearning marrig Contrary to the Rulles of friends and allso his Wife Being with Chilld Before marridge wars Rell & aproved at this meeting and wars orderd to be Red at the Close of a first Days meeting which wars Dun at this meeting Colected 5s 6 penc at the same meeting John Haugood Broght 14 Shillings for half a years Rent for the Dwelling House at Whittelbury Due the 25th 3d month 1764[61]

at our mens monthly meeting held at Chackmoore 27:8th month 1764[62]

wars pressent John Haugood J<no> Gray Will[ia]m Colless at this meeting Colected 4s 6 penc

/ [...]

at our mens mo[nthly] meeting held at Chackmoore

28: 7 month 1773[63]

wars pesent Jn<o> Haugood Jn<o> Butcher Jn<o> Eaton at this meeting Jn<o> Haugood made Report that the too friends appeinted to Go to the Quarterly meeting wars Berth Thare Broght the yearly meeting Epissels[64] which wars Disstributed to Ech family one & Likewise Broght a form & Deckleration of fidelity p[ai]d Samuell Coles 11s 3 penc for Bread & flower for W[illia]m Haugoods family at this meeting Colected 10 Shiling<s> at this meeting Sent Sarah Peercifull 10s 6 penc oute of the Colection mony

/ [...]

at our mens monthly meeting held at Chackmoore
23:2 month 1774[65]

Wars present J[oh]n Haugood J[oh]n Gray J[oh]n Munday the minute Respecting alltering the Quarterly meeting to the forth Day at Aylsbury wars agreearedn and afew Lines Sent to the Quarterly meeting Giving our Consent to the Sum at this meeting paid Samuell Coles Senor a bill for Bread & flower for W[illia]m Haugoods family one pound 4 Shillings 2 penc oute of the Colection mony

at this meeting collected 1300

at this meeting Thomas Ball with the Asistance of Samuell Coles Juner is Desiered to Draw up A Testimony against the next monthly meeting

for the approbation of the said meeting Respecting William Haugoods Conduct in not Indevering to Do what he Can for his family which is Contrary to the Truth he makes profession of

[NQ 4/1/3]

Chackmore and Buckingham 1780–1798

/

This Book Belongeth to the Friends of Chackmore Monthly Meeting 1780

/ [...]

At our Monthly Meeting held at Buckingham the 24th of the 12th Month 1794[66] Was presant William Coles Joseph Gilkes Jun[io]r William Richardson John Munday and Others

The four Quiries to be Answerd to the Ensuring Quarterly Meeting where read and Written Answers prepard and agreed to and the following friends are apointed Representitives. Samuel Coles Joseph Gilkes Jun[io]r, William Richardson and Joseph Coles

At this Meeting was Receiv'd a request from Martha Greaves to be readmitted with her Children into Membership[67]. Therefore this Meeting apoints William Coles and Joseph Gilkes Jun[io]r to pay her a Visite on that Account– [...]/

The Minute respecting Colecting the Books belonging to this Meeting Continued –

SARAH RYAN TO MARY FLETCHER (1762 AND 1763)

Sarah Ryan to Mary Fletcher (April 1762 and January 1763), Fletcher-Tooth Collection, John Rylands Library, Manchester, England.

In the late 1730s, John Wesley – the father of Methodism – began to envision a religious community that 'centered on the conversion experience, social discipline and spiritual fellowship.'[1] This vision began to take shape in 1738 when he organized the Fetter Lane Society in London in partnership with the Moravians. The society became a gathering place for converts: it organized believers into bands, provided them with social structure and detailed the rules of religious discipline that should guide their lives.[2] For a time, it seemed that this collaborative venture could result in the merging of the Moravians and the Methodists into a single family. However, this possibility dissolved in 1740 when John and Charles Wesley decided to sever ties with the Moravians as a result of their radical approach to sexuality, their commitment to forming a bounded community and their antinomian views.[3] Likewise, the Moravian leader, Count Zinzendorf, was opposed to certain elements of Methodist theology and practice. He disagreed with their teachings on the possibility of sanctification or Christian perfection, as well as their enthusiastic style of worship and their belief in conversion as a process rather than an instantaneous event.[4]

As early as 1739, John Wesley began preaching in open-air settings in an attempt to emulate the preaching style of George Whitefield. In the years that followed, he organized a small number of ministers as well as an ever-expanding group of lay preachers, most of whom lacked formal training, to serve as itinerant preachers. As the movement grew, Wesley carefully regulated the evangelistic work in which his preachers engaged: they were expected to cover large geographic areas, moving from one location to the next in quick succession. On the local level, the Methodist laity was organized into classes and bands; itinerant preachers served as the liaison between local societies and Wesley and other church leaders.[5]

Although Wesley carefully organized and regulated the Methodist movement, he also, as Anna Lawrence notes, 'established important sources of power within the laity.'[6] Indeed, in both England and America, early Methodist societies were often dominated by lay leadership, which included women as well as men. In Bristol, the central location for Wesley's revivals, for example, more women served as lay leaders than men. The same would be true of the London Foundry Society – the first society under the direct control of Wesley, which ultimately replaced the Fetter Lane Society. It was located in an old cannon factory with room for meetings, gatherings, publishing and social ministering – here women outnumbered men by forty-seven to nineteen in 1742. Similarly, women in early American Methodism outnumbered men by two to three in some areas.[7]

As Methodism continued to grow and develop, bands and classes became the key units of lay organization.[8] Lawrence explains, 'Bands were usually single sex and formed of like-minded people from similar backgrounds and shared marital status'.[9] These 'little families of love', as Francis Asbury dubbed them, fostered intimate spiritual fellowship between those who shared similar commitments.[10]

In contrast, classes 'were the basic unit of official Methodist membership' and were thus reserved for those deemed worthy of this association.[11] Indeed, one had to obtain a class ticket – a piece of paper that included the person's name and location – in order to become a member of and a participant in a class meeting. Classes were usually larger than bands, typically consisted of about a dozen members and could be composed of both sexes. In the context of such meetings, Methodists shared conversion experiences and received instruction about appropriate conduct.[12] Those invited to participate often considered the opportunity an invitation to become a part of the Methodist family.[13]

Sarah Ryan and Mary Bosanquet Fletcher (see also Volumes 1 and 4) are examples of women who accepted the invitation to become a part of, and who eventually became leaders within, the Methodist family. Upon meeting at the Foundry in 1762 – 'the centre of the evangelical revival during the early 1760s' – [14] the two women became instant friends, notwithstanding their distinctively different backgrounds and ages: Ryan was a working-class servant (she worked as housekeeper for the Methodist centres in London and Bristol), laundress and bigamist, whereas Bosanquet was a 'wealthy gentlewoman' who would eventually become an 'eminent leader and preacher' within the Methodist movement.[15] At the time of meeting, Ryan was thirty-three and Bosanquet was eighteen.

When Ryan and Bosanquet first met, Ryan had just resigned her position as housekeeper at Wesley's New Room in Bristol, as a result of poor health.[16] Through participation in band meetings at the Foundry, where Ryan had accepted another housekeeping position, the two women converted fully to Methodism as they nurtured one another's religious development, discovered their commitment to a shared spiritual mission and came to see each other as family.[17] Eventually, Bosanquet and Ryan were able to establish an orphanage and Methodist community at Leytonstone, enabled by a legacy left by Bosanquet's grandmother.[18] Between 1763–68, thirty-four adults and thirty-five children found a home there. Leytonstone also served as a lodging place for itinerant ministers, as well as the location of weekly band and class meetings. Wesley often referred to the community Bosanquet and Ryan formed as a 'little family.'[19] In 1768, the community relocated to Cross Hall due to financial struggles and Ryan's poor health. Notwithstanding the move, Ryan passed away a short time later. In many ways, Ryan served as a maternal figure in Bosanquet's life. Her spiritual experiences and influence shaped the young woman's view of Christ, as well as her preaching, service and family life.[20] Bosanquet believed that their friendship extended beyond the grave and that they would always be united as spiritual kin.[21]

The following two letters, written from Ryan to Bosanquet, capture early Methodist views of spiritual kinship. Ryan wrote the first letter in 1762, the very year in which she met Bosanquet. The other letter was composed a year later, in 1763. Both demonstrate that they, like many other women, were able to witness, experience and describe spiritual experiences in an effort to establish the 'best bonds' – language Methodists often used to describe 'their relationships to their religious brothers, sisters, mothers, and fathers' – with one another.[22] To Ryan and Bosanquet, their association extended far beyond common beliefs and goals – they were spiritual kin, joined together by divine will.

Notes
1. A. Lawrence, *One Family Under God: Love, Belonging, and Authority in Early Transatlantic Methodism* (Philadelphia, PA: University of Pennsylvania Press, 2011), p. 36.
2. Lawrence, *One Family Under God*, p. 36.
3. A. Fogelman, *Jesus is Female: Moravians and Radical Religion in Early America* (Philadelphia, PA: University of Pennsylvania Press, 2007), pp. 158–9.
4. D. Hempton, *Methodism: Empire of the Spirit* (New Haven, CT: Yale University Press, 2005), p. 14; D. B. Hindmarsh, *The Evangelical Conversion Narrative: Spiritual Autobiography in Early Modern England* (Oxford: Oxford University Press, 2008), pp. 162–3; D. Andrews, *The Methodists and Revolutionary America, 1760–1800: The Shaping of an Evangelical Culture* (Princeton, NJ: Princeton University Press, 2002), pp. 25–6.
5. Lawrence, *One Family Under God*, pp. 36–7; F. Baker, *John Wesley and the Church of England* (London: Epworth Press, 2012), p. 185.
6. Lawrence, *One Family Under God*, p. 38.
7. Lawrence, *One Family Under God*, p. 38. See also Andrews, *The Methodists and Revolutionary America, 1760–1800*, p. 247.
8. Lawrence, *One Family Under God*, p. 38.
9. Lawrence, *One Family Under God*, p. 38; see also J. Wesley, *Rules of the Band Societies* (London, 1738).
10. D. Sherman, *History of the Revisions of the Discipline of the Methodist Episcopal Church* (Charleston, SC: Nabu Press, 2010), p. 139.
11. Lawrence, *One Family Under God*, pp. 38–39.
12. Hempton, *Methodism: Empire of the Spirit*, p. 78; Andrews, *The Methodists and Revolutionary America, 1760–1800*, p. 93.
13. Lawrence, *One Family Under God*, p. 39.
14. Lawrence, *One Family Under God*, pp. 32–3; C. Yrigoyen, *John Wesley: Holiness of Heart*

and Life (New York, NY: Abigndon Press, 2010).
15. P. Mack, *Heart Religion in the British Enlightenment* (Cambridge: Cambridge University Press, 2008), p. 157; A. Culley, *British Women's Life Writing, 1760–1840: Friendship, Community, and Collaboration* (New York, NY: Palgrave Macmillian, 2014), p. 25.
16. Culley, *British Women's Life Writing, 1760–1840*, pp. 25, 33.
17. Mack, *Heart Religion in the British Enlightenment*, p. 158.
18. Culley, *British Women's Life Writing, 1760–1840*, p. 33.
19. *Letters of John Wesley*, vol. 7, p. 67.
20. Mack, *Heart Religion in the British Enlightenment*, pp. 158–61.
21. Mack, *Heart Religion in the British Enlightenment*, pp. 158–63.
22. Lawrence, *One Family Under God*, p. 72.

Sarah Ryan to Mary Fletcher (1762 and 1763)

64

Dear love farwell in the best Bonds[1]– S. Ryan

I think it was in May, or June, She came to London_ The account of her Illness – and the Manner of her being led to settle with me I need not Repeat As it is expressed at large in my Life – But to shew the Spirit She came up in – I will just Mention with what satisfaction She saw and heard the Progress of that great work then in London[2] – as She had but one Interest – that of the Glory of God – So no news Could delight her soul <like> that of his Glory being promoted – She came in the Spirit of a Little Child Ready either to teach or to Learn as God should appoint – And to Her Friday Band in Bristol She Wrote in these words.–

London – 1762–

My Dearly beloved in our Common Lord.

After a Safe though Painful Journey, My Blessed Guide brought me Safe in Peace on Wednesday Night to my Dear Friends. He hath never failed me Yet, and I will Trust Him for ever. On Friday at Twelve O'Clock they took me to the Foundry Meeting[3] where there was about a Hundred Simple Men and Women, who could Testify, the Blood of Jesus had cleansed them from all Sin—I Sat with Astonishment! And Like the Queen of Sheba[4] said the one half hath not been told me! As they spoke, the Fire seemed to fall from Heaven! These are little Children indeed! O Let us adore our Almighty King and Say was ever love like His— O my dear friends my heart burnt for Bristol[5] how did I long to have that Society Partake of the Same, But you my dear Sisters are very near my heart indeed! for you what do I not desire!

/

65

I am in a Strait and Could wish You in London for one Month – You would get Clearer light into the way of Faith—but my dear master's will is best, I dare not Chuse – On Saturday Night we meet at Mr. Maxfields[6]– Such Faith, Love, and Simplicity – I sat in Silence, twas Enough for me to hear and Rejoice.—Sunday I went to Chapple expecting a great Blessing, and surely I was not disappointed – I was Amazed at the People, hearing their Groans-and fervent Amens! – And

Still I wonder and Adore the great I am! the faithful and true Witness – At night we had a Love feast[7] – The Preachers said little but left Room for the witnesses to tell how the Lord had wrought the great Work on their Soul such Prayers and Groans for them, who had not Received the Liberty would have Pierced your Hearts, It appeared to me there was nothing but simplicity

O! is not this the Lords doing, and marvelous in our Eyes – I cannot doubt of the Experience of any one, I have yet spoke to- Glad was I to find my- self one of the ~~members~~ <number> of Jesus's Little Children – My dear friends may you Increase abundantly in Love, and be as fire among stubble &c

> Having still a few more Odd Papers wrote at different times –
> some with, and some without Bates-I will add a Little more
> by way of Diary.

January 1763

MARY FLETCHER, ACCOUNT OF SARAH LAWRENCE, METHODIST MINISTER (1801)

The Fletcher-Tooth Papers, Journals, MAM/FL/34–35, Methodist Archives and Research Centre, John

Rylands University Library, University of Manchester, Manchester, England.[1]

In the eighteenth century, the terms family, kinship and friendship were applied to 'diverse social relations'.[2] An example of the expansion of familial ties is illustrated in the life and the writings of Mary Bosanquet Fletcher (see also Volume 1; Volume 4). Indeed, Amy Culley argues, Bosanquet Fletcher wrote about friendships in familial terms 'by drawing on scriptural tropes and Methodist conceptions of religious community'.[3] Such fictive ties often served as alternatives to consanguineous family relationships.

In addition to preserving the life story of her 'spiritual mother', Sarah Ryan, Bosanquet Fletcher also kept a record about Ryan's niece, Sarah or 'Sally' Lawrence (1759–1800). Orphaned at the age of four, Lawrence entered the Leytonstone Orphanage that Bosanquet Fletcher and Ryan had founded together, thus becoming a part of their Methodist family.[4]

Following Ryan's death, Lawrence became Bosanquet Fletcher's companion and spiritual protégé.[5] Near the age of ten, Lawrence converted to Methodism. She joined the Leeds Methodist society when she was eighteen years old and later became the leader of the children's meetings at Madeley (John Fletcher's estate).[6]

After Mary Bosanqut married John Fletcher on 12 November 1781, Lawrence moved to Madeley with her spiritual mother.[7] The Fletchers considered Lawrence their adopted daughter.[8] A letter written shortly following John Fletcher's death demonstrates Lawrence's relationship with her 'adopted' parents. She proclaimed:

> I have lost the best of Masters and a kind, affectionate tender Father! But should I lose my dear Mistress who hath been such an Indulgent Mother to me for near twenty five years! I should Indeed become a desolate Orphan![9]

When Sarah Lawrence passed away in 1815, Bosanquet Fletcher was comforted by a vision of her 'little girl' in the next world. Bosanquet Fletcher dreamt she crossed a river and saw a community of believers in heaven. She continued:

> [T]hen I saw two Young Women who died in the Lord sometime since and Betty Humpaces with my Little Girl and Mr Fletcher they were in the most Lovely White I ever Saw and Mr. Fletcher held up his hands and Looked most heavenly. My Little Girl said with a Sweet voice My mummy is coming my mummy is coming ... O how many ways hath the Lord to comfort his children and to Let us know the family above and below are but one.[10]

Bosanquet Fletcher preserved the life story of her spiritual daughter, Sarah Lawrence. While composing biographical sketches of the young woman's life, Bosanquet Fletcher drew upon the subject's personal reflections on her relationship with God, transcriptions of her diary entries and accounts of her dreams (which Bosanquet Fletcher had written down). In addition to the manuscript source that is printed below, Bosanquet Fletcher also wrote a funeral sermon, epitaph and a biographical account about Lawrence that was published in the Methodist Magazine in 1803. Of these sketches, Amy Culley declared,

> Lawrence's personal history is therefore mediated by Fletcher and refracted through a range of texts, which are a confusion of autobiography, biography, private and public, self reflection and communal memories. As a collection they suggest the ways in which the representation of life and death is shaped by the women's personal relationships and their sense of belonging to an ongoing spiritual history that might be perpetuated beyond their own lifetimes.[11]

Notes
1. The manuscript writer used dashes to indicate pauses, breaks or end of lines instead of the usual punctuation. These dashes were retained in poetry and epistolary text, but otherwise were eliminated. Almost all superscript text was preceded by a caret. Excepting the first and last pages of the manuscript, all the pages were headed with the year 1801 in the centre and numerical pagination in the right-hand corner.
2. N. Tadmor, *Family and Friends in Eighteenth Century England: Household, Kinship and Patronage* (Cambridge: Cambridge University Press, 2001), p. 275.
3. A. Culley, *British Women's Life Writing, 1760–1840: Friendship, Community, and Collaboration* (London: Palgrave, 2014), p. 40.
4. H. Moore, *The Life of Mrs. Mary Fletcher, Consort and Relict of the Rev. John Fletcher* (New York, NY: J. Soule and T. Mason, 1818), p. 55.
5. Culley, *British Women's Life Writing, 1760–1840: Friendship, Community, and Collaboration*, p. 55.
6. P. Mack, *Heart Religion in the British Enlightenment: Gender and Emotion in Early Methodism* (Cambridge: Cambridge University Press), p. 305. The children's meetings were one of a few examples of Methodist religious meetings aimed at children. A. M. Lawrence, *One Family Under God: Love, Belonging, and Authority in Early Transatlantic* (Philadelphia, PA: University of Pennsylvania Press, 2011), p. 150.

7. Mack, *Heart Religion in the British Enlightenment*, p. 254.
8. She described her as 'an eternal child and obedient to a fault'. A. Lawrence, *One Family Under God*, p. 150.
9. 'An Account of Sarah Lawrence', Fletcher-Tooth Collection, John Rylands Library, Manchester, Sarah Lawrence, Box 24, Folder 5i.
10. MBF Journal, 22 December 1802, Fletcher-Tooth Collection, John Rylands Library, Manchester, Sarah Lawrence, quoted in *One Family Under God*, p. 181.
11. Culley, *British Women's Life Writing, 1760–1840: Friendship, Community, and Collaboration*, p. 55.

Mary Fletcher, Account of Sarah Lawrence, Methodist Minister (1801)

An Account of Sarah Lawrance, many years a Servant of adopted daughter rather of Mr & Mrs Fletcher/written by Mrs. Fletcher[1]

Sarah Lawrance was the Niece of my dear friend Sarah Ryan[2] ; A Providence Cast her into our hands, when a little Child.[3] as she Increased in Reason we observed a remarkable Upright Obedient <spirit in her,> and a great Attachment to us. When very young she would often cry to the Lord with great E₍ₐ₎arnestness that she might never be Seperated from me. One thing was Remarkable; If her Aunt and I were Conversing about <anything of a private> We had not need to Caution her, If if Present, / for I never knew that Child, Repeat anything: such a sense she seemed always to feel of the duty of keeping a secret; and such a Watchfulness even at that age, over her Words. And in above forty years, she has lived with me, I have never found any Change in <in her, any declension from> this spirit of Faithfulness: and since she has <from the time> became my Friend as well as Child, I could Consider every Word spoke to her as secure as in my own Bosom.[4] The marks of a work of grace beginning on her soul, might be observed very Early. before she was Eight years old she was often under strong Convictions for sin as she has since <afterwards> told me and frequently was affraid when she lay down in bed that she should awake in Hell! <When she was> About ten years old <of age> she found a strong desire to be devoted to God; and when she heard us Read in the Family[5] of the sufferings of our Lord or of the Martyrs, <it> would kindle in her breast an Intense desire to suffer something for Him who had borne so much for her. And she used to do many Actions, According to her Childish Ideas to satisfy that desire, such as tying her arms behind her all night, and lying in the most uneasy posture she could &tc. Often she was filled with thank fullness for being cast when <the opportunity> she had <of receiving> a Religious Education! And determined if ever she was brought <carried> into the World she never would be like them others – 'No (said she,) not so much as my Cap will I Change.' I will always walk by the Rules and Plan I have been brought up on by; and if I have anything to do with Children I will strive to teach them as I have been taught:'

And truely [sic] in this she made good her Words She did Labour and delight in ~~her~~ ^{the} Childrens meetings,⁶ which she held in Different
/
1801
Places.⁷ And such a Gift of Wisdom for the Instruction of youth, as she has been blest with for these seven years past, I have seldom ~~seen~~ <observed> . When about sixteen, Conviction <for sin was> fastened more deeply on her mind; and I have heard her ~~say~~ <tell> with what earnest Cries and Tears she used to Wrestle with the Lord' that He would make her a Christain †indeed, and ǂjoin her to his People here, and hereafter. She had such a sens of the sin of her fallen Nature, that she Carried ~~a~~ Constant Condemnation in her own Breast; ǂ And was Continually acknowledging how Just it would be in God, to send her to Hell! <she> thought she ~~should~~ never <would> be accepted! When near Eighteen, she was taken into the society and the June following, she went to Leeds old Church, to be Confirmed.⁸ She walked home again alone, (about five miles,) & all the way ~~she~~ was pleading with the Lord that she might never grow Slack again! When she got near home, The Word Came to her with much Power 'I will keep thee as the Apple of Mine Eye'⁹ This filled her soul with delight and Consolation, now firmly believing she should be made a true Child of God (The following I take from her own Account) 'For two or three Weeks after this, I ~~remained~~ <continued to be> much in Earnest; and <was> Encouraged to believe; the Lord would give me a dear Evidence <that> I was forgiven. One Tuesday night before I came into [2 illeg. words] <meeting> I thought I will ~~be~~ determined to speak quite free to night; (a thing I had been quite Backward <to do>) My Mistress met the Class,¹⁰ and begun with that word 'Rejoice evermore, and in every thing give thanks'.¹¹ When / She came to speak to me she said 'Sally,¹² have you nothing to give thanks for?' I answered 'Yes many things,' and named the above Promise In doing which I felt my Faith a little Increased. Next day Coming into her Room she asked me If I could Trust in the Lord now? adding, 'All is done on his side 'Tis only for you to Accept it by believing' I Replied, 'I think I can; But as I left the Room a doubt started up, 'I do not know my Sins <are> forgiven' Yet I thought I do feel a Change The Friday following as she was meeting the Children,¹³ my hope Increased and while she was Repeating those Words in Prayer 'There is now no Condemnation to those who are in Christ Jesus' I felt such a Confidence There was no Condemnation for me As filled my whole Soul with Joy and Love. Now I did feel the Liberty of God's dear Children and, I think, If all Earth and Hell had opposed It ~~seemeds~~ to me Impossible ~~for~~ a doubt ~~to~~ <should have> entered in In this sweet Liberty, keeping the Peaceful Presence of God, I Continued to Walk for some months. One day meeting with something that was Trying I spoke a hasty Word to one of the Family. Immediately I felt a Cloud <on my mind> and could not Rejoice in the Lord as before, though I sought <it> with Prayers and Tears. From that Day I received

a deeper Conviction than ever before of the Necessity of all Evil Tempers being removed out of my heart. And for the next four months my whole soul seemed Engaged in the pursuit of that deliverance; And <was> often in the daily Expectation thereof. & I now looked for it ~~at~~ <in> every means of Grace. One Wednesday Night in that blessed meeting / We used to have once a fortnight at CrossHall[14], where so many were blest; while I was waiting on the Lord and saw myself, as laying at the Pool side, longing for the Lord to say, <u>Be Clean</u>. My soul was engaged in ~~Wrestling~~ <fervent> Prayer that I might that night be bught into dear Liberty. And while my dear Mistress[15] was Praying, several Promises were applied to my mind such as, 'Thou art clean through the Word I have spoken unto thee' &ce I now felt unbelief give way and was enabled to Cast my Soul on the perfect Atonement and felt the Divine Efficacy of that Blood which Cleanseth from all Sin.[16] (This was ~~on the Thirtieth of~~ December <30th> 1778) From that night I felt a very great Change, and ~~a which closer walk~~ <begun to walk much more closely> with God than I had ~~known~~ <done> before. That which I enjoyed in Justification[17] was Precious, but this far exceeded. Now I could begin the New Year with a New Heart and so Powerfully did the Love of God fill and enlarge my Soul that I was Constrained many ~~and many a~~ times to Cry out in the fullness thereof 'Whom have I in heaven, but thee and but thee and there is None upon Earth I desire in Comparison with thee.' I could Truly say 'all slavish fear is gone: I have but one Fear To displease that Gracious God who hath done so much for me' Now I could rejoice in Tribulation, Crosses and Provocations. I felt the Love which never faileth and a delight in the Thought <that> I had any thing to bear for God. I found a Continual Watchfulness and such an <u>Invariable</u> Sense of the Lord's approval that I was every Moment as it were afresh accepted in the beloved!

After walking in the Liberty for some months[,] A Circumstance Occurred which Proved to me a source of Many Sorrows. Being one / Day falsely accused by some I was Conversing with, I answered The Truth, but perceiving ~~it~~ <what I said> was not Received, I felt grief, ~~as it was~~ <being> a near Point, <& one> in which I was perfectly Clear. I did not speak An Unkind word nor Indeed <feel.> any thing Contrary to Love But I burst into Tears. On which one, said <who at that time live with us,> 'Well Sally, don[']t you feel Sin <u>now</u>? If you don[']t what makes you Cry'? A Cloud ~~I~~immediately fell on my Mind, and I began to Reason. 'What was it made me Cry? do I not feel som[e]thing wrong? Shall I not again be as before; with many Fiery darts which Satan took the Opportunity to throw in and looking at the Waves, I began to sink, and unbelief once more Lifted up its head, And I was ~~drove~~ <driven> into many fears and needless Scruples. I now felt the most anxious desire to Recover the Ground I had lost but, ~~did~~ not Clearly see <into> the way of Faith, I <u>but</u> strove to go Great Lengths in fasting and Self denial. And here in the Devil got the advantage and ~~Teased~~ <Tossed> my Soul with sore Temptation I was, as I thought, Condemned in every thing. I went about, fearing I Sought my own Will And afraid to eat my bread or put on my Clothes Least ~~It~~ it should be an Indulgence. By this I much hurt my health, and more my Soul. ~~For~~ <For> my Mind was so taken up with Reasoning about every thing I did that it kept me in Continual Temptation and prevented that quick attention to the Lord which is the only Posture for the Soul to grow in. And I have since Clearly discovered <that> that was the very thing Satan strove for. I found, however, at times, many Gracious Vissits [sic] from the Lord, and had ~~at Seasons~~ Sweet Communion with Him. My desire to do his Will in every Point was Strong and Ardent, and my heart was Ready to Break – ~~one who at that time lived [with/for?] us.~~

/

At the thought of having ~~sunk away~~ <declined> from that Intimate Union I once Enjoyed. About this time I dreamed[18] <that> I saw a bright Cloud, as I looked on it, It grew more and more Glorious & there appeared in it a Company of the heavenly host which I saw as far as the head, shoulders [sic] and Breast But one among them I saw quite to the feet, of Exquisite Beauty. He Came thro' the Cloud and appeared in a field near our Garden I Cried out: 'O Nanney Walker! there is the Lord Jesus.'[19] I ran to the garden door and oppened [sic] it. He took hold of my hand and helped me, and Came with me into the Parlour I run to tell my Mistress the Lord Jesus was in the Parlour! She went in and after a time, they Came out together and went into the Red Room where I thought Mr Wesley[20] was sitting. Our Lord touched his forehead and said 'You are in the Presence of God, and the Holy Angel of He then Came into the Parlour again. I thought, I long to go in and, opening the door, I met him He kissed me and said[, ']Before I come again you will be taken' To which I answered[, ']Ah Lord I often fear I shall never hold out. I shall never Come there' He then Stooped down and took up my Right foot and set it down again. It was explained to me He would order my steps then He went thro' the garden and gradually ascended till I saw Him no more'

I would here observe some time after my dear Mr. Fletcher[']s[21] Death[22] as I was one day Pleading with the Lord to raise up more helpers in the Work, ~~The~~ Word came to me The Spirit of Elijah shall Rest on Elisha'[23] I thought it meant her and soon after a Vissible [sic] Concern arose on her Mind, more forceable [sic] than ever for the Souls of the People In Particular the Rising Generation and such a Gift was then given her for Children, as I have hardly seen

/

In any one and a Love like that of a Parent Next, the sick were Laid on her heart and she ran far and near to seek and relieve them both <in> Soul and Body insomuch, that It greatly broke ~~out~~ her Little Strength, which was always but small One night she dreamed she was looking out at our Chamber Window on a Parcel of Fowls of all sorts and sizes, in the yard When she saw a very Little Bird flying to and fro over them And as each put up its Head the little Bird put a bit into its mouth after looking on them some time she thought she Called me, and said, 'Only look how that Little Creature feeds these great Fowls' She then saw a most beautiful Pillar in the sky It appeared like Gold exceeding bright. She was solemnly affected at the sight, and awoke with the application of these words to her heart I have made thee as that little bird follow me and I will make thee a Pillar This brought to her mind a Promise given her many years back: 'I will make thee a Pillar in my house to go out no more' But though she had many sweet times of encouragement her mind had usually a dejected Turn! To hear her speak of her state in the meetings you would almost have thought she had been Cold, Careless and Unfaithful, Idle, and good for nothing: so frequently was she Buffeted with Fiery darts of Accusation but at that very time, how have I been humbled to the Dust, at the Ardent Zeal and diligent Application wherewith she sought after the good of her fellow Creatures. For ~~Repressing~~ <Reproving> Sin, and Inviting to the means of Grace few Could Equal Her. Here I did indeed see the spirit of my dear Mr. Fletcher[24] I ~~seemed~~ to Rest on Her and like him, she began a Meeting in a very hardened Part of the Parish with a Bell in her hand, the Occasion of which / was as follows. About this time there was a Play Began of a very loose sort, which drew in many of the young People.[25] They used each night to Pass by our door like mad ~~things~~ <creatures> she was greatly afflicted at this, as it appeared likely to be an Inlet to much sin of Many kinds. While she was Continually Laying the Matter before the Lord, Some men also began a game each night in the Church yard She felt a Conviction to reprove These but found her Nature very averse to such a Cross however as her greatest fear was that of not being faithful to what the Lord Required She ventured out among them And strove to turn their Minds to a better Purpose, ~~I~~intreating them with Tears of love and Pity to take some thought for their Souls for whom the Blood of Jesus had been shed. And so did the Lord bless her Feeble endeavours that It was quite brok[en] up from that very night.

Encouraged by this she still made her Requests known to the Lord that He might overturn the other evil sport also and one night standing at the door of our meeting Room by which they used to Pass she began to speak to them but alas! it was like stoping[sic] mad Bulls then she said If I cannot stop you I will break your Ranks and laying hold of Five young Women She held them while she conversed with them Several more of the Company passing by at the time, both men and women And Blessed be God we saw no more of It for two years When some whom we knew made an attempt to renew it. We again Cried to the Lord and to some of the heads of it we sent this message 'As I was standing at the Window looking on them, the thought passed my mind Ah! Poor things! This is all the Pleasure they will have / to all Eternity unless they Repent: 'The Message was Carried and we have Cause to Praise God ~~It~~ <the sinful custom> was quite broke off After the night above mentioned, when she spoke to the young Women and the Play was given up, She took the first oppertunity [sic] to go

down the Town and Enquire who were the Ringleaders of the affair and found it to be some Navigators who were lately Come into the Parish to work at the new Cut. She went to the Houses where they Lodged, and Conversed with them and observing to them the Blessing Promised on Family Prayer She persuaded them to join with her therin [sic]. The thought then struck her mind, If she could once a week come to some house and spend a Little time with the Children. And then about half an hour with the Grown People, that It would be a Blessing a Place Immediately Opened and Each Thursday Night for near five years, she Constant by attended them. But as she Strove to suit their time, which Varied as different Parts of the year She took the little Bell in her hand, because they were not to gather 'till they heard It This Called out a number of Children; and O'may her Labours on them as well as the Parents be found to Everlasting Life in that Day. Madeley Town[26] is a hardned [sic] Spot. {-I do not know I ever found more discouragement in Speaking any where than there } and she has been brought to <shed> tears over them many times when going from door to door She has Intreated them to Come, and in Return met with only Reproach and Rudeness. But that was nothing to her, who sought no honour but from God. Sometimes Satan would Represent, how Rediculous she appeared in their Eyes. And when Carnal Stranger Passed by in Carriages &ce that they would think her mad.
/
But as these means she ~~Use Rose~~ <knew> had ~~Call~~ <been instrumental in calling> some, and <had> been blest to many as well as Prevented much Sin, she Rejoiced to have the honour of ~~becoming~~ <being thought> a fool for Christ! And such an intense Love did she feel towards them, at the very time they were ~~making a~~ Ridiculing ~~of~~ Her that she has told me 'It seemed, she could, with Pleasure <submit to> be bound to a Stake and burned, if it might but draw these souls to Choose the Way of Life.

It has been long very greevious [sic] to us, that at Christmas[,] Easter, and Whitsuntide, the Carnal <People> would frequently Introduce dancing, shews &ce And much did she Labour to prevent This Gross abuse of those holy Seasons one night Passing <illeg.> by a Publick house,[27] where they were dancing, she looked to the Lord for Power and going in among them begun to plead with them, and in a very moving and tender manner to Express the Love and Concern she felt for their Souls! And Glory be to God, we have some in heaven who dated their first Conviction from that hour. Indeed her whole soul seemed to be drawn out after the Salvation of all around her. She began meetings in different Places on which numbers attended. Her method was, after Singing and Prayer, to Read some Life Experience, or some Awakening Author stoping [sic] now and then, to explain and apply it ~~It~~ as the Lord gave her Utterance. And several, <who are> now lively believers In our Connextion[28] [sic], were brought in through that means. But in every Step she inquired of the Lord, fearing much to take one out of his Order! She has mentioned to me a dream <she had:> (I don[']t Exactly know the time) <in which> she thought, she was ~~t~~informed her Father, (who Died in the Lord many years ago.) was in a Certain Place and desired to see her; and that / she and I went together for that purpose:[29] But <but that,> in the way, I asked her to go and look at a Dial, and tell me what hour it was[.] She went down a Step Stone Walk, and saw it was just Eleven; and came to a Place which struck her with a solemn Impress[i]on that God had a work to do there[,] and having a Dish of Corn in her hand[.] She stopt[sic] and said, I will throw some of this Corn about; in token the Lord will some time sow his Gosple [sic] in this Place[.] As she went a Woman came out of her door and abused her much: but in her Return[,] the same woman Bestowed many Blessings upon her! She thought we went on till we came to an house, where we found her Father: He shewed her much affection, and said, 'My dear Child, I could not Rest till I saw you.' (A Little before his death he had a Promise of Salvation for all his Chilodren) After this she awoke. The Dream made a strong Impression on her mind, and often has she told me[,] she did believe she was to be called to some place she had never seen. But as it had a Resemblence [sic] to some we Passed through in Wales, she rather thought it would be in that Country. When the Works Commenced in Coal Port[,][30] and the Inhabitants began to encrease ; she was strongly Invited to come and hold a meeting there[.] I <And> found her mind drawn to accept the offer. But how was she struck[,] when the very Stone Walk and all the Place where she had sown the Corn, was as Plain to her Natural Eye[,] as before she had seen it Represented in her dream. On her Return she said 'The Houses and every Part is as exact as if I had had it drawn in a Picture.'

/

Here she Continued to attend every other Sunday Night <for> four years, and much of the Power of God was felt there. The Sinners would scoff, but her word was amazingly Received by Numbers, and deeply did they Lament when she could no longer meet with them as usual! and many an Earnest Prayer did they put up that she might be Restored to them again.

I have before observed she had a Natural tendency to be low[,] which was in Part Constituional, and Indeed I think she Possessed the full answer of that Prayer[,] 'Quick as the Apple of an eye, O God my Conscience make!' She Thirsted after a full Conformity <to God> and Panted to Worship him in the Beauty of Holiness[,] often would she plead with the Lord to let her know what she was in his sight[.] One night she dreamed she was in a Room with another Person[,] but did not Remember <with> whom They were <both> much taken up with admiring a Beautiful Picture. As they were about to leave the Room[,] she turned her Head to have another Look and was surprised to see it move when going before it she percieved [sic] its motions were similar to hir[sic] own[.] She then saw her whole Person from head to foot as In a looking Glass[,] and of Exquisite beauty[.] Then lifting up her mind to the Lord with Inquiring Wonder! She was answered I have made thee Comely by <through> my Comeliness, which I have put upon thee[.]' On which she awoke Praising the Lord[,] as she

Lay in the same Room with me[.] She told me of it and has since Remembered me [.] I made answer[,] Well it is the Glass of Faith[,] and when you steadily look thro' it[,] it shews you what you are in the Reflected Beauties of the <your> Lord. I must here / observe from the time she thought she had lost that salvation[.] I could never decern [sic] in her my spirit but that of the most Perfect deadness to Earth.' And such a submission to Crosses of every kind as augured to me, her will was truly lost in that of God.

I Lament she did not keep a Diary but some little Seraps [sic] I have found in her Desk[,] one is a Letter she wrote to a Friend on her dear Masters Death[31]

'Sep. 6 1785

'My dear Friend–

'In much Trouble and grief of mind I now write to you. I have for a long time had many deep Waters to Wade through! My dear Mistress[32] was taken Ill of a Fever, and Came out In Spots[.] My Master and I suffered much in the Fear of her being taken from us[,] but our Gracious Lord in mercy to us hath Raised her again[.] But before she was quite Recovered my dear Master was taken Ill[.] And, O what Tongue Can tell the Patience with which he endured his affliction? <He was> all Resignation to the will of God. Life or death seemed Eaqual [sic] to him: Indeed He had lived in such an holy Familiarity with death, that every day He would be talking of it[,] and at night when Lying down in his Bed, He <he> used to say[,] 'I seem to see myself as a corps stretched out on this Bedstead[.]' Then he would add <xxx> Lord give us dying grace[,]' and Indeed he had it: O had you been favoured with waiting on my dear Master in his Dying moments as I was[,] you would have seen how He passed through the Valley of the Shadow of Death and did fear<ed> no / Evil.[33] Satan seemed to have no Power to Tempt Him: No, he had fought the Good fight![34] and had then nothing to do but stop quietly out of this into a better world. Never did I see One so filled with the Love of God as he was. His whole soul seemed wrap<p>ed up in Love! <so> that he often cried aloud 'God is Love!' He hath given me such a manifestation of Himself in that Character, as quite fills me! I cannot tell you half I feel!' He strove to Comfort my dear Mistress, saying, 'My dearest; What Canst thou fear when 'God is Love!' He hath given me such a manifestation of Himself in that Character, as quite fills me! I cannot tell you half I feel!' He strove to Comfort my dear Mistress, saying, 'My dearest, what canst thou fear when God is Love!' He would often express great thankfulness for their Union[,] and sure never were two more Closely United[.] When on his Death bed, how would He look at her and say[,] 'My dear[,] my Preacious[,] my Generous Polly[,] God will open all thy way before thee,' She nursed him most Tenderly, night and day and never left him at all[,] and He often Expressed his great Satisfaction in having her so Constantly about him[.] Indeed the Lord wonderfully gave her strength for the Day. But O the stroke is very heavy upon her! No one can tell what she goes through. She seems Rippening for Glory; and I often fear her stay will be short. Lord prepare me for that Day. Truly it is a heavy stroke to me. I have lost the best of Masters and a kind, affectionate tender Father! But should I lose my dear Mistress who hath been such an Indulgent Mother to me for near twenty five years! I should Indeed become a desolate Orphan!

But the Lord knowes what will be best. I desire to give Myself wholly up to Him[.] I find nothing will do but a Constant looking up to Jesus through all. Satan thrives to oppress me, but the Lord gives me many Precious Promises; and I find him very near me. I often Rejoice in the thought of one day / Seeing my dear Redeemer face to face[,] and there meeting my dear Friends never to Part again.[35] O! it will not be long before we shall have done with this weary world! and Tempting Devil, hold out faith and Patience a Little longer!

How little did I think on August 14[,] 1783[,] When, on our Journey to Ireland[36] that this day two years, the Convoy of Angels the Chariots of Israel, that seperated [sic] Elijah from Elishai[37] would take my dear: dear: Master from my head that day! Yes he is gone from me! but I still comfort myself with that thought[,] He who late my Friend Received[,] will send the Chariot soon for me

'Yes—For us is prepar'd
'The Angelical Guard
'The Convoy attends!
'A ministring [sic] host of Invisable [sic] Friends
'Ready Wing'd for their Flight
'To the Regions of Light
'The horses will Come –
'The Chariot of Israel to Carry us home!'

One more little Fragment[] I find wrote <written> in the White Page of a Book[.] <illeg.> August[,] 1795[,] Yesterday being the Second Sunday in the month[,] I found it a Solemn Season, a day much to be Remembered as it was just Ten years since <when> my dear Master was Called to enter an Eternal Sabbath of Rest[.][38] I felt my heart greatly drawn out in Prayer, that I might enter into a further <larger> measure of that Rest which Remains for the People of God. For – though, Glory be to his dear name, I have Clearly felt Hhis Pardoning Love for more than Eighteen years [,] and have often found Seasons, When I could Truely feel / I did Love God with all my heart. Yet those happy moments were but short[.] Unbelief would Creep in, and too, too often my unwatchful heart would give way to discouragement, and let go its little hold of <on> that Glorious Liberty[.] But Yesterday how did my soul long and Pant for my dear Lord, to come and make his abode in my worthless heart[.] I feel Him mine[.] I can Indeed say

'With me thou doest Ev'n now Reside
'But in me thou shall soon abide.'

As I flattered myself that she would Close my Eyes, I tenderly felt for the Pain she would suffer in the Loss of me; and wished to alleviate it to the Utmost of my Power. I therefore wrote now and then a few Lines, for her to Open when I should be no more on Earth, and as they express my real Sentiments Concerning her[.] I am not free to destroy[,] but have them as a Testimony of my sincere Acknowledgements [sic] of what she was to me.

October 2[,] 1786[39]

'My very dear Sally—

I Charge you never give way to the thought that you could have been to me any thing more than you have, for it is a Temptation! You have been to me a <u>faithful Child</u>, and a great Comfort __ From the time I lost your dear and Precious Master; you have, under God, been my greatest Temporal Consolation. Give me now up to the Lord in full Confidence you shall come to us: and abide with us for ever! Sorrow not as those who have no hope of seeing their friends again, for you shall / Shortly be with us in Glory __ 'and the days which in heaven we spend for ever and Ever shall Last'

In the year 1790 being Ill, I wrote a Postscript to Confirm the above & three years after as follows

June 19[,]1793__

'My dearest Child—

I have been reading over my first Letter to you[,] Wrote in 86 and that of 90[,] and do, with all my heart, Confirm every word therin[sic]: you are to me a most Precious Gift of the Almighty! and the Greatest Comfort (next to God) of my Life[.] It is my sorrow and Sin that over I <have> grieved you in any thing[,] for I am witness how tenderly and Constantly you have strove in every thing, to add to my happiness[.] and your Labour has not been lost. What a support and Comfort have you been to me in all my Trials and afflictions! I wish I could do more for you in Temporals. But you know I have made my Will as I thought Conscience Dictated[.] And I thank God for being able to do for you, as I have done[,] and now I can with Confidence Commit my dearest Child, to the arms of the Almighty and am sure He will Preserve both Soul and Body[,] for the Lord hath said to me, [']I will Bless those that bless thee[.]' And never could I claim that Promise more fully for any One than I can for <u>you</u>, In firm Confidence It shall be answered. And now Believe you are <u>still</u> one with me, in the Lord[.] Remember forgetfulness is mortal! And Gratitude is Immortal! I <u>can</u> / <u>Therefore never forget you</u>: Believe you dear Master and I, are ready to Receive and Welcome you to the Mansions of Glory![40] I Pray and believe, the head of the Church to be your head: as my dear – <u>dear</u> Husband Prayed for me. And I Pray that the Lord may Cause His Spirit to Rest on you in such a way, as shall help on the souls of the dear People United in these Societies[.] And I think our Spirits will be with you, whenever you are led to tell them of the Love of Jesus! They are also our kindred Spirits, and Cannot be forgotten in heaven!

What I wrote for her Funeral Sermon was as follows[:]

My dear friend Sarah Lawrance has for many years been Weak and Infirm.[41]
[…]

One day Conversing with my husband Concerning our Burial, He said[,] she might be laid to us, if she Died here[,] for she w[as][42] our adopted Child[,] Remembering that, I have given Her the Ti{fold or tear} on one side of our Tomb Stone in these Words

Also

Sarah Lawrance

The adopted Daughter of John ~~William~~ and Mary de la Flechere

Who Died December 3, 1800.

Aged 44 years.

She Loved God, with all her Heart {illegible} Gloried in Christ Jesus

Was Zealous in His Cause

Suffered with Unwearied Patience

And Finished Her Course with Joy.

'These overcame by the Blood of the Lamb, and the Word of their Testimony[.]

QUAKER FICTIVE FAMILIES

Wilson, Rachel, Letter to R. Jones and H. Cathrall (1770), Quarterly Meeting of Ministers, 1769, Allinson collection, Haverford College, Haverford, PA. 968 HOC #7

Jones, Rebecca, Letter to Edward Cathrall (1782), Allinson Collection, Haverford College, Haverford, PA. 968 HOC #7

In urban settings such as colonial Philadelphia, it was not uncommon for unmarried women to form a household together.[1] Although such arrangements usually involved sisters who had never married, a widowed and an unmarried sister, or a widowed mother and her unmarried or widowed daughter, some unmarried friends also established and maintained long-term households with one another. As household partners they shared economic and domestic responsibilities, dividing chores 'according to individual skills and inclinations'.[2]

Quakers Rebecca Jones and Hannah Catherall – both schoolteachers – serve as an example of women who formed a household together, in their case, for at least twenty years. Through the fictive ties they created, they 'blended emotional and economic interests'.[3] Together, they engaged in numerous social activities and became leaders of the Quaker community. In particular, they had opportunities to form 'special bonds with other independent women'.[4]

Although the two women shared similar views and interests, they came from very different backgrounds. Jones had been raised in Philadelphia in the Anglican faith. At the age of twelve, she began attending Quaker meetings. In this context, she became acquainted with the visiting English Friends, Catherine Peyton and Mary Peisley. Deeply affected by their preaching, Jones requested spiritual guidance from Peyton. As a result, she became friends with several other ministers, as well. In 1758, at the age of nineteen, Jones began her own ministerial career. Catherall, on the other hand, was the daughter of a prominent Burlington Quaker family; consequently, she served as the clerk of the Philadelphia Yearly Meeting from 1778 to 1794.[5]

Jones and Catherall opened a school together in 1763. Through this venture, the two friends taught boys and girls for a span of twenty years.[6] Many of their students, some of whom came from prominent Quaker families, stayed with them for extended periods of time, often spanning several years. Catherall and Jones thus helped shape the lives of many young Quakers.

In addition to sharing a home and a career, Jones and Catherall also shared religious and social commitments. They had many friends in common and attended parties and dinners together. For example, the English Quaker, Rachel Wilson and her daughter Rachel, 'corresponded with Jones and Catherall jointly'.[7]

The following two letters capture the web of relationships that developed around the fictive ties that bound Jones and Catherall to one another as well as to their extended family members and friends. The first, written from Rebecca Jones to Edward Catherall, suggests that friends and family 'accorded [Jone's and Catherall's] relationship a respected status'.[8] It is particularly interesting to note that Jones signed this note to Hannah's nephew as 'Aunt R Jones'. The second letter, written from Rachel Wilson (junior) to Catherall and Jones, celebrates the fictive ties her biological mother, Rachel Wilson, made as she toured much of colonial America from Philadelphia to Boston to North Carolina and Virginia as an 'eminent' and 'celebrated'[9] Quaker preacher from 1768–9.[10]

Notes
1. K. Wulf, *Not All Wives: Women of Colonial Philadelphia* (Ithaca, NY: Cornell University Press, 2000), p. 110.
2. Wulf, *Not All Wives*, p. 111.
3. Wulf, *Not All Wives*, p. 111.
4. Wulf, *Not All Wives*, p. 111.
5. I. A. Brendlinger, *To Be Silent ... Would be Criminal: The Antislavery Influence and Writings of Anthony Benezet* (Lanham, MD: Scarecrow Press, 2006), p. 110, n. 76.
6. 'Overseers of the Friends Public Schools to Rebecca Jones and Hannah Catherall Dr from 4 mo. 5. 1763 to 4th moth 5th 1764', Teachers' Accounts, Box 1, William Penn Charter School Archives, Quaker Collection, Haverford College.
7. Wulf, *Not All Wives*, p. 113.
8. Wulf, *Not All Wives*, p. 113.
9. News articles as quoted in R. Larson, *Daughters of Light: Quaker Women Preaching and Prophesying in the Colonies* (Chapel Hill, NC, and London: The University of North Carolina Press, 1999), pp. 233–9.
10. J. Somervell, *Isaac and Rachel Wilson, Quakers of Kendal, 1714–1785* (London: Swarthmore Press, 1924), p. 5; Larson, *Daughters of Light*, pp. 33–9; G. Braithwaite, *Rachel Wilson and Her Quaker Mission in 18th Century America* (UK: Sessions Books, 2012), p. 1.

Rachel Wilson, letter to R. Jones and H. Cathrall (1770)

Dear Friends Kendal 10th 3rd mo 1770[1]

R. Jones of the Catherall/My mind is feelingly sensible of your kind disinterested motive in writing me, and the unfeigned acknowledgements of a Grateful heart, have often been breathed in secret, upon the repeated perusal of your Affectionate Sentiments, and friendly advice, with ardent Desires, that neither the flattering Blandishments of Pleasure, nor all the Glittering Allurements, of Youthful fancy, may ever erase from my remembrance, the humbling Consideration of the high Privileges I enjoy, above many, more Worthy, and freely Amicable or My Situation in Life, preserving me from many Snares, which numbers at an inexperienced Age, have mournfully witnessed – Yet through the various allotments of Providence, there's no State totally exempt from Trials; the unwary Mind is ever liable to be diverted from its most necessary Pursuit, by a variety of gilded Baits, and fallacious Prospects of temporal Joys. At least I find it so, and painfully feel that I am frail – Yet at times, the feeble perspirations of grateful Praise ascend from a Contrite Spirit, deeply impressed with the unmerited, Unbounded Love of the omnipotent Father, and Friend of Men – I expect before this, you will have heard of my Dear Mother's safe arrival in England.[2] She has been now at home ten weeks, and is much favoured with the enjoyment of Health; and appears less altered, than we might reasonably expect, by her many long journeys and Laborious engagements. The great Master whom she served amply supplied with Strength in the needful hours, sweetening every bitter cup of afflicting Exercise, and supporting frail Humanity under almost insuperable Difficulties – She often mentions you with an affectionate Regard, bearing in remembrance the near Sympathy of her friends, whilst she was far separated from every endeared connection in Life, and had to pass through many painful Conflicts and Arduous trials.

Her American Friends are frequently the Subject of our Conversation, to whom tho to us personally unkown, we feel our minds nearly united, in that Love which cant be Circumscribed by time, or space, nor can the wide Atlantic set bounds to our thoughts. In Idea we often visit you, enquiring of our Dear Parent, after many whom we only know by Character—Of you my Dear friends more particularly, whose agreeable Letters were as acceptable, as unexpected, and have pressed my mind with Sentiments of Gratitude and Esteem, and be assured at any time a few Lines from either of you, would be received with Pleasure.

By your Affectionate and Obliged friend,

R. Wilson Jones

R. Wilson's Dear Love attends her Esteemed friend P. J. of H. C. whom she affectionately remembers, with many more at Philadelphia, to whom she presents her Dear Love, as in your freedom – particularly to Tho. Clifford and Wife, and let them know, I have not seen their Son since my Return, but am in hopes ere long to see both him, and Abel James; as Spring draws nigh they may venture into the North without harm, where we shall some of us, be pleased to see them. I had a Letter from R. James, lately, wherein he gives a good Acct. of his Health, that am in hopes his coming to England, may have the desired effect. My Mind Salutes his Dear Wife & Children, in pure love – as my Daughter hath wrote pretty fully, there is the less for me to do.

Farewell Dearly,

Rachel Wilson

Wilson 10 mon. 1770[3]

To R. Jones & H. Cathrall

Philadelphia

In a Quarterly Meeting[4] of Members & Elders, held at the Falls in Buchs County[5] – the 30th of 8th mon. 1769[6] —

Our Dear Friend Rachel Wilson had an open, encouraging time. And first to Ministers– She used a familiar Proverb 'Strike while the Iron is hot' and prepared the Necessity of minding the right Time for standing up;[7] reminding them of the fruitful labour attending Striking when the Heat was gone out – And in particular to those who were Young in the Ministry, that they might not let in the Reasoner, and think because such and such frds[8] were at Meeting, they had best Smother their little Matter. She had been often helped by a few Words in the Simplicity, in the forepart of a Meeting, and it was like opening a Door to further Service – But some, when they had something to offer, kept it to themselves, and chewed it, and chewed it, till they had got all the Substance out, and perhaps just at the close of a Meeting (when they found themselves uneasy with leeting the right time Slip) had stood up and like Spit it out, and it was of no use to anybody else – She observed to the Elders, that the Snuffers under the Law, were to be made of the same beaten Gold with the Lamps, and enlarged on the Use of Snuffers – that often times without them, the Fallow, the Life of the Candle would be in danger of wasting, and that they were of great Service, when skillfully used to take of all Superfluous Snuff, and remarked when done with Judgment, how much brighter the Light burned. But cautioned against too frequent use of them, for she had seen the Disadvantage attending it; Some People were seldom easy unless they were Snuffing.

In the Yearly Meeting of Ministers & Elders at Philadelphia 9th mo. 1769[9]

At the Opening of the Meeting she delivered herself in these Words.

'If I have a right Sense in this Meeting, there is a withholding more than is meet, By which the Work is retarded, Individuals suffer, and the General are sensible of the Loss'—In the several Meetings she appeared divers times, and once, when she was about expressing something relative to herself, she signified she was led from her own Concern, to speak to out friend John Woollman[10], who was under a concern to visit some of the Islands. She addressed him with much Sympathy, and ardently wished the good Hand might be with him, and enable to divide the Word aright, to the Honour of the great Name, the Comfort of those among whom he had to Labour, and his own lasting Peace. And for his Encouragement, she testified she had found as she steadily eyed her great Master, from Day to Day. She had been in no Lack of any thing, but He had been altogether Sufficient—And in the concluding Meeting she imparted much Solid advice, particularly to Elders whom she compared to the Golden Snuffers under the law, that were made of the same beaten Gold with the lamps, and remarked that if a proper use was made of Snuffers, by taking away that, that dimmed the lustre and was Superflous, the Light would burn and Shine clearer and brighter, but some were so fond of snuffing, that they had at length wasted the Life of the Candle and had sometimes put it quite it out—And further she said she had been comforted with every appearance in the Several Meetings, that had been in the line of Truth and that no such has ever been in her Way, but had been helpful to her, and that she was free to say. She had not opened her Mouth by way of Reflection against any friend and towards the conclusion signified. She had as much or more Need than any other to live near the Truth and rquested the Prayers of her friends for her Preservation ahd Help for she expected to meet with Trials and Exercises if she should live, &c, &c, &c.

In the concluding Women's Meeting of Business[11] our said friend was led to speak very encouragingly to us respecting the attendance of religious Meetings: She said she had not abundance of this World's wealth, yet Sufficient and enough, and that her outward outward Affairs never suffered by attending them, and further she had this Testimony for herself, that she never since she knew the Truth neglected going to Meeting, unless prevented by Sickness in her family, or on account of the care of Infants, which she allowed reasonable excuses—And expressed her Satisfaction of Mind throughout this Yearly Meeting[12], that she had been comforted in the several Sittings thereof, and concluded on leaving the Meeting to adjourn in a solid weighty frame, which they did after Ann Moor[13] had appeared in fervent Supplication.

Rebecca Jones, Letter to Edward Cathrall (1782)

Dear Edward[14] Philada 7th Mo. 25th 1782.[15]
    Since thou left thy Father's house, my Mind has been many times turned toward thee, sincerely desiring thou may not only witness preservation from every temptation that may present with design to draw thee still further from the Path of Innocence but that by a steady adherence to the quick & powerful Word in the Secret of thy own Mind, thou may be brought into an Acquaintance with a State of true inward Stillness in which thou may be favoured to understand the things that belong to thy Souls peace, which is of the greatest Consequence both to Age & Youth, especially when we consider that our Stay in this World is very uncertain, and that after we have done with things below, we must appear before a Righteous tribunal, there to give an Account of the deeds done in the body, whether good or Evil. How careful then ought we to be in our Steppings thro time? How watchful over our Words & Actions, Retirement of Mind is such an excellent Situation. I have found it so. That I can not but recommend it to thee, may thou often retire alone, & rather choose to be alone, than in such Company as may have a tendency to do thee hurt. Young People who are inexperienced are often drawn into things highly improper, if not offensive, in the Light of Heaven, for want of keeping on their Guard in this very Spot – when as if they did but love Silence, and hearken to the Monitors of divine Grace in their own Hearts, they would grow up in good liking, yea in favour both with God & Man. My Heart with thy Dear Aunt Hannah[16] prays for thy preservation, and that thou may now in a State of Separation from all thy tender Connections, be met with by him, who is willing to do thee good, and is waiting to be gracious to the Children & Grand Children of those who have loved & served him, as thy Grandparents did.[17] Now keep this Letter to thy Self – and read it over leisurely. It is the longings of one of thy best friends and whom thou call thy Aunt. R. Jones

To. E. Catherall

VOLUNTARY ASSOCIATIONS

Female Society and Female Association of Pennsylvania, Minutes (1805–15), Quaker Collection, Haverford College, Haverford, PA.

Articles of Association of the Female Hospitable Society (1814), Quaker Collection, Haverford College, Haverford, PA.

The initial voluntary associations that emerged in eighteenth-century Philadelphia were primarily composed of 'assemblies of men'.[1] By the end of the century, however, American women began to emulate the example of evangelical English women by organizing their own benevolent societies.[2] The voluntary associations they created and operated, Bruce Dorsey observed, 'grew exponentially in the early republic'.[3]

In 1793, free African-American women in Philadelphia organized the Female Benevolent Society of St Thomas at the African Church.[4] This mutual assistance society provided relief benefits to due-paying members; however, they lacked the resources to provide charity for the city's poor.[5] Two years later, a group of Quaker women determined that they wanted to assist women and children who had been impoverished as a result of the yellow fever epidemics that had swept through 1790s Philadelphia. They established the Female Society for Relief and Employment of the Poor, which was 'the first female charity organized independent of a church and providing general assistance to the poor rather than to due-paying members'.[6] Within a year of founding the Female Society, some women Quakers also established separate charity school societies for black women and poor white women.[7] Members of the Female Society visited the homes of poor women each week and brought much needed food and medicine with them. On occasion, they also provided childcare so mothers could make money spinning. Between 1800 and 1818, this society employed fifty to eighty women per year; it also provided assistance to approximately one hundred additional families.[8]

Over the succeeding decades, groups of white Protestant women created other charitable associations. In 1800, for example, women in Philadelphia organized the Female Association for the Relief of Women and Children in Reduced Circumstances.[9] Members of this group visited the poor and provided them with monthly cash pensions. Until 1807, when the almshouse took over work-relief projects, they also paid women for spinning that they completed in their own homes.[10] In addition, they maintained a soup house between 1802 and 1807; they later converted it into an asylum for destitute widows and children, and then into a private school for girls. Through the various relief efforts this society engaged in, they were able to assist between 500 and 600 women annually until the 1820s.[11]

In 1808, the wives of several prominent ministers formed the Female Hospitable Society. Responding to the embargo, which left a number of men unable to support their families, members of this society provided assistance for such families, as well as to widows and orphans.[12] They also visited poor families and accessed their needs. They would then issue 'orders that entitled the women to cash relief, payment for home spinning, medical assistance ... or relief in kind from the hospitable society's storeroom'.[13]

In speaking of the first white women's charitable organizations in Philadelphia, Dorsey observed that they 'emanated from the labors of young, unmarried Quaker women: women without sons to raise up as good republican citizens or husbands to soften and influence toward compassion and sympathy'.[14] The women involved in these societies kept careful records that detailed the acts of service they performed, but their records also reflect the bonds they established with one another as they united – committed to making a difference for families who were struggling.

Notes
1. B. Dorsey, *Reforming Men and Women: Gender in the Antebellum City* (Ithaca, NY: Cornell University Press, 2002), p. 12.
2. P. Ferguson Clement, *Welfare and the Poor in the Nineteenth-Century City: Philadelphia, 1800–1854* (Rutherford: Fairleigh Dickinson University Press, 1985), p. 144.
3. Dorsey, *Reforming Men and Women: Gender in the Antebellum City*, p. 12.
4. S. J. Kleinberg, *Women in the United States, 1830–1945* (New Brunswick, NJ: Rutgers University Press, 1999), p. 82; Dorsey, *Reforming Men and Women*, p. 12.
5. Dorsey, *Reforming Men and Women*, p. 28.
6. Dorsey, *Reforming Men and Women*, p. 12.
7. Dorsey, *Reforming Men and Women*, p. 12.
8. Ferguson Clement, *Welfare and the Poor in the Nineteenth-Century City: Philadelphia, 1800–1854*, p. 144; O. A. Pendleton Jr, *Influence of Evangelical Churches upon Reform: A Case-Study Giving Particular Attention to Philadelphia, 1790–1840* (Lancaster, PA: Lancaster Press, 1947), p. 276; Female Society of Philadelphia for the Relief and Employment of the Poor Report, 1871, pp. 4–10.
9. E. S. Wistar, *The History of the Female Association of Philadelphia for the Relief of Women and Children in Reduced Circumstances*; Ferguson Clement, *Welfare and the Poor in the Nineteenth-Century City*, p. 144.
10. Ferguson Clement, *Welfare and the Poor in the Nineteenth-Century City*, p. 144.
11. Ferguson Clement, *Welfare and the Poor in the Nineteenth-Century City*, p. 144; Wistar, *The History of the Female Association of Philadelphia for the Relief of Women and Children in Reduced Circumstances*, pp. 3–15.
12. Ferguson Clement, *Welfare and the Poor in the Nineteenth-Century City*, p. 145.
13. Ferguson Clement, *Welfare and the Poor in the Nineteenth-Century City*, p. 145.
14. Dorsey, *Reforming Men and Women*, p. 28.

Female Society and Female Association of Pennsylvania, Minutes (1805–15)

You are requested to attend a meeting of the Board of Direction *of the* Female Association, *on* ___ *at the house of Mrs.*___ *at* ___ *o'clock in the morning. By order of the President,*

                                                                               Secretary

/

To The Ladies of the Female Association[1]
Philadelphia March 5th 1805

    I fear, that silence upon a subject, which merits the highest acknowledgment of gratitude, might appear to the worthy ladies of the female association as if I were insensible to the favour they have had the goodness to confer on me; I Therefore take the liberty of addressing Them to say, how thankful I am for Their considerate kindness, and however poor the compensation of mere acknowledgment may be, for generosity so nobly evinced to a stranger, apparently friendly as I am, yet I must add to the obligation, by saying, that I am impressed with the {smudge} deepest sense of gratitude; that in this way only I can discharge a duty I owe the excellent ladies; and that I have no other means of disencumbering my heart from a sentiment which otherwise would become oppressive to my self. I must also add this, that, tho' the pecuniary debt is discharged, by the receipt which my dearest Mrs. Bradford[2] so condescendingly brought me, and was <that> greatly eases my mind on a subject, which in some lenth of time might have made my honesty questionable, yet I am far from considering myself honorably free from the bond, for if in future Heaven should prosper me with better circumstances I will joyfully return the loan – That may be done – But the impressive sentiment of gratitude no time; nor no return of pecuniary matters can ever eradicate from the heart of

                                                            Ladies
                                                      Your most grateful
                                        Most obedient humble Ser[vant]
                                                          Mary Ralston[3]

/

The Female Association
Letter from Mrs. Hannah Boudinott[4]
dated Burlington 18th Nov[embe]r 1805

Burlington November 18th 1805

Most respected Ladies

The separation that has, in the course of Providence, taken place between us, by my removal from your City, renders it impracticable for me, longer to fill the honourable place your confidence has favour'd one with.

It is with regret that I reflect on the small assistance I have afforded you since my appointment; but be assured, that where ever I am, my prayers, and best wishes, shall attend you, for Success in your laudable and benevolent exertions, in behalf of the poor and distressed.

I am ready to transfer the stock, in my name, to such Person as you shall order and direction.

With the sincerest desire for your individual happiness, and a blessing on all your charitable labours.

I have the honour to be with
sentiments of esteem
Ladies your much obliged
humble servant
Hannah Boudinot

/

Resolved – That Mrs. Stocker[5] be requested on behalf of the Members of this Institution, to reply to the communication rec[eive]d from Mrs. Boudinot expressing their regret that she should have found it necessary to resign the office of President of the Society; and directing her to put into the hands of Mrs. S.V. Bradford, as her successor, all papers belonging to the Female Association.

Resolved – That the thanks of the Society be return'd to Mrs. S.V. Bradford[6] for her zeal & fidelity in discharging the duties of her late office, & for the various instances of patronage & personal service she has so perseveringly render'd the Institution. The following resolutions were laid before the Society and unanimously adopted –

Nov 1805

Mrs Pres

/

I am directed to transmit you my dear Mrs. Bradford a copy of the following resolution from the minutes of the society at their meeting Nov 24th 1805 and to beg you to deliver the enclosed to your Mamma.

Resolv'd – That Mrs. S.V Bradford receive the thanks of their society for her zeal and fidelity in discharging the duties of her late office, and for the various instances of patronage and personal service she has so perseveringly rendered the institution.
/
Mrs. Boudinot,
Madam,
Agreeably to a resolution of the members of the Female Association of Philadelphia present at their annual meeting in November 1805, I have the honor to communicate to you the expression of their regret on receipt of your resignation, their thanks for the affectionate and pious wishes which accompanied it, and their request that you deliver over to Mrs. S.V. Bradford (who is duly and unanimously elected President of the society) all books or papers in your hands relative to the business of the institution. The Committee appointed by the Board of direction to examine the late Treasurer's Act report[7] – that they have examin'd the same and find them Correct –

Mary Hodge[8]
Sarah Stille[9]

April 16th 1806
/
Princeton NJ Apr 14 Paid 10
Mrs Stocker[10]
Front Street,
Philadelphia
letter {tear} from Mrs S. V Bradford
dated Princeton
13 – April 1807 –
to Mrs Stocker
Mrs Stocker –
President of the Board of Direction

Princeton April 13th 1807

My dear Madam,
I have been under the necessity of attending my father to this place – the storm to day has prevented my return home – and of course I must relinquish the pleasure of meeting the ladies – you will be good enough to make my apology, and take my place.

Make my compliments acceptable to Mrs. and Miss Potts.[11] I must make my letter short (although I have several things to say) as I find great difficulty in writing by candlelight.

I am my dear Madam with
Respect and esteem yours &c

Susan V Bradford

Mrs Stocker.

/

Geo[rge] Taylin Jr presents his compliments to Mrs. Hodge and informs her that he has purchaced four shares Phil[adelphia] Bank stock a 125 which will amount to exactly 500 Dollars. and he will be much obliged to Mrs. Hodge to inclose him a check for that sum by the Bearer.

Friday Morning
1 May 1807
I subjoin a Bill & a receipt on it
/
Mrs Mary Hodge

Phila[delphia] 1st May 1807

Mrs. Mary Hodge

Bo cf of Geo[rge] Taylin Jr 4 Shares Phila[delphia] Bank stock a 125 p[er] c[en]t $500 –

Transferred to Mary Hodge Treasurer in trust for the female Association of Phila[delphia]

Rec[eive]d payment
Geo[rge] Taylin Jr

/

Philadelphia August 1st 1807

Enclosed I have the pleasure of sending you Twenty five dollars, a donation from the Managers of the last Cotillon Party,[12] for the use of the Female Association – There is still a balance due of some 40 or 50 dollars which if received shall be appropriated to the same person.

I remain
Your
respectfully,
J[a]m[e]s R C Smith
/

My dear Miss Gratz,[13]

I receiv'd your exclosure with peculiar pleasure – it was promised some time since – and I was apprehensive it had been otherwise appropriated – I have also to acknowledge the receipt of a donation of five dollars forwarded by you – it will be certainly proper to so return an acknowledgment to Mr Smith as it has been customary on these occasions – yours with sincere esteem

M Hodge

August 3rd 1807

/
My Dear Miss Gratz–

You will oblige me by lending me your Book of Minutes[14] to assist me in my undertaking of replaceing the Book belonging to the Society – As the papers remaining are without name or date I find it difficult to arrange them correctly – Yours with esteem

M Hodge

Monday Oct 4th 1807

/

Philadelphia Nov 3rd 1807

Sir ___

The Board of Direction[15] of the Female Association having ordered a statement of the funds to be prepared for the general meeting of the Society[16] and the interest on the public stock to be collected – I must intreat you to furnish me with a power of attorney to send to Washington, for two quarters interest laying in the office there[,] and which the clerk of the Bank here informs me can be procured in no other way – he also hinted that a similar power would have been more acceptable to the Bank than the certificate which I presented – As it is my wish to comply with all the forms of business {tear} would oblige me extremely by enabling me to do so –

The Ladies hope to have the pleasure of seeing Mrs Bradford[17] at the general meeting – please to present my respects to Mrs Boudinot[18] and believe me I've respectfully yours – Mary Hodge[19]

/

Miss R. Gratz
Philadelphia

Philadelphia Jan[ua]ry 6th 1808

Dear Miss

Your very polite Letter came only to hand, and I meant to have done th̶myself the pleasure of waiting on you in person, and mentioning, what I must now do by letter, being obliged suddenly to leave Town, to prevent being detained by the Ice –

My design is to appropriate that House, to charitable purposes; if therefore the female association can improve it for a free school, or any other useful purpose for the benefit of the poor, I will enlarge or Continue the lease for 2 or 3 years more – Otherwise I will, on my first coming again to this City, comply with the Condition of the Lease –

Whenever the Director determine on the business, I will be much obliged by a line of information –

I am with great respect
You very H[um]ble Serv[an]t
Cha[rle]s Boudinot[20]

Miss R. Gratz
/

Burlington Feb[ruar]y 5 1808

Miss Gratz

    I was honored with your very polite Letter the 31st of January a day or two ago. It will give one great pleasure to lend my aid to your worthy association, in promoting the happiness of the Orphan & Widow – They may depend on my agreeing to any plan they may think proper to advocate – I will therefore readily consent to enlarge the Lease, three or four years long as may best suit their plan.

    I send at fort an Order for Lydia Coleman to remove from the premises – I have left a blank for the day which you will fill up so as to answer your purposes; but I could wish it should not be before the 1st March next.

                        I have the honor to be with due regard
                                 Yours most respectfully
                                   Cha[rle]s Boudinot

Miss Gratz
/

    I am gratified my dear Miss Gratz with the hope held out in your note that we shall not eventually lose you as Secretary – there will be no claim upon your attention for three weeks to come which time I trust will prove effectual in restoring your health and soothing your spirits – at least it may enduce you to try the experiment of employment as a remedy for affliction & I am the mo[re] solicitous you should try it no experience has convinced me of its efficacy – If there are any reports respecting the soup house among your papers please to send them to me as I wish to make some extract from them – Yours with sympathy & affection

                                           M Hodge–

Nov 1st 1808–
/

Madam

    I have great pleasure in requesting your acceptance of ninety eight Dollars and thirty seven Cents for the use of the <School under the direction of the> 'Female Association for the releif of indigent Single Women and Children', being the residue of the Sum of many bequeathed to me by the late Mr. Charles Nicholes[21] to be applied to charitable purposes.

    With great regard, and best Wishes for the prosperity of the excellent institution over which <you> preside, I am Madam very respectfully your sincere friend
                                               Benj[ami]n Rush[22]

Novem[ber] 15.
   1808
   /

Madam

Since you did me the honor to call upon me Mrs Latimore & Mrs McLane have had the goodness to request the same favor, as these Ladies are probably among your acquaintance you would lay no under particular obligation by informing them you have heard from no since their visits on the subject of their inquiries. in apology for which they have afford with equal delicacy & propriety their motives for scrutinizing so closely into my family affairs, observing it was only in conformity with their usual rules of their association.

Having already mentioned to you the name of M Breeck I did suppose any member of the <female> society might through him receive every requisite information on the subject of my family connections.

Mrs. McLane has been pleased to express some surprize that Mr. Spears misfortunes should have preceeded to such a length, while his family connections in Boston are so competent to administer to his relief. Among the many evils of this troublesome world, perhaps that of becoming an object of commiseration of relief may be conscious as one of the greatest misfortunes & which demands our highest sympathy – In visits of this nature it is also greatly to be regretted that some domestic affairs will unavoidably be brought to light which otherwise might have remained forever concealed from public view.

The fact is Madam, Mr. Spear has withdrawn from his family. & not that they have abandoned him or that any personal quarrel has taken place, but the division of a Fathers estate which was the fruit of his industry & hard earnt labors for more than 40 years has been the just grounds as he conceives of his resentment – This property having been wrested from him while in a state of insanity by a capricious & avaricious Son & afterwards given to three children in a manner equally wicked & unjust, one sister already in affluence receiving 25000$ while another received only $5000 – One brother receiving $10,000 & two others nothing appears to Mr S. sufficient grounds of dissatisfaction & estrangement from those who were in proporsion of what belongs to others

On the part of Mrs Spear, I will forbear going into a detail of her family affairs which however in point of justice & equity have scarcely a shadow of preference from that already related. Her mother having no other child has made a very injudicious disposition of a very handsome property this connected with other circumstances seems to have laid the foundation of disquietude & disaffection which at length produced a separation since which no correspondence & social intercourse has erased.

Mrs Spear has till within the last twelve month been in the habit of receiving frequent aid and assistance from her two sons who follow the Sea – but since the Embargo she is of necessity deprived that benefit.

I must beg your pardon for thus disturbing you in a business in which I am sensible you have so little interest or concern, but having an opinion it might satisfy those Ladies who have been pleased to consider me an object of their care & attention I have chearfully submitted my story for their inspection & pray you would make such use of it as you may think proper.

Being with great esteem & respect
Your very obliged friend.
M SPear

Phila[delphia] Jan 16. 1809
/

A Letter from
Mrs Bradford
Nov. 1809

The Ladies of the female Association of Philadelphia
Mr Higginson
Miss Gratz

Burlington November 18th 1809

Ladies,

I have delayed writing until the last moment in the hope that my other duties would have permitted me once more, to meet you in our Society, and personally to have offered you my thanks, for the honour you have done me in so long continuing my <u>name</u> as your President; when it has been wholly out of my power to render you the least assistance. This consideration alone, prompts me now, thus to send in my resignation. It is an act of judgment, not of feeling, for be assured it is with the greatest regret that I leave you – it occasions sensations I neither can, or wish to express – Were I to remain with you, my fathers present state of health, together with my distant residence from the city, would make it improbable, that I should ever have the satisfaction of making any amends for my past deficiencies I am however persuaded you will not doubt my sincerity when I say, that I shall ever feel the most lively interest in all the concerns of the society, and be ready at all times, to afford them any assistance that may be in my power –

With the most grateful sense of your attention,

I am ladies, with the highest
Respect and esteem –

Your most obedient

And humble servant –

Susan V Bradford –

The ladies of the Female association of Philadelphia
/
Miss Rebecca Gratz

Market Street

In reply to your polite, and very flattering communication from the Board of Directors, Miss Gratz, I have to ~~reply~~ <remark> that when informed of my nomination to the office of President, I disclaimed, most honestly, the intended honor, strongly urg'd the appointment of another, and promised to make up a ticket and to attend the meeting but actually forgot both the business & the time until the election was over and my appointment was announced. An inattention which I may confess to you, Miss Gratz, who have felt the presence of affliction, and know how sorrow, regret, & painful retrospection monopolize the thoughts & absorb the faculties, tho' you know not the effect of reiterations – and may you never know! But I wander – The point is, if I am elected President I <u>must</u> hold the office during one year, agreeably to the Constitution; it is not optional with me to accept or to refuse it, as I before observed; and I would not choose to retain a place in the direction of the same time, tho the Ladies, with a delicacy which has always mark'd their conduct, have proposed it.

Have the goodness therefore to offer them my thanks for this, & all former attentions, with a request that the vacancy may be fill'd; and my earnest wishes that my successor, no less than the other Directors recently appointed, may prove a valuable acquisition to their Board.

Yours respectfully
S. Stille[23]

December 16th 1809

/

D –

Dear Madam

I have taken the liberty of placing in your hands the sum of thirty dollars – as a donation from me, for the use of that very Benevolent Institution the Female Society, for the relief of distressed Women – I am Madam

With the greatest respect your obedient servant
Hannah Lardner[24]

Dec the 18th 1809

/

Miss Gratz
High Street

Mrs B Chew presents her compliments to Miss Gratz, & returns the report sent, with her entire approbation Mrs C[hew] begs Miss Gratz will have the goodness to excuse her not returning an earlier Answer, As she has been engaged by the indiposition of her Children –

Mrs. C[hew] some time since presented a report from the Committee of the widow & orphan House, part of which she thinks will answer to subjoin – as no alteration has since taken place. Mrs. C[hew] believes Miss Gratz has this report with the Books of the Board

As Miss G[ratz] is so highly gratified, She will be so Obliging as to put in her own Language the necessary report.

Jan[uar]y 18th 1810

/

February 14th 1810. Received from Mrs. Hodge Treasurer of the Female Association Seven dollars fifty Eighty seven & a half cents, being the amount paid by me for having the water pumped out of the Soup House cellar, & the same repaid, while occupied by the Association –

John B. Wallace

Dec 7, 09

/

To the Board of Direction Of the Female Association of Philadelphia

The following statement is respectfully submitted to the consideration of the Board of Direction under the impression that possibly they may deem the <peculiar> circumstances sufficiently urgent to authorise a departure from a general rule. But as the object for whom releif is solicited resides out of the State there are certainly many objections that my be reasonably urged and if after the particulars are stated the Board deem it inexpedient to comply with the request the petition is respectfully withdrawn with a firm conviction that their decisions are guided by wisdom as well as Benevolence –

There is now residing in Burlington a widow by the name of Ann Mitchell – <whose character is well> a native of Santa Cruz, but residing who has been many years in this country formerly lived in this city and was a communicant in Dr Greens congregation. About 5 years ago she went to Santa Cruz to arrange her affairs and after suffering many losses and difficulties she sunk her <property> into an annuity of 300$ <appointed an agent to remit her income> and returned to this country as a every year and returned to this country as living is so much cheaper here than there she brought with her a small sum on which [illeg.] supported her for sometime daily expecting the promised supply two years have now lapsed since she has received one cent and the proper measures have been taken to procure redress yet the difficulty of supporting her in the mean time is very considerable. The inhabitants of the town where she lives have exerted themselves in her behalf subscriptions have been raised and releif afforded in many ways till all reserves are exhausted and charity itself seems at a pause any sum therefore however small would be acceptable. a in the mean time a reasonable hope is entertained that some supply may be received from the West Indies. As Mr. Yard has and two other gentleman have interested themselves in her behalf – the present releif therefore is solicited in the form of a loan to be strictly refunded in t if ever circumstances will admit. if upon enquiry her affairs are found desperate the

poor-house must be her final resort but to delay that painful moment as long as possible seems highly desirable for tho never in the higher walks of life yet she has been accustomed to live creditably and to associate with <very> decent society She is now above seventy years of age in addition to the usual infirmities of that advanced period she is totally blind. her only child a daughter fifty years ~~of age~~ <old> is an entire ideot and ~~now~~ poverty is <now> advancing with hasty steps for by the 1st of May her little fund will be entirely exhausted The character of this person is well known to the writer of this article and she believes her to be a very worthy good woman and if upon consideration of her peculiar misfortunes, <the Board> ~~they~~ may judge proper to extend relief however small, it will be most gratefully received and shall be very frugally expended—
Philadelphia
April 1st 1810
/
Philadelphia 16 Jan[uar]y 1811
Madam

I take the Liberty of informing the benevolent & valuable Society of Ladies of which you are president that in the will of Mrs Mary Cobb formerly Housekeeper of Chief Justice Shippen[25] is the following Clause

'I hereby appoint Edward Burd[26] of the City of Philadelphia Executor of this my last Will and Testament & bequeath to him all the Rest and Residue of my Estate upon this special Confidence & Trust that he will apply the same to the purchase of any Stock whatever that he shall approve of and pay the Dividends thereof as the same shall become due to the president for the Time being of an Association of Ladies in the City of Philadelphia stiling themselves 'The Female Association of Philadelphia for the Relief of Women and Children in reduced Circumstances' and if they shall obtain a charter of Incorporation then the said Edward Burd is to be at Liberty if he shall think proper to assign the principal monies of said stock to such incorporated Society by whatever name they shall be incorporated in trust to apply the Dividends thereof only to the charitable purposes of the same society'

I have lately settled the Accounts of the Estate in the Registers Office and the Residue of the Estate after payment of Debt, & Legacies amounts to $678 36/100 in Cash & one Share of Stock in the Bank of North America – If the Society have been incorporated & they will favor me with a Sight of the Articles of Incorporation that I may know their corporate Name I will assign to them ~~Society~~ the Share of Bank Stock & pay them the Cash balance – otherwise I will invest the money in any kind of Stock that may be agreeable to the Society

The half years Dividend on the Share of Stock in the Bank of N. America due the 11 January instant amounting to $20 is exclusive of the Bal[ance]s I have mentioned & being only Dividend may be immediately applied to charitable purposes

                                I am Madam
                                With great respect
                                Your most obed[ient] Serv[ant]
                                Edw[ard] Burd

Mrs. Stocker
/
Mrs Katherine Chew[27]
112 Spruce Street

Mr Chauncey[28] presents his most respectful compliments to Mrs Chew, and solicits from her the favour, to make known to The Female Association, that he has experienced the sincerest satisfaction from a perusal of their resolution, politely communicated by their Secretary. He also respectfully requests, that The Association may be assured, that his services are at their command, whenever it shall be thought that they may be usefully employed, in promoting the views of the Institution.

Mr Chauncey is sensible of the polite attention shown for his professional services; and cheerfully accepts the compliment, – but upon condition, that he may be allowed, to devote the inclosed to the liberal purposes of the Association.

48 Walnut Street
Jan[uar]y 31. 1811.
/

                                            2nd February 1811
Madam

I return the Charter of Incorporation with which you were pleased to intrust me having taken the Corporate name to enable me to vest the Interest of the Share of Bank Stock in the Corporation which has been bequeathed to them by Mrs. Cobb.

Permit me to express my grateful Sense of the light in which the Conduct of Mrs. Burd & myself[29] has been viewed by your amiable Society which has been greatly heightened by the manner of the Communication by a Lady whom we both so highly esteem –

Mrs. Cobb[30] has been so long in this Country without any Correspondence with her friends in Germany that she had lost all Knowledge of them & she had no Relations here that had any Claims on her Bounty & if she had been in distress she w[oul]d have been one of the Persons to whose Relief the Benevolence of the Society would have been extended There therefore appeared to be a peculiar propriety in the Donation both in the Person making it & the object of its application I sincerely wish that the society may receive additional fund commensurate with the Extent of their charitable purposes & with the best wishes to the Association

    I am Madam
    Your most humble Serv[ant]

Edw[ard] Burd
/
Mrs Stocker President
Of the Board of direction
Of the female association Of Philadelphia

Phi[ladephi]a Feb[ruar]y 13 1811

Dear Madam,

I have just received from an unknown hand the inclosed six dollars. It is no doubt – from some friend to the Institution, which owes so much to your unremited and praiseworthy exertions. This is all I know with certainty of the benevolent Donor. I suspect, however, that it is from a gentleman who has before handed, through me, monies to the association. I have sincerely regretted that my Health heretofore, and a violent rheumatic affliction this winter has put it out of my power to be useful to the Society. I have wished to forward to you my resignation, and should long ere this have done so but for the persuasion of my friends. I can no longer see it my duty, however, to withhold it, and sincerely regret that I have been so long a useless member of the Board, the pressure of active duties thereby falling on a few of the Ladies, of which it would have been a pleasure to me had Heaven permitted to have borne a considerable part. my Health not [illeg.] having allowed me to leave my chamber for 5 months, seeing little prospect that it will, shortly, and feeling borne, down by domestic afflictions which have in a rapid degree succeeded each other – with sensations I am unable to describe and best wishes for the happiness of each benevolent individual, comparing your highly respectable Board, (ardent and feelingly interested for the pro[s]perity of the association) which must ever continue, and wishing you the reward of your labors, permit me to take my leave with affection

Yours –
Eliz[abe]th Taylor[31]

/
Report of the Board of Directors in April 1811

Philadelphia April 17th 1811

The Board of Direction respectfully submit the following statement to the Female Association. That they convened at the usual time in November have met statedly once a fortnight. and received monthly the reports of the Managers in which they are happy to say are exhibited an interesting list of Pensioners and a judicious application of the funds appropriated to their relief. Ninety Six women and Forty Children have been assisted by them during the winter, several of the former are afflicted with incurable diseases, some are very aged – and two or three have closed their mortal career! While on the bed of sickness, these were cherished by your bounty, who must else have felt the pressing hand of want added to the pangs in which departing nature yields to fate. All conditions of human life are subject to sorrow and suffering but when old age, disease, and poverty are united, all hope save that beyond the grave would disappear did not the touch of Charity waken our hearts and impell us to offer the little relief which food & raiment and consoling words can afford.

In Congratulating you on their success in obtaining a charter, the Board must apprise you that the Female Association can no longer indulge in that privacy which has hitherto been so consonant to their places & wishes. Yet the advantages they derive from it greatly exceed those they relinquish, in the infancy of the society they feared to exhibit their unwise proceedings to the public eye. but 10 Years experience – the reputation they have acquired and the confidence, success has given them, tend to lesson the regret they should have felt at an earlier period, on being forced into notice. And they pledge themselves to fulfil with encreasing energy the duties of their office. The Articles of Incorporation together with the constitution[32] is preparing for the press and will be presented to you at our board meeting in November. The Treasurer published an account of a liberal Legacy bequeathed by Mrs Mary Cobb.

Hoping that essential benefit has been received by the unfortunate objects of our care the Board of Direction tender their grateful thanks to the Managers – and the members generally whose <for their> co operation and patronage <which> can alone sustain the Female Association. and thereby presents the welfare of that helpless class of society who having none to help them are ready to perish amidst the storms of winter, the easing of hunger, and the train of ills to which their destitute situation enforce them and beg leave to convince you that

'Blessings always trail on virtuous deeds
Had tho' a late, a sure reward succeeds'
/

Report of the Directors

Dear friends and Companions, We assemble this Morn[in]g

Upon the recurrence of another anniversary which completes the period of a quarter of a Century, since this Association was form[e]d, by a few of those highly favour & Individuals, that occaisonally appear in society to improve and adorn it – They have long since pass'd away – leaving but a small remnant of their Associates(as this meeting plainly evinces) to follow in the path of usefulness they had traced and – It was at that period an untried experiment for a female to attempt extending her the sphere of her exertions beyond the narrow limits of her own household. The result has proved that it not only may be done <u>to a certain extent</u> without infringing on the duties of domestic life but by affording a diversity of occupation render her more capable of fulfilling them – The success attending this attempt lead the way to various similar Associations, tending to, the same object – The Instruction, and ameloration of the condition of the Poor – So numerous indeed have they become – that the question is <frequently>

agitated whether they do not create in some degree the evils they were intended to remedy as the object of Charity seem to increase in proportion to the exertions made for their relief. But as this objection may be urged not only against the association of Individuals but also against the numerous & extensive plans ~~with~~ which this Age of benevolent enterprise have elicited, <that> there seems to be no alternative but to wast[e] the effects of Time, whose qualifying influence will doubtless mature those attempts to that happy medium in which real usefulness consists – In the mean time it is incumbent on the managers of those various Societies to use great discrimination in the distribution of the Charity entrusted to their charge the less they should become amenable to the accusation of encouraging idleness instead of relieving the indistrious Poor – With, <the> Tide of prosperity which has overflow'd the Country there is an under current of Idleness disapation & intemperance, which undermining the sober habits of the labourous Class of the community is a fruitful source of the wretchedness ~~we~~ that continually presents itself for relief; and it requires, not only the exercise of Judgement, but great self controul to select from this number the really deserving Objects of attention – These have a special claim to our sympathy and aid as we are assured by the mouth of unerring Wisdom that they will now compose a large portion of the human family. The very constitution of our nature ensures it – For what prudence at Industry, as sagacity, can arest decrease or shield from those calamities that the very elements inflict and the fluctuations of Society unavoidably produce. These are the Dispensations of Heaven sent in mercy to purify Humanity from the Dross that binds it to earth – and by calling into exercise the <best> principles of our Nature in imparting relief and consolation to the sufferer, brings into contact the different classes of society and strengthens that Bond of Union on which their mutal well being depends.

The reports of the managers for the past year ~~which is~~ exhibit the usual number of Pensioners and evince the same persevering care and sympathy which has ever accompanied their endeavours to relieve the suffering Objects recommended to their attention. The Treasurer <after will show> that notwithstanding the great diminution of receipts compared with former years yet the share of public favour they ~~are~~ still ~~favored~~ enjoy enables them to impart reliev & consolation to many a Desolate Widow <u>with a Family of helpless Children</u>.
/
To the Ladies of the Female Association

The Season has again arrived when it is the duty of the Board of Direction to lay before you the business which has engaged their attention and engrossed the labour of the Managers during the winter, and they come prepared like 'faithful Stewards' to render in their accounts cheerfully because they are animated with the hope that they have been successful, and they anticipate the benevolent glow that will suffuse your bosoms, while you listen to the detail of misery relieved through your bounty – Of old age reclining on the staff you have provided – of destitute natrons sustained on the bed of languishment, and suffering, by your means – Of the lonely widow cherished and encouraged to exert remaining strength, while an helping hand is stretched out with Your contribuition to raise her up – of Youth whose morn of life is overcast by clouds of adversity, and sorrow through which your charity pours the rays of comfort – and of lisping infancy rescued from those wants which pressed so heavily on its mothers breast until you appear, and lighten her load – All these have our Managers recited to us in a manner that must find its way to every heart and from these reports we shall select a few instances to place before you

An aged Female who had for twelve years tenanted a miserable hovel in the Northern Liberties – was wholly confined to her bed – scarcely strong enough to bear her palsied limbs – and furnished only with a tattered covering through which the wintry wind found many a passage – her only support was derived from the daily labour of a kind-hearted daughter, who was herself a widow, and the mother of five children, all depending on the labour of her hand, which she was obliged to seek from day-to day through this extensive city – happily for this afflicted family they had been taught to place their hopes beyond the turmoil of this troubled life – and the lonely invalid could beguile both pain and solitude in the perusal of the Holy Bible which was her constant companion – the pillar of her strength!

Your agent visited them – she clothed them comfortably – and fed them plentifully – she procured work at home for the old womans daughter – bound out her little boys to profitable Trades and sent the younger children to a charity school – and thus by a little timely assistance rescued a worthy family from extreme misery – The old woman lived two years after this period, a most grateful pensioner of the Society, and had the consolation at her death of leaving her pious daughter in a comfortable situation – industriously maintaining herself & family – and enjoying the prospect of seeing her children respectably provided for –

Again our Manager was called on to assist a widow and nine children, her husband had once been prosperous – but failed shortly before his death, and left his family entirely destitute – It is easier to imagine than to describe the distress of such a situation! The hardships of the poor are great indeed – and Providence Mercifully proportions their strength to the burthens they are allotted to bear – but the hapless widow – thus bereft of a beloved partner & protector – and deprived of the means of supporting existence, while a numerous family of little dependents are looking up to her for bread – is an object of the deepest interest to every mind of sensibility – this unfortunate woman's claims were not unheeded, the funds of the society contributed to her relief – our judicious manager formed means without wounding the delicacy of her feelings to engage her talents in some useful occupation by which, with the assistance of her two eldest daughters she was enabled to keep want from her door – and we are happy to add, that as the younger children advanced in life, they contributed their aid to lighten their mothers toil – and that their industry has been so successful that they are now all enjoying a very confortable & respectable rank in society – were we to detain you Ladies, to enumerate the various distressful cases which are recorded by our Managers – we should lead you to the bedside of many sufferihg invalids where you would behold some wasting away in consumptions – some enduring the pain of lingering Cancers – others crippled with Rheumatisms – and many with other infirmities, which would make life a burthen were they shielded from the evils of poverty – but alas! all these sufferers would be in want of the common necessaries of life – but for the assistance they derive from this Institution.

The number of Pensioners reported this winter is Two Hundred and Thirty. One Hundred & Nineteen women & One Hundred & Eleven Children – to which must be added several transient applicants who in the severity of the season were benefitted by the society – One, a stranger – sick & in trouble – & two, or three others – who had known better days, and often times when fortune was more kind, had freely bestowed on others, what they now (experiencing the changeableness of earthly riches – were obliged to solicit from the hand of Charity.

The Board have the pleasure to state, that the Association has never been in a more flourishing situation than at present – That they have received several Liberal donations and that these subscribers are more numerous than they were last year – They feel deeply impressed with a sense of the responsibility devolving on them, and trust they shall ever, to the best of their abilities discharge their duty with impartiality and effect.

With respect do the Orphan House[33] the Board refers you, to the very interesting report prepared by the Committee of Superintendence which accompanies this – they commit forbear cherishing the same wishes, & the same hopes respecting this little establishment which one so warmly expected by the zealous Committee These hopes they rest – Praying that the Almighty God 'who is a friend to the widow – and a father to the Orphan' may strengthen us in all our endeavours to promote their welfare and happiness –

April 15th 1812
Report of the Board Of Direction
/
PRINCETON DEC 30
Miss Rebecca Gratz
Chesnut St
Philadelphia

Princeton Dec 30th 1812

My dear Miss Gratz –
I have just receiv'd your letter containing the request of the Board of Direction and regret that I have occaisoned any difficulty by leaving the business

unsettled in Nov but being prone upon all occaisons to attend more to the Spirit than the letter of the Law, probably do not give the attention to <u>form</u> that is due and having transacted the business myself sometime without a transfer of the Stock of the Society suppos'd that my Successor would be equally indifferent – But there was a less reprehensible motive that influenced me. The Charterly that the property of the Society shall be invested in the Trustees – and being one of the number it did not appear to me necessary to the business of the Treasurer that the transfer should be made immediately – the event has proved otherwise and added one more memento <against> the danger of procrastination –

When I tooke the pen it was with the intention of informing you that I should be in Phila[delphia] to morrow even't but my Son is so extremely reluctant to my taking the Journey that I begin to ~~preparing~~ pause and as Mr. Ralston his kindly favoured me these powers of Attorney papers I ought to first t[r]y if those will answer the purpose – But if these should prove insufficient to being the Accounts to complete adjustment and give <u>intire</u> satisfaction to my Successor the Season will be no impediment to my meeting the Ladies –

Accept my dear Miss Gratz the compliments of the Season and may each returning year bring with it the sweetest of pleasures the approbation of your own Kind–

Yours with esteem

M Hodge

/

President of Directors Female Association

The President of Directors of The Female Association

Respected Ladies

I am authorised by the Committee appointed by the Select of Commen Councils[34] to take charge, this year, of the Fund for the supply of the Poor <u>of the City</u> with Fuel, to inform you, that, <at> a meeting held last evening, it was determined to place at the disposition of the Three Female charitable Institutions of the City, the Wood that has been purchased in equal proportions, as near as may be – you have therefore inclosed an authority to draw orders upon the Person of whom the Wood was brought to the amount of twenty three Cords, being one third of the whole quantity – The Councils in appointing the Committee gave them discretionary power, either to distribute the Wood themselves, or avail of the agency of others, as the Committee might deem best calculated to carry into effect the benevolent objects of the Donors of the Fund: which as far as they can be collected were the relief of Widowed house-holders, or indigent Women with Children, deserted by their husbands – or generally speaking Females in distress, whose sense of delicacy deter them from being Public Claimants of Charity Hence I take it upon myself to say the Committee have judged wisely, in selecting as their almoners, Insitutions that are peculiarly adapted to fulfil these views for the Committee was aware of not only the zealously active benevolence of the members but of the scrupulously careful discrimination exercised in bestowing of their alms. I have only to add that a small portion of the Fund seems assigned to the relief of coloured people, which will hold them up partially as object of your bounty.[35] By direction of the Committee I request that a Register be kept of the various draws upon Mr Rodgers with the respective sales and quantities, and that a copy thereof be sent to me when the wood is all delivered – also that any recommendation coming from either of the members of the committee claim your attention.

                                                                        I am with great respect
Your Ob[dient]H[u]m[ble] Serv[ent]
Rob[ert] Petshie Chairman

Committee
Robert Petshie
Thomas Latimer } Select Council
John Hart
Liberty Brownes
F. Mitchell} Common Council
Samuel Witherell

                                      Philade[lphi]a Jan[uar]y 9th. 1813.

/
Report of the board Of Direction April, 1813
Report of the Board Of Direction –
Ladies

As the season of active duty again closes the Board of Direction of the Female Association is called on to present you a statement of the application made of your bounty is doing which they hope to afford you that satisfaction which naturally arises in the kind of benevolence, contemplating its own work

If you will allow them to conduct you into the abodes of penury and disease, where, the forlorn widow and destitute orphan pines in solitude & pain – Your sympathy shall be allocated by tracing the footsteps of the Manager[36] who, has sought (<u>as your Almoner</u>) the humble dwelling to relieve the wants and cheer the drooping Spirit of its suffering inhabitants – You shall hear the overflowing of their gratitude, whose hearth has been warm'd during the inclement season – and whose board has been supplied – you will often recognize aged women who have long depended on you for their chief comforts during the winter, and who are enabled to struggle with severe trials from the conviction that they will not be deserted in the hour of need – and that these Children will be clothed and fed so long as they merit or need such supplies – Young children shall meet you on the threshold with blessings for the decent wrapper and warm flannel that has protected their grandmothers aching limbs from the storms of winter. And you will be surprised to hear how small a sum may serve to alleviate the calamities of indigence – One Hundred and Thirty Two Women, and One Hundred and fourteen Children have been relieved by the association with the sum of 882 <932> Dollars exclusive of the Orphan House 'establishment for the support of which there is an annual appropriation of four hundred Dollars

There is a point beyond which human erection fails, continued suffering enervates both the body & the mind, and they must risk together useless strengthen'd & enouraged by the timely aid of kindess and of charity, let no one imagine these single contribution is of small importance.

Less than a single subscription has often raised a dejected family – supplies the pressing want, and rendered the mother capable of maintaining herself and children. Many among our Pensioners are being aged and infirm – their wants are few – but the helplessness of their stage of life makes the little they receive indispensable – the interest these excite in the breast of those who are accustom'd to distribute your alms – amply rewards their toil – a few of this class have departed since last we met, acknowledging with their latest breath the benefit received from the Society. Let us then continue our united efforts we re-assemble at the Anniversary Meeting[37] with new kindled zeal in so urgent a cause – assured that one of the most important duties we owe Society & Religion is to cherish the widows & destitute orphan – and May ye, Ladies, each experience how 'Blessed are the Merciful.'[38]

/

Mrs. Stocker President
of the Board of Managers of the Female Association

Philad[ephi]a January 14 1814

Madam,

A Committee of the City Councils is appointed for the distribution of Fund to the Poor of the City during the inclemency of this Season; but as this committee feel themselves inadequate to the trust, from want of knowledge of those poor who are the fittest objects of this Charity, they have resolved to tender this Task to the Female Association and to request the Ladies, composing the Board of Managers to accept of the trouble of distributing, to first of the poor, residing exclusively from the South side of Walnut street to the North side of Cedar first & between the two Rivers, part of the wood.

Should the Ladies, of your benevolent Institution, over whom you preside, be willing to undertake this act of kindess, the committee will be highly flattered to receive your answer and shall provide you with the necessary orders for the delivery of the Firewood.

In behalf of the Committee, I have the honor to be with the highest respect, Madam

Your most obed[ien]t humble Servant

James Vanuxem Chairman
Mrs. Stocker President
/
                                            Philadelphia Jan[uar]y 17th. 1814
Madam,

I am charged by the Committee to acknowledge the receipt of your obliging answer with which you have been pleased to honor me, in behalf of the Board of Managers of Your Charity, for which the Committee beg you to receive their expressions of gratitude –

In order to guard against impositions, I am directed & enclose Ninety Orders for the wood; which you Madam, will please to sign as President of the Board, and to request the Lady Manager to fill up the name, of the poor Object, who is to receive the supply, in the order; recommending the person, to whom it is given, to attend at the depost of the wood, in the Public Square of Walnut street, between Seventh of little Seventh streets, on Tuesdays, Thursdays & Saturdays and to accompany the Cart to his or her dwelling –

To avoid confusion and to obtain greater dispatch the Ladies Managers are respectfully invited, not to issue more than ten or twelve of the orders in one day –

Be pleased to accept the Sincere thanks of the Committee for all the trouble & attention which you & the Managers will be at; to believe them with respectful sentiments for your benevolent Zeal towards suffering humanity; and with their unfeigned regard.

I am Madam, with the utmost respect –
Your very obed[ient] humb[le] Servant
James Vanuxem Chairman
Madam M Stocker, President
/
Mrs Margaret Stocker President Of the Female Association –
                                            Philadelphia Feb[ruar]y 12th. 1814
Madam,

I am honored with a Letter of the 10th Instant, signed Rebecca Gratz Secretary of the Board of Directors of the Female Association: Informing 'that the portion, of firewood, committed to their charge has all been distributed within the District prescribed, to such applicants as appeared to them more deserving and more distressed.'

The Committee feel themselves much obliged that the intentions of the Donors, have so effectually been realized, by the active goodness of the Ladies composing the different Boards of the benevolent Societies, under whose care the fire wood has been divided; for which the Committee express, through me, their unfeigned acknowledgments for your trouble & their wishes that the blessings of those poor objects who obtained this small relief may fall on you Madam and the Ladies, who devote so much of their time in alleviating the distresses of human Beings.

May your eminent vertues be rewarded, here, with an uninterrupted continuation of health and prosperity and with everlasting Bliss here after, is the prayer of the Committee and of
Madam,

Your most respectful & obed[ient] Servant
James Vanuxen Chairman

Mrs. Margaret Stocker President
/
Report of the board Of Direction 1814
Ladies,

If ever the Board have had reason to look back with satisfaction on the labours of a season, they confidently trust this may be accorded to their retrospection of the closing Session.

The calamities of war are spoken of with sympathizing regret at the fireside of almost every domestic circle, but they are felt – keenly felt by the unfortunate class of society for whose relief you are humanely associated. Many new made widows, and sorrowing Orphans swell the Managers list. The aged Mother whose only Son has fallen in his countrys cause puts in an affecting appeal and the soldiers family made destitute by his loss claims more than the ordinary offices of Charity – unhappily, at a period that so many are added to the number of poor – the means of support are less attainable, the price of every article of use is beyond their reach – and honest industry languishes for employment –

The Labourer who formerly could daily bring home to his family ample provision for the morrow must witness their wants or leave them for the hardships and perils of a winter campaigne and many of these for the <u>first time</u> are obliged to seek relief from public Charity. Declining invalids too, whose receeding strength baffle exertion depend upon you – we have several pensioners[39] whose sufferings are indescribable – painful and incurable disease slowly bears them to the tomb – the darkness of which they already experienced in blindness occasioned by cancer in their faces – one aged widow dreadfully maimed by a fall, painfully lingers out the remainder of her days with two broken ribs. She has passed his 86th year and has no support but you – To enumerate the <interesting> cares recorded in the Manager Report could too long retain you here – and too severely for your feelings suffice it that the Hundred and Twenty Six Women and the Hundred and Twelve Children have been relieved during the Winter by the Managers that several by especial for mission of the Board have received assistance thro' their members from the power of the society – that the Select Committee has also been employed and that the Orphan House still shelters the innocent little charge first placed there – these destitute babes are solely dependent on the association – they are fed and clothed and instructed at your expense, and the aged women employed for their use would be as destitute as their helpless protegés but for the Assylum that shelters them –

So greatly has the extraordinary hardships of this season pressed on the defenseless poor that we fear Ladies, our means would have fallen far short of our wishes or their necessities had not the Blessing of Providence open'd new sources of benefaction to us – The City Councils by making us their willing agents in the distribution of fuel enabled us to enliven the cheerless hearth of many shivering persioner. Several liberal donations two Legacies from departed Friends and the proceeds of a Trust generously presented by [illeg.] gentleman <(Mr Lechlitmer)> have enlarged their funds to meet the exigencies of this oppressive season and taught us to rejoice that on the humble Sphere to which female duties is confined the Eye of Conscience turns, and the beam of Mercy shines.

Let us then persevere and experience that the advantage of Charity is twofold blessing those who give and those who receive.

April 20th 1814
/

Philad[elphi]a Dec[embe]r 14th – 1814

Madam –

I beg leave through you to offer to the Trustees of the Female Association of Philad[elphi]a for the relief of Women and Children in reduced circumstances my resignation of the office of Secretary to the Society. My best wishes for the success of the Society still continues, and while I feel every disposition to write my exertions with those of Others, to carry into effect the benevolent views of the Association, I regret that various circumstances, with the detail of which it is unnecessary to trouble the Trustees, put it out of my power to discharge any longer, the duties of the appointments with which they have honored me, with advantage to the Society, or Satisfaction to myself.

I feel the less reluctance in making known this determination on my part, from the belief that, the Trustees will have little difficulty in selecting some other person better qualified to fill the Office, and who will have it more in her power than I have had, to give the requisite attention to the discharge of its duties.

Very Respectfully Yours

Mary Robertson[40]

/

Mrs Mary Robertson
8th Between Walnut & Spruce
Madam,

The late Mrs Cox, having by her will bequeathed One Hundred dollars to the Directors of the Female Association in the city of Philad[elphi]a for the Releif of

Women and children in distress, I shall pay it at any moment, without the usual delay, to any person who may be authorized to receive it.

May I ask the favor of you to communicate this note, to the person or persons who are empowered by the Association to receive the legacy?

I am
with great Respect
your mo[st] ob[edient] serv[an]t

Hor[ace] Binney[41]
7 Mar. 1814

Mrs. Robertson

/

Mrs. Margaret Stocker
President of the Female Association
For the Relief of the Poor

Philad[elphi]a Jan[uar]y 9, 1815

Madam,

Councils have appointed a Committee from their Body, for the purchease of Firewood and to have the same distributed to the most necessituous Poor of the City of Philad[elphi]a during the inclemency of this winter, according to the intentions of the Donors of the Fund for that purpose; the members composeing this committee with diffidence address themselves to the Female Association and respectfully request them to be at the trouble to take charge of part of the firewood to be divided among such of the Poor residing on the North side of Cedar to the South side of Walnut streets and throughout said District from River to River. −

The great attention bestowed by the Ladies Managers of Your benevolent Institutuion has claimed the gratitude of former Committees on like Occasions and the present one shall feel highly gratified and thankful, should the Ladies Managers acquiesce in accepting this humane task at this Season. In that case, upon the answer which you will please to honor me with, the necessary orders, for the delivery of the wood, shall be prepared.

I have the honor to be with the greatest Respect,
Madam

Your most obed[ient] & humble serv[ant]
James Vanuxem Chairman

Mrs. Margaret Stocker.[42]

/

Philad[elphi]a January 13 1815

Madam,

I had the honor of receiving the obliging Letter which you were pleased to have directed to me on the 11th Inst. By the Fair Secretary of the Board, over which you preside, assuring the Committee that the Ladies of the Female Association cheerfully accept the distribution of part of the Firewood, provided for the Poor; in conformity therewith, I take the liberty to enclose Eighty two orders on the Carter who is to attend at the delivery on the next Mondays Wednesdays and Fridays in each & every week, at the Public Square, in Walnut Street.

I beg leave to request the ladies to fill up, the Blanc, with the name & residence of the Poor Object who is to receive it, of the ordert; and not to subject the Bearer to wait longer than necessary, at the deposit of the wood, if only Ten or Twelve orders issue in one of those days, this measure would facilitate the delivery and not expose the person.

I must not assure you Madam, how much the Committee are indebted to the Ladies of the benevolent Female Societies for their distinguished alacrity in this undertaking, as the Committee are well aware of their incapacity to fulfill, in an adequate manner, the intentions of the Donors of that Fund, no[t] having the qualification to discriminate those objects most deserving the charity, which the Ladies of your inestimable Institution so conspicuously possess.

I remain with the utmost respect,
Madam

> Your most obedient and humble Serv[ant]
> James Vanuxem Chairman[43]
> Of the Committee for the distribution
> Of fuel to the Poor of Philad[elphhi]a

Mrs. Rush, President
Of the Female Association
/
Miss Gratz –
Secretary of the Female Association

Dear Madam,

It is with sensations of the most heartfelt satisfaction that I acknowledge the receipt of your communication of the 14th. The approbation of a Board with whom I have been so long associated in habits of friendly intercourse and united ascertions to alleviate the miseries of many of our suffering fellow citizens, is highly gratifying to me, the station which declining health and domestic cares rendered it necessary for me to resign, I always endeavoured to execute the duties of, to the best of my ability, at same time I feel that in the Resolution of the Board, they have much overestimated my services which I had it in my power to render; the success of which must be imputed under divine Providence to the unmerited attention and support I received from the members of the Board – I beg they will be informed of my constant Prayers for their individual propserity, and that any advice or assistance which it may yet be in my power to render, shall ever be most cheerfully offered – with sentiments of unfeigned regret

Believe me –
Dear Madam

          Your Affec[tionate] Humble Serv[van]t
              Margaret Stocker

Philad[elphi]a January 23[r]d 1815
/
To the President & Board of Direction Of the Female Association
              January 24 1815
 President & Board of Direction Of the Female Association
Ladies

It is with regret that I am compelled to decline acting any longer as a Member of the Board of Direction of your Society my late indisposition and my still delicate state of health renders me unable to meet you & take that share in your labours which I otherwise would, I therefore beg leave to tender you my resignation with my best wishes for the prosperity of the Association and the happiness of each individual member – I am –

            Ladies Yours Respectfully
              R Leaming –

NB should the enclosed be insufficient to discharge my fines for nonattendance on the Board the Baliance shall be immediately paid, as soon as the Secetary informs me of it – RL

Articles of Association of the Female Hospitable Society (1814)

ARTICLES
OF
ASSOCIATION
OF THE
FEMALE HOSPITABLE SOCIETY;
ENTERED INTO, AND AGREED ON, AT ONE OF THEIR ANNUAL MEETINGS.
PHILADELPHIA:
PUBLISHED BY ORDER OF THE SOCIETY.
William Fry, Printer.
1814. /

ARTICLES, &c.

AS it hath pleased Divine Providence to bless with success the exertions which have been made to advance the purposes, and increase the funds of the Female Hospitable Society, its usefulness has consequently become infinitely more extensive. And, that harmony, order, and rectitude may be preserved, and its numerous members, and beneficent donors, be made fully acquainted with the rules by which it is governed, it is deemed expedient for their information, and the well being of the Society, to publish the following form of a Constitution.

ARTICLE I.

This Society shall be established under the name of 'The Female Hospitable Society of Philadelphia,' for the relief of the sick, the aged, the indigent, the widow, the orphan, and the destitute stranger.

ARTICLE II.

Each person shall pay at the time of subscribing, fifty cents into the hands of the Treasurer, and two dollars annually. Males to be admitted as subscribers and donors.[44] /

ARTICLE III.

There shall be two general meetings in a year; one on the first Monday in May, and the other on the first Thursday in November; the latter to be considered the Anniversary. The time and place of every meeting, except the times mentioned in this article, shall be determined by the Governess, of which due notice shall be given to the members by the Secretary. Twenty-four members shall constitute a quorum to transact business.

ARTICLE IV.

The transactions of the Society shall be conducted by a Governess, a Board of Managers, a Treasurer, a Secretary, and a Special Visiting Committee, who are to be elected annually by ballot, at the Anniversary.[45]

ARTICLE V.

The Governess shall preside at all meetings, or, in her absence, one to be chosen *pro tempore*.[46] It shall be her duty to preserve order, declare the decisions of the Society when made, and be the organ of all communications to or from the Society. She shall have power to call a special meeting whenever it appears in her judgment necessary; and it shall be her duty to use her best endeavours to support the interests of the Society, and to procure employment for the industrious poor. She shall also preside at the store-room[47] twice a week during the winter season, on Mondays and Fridays, from nine o'clock until twelve, A. M. to receive and attend to all applications for employment and relief. She shall, also, with /

the consent of the Board of Managers, solicit the preaching of charity sermons[48] for the replenishment of the funds, when requisite and practicable.

ARTICLE VI.

The Special Visiting Committee shall consist of five members, who may be able to administer spiritual as well as temporal relief, to the sufferers who are without earthly support; not excepting persons of any nation, colour, or profession. It shall also be particularly their duty to visit and instruct distressed widows, orphans, and wretched females in the Almshouse, Hospital, and Prison, as often as permission to that effect can be obtained. They shall also pray with the sick, and exhort the healthy to seek the Lord while he may be found; and, at all times, when practicable, read a portion of the Holy Scriptures to the ignorant and miserable daughters of poverty and affliction. It shall further be their duty to put into the hands of those who can read, and are destitute of the word of life, a copy of the Sacred Scriptures, and to use every prudent means to bring back lost sheep to the fold of Christ.[49]

They shall have power to draw on the Treasurer monthly, during the winter season, for a sum not exceeding fifteen dollars, to be distributed for the relief of the sick, as they may deem proper. They may also recommend to the Governess and Managers, at the store-room, on Mondays and Fridays, those to whom they suppose further relief necessary; the persons bringing a written order specifying the kind of relief, and signed by one of the committee. All orders of the Special Visiting Committee on the Treasu- / rer, must be signed by the Governess, and countersigned by the Secretary, and shall be considered as the Treasurer's voucher for monies so appropriated.

ARTICLE VII.

The Board of Managers shall consist of twenty-four ladies, twelve of whom shall be considered as Principals, and twelve as Assistants. That they may proceed without confusion, the Governess shall, at one of the monthly meetings, appoint to them their different wards as may best suit their convenience. And, as immorality is too often the companion of poverty, it shall be their duty to visit all applicants for relief or employment, and by discovering, as far as lies in their power, the worthiness or unworthiness of such persons, prevent the Society from being constantly liable to imposition. They shall also advise and persuade all whom they discover to be vicious, to refrain from the evil of their ways; as they cannot be objects of the Society's benevolence whilst they continue unjust to the community at large, and to themselves. The Managers shall give to every person whom they consider worthy of employment, or relief, a written or printed card of recommendation, signed by the manager of the ward in which such person resides; and the Governess, or presiding Managers, shall not relieve any applicant without such card of recommendation. It shall further be the duty of the Managers to attend at the store-room in rotation, a Principal and an Assistant Manager every Monday and Friday, until the whole shall have assisted in attending to, and relieving the wants of the several applicants. The applicants above High street shall be / directed to call at the storeroom on Mondays; and those below it, on Fridays.

ARTICLE VIII.

All orders for the use of the Governess and Board of Managers, shall be drawn on the Treasurer by the Secretary, and signed by the Governess and one of the Principal Managers.

ARTICLE IX.

The Governess and Board of Managers may appoint, at any of the monthly meetings, collectors to solicit subscriptions and donations from charitably disposed persons.

ARTICLE X.

The Treasurer shall give security for the faithful discharge of her trust, and it shall be her duty to receive, and keep a regular account of all monies belonging to the Society, and pay all orders regularly drawn and signed; receiving, at the time of payment, a receipt, except from the Special Visiting Committee, whose orders, regularly drawn and signed, shall be considered as sufficient vouchers. She shall keep a fair statement of all monies expended, and of what remains in her hands, and settle her accounts once a year with a Committee appointed by the Board of Managers for that purpose. She shall deliver over all books, monies, and papers in her possession belonging to the Society, into the hands of her successors within one week after the expiration of her office. /

ARTICLE XI.

It shall be the duty of the Secretary to attend all the meetings of the Society, and keep a fair record of all their proceedings. She shall notify the members of the Society of all general and special meetings, and keep a regular account of the members and benefactors of the Society. She is to prepare a statement of the funds, and how they have been expended for the satisfaction of donors and subscribers.

ARTICLE XII.

The Special Visiting Committee, and Board of Managers, shall meet once a month, the time and place specified by the Governess, to examine the state of the funds and expenditures, and make such by-laws as may become necessary, providing that the said by-laws are not inconsistent with the express intentions of this institution. The Governess and one third of the Managers shall constitute a quorum[50] for transacting business.

ARTICLE XIII.

Females of every Christian denomination shall be admitted as Members of this Society, and the rights of membership shall always be equal. Each subscriber shall have the privilege of recommending to the care of the Society any poor person, with whose situation and character they are acquainted.

ARTICLE XIV.

In case of the death or resignation of any person holding an office in this Society, the Governess shall call a meeting to elect a suitable person to fill the vacancy. /

ARTICLE XV.

No debts shall be contracted in the name of the Society, except by the consent of the Governess, and Board of Managers.

ARTICLE XVI.

The store-room, which shall be procured by the Governess on the cheapest possible terms, shall be used for depositing all articles whatever belonging to the Society, which shall be at the discretion and disposal of the Governess and Board of Managers, who shall keep a fair statement of their proceedings, with a list of the names and number of persons employed and assisted, which shall always be open for the inspection of any member.

ARTICLE XVII.

The Governess shall nominate the candidates to be elected for, and to compose the Special Visiting Committee, and Board of Managers. The Special Visiting Committee and Board of Managers, shall nominate the candidates for Governess, Treasurer, and Secretary.

ARTICLE XVIII.

In case of the death or resignation of the Governess, the Board of Managers shall appoint one of their own body to act until the constitutional time of election; and all persons who hold the different offices of the Society, may be re-elected if nominated for re-election. /

ARTICLE XIX.

Each of the members who compose the Special Visiting Committee and Board of Managers, shall have a paper with the impression of a spinning wheel, and signed by the Governess, Treasurer, and Secretary, to obtain donations and subscriptions from all who are disposed to relieve the wants and woes of their suffering fellow creatures. The subscription paper shall be entered by the Secretary on the books of the Society, and shall be settled on or before the general meeting to be held the first Monday in May.

ARTICLE XX.

As females and children are considered as being more particularly the objects of this Institution, the medical gentlemen who have offered, or may hereafter gratuitously offer their services to this Society, shall not be expected to attend, except when a sick husband involves a wife and children in distress; and even in those cases, it shall be left to the physician's philanthropic feelings to determine. All applicants for medical assistance must be furnished with a written recommendation to the physician, from the Managers in the ward in which such applicants reside. No other communication will be attended to, except the personal solicitation of the managers.

ARTICLE XXI.

As the Spiritual as well as temporal relief of all poor and needy desolate Females, who have no human eye to pity nor hand to help them, are the general objects of the Charity of this Institution, yet the preference is generally to be given to those of the / Household of Faith, who are sick and afflicted; and as this Society is solemnly impressed with a conviction, that it is their duty to inculcate religion and morality as far as lies in their power, it shall be the duty of every member of this Institution to give general information of the purposes for which the Society was formed; so that the sorrowing and the dying, who on beds of pain are under concern for the eternal welfare of their souls, may know where to send for consolation.

ARTICLE XXII.

The Governess, with the assistance of the Board of Managers, shall provide a suitable person, and one in whom the Society can place confidence, to occupy the store-room, upon such terms as may be resolved on at one of the monthly meetings. A receipt must be given for all articles left in her charge; and she shall also keep the store-room open for the inspection of the Society at all times, when required, and receive and take charge of all donations that may be sent to the store-room, for the use and benefit of the poor under the care of the Society.

ARTICLE XXIII.

All meetings of the Society to begin and end with prayer and praise.[51]

ARTICLE XXIV.

Any lady, who, not attending the annual meeting in November, shall send her subscription at that time, shall be entitled to vote by proxy, for the candidates to fill the different offices of this Society. /

ARTICLE XXV.

If it can be satisfactorily proven at any of the monthly meetings, that a person filling any one of the different offices of this Society, has been unfaithful to her trust, she may be expelled by a majority of the Special Visiting Committee and Board of Managers, and a person appointed through the same medium to fill the vacancy. The Governess, Treasurer, and Secretary may vote as the truth shall influence their judgment.

ARTICLE XXVI.
No young lady to be nominated to fill any of the offices of this Society, without the full and entire consent of her parents or guardians.

ARTICLE XXVII.
No person, unless in extraordinary cases, shall continue to be relieved by this Society, who, having children, shall refuse to put such of them as are of a proper age, to good trades, or eligible service, or to send them to a charitable school, when in their power.

ARTICLE XXVIII.
And whereas, the manufacturing of articles of clothing for the poor has been carried into effect, and, from the late experience of the Society, it appears that the future benefit arising from it will be more extensive and general, the Governess shall appoint fifteen Directors to assist her in taking charge of that department. An account of their proceedings must be rendered to the Managers at any of the / monthly meetings. They shall have power to appoint a secretary, who shall keep a fair statement of all their proceedings relative to the manufactory, in a book to be kept for the purpose, which must be laid before the board at their monthly meetings in the manufacturing room.

ARTICLE XXIX.
When there shall be a sufficient fund obtained to enable the Directors to have in stock two thousand dollars, the said sum shall be kept full and entire (in cash) for the above-mentioned purpose–that the manufactory may meet with no interruptions from a pecuniary source.

ARTICLE XXX.
At the monthly meetings in May and November, the Governess shall exhibit to the Society, a just and full statement of her proceedings for the six months past, which statement shall be recorded in the books of the Secretary. /

NAMES OF THE OFFICERS.
Governess–Mary A. Snyder. No. 321 High St.[52]
Treasurer–Elizabeth Van Pelt, No. 149, Chesnut Street.[53]
Secretary–Eliza Norman, No. 41, North Fifth St.
Managers.
Catharine Baker, No. 23, Cherry Street.

Elizabeth Krips, No. 71, Walnut Street.
Mary Kay, No. 113, Lombard Street.
Elizabeth Monnington, No. 206, North Sixth Street.
Hester Hayward, No. 109, Vine Street.
Marham Jones, No. 43, Almond Street.
Mary Kelsey, No. 79, South Fifth Street.
Eliza Tice, No. 94, South Fifth Street.
Kesiah Sweetman, High Street, second door from the west corner of Eighth.
Mary Sneething, corner of Callowhill and Garden Street.
Margaret Silver, No. 7, North Fifth Street.
Mary A. Halberstadt, No. 214, North Front Street.
Collectors.
Rebecca R. Rush, No. 77, North Seventh Street.
Mary Hopple, No. 80, Vine Street.
Eliza Vanneman, No. 27, Branch Street.
Board of Directors for the Manufactory.
President–Mary A. Snyder.
Vice-President–Margaret Silver.
Rebecca Wilmore, No. 120, North Fourth Street.
Catharine Baker, No. 23, Cherry Street.
Martha Patterson, No. 65, North Fourth Street. /
Mary C. Potts, No. 65, Locust Street.
Frances Holcombe, No. 21, Branch Street.
Susan Poulson, No. 106, Chesnut Street.
Helen P. Burch, Mantua Village.
Eliza Brodhead, No. 49, Filbert Street.
Martha G. Janeway, No. 208, Mulberry Street.
Barbary Lentz, No. 236, North Second Street.
Julia Knight, No. 173, North Front Street.
Ann Cook, No. 140, North Fourth Street.
Christiana Campbell, No. 8, South Third Street.
Elizabeth Heyl, No. 106, North Second Street.
Mary Wiltbank, corner of Eighth and Walnut Streets.
Superintendant at the Store Room–M. D. Burke, No. 5, Apple-tree Alley.
Committee to Visit and Pray with the Sick.
Ann Cook, No. 140, North Fourth Street.
Mary Douglass, No. 251, Vine Street.
Martha Taylor, No. 47, Penn Street.
Cornelia Cooper, No. 21, Race Street.
Mary Buckman, No. 45, North Eighth Street.
Sarah Symington, No. 4, North Seventh Street.

Jane Bell, No. 79, Lombard Street.
Physicians for 1814.
Dr. George S. Schott, From the river Schuylkill to the east side of Delaware Eighth Street.

Dr. A. B. Tucker, From the east side of Eighth Street, to the east side of Fourth Street.

Dr. Joel Martin, From the east side of Fourth Street, to the east side of Second Street.

Dr. Alexander Knight, From the east side of Second Street, to the river Delaware. /

THE following summary of the expenditures of the Female Hospitable Society since its commencement in 1808, serves to show that whatever is undertaken in the fear of the Lord is sure to prosper and increase even to an hundred fold; and although our desires to benefit the poor and needy may meet with many checks and discouragements, we ought to bear all things and persevere to the end, for the sake of Him who is no respecter of persons.

Amount of moneys expended for the relief and employment of the poor in the years following, viz.

-	D.	C.
In 1808,	92	21 1/2
1809,	510	73 1/2
1810,	1918	81
Sales of manufactured articles in 1810,	186	10 1/2
In 1811,	1767	85
Sales of manufactured articles in 1811,	269	–
In 1812,	2180	68
Sales of manufactured articles in 1812,	223	43
In 1813,	2035	25 3/4
Sales of manufactured articles in 1813,	290	
For machinery and manufactory,	1489	37
In 1814 to the first of April,	393	74
For employment at the Factory room,	408	99 1/2

	D.	C.
Stock in manufactured articles,	600	88
Total,	$12366	98 3/4 /

Amount of moneys paid to poor women for spinning flax and tow at their own places of abode, in the years following, viz.

	D.	C.
In 1809 and 1810,	154	22
1811,	433	82
1812,	386	17
1813,	200	73 1/2
1804 to the first of April,	212	77
Total,	$1387	71 1/2
Whole amount brought forward,	$12366	98 3/4

Four hundred and forty-four yards of shirting muslin have been manufactured at No. 5, Apple-tree Alley and given to the poor since May, 1813.

The Books of the Society are at all times open to investigation as to the correctness of the above statement.

Amount paid in Medicine in 1813.

	D.	C.		D.	C.
By Jackson,	36	–		194	–
S. Say,	37		By Zollickoffer,	6	–
Jos. Coates,	17		Cave,	10	–
Harris,	30		Cutbush,	10	–
Dyott,	25		Beck,	2	50
Smith,	20		Moland,	2	–
Morris,	10		Lee,	2	50
Ecky,	1		M'Corkle,	3	–
Milnor,	10		Heimberger,	3	–
Allen,	8		Jos. Lehman,	5	–
	194			238 /	–

Subscribers in Medicine for 1814.

–	D.	–	D.
Mr. Milnor,	10	–	145
Schweley,	10	J. W. Sims,	8
Jackson & Co.	30	Gilfillan,	7
North & Cave,	20	Heimberger,	5
Wiltberger,	10	Dyott,	20
M'Clintock,	10	Plies,	6
J. Morris,	10	R. Moland,	5
J. Cutbush,	10	Burns,	5
J. Lehman,	10	Lowber,	10
C. Marshall,	25	Morris&Brothers,	10
–	145	–	221

REPORT OF THE PHYSICIANS.

Patients attended by A. B. Tucker for the Female Hospitable Society in 1813.

The number cured, are	74
Relieved,	15
Dead,	7
Removed, &c.	5
Vaccinated,	12
Remaining under care,	7
–	120 /
Brought forward,	120

Patients attended by Dr. Knight in 1813.

Cured,	71
Relieved,	5
Dead,	7
Removed, &c,	5
Vaccinated,	28
	116

By Dr. Lawton do.	–
Cured,	30
Relieved,	16
Dead,	3

Removed, &c.	13
Vaccinated,	3
–	65
By Dr. Cox do.	–
Relieved,	1
Remaining,	2
–	3
By Dr. Lambert do.	–
Cured,	20
Relieved,	6
Dead,	2
–	28
By Dr. Martin do,	–
Cured,	17
Relieved,	7
Removed, &c.	5
Vaccinated,	10
–	39
–	271 /

From the foregoing Report it appears, that three hundred and seventy-one patients have been attended by the Physicians of the Female Hospitable Society, of which the number

Cured, are	210
Relieved,	50
Dead,	19
Removed, &c,	30
Vaccinated,	53
Remaining,	9
Total,	371

The charitably disposed who may wish to contribute to the funds of the Society, either by becoming members or contributors, are respectfully informed that subscription papers are held by all the officers of the Society, who will gratefully receive any donation or subscription.

ARTICLES, TO BE OBSERVED AND KEPT BY ALL THE MEMBERS OF THE BENEVOLENT FEMALE SOCIETY (1790)

Articles, to be Observed and Kept by All the Members of the Benevolent Female Society, begun December, 7th, 1789. And Now Held at the House of Mr. T. Warton, in Dagger-Lane, Kingston-Upon-Hull (Hull: J. Ferraby, in the Butchery, 1790), ECCO, ESTC Number T146326, ECCO Range 7058.

'Friendship relationships,' according to Naomi Tadmor, 'were major social relationships in eighteenth-century England.'[1] That friendship ties in fictive family associations were important was evidenced by the many societies with 'friend' in their title.[2] These 'friendly societies' as they were known, provided mutual assistance, offered an early version of insurance and were often formed by members from a particular occupation, religious affiliation, or according to a common objective.[3] These societies met once a week in alehouses, private homes or in churches, and collected dues or fines to care for the needy within the organization or for objects of charity.[4]

In addition to the benevolent societies formed by shared religious beliefs or similar occupations, many were organized along gender lines. For instance, in Newcastle-Upon-Tyne and Gateshead, Eneas Mackenzie published a history of their benevolent societies, and out of the 165 benevolent societies Mackenzie listed, at least forty-one were female benefit societies.[5] Mackenzie observed, 'There are several *Congregational Charities* in this town, for relieving the distressed poor belonging to their own body; and also some *Public Associations*, chiefly for giving pecuniary assistance to persons who cannot be benefitted by the poor-laws of England.'[6]

Born out of a collective desire to help beyond denominational and parish resources, religious, secular and gender-based benevolent organizations formed fictive families to care for their needy. These friendly societies offered their members more than the pecuniary assistance recorded by Mackenzie, because they acted as the member's instrumental family by offering aid when the consanguineal family was unable. As Margaret Hunt observed, 'the Societies show many of the features of a surrogate family. Like families they were insular and highly selective about who gained entrance.[7] Unsurprisingly, therefore, the language of address these friendly societies adopted was familial, as demonstrated in the unattributed poem at the conclusion of the preface to the *Articles, to be Observed and Kept by All the Members of the Benevolent Female Society* (1790).

Notes
1. N. Tadmor, *Family and Friends in Eighteenth-Century England: Household, Kinship, and Patronage* (Cambridge: Cambridge University Press, 2001), p. 171.
2. Tadmor, *Family and Friends in Eighteenth-Century England*, p. 168.
3. Tadmor, *Family and Friends in Eighteenth-Century England*, p. 169.
4. M. R. Hunt, *The Middling Sort: Commerce, Gender, and the Family in England, 1680–1780* (Berkeley, CA: University of California Press, 1996), p. 104.
5. E. Mackenzie, 'Charitable Institutions: Benevolent Societies', *Historical Account of Newcastle-Upon-Tyne including the Borough of Gateshead* (Newcastle-upon-Tyne: Mackenzie and Dent, 1827), pp. 546–68, British History Online, at http://www.british-history.ac.uk/no-series/newcastle-historical-account/ [accessed 9 December 2014].
6. Mackenzie, 'Charitable Institutions: Benevolent Societies'.
7. Hunt, *The Middling Sort*, p. 105.

Articles, to be Observed and Kept by All the Members of the Benevolent Female Society (1790)

ARTICLES, TO BE OBSERVED AND KEPT BY ALL THE MEMBERS OF THE Benevolent Female Society, BEGUN DECEMBER, 7th, 1789. And now held at the House of Mr. T. WARTON, IN DAGGER-LANE, *KINGSTON-UPON-HULL.*[1]
HULL: PRINTED BY J. FERRABY, IN THE BUTCHERY. MDCCXC. /

BENEVOLENT FEMALE SOCIETY.[2]
THIS Society *is formed for the support of their members when afflicted with disorders to which the human Race are subject to, and now so numerous, that few provident people, (particularly those dependant on a livelihood from labour) but who are engaged in those valuable Institutions; and even persons in a sphere of life superior to that of the mechanic*[3] *have associated therein chearfully lending assistance towards alleviating the wants, and distresses of their fellow-creatures, when rendered incapable of prosecuting their respective occupations. Every benevolent mind therefore, who sincerely delights in the good of others, will not fail to improve every opportunity to promote the happiness and comfort of those in particular who are afflicted with sickness, lameness, blindness, or any other calamity, by which they are deprived of the means and power of supporting not only themselves, but perhaps a numerous family. That this is the true and laudable intention of this Society, the following Articles will sufficiently explain, where every disorder with which any member may be afflicted, is, as far as is consistent with the general good of the whole Society, so far relieved, as at least to prevent want from coming within her doors. And we do entreat our Sisters,*[4] *who become Members, strictly to observe the following* RULES *and* ORDERS, *whereby they may be thought worthy of the benefits therein-mentioned, when they are justly intitled thereto.*

Let us like Sisters chearful be,
Unite in love when we each other see;
And lend our assistance when sickness crave,
There is no respect of persons in the GRAVE.[5] /
RULES AND ORDERS.

ARTICLE I.

[...] THAT four Stewardesses[6] shall be chosen every half Year, and that the Stewardesses business shall be to take care the following Articles be duly observed, on forfeiture of One Shilling, or be excluded.[7][...]

IV. [...] THAT a Feast[8] shall be held on the third Wednesday in *June*, in the year 1791, and so forwards; and every member to pay on the meeting night before the Feast, One Shilling towards the Feast, and Two-pence to the servants, or forfeit One Shilling [...] No business to be done on the Feast-day on any account. [...]

VI. [...] THAT a Register Book[9] shall be kept, wherein shall be inserted the name of every member, with her age, and her Husband's trade and place of abode, which she shall give the Clerk an account of, at the time of her entrance; likewise when she removes to another habitation, she shall give notice of it the next club-night to the Clerk, or forfeit Six-pence. [...]

IX. [...] NONE to be admitted a member of this Society above 45 years of age; and should any person be disputed, she shall procure a baptism register. Neither shall any person be admitted that hath any infirmity, or natural distemper on her at spring or fall;[10] and should any person obtain admission, and / it be proved that she had an infirmity at the time of her entrance, and request any benefit for the same, she shall be excluded, and all her money forfeited to the box. Any person who means to become a member of this Society, shall come to the club-room, and give her name, her age, and her husband's trade and place of abode, and then withdraw into another room, whilst the Clerk asks the necessary questions, previous to her admission ; and if any one of the Society shews just cause why she may not be admitted, that member who shall divulge to such person, who it was that made the objection, shall forfeit Five Shillings, or be excluded; and each person shall have the Articles of admission read over to them by the Clerk, or she shall forfeit One Shilling. [...]

XII. [...] THAT when any member shall become sick, lame, or blind, and thereby rendered incapable of doing the housewifery,[11] shall be allowed Seven Shillings *per* week, and shall have her allowance every week, but no odd days to be paid for, and nothing shall be allowed to those members who may be troubled with the breeding-sickness,[12] nor lying-in women. But should any member be not able to do her work at the expiration of the month, she shall be allow'd the weekly benefit of Five Shillings *per* week ; but she must send a note to the Clerk, to acquaint him of her sickness, and a punctual direction where she lives, that the Stewardess may not be put about to find her; should any neglect this, they shall be fined Six-pence; and should the Stewardesses neglect their duty, after they have had notice given them by the Clerk, of the sickness of any member, they shall pay Two Shillings and Six-pence for each neglect, or be excluded. [...]

XIV. [...] THAT if any member of this Society knows of any impostor receiving the benefit from this Society, she shall disclose it the first meeting night, or forfeit Five Shillings, and the member giving such information, upon due proof being made, shall be allowed Five Shillings out of the joint-stock, and the said impostor shall forfeit Five Shillings, or be excluded.

XV. [...] THAT should any member of this Society cause any quarrel, and thereby receive any hurt, she shall not receive any benefit from this Society during her illness, if she does, and it be proved, she shall be excluded, and the same for any that claims benefit for the Venereal Disease. [...]

XVIII. [...] THAT if any member brings a stranger into the club-room without leave of all the Stewardesses, she shall forfeit Three-pence; if they obtain leave and such stranger causes any quarrels, or swears, or calls any member in the club-room, those who brought them shall be answerable for all Fines they may be subject to. [...]

XIX. [...] THAT if any member of this Society shall think proper with a view of obtaining a better livelihood, to remove into any other part of Great-Britain, upon making their payments as usual, the aforesaid allowance in case of sickness, lameness, or blindness, shall be punctually remitted them on sending a Certificate, (as in the appendix) setting forth her disorder, signed by the Doctor, Minister, and Churchwardens of the Parish where she resides, which certificate must be renewed every month during her illness, and the allowance as in the 20th Article in / case of death, shall be paid to her husband or executors, upon their sending a certificate as above.

XX. [...] THE four Stewardesses and Clerk shall attend the Funeral, and the Stewardesses shall each of them have a hood, scarf, and gloves, at the expence of the Society [...] when one of the Stewardesses assistant shall go to the house where the deceased Sister's corpse is, and bring notice to the Stewardesses the time they are to attend their Sister's corpse to the grave, and then return back before her husband, or executors, and then to the club-room, where they shall be allowed to expend One Shilling and Six-pence [...] Every member who doth not attend shall contribute One Shilling to the box at the death of every free member, or member's husband, and must be paid the next meeting night after the Stewardesses give notice so to do. Every free Sister at the death of her first lawful husband shall receive Ten Guineas, and at the death of her second shall receive but nothing for the third. A certificate of the / member's marriage to be produced if required. – Any member dying before she has been one year in the Society, shall receive Thirty Shillings, each member to subscribe Six-pence, and all the overplus money to go into the box.

XXI. [...] THAT should any member of this Society, lay violent hands on herself, after she is free of the box, if she leaves a husband, or children, they shall be allowed $7\text{-}7=0$ but no other person shall be intitled to it, neither shall her funeral be attended as above; and if any member be convicted of felony, she shall be for ever excluded.

XXII. [...] THAT when any member of this Society who is intitled to the benefits die, and leaves a husband, he may have a coach and hearse, as also any who may have power to receive the same; and as the allowance is properly meant for a decent interment, should any fault be found, the Stewardesses shall have power to order it to be amended, and a Pall[13] shall be provided at the Society's expence. And it is expected that every Sister when it may please God to call her from this transitory life, that she shall have a psalm sung before her to Church, and in the Church/ .[...]

XXVI. [...] THAT if at any time of monthly meetings there should be more liquor than every member's Two-pence, it shall be made good by the Stewardesses, if they neglect giving each member their ticket, as they pay their monthly contribution [...] and should any member call for more after she has had her share, she must pay for it herself. [...]

XXIX. [...] IF any member should become Sick, Lame, or Blind, and thereby requests the benefit of this Society, they must be very careful in complying with those Articles, as no member shall do any sort of work, only giving breast to a child, or verbal orders to servants, or sign a receipt, or other writings; should any member be found doing contrary to this Article, she shall be fined as the Society may think proper, and on refusal of this Fine, they shall be excluded.

XXX. [...] SHOULD any member of this Society become Blind, such member shall have Three Shillings *per* week, so long as their Blindness continues. And if any member be confined for debt, she shall have such weekly allowance as the Society may think proper, but not to exceed Two Shillings *per* week,

HANNAH BENTLEY, Mother.
CATHARINE MOODY,
MARTHA JOBLIN, } Stewardesses.
SARAH LATIMOOR,
JANE HEDGILL, } Assistants.
JOHN ROBINSON, Clerk.[14]

CLARA REEVE, 'LETTER XIV' ('THE PLAN OF A FEMALE COMMUNITY')

Clara Reeve, 'Letter XIV', *Plans of Education; with Remarks on the Systems of Other Writers. In a Series of Letters between Mrs Darnford and her Friends* (London: Printed for T. Hookham, and J. Carpenter, New and Old Bond-Street, 1792), pp. 130–67, ECCO, ESTC Number T110125, ECCO Range 1299.

During the long eighteenth century, English Protestant female educational utopias promised to fulfill the fictive family role previously performed by Catholic nunneries. These utopias created families based not on relationships of blood and marriage, but through co-residence and some form of authority.[1] Mary Astell, in *A Serious Proposal to the Ladies* (1694), proposed 'to erect a *Monastery*, or if you will ... a *Religious Retirement*' for women.[2] Ever the assimilator, Daniel Defoe borrowed Astell's idea in his *Essay on Projects* (1697).[3] In the mid-eighteenth century, Samuel Richardson, in *The History of Sir Charles Grandison* (1753), posited

> We want to see established in every county, *Protestant Nunneries*; in which single women of small or no fortunes might live with all manner of freedom, under such regulations as it would be a disgrace for a modest or good woman not to comply with, were she absolutely on her own hands; and to be allowed to quit it whenever they pleased.[4]

The bluestocking Sarah Scott created a female educational utopia in *A Description of Millenium Hall, and the Country Adjacent* (1762).[5] Scott's communal charitable and educational projects in *Millenium Hall*, Gary Kelly noted, 'were paralleled or imitated by others, and by increasing numbers of middle-class women in particular, as the bluestocking reform impulse spread down the social scale.'[6]

One such imitation of Scott's communal project was Clara Reeve's (see also 'Racial Diversity of Families') *Plans of education; with remarks on the systems of other writers; in a series of letters between Mrs. Darnford and her friends* (1792). Reeve wrote her educational treatise in response to the early years of the French Revolution, upon which she had cast an approving and sympathetic eye: 'The Revolution in France will be a ... warning to Kings, how they oppress and impoverish their people'.[7] 'According to Reeve, women would play an important role in the 'national regeneration' of a morally and politically corrupt England, through improved female education and by maintaining 'discipline, order, and hierarchy.'[8]

Female education and independence were valued by Reeve. The eldest of eight children born to William Reeve, an Ipswich rector, and Hannah Smithies, Reeve read to her father from the newspaper and the works of Classical authors in translation.[9] When her father died, Reeve, two sisters and her mother moved from Ipswich to Colchester. Reeve never married and moved back to Ipswich to live in lodgings and support herself by her writings, which was against her family's wishes.

Reeve's first publication was a collection of poetry (see also Volume 2); three years later she published an English translation of a seventeenth-century Latin prose Romance about Henri IV, which she felt was an allegory applicable to the political and religious divisiveness of English politics. Reeve's most popular work, *The Champion of Virtue*, which was republished a year later under her name as *The Old English Baron: a Gothic Story* (1778), was one of the first gothic novels written by a woman. Reeve continued to publish gothic novels and romances (novels set in exotic locations about courtly life). Reeve turned to educational writing in 1791, when she published *The School for Widows: a Novel*; the 'school' of the title was adversity, which taught women unique skills and knowledge useful in private and local life, but that were ignored by male-dominated learned culture.[10] This novel was a departure from Reeve's earlier fiction, because she wrote about 'common life from women's perspective'.[11]

In the selection below, Reeve set forth the rules and procedures of her Female Community, which would oversee the Seminary of Female Education. As a fictive family, Reeve's Female Community utilized the language of kinship, since the twelve founding women were to be called the 'Council of Sisterhood'. Reeve also invoked (and borrowed from female Catholic monastic terminology) titles of authority in the construction of her co-resident household family: the 'Superior' was in charge of the community, and was called 'Mother'. Reeve's Female Community created a fictive family bound by the relationships of gender, matriarchal authority and shared household management.[12]

Notes
1. N. Tadmor, *Family and Friends in Eighteenth-Century England: Household, Kinship, and Patronage* (Cambridge: Cambridge University Press, 2001), p. 20.
2. 'Mary Astell 1666–1731', in K. M. Rogers and W. McCarthy (eds), *The Meridian Anthology of Early Women Writers: British Literary Women from Aphra Behn to Maria Edgeworth 1660–1800* (New York, NY: Meridian, 1987), pp. 112–41, on p. 117.
3. *ODNB*.
4. S. Richardson, *The History of Sir Charles Grandison*, ed. J. Harris (London: Oxford University Press, 1972), part 2, p. 355.
5. *A Description of Millenium Hall, and the Country Adjacent: Together with the Characters of the Inhabitants, and such Historical Anecdotes and Reflections, as May excite in the Reader proper Sentiments of Humanity, and lead the Mind to the Love of Virtue. By A*

    Gentleman on his Travels (London: J. Newbery, 1762).
6. G. Kelly (ed.), 'Introduction: Sarah Scott, Bluestocking Feminism, and Millenium Hall', *A Description of Millenium Hall. By Sarah Scott* (Peterborough: Broadview Literary Texts, 1995), pp. 11–43, on p. 41.
7. *Plans of Education*, p. 214. Quoted in Gary Kelly's article on 'Clara Reeve', in *ODNB*.
8. *ODNB*.
9. *ODNB*.
10. *ODNB*.
11. *ODNB*.
12. Tadmor, *Family and Friends in Eighteenth-Century England*, p. 24.

Clara Reeve, 'Letter XIV' ('The Plan of a Female Community')

LETTER XIV.

MRS. DARNFORD TO LADY A –.
I send, enclosed, my principal Plan for your ladyship's inspection.
F.D.
THE PLAN OF A FEMALE COMMUNITY, AND A SEMINARY OF FEMALE EDUCATION.

THE defects of the present system of female education in this country, are generally acknowledged, by all who have considered and remarked upon it; they are, indeed, too apparent in the manners of English women of the present times. – They have formerly been celebrated for / the modesty of their dress and deportment, for the purity and even sanctity of their manners. It is believed that there are still a great number of individuals, who deserve and support the national character; but it is indisputable, that the manners of our country women in general have sustained a great and alarming alteration in the course of the present century.

The decrease of marriages, the increase of divorces, the frequency of separations,[1] bear melancholy testimony to the truth of these assertions. The great number of public victims of pride, vanity, and dissipation, are too apparent and frequent, to leave any doubt remaining of this general declension of manners.

Among those respectable women who support the national character, there are many who lament this alarming alteration; who are ardently solicitous to stop / the torrent of vice and folly, to investigate the causes of it, and to seek out for a remedy.

They think this must be found in a better system of education, by which the rising generation may be preserved from the contagion of bad example, and be enabled to restore the national character of virtue, modesty, and discretion.

It is certain, that the principal causes of this declension of manners, are, first, a bad method of education; and, secondly, a series of bad examples after this education is completed. Leaving the latter article to the investigation of abler hands, we shall pursue the first, as the object of our present enquiry.

It is the general method of people of condition to give their children, from the state of infancy, to the care of nurses, and servants of a low class; to persons generally ignorant and mercenary, frequently / unprincipled. These preceptors prevent the seeds of virtue from germinating, and cultivate in the young and flexible heart the weeds of pride, self-consequence, fraud, and artifice, and every bad propensity.

Those parents can never be too highly honoured, who themselves superintend the education of their children; for though they only fulfil their duties, yet, considering the great numbers who neglect them, they are entitled to praise and respect; there is no kind of education equal to that of a wife and virtuous mother;[2] but this character is every day less common among us.

When the children are taken out of the nursery, they are sent to some school, where they are supposed to learn the rudiments of language, morals, and manners; every useful kind of knowledge, and every ornamental accomplishment. – / These depend, however, upon the chance of the merit and abilities of the persons who are intrusted with this very important charge.

When we consider how few persons are duly qualified for this sacred trust, we need not wonder at the mischiefs arising from the abuse in the discharge of it; they have been remarked by many who have been sufferers by them, or who have felt their effects in those who were the most dear to them.

It is not in this Essay, that we shall enumerate these abuses and corruptions; none who think seriously are ignorant of them; we only just hint the causes and seek for the remedy.

When we consider the great increase of boarding schools, we ought not to be surprised at the increase of the evils arising from them. [...]

How often do we see the young girls come from those schools, full of pride, vanity, and self-consequence!– ignorant of the duties and virtues of a domestic life, insolent to their inferiors, proud and saucy to their equals, impertinent to their parents; without that sweet modesty and delicacy of mind and manners, which are the surest guards of female virtue, and the best omens of their future characters as wives, mothers, and mistresses of families; and which nothing can compensate for the want of.

To this source, we have traced one of / the great causes of the present degeneracy of female manners, which our undertaking is intended to reform and to remedy.

We conceive, that it is very practicable to inculcate the highest principles of religion and virtue, and to blend them with the most elegant female accomplishments, and the most useful social and domestic qualities; this, therefore, is the design and purpose of our new plan of female education:[3] but this is not our only purpose; we propose to extend the advantages of it still further, to the general utility of the whole community.

We have observed from the increase of boarding schools, and from the general stile of education among the middling and lower ranks of people, every degree educating their children in a way above their present circumstances, and future expectations; / that a great number of young women come into the world without fortunes suitable to their educations, and afterwards, by the death or misconduct of their friends, are exposed to all the dangers of a deserted and friendless situation. [...]

Our present undertaking is partly designed to provide for these helpless, friendless, destitute young women, to take them from the dangers that surround them, to give them habits of industry and employment, to give them some business for their future support, and, finally, to make them useful and happy members of society.

These, and many other noble and useful purposes, are designed in this our Plan of Female Education, which is here offered to the public consideration; if they appear worthy of encouragement, it is hoped they will meet with the assistance necessary to carry so great a design into execution; / we claim the patronage and protection of the virtuous and generous, and we despise the attacks of the ignorant and malignant censurers of our Plan, conscious of the rectitude and integrity of our intentions.

Influenced by the considerations above-mentioned, several Ladies of unquestionable characters and abilities, have determined to form a community, for the purpose of founding a Seminary of Female Education upon the following Plan:

They will enter into a voluntary engagement for three years, to be renewed at the end of the term; or, in case any person chooses to be released from her engagement, she may then be freed from it.

They will each subscribe a certain part of their respective fortunes, for the support / and service of the said Community.

The Community thus united, shall hire or purchase a large and commodious house, in a convenient situation; at a limited distance from a market town, but not in it; which they shall furnish and prepare for the reception of boarders.

Each of the Ladies shall apply for the particular department which she desires to undertake; and her pretensions shall be examined, and decided by the majority of the Community.

As soon as every department is filled up, the Ladies shall hold a Council every Monday morning, to compose the Rules for governing the Society, and to consult on the best methods of putting them into execution. /

The Offices of the Ladies of the Female Community.

I. THE Superior, or Governess of the Community,[4] who shall be the head of it, she shall have two votes on every question, and many privileges to be explained hereafter.

II. The Treasurer, who shall receive and disburse the revenue of the Community, and give a regular account of it.[5]

III. The Superintendent of the Household, who shall regulate and inspect every department in it.

IV. The Governess of the Young Pupils, who shall direct their morals, manners, and studies.

V. The Sub-Governess, who shall superintend all their works, and constantly attend in the school at certain hours. /

VI. The House-keeper, who shall order in all the provisions, direct the tables, and keep the weekly account.

VII. The Intendant of the Garden, and all its productions.

VIII. The Intendent of the Cellar, and the Liquors of all Kinds, and who keeps an account of them.

IX. The Intendant of all the Works done in the Community, particularly those made and sold for the benefit of the poor young women in it.

X. The Secretary to the Community, who shall write all the letters in the name of it, and keep a journal of all the transactions in it from its foundation.

XI. The Accomptant, who shall keep a Ledger, and enter an account of the receipts and disbursements.

XII. The Intendant of the Dairy[6] and / Poultry-yard, who shall keep an account of their Productions.

After the Community shall be established, there shall be as many young ladies received and educated, as can be accommodated [...] – The strictest attention shall be paid to their moral, and mental, as well as personal improvements; and they shall be taught every branch of useful knowledge in common life, to qualify them to govern and conduct a family.[7]

These young ladies must, in all respects conform to the Rules of the Community, and they must have every thing they wear made by the servants of it. /

[...] It is proposed, that a certain number of young girls, the daughters of clergymen, officers in the army and navy, placement, or any profession whose parents have died in indigent circumstances, and left them entirely destitute of any provision, shall be received into this community for the term of seven years; to be employed in the service of it during that time; and if their behavior is approved, they shall receive proper testimonials, and other tokens of approbation, in proportion to the ability of the Community to confer them, in order to promote their establishment in their respective business or employment.

During the time of their residence in the Community, they shall receive all the advantages of tuition which are given to the / pupils of condition, and shall be constantly employed in their assigned departments; and every one shall learn a trade, or business, for their future support and provision.

There shall be one of each business here mentioned:

1. – The Milliner to the Community, and teacher of her art.[8]

2. – The Mantua-maker,[9] and teacher of the same.

3. – The Clear-starcher,[10] and teacher of the same.
4. – The Lace-maker, and teacher.
5. – The Stay-maker, and teacher.
6. – Embroiderer, and teacher of curious works.
7. – Plain-worker,[11] and teacher.
8. – Spinner of hemp and flax, and teacher.
9. – Knitter of thread, cotton, and worsted hose, &c. /
10. – The Florist, who makes flowers, and draws patterns for work.
11. – Assistant to the Sub-governess, and teacher in the school.
12. – Second Assistant to the same, and teacher.
13. – Assistant to the House-keeper.
14. – Assistant to the Intendent of the Dairy, &c.

[...] In order to avoid every incitement to pride, vanity, and self-conceit, it is proposed, that all the young pupils of this Community shall be cloathed in a neat plain uniform; and that neatness in the wearing it, shall be the only mark of distinction. /

The Assistants to wear an inferior uniform.

The servants, another uniform of inferior materials.

No kind of distinction shall be shewn to children of birth, fortune, or any accidental advantages.[12]

[...] Each of the Assistants shall have a certain portion of time allotted them to work for the benefit of the community, and the money arising from this allotment, shall be employed for the purpose of settling the Assistants, when they are sent into the world; either as a marriage portion, or to establish them in their respective businesses. /

The young ladies are to be encouraged to devote some part of their time to this laudable purpose, but at their own option, that they may have the full merit of it.

It will be necessary to appoint a Chaplain to the Community, and to have a Chapel within the house. The Chaplain to attend on Sundays and holydays, but not to reside in the house.

One of the Ladies, Governesses of the Community, shall read prayers every morning at stated hours. The prayers shall be selected from the Liturgy of the Church of England, with such other occasional ones as shall be appointed by the Superior.

The servants of the Community shall be chosen from the industrious poor, or such persons as have suffered by misfortunes. It is presumed that such persons being under particular obligations to the / Community, would be likely to serve it faithfully.

[...] None of the Pupils or Assistants shall receive or send any letters,[13] without the inspection of one or more of the ladies of the Community. /

[...] The Community shall hire or purchase lands contiguous to it, for every convenient purpose. [...]

It is supposed, that ladies in the first year of their widowhood – Ladies, whose husbands are sent abroad in public offices – Single ladies, who have not settled their plan of life – Ladies of more advanced age, who have met with misfortunes or disappointments, and wish to retire from / the world: – It is supposed, that many ladies of these, or other situations, would be glad to retire to such an asylum. [...]

Hints for the Government of the Female Community.

[...] The first twelve persons shall compose the Sisterhood; and to succeed in turn to the office of superior, in preference to any that shall afterwards be admitted. /

Every one of the Sisters shall advance, at the least, one hundred pounds for the outset; and shall pay, yearly, twenty pounds into the treasury of this Society.– It is supposed that it will, in due time, maintain itself, and provide for others. [...]

[...] A Council of the Sisterhood shall be held every Monday morning, at ten / o'clock,[14] to consult on the best method of putting the Rules into execution; and afterwards for the well-governing of the Community.

[...] All the teachers in the Seminary are to be females, whether of dancing, drawing, music, language, &c.

[...] Each of the Assistants is to have a young person under them, in training to their particular art, and as a successor to them, whenever they shall leave the Community.

[...] Every Sunday after morning service, there shall be a collection of alms, for the relief of the unfortunate poor.

[...]

The Superior shall be called the Mother of the Community.

The Sisterhood, by the name of Sister, with the proper addition.

The Assistants, by their proper names, without any addition.

The Young Pupils, Miss, or Mademoiselle, with their proper names.

The Superior, or one of the Sisterhood by her appointment, shall read prayers twice every day;[15] at ten o'clock in the morning, and at eight in the evening, when all the Community (except such as cannot be spared from their respective offices) are to attend.

[...] The Superior shall on Wednesdays and Fridays, either before or after prayers, read an exhortation to those who attend, upon the religious, moral, and social duties, and enforce the strictest observance of them; she may select from the works of the best writers, or occasionally give observations of her own.

There shall be a room appointed for a school-room, another for the refectory.[16]– / The pupils shall dine at an early hour, suppose one o'clock, and then return to the school room; after they rise, the Teachers and Assistants shall sit down at the same table, and then all retire to the school room, or walk in the garden with the pupils, if the weather permits; and all of them shall be allowed an hour for exercise and amusement before they return to their work; and the same before dinner. – There shall be a second dinner ready at three o'clock for the Boarders and the Sisterhood, excepting such of them as shall choose to dine early, and such as are appointed to preside over the early tables, which shall be taken in rotation by all the Sisterhood, excepting the Superior.

[...]

When the rules of the Community are established, certain penalties shall be enjoined for every infringement of them. – If any Pupil, Teacher, Assistant, or Servant, shall commit a fault of consequence, the Superior shall reprove her privately for the first offence; for the second, before the whole Sisterhood; for the third, she shall be expelled the Community.

If any of the Sisterhood shall desire to leave the Community, she shall declare it, and her reasons, before the Sisterhood; and if fully resolved to go, she shall be released by the Superior, and another chosen to supply her place; and if any of them should behave so as to give offence to all the rest, she should be exhorted by the Superior to amend, or else to withdraw from the Community; and the reasons shall not be declared, or known, except to / the Sisterhood, so that her retreat shall appear to be voluntary, to the rest of the Community.

[...]

LETTER XV.

LADY A –, TO MRS. DARNFORD.

[...] The only doubt is of the practicability: is it possible to draw together twelve women all of one mind? – Will they unite in the executive parts you have allotted them? – I heartily wish that such Communities could be established; but I fear the passions and prejudices of both sexes, would unite to depreciate the scheme, and to defeat your designs.

[...] All that are dear to me wish to be so to you, but especially
Your obliged and affectionate friend,
LOUISA A –,

ELIZABETH BENTLEY, 'ON THE RENEWAL OF VIRTUOUS FRIENDSHIP IN A FUTURE STATE. JULY, 1790'

Elizabeth Bentley, 'On the Renewal of Virtuous Friendship in a Future State. July, 1790', *Genuine Poetical Compositions, on Various Subjects* (Norwich: Crouse and Stevenson, 1791), pp. 47–9, ECCO, ESTC Number T040772, ECCO Range 5526.

Having been orphaned at a young age and as an only child, Elizabeth Bentley (1767–1839) would have looked to friends to fulfil the role of emotional and intentional family. In her poem, 'On the Renewal of Virtuous Friendship', Bentley used the term 'friend' to refer to both biological ties of family and fictive bonds through affection. Naomi Tadmor explained that the term, 'friend' could encompass kinship, spiritual attachments, sentimental relationships and patronage.[1]

Kinship, sentimental relationships and patronage all played a part in Bentley's career as a poet. Bentley was the only child of Daniel Bentley, 'a journeyman cordwainer' and Elizabeth Lawrence, the daughter of a cooper. In a letter to her literary benefactor, the Rev. Dr Walker, Bentley credited her father, who 'received a good education himself', as her primary educator in reading and spelling, but not grammar.[2] After her father's stroke, which occurred when Bentley was ten, he taught her 'the art of writing'. After the death of her father, and with the encouragement of her mother and friends, Bentley purchased 'a small grammar-book, second hand', which enabled her to attain 'the art of expressing myself correctly in my native language'.[3] In order to publish her poetry, Bentley needed a patron to solicit subscribers to her poetry. An advertisement for subscribers included one of her poems, to help 'secure to her the Patronage of those who have perused the foregoing genuine Specimens of her Poetry'.[4] Qualifying her poem as 'genuine' ensured the potential subscriber that Bentley, a labouring poet had undergone some form of literary aptitude investigation, though perhaps not on the scale of Phillis Wheatley's (see also 'Racial Diversity of Families') strange tribunal in Boston. The appeal worked, since Bentley's *Genuine Poetical Compositions, on Various Subjects* was published in 1791.

Bentley died in a Norwich almshouse for the aged poor. In her will she bequeathed the residue of her estate, to cover funeral expenses, to Elizabeth Lawrence Whiting. Elizabeth Whiting might have been a maternal cousin or a non-relative friend. The strong bond of friendship, with friends such as Elizabeth Whiting and beloved family members, is the subject of Bentley's poem included below.[5]

Notes
1. N. Tadmor, *Family and Friends in Eighteenth-Century England: Household, Kinship, and Patronage* (Cambridge: Cambridge University Press, 2001), p. 167.
2. *ODNB*.
3. E. Bentley, *Speedily will be Published, Price Two Shillings and Sixpence, the Poetical Compositions of Elizabeth Bentley; who, Unimproved by Education, Has Given Proof of a Strong Natural Genius; and Uses her Best Endeavours to Obtain a Livelihood by Honest Industry, Living Irreproachably with her Aged Mother, Near St. Stephen's Gates, Norwich. The Encouragers of Indigent Merit are Entreated to Favor the Authoress with their Names and Subscriptions; Which will be Taken by W. Stevenson, at the Norfolk Arms; and all the Booksellers in Norwich* (Norwich, 1790), Eighteenth Century Collections Online. Gale. Brigham Young University – Utah [accessed 12 November 2014].
4. Bentley, *Speedily will be Published*.
5. Elizabeth Lawrence Whiting, a spinster, died 25 August 1865 in Norwich in Norfolk. See online database at Ancestry.com, England & Wales, National Probate Calendar (Index of Wills and Administrations), 1858–1966. Provo, UT, USA: Ancestry.com Operations Inc, 2010 [accessed 6 December 2014].

Elizabeth Bentley, 'On the Renewal of Virtuous Friendship in a Future State. July, 1790'

Dedicated, by permission, to WM. DRAKE, JUN. ESQ. M.P.
GENUINE Poetical Compositions, ON VARIOUS SUBJECTS.
By E. BENTLEY.
NORWICH: PRINTED BY CROUSE AND STEVENSON, FOR THE AUTHORESS, AND MAY BE HAD OF HER NEAR THE NORFOLK AND NORWICH HOSPITAL; OR OF W. STEVENSON, IN THE MARKET-PLACE. MDCCXCI. *Entered at Stationers' Hall* /

ON THE RENEWAL OF VIRTUOUS FRIENDSHIP[1] IN A FUTURE STATE.
JULY, 1790.

IF, when the Spirit quits her day-built cell,
With incorporeal essences to dwell,
Attachments form'd on earth their force retain,
And with increasing ardour still remain;[2]
What raptures must possess the virtuous mind,
Virtue alone those joys can hope to find, /
To meet in worlds of never-ending bliss,
All whom we lov'd, esteem'd, rever'd in this.
The long-lost Child shall glad the Parents' sight,
Deck'd in refulgent robes of spotless light;
Children with grateful smiles their Parents greet,
Who fled before them to the blissful seat.
They whom th' untimely stroke of Death disjoin'd,
The faithful Pair, by sacred vows combin'd;
Met in the realms of happiness, shall prove
The true delights of pure celestial love.
But when two hearts whom tender Friendship sways,
On virtue founded in their earliest days;
(Union which sympathy of soul endears,
Its strength maturing with increasing years)
Who ne'er could wish one pleasure to conceal,
Nor knew one grief but Friendship's balm could heal;

Sincerely anxious for each other's good,
By mutual counsel, sweet reproof they stood:
When two such Spirits wing their airy way,
And reach the bright abodes of endless day;
Enraptur'd, each the dear-lov'd friend shall view,
And ardently the solemn league renew;
Ecstatic transports feel, without alloy,
Sublimest friendship height'ning ev'ry joy;
They part no more, nor change their glorious state,[3]
Completely blest beyond the power of Fate. /
Should we not form such friendships here below,
As only can survive the destin'd blow?
Since Vice, though leagu'd,[4] her trust shall soon betray,
And Folly's airy vows flee swift away;
Whilst virtuous Union scorns th' attacks of Time,
And hopes to flourish in a nobler clime;
Of never-fading happiness possest,
In heav'nly mansions[5] of eternal rest.

EDITORIAL NOTES

John Romans, Deed (1766)

1. *John Romans of Rickall*: It is possible that the elder John was the same person christened in 1685 in Wheldrake, Yorkshire. Church of England, Wheldrake Parish Registers, christening of John Rummans, son of William Rummans, 27 September 1685, *England and Wales Christening Records, 1530–1906*, at www.ancestry.co.uk [accessed 1 December 2014].
2. *Appurtenances*: buildings (other than a dwelling) and physical additions to the land.

Ward Hallowell, Licence [*sic*] to Change His Name to Ward Nicholas Boylston (1770)

1. *Richard Earl of Scarborough*: Richard Lumley-Saunderson, fourth Earl of Scarbrough (1725–82) was the Cofferer of the Household and deputy Earl Marshal in 1765.
2. *Edward Duke of Norfolk*: Edward Howard, ninth Duke of Norfolk (1686–1777) was Earl Marshal from 1732 to 1777.
3. *Earl Marshall*: The office of royal marshall, first held by John FitzGilbert the Marshal, who was to manage the royal family's horses and protect the monarch, became hereditary in the twelfth century, and soon passed to the Earls of Norfolk's family, when it became the Earl Marshal.
4. *Nicholas Boylston*: Nicholas Boylston (1716–71) was the oldest son of Dr Thomas Boylston and Mary Gardner.
5. *His Mother's Side*: Ward Hallowell was the oldest son of Benjamin Hallowell (1724–99), a captain, and Mary Boylston (1722–95), who was the sister to Nicholas Boylston.
6. *St. James's*: St James' palace became the administrative centre of the British monarchy under the reign of William III and Mary II in 1698.
7. *Wemouth*: may refer to Thomas Thynne, first Marquess of Bath and The Viscount Weymouth (1734–96) served as a secretary to George III.
8. *Ralph Bigland, Somerset of Reg.*: Ralph Bigland (1712–84) was an antiquarian who, when working in the office of Somerset Herald of Arms in Ordinary, advocated that greater genealogical information should be included in church registers.

Jane Parminter, Will (Written 1807, Proved 1812)

1. *Spinster*: In the seventeenth century, the occupation of spinning became a legal category to separate never-married women from other single women who had previously been married. See J. Bennett and A. Froide (eds), *Single Women in the European Past, 1250–1800* (University of Pennsylvania Press, PA, 1998).
2. *my Brother John Parminter*: Single women often bequeathed money to their siblings and to extended kin, such as cousins, nephews and nieces. See A. L. Erickson, *Women and Property in Early Modern England* (London and New York: Routledge, 1993).
3. *Navy five per cents*: The Bank of England was established in 1693, and was partially financed through selling stocks with a fixed return rate per annum. These 'annuities' were first called Consolidated Annuities (1780–1880) and paid 3 per cent per annum. Navy annuities, or 'Navy five per cents', were the third type paid by the English military and were begun the year before Jane's death, in 1810.
4. *Messuage*: 'a dwelling house together with its outbuildings and the adjacent land assigned to its use' (*OED*).
5. *Great Courtlands*: Great Courtlands was comprised of five fields upon which A la Ronde was built.

John Drayton, Letter to James Glen (1761)

1. *Glennie*: Glen Drayton is the son of John Drayton, James Glen's nephew.
2. *Bill of Exchange*: A bill of exchange is a written, unconditional order by one party to another to pay a certain sum.
3. *Gazettes*: The South Carolina Gazette includes marriages, deaths, passenger arrivals, military operations, estates, advertisements and much more.
4. *Yellow fever*: Charleston faced a yellow fever outbreak that spread up through Massachusetts, Pennsylvania and other parts of the United States from 1742 to 1793.
5. *Mr. Rattray*: John Rattray was a member of the twenty-fourth Commons House of Assembly in the Royal Colony of South Carolina. John Rattray died from yellow fever on September 30 1761, leaving his seat vacant.
6. *William Loyd*: William Lloyd was a merchant living in Charleston, South Carolina. He died from yellow fever on August 30 1761.
7. *Mr. Numan*: Edward Newman was a merchant living in Charleston, South Carolina. He died on 10 October 1761.
8. *Mr. Bullock*: James Bullock managed James Glen's affairs in Carolina while he was away in London.
9. *Rice has been a Drug ever Since you left this*: The sale of rice was quite disappointing to John Drayton because the market price was much lower than expected. Glen did not make as much money from the crop of rice than he intended to make.
10. *a Charge and Expence*: Drayton is referring to one of Glen's Negro workers as a charge and expense because she is incapable of working. Drayton believes that Glen would be better off getting rid of her from the plantation.
11. *nineteen hands*: This is a reference to the nineteen Negroes James Glen purchased in 1765.
12. *Billy Drayton*: Billy is the son of John Drayton. Billy struggled with college, and particularly the law, so he became a planter.
13. *Pender, Tattamore, Nanny, Tom and Jammie*: These are the names of five of James Glen's

slaves on his plantation.
14. *money for my Childrens use in England*: John Drayton sent his children to London for their education. James Glen took care of them while they were there.
15. *Tom Middleton*: Thomas Middleton lived from 1734–1813, the son of Henry Middleton. Thomas Middleton was a plantation owner in South Carolina.
16. *carage*: carriage refers to a person's bearing, deportment or manners.
17. *Charles:* Charles Drayton was the son of John Drayton.
18. *Mr. Izard*: Ralph Izard lived from January 1742–May 30 1804 in South Carolina. He was a US politician and served as President of the United States Senate *pro tempore* in 1794. In 1764, Izard married Alice DeLancey of New York, and had thirteen children.
19. *Tomie*: Thomas Drayton, the son of John Drayton.
20. *Uncle and Aunt*: This refers to James Glen and his wife. John Drayton was married to Glen's sister, Margaret Glen.
21. *why don't they come to Mr. Drayton*: This is simply the way of asking when the Glens will return to South Carolina from London.
22. *Mrs. Glen*: Elizabeth Wilson Glen, the wife of James Glen.
23. *Buchanan*: Andrew Buchanan was a merchant in Glasgow.
24. *Simson*: William Simpson, a merchant in Glasgow.

A. W. Rumney (ed.), *From the Old South-Sea House* (1914)

1. *Miss Holyoak*: Charlotte Holyoak married William in 1799.
2. *Mr. Clark*: Most likely their maternal uncle, Edward Clark, or perhaps another Clark relative.
3. *Old South Sea House*: headquarters for the South Sea Company (founded 1711), a joint-stock company that was used to manage government debt.
4. *Mr. Martin friend*: It is unclear who Martin, Johnson, Francis or Combe were.
5. *brother Anthony*: Anthony Rumney, born 1762.

Chesnut and Cox Families, Correspondence (1797, 1800, 1810)

1. *Mrs. Stockton*: Catherine, Mary's sister. She was the wife of Samuel W. Stockton, of Trenton, New Jersey.
2. *Miss Sally*: Mary's sister, Sarah. She later married Dr John Redman Coxe, of Philadelphia.
3. *James*: James Chesnut, Mary's husband.
4. *John Chesnut*: Mary's father-in-law. Mary's father John Cox had died in 1793 during the yellow fever epidemic.
5. *Betsy*: Elizabeth (b. 1783), wife of Horace Binney (1780–1875), lawyer and director of the first Bank of the United States.
6. *Nephew*: Refers to Mary and James's son, James Jr.
7. *Theodosia*: Theodosia Sayre Coxe, niece of Esther Cox, cousin to Mary Bowes Cox Chesnut. Her letters with her father are included in Volume 2, 'Childhood'.
8. *Mr. Barton*: Matthias Barton husband of Mary's sister Esther.
9. *Her Fathers Will*: The will of John Cox (Late of Bloomsbury, New Jersey), City of Philadelphia, was signed 7 February 1792. It notes a large Estate on the Susquehanna. Executors were Esther Cox, John Stevens, Samuel W. Stockton and Mathias Barton.
10. *Mr. Cox*: John Cox (1732–93), Mary's father.

11. *Little John*: John Chesnut (1799–1839), grandson of John Chesnut, son of Mary Bowes Cox and James Chesnut.
12. *Serena*: Esther Serena Chesnut (1797–1822), granddaughter of John Chesnut, daughter of Mary Bowes Cox and James Chesnut.
13. *Mrs. Kennedy*: Jane Kennedy, family friend to the Chesnuts.
14. *Hetty Barton*: Esther (Hetty), b. 1767, wife of Matthias Barton, daughter of Esther Cox, sister of Mary.
15. *Francis Stevens*: Son of Rachel Cox Stevens (Mary's sister) and Colonel John Stevens.

Lovejoy Family Correspondence (1817–19)

1. *Meredith*: Meredith was formerly New Salem, and was incorporated under its new name on 13 June 1769 (Genealogy and History of New Hampshire and its counties, available at http://www.nh.searchroots.com [accessed 7 January 2015]).
2. *Dear Sir*: The brothers were four years apart in age, so as the younger brother, Henry would be expected to show deference to birth order in his family.
3. *Havannah*: From 1798 to 1800, the United States waged the 'Quasi-War' with France in the Caribbean. The French Directory, its final revolutionary government, had been unable to finance its European wars, and consequently seized several American merchant ships. On 28 May 1798, the US responded with Naval attacks against the French privateers. President John Adams had sent American ambassadors to negotiate peace, which was accomplished in the Treaty of Mortefontaine during the Convention of 1800. (US Department of State, Office of the Historian, available at https://history.state.gov) [accessed 7 January 2015].
4. *Buried in 20 fathoms Water*: The USS *Warren* was commissioned from New England in late 1799 and from January to June 1800, was stationed off Havana, Cuba. The crew experienced several deaths from the yellow fever epidemic during June in Havana and July 1800 near Veracruz, Mexico. The Master Commandant Newman and his son John also died in August (Dictionary of American Naval Fighting Ships, available at: www.history.navy.mil) [accessed 7 January 2015].
5. *Sandbornton*: Sandbornton, New Hampshire, was renamed from Crotchtown in 1748 when Governor Benning Wentworth granted land to sixty settlers, several of whom were surnamed Sandborn (A. Coolidge and J. B. Mansfield, *A History and Description of New England* (Boston, 1859)).
6. *Mr Joshua Lovejoy Esq-*: Joshua Senior had been born in Andover, New Hampshire, on 8 January 1743 or 1744 and died 28 January 1832. He had served as a sergeant in the Continental Army under Captain Benjamin Ames' Company in Colonel James Frey's Massachusetts Militia Regiment.
7. *Buffalo New York Niagara County*: Niagara County had been created in 1808, and Buffalo was a part of that county until the creation of Erie County in 1821.
8. *your Mother*: On 30 April 1769 Joshua Lovejoy Sr had married Sara Perkins (1744–1828).
9. *Taylor & Family*: Joshua Jr's sisters were Sarah (b. 1773) who married Vine Bingham (1765–1813) on 4 March 1805; Phebe (b. 1778) who married Joseph Conner (1764–1806) and then George Blanchard in 1810; Mary 'Molly' (1781/2–1849) who married Thomas Taylor (1781–1853) on 3 November 1804; and Lydia (1786–1859) who married Daniel Lane (1778–1814).
10. *Andrew*: Andrew James Lovejoy (1772–1856).
11. *Jonathan*: Jonathan Lovejoy (1780–1845) married Sally Taylor, the sister to Thomas

Taylor, who was the husband of Molly Lovejoy, on 14 March 1812.
12. *Warrin*: Warren was probably named for General Warren, who had died near Joshua in the battle of Bunker Hill.
13. *Compinsation from Government for your Losses by the enemy in the time of Our War*: The *Buffalo Gazette* on 28 January 1817 ran an article in which Smith Salisbury, the newspaper editor, called for the government to 'amply remunerate their losses'. The United States Government had appointed a special commissioner, Richard Bland Lee, to distribute federal compensation to the innocent victims of the War of 1812.
14. *Bankrupt Act*: The two acts that passed the 15th United States Congress in April 1818 were the Flag Act (Sess. 1, ch. 34, 3 Stat. 415) and the Navigation Act (Sess. 1, ch. 70, 3 Stat. 432). The 14th US Congress passed the Second Bank of the United States (Sess. 1, ch. 94, 3 Stat. 266) and the Dallas tariff (Sess. 1, ch. 107, 3 Stat. 310).
15. *Buffalo Glens Falls*: Glens Falls was originally called Wing's Falls in 1766, named after Abraham Wing, a prominent leader of the Quakers settled there. Colonel Johannes Glen changed the name in 1788, and a post office was established in 1808. See R. King, *Bridging The Years: Glens Falls, New York 1763-1978* (Glens Falls, NY: Glens Falls Historical Association, 1978).
16. *Jabesh*: Identity is unknown.
17. *Canan*: Canan could refer to Canaan, New York, which was established in 1759; Canaan, New Hampshire, which was chartered in 1761; or Canaan, Connecticut, which was incorporated in 1739.
18. *Mariah*: Identity is unknown.
19. *W[illia]m Wing*: William Wing's relationship to the Lovejoy family is unknown.
20. *To Joshua Lovejoy & Sally Lovejoy*: Sally could be the nickname of Joshua the younger's sister, Sarah, or his sister-in-law, the wife of Jonathan, or an unrecorded wife.

Anna Letitia Barbauld, *Hymns in Prose for Children* (1781)

1. *Dr. Watts' Hymns / for Children*: Isaac Watts (1674-1748) was a dissenting minister and prolific hymn writer. Watts considered poetry a divine gift, and wanted to elevate and improve the hymns sung at church. He published his *Horae Lyricae: Hymns and Spiritual Songs* (1707) which were biblical paraphrases, religious and eucharist hymns. The poems Watts wrote for children was published in 1715: *Divine Songs Attempted in Easy Language for the Use of Children*. Watts was influenced by the writings of John Locke regarding the education of children, and in particular that reading should delight the child, as well as the Calvinist view that children needed to be disciplined against their being wilful, deceitful and corrupted by sin.
2. *A.L.B.*: Anna Letitia Barbauld.
3. *Negro woman*: Barbauld had been antislavery before William Wilberforce started his abolition campaign in Parliament in May 1789 (McCarthy, *Anna Letitia Barbauld*, pp. 292–3).

Ann Murry, *Mentoria: Or, the Young Ladies Instructor* (1799)

1. *Mentoria*: Mentoria was a feminized version of the masculine mentor, or teacher. Ann Murry's *Mentoria* was reissued in twelve editions, inspired her to write a sequel in 1799, which appears only to have been printed once, and an American edition by Mrs. (Susanna) Rowson in 1794.
2. *by paying implicit obedience to their commands*: Murry utilized the Biblical injunction for

children to honour and obey their parents, as expressed in Moses' Decalogue, the fifth commandment. References to the fifth commandment are found in Exodus 20:12 and in the New Testament epistle, Ephesians 6:2.
3. *imitation to those who are younger*: Sibling relations in prescriptive literature emphasized love and kindness rather than the honour and obedience from children towards their parents. See A. Harris, *Siblinghood and Social Relations in Georgian England: Share and Share Alike* (Manchester: Manchester University Press, 2012).
4. *Maintain your own dignity, nor ever lose it, by permitting a servant to joke with you, or partake of your recreations*: A concern within household families was the preservation of hierarchical relationships between the nuclear family and the contractual dependents such as servants. See N. Tadmor, *Family and Friends in Eighteenth-Century England: Household, Friendship, and Patronage* (Cambridge: Cambridge University Press, 2001).
5. *comfort the afflicted, and clothe the naked*: In the New Testament gospel of Matthew, Jesus taught the parable of the sheep and the goats, in which he differentiates the behaviour and opinion of people towards the poor. The sheep will be invited to stand on the shepherd's right hand, and the goats will be divided on the left because the former cared for the physical needs of the poor while the latter did not. Matthew 25:36 'Naked, and ye clothed me'.
6. *there can be no love, as love casteth out fear*: Murry referred here to 1 John 4:18, 'There is no fear in love; but perfect love casteth out fear'.
7. *Politeness*: Conduct books were also known as courtesy books, since they had derived from the Renaissance handbooks on courtly, masculine behaviour for aristocratic men. During the eighteenth century, more courtesy books began to address women and defined the features of femininity. An important quality both men and women desired to acquire was politeness, which meant courtesy, good manners, respectful behaviour as well as polish, elegance and good taste. See P. Carter, *Men and the Emergence of Polite Society, Britain 1660–1800* (London: Longman, 2001) and I. H. Tague, *Women of Quality: Accepting and Contesting Ideals of Femininity in England, 1690–1760* (Woodbridge: Boydell Press, 2002).
8. '*To do to others, as you would they should do unto you*': Murry freely quoted from the New Testament gospels, Matthew 7:12 and Luke 6:31 which contain Jesus' 'Golden Rule'.

Jane Davis, *Letters from a Mother to her Son, on his Going to Sea: And a Letter to Capt. S.* ([1799])

1. *TO SIR RICHARD HILL, BART., M. P*: Sir Richard Hill, second Baronet of Hawkstone (1732–1808) was a Methodist convert in Oxford. His younger brother, Rowland Hill (1744–1833) was an evangelical preacher. Starting in 1780 Hill represented Shropshire in Parliament for twenty-six years. Hill wrote several religious pamphlets.
2. *a numerous infant family*: Infant often referred to young children under the common law legal age of twenty-one.
3. *Accompts*: numeracy and accounting.
4. *Hebrews 4:9*: 'There remaineth therefore a rest to the people of God'.
5. *Lamb*: Another symbolic name for Jesus was the Lamb of God. In John 1:29, John the Baptist stated when he saw his cousin, Jesus, 'Behold the Lamb of God, which taketh away the sin of the world'.
6. *For neither sickness, nor pain, nor death, nor parting*: In Romans 8:38–9 a similar construction was used to describe the power of spiritual bonds: 'For I am persuaded, that

neither death, nor life, nor angels, nor principalities, nor powers, nor things present, nor things to come, Nor height, nor depth, nor any other creature, shall be able to separate us from the love of God, which is in Christ Jesus our Lord'. Similarly, John Wesley preached 'there shall be no more death, neither sorrow nor crying: neither shall there be any more pain; for the former things are done away' (W. Carpenter (ed.), *Wesleyana, Or, A Complete System of Wesleyan Theology* (New York, 1840), p. 296).

Recusant Returns, Diocese of York (1767, 1780)

1. Archbishop Drummond probably misunderstood or misinterpreted the earlier returns because the Catholic population was increasing in the middle of the century. J. Jago and E. Royle, *The Eighteenth-Century Church in Yorkshire: Archbishop Drummond's Primary Visitation of 1764* (York: Borthwick Institute of Historical Research, 1999), p. 27.

William Tennent III, On the Dissenting Petition, House of Assembly, Charleston, South Carolina (1777)

1. *the important moment of forming a Constitution for this most righteous purpose*: Tennent addressed the General Assembly of South Carolina as they were preparing to revise their colonial constitution to accommodate their post-revolutionary government. Tennent's speech to the General Assembly initiated the disestablishment of the Anglican Church as the state religion in South Carolina, which was enacted when the South Carolina state Constitution was ratified in 1790.
2. *the law knows not the other Churches*: The Church Act of 1706 established the Anglican Church as the government's official religion. Following Parliament's act in 1711 to fund the construction of fifty Anglican churches in London, the first Anglican church building was constructed in South Carolina by an act of the General Assembly,
3. *the law knows not the Clergy of the other churches, nor will it give them a license to marry their own people*: The Church Act of 1706 also denied Dissenting faiths the legal ownership of their church property, and the legal recognition of their ministers marrying brides and grooms.
4. *the Ordinary*: a county judge having jurisdiction esp. of a court of probate (*OED*).
5. *suit in Chancery*: In South Carolina, the Court of Chancery heard petitions from individuals who alleged that the normal judicial procedures had failed to treat them fairly. Chancery determined its rulings based not on precedent, such as in Common Law procedures, but on equity according to particular situations. See South Carolina History of Court of Equity, at http://www.carolana.com/SC/Courts/SC_Court_of_Equity.html [accessed 8 January 2015].
6. *The law vests the Officers of the Church of England ... for the support of the poor: an enormous power*: In the British colonies, some colonial governments elected to follow the British model of poor relief through ecclesiastic parish officials, and others administered poor relief through the civic organizations in town (see 'Poor Families').
7. *Machiavelian*: Niccolò Machiavelli (1469–1527) was considered the father of modern political theory. Machiavelli wrote *The Prince* (1532) as an instructional treatise to Lorenzo de' Medici, in which he advocated actions that he believed would free the Florentine Republic from the Emperor Charles V's army as it advanced towards Rome. With the overarching theme of Florentine independent rule, Machiavelli wrote that since all

men were not good, virtuous and loyal, then their leader must not act according to religious principles, but rather act according to situation in order to maintain his control, without incurring the hatred of his subjects. His precepts, which demonstrated that the ends justified the means associated his name, which became utilized adjectivally, with negative political power.

8. *is the tax which it makes all other denominations pay to the support of the religion of one*: The Fundamental Constitution of 1669 stipulated that any seven persons could unitedly form their own church and any other religious denomination must declare a belief in and publicly worship God. After the Church Act of 1706, the colonial government could levy taxes to support the building and maintenance of the Anglican churches.

9. *In this respect they stand upon the same footing with the Jews*: The Fundamental Constitution of 1669 allowed any other religious denominations the freedom of worship in South Carolina, as long as they declared a belief in and publicly worship God. Many Jewish families emigrated from England to Charleston during the eighteenth century, and by the early nineteenth century, South Carolina had the largest concentration of Jews in America. See the Jewish Encyclopedia (1901–6), at http://www.jewishencyclopedia.com [accessed 8 January 2015].

10. *Sir, you very well know, that it was not the three pence on the pound of tea, that roused all the virtue of America*: The Sons of Liberty in Boston, Massachusetts, protested the Tea Act of 1773 by tarring and feathering John Malcolm, the British Excise Man in November; on 16 December they boarded three ships in the Boston harbour and hurled 342 chests of tea into the Boston harbour.

11. *Catholicism*: Catholicity referred to 'The quality of being comprehensive in feeling, taste, sympathy, etc.; freedom from sectarian exclusiveness or narrowness' (*OED*).

Zina Baker Huntington Correspondence (1808–13)

1. *we had a verry agreeable journey*: They are travelling to Watertown, New York from Plainsfield, New Hampshire.
2. *my new father*: William Huntington.
3. *My new Mother:* Presendia Lathrop Huntington.
4. *all the family I like verry well*: The Huntington family had seven children: John Lathrop Huntington, Ambrose Woodward Huntington, Hiram Huntington, Dyer Huntington, Precendia Huntington, Cyrus Thompson Huntington and William Huntington.
5. *I went to meeting last Sunday*: She is referring to church.
6. *Co. Prices wife she that was Ruth Grant*: Rufus Price was a colonel in the Revolutionary War, an aide to General George Washington. Price married Ruth Grant on 7 May 1778. The Huntingtons met them in New York.
7. *tolland:* a small town in Connecticut where Dorcas Baker lived.
8. *ADIEU:* another term for goodbye or farewell.
9. *daddy:* Oliver Baker.
10. *Wm. Huntington, Jr.:* William Huntington, Jr is Zina's husband.
11. *My Honored Parents*: Oliver and Dorcas Baker.
12. *Zina*: referring to her daughter/namesake.
13. *akes*: aches.
14. *growing stupid:* Stupid in this context means spiritual laziness or sluggishness of understanding.
15. *William*: Zina's husband.
16. *My babe*: Dimick Baker Huntington.

17. *Wm:* Zina's husband, William.
18. *my Mother:* Dorcas Baker.
19. *now sympathize with you on a solemn occasion, being well satisfied our Honored Father:* Oliver Baker, Zina's father, died on 3 October 1811.
20. *Death of a sister:* Zina's twin sister, Lina Baker, died on 27 August 1808.
21. *my tender Mother and brothers and sisters I am yet spared to speak to you once more in this silent way:* Zina has eleven siblings. As of 1811, when this letter was written, only Heman Baker, Oliver Baker, Semantha Baker, Dimick Baker, Dorcas Baker, Lodema Baker Elizabeth Baker and Mary L. Baker survive.
22. *Therefore let my speech be to warn and advise you to prepare to follow our near and tender Father:* She is encouraging her family to become more religious.
23. *village of Watertown:* Watertown, New York.
24. *Honored Parent ... this from yours:* This is a quick note from William Huntington, Zina's husband, to the Baker family.
25. *Semantha:* Zina's sister.
26. *Burrs Mills:* a city in New York near Watertown.
27. *among the Soldiers and is yet there has been several Deaths there this week past, you live where you do not see the effects of war, we have had some alarms this season past:* Four major battles of the War of 1812 were fought in New York. New York supplied a total of 77,000 men to fight in the war.
28. *abominable war:* this is referring to the War of 1812.
29. *Semantha:* Zina's sister.
30. *I am stupid:* referrs to spiritual laziness or lacking skill or genius.
31. *as great a union among the church as I have seen at any time:* She is referring to the Presbyterian Church.
32. *Adieu:* 'goodbye' (French).
33. *Presendia:* Zina's daughter.
34. *had a fine boy:* There do not seem to be any records that contain the name of this baby boy. He was born on 11 Feburary 1813.
35. *expired the day before it was 3 weeks old:* 2 March 1813.
36. *gave me some pukes:* medicine that caused vomiting.
37. *My girl:* This term is ambiguous. She could either be referring to her hire girl/servant, or to one of her daughters.
38. *I expect you heard of a battle in June or July:* The First Battle of Sacket's Harbor was a naval battle fought between the Americans and the British. The Village of Sacket's Harbor is just west of Watertown, where Zina lived.
39. *religion in this place it is not so dull and stupid:* Dull and stupid refers to spiritual laziness or sluggishness.
40. *appearance of a reformation:* interest in and commitment to religion.
41. *Louville:* Lowville is a village in New York near Watertown, New York.
42. *Denmark:* a city in New York just east of Watertown, New York.
43. *there is a great work going on and we hope it will spread and overshadow us:* She is referring to revival movements and a renewal of religious interest.
44. *opened the eyes of my husband:* She is referring to the conversion experience of her husband, William.
45. *Wm:* William.
46. *Ambrose:* Ambrose Woodward Huntington is William Huntington's brother, Zina's brother-in-law.

47. *Lodema:* Zina's younger sister.
48. *adieu:* 'goodbye' or 'farewell' (French).
49. *to speak to you in this silent way:* She is referring to their communication through the correspondence they write back and forth.
50. *stupid time:* a time of spiritual laziness.
51. *babe:* William Dresser Huntington.
52. *adieu:* 'farewell' (French); serves as an expression of kind wishes at parting.

Robert Nelson, *An Earnest Exhortation to House-Keepers, to Set Up the Worship of God in their Families* (1739)

1. *give a strict Account at the Day of Judgment ... and how you have exercised it*: In the New Testament gospels of Matthew and Luke, Jesus taught that the kingdom of Heaven was like the parable of the talents, in which a man portions out his goods to three of his servants before he travelled into a far country. A talent was an ancient unit of value. To the first servant, the man gave five talents, to the second, two talents, and the third one talent. The first two increase their number of talents through trade, while the last servant buried his in the earth. When the master returns, he rewards the first two servants and condemns the third because he acted in fear.
2. *Never omit carrying them ... and see that they behave themselves reverently at the Publick Worship*: Nelson's view of children reflected Calvinist and contemporary views: children were wilful, deceitful and corrupted by sin. Catechizing the child taught religious belief as well as provided a means of enforcing proper discipline.
3. *reading a Psalm*: Psalms were Hebrew poetry from the Old Testament. Unlike English poetic forms, psalms utilize parallelism and chiasmus instead of rhyme and meter.
4. *we are obliged to use our utmost Endeavours to obtain*: Nelson referred to Jesus' sermon on the mount, in which the Lord stated 'Ask, and it shall be given you; seek and ye shall find; knock and it shall be opened unto you' (Matthew 7:7; Luke 11:9).
5. *will always be ready to assist and strengthen us in the doing and suffering his holy Will*: To the Hebrews the New Testament contained writings about the role of Christ as the mediator between God and man; Hebrews 13:21 'Make you perfect in every good work to do his will, working in you that which is wellpleasing in his sight, through Jesus Christ; to whom be glory for ever and ever. Amen'.
6. *and afterwards for receiving the blessed Sacrament*: In the Church of England, confirmation was administered by the laying on of hands to previously baptized members when they felt ready to affirm and live their faith. After confirmation, the worshipper would partake of the eucharist symbols of wine and bread.
7. *That we may herein exercise ... Consciences void of Offence both towards God and towards Man*: The apostle Paul declared his feelings regarding his ministry with these words from the Acts of the Apostles 24:16.
8. *that we may love Thee, the Lord our God ... shall do unto us, that we may do likewise unto them*: The great commandment and the golden rule were found in Matthew 22:36–40 and Mark 12:28–34.
9. *denying Ungodliness and worldly Lusts ... and purify unto himself a peculiar People, zealous of good Works*: Paul wrote these words to Titus, in Titus 2:12.
10. *Let our Loins always be girded about*: 'Loins girded about' was a biblical expression of readiness.

11. *our Lamps burning*: In Jesus' parable of the ten virgins, which, like the parable of the talents, is about the kingdom of Heaven, five young women bring extra oil for their lamps and are wise since they are ready for the arrival of the bridegroom, and five are foolish because they did not bring enough for the wait (Matthew 25:1–13).
12. *Bless all our Friends, Relations and Benefactors*: For a discussion on the relationships between kinship, friendship and patronage, see N. Tadmor, *Family and Friends in Eighteenth-Century England: Household, Friendship, and Patronage* (Cambridge: Cambridge University Press, 2001).
13. *Our Father, &c*: The Lord's Prayer.
14. *that I may keep my Hands from picking and stealing, and my Tongue from Evil-speaking, Lying, and Slandering*: Nelson used the language of the Anglican Prayer Book catechisms taught at school for the children's prayer.

Anon., *A Persuasive to Family Religion* (1736)

1. *the great High-priest*: Paul in Hebews 4:14 explained that Jesus was the 'great high priest'.
2. *him that is ashamed of me before men, of him will I be ashamed before my father and his holy angels*: After Jesus predicted his death and resurrection, he invited his followers to 'take up' their 'cross' and then his words in Mark 8:38 and Luke 9:23–7.
3. *There is no safety in our goings out and comings in*: Psalm 121:8, 'The LORD shall preserve thy going out and thy coming in from this time forth, and even for evermore'.
4. *'Tis the blessing of the Lord makes rich*: Proverbs 10:22, 'The blessing of the LORD, it maketh rich, and he addeth no sorrow with it'.
5. *rise up early, sit up late, and eat the bread of carefulness*: Psalm 127:2, 'It is vain for you to rise up early, to sit up late, to eat the bread of sorrows: for so he giveth his beloved sleep'.
6. *he shall give his Angels charge concerning thee, to keep thee in all thy ways*: Psalm 91:11, 'For he shall give his angels charge over thee, to keep thee in all thy ways'.
7. *conscience of closet religion*: Jesus, before he taught his disciples the Lord's Prayer, he warned in Matthew 6:6, 'But thou, when thou prayest, enter into thy closet, and when thou hast shut thy door, pray to thy Father which is in secret; and thy Father which seeth in secret shall reward thee openly'.
8. *tasted that the Lord is gracious*: 1 Peter 2:3, 'If so be ye have tasted that the Lord is gracious'.
9. *'tis good to draw nigh to God*: Psalm 73:28, 'But it is good for me to draw near to God: I have put my trust in the Lord GOD, that I may declare all thy works.'
10. *France, Piedmont, the Palatinate*: France, Piedmont and the Palatinate were involved in the Nine Years' War (1688–97), which involved the persecution of Protestants, and in particular the Huguenots who fled France in the thousands.
11. *Thorn*: unidentified city, unless Thorn is an Anglicized version of Turin, which is a city in the Piedmont. The War of the Polish Succession was waged from 1733 to 1738, with the French and the Duke of Savoy, who governed the Piedmont, supporting the Polish against the Russians and Austrians.
12. *the seat of the scorner*: Psalm 1:1, 'Blessed is the man that walketh not in the counsel of the ungodly, nor standeth in the way of sinners, nor sitteth in the seat of the scornful'.
13. *thrice happy is that people whose God is the Lord*: Psalm 144:15, 'Happy is that people, that is in such a case: yea, happy is that people, whose God is the LORD'.

Abbé d'Ancourt, 'Of Politeness in Religion, and against Superstition', 'Of Devotion', 'Of Behaviour at Church', *The Lady's Preceptor* (1743)

1. *that Earth or Heaven could bestow ... In every Gesture Dignity and Love.* / *MILTON*: The epigraph is from John Milton's *Paradise Lost*, book 8, ll. 482–4, 488–9, in which the creation of Eve from Adam's rib is described. The lines missing are: 'Led by her Heav'nly Maker, though unseen, / And guided by his voice, nor uninformd / Of nuptial Sanctiie and marriage Rites'.
2. *Monster*: the Latin root of monster – *monere*, 'to warn', revealed the ideological function of the misbehaving woman to appositely define appropriate feminine behaviour. 'Monster' in this sense functions as its etymologically related word, to admonish or show what a young women ought not to do. See F. Botting, *Gothic (the New Critical Idiom)* (London: Routledge, 2013).
3. *Enthusiastical*: during the eighteenth century, the Church of England was suspicious of Dissenting 'enthusiasm'. Samuel Johnson defined enthusiasm as 'a vain confidence of divine favour or communication'. Philip Doddridge warned, 'There is really such a Thing as Enthusiasm, against which it becomes the true Friends of the Revelation to be diligently on their Guard' (*Life of Gardiner*). Enthusiasm was considered 'Ill-regulated or misdirected religious emotion, extravagance of religious speculation' (*OED*).
4. *TO behave with Modesty*: Conduct literature such as *The Lady's Preceptor* taught young women the importance of modesty and chastity in the preservation of their virtue. See I. H. Tague, *Women of Quality: Accepting and Contesting Ideals of Femininity in England, 1690–1760* (Woodbridge, Suffolk: Boydell Press, 2002).

David Muir, *An Humble Attempt toward the Revival of Family-Religion among Christians* (1749)

1. *JOSHUA xxiv. 15*: Joshua 24:15.
2. *Tabernacles*: In Exodus 31, the Lord commanded Moses to build a Tabernacle to house the ark of the covenant and perform religious rituals until they could build a temple in the promised land. St Paul related the human body to the tabernacle or temple of the Holy Spirit (1 Corinthians 6:18–20).
3. *Altars*: In Genesis 8, Adam built an altar and burned offerings to the Lord. St Paul also described the Christian as the new altar of the covenant that housed the ten commandments: 'fleshy tables of the heart' (2 Corinthians 3:1–3).
4. *PROPHET*: Muir uses the three-fold office of Jesus Christ as prophet (Deuteronomy 18:14–22), and priest (Psalm 110:1–4), and king (Psalm 2) to model the role of the father in his household family.
5. *KING*: The language of kinship was used in political and ecclesiastical discussions of leadership. The king of the country was also referred to as its father, and the God of Christianity was addressed as Father in Heaven. The King of England was also an ecclesiastical leader through his position as the head of the Church of England. See N. Tadmor, *Family and Friends in Eighteenth-Century England: Household, Kinship, and Patronage* (Cambridge: Cambridge University Press, 2001).
6. *Adam's sinful Race*: the belief in original sin, which resulted from Adam's transgression in and subsequent expulsion from the Garden of Eden, was shared by Catholics and most Protestant sects. Protestant sects differed in their approach to the effects of original sin,

since some, like the Catholics, practised infant baptism to save the child tainted by original sin, and others did not. The use of race in this context refers to the lineage concept of genealogy and not to the emerging concept of biological and phenotypical difference. See E. C. Eze, *Race and the Enlightment: A Reader* (Cambridge, MA: Blackwell Publishers, 1997).

7. *praying with his twelve Disciples, which was then his little Family*: Muir referred to Jesus and his disciples as a family bound not by consanguineal but rather by spiritual ties.

8. *the Children of the Covenant made with Abraham and his Seed*: In Genesis 12–17, God granted to Abraham and his progeny the land of Israel, known as the Promised Land, if he and they worshipped him and offered animal sacrifice. The sign of this covenant was male circumcision. They were to become a great nation and a blessing to all peoples on the earth. Those who entered into the covenant were called the Children of the Covenant. In Hebrews 8, Christians participated in the 'new covenant' through the Eucharist, which represented the body and blood of Christ, who was called the Lamb of God. Also, circumcision became symbolic for early Christians, as Paul expressed in Romans 2:29, 'and circumcision is that of the heart, in the spirit, and not in the letter; whose praise is not of men, but of God'.

9. *if there be a hotter Place in Hell*: Unlike Dante's icy-cold centre of Hell, Muir's concept referred to John Calvin's teachings of Hell as a place of fiery eternal torment, based upon Matthew 25:41, 'Then shall he say also unto them on the left hand, Depart from me, ye cursed, into everlasting fire, prepared for the devil and his angels'.

Anon., *Cheap Repository Tracts for Sunday Reading* (1800)

1. *The Lord's Prayer*: Jesus taught this prayer to his disciples in Matthew 6:9–13 and Luke 11:2–4, '9After this manner therefore pray ye: Our Father which art in heaven, Hallowed be thy name. 10Thy kingdom come. Thy will be done in earth, as it is in heaven. 11Give us this day our daily bread. 12And forgive us our debts, as we forgive our debtors. 13And lead us not into temptation, but deliver us from evil: For thine is the kingdom, and the power, and the glory, for ever. Amen.' The Lord's Prayer was included in the Book of Common Prayer in the Church of England.

2. *the Belief*: may refer to the Nicene Creed, which was included in the 1662 Book of Common Prayer: I believe in God the Father Almighty, Maker of heaven and earth: And in Jesus Christ his only Son our Lord, Who was conceived by the Holy Ghost, Born of the Virgin Mary, Suffered under Pontius Pilate, Was crucified, dead, and buried: He descended into hell; The third day he rose again from the dead; He ascended into heaven, And sitteth on the right hand of God the Father Almighty; From thence he shall come to judge the quick and the dead. I believe in the Holy Ghost; The holy Catholick Church; The Communion of Saints; The Forgiveness of sins; The Resurrection of the body, And the Life everlasting. Amen.

3. *the vain repetitions used in prayer by the Pharisees*: Before Jesus taught the Lord's Prayer, he warned in Matthew 6:5–7, 'And when thou prayest, thou shalt not be as the hypocrites are: for they love to pray standing in the synagogues and in the corners of the streets, that they may be seen of men. Verily I say unto you, They have their reward. But thou, when thou prayest, enter into thy closet, and when thou hast shut thy door, pray to thy Father which is in secret; and thy Father which seeth in secret shall reward thee openly. But when ye pray, use not vain repetitions, as the heathen do: for they think that they shall be heard for their much speaking.'

4. *IF all Masters and Mistresses of Families*: During the eighteenth century, the concept of

a family included a household unit comprised of a nuclear family and co-habitant dependents such as servants and apprentices. This household family was bound not only by ties of blood and marriage, but also by co-residence, and organized under some form of authority. This authority figure, or head of the household, was expected to direct household management, provide and administer household finances, and oversee household religious observance. See N. Tadmor, *Family and Friends in Eighteenth-Century England: Household, Kinship, and Patronage* (Cambridge: Cambridge University Press, 2001).

5. *Sunday Schools*: Sunday schools, or Sabbath schools, were established in the 1780s, first by Robert Raikes and Thomas Stock in Gloucester to educate 'deserving' plebeian children on the day they were not required to labour. Students were taught reading, arithmetic, catechism and sometimes writing. Many of these schools were financed by subscribers; Hannah More established several Sunday schools.

6. *"the Holy Spirit that helpeth our infirmities."*: The author quotes from Romans 8:26, 'Likewise the Spirit also helpeth our infirmities: for we know not what we should pray for as we ought: but the Spirit itself maketh intercession for us with groanings which cannot be uttered'.

7. *Holy Spirit which God hath promised to them that ask it*: In Hebrews 2:4, Paul encouraged the early Christians to seek for salvation: 'God also bearing them witness, both with signs and wonders, and with divers miracles, and gifts of the Holy Ghost, according to his own will?' In Acts 8:14–15, after the day of Pentecost, the apostles prayed for the gifts of the spirit for other believes: 'Now when the apostles which were at Jerusalem heard that Samaria had received the word of God, they sent unto them Peter and John: Who, when they were come down, prayed for them, that they might receive the Holy Ghost'.

Isle of Wight County, Virginia, Deeds (1720–36 and 1741–9)

1. *Indenture*: any deed, written contract, or sealed agreement (*OED*).
2. *King Edmunds*: In 1711, Colonial Lieutenant Governor Alexander Spotswood met with the Teerheer (Chief) of the Nottaways. The Teerheer was Occuraass, who was called William Edmund by the colonial officials, and in return for not joining the Tuscaroras Indians in their fight with the Virginians, two of the chief's sons were sent to college. King Edmunds was William Edmond.
3. *James, Harrison, Peter, Wansake Robin, Frank, Wonoak Rigin, Robin Scholler, Sam*: Under the Chief or Teerheer of the tribe, were the Great Men, eight in number, of the Cheroenhaka. See the *Executive Journals of the Council of Colonial Virginia*, vol. 3, 1 May 1705–23 October 1721 (Richmond, VA: Virginia State Library, 1928).
4. *Nottaway Indians*: The Nottoways (Cheroenhaka – People at the Fork of the Stream) were an Iroquoian speaking tribe, who lived in Isle of Wight County along the shores of the James River. Their first contact with Anglo-colonists was in 1608/9. The name 'Nottoway' derived from the name by which the Algonquian tribes called the Cheroenhaka: 'Nadawa' or snakes, adder, enemy.
5. *John Simmons*: John Simmons of Surry County received permission to survey and patent Raccoon Island, which was around 300 acres, on 13 June 1728. He continued to purchase lands from the Cheroenhaka.
6. *Tho[ma]s Coche and Benj[amin] Edwards*: Benjamin Edwards and Thomas Cocke also purchased land with John Simmons on 7 August 1735.
7. *Act to Enable the Nottaway Indians to Sell Certain Lands*: The Virginia General Assembly passed several acts to enable the Nottoway Indians to sell tracts of their lands to white settlers on 7 August 1735 and again in February 1772, and 17 February and 11 May 1809.

8. *Tract of land*: The Treaties of 1646, 1677 and 1705 granted the Cheroenhaka the Circle and Square Tract of 41,000 Acres in Southampton County, which was created from a portion of the Isle of Wight County in 1749–50. See Red Hawk 'Teerheer,' Chief, Cheroenhaka (Nottoway) Indian Tribe, Southampton County, Virginia, at http://www.cheroenhaka-nottoway.org/nottoway-history [accessed 15 January 2015].
9. *Feofm[en]t*: feoffment 'The action of investing a person with a fief or fee. In technical lang. applied esp. to the particular mode of conveyance (originally the only one used, but now almost obsolete) in which a person is invested with a freehold estate in lands by livery of seisin (at common law generally but not necessarily evidenced by a deed, which however is now required by statute)' (*OED*).
10. *Enfeofed*: enfeoff: 'To invest with a fief; to put (a person) in possession of the fee-simple or fee-tail of lands, tenements' (*OED*).
11. *Livery and Seisin*: a transfer of possession of freehold estates (*OED*).
12. *Quitrent*: a tax or rent paid to the king (*OED*).
13. *Patent*: a tract of land conferred by letters patent (*OED*) or public land granted by a governing body, at http://freepages.genealogy.rootsweb.ancestry.com/~jcat2/18centvalaw.html [accessed 5 December 2014].
14. *soccage*: socage was the tenure of land by certain determinate services (*OED*).
15. *in Cupite*: in capite (Latin): 'directly from the Crown' (*OED*).
16. *Knights service*: 'Under the Feudal System: The military service which a knight was bound to render as a condition of holding his lands; hence, the tenure of land under the condition of performing military service' (*OED*).

James Dolbeare, Bills of Sale (1732 and 1743)

1. *William Richardson*: William Richardson was a yeoman and Loran's high price may indicate that he had cultivated a variety of skills. See J. Adams Vinton, *The Richardson Memorial* (1876), p. 537.
2. *Nintey pounds*: ninety was among the highest prices quoted at a time when slaves typically cost £40.
3. *Brazier*: a brazier was an artisan who worked with brass.
4. *To warrant and defend*: 'to guarantee security of possession to a person or institution by freeing (land, services, etc.) of earlier claims or charges, and promising to protect or vindicate against future claims or claimants' (*OED*).

Birth of Negroes, Galbreath Moore Family Bible (1819–56)

1. *Margarat Galbreath*: Neil Galbreath was born on 24 September 1739 in Argyllshire, Scotland and died on 4 September 1810 in Christian, Kentucky, United States of America. His wife, Eufemia Effie Blue, was born in Scotland and they had thirteen children. Margaret Galbreath (1770–1822).
2. *Dan[ie]l Galbreath Born*: Daniel Galbreath married Mary Galbreath on 3 March 1814 in Christian, Kentucky.
3. *Marron Galbreath Born*: Marian Galbreath married Daniel Mcswain on 12 November 1818 in Christian, Kentucky.

Lancaster, Pennsylvania Clerk of Courts, Returns of Negro and Mulatto Children (1788–93)

1. *the Gradual Abolition of Slavery*: On 1 March 1780, the Pennsylvania legislature passed 'An Act for the Gradual Abolition of Slavery' and on 29 March 1788 'An ACT to explain and amend an act, entitled "An Act for the Gradual Abolition of Slavery"' was passed.
2. *John Hubly Cl[er]k*: After 1 March 1780 all children of enslaved mothers had to be registered by the slaveholder with the appropriate clerk of peace or clerk of the court where they resided. These records had to be submitted by 1 April 1789, and thereafter within six months of each subsequent child; the penalty for negligence in filing was the immediate emancipation of the unregistered child(ren).
3. *the Children to Serve until the age of twenty Eight years of age*: Children born after 1 March 1780 would become indentured servants instead of slaves, and would be bound in service until their twenty-eighth birthday.
4. *Subscriber President of the Court of General Quarter Sessions of the Peace*: The quarter sessions court was established by Governor John Evans in 1707, for each county. See the Pennsylvania State Archives, http://www.phmc.state.pa.us/bah/dam/rg/coffices.htm [accessed 12 January 2015].
5. *Ead[em] Die*: 'same day' (Latin).
6. *Pruthonitors*: A prothonotary was a chief clerk or administrative officer of a county court of law in the United States (*OED*).
7. *May 1st 1790*: The 29 March 1788 amendment was passed that any child born to a slave or 'servant for term of years' mother after 1 March 1780 must be registered by the slaveholder with the appropriate clerk of peace or clerk of the court where they reside. These records had to be submitted by 1 April 1789 and thereafter within six months of the birth of each subsequent child; the penalty for negligence in filing was the immediate emancipation of the unregistered child(ren). The records after 1 April 1789 do appear to slowly diminish.

Vick Family Deed of Emancipation (1789)

1. *Deed*: In May 1782 the House of Delegates passed 'An Act to Authorize the Manumission of Slaves'. Before this Act, it was illegal for slaveholders to emancipate their slaves without legislated approval; now the Act allowed slaveholders to liberate their slaves if two witnesses certified the 'instrument of emancipation' in the county court. See E. S. Wolf, *Race and Liberty in the New Nation: Emancipation in Virginia from the Revolution to Nat Turner's Rebellion* (Baton Rouge, LA: Louisiana State University Press, 2006); A. Levy, *The First Emancipator: The Forgotten Story of ROBERT CARTER the Founding Father Who Freed His Slaves* (New York, NY: Random House, 2005).
2. *Jesse Vick*: Jesse Vick was born in Southampton County, Virginia around 1755, the second son of Simon and Patience Vick.
3. *full freedom without any interruption from us or from any person claiming for by or under us*: Vick's deed of emancipation redefined Rose and Simon's family relationship since they were now a free black family instead of heritable property of Vick's heirs.
4. *Lenrie Vick*; *William Newsom*; *Pilgrim Vick*; *Josah W. Cathon*; *Joshua Vick*; *Sarah Vick*; *Giles Vick*; *Piety Vick*: unidentified.

John Beall, Will (1803)

1. *John Beall*: John Bradley Beall was born on 23 November 1760 in Montgomery, Maryland.
2. *Wilkes County*: In 1777 Wilkes County had been created from former Cherokee and Creek Indian lands.
3. *devise*: To assign or give all kinds of property that could be disposed of by will (*OED*).
4. *Mary Bell Beall*: Mary died in 1820. See http://trees.ancestry.com/tree/44909445/person/6276360439 [accessed 19 January 2015].
5. *to have her Maintainance out of the plantation and stock during her life ... utinsels and House hold furniture*: Like most eighteenth-century Georgia land owners, Beall left his wife a maintenance instead of an estate in 'fee simple', which would have given her ownership and hence power to bequeath it according to her desires. Male testators primarily bequeathed commodities to women and land to men.
6. *maintain the family and School*: Male testators also entrusted the overseeing of young children's education to sons instead of wives.
7. *Betsy Beall*: Elizabeth Beall (1782–1833).
8. *Richard Rivear; Daniel Gafford; John Hatieay; D Farrell*: unidentified.

George Walker, Leeward Plantation Appraisal (1781)

1. *Deed*: An instrument in writing (which for this purpose includes printing or other legible representation of words on parchment or paper), purporting to effect some legal disposition, and sealed and delivered by the disposing party or parties (*OED*). William Blackstone defined a deed as 'a writing sealed and delivered by the parties ... it is called a deed ... because it is the most solemn and authentic act that a man can possibly perform, with relation to the disposal of his property' (*Common Laws of England*, II.295).
2. *Honourable Frenans Moe*: unidentified.
3. *George Walker*: George Walker might have lived in the St Michael Parish, which has on record the baptisms of his slaves.
4. *Clayed*: 'sugar, refined with clay' (*OED*).
5. *Abraham Cumberbatch*: may be Abraham Cumberbatch (1754–96) or his father, Abraham Carleton Cumberbatch (1726–85), who were associated with slaveholding plantations in Barbados. University College of London, Legacies of British Slave-Ownership, at https://www.ucl.ac.uk/lbs/person/view/2146630501 [accessed 19 January 2015].
6. *Cumberbatch Sober*: Cumberbatch Sober (1742–1827).
7. *Samuel Hinds... Benjamin Seale... John Boyce*: unidentified.

John Williams and Elizabeth Williams, his Wife, and their Children, Removal Orders (1818)

1. *Midd[lese]x General Session*: Instead of the quarter sessions held four times a year in other counties, the Middlesex sessions met eight times a year. See www.londonlives.org [accessed 12 January 2015].
2. *Parish of SAINT MARGARET*: The parish of Saint Margaret encompassed the Palace of Westminster and administered the parish concerns for Saint John, which had been created in 1727.
3. *City and Liberty of Westminster*: In 1585 the Westminster Court of Burgesses was established after the dissolution of Westminster Abbey. Westminster was divided into twelve

wards, including a portion of the parish of Saint Margaret, as well as the parish of St Martin in the Fields.
4. *Saint Marylebone*: The parish of Saint Marylebone is in central London, within the City of Westminster.

Dido Elizabeth Belle Davinier

1. *Dido Elizabeth d[aughte]r of Bell*: 'Bell' is most likely Sir John Lindsay – the son of Lord Mansfield's sister, Amelia Murray Lindsay. John Lindsay was stationed in the West Indies on the warship, the HMS *Trent*, which had taken Maria Belle from a Havana from Spain in 1762. Most likely Lindsay met Dido's mother, Maria Bell(e), on one of the Spanish ships. According to the date of the baptismal entry, Dido would have been born either in 1760 or 1761. See P. Byrne, *Belle: The Slave Daughter and the Lord Chief Justice* (New York, NY: Harper, 2014) and Slavery and Justice at Kenwood House, at https://www.english-heritage.org.uk [accessed 9 January 2015].
2. *Maria his Wife*: This is the only mention of Dido's mother in civil documents. The entry has obscured Dido's illegitimacy by referring to her father by her mother's surname, as well as by describing Maria as a wife. As Lindsay's illegitimate daughter, Dido would not legally be known as Dido Lindsay.
3. WILL: The will of Mansfield was executed in 1782, before his wife's death, and his nephew's, Sir John Lindsay's.
4. *Earl of Mansfield*: William Murray (1705–93) was born at Scone Palace in Perthshire, Scotland to David Murray, the fifth viscount of Stormont, and his wife, Margaret Scott. Murray became Baron Mansfield when he was appointed lord chief justice in 1756. In 1776 Mansfield was elevated to an Earldom. See N. S. Poser, *Lord Mansfield: Justice in the Age of Reason* (Montreal: Mcgill Queens University Press, QC, 2013).
5. *Westminster Abbey*: Murray was buried in the north transept of Westminster Abbey on 28 March 1793. Murray arrived in London in 1718 to attend Westminster School. See Poser, *Lord Mansfield*.
6. *Ann and Marjory*: Ann and Marjory Murray were Mansfield's brother David's daughters.
7. *dear Wife*: On 20 September 1738, Murray married Lady Elizabeth Finch (1704–84), the daughter of Daniel Finch, the seventh earl of Winchilsea, and his second wife, the Hon. Anne Hatton. Lady Elizabeth was a distant relation of Heneage Finch, husband to the poet, Anne Finch (see Volume 2).
8. *Elizabeth Murray*: Elizabeth Murray (1760–1825) was the eldest daughter of David Murray, Lord Stormont, and Henrietta Frederica de Berargaard.
9. *Sir David Lindsay*: Lindsay (1724–97) was a maternal nephew to Lord Mansfield and elder brother to Sir John Lindsay, the father of Dido Elizabeth. See www.ancestry.com [accessed 9 January 2015].
10. *Sir John Lindsay*: Lindsay died when travelling to Bath in 1788.
11. *Mrs. Murray*: identity unknown.
12. *my Sister Margaret*: William Murray had an eldest sister, Marjory, who might be this sister.
13. *John Way*: John Way was Mansfield's property manager who kept his accounts for thirty-five years.
14. *confirm to Dido Elizabeth Belle her freedom*: Mansfield ensured that Dido would be independent and not legally liable to being treated as a slave by her father's family.
15. *Dutchess Dowager of Portland*: Margaret Cavendish Bentinck, duchess of Portland (1715–85), was a member of the Bluestocking Circle and friends with Elizabeth Carter

(see Volume 4).
16. *Vanlo*: Lord Mansfield had his portrait painted by Jean-Baptiste van Loo (1684–1745) while he was in England in 1737.
17. *Lady Mary Milbank*: Lady Mary Watson-Wentworth was the daughter of Thomas Watson-Wentworth, first marquess of Rockingham, and Mary Finch, sister to Elizabeth Finch. Lady Mary married John Milbanke.
18. *Lady Charlotte Wentworth*: The Right Honorable Lady Charlotte Wentworth's will was proved 26 May 1810 in St Marylebone, Middlesex, England. Her relationship to Lord Mansfield is unidentified.
19. *Lord Kinnoul, the Archbishop of York, and the Bishop of Worcester*: George Henry Hay, eighth earl of Kinnoull was a childhood friend of Mansfield. His son Thomas Hay, ninth earl of Kinnoull, who died in 1787 could be the earl of Kinnoull or the younger son, Robert Hay Drummond, who became the archbishop of York (1761–76). The archbishop of York could also be William Markham, who was the archbishop from 1776 to 1807, and who was the bishop from 1781 to 1808.
20. *Lady Stormont*: in 1776 the Honourable Louisa Cathcart married David Murray, Lord Stormont, who was William Murray's heir.
21. *Lady David Lindsay*: Sir David Lindsay's wife was Susanna Long (d. 1818).
22. *Lady John Lindsay*: Mary Milner (1740–99) was Sir John Lindsay's legal wife, and was charged by Lindsay to care for his illegitimate children in his will.
23. *my Nephew David Viscount Stormont*: David Murray was William Murray's nephew, and father to Elizabeth Murray Finch-Hatton.
24. *Nieces, Anne and Margery*: Mansfield added nineteen codicils, which increased the allowances to his nieces, Dido Elizabeth, and faithful servants.
25. *marriage of my niece Elizabeth*: on 10 December 1785, Elizabeth married George Finch-Hatton, who was related to Lady Mansfield as the son of her brother, Edward. Lord Mansfield bestowed her inheritance upon her at the time of her marriage.
26. *John Davinier*: Davinier, a senior servant as a gentleman's Steward, emigrated from France around 1783.
27. *above the age of Twenty one Years*: after Lord Hardwicke's Marriage Act, brides under the age of consent, twenty-one, must have parental approval.
28. *License*: The 1694 and 1695 Marriage Duty Acts required that banns or marriage licences must be obtained before a marriage ceremony. Dido's comfortable financial situation enabled her to marry John Davinier in St George's, Hanover Square, London, which was 'one of the most fashionable churches in greater London'. Marrying by an expensive license, instead of by banns also revealed her well-connected status.
29. *the Right Reverend Father in God, Beilby by Divine permission, Lord Bishop of London*: Beilby Porteus (1731–1809) was the bishop of London who started the Cheap Repository Tracts, and also advocated abolition.
30. *Plaint*: 'A (spoken or written) statement of grievance, submitted to a court of law for the purpose of obtaining redress; an accusation, a charge' (*OED*).
31. *between the Hours appointed in Constitutions Ecclesiastical confirmed*: the Church of England, as per Canon 62 of the 1603 Canons, required clergy to conduct the marriage ceremony between 'hours of eight and twelve in the forenoon' and 'at the church door.' See http://www.anglican.net/doctrines/1604-canon-law [accessed 9 January 2015].
32. *now by Law established*: Lord Hardwicke's Marriage Act (1753), or 'An act for the Better Preventing of Clandestine Marriage' required marriages to be performed by an Anglican minister in a parish church or chapel with two witnesses. Jews and Quakers were exempt

from this law, but all Dissenting and Catholic brides and grooms had to be married in Anglican churches, in order for it to be legally binding. See www.parliament.uk [accessed 9 January 2015].

Olaudah Equiano, or Gustavus Vassa, 'The African'

1. *Isa. xii. 2. 4*: Isaiah 12:2, 4.
2. *Governor Macnamara*: Matthias MacNamara (November 1775–8 April 1777) was the lieutenant governor of James Island in 1775, and the next year was appointed governor of Senegambia, both British possessions on the West coast of Africa.
3. *thirty-nine articles*: In 1563 the tenets or articles of belief of the Anglican Church were condensed from the forty-two articles of Thomas Cranmer.
4. *missionary to Africa*: Equiano could not receive the approval of the bishop of London, Robert Lowth. See Walvin, 'Equiano, Olaudah'.
5. *I was glad to hear that an edition of my Narrative*: The year before he published his autobiography, Equiano sent a petition to Queen Charlotte promoting abolition on 21 March 1788. Equiano's *The Interesting Narrative of the Life of Olaudah Equiano* raised awareness of the abolitionist cause on both sides of the Atlantic, and was reprinted in eight editions during his lifetime.
6. *I remained in London till I heard the debate in the House of Commons on the Slave Trade, April the 2d and 3d*: On Monday, 2 April 1792, William Pitt delivered his speech to abolish slavery to the House of Commons. A total of 519 petitions against slavery were also submitted and on Tuesday, 3 April 1792, the gradual abolition of slavery passed. See The Schomburg Center for Research in Black Culture, available at http://abolition.nypl.org/print/abolition [accessed 12 January 2015].
7. *Gustavus Vassa (an African)*: Starting in 1787, 'Gustavus Vassa the African' wrote articles and reviews of treatises in London newspapers. See P. Fryer, *Staying Power: The History of Black People in Britain* (London: Pluto Press, 1984).
8. *Licence*: The 1694 and 1695 Marriage Duty Acts required that banns or marriage licences must be obtained before a marriage ceremony. Equiano's writings contributed to his accumulating wealth; marrying by an expensive license, instead of by banns, also revealed his celebrity status.
9. *Cha[rle]s Hill Curate*: Anthony Hamilton was the vicar of St Martin's in the Fields Parish Church, but often vicars utilized the services of curates to perform pastoral duties.
10. *Thomas Cullen*: unidentified.
11. *Aldermanbury*: Aldermanbury was in central London near St Paul's Cathedral, in the Bassinghall ward.
12. *City of London*: London was subdivided into twenty-six wards or aldermanry, which were self-governing entities during the eighteenth century.
13. *John Audley and Edward Ind*: John Audley and Edward Ind were gentlemen from Cambridge and, along with Equiano, members of the Society for Effecting the Abolition of the Slave Trade (SEAST). See V. Carretta, *Equiano, the African: Biography of a Self-Made Man* (Athens, GA: University of Georgia Press, 2005).
14. *infant*: Children under the age of legal accountability were called infants.
15. *Anna Maria*: Anna Maria was born on 16 October 1793 and baptized in St Andrew's Church, Soham on 30 January 1794. She died on 21 July 1797.
16. *Johanna Vassa*: Joanna Vassa was born on 11 April 1795 and baptized in St Andrew's Church, Soham on 29 April 1795, and was by 1797 the sole surviving member of Equi-

ano's family. Joanna married the Rev. Henry Bromley on 29 August 1821 in the church of St James, Clerkenwell. In 1857, Joanna passed away and was buried in Abney Park Cemetary, London. See A. Osborne, *Equiano's Daughter: The Life and Times of Joanna Vassa* (London: Momentum Arts, 2007).

17. *Moiety*: Either of two parts into which something is divided; one's share or portion (*OED*).
18. *Treasuror and directors of the Sierra Leone Company*: In 1786, Equiano was appointed the commissary of provisions and stores for the 'resettlement' scheme of the black poor to Sierra Leone (see 'Williams Settlement'). Though Equiano was dismissed, his will indicated his continued interest in the success of the colony.
19. *Treasurer and Directors of the Society instituted at the Spa Fields Chapel*: Though Equiano had been denied the opportunity to go as a missionary to Africa, he still valued missionary work. The society at Spa Fields Chapel was interdenominational and later became the London Missionary Society.
20. *Elizabeth Melliora Cross No. 9 Adam Street*: unidentified, though her address was the same as James Gillham, the lawyer, and could be a member of his household family.
21. *J. Gillham No. 9 Adam Street Adelphi*: James Gillham was Equiano's lawyer. The address, Adam Street, Adelphi was in the Neoclassical Adelphi Terrace, which the Adam brothers (Robert and James) constructed from 1768 to 1772.
22. *Copyhold*: A kind of tenure in England of ancient origin – tenure of lands being parcel of a manor, 'at the will of the lord according to the custom of the manor', by copy of the manorial court-roll (*OED*). As copyhold and not freehold, the land was owned by the tenant for his or her lifetime and that of his or her immediate heirs, but could be reclaimed by the lord of the manor at the time of the lease's renewal.
23. *Isle of Ely and County of Cambridge*: The city of Ely was surrounded by marshy fenland, and supposedly the name 'Isle of Ely' derived from the Venerable Bede's description of the area as the 'island of Eels'. The Isle of Ely was a county palatine, of which an earl, lord – or in the case of Ely – the bishop, had royal permission to administer autonomously civil and criminal jurisdiction within that territory (*OED*).
24. *Mrs. Ann Cullen*: Ann Jones married James Cullen and was the mother of Susanna Cullen Vassa. Ann died in 1820.
25. *by the last Will and Testament of my late wife Susanna Vassa*: Susanna died on 21 February 1796 and had been buried at St Andrew's Church, Soham, where she had married Equiano and where her daughters had been baptized. Susanna had written a will on 12 December 1795 in which she bequeathed to Equiano the lands her sister Mary had willed to her, upon the anticipated death of their mother. See V. Carretta, *Equiano, the African: Biography of a Self-Made Man* (Athens, GA: University of Georgia Press, 2005). As a married woman, Susanna could only write a will with her husband's consent, which indicated Equiano's egalitarian and loving treatment of his wife. Perhaps Equiano's experiences as a slave enlarged his empathy toward his wife's subordinate legal position as a married woman. See S. Staves, *Married Women's Separate Property in England, 1660–1833* (Cambridge, MA: Harvard University Press, 1990); A. Erickson, *Women and Property in Early Modern England* (London: Routledge, 1993).
26. *James Parkinson Esquire*: James Parkinson (1730–1813) acquired the Lever collection through lottery on 23 March 1786. He was a land agent and accountant, and one of the proprietors for the Ranelagh Gardens in London. See *ODNB*.
27. *Leverian Museum Blackfriars Road*: Ashton Lever collected natural historical items such as fossils, shells and animals – many from the travels of Captain James Cook – and displayed them at the Holophusikon at Leicester House in London until 1786, at which

time it was moved by James Parkinson to the Rotunda at No. 3 Blackfriars Road until 1806.
28. *Francis Fokes and Frances his wife*: unidentified.
29. *Mrs Ann Seborne of Westwell*: unidentified.
30. *Plaisterers Hall*: The Plasterers Hall according to an advertisement in *The Times* was a brick building with 'numerous convenient apartments, a spacious Hall ... a Music Gallery, a large yard, a store cellar' and was 'particularly suitable for many businesses'. At the time of his death, Equiano was living on Paddington Street, Middlesex. See V. Carretta, *Equiano, the African: Biography of a Self-Made Man* (Athens, GA: University of Georgia Press, 2005).
31. *Master or Commissary of the Prerogative Court of Canterbury*: the Prerogative Court of Canterbury and of York had jurisdiction over the estates of deceased persons and to grant probate if the deceased had possessed goods above a set value in two or more dioceses. When the archbishop of Canterbury was not presiding at the Prerogative Court, the master or commissary was in charge.
32. *passest by*: The epitaph was composed in heroic couplets.
33. *foul disgrace*: The poet alluded to the abolitionist view towards slavery.

Clara Reeve, 'Letter X' and 'Letter XI'

1. *Fenelon*: The early eighteenth-century French theologian and philosopher, François de Salignac de la Mothe-Fénelon, wrote influential treatises about education for women and for his specific charge, the duke of Burgundy.
2. *delivered from the yoke of tyranny, and become freemen*: Reeve supported the early years of the French Revolution. See G. Kelly, *National Biography* (Oxford University Press, 2004); online edition (May 2010), at http://www.oxforddnb.com.erl.lib.byu.edu/view/article/23292 [accessed 10 November 2014].
3. *the Helotes*: The Helots were an intermediary serf class between slaves and the free Spartan citizens.
4. *sugar islands*: The British West Indies were part of the triangle trade, receiving slaves from Africa and exporting sugar to England.
5. *hewers of wood and drawers of water*: The Gibeonites were a people conquered by Joshua. See Joshua 9:21.

Phillis Wheatley, 'Preface' and 'Letter of Attestation', in *Poems on Various Subjects* (1773)

1. *Negro Servant*: In England slaves were often called servants, which may be why Phillis was referred to as a servant rather than a slave in the London publication of her poems in 1773. See G. Gerzina, *Black London: Life before Emancipation* (New Brunswick, NJ: Rutgers University Press, 1995).
2. *Mr. John Wheatley*: John purchased the seven-year-old Phillis for his wife, Susanna Wheatley. See V. Carretta, *Phillis Wheatley: Biography of a Genius in Bondage* (Athens, GA: University of Georgia Press, 2011).
3. *London*: Boston printers refused to publish Wheatley's poems, so she sailed to London with Nathaniel Wheatley, the oldest surviving son of John and Susanna.
4. *most generous Friends*: Many female writers, when publishing their work, emphasized their reticence to publish as well as the reassurance that their work did not compromise

their feminine amateur status. See V. Jones (ed.), *Women in the Eighteenth Century: Constructions of Femininity* (London: Routledge, 1990); F. Donoghue, *The Fame Machine: Book Reviewing and Eighteenth-Century Literary Careers* (Stanford, CA: Stanford University Press, 1996).

5. *taught in the Family*: New England allowed slaves the right to be baptized, to marry and to acquire literacy. Education, however, was dependent upon the master's generosity. While the Wheatley's white children would most likely have attended a 'petty' or elementary school, Phillis, as a slave, would not have been able to attend.

6. *Rev. Mr. OCCOM, the Indian Minister*: One of Phillis's first letters was to Samson Occom, a Mohigan convert to Christianity and a minister. Occom was trying to raise funds for schools to educate Native Americans, who were disadvantaged because 'despised on earth on account of [their] colour'. *The Collected Works of Phillis Wheatley*, ed. J. C. Shields (Oxford: Oxford University Press, 1988).

7. *Latin Tongue*: Shields posited that Phillis learned Latin, usually only taught to boys, from the neighbour across the street, Mathew Byles.

8. *is thought qualified to write them*: the 'Attestation' further inscribed the challenges of Wheatley's race, labouring status and gender to write and publish poetry. Other labouring female poets wrote poems defending their literary abilities, but no white labouring poet – male or female – was ever interviewed by eighteen men to determine if s/he had the knowledge to compose the kind of poetry s/he wrote.

9. *His Excel'ency THOMAS HUTCHINSON, Governor*: Thomas Hutchinson (1711–80), a Loyalist, lived in exile in England during the American Revolutionary War, where he met Dido Elizabeth at Kenwood house (see 'Dido Elizabeth Belle').

10. *The Hon. ANDREW OLIVER, Lieutenant-Governor*: Thomas Oliver (5 January 1733/4–20 November 1815) was the last royal lieutenant-governor of the Province of Massachusetts Bay. See L. R. Paige, *History of Cambridge, Massachusetts: 1630–1877* (Boston, MA: H.O. Houghton and Company, 1877).

11. *The Hon. Thomas Hubbard*: Thomas Hubbard was the treasurer for Harvard and commissary general of the Province of Massachusetts Bay.

12. *The Rev. Charles Chauncy, D.D.*: Charles Chauncy (1705–87) was a Congregationalist minister and member of the American Academy of Arts and Sciences. See http://www.amacad.org/publications/BookofMembers/ChapterC.pdf [accessed 19 January 2015].

13. *Hon. John Erving*: John Erving (1693–1786) was a merchant and a loyalist governor of Boston. See http://www.geni.com/people/Hon-John-Erving/6000000002589269550 [accessed 19 January 2015].

14. *Rev. Mather Byles, D.D.*: Mather Byles was a pastor of the Hollis Street Church from 1733 to 1776 in Boston. See *The New England Historical and Genealogical Register*, volume 26 (1872) via books.google.com [accessed 19 January 2015].

15. *Hon. James Pitts*: James Pitts (1712–76) graduated from Harvard in 1727. See D. Goodwin, Jr, *Memorial of the Lives and Services of James Pitts and his Sons, John, Samuel and Lendall, during the American Revolution, 1760–1780* (Chicago, IL: Culver, Page, Hoyne & Co., 1882).

16. *Ed Pemberton*; *Harrison Gray*; *Rev. Andrew Elliot, D.D*; *Joseph Green*, Esq: unidentified.

17. *Hon. James Bowdoin*: James Bowdoin (1726–90) was the president of the American Academy of Arts and Sciences. See: *An Eulogy on the Honourable James Bowdoin, Esq. L.L.D. Late President of the American Academy of Arts and Sciences*, (Boston, MA: John Eliot, Jun., 1812) at https://archive.org/details/eulogyoflatehonj00jenk [accessed 19 January 2015].

18. *John Hancock, Esq*: John Hancock (1737–93) was a prominent patriot in the American

Revolutionary War and, as the president of the Second Continental Congress, was a signer of the Declaration of Independence.
19. The Rev. Mr. *Samuel Mather*: Samuel Mather (1706–85) was the son of Cotton Mather. See *The New England Historical and Genealogical Register*, volume 26 (1872) via books.google.com [accessed 19 January 2015].
20. Rev. Mr. *John Moorhead*: John Moorhead was the minister of the Arlington Street Church in Boston until his death in December 1773. Moorhead's slave, Scipio Moorhead, drew the frontispiece portrait of Wheatley for her *Poems on Various Subjects* (1773). Wheatley wrote a poem to his daughter, 'An Elegy, To Miss Mary Moorhead, On the Death of her Father, The Rev. Mr. John Moorhead'.
21. *Richard Carey*: Carey wrote a letter of introduction for Phillis Wheatley for the countess of Huntingdon. See V. Carretta, *Complete Writings by Phillis Wheatley* (London: Penguin, 2001).

Diocese of Exeter Visitation Records, Stockley Pomeroy (1744)

1. *N. EXON*: Nicholas Clagett, bishop of Exeter (Exon), 1742–6. See Nicholas Clagett (CCEd Record ID 3222060) in: *The Clergy of the Church of England Database, 1540–1835*, at http://www.theclergydatabase.org.uk [accessed 10 January 2015].
2. *Rich[ar]d Foot Minister*: Richard Foot was rector of Stockley Pomery until his death in 1755. See under CCEd Record ID 323186, in *The Clergy of the Church of England Database, 1540–1835*, at http://www.theclergydatabase.org.uk [accessed 10 January 2015].

Stoke Abbott, Dorset, Bastardy Papers (1780–1820)

1. *chargeable*: meaning the person would require parish assistance.
2. *d*: the abbreviation for pence, from 'dinare', a reference to an early Roman coin that came to be used for pence.

St Katherine Cree Parish Apprenticeship Indentures (1693–1753)

1. *Thomas Jewry*: most likely Thomas Jury, a 'Parish Child taken up in poor Jury Lane' and baptized 28 January 1684. Church of England, St. Katherine Cree, baptisms 1663-1727, P69/KAT2/A/001/MS07889, item 001, digital image at www.ancestry.co.uk [accessed 1 December 2014].
2. *Elizabeth Osborne*: Elizabeth was nearly twelve years old when the indenture was written. Church of England, St Katherine Cree, Church of England, St Katherine Cree, baptisms 1663-1727, birth and baptism of Elizabeth Ossburne, daughter of John and Ann, 28 December 1682.
3. *Hannah Synagogue*: Hannah Sinnogogue 'taking upp at the Sinnoggue doore' on 18 January and baptized 24 January 1699. Church of England, St Katherine Cree, Church of England, St Katherine Cree, baptisms 1663-1727.
4. *Frances George*: most likely Frances George, 'taking upp in george ally' 2 March and baptized 3 March 1702. Church of England, St. Katherine Cree, Church of England, St. Katherine Cree, baptisms 1663-1727.
5. *Anne Gray*: likely Anne Gray 'taking upp in grayhound ally' on 23 April and baptized 24 April 1703. Church of England, St. Katherine Cree, Church of England, St. Katherine Cree, baptisms 1663-1727.

6. *Prissillia Pumps*: likely Priscillia Pump, 'taking up at Richard Farnborow door' on 8 April and baptized 10 April 1707, Church of England, St Katherine Cree, Church of England, St Katherine Cree, baptisms 1663-1727.

Hints for the Institution of Sunday-Schools and Parish Clubs, for the Benefit of the Poor (1789)

1. *Martinmas and Candlemas*: St Martin's Day (11 November) and the Presentation of Christ in the Temple (2 February).

Society of Friends, Buckingham Monthly Meeting, Men's Minute Books (1735–98), Women's Minute Books (1670–1822)

1. *Hogshaw house*: Hogshaw is a civil parish in Buckinghamshire, England
2. *25 day of the 5 mo[nth] 1720*: The Quaker calendar differed from today's traditional calendar because it was a Julian calendar up until 1752. This meant that the Quaker year began in March, rather than in January. The Quakers were opposed to the use of the names of months based on pagan gods, so they referred to the months simply by numbering them. This date refers to 25 July 1720.
3. *Make in quire consarn hur clernes*: Friends (Quakers) who are ready to marry must inquire about their clearness. The Marriage Clearness Committee determines if a couple is ready for marriage. This ritual includes question asking, prayer and worshipful silence. It was necessary for a couple to marry. See E. Michener, *A Retrospect of Early Methodism* (Philadelphia, PA: T. Ellwood Zell, 1860), p. 224.
4. *29 day of 6 mo[nth] 1720*: 29 August 1760.
5. *The 26 of the 12 mo[nth] 1721*: 26 February 1721.
6. *Ann Haugood*: Ann Hawgood married Joseph Tomson on 6 November 1720.
7. *The 26 day of the first 1722*: 26 March 1722.
8. *The 26 day of the first month 1722*: 26 March 1722.
9. *The 31 of the 12 month 1753*: In 1753, the Quaker calendar shifted from the Julian calendar to the Gregorian calendar. With this change, the first month of the year was now January. This date is December 31, 1753.
10. *The 29 of the 9 month 1755*: 29 September 1755.
11. *The 27 of the 10 month 1755*: 27 October 1755.
12. *Wickham*: Wickham, or Wykeham, is a small historic village and civil parish in Hampshire, in southern England.
13. *the 7th of the 14th Month 1761*: This likely should read the 7th of the 4th month 1761, referring to 4 April 1761.
14. *A Womens Quarterly Meeting*: Quarterly meetings are made up of the representatives of the monthly meetings from within the same region. These meetings address the basic pastoral and business affairs for the Society of Friends.
15. *7th of ye 4th Month 1761*: 7 April 1761.
16. *Yearly Meeting*: Yearly meetings were annual gatherings of Quakers from different regional areas. The Yearly Meeting oversaw the smaller monthly, quarterly and regional meetings to discuss issues and concerns, set guiding principles and publish expressions of Quaker faith.
17. *Friends*: Friends is a term that refers to Quakers.

18. *Plainness of Speech Behaviour and Apparel*: Quakers were well known for their emphasis on plan speech, behaviour and apparel. Quakers were encouraged to display simplicity in their outward appearance, including fancy clothing and possessions. Simplicity in speech also encouraged equality among the Friends (Quakers). See S. Fatherly, *Gentlewomen and Learned Ladies: Women and Elite Formation in Eighteenth-Century Philadelphia* (Cranbury, NJ: Rosemont Publishing, 2008), p. 64.
19. *Paying Tithes*: Quakers rejected tithing as unjust, as well as declining to support a system from which they were dissenting. George Fox, the Society's founder, often preached against tithing. It has been estimated that between 20,000 and 30,000 Quakers spent periods in prison for non-payment of the tithe. S. Murray, *Beyond Tithing* (Eugene, OR: Wipf and Stock Publishers, 2002), p. 170.
20. *Inclinable*: to be inclined or willing to do something.
21. *Education of their Offspring*: One of the major emphases of monthly, quarterly and yearly meetings was to take care of the poor of the Society. All the members of the Society were considered as brethren and were entitled to support from one another.
22. *Rules of Discipline*: the Society of Friends established the Rules of Discipline in Yearly Meetings. They set out the rules for what it means to be a Quaker.
23. *Chackmore*: Chackmore is a parish in north Buckinghamshire, England.
24. *29 of the 3 Month*: 29 March 1755.
25. *Buckingham*: Buckingham is a town in north Buckinghamshire, England.
26. *Nash*: Nash is a village and civil parish within the Vale District in north Buckinghamshire, England.
27. *Date? 27th of 9th Month 1793*: 27 September 1793.
28. *Meeting Queries*: These are the questions and issues addressed in the meetings.
29. *The 30th of 7 Month 1794*: 30 July 1794.
30. *The Yearly Meeting Epistle*: This document is written at the Quaker Yearly Meeting held in London, England. It is a letter addressed to the different Quaker parishes throughout England and America.
31. *the 27th of 8th Month 1794*: 27 August 1794.
32. *A Certificate was produced*: Part of the Quaker ritual of Marriage Clearness could include a certificate that explained that the couple has been found ready for marriage. This certificate could have been provided to the parents of the couple who intended to marry.
33. *Conversation and Clearness of all others respecting Marriage*: Friends (Quakers) who are ready to marry must inquire about their clearness. The Marriage Clearness Committee determines if a couple is ready for marriage. This ritual includes question asking, prayer and worshipful silence. It was necessary for a couple to marry. See E. Michener, *A Retrospect of Early Methodism* (Philadelphia, PA: T. Ellwood Zell, 1860), p. 224.
34. *the 24 of 9th Month 1794*: 24 September 1794.
35. *28th of the 1st Month 1795*: 28 January 1795.
36. *25th of 2^{d} Month 1795*: 25 February 1795.
37. *The 25th of 3^{d} Month 1795*: 25 March 1795.
38. *Mens Meeting*: Quakers held separate monthly meetings for both men and women. The men's meetings took care of Quaker business in their interaction with the outside world, while the women's meetings had the task of maintaining discipline within the ranks of the female members of the Quakers.
39. *Sarvise*: service.
40. *Bidlesdon Meeting*: Biddlesden is a village and civil parish in Aylesbury Vale distict in north-west Buckinghamshire, England. Many of the meetings of the Society of Friends

were held in Biddlesdon.
41. *Whitlebury*: Whittlebury is a village and civil parish in the south of the county of Northamptonshire close to its border with Buckinghamshire, England.
42. *Chackmore*: Chackmore is a village and civil parish in north Buckinghamshire, England.
43. *The County of Buck's*: Buckinghamshire.
44. *Incurage the Running of Goods*: This refers to the smuggling and illegal selling of different goods.
45. *6 mo 1*: 1 August 1743.
46. *7 mo 6*: 6 September 1743.
47. *Her keeping Company with on that is not a Br[other]*: This is in reference to the fact that one of the women was keeping company with a man who was not a Quaker. Quakers are expected to marry other Quakers so they can teach their children the proper way to live.
48. *9 mo 26*: 26 November 1744.
49. *10 mo 31*: 31 December 1744.
50. *Defray*: provide money to pay a cost or expense.
51. *Oxfordshire*: Oxfordshire is a county in south-east England.
52. *11 mo 28*: 28 January 1744.
53. *26th 3 month 1753*: 26 March 1753.
54. *Quarterly meeting*: Quaker Quarterly Meetings were held four times a year. These meetings oversaw and dealt with the issues of Quaker monthly meetings and included worship, fellowship and items of business.
55. *30th 4 month 1753*: 30 April 1753.
56. *Richard Lounds of Winsllow*: Richard Lowndes lived from 1707–75 and served as the Master of Parliament from Buckinghamshire.
57. *20: 6 month 1764*: 20 June 1764.
58. *25 of the 3 month 1764*: 25 March 1764.
59. *Sherington*: a village and civil parish in the Borough of Milton Keynes in Buckinghamshire, England.
60. *30: 7th month*: 30 July 1764.
61. *25th 3d month 1764*: 25 March 1764.
62. *27:8th month 1764*: 27 August 1764.
63. *28: 7 month 1773*: 28 July 1773.
64. *Yearly meeting Epissels*: These epistles were created at the Yearly Meeting held in London. The epistles were delivered to Quaker families and parishes.
65. *23: 2 month 1774*: 23 February 1774.
66. *24th of the 12th Month 1794*: 24 December 1794.
67. *Readmitted with her Children into Membership*: Readmission into Quaker society is determined by monthly meetings.

Sarah Ryan to Mary Fletcher (1762 and 1763)

1. *best Bonds*: This phrase came up often in relation to the relationships that were forged between Methodists. This idea captures their sense of fictive family ties. For more details, see A. Lawrence, *One Family Under God: Love, Belonging, and Authority in Early Transatlantic Methodism* (Philadelphia, PA: University of Pennsylvania Press, 2011), pp. 72–95.
2. *Progress of that great work then in London*: She is referring to the success of Methodist revival meetings.
3. *Foundry Meeting*: located in an old cannon factory in London that the Wesleys con-

verted into a chapel. The purpose of this meeting was to minister, gather, decide on how Methodism should be taught and decide what Methodism should teach.
4. *Queen of Sheba*: according to biblical tradition, travels northward to the kingdom of Israel to test the wisdom of King Solomon. She tests Solomon's knowledge and wisdom by asking him difficult questions and presenting him with complex riddles. The Queen of Sheba, impressed with Solomon's answers and wealth, remarks that 'the half was not told' her regarding Solomon's wisdom and prosperity. For more details, see 1 Kings 10:1–7.
5. *Bristol*: John Wesley formed the first Methodist Society in Bristol in the spring of 1739. A 'society' was the term used to describe a group of Methodists gathering together for the purposes of worship and fellowship.
6. *Mr. Maxfields*: Thomas Maxfield was a native of Bristol, and was converted to Methodism by John Wesley. He later travelled with Charles Wesley for a period. When Wesley left London, he left Maxfield in charge of the Foundry Society with the responsibility to pray with and advise the members.
7. *Love feast*: John Wesley adopted the Love Feast from the Moravian Agape Meal – a communal meal inspired by biblical accounts. Love Feasts consisted of prayer, song, testimony and the sharing of food and water.

Mary Fletcher, Account of Sarah Lawrence, Methodist Minister (1801)

1. *An Account ... their Testimony [.]*: The manuscript writer used dashes to indicate pauses, breaks or end of lines instead of the usual punctuation. These dashes were retained in poetry and epistolary text, but otherwise were eliminated. Almost all superscript text was preceded by a caret. Excepting the first and last pages of the manuscript, all the pages were headed with the year 1801 in the center and numerical pagination in the right-hand corner.
2. *Sarah Ryan*: an early convert to Methodism, and Mary Bosanquet Fletcher's closest friend.
3. *Providence Cast her into our hands, when a little Child*: Following the deaths of her parents, Sarah Lawrence lived in the orphanage founded by Mary Bosanquet and Sarah Ryan in Leytonstone.
4. *became my Friend as well as Child*: Mary Bosanquet referred to Sarah Lawrence as her adopted daughter. Sarah lived with her until she passed away.
5. *the Family*: She is referring to other individuals living in the orphanage. They referred to one another as family. They read, studied and prayed together.
6. *Childrens meetings*: one of a few examples of Methodist religious meetings aimed at children. A. M. Lawrence, *One Family Under God: Love, Belonging, and Authority in Early Transatlantic* (Philadelphia, PA: University of Pennsylvania Press, 2011), p. 150.
7. *held in Different ... places*: Lawrence held children's meetings at Madeley, at Fletcher's parish and estate.
8. *She had such a sens of the sin of her fallen Nature ...* : This is an account of Sarah's desire for a conversion experience.
9. 'I will keep thee as the Apple of Mine Eye': Psalm 17:8.
10. *met the Class:* Methodist 'Class Meetings' were composed of a group of around twelve Methodists. These classes gathered for weekly prayer, Bible study and mutual encouragement.
11. '*Rejoice evermore, and in every thing give thanks*': 1 Thessalonians 5:16–18.
12. *Sally*: Sarah Lawrence went by the name Sally.

13. *meeting the Children*: She led the children's meeting in Leeds.
14. *CrossHall:* a farm just outside of Leeds. Mary Bosanquet Fletcher transformed the farm at Cross-Hall into a thriving center for Methodist worship.
15. *my dear Mistress*: She is referring to Mary Bosanquet.
16. *Cast my Soul on the perfect Atonement ... Cleanseth from all Sin*: This is an account of Sally's conversion experience.
17. *Justification*: a belief that the grace of Jesus Christ has resulted in forgiveness of sin.
18. *I dreamed*: Many early Methodists believed that spiritual direction from God came in the form of dreams. For more details about this, see P. Mack, *Heart Religion in the British Enlightenment: Gender and Emotion in Early Methodism* (New York, NY: Cambridge University Press, 2008), p. 245.
19. *'O Nanney Walker! there is the Lord Jesus'*: It was not uncommon for early Methodists to have dreams and visions of Jesus Christ.
20. *Mr. Wesley*: John Wesley.
21. *Mr. Fletcher*: John Fletcher; Mary Bosanquet's husband and Sarah Lawrence's 'spiritual father'.
22. *Mr. Fletcher's Death*: 14 August 1785.
23. *Spirit of Elijah shall Rest on Elisha*: 2 Kings 2:15.
24. *I did indeed see the spirit of my dear Mr. Fletcher*: This is referencing a vision of John Fletcher, who was deceased.
25. *a Play Began of a very loose sort*: Methodists were opposed to light-hearted entertainment, like plays and dancing. They considered such activities sinful.
26. *Madeley Town*: After Mary Bosanquet married John Fletcher, she and Sarah Lawrence moved to his home in Madeley.
27. *Publick house*: A public house is a tavern or drinking establishment, more commonly referred to as a pub.
28. *In our Connextion*: A connexion was a circuit of prayer groups who would employ travelling ministers in conjunction with the regular ministers attached to each congregation
29. *she and I*: Both Mary Fletcher and Sarah Lawrence had dreams of John Fletcher following his death.
30. *Coal Port*: Coalport is a village in Shropshire in England.
31. *dear Masters death*: John Fletcher.
32. *My dear Mistress*: Mary Bosanquet Fletcher.
33. *Valley of the Shadow of Death*: Psalm 23:4.
34. *fought the Good fight*: 2 Timothy 4:7.
35. *there meeting my dear Friends never to Part again*: This statement captures the Methodist sentiment that Heaven was relational.
36. *our Journey to Ireland*: The Fletchers travelled to Ireland and England as part of John Fletcher's spread of Methodism. Sarah Lawrence accompanied the Fletchers on this trip. Lawrence and Bosanquet Fletcher rode ahead of John Fletcher on this trip.
37. *the Convoy of Angels the Chariots of Israel, that seperated [sic] Elijah from Elisha*: Elijah, instead of dying, was translated or taken up to heaven by a convoy of angels and a chariot, while Elisha was left to be the prophet on Earth. See 2 Kings 2: 1–11.
38. *it was just Ten years ... Called to enter an Eternal Sabbath of Rest*: In the eighteenth century, people commonly marked the anniversaries of loved one's deaths with sentimental journal/diary entries.
39. *October 2[,] 1786*: This letter was written by Mary Bosanquet Fletcher.
40. *Believe you dear Master and I, are ready to Receive and Welcome you to the Mansions of*

Glory!: This captures Mary Bosanquet Fletcher's sentiment that she would be reunited with John Fletcher and Sarah Lawrence in heaven.
41. *My dear friend Sarah Lawrance has for many years been Weak and Infirm*: Sarah Lawrence died on 3 December 1800.
42. *One day ... she w[as]*: Right-side edge of document is either folded under or ripped off, which obscures a few words.

Quaker Fictive Families

1. *10th 3rd mo 1770*: 10 March 1770.
2. *My Dear Mother's safe arrival in England*: Rachel Wilson was a travelling Quaker preacher. She spent time preaching in America.
3. *10 mon. 1770*: October 1770.
4. *Quarterly Meeting*: Quaker Quarterly Meetings were held four times a year. These meetings oversaw and dealt with the issues of Quaker monthly meetings and included worship, fellowship and items of business.
5. *Falls in Buchs County*: Falls Township is a township in Bucks County, Pennsylvania. Bucks County is immediately northeast of Philadelphia.
6. *8th mon. 1769*: 30 August 1769.
7. *'Strike while the Iron is hot'*: This alludes to the imagery of a blacksmith forging the metal before it cools and hardens.
8. *Friends*: Quakers were often referred to as Friends.
9. *9th mo. 1769*: September 1769.
10. *John Woollman*: John Woolman was an itinerant Quaker preacher who travelled throughout North America and England particularly focused on convincing Quakers that slavery was contrary to Christianity.
11. *Women's Meeting of Business*: Separate meetings were held exclusively for Quaker women. These meetings including the Women's Meeting of Business gave Quaker women greater leadership roles within the community. This meeting incorporated aspects of worship and fellowship, but also addressed concerns within the Quaker community.
12. *Yearly Meeting:* annual gatherings of Quakers from different regional areas. The Yearly Meeting oversaw the smaller monthly, quarterly and regional meetings to discuss issues and concerns, set guiding principles and publish expressions of Quaker faith.
13. *Ann Moor*: Ann Moore (1710–83) was an itinerant Quaker minister.
14. *Dear Edward*: Hannah Cathrall's nephew.
15. *7th Mo. 25th 1782*: This letter is dated 25 July 1782. The Quakers objected to using the names of months derived from pagan gods, so the months were typically numbered. Up until 1752, the Quakers used the Julian calendar beginning on 25 March, as opposed to the Gregorian calendar, which began on 1 January.
16. *Aunt Hannah*: Hannah Cathrall.
17. *as thy Grandparents did*: Edward's grandparents were the prominent Quakers, Edward Cathrall and Rachel Herring Cathrall.

Voluntary Associations

1. *To The Ladies of the Female Association*: This is a letter from someone who benefitted from the help of the Female Association of Philadelphia.
2. *Mrs. Bradford*: Mrs Bradford was the treasurer of the Female Association of Philadelphia.

3. *Mary Ralston*: Mary Ralston lived from 1772 to 1850 in Philadelphia. Little information can be found on her husband, however it appears that Ralston was widowed early in her marriage. It is likely at this point that she benefitted from the Female Association of Philadelphia. A few years later, in 1812, Ralston established a private girls' school in her home.
4. *Mrs. Hannah Boudinott*: Hannah Stockton Boudinot lived from 1736 to 1808 in New Jersey. She was married to Elias Boudinot, a lawyer and statesman from Elizabeth, New Jersey. Elias Boudinot was a delegate to the Continental Congress, later served as a US Congressman and Director of the US Mint. The Boudinots were a well-to-do family with connections to George and Martha Washington. Boudinot was not able to serve in the position of president of the Female Association of Philadelphia once she and her husband moved to Burlington, New Jersey in 1805.
5. *Mrs. Stocker*: Margaret Stocker was a member of the Female Association of Philadelphia. She was later tasked with writing 'The Constitution and By-laws of the Female Association of Philadelphia for the Relief of Women and Children in Reduced Circumstances'.
6. *Mrs. S. V. Bradford*: Mrs. Susan V. Bradford became the president of the Female Association of Philadelphia in 1805. She was the daughter of Hannah and Elias Boudinot.
7. *Treasurer's Act report*: The Female Association of Philadelphia appointed a committee to examine the account report of the previous treasurer. This was done to ensure that the budget was balanced and all the funds were accounted for.
8. *Mary Hodge*: Mary Hodge was married to Major Samuel Hodgdon of Philadelphia. She was a member of the Female Association of Philadelphia. She later served as the treasurer of the society.
9. *Sarah Stille*: Sarah Stille was born in Philadelphia in 1738. In 1762 Stille married Edward Yorke at Christ Church. Yorke died in 1791 leaving Sarah Stille a widow. She later married Thomas Vanderpool, a West Indian merchant. Stille became an officer in the Female Association of Philadelphia.
10. *Mrs. Stocker*: Margaret Stocker was a member of the Female Association of Philadelphia. She was appointed as the president of the board of direction. Stocker later wrote 'The Constitution and By-laws of the Female Association of Philadelphia for the Relief of Women and Children in Reduced Circumstances'.
11. *Mrs. And Miss Potts*: Mrs Ann Potts and Miss Ruth Potts were members of the Female Association of Philadelphia.
12. *Cotillion Party*: Cotillion Party refers to a nineteenth-century party dance or game. The term is also synonymous for a 'ball'.
13. *Miss Gratz*: Rebecca Gratz was appointed to be the secretary of the Female Association for the relief of women and children in 1801. In 1815 she founded the Philadelphia Orphan Asylum. In 1838 she organized the first Jewish Sunday school in America, and played a leading role in in the Female Hebrew Benevolent Society of Philadelphia.
14. *Book of Minutes*: A book of minutes is a book kept by the secretary of an organization that contains detailed notes and dates about the deliberations of and resolutions adopted at a meeting.
15. *The Board of Direction*: A board of directors ran the Female Association of Philadelphia. This board consisted of thirteen women and a treasurer. In 1805, the board of directors was made up of: Mrs Cox, Mrs Bayard, Mrs Bunner, Mrs Green, Mrs Griffith, Mrs Murray, Mrs Montgomery, Mrs Miller, Mrs Stille, Mrs Stocker, Miss Sproat, Miss Smith and Mrs Taylor.
16. *the Society*: The Female Association of Philadelphia held two general meetings each year; one was held on the third Wednesday of April and the other was held on the third Wednesday of November. At these meetings, reports were received about the effects of

the charity of the society and the state of the funds. At the November general meeting, elections were held for the president and the board of directors.
17. *Mrs Bradford*: Mrs Bradford was the treasurer of the society and later replaced Mrs Boudinot as the president of the society.
18. *Mrs Boudinot*: Mrs Boudinot was the president of the society until 1805. She was succeeded by Mrs Bradford.
19. *Mary Hodge*: Mary Hodge was the treasurer of the society in 1807.
20. *Cha[rle]s Boudinot*: Charles Boudinot managed the leases.
21. *Mr. Charles Nicholes*: Charles Nicholes was a benefactor of many organizations, including the Female Association of Philadelphia and many Pennsylvania hospitals.
22. *Benj[ami]n Rush*: Benjamin Rush lived from 1746 to 1813 in Philadelphia, Pennsylvania. Rush was a Founding Father of the United States, a physician, politician, social reformer, educator, humanitarian and founder of Dickinson College.
23. *S. Stille*: Sarah Stille was born in Philadelphia in 1738. In 1762 Stille married Edward Yorke at Christ Church. Yorke died in 1791, leaving Sarah Stille a widow. She later married Thomas Vanderpool, a West Indian merchant. Stille became an officer in the Female Association of Philadelphia and is later appointed to be president of the society.
24. *Hannah Lardner*: Hannah Lardner was married to Captain Charles Biddle of Philadelphia, a Revolutionary War privateer. The Lardner family was quite prominent in Pennsylvania.
25. *Chief Justice Shippen*: Edward Shippen lived from 16 February 1729 to 15 April 1806. He served as the chief justice of the Pennsylvania Supreme Court in Philadelphia from 1799 to 1804.
26. *Edward Burd*: Edward Burd lived from 5 February 1749 to 24 July 1833. He was a revolutionary war officer and later worked as a clerk of the court in the Pennsylvania Supreme Court. Burd was the nephew of Chief Justice Edward Shippen and married Shippen's daughter, Elizabeth.
27. *Mrs Katherine Chew*: Katherine Banning Chew lived from 1770 to 1855 and was the wife of Benjamin Chew Jr. Chew was widowed in 1844, with nine surviving children.
28. *Mr Chauncey*: Charles Chauncey was a lawyer in Philadelphia.
29. *Mrs. Whitefield*: Edward Burd was married to Elizabeth Shippen Burd.
30. *Mrs. Cobb*: Mary Cobb was the housekeeper of Chief Justice Edward Shippen, the father-in-law of Edward Burd.
31. *Eliz{abe}th Taylor*: Elizabeth Taylor was a member of the board of the society.
32. *the constitution*: The constitution of the Female Association of Philadelphia was written in 1803. This document dictated how the society was to run, particularly in terms of leadership and meetings. The articles of incorporation were additional rules that governed the management of the society – particularly financially.
33. *Orphan House*: The Philadelphia orphanage was founded in 1793 following an epidemic of yellow fever. However, this orphanage eventually closed and moved all of the orphans into the almshouse. Rebecca Gratz, however, saw a need for an institution of orphans. In 1815, she founded the Philadelphia Orphan Asylum. See D. Schneider and S. M. Macey, 'Foundings, Asylums, Almshouses and Orphanages: Early Roots of Child Protection', *Middle States Geographer*, 1:35 (2002), pp. 92–100, on p. 98.
34. *The Select of Commen Councils*: A twelve-man select council, chosen by the freeholders, was created by an Act of 4 April 1796. This select council was a part of the common council held in Pennsylvania to manage the city.
35. *bounty*: This term refers to generosity and liberality.
36. *Manager*: The board of the Female Association annually appointed a manager of charity.

37. *Anniversary Meeting*: The anniversary meeting is the second general meeting held by the Female Association of Philadelphia on the third Wednesday of November.
38. *'Blessed are the Merciful'*: Matthew 5:7.
39. *pensioners*: Pensioners are people who receive regular payments from the government or employers.
40. *Mary Robertson*: Mary Robertson was married to James Robertson.
41. *Hor[ace] Binney*: He was a lawyer and congressman in the United States House of Representatives from Pennsylvania.
42. *Margaret Stocker*: Margaret Stocker was a member of the Female Association of Philadelphia. She was appointed as the president of the board of direction. Stocker later wrote 'The Constitution and By-laws of the Female Association of Philadelphia for the Relief of Women and Children in Reduced Circumstances'.
43. *James Vanuxem Chairman*: He immigrated from France in 1760 and became a wealthy merchant in Philadelphia and Bristol. He worked as the chairman of the Committee for the Distribution of Fuel to the Poor of Philadelphia.
44. *subscribers and donors*: Subscribers paid the society two dollars annually. Donors were women and men who made occasional donations to the society.
45. *the Anniversary*: This refers to the meeting held by the Female Association in November for elections of officers and other business.
46. pro tempore: temporarily, in the place of, for the time being (Latin).
47. *store-room*: The Female Association provided a storeroom for the reception of articles of clothing, groceries and other contributions.
48. *charity sermons*: The Female Association hired professional fundraising orators who delivered charity sermons from Salem, Massachusetts to Philadelphia. These sermons often repeated the contrast between benevolence and luxury, suggesting the proper way to dispose of wealth. These sermons were employed to encourage donations to benevolent societies such as the Female Association. See B. Dorsey, *Reforming Men and Women: Gender in the Antebellum City* (Cornell, NY: Cornell University Press, 2006), pp. 32–3.
49. *to bring back lost sheep to the fold of Christ*: Although this was an inter-denominational society, the Christian language and theology that formed the basis of American culture was also evidenced in society constitutions and goals.
50. *quorum*: A quorum is the term for the minimum number of members of an assembly or society that must be present at the meeting to make the meeting valid. In the case of the Female Hospitable Society, a quorum is made up of the governess and one third of the managers.
51. *begin and end with prayer and praise*: This provided women with spiritual and social power. It gave a sense of strength and encouragement to persevere.
52. *Mary A. Snyder*: Mary A. Snyder was married to a grocer and served as the governess of the Female Hospitable Society of Philadelphia. This society was designed for the relief of the sick, the aged, the indigent, the widow, the orphan and the destitute stranger.
53. *Elizabeth Van Pelt*: Elizabeth Van Pelt was married to a dentist and served as the treasurer of the Female Hospitable Society.

Articles, to be Observed and Kept by All the Members of the Benevolent Female Society (1790)

1. KINGSTON-UPON-HULL: Hull was the birthplace of William Wilberforce, who had been elected as the city's member of parliament in 1780. See *ODNB*.

2. *BENEVOLENT FEMALE SOCIETY*: These 'friendly societies', or benevolent societies, provided mutual assistance, offered an early version of insurance and were often organized along gender lines. See N. Tadmor, *Family and Friends in Eighteenth-Century England: Household, Kinship, and Patronage* (Cambridge: Cambridge University Press, 2001).
3. mechanic: 'one who works with his or her hands, an artisan, and also belonging to or characteristic of the lower part of the social scale or the lower classes' (*OED*).
4. our Sisters: The language of address these friendly societies adopted was familial. By addressing each other as 'sister', the members demonstrated the equal relationship they shared within the fictive family. See C. Dallett Hemphill, *Siblings: Brothers and Sisters in America* (Oxford: Oxford University Press, 2011).
5. Let us like Sisters chearful be, / Unite in love ... sickness crave, / There is no respect of persons in the GRAVE: The poem's attribution is unknown.
6. *Stewardesses*: 'female officials who control the domestic affairs of a household, directing the domestics, and regulating household expenditure' (*OED*).
7. *One Shilling, or be excluded*: Benevolent societies had fines and dues to generate income for the group, that when paid insured the continuing membership of individuals, or if neglected ejected the member from the society.
8. THAT *a Feast*: Benevolent societies also celebrated anniversaries of their founding, which helped strengthen their ties of friendship. See A. Harris, *Siblinghood and Social Relations in Georgian England: Share and Share Alike* (Manchester: Manchester University Press, 2012).
9. *Register Book*: 'A book or volume in which information of any kind is regularly and accurately recorded; esp. any of various official or authoritative books of record having some public or commercial importance' (*OED*). The register also participated in the fictive family's household economy by listing who was a member and therefore would be part of the exchange of goods and services.
10. *natural distemper on her at spring or fall*: The medieval belief that the body was composed of various 'humours' or 'tempers' still influenced British medical practice. Hence a distemper was a disorder, a disease, an ailment of the mind or body from the excess of particular humours. This distemper appeared to relate to allergies, since it was associated with specific seasons.
11. *housewifery*: 'The activity or occupation of being a housewife and in particular the management of the household and the performance of domestic tasks' (*OED*). The term 'housewifery' equated marriage with female maturity, and also elided marriage with a woman's primary occupation of housekeeper. See A. Froide, 'Marital Status as a Category of Difference: Singlewomen and Widows in Early Modern England', in J. Bennett and A. Froide (eds), *Single Women in the European Past, 1250–1800* (Philadelphia, PA: University of Pennsylvania Press, 1998), pp. 237–69.
12. *breeding-sickness*: breeding in this case refers to pregnancy up to birth, which then becomes lying-in at the moment the pregnant woman gives birth. Breeding sickness would refer to 'morning sickness' also known as *nausea gravidarum* or its more severe condition, *Hyperemesis gravidarum*.
13. *Pall*: 'A cloth, usually of black, purple, or white velvet, spread over a coffin, hearse, or tomb' (*OED*).
14. *HANNAH BENTLEY ... CATHARINE MOODY ... MARTHA JOBLIN ... SARAH LATIMOOR ... JANE HEDGILL ... JOHN ROBINSON*: unidentified.

Clara Reeve, 'Letter XIV' ('The Plan of a Female Community')

1. *the increase of divorces, the frequency of separations*: see Volume 4.
2. *there is no kind of education equal to that of a wife and virtuous mother*: In the late eighteenth century, educational writers stressed the importance of a practical education for women. These 'virtuous citizen-mothers' would improve the state of marriage, the family and by extension, society. See P. J. Miller, 'Women's Education, "Self-Improvement" and Social Mobility – A Late Eighteenth Century Debate', *British Journal of Educational Studies*, 20:3 (October 1972), pp. 302–14, on p. 302, at http://www.jstor.org/stable/3120775 [accessed 20 December 2014].
3. *the design and purpose of our new plan of female education*: The late eighteenth century was a time of intense interest in educational innovation and experimentation. Reeve's *Plans* was one of many texts that promoted the power of formal education to improve women's lives. While improvement was acceptable, social advancement was considered more problematic, since a girl educated above her station would no longer be satisfied with the marital or the limited employment options available to her. To address this problem of inappropriate education, Reeve proposed practical training in trades acceptable for women. See Miller, 'Women's Education'.
4. *THE Superior, or Governess of the Community*: Reeve borrowed from female Catholic monastic terminology her titles of authority in the construction of her co-resident household.
5. *The Treasurer … and give a regular account of it*: Fictive families managed a fictive family economy, which recorded the goods and services collected and disbursed. See A. Harris, *Siblinghood and Social Relations: Share and Share Alike* (Manchester: Manchester University Press, 2012).
6. *Intendent of the Dairy*: Some domestic chores were performed by the mistress of the household family (see 'Dido Elizabeth Belle'); see also A. Vickery, *The Gentleman's Daughter: Women's Lives in Georgian England* (New Haven, CT: Yale University Press, 1998).
7. *to qualify them to govern and conduct a family*: The purpose of a young genteel woman's education was to prepare her to run a household (see Volume 2, 'Childhood', and Volume 3). See also Vickery, *The Gentleman's Daughter*.
8. *The Milliner to the Community, and teacher of her art*: This occupation and those following were acceptable trades for middling to plebeian women because they dealt with female clientele for female textiles and fashion. A milliner made articles of women's clothing, and in particular hats (see Volume 2, 'Mary Chandler').
9. *The Mantua-maker*: A seamstress who sewed 'a kind of loose gown worn by women, fashionable esp. in the late 17th and early 18th centuries' (*OED*). See E. Ribeiro, *The Art of Dress: Fashion in England and France, 1750–1820* (New Haven, CT: Yale University Press, 1995), and A. Hart and S. North, *Seventeenth and Eighteenth-Century Fashion in Detail: The 17th and 18th Centuries* (London: Victoria and Albert Museum, 2009).
10. *The Clear-starcher*: 'one who stiffens dress linen with clear or colourless starch' (*OED*).
11. *Plain-worker*: Unlike the elaborate and decorative designs with varied stitches for embroidery, plain needle-work was neat straight stitches for sewing seams.
12. *No kind of distinction shall be shewn to children of birth, fortune, or any accidental advantages*: Reeve believed in social hierarchies based on labour and merit, but not in the vestiges of a politically corrupt England that provided benefits solely according to birth.
13. *None of the Pupils or Assistants shall receive or send any letters*: The censorship of young ladies' letters was to prevent correspondence between young men and women (see Volume 2, Lady Mary Wortley Montagu).

14. *A Council of the Sisterhood shall be held every Monday morning, at ten o'clock*: Fictive families maintained a family calendar similarly to household families as part of their fictive family economy. See Harris, *Siblinghood and Social Relations*.
15. *The Superior ... shall read prayers twice every day*: Just as fathers and mothers were charged with directing religious observances with in the home, so too was the authority figure of fictive families. See 'Religious Diversity'.
16. *refectory*: Both Reeve and Mary Astell drew upon Catholic models of convents to fashion their female educational communities. Astell, in *A Serious Proposal to the Ladies* (1694), proposed 'to erect a Monastery, or if you will ... a Religious Retirement' for women. Reeve here refers to the dining hall by its monastic name, refectory: 'A room used for communal meals or refreshment, esp. in an educational or religious institution' (*OED*).

Elizabeth Bentley, 'On the Renewal of Virtuous Friendship in a Future State. July, 1790'

1. *FRIENDSHIP*: Bentley used the term 'friend' to refer to both biological ties of family and fictive bonds through affection. The term 'friend' could encompass kinship, spiritual attachments, sentimental relationships and patronage. See N. Tadmor, *Family and Friends in Eighteenth-Century England: Household, Kinship, and Patronage* (Cambridge: Cambridge University Press, 2001).
2. *Attachments form'd on earth ... increasing ardour still remain*: David Cressy explained how sixteenth- and seventeenth-century Christian belief comforted the bereaved with the 'prospect of eventual reunion in heaven' (*Birth, Marriage and Death: Ritual, Religion and the Life-Cycle in Tudor and Stuart England* (Oxford, Oxford University Press, 1997), p. 388). Bentley affirmed the durable bonds not only between family but also between friends in this poem.
3. *They part no more, nor change their glorious state*: Bentley compared the eternal nature of conjugal bonds to the spiritual bonds through religious friendship.
4. *leagu'd*: Leagued is 'to form or join into a league; to band together with; to confederate' (*OED*).
5. *heav'nly mansions*: In John 14:2, Jesus stated to his disciples: 'In my Father's house are many mansions: if it were not so, I would have told you. I go to prepare a place for you.'

LIST OF SOURCES

Text	Source
Berkeley Seymour, Will (Written 1744, Proved 1744)	Bitton, Gloucestershire, proved in the Prerogative Court of Canterbury. The National Archives, PROB 11/735.
Jane Seymour, Will (1762–70)	Proved in the Prerogative Court of Canterbury. The National Archives, PROB 11/959.
John Romans, Deed (1766)	University of York, Borthwick Institute of Historical Research, Rom. 47.
Ward Hallowell, Ward, Licence [sic] to Change His Name to Ward Nicholas Boylston (1770)	Boylston Family Papers, 1704–1770, Ms n-4 Box 3 of 86 Folder Jan–June 1770, Massachusetts Special Collections.
Jane Parminter, Will (Written 1807, Proved 1812)	The National Archives, Kew, England, Prerogative Court of Canterbury and Related Probate Jurisdictions: Will Registers, Class: PROB 11, Piece: 1530.
John Drayton, Correspondence with James Glen (1769–75)	James Glen Papers, University of South Carolina Digital Collections, at http://library.sc.edu/digital/collections/glen.html
A. W. Rumney (ed.), *From the Old South-Sea House* (1914)	*From the Old South-Sea House, being Thomas Rumney's Letter Book, 1796–1798* (London: Smith, Elder, and Co., 1914), pp. 9–14.

Text	Source
Chesnut and Cox Families Correspondence (1797, 1800, 1810)	Papers of the Cox and Chesnut Families, 1792–1858, University of South Carolina Digital Collections, Folder 5: 1 June 1797–11 July 1797, Call Number: Manuscripts Plb 5-FWS-9-2, Folder 9: 14 March 1800–28 October 1800 Call Number: Manuscripts Plb 5-FWS-9-2, Folder 29: 23 August–28 October 1810 from Papers of the Cox and Chesnut Families located in South Caroliniana Manuscripts Division. Call Number: Manuscripts Plb 5-FWS-9-2http://library.sc.edu/digital/collections/coxches.html.
Lovejoy Family Correspondence (1817–19)	Ferris and Lovejoy family papers, Harold B. Lee Library (hereafter HBLL), Provo, UT.
Anna Letitia Barbauld, *Hymns in Prose for Children* (1781)	(London: Printed for J. Johnson, No. 72, St. Paul's Church-Yard, 1781). ECCO, ESTC Number T053117, ECCO Range 1931.
Ann Murry, *Mentoria: Or, the Young Ladies Instructor* (1780)	(London: Printed by Frys, Couchman, and Collier, for Charles Dilly, in the Poultry, 1780), ECCO ESTC Number:T231307, ECCO Microfilm Reel#:Range 14525.
Jane Davis, *Letters from a Mother to her Son, on his Going to Sea: And a Letter to Capt. S.* ([1799])	(Stockport: Printed by J. Clarke, [1799]), pp. 29–33. ECCO, ESTC Number N019975, ECCO Range 11710.
Church of England, Haselbury Plunknett, Somerset, Parish Registers (1680s, 1754, 1813)	Family History Library Brit film 1526637, original at Somerset Record Office 88360378, 51920 HRP, 87 20.
Recusant Returns, Diocese of York (1767, 1780)	Borthwick Institute, University of York, Ep.Rec.Ret. 1780/569.
William Tennent III, On the Dissenting Petition, House of Assembly, Charleston, South Carolina (1777)	Travel Journal and Album of Collected Papers of William Tennent III (1740–1777), University of South Carolina Manuscripts Division, Digital Collection, at http://digital.tcl.sc.edu/cdm/ref/collection/wtj/id/378
Zina Baker Huntington Correspondence (1808–13)	Zina Brown Card Family Collection, LDS Church History Library, Salt Lake City, UT.

List of Sources

Text	Source
Robert Nelson, *An Earnest Exhortation to House-Keepers, to Set Up the Worship of God in their Families* (1739)	(London: Printed and sold by M. Downing, in Bartholomew-Close near West-Smithfield, 1739), pp. 3–20, ECCO, ESTC Number T225141, Ecco Range 13126.
Anon., *A Persuasive to Family Religion* (1736)	(London: Printed for Richard Hett, at the Bible and Crown in the Poultry; and sold by T. Cadell, Bookseller, in Bristol, 1736), pp. 3–11, ECCO, ESTC Number T079346, ECCO Range 3749.
Abbé d'Ancourt, 'Of Politeness in Religion, and against Superstition', 'Of Devotion', 'Of Behaviour at Church', *The Lady's Preceptor* (1743)	(London: Printed for J. Watts, 1743), pp. 3–8, ECCO, ESTC Number T068927, ECCO Range 11641.
David Muir, *An Humble Attempt toward the Revival of Family-Religion among Christians* (1749)	(London: Printed for the Author, and Sold by J. Oswald at the Rose and Crown in the Poultry, Cheapside, 1749), ECCO, ESTC Number T091605, ECCO Range 5786.
Anon., *Cheap Repository Tracts for Sunday Reading* (1800)	(London: Sold and printed by Bye and Law, 1800), pp. 356–61, ECCO, ESTC Number T184326, ECCO Range 10538.
Isle of Wight County, Virginia, Deeds (1720–36 and 1741–9)	Isle of Wight County Deed Book 7, 1744–7 (Richmond, VA: Southside Virginian Pub. Co.: Orders to W.L. Hopkins, c. 1994).
James Dolbeare, Bills of Sale (1732 and 1743)	Dolbeare Family Papers 1685–1745, MassHS, Box 1 of 7, Folders 1655–1725, 1726–32, 1733–34, 1742-4
Birth of Negroes, Galbreath Moore Family Bible (1819–56)	Moore Family Notes (1770–1950), HBLL, Brigham Young University, Provo, UT. MSS 1306.
Lancaster, Pennsylvania Clerk of Courts, Returns of Negro and Mulatto Children (1788–93)	Returns of Negro and Mulatto Children and Index of Slaves, 1788–1793, FHL 1433968.
Vick Family Letter of Emancipation (1789)	Archival Manuscript, HBLL MSS SC474.
John Beall, Will (1803)	Wilkes County, Georgia, Georgia, Probate Records, 1742–1990, Wilkes County, 1790–1852. 1803 John Beall will.
George Walker, Leeward Plantation Appraisal (1784)	London Metropolitan Archives (hereafter LMA), London, United Kingdom, 4301.A.001.

Text	Source
John Williams and Elizabeth Williams, his Wife, and their Children, Removal Orders (1818)	Middlesex Sessions of the Peace: Court in Session, LMA, London.
Dido Elizabeth Belle Davinier	Baptism Record (20 November 1766) St George's Church, Bloomsbury, LMA P82/GEO1/001.
'The Earl of Mansfield's Will', *Diary or Woodfall's Register* (1793)	issue 1274, 17th–18th Century Burney Collection Newspapers, Gale Document Number: Z2000306912.
Dido and John Davinier Marriage Allegation and Bond (1793)	St George, Hanover Square and St Martin's in the Fields, LMA DL/A/D/24/MS10091E/106.
Susannah Cullen and Gustavus Vassa, Marriage Certificate (1792)	Soham Cambridgeshire, FHL.
Olaudah Equiano, *The Interesting Narrative of the Life of Olaudah Equiano, or Gustavus Vassa, the African* ([1794])	(Norwich: Printed for, and sold by the author, 1794) Eighth edition enlarged, pp. 333–5, 358–60. ECCO, ESTC Number T136630, ECCO Range 3549.
Gustavus Vassa, Will (1797)	The National Archives, Kew, Prerogative Court of Canterbury and Related Probate Jurisdictions, PROB 11, Piece: 1289.
Anna Maria Vassa, Epitaph (1796)	St Andrew's Church, Chesterton, Cambridge http://trees.ancestry.co.uk/tree/31080769/person/12488423511/photox/006de799-356f-4408-9095-0dee20024f3c?src=search
Daniel Renaud, commonplace book selections from *The Ladies Oracle* (c. 1750)	William Andrews Clark Memorial Library, UCLA, MS 1977.007.
Clara Reeve, 'Letter X' and 'Letter XI'	(London: Printed for T. Hookham and J. Carpenter, New and Old Bond-Street, 1792), pp. 76–96, ECCO, ESTC Number T110125, ECCO Range 1299.
Adolph B. Benson, *Peter Kalm's Travels in North America* (1937)	(New York: Wilson-Erickson, 1937), pp. 129–30, 142–3, 204–11.
Phillis Wheatley, 'Preface', and 'Letter of Attestation', in *Poems on Various Subjects* (1773)	(London: Printed for A. Bell, 1773), pp. 5–8, ECCO, ESTC Number T153734, ECCO Range 1280.
Catherine Sedgwick to Frances Sedgwick (1807) on Elizabeth Freeman – 'Mumbet'	Robert Sedgwick Family Papers, Massachusetts History Society MS N-851, Box 77 of 117, Folder 24.

Text	Source
Diocese of Exeter Visitation Records, Stockley Pomeroy (1744)	Exeter Record Office, Devonshire, Chanter 225a.
Haselbury-Plucknett, Somerset, Settlement and Removal Papers (1723–1801)	FHL Brit film 1596989, citing Somerset Archives and Local Studies D/P/ha.pl/13/3.
Stoke Abbott, Dorset, Bastardy Papers (1780–1820)	Dorset History Centre, PE/STA: OV/4/2, digital images at www.ancestry.co.uk.
John Sibley, Settlement Examination (1753)	Mosterton, Dorset, Poor Law Records, Dorset History Centre PE/MSN: OV 3/2, digital image www.ancestry.co.uk.
St Katherine Cree Parish Apprenticeship Indentures (1693–1753)	Saint Katherine Cree: City Of London, LMA P69/KAT2/B/038/MS07701/001.
Ashton in Makerfield, Lancashire, Census of the Poor (1816)	FHL British Film 1701023, items 1–2, original at Warrington Library, Archives and Museum, WMS 735 Sibson Papers, Brym End Census of the Poor.
St Ann's Parish (Albemarle County, Virginia), Vestry Book (1772–85)	FHL US/Can Q 925.5482 K2s, Reproduced from the original in the Henry E Huntington Library and Art Gallery.
London Society for Educating Poor Children in the Protestant Reformed Religion (1782)	(London: R. Denham, 1782), ECCO, ESTC Number T0128247, ECCO Range 6936.
Hints for the Institution of Sunday-Schools and Parish Clubs, for the Benefit of the Poor (1789)	(York: W. Blanchard, 1789), ECCO, ESTC Number T028247, ECCO Range 6936.
Ferdinando Tracy Travell, *The Duties of the Poor* (1793)	(London, 1793), British Library, 224.c31 (excerpts).
Society of Friends, Buckingham Monthly Meeting, Men's Minute Books (1735–98), Women's Minute Books (1670–1822)	Buckinghamshire Record Office, NQ/4/3/1.
Sarah Ryan to Mary Fletcher (1762 and 1763)	Fletcher-Tooth Collection, John Rylands Library, Manchester, England.
Mary Fletcher, Account of Sarah Lawrence, Methodist Minister (1801)	Fletcher-Tooth Collection, John Rylands Library, Manchester, Sarah Lawrence, Box 24, Folder 5.
Rachel Wilson, Letter to R. Jones and H. Cathrall (1770)	Quarterly Meeting of Ministers, 1769, Allinson Collection, Haverford College, Haverford, PA. 968 HOC #7.
Jones, Rebecca, Letter to Edward Cathrall (1782)	Allinson collection, Haverford College, Haverford, PA. 968 HOC #7

Text	Source
Female Society and Female Association of Pennsylvania, Minutes (1805–15)	Quaker Collection, Haverford College, Haverford, PA.
Articles of Association of the Female Hospitable Society (1814)	Quaker Collection, Haverford College, Haverford, PA.
Articles, to be Observed and Kept by All the Members of the Benevolent Female Society (1790)	(Hull: J. Ferraby, in the Butchery, 1790), ECCO, ESTC Number T146326, ECCO Range 7058.
Clara Reeve, 'Letter XIV'	(London: Printed for T. Hookham, and J. Carpenter, New and Old Bond-Street, 1792), pp. 130–67, ECCO, ESTC Number T110125, ECCO Range 1299.
Elizabeth Bentley, 'On the Renewal of Virtuous Friendship in a Future State. July, 1790', *Genuine Poetical Compositions, on Various Subjects* (1791)	(Norwich: Crouse and Stevenson, 1791), pp. 47–9, ECCO, ESTC Number T040772, ECCO Range 5526.